PHP 7 Programming Cookbook

Over 80 recipes that will take your PHP 7 web development skills to the next level!

Doug Bierer

BIRMINGHAM - MUMBAI

PHP 7 Programming Cookbook

First published: August 2016

Production reference: 1260816

Published by Packt Publishing Ltd.
Livery Place
35 Livery Street
Birmingham B3 2PB, UK.

ISBN 978-1-78588-344-6

www.packtpub.com

Credits

Author
Doug Bierer

Reviewers
Salvatore Pappalardo
Vincenzo Provenza

Commissioning Editor
Kunal Parikh

Acquisition Editor
Kirk D'costa

Content Development Editor
Merint Thomas Mathew

Technical Editor
Madhunikita Sunil Chindarkar

Copy Editor
Safis Editing

Project Coordinator
Suzanne Coutinho

Proofreader
Safis Editing

Indexer
Rekha Nair

Production Coordinator
Melwyn Dsa

Cover Work
Melwyn Dsa

Foreword

With PHP 7, we get a host of new features and improvements, such as abstract syntax tree, throwable errors, scalar type hints, return type declarations, speed improvements, and so much more.

The question facing PHP developers these days is not "Should I use the new features?", but "How do I implement these features to build better applications faster?"

I remember building applications in PHP 4. It was a simpler time for PHP developers as it could be intermingled with HTML and everything was in one file. Instead of frameworks, we had libraries of functions that got included. Applications were basically just CRUD desktop applications that we figured out how to shovel onto the web.

Application development has changed several times since then. New frameworks, such as AJAX, PHPUnit, composer, and API-First, were introduced.

All of these things, and many others, have influenced how PHP developers build applications. Today, you will be laughed out of a job if you have a paged-based application that mixed HTML and PHP. So, what will you do? How will you build modern PHP applications and APIs? How will you leverage all the new tools that PHP gives you to build faster, better, stronger applications? I am so glad you asked.

My friend Doug Bierer has the answer for you. This isn't YAUT (Yet Another Useless Tome) of information that you will put on a shelf and never use. The book you are holding in your hands is destined to, quickly, be a part of your `ducktape` library. (Every developer has a `ducktape` library. It is made up of those books you refer to so often that they are now held together by `ducktape`.)

Doug takes the time to show you the new features that you need to understand, like so many developer books out there. Where this book is different is that the author takes the time to show you how to solve real-world problems using these new tools. Not only do you learn, but you can immediately solve problems with what you learn.

You don't have to be an expert in PHP to use advanced concepts. However, you do have to learn, understand, and use these advanced concepts if you ever hope to grow as a programmer. This book will help you down your path to becoming a better programmer.

Cal Evans

Nomad PHP
Nerd Herder for the World Wide Herd

About the Author

Doug Bierer has been hooked on computers since his first program, written in Dartmouth BASIC on a DEC PDP-8, in 1971. In his wide-ranging career, this author has been a professional contract programmer since 1978, having written applications in BASIC, PL/I, assembler, FORTH, C, C++, dBase/FoxBase/Clipper, Pascal, Perl, Java, and PHP. He deployed his first website in 1993 while living in San Francisco. He speaks four languages, has traveled extensively, and has lived in the USA, France, the Netherlands, England, Sweden, Scotland, and Thailand. He also spent some years doing Linux system administration and TCP/IP networking. He is also an accomplished musician (he has written over 60 songs) as well as a writer, under the pen name of Douglas Alan.

Doug's own company is unlikelysource.com, which specializes in consulting, PHP programming, website development, and training (primarily for Zend Technologies Ltd and Rogue Wave Software Inc.

His works of fiction published on `https://www.lulu.com/` are *The End, And Then?* and *Further Indications*. Some of his technical works for O'Reilly Media are *Learning PHP and MySQL*, *Learning PHP Security*, *Learning MongoDB*, and *Learning Doctrine*.

First and foremost, I would like to dedicate this book to my mother, Betty Bierer, who passed away in May 2016. She encouraged me all my life, and applauded my accomplishments (no matter how bad!). She attended all my music concerts, bought all my CDs, and read all my books (even if she did not understand them). I would also like to thank my long-suffering wife, Siri, who patiently endured the hours it took me to write this book without complaint. (She did, however, make threats if I agreed to take on another one... negotiations are ongoing.) Finally, I would like to thank a number of notables in the PHP community who let me bounce ideas off them or offered inspiration. These include, Matthew Weir O'Phinney, Cal Evans, Daryl Wood, Susie Pollock, Salvatore Pappalardo, Slavey Karadzhov, and Clark Everetts.

About the Reviewers

Salvatore Pappalardo, a tech geek from birth, has been a software engineer since 2002. He loves "from scratch" development. He's a tech lover, sci-fi reader, movie enthusiast, and a TED talks addict.

Vincenzo Provenza is a web developer with more than 5 years of experience with different technologies and programming languages (mainly PHP and JavaScript). He loves to travel and read.

www.PacktPub.com

eBooks, discount offers, and more

Did you know that Packt offers eBook versions of every book published, with PDF and ePub files available? You can upgrade to the eBook version at `www.PacktPub.com` and as a print book customer, you are entitled to a discount on the eBook copy. Get in touch with us at `customercare@packtpub.com` for more details.

At `www.PacktPub.com`, you can also read a collection of free technical articles, sign up for a range of free newsletters and receive exclusive discounts and offers on Packt books and eBooks.

`https://www2.packtpub.com/books/subscription/packtlib`

Do you need instant solutions to your IT questions? PacktLib is Packt's online digital book library. Here, you can search, access, and read Packt's entire library of books.

Why Subscribe?

- Fully searchable across every book published by Packt
- Copy and paste, print, and bookmark content
- On demand and accessible via a web browser

Table of Contents

Preface

PHP 7 has taken the open source community by storm, breaking records for speed, which is, metaphorically, causing heads to turn. In its most fundamental sense, the core engineering team has effected a major rewrite of the language but has still managed to maintain backward compatibility to a high degree. The impact of these internal changes is outwardly manifested in an almost 200% increase in speed, with significant savings in memory usage. From a development perspective, changes in how commands are parsed along with a uniform variable syntax have introduced new ways to write code which were simply not possible in the earlier versions of PHP. By the same token, any developer who is unaware of how commands are interpreted in PHP 7 can fall into unseen traps, which causes the code to malfunction. Accordingly, the mandate of this book is to illustrate new and exciting ways to write code and to point out any areas of incompatibility with previous versions of PHP. It is also important to note that this book addresses both PHP 7.0 and 7.1.

What this book covers

Chapter 1, Building a Foundation, helps you get started with the initial setup and configuration of your PHP 7 development environment. We will also present a few hard-hitting initial recipes, which show off new features of PHP 7.

Chapter 2, Using PHP 7 High Performance Features, takes a deep dive into the new features of the language. You will be introduced to the concepts of the abstract syntax tree and uniform variable syntax, among others, and you will learn how these can affect day-to-day programming. This is followed by recipes that take advantage of PHP 7 performance improvements, including significant new changes in the `foreach()` loop handling.

Chapter 3, Working with PHP Functional Programming, emphasizes how PHP has always had the capability of working with programmer-defined libraries of functions rather than classes, and PHP 7 is no exception. In this chapter, we will take a closer look at improvements in the handling of functions, including the ability to provide "type hints" involving basic data types, such as integer, float, Boolean, and string for both input and output. We will also provide extensive coverage of iterators from the Standard PHP Library, as well as how to write your own iterators by taking advantage of improved handling of generators.

Chapter 4, Working with PHP Object-Oriented Programming, explores the basics of PHP object-oriented programming. Quickly getting beyond the basics, you will learn how to use PHP namespaces and traits. Architectural considerations will be covered, including how to best use interfaces. Finally, an exciting new PHP 7 feature, anonymous classes, will be discussed along with practical examples of its use.

Chapter 5, Interacting with a Database, explores the ability to have your application read from and write to a database, which is a critical part of any modern website. What is widely misunderstood, however, is the proper use of the PHP Data Objects (PDO) extension. This chapter will present thorough coverage of PDO, which in turn will allow your applications to interact with most major databases, including MySQL, Oracle, PostgreSQL, IBM DB2, and Microsoft SQL Server, without having to learn any other set of commands. In addition, we will cover advanced techniques, such as working with Domain Model Entities, performing embedded secondary lookups, and implementing jQuery DataTable lookups using PHP 7.

Chapter 6, Building Scalable Websites, delves into one of the classic problems faced by PHP developers building interactive websites—hardcoding HTML forms and later having to perform maintenance. A neat and efficient object-oriented approach is presented in this chapter, which, with a minimal amount of code, lets you generate entire HTML forms that can easily be changed in the initial configuration. Another equally vexing problem is how to filter and validate data posted from a form. In this chapter, you will learn how to develop an easily configurable filtering and validation factory, which can then be applied to any incoming post data.

Chapter 7, Accessing Web Services, covers something that is becoming more and more important to web development—the ability to publish or consume web services. This chapter covers the two key approaches: SOAP and REST. You will learn how to implement SOAP and REST servers and clients. Further more, the recipes presented use the Adapter design pattern, which allows a considerable degree of customization, meaning that you are not locked into a specific design paradigm.

Chapter 8, Working with Date/Time and International Aspects, helps you cope with the fierce competition owing to the growth of the World Wide Web (WWW), leading to more and more customers looking to expand their business into international markets. This chapter will get you up to speed on all aspects of internationalization, including the use of emoticons, complex characters, and translation. Further more, you will be shown how to acquire and handle regional information, including language settings, number and currency formatting, as well as date and time. Additionally, we will cover recipes that show you how to create internationalized calendars, which can handle recurring events.

Chapter 9, Developing Middleware, deals with the hottest topic in the open source community right now—middleware. As the name implies, middleware is software that can be *snapped* into place, which adds value to an existing application without having to alter the source code of that application. In this chapter, you will be shown a series of recipes, implemented as PSR-7-compliant middleware (see *Appendix, Defining PSR-7 Classes*, for more details), which perform authentication, access control, caching, and routing.

Chapter 10, Looking at Advanced Algorithms, helps you understand that, as a developer, given the tremendous number of programmers and companies competing for the same business, it is extremely important that you gain mastery of key advanced algorithms. In this chapter, using PHP 7, you will learn the theory and application of getters and setters, linked lists, bubble sorts, stacks, and binary search. In addition, this chapter examines how to use these techniques to implement a search engine, and how to handle multi-dimensional arrays.

Chapter 11, Implementing Software Design Patterns, works on an important aspect of object-oriented programming, that is, an understanding of key software design patterns. Without this knowledge, when applying for a new position or attempting to attract new customers, you, as a developer, will be at a severe disadvantage. This chapter covers several critically important patterns including Hydration, Strategy, Mapper, Object Relational Mapping, and Pub/Sub.

Chapter 12, Improving Web Security, addresses issues arising from the pervasive nature of the Internet today. We see cyber attacks being launched with greater and greater frequency, often with devastating financial and personal loss. In this chapter, we will present solid practical recipes that, if implemented, will give your websites an exponential boost in terms of safety and security. Topics covered include filtering and validation, session protection, secure form submission, secure password generation, and the use of CAPTCHAs. In addition, a recipe is presented that will show you how to encrypt and decrypt data without using the PHP mcrypt extension, which is deprecated in PHP 7.1 (and will ultimately be removed from the language).

Chapter 13, Best Practices, Testing, and Debugging, covers best practices and debugging of your code to produce well written code that works. In this chapter, you will also learn how to set up and create unit tests, handle unexpected errors and exceptions, and generate test data. Several new PHP 7 features are presented, including how PHP 7 can "throw" errors. It is important to note that *best practices* are identified throughout the book, not just in this chapter!

Appendix, Defining PSR-7 Classes, addresses recently accepted PHP Standards Recommendation 7, which defines interfaces used in conjunction with middleware. In this appendix, you will be shown solid implementations of PSR-7 classes that include value objects, such as URI, body, and file upload, as well as request and response objects.

What you need for this book

All you need to successfully implement the recipes presented in this book will be a computer, 100MB of extra disk space, and a text or code editor (not a word processor!). The first chapter will cover how to set up a PHP 7 development environment. Having a web server is optional as PHP 7 includes a development web server. An Internet connection is not required, but it might be useful to download code (such as the set of PSR-7 interfaces), and review PHP 7.x documentation.

Who this book is for

This book is for software architects, technical managers, developers from intermediate to advanced, or just the curious. You will need to have a basic knowledge of PHP programming, especially OOP.

Sections

In this book, you will find several headings that appear frequently (Getting ready, How to do it, How it works, There's more, and See also).

To give clear instructions on how to complete a recipe, we use these sections as follows:

Getting ready

This section tells you what to expect in the recipe, and describes how to set up any software or any preliminary settings required for the recipe.

How to do it...

This section contains the steps required to follow the recipe.

How it works...

This section usually consists of a detailed explanation of what happened in the previous section.

There's more...

This section consists of additional information about the recipe in order to make the reader more knowledgeable about the recipe.

See also

This section provides helpful links to other useful information for the recipe.

Conventions

In this book, you will find a number of text styles that distinguish between different kinds of information. Here are some examples of these styles and an explanation of their meaning.

Code words in text, database table names, folder names, filenames, file extensions, pathnames, dummy URLs, user input, and Twitter handles are shown as follows: "Finally, take the class `LotsProps` defined in the third bullet point and place it in a separate file, `chap_10_oop_using_getters_and_setters_magic_call.php`."

A block of code is set as follows:

```
protected static function loadFile($file)
{
    if (file_exists($file)) {
        require_once $file;
        return TRUE;
    }
    return FALSE;
}
```

When we wish to draw your attention to a particular part of a code block, the relevant lines or items are set in bold:

```
$params = [
  'db'   => __DIR__ . '/../data/db/php7cookbook.db.sqlite'
];
$dsn  = sprintf('sqlite:' . $params['db']);
```

Any command-line input or output is written as follows:

```
cd /path/to/recipes
php -S localhost:8080
```

New terms and **important words** are shown in bold. Words that you see on the screen, for example, in menus or dialog boxes, appear in the text like this: "When the **Purchases** button is clicked, initial purchase info appears."

Warnings or important notes appear in a box like this.

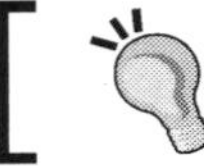

Tips and tricks appear like this.

Reader feedback

Feedback from our readers is always welcome. Let us know what you think about this book—what you liked or disliked. Reader feedback is important for us as it helps us develop titles that you will really get the most out of.

To send us general feedback, simply e-mail `feedback@packtpub.com`, and mention the book's title in the subject of your message.

If there is a topic that you have expertise in and you are interested in either writing or contributing to a book, see our author guide at `www.packtpub.com/authors`.

Customer support

Now that you are the proud owner of a Packt book, we have a number of things to help you to get the most from your purchase.

Downloading the example code

You can download the example code files for this book from your account at `http://www.packtpub.com`. If you purchased this book elsewhere, you can visit `http://www.packtpub.com/support` and register to have the files e-mailed directly to you.

You can download the code files by following these steps:

1. Log in or register to our website using your e-mail address and password.
2. Hover the mouse pointer on the **SUPPORT** tab at the top.
3. Click on **Code Downloads & Errata**.
4. Enter the name of the book in the **Search** box.
5. Select the book for which you're looking to download the code files.
6. Choose from the drop-down menu where you purchased this book from.
7. Click on **Code Download**.

You can also download the code files by clicking on the **Code Files** button on the book's webpage at the Packt Publishing website. This page can be accessed by entering the book's name in the **Search** box. Please note that you need to be logged in to your Packt account.

Once the file is downloaded, please make sure that you unzip or extract the folder using the latest version of:

- WinRAR / 7-Zip for Windows
- Zipeg / iZip / UnRarX for Mac
- Using built-in Linux utilities or 7-Zip / PeaZip

The code bundle for the book is also hosted on GitHub at `https://github.com/PacktPublishing/PHP-7-Programming-Cookbook`. We also have other code bundles from our rich catalog of books and videos available at `https://github.com/PacktPublishing/`. Check them out!

Errata

Although we have taken every care to ensure the accuracy of our content, mistakes do happen. If you find a mistake in one of our books—maybe a mistake in the text or the code—we would be grateful if you could report this to us. By doing so, you can save other readers from frustration and help us improve subsequent versions of this book. If you find any errata, please report them by visiting `http://www.packtpub.com/submit-errata`, selecting your book, clicking on the **Errata Submission Form** link, and entering the details of your errata. Once your errata are verified, your submission will be accepted and the errata will be uploaded to our website or added to any list of existing errata under the Errata section of that title.

To view the previously submitted errata, go to `https://www.packtpub.com/books/content/support` and enter the name of the book in the search field. The required information will appear under the **Errata** section.

Piracy

Piracy of copyrighted material on the Internet is an ongoing problem across all media. At Packt, we take the protection of our copyright and licenses very seriously. If you come across any illegal copies of our works in any form on the Internet, please provide us with the location address or website name immediately so that we can pursue a remedy.

Please contact us at `copyright@packtpub.com` with a link to the suspected pirated material.

We appreciate your help in protecting our authors and our ability to bring you valuable content.

Questions

If you have a problem with any aspect of this book, you can contact us at `questions@packtpub.com`, and we will do our best to address the problem.

1

Building a Foundation

In this chapter, we will cover the following topics:

- PHP 7 installation considerations
- Using the built-in PHP web server
- Defining a test MySQL database
- Installing PHPUnit
- Implementing class autoloading
- Hoovering a website
- Building a deep web scanner
- Creating a PHP 5 to PHP 7 code converter

Introduction

This chapter is designed as a *quick start* that will get you up and running on PHP 7 so that you can start implementing the recipes right away. The underlying assumption for this book is that you already have a good knowledge of PHP and programming. Although this book will not go into detail about the actual installation of PHP, given that PHP 7 is relatively new, we will do our best to point out the quirks and *gotchas* you might encounter during a PHP 7 installation.

PHP 7 installation considerations

There are three primary means of acquiring PHP 7:

- Downloading and installing directly from the source code
- Installing *pre-compiled* binaries
- Installing a *AMP package (that is, XAMPP, WAMP, LAMP, MAMP, and so on)

How to do it...

The three methods are listed in order of difficulty. However, the first approach, although tedious, will give you the most finite control over extensions and options.

Installing directly from source

In order to utilize this approach, you will need to have a C compiler available. If you are running Windows, **MinGW** is a free compiler that has proven popular. It is based on the **GNU Compiler Collection** (**GCC**) compiler provided by the **GNU** project. Non-free compilers include the classic **Turbo C** compiler from Borland, and, of course, the compiler that is preferred by Windows developers is **Visual Studio**. The latter, however, is designed mainly for C++ development, so when you compile PHP, you will need to specify C mode.

When working on an Apple Mac, the best solution is to install the **Apple Developer Tools**. You can use the **Xcode IDE** to compile PHP 7, or run `gcc` from a terminal window. In a Linux environment, from a terminal window, run `gcc`.

When compiling from a terminal window or command line, the normal procedure is as follows:

- `configure`
- `make`
- `make test`
- `make install`

For information on configuration options (that is, when running `configure`), use the `help` option:

```
configure --help
```

Errors you might encounter during the configuration stage are mentioned in the following table:

Error	Fix
`configure: error: xml2-config not found. Please check your libxml2 installation`	You just need to install `libxml2`. For this error, please refer to the following link: `http://superuser.com/questions/740399/how-to-fix-php-installation-when-xml2-config-is-missing`
`configure: error: Please reinstall readline - I cannot find readline.h`	Install `libreadline-dev`

Error	Fix
`configure: WARNING: unrecognized options: --enable-spl, --enable-reflection, --with-libxml`	Not a big deal. These options are defaults and don't need to be included. For more details, please refer to the following link: `http://jcutrer.com/howto/linux/how-to-compile-php7-on-ubuntu-14-04`

Installing PHP 7 from pre-compiled binaries

As the title implies, **pre-compiled** binaries are a set of binary files that somebody else has kindly compiled from PHP 7 source code and has made available.

In the case of Windows, go to `http://windows.php.net/`. You will find a good set of tips in the left column that pertain to which version to choose, **thread safe** versus **non-read safe**, and so forth. You can then click on **Downloads** and look for the ZIP file that applies to your environment. Once the ZIP file has been downloaded, extract the files into the folder of your choice, add `php.exe` to your path, and configure PHP 7 using the `php.ini` file.

To install the pre-compiled binaries on a Mac OS X system, it is best to involve a package management system. The ones recommended for PHP include the following:

- MacPorts
- Liip
- Fink
- Homebrew

In the case of Linux, the packaging system used depends on which Linux distribution you are using. The following table, organized by Linux distribution, summarizes where to look for the PHP 7 package.

Distribution	Where to find PHP 7	Notes

Debian	`packages.debian.org/stable/php`
	
	`repos-source.zend.com/zend-server/early-access/php7/php-7*DEB*`
		Use this command:
		`sudo apt-get install php7`
		Alternatively, you can use a graphical package management tool such as **Synaptic**.
		Make sure you select **php7** (and not php5).

Distribution	Where to find PHP 7	Notes
Ubuntu	packages.ubuntu.com repos-source.zend.com/zend-server/early-access/php7/php-7*DEB*	Use this command: `sudo apt-get install php7` Be sure to choose the right version of Ubuntu. Alternatively, you can use a graphical package management tool such as **Synaptic**.
Fedora / Red Hat	admin.fedoraproject.org/pkgdb/packages repos-source.zend.com/zend-server/early-access/php7/php-7*RHEL*	Make sure you are the root user: **`su`** Use this command: **`dnf install php7`** Alternatively, you can use a graphical package management tool such as the GNOME Package Manager.
OpenSUSE	software.opensuse.org/package/php7	Use this command: **`yast -i php7`** Alternatively, you can run `zypper`, or use **YaST** as a graphical tool.

Installing a *AMP package

AMP refers to **Apache**, **MySQL**, and **PHP** (also **Perl** and **Python**). The * refers to Linux, Windows, Mac, and so on (that is, LAMP, WAMP, and MAMP). This approach is often the easiest, but gives you less control over the initial PHP installation. On the other hand, you can always modify the `php.ini` file and install additional extensions to customize your installation as needed. The following table summarizes a number of popular *AMP packages:

Package	Where is it found	Free?	Supports*
XAMPP	www.apachefriends.org/download.html	Y	WML
AMPPS	www.ampps.com/downloads	Y	WML
MAMP	www.mamp.info/en	Y	WM
WampServer	sourceforge.net/projects/wampserver	Y	W

Package	Where is it found	Free?	Supports*
EasyPHP	www.easyphp.org	Y	W
Zend Server	www.zend.com/en/products/zend_server	N	WML

In the preceding table, we've enlisted the *AMP packages where * is replaced by **W** for Windows, **M** for Mac OS X, and **L** for Linux.

There's more...

When you install a pre-compiled binary from a package, only `core` extensions are installed. Non-core PHP extensions must be installed separately.

It's worth noting that PHP 7 installation on cloud computing platforms will often follow the installation procedure outlined for pre-compiled binaries. Find out if your cloud environment uses Linux, Mac, or Windows virtual machines, and then follow the appropriate procedure as mentioned in this recipe.

It's possible that PHP 7 hasn't yet reached your favorite repository for pre-compiled binaries. You can always install from source, or consider installing one of the *AMP packages (see the next section). An alternative for Linux-based systems is to use the **Personal Package Archive** (**PPA**) approach. Because PPAs have not undergone a rigorous screening process, however, security could be a concern. A good discussion on security considerations for PPAs is found at `http://askubuntu.com/questions/35629/are-ppas-safe-to-add-to-my-system-and-what-are-some-red-flags-to-watch-out-fo`.

See also

General installation considerations, as well as instructions for each of the three major OS platforms (Windows, Mac OS X, and Linux), can be found at `http://php.net/manual/en/install.general.php`.

The website for MinGW is `http://www.mingw.org/`.

Instructions on how to compile a C program using Visual Studio can be found at `https://msdn.microsoft.com/en-us/library/bb384838`.

Another possible way to test PHP 7 is by using a virtual machine. Here are a couple of tools with their links, which might prove useful:

- **Vagrant**: `https://github.com/rlerdorf/php7dev` (php7dev is a Debian 8 Vagrant image that is preconfigured for testing PHP apps and developing extensions across many versions of PHP)
- **Docker**: `https://hub.docker.com/r/coderstephen/php7/` (it contains a PHP7 Docker container)

Using the built-in PHP web server

Aside from unit testing and running PHP directly from the command line, the obvious way to test your applications is to use a web server. For long-term projects, it would be beneficial to develop a virtual host definition for a web server that most closely mirrors the one used by your customer. Creating such definitions for the various web servers (that is, Apache, NGINX, and so on) is beyond the scope of this book. Another quick and easy-to-use alternative (which we have room to discuss here) is to use the built-in PHP 7 web server.

How to do it...

1. To activate the PHP web server, first change to the directory that will serve as the base for your code.
2. You then need to supply the hostname or IP address and, optionally, a port. Here is an example you can use to run the recipes supplied with this book:

```
cd /path/to/recipes
php -S localhost:8080
```

You will see output on your screen that looks something like this:

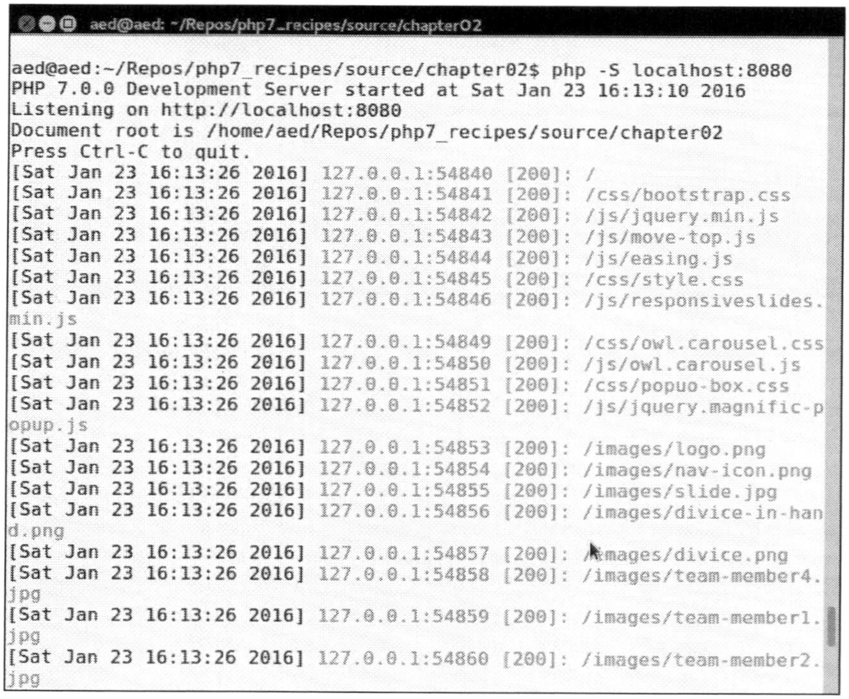

```
aed@aed: ~/Repos/php7_recipes/source/chapter02
aed@aed:~/Repos/php7_recipes/source/chapter02$ php -S localhost:8080
PHP 7.0.0 Development Server started at Sat Jan 23 16:13:10 2016
Listening on http://localhost:8080
Document root is /home/aed/Repos/php7_recipes/source/chapter02
Press Ctrl-C to quit.
[Sat Jan 23 16:13:26 2016] 127.0.0.1:54840 [200]: /
[Sat Jan 23 16:13:26 2016] 127.0.0.1:54841 [200]: /css/bootstrap.css
[Sat Jan 23 16:13:26 2016] 127.0.0.1:54842 [200]: /js/jquery.min.js
[Sat Jan 23 16:13:26 2016] 127.0.0.1:54843 [200]: /js/move-top.js
[Sat Jan 23 16:13:26 2016] 127.0.0.1:54844 [200]: /js/easing.js
[Sat Jan 23 16:13:26 2016] 127.0.0.1:54845 [200]: /css/style.css
[Sat Jan 23 16:13:26 2016] 127.0.0.1:54846 [200]: /js/responsiveslides.
min.js
[Sat Jan 23 16:13:26 2016] 127.0.0.1:54849 [200]: /css/owl.carousel.css
[Sat Jan 23 16:13:26 2016] 127.0.0.1:54850 [200]: /js/owl.carousel.js
[Sat Jan 23 16:13:26 2016] 127.0.0.1:54851 [200]: /css/popuo-box.css
[Sat Jan 23 16:13:26 2016] 127.0.0.1:54852 [200]: /js/jquery.magnific-p
opup.js
[Sat Jan 23 16:13:26 2016] 127.0.0.1:54853 [200]: /images/logo.png
[Sat Jan 23 16:13:26 2016] 127.0.0.1:54854 [200]: /images/nav-icon.png
[Sat Jan 23 16:13:26 2016] 127.0.0.1:54855 [200]: /images/slide.jpg
[Sat Jan 23 16:13:26 2016] 127.0.0.1:54856 [200]: /images/divice-in-han
d.png
[Sat Jan 23 16:13:26 2016] 127.0.0.1:54857 [200]: /images/divice.png
[Sat Jan 23 16:13:26 2016] 127.0.0.1:54858 [200]: /images/team-member4.
jpg
[Sat Jan 23 16:13:26 2016] 127.0.0.1:54859 [200]: /images/team-member1.
jpg
[Sat Jan 23 16:13:26 2016] 127.0.0.1:54860 [200]: /images/team-member2.
jpg
```

3. As the built-in web server continues to service requests, you will also see access information, HTTP status codes, and request information.
4. If you need to set the web server document root to a directory other than the current one, you can use the `-t` flag. The flag must then be followed by a valid directory path. The built-in web server will treat this directory as if it were the web document root, which is useful for security reasons. For security reasons, some frameworks, such as Zend Framework, require that the web document root is different from where your actual source code resides.

   Here is an example using the `-t` flag:

   ```
   php -S localhost:8080 -t source/chapter01
   ```

   Here is an example of the output:

```
aed@aed: ~/Repos/php7_recipes
aed@aed:~/Repos/php7_recipes$ php -S localhost:8080 -t source/chapter01
PHP 7.0.0 Development Server started at Sat Jan 23 16:17:57 2016
Listening on http://localhost:8080
Document root is /home/aed/Repos/php7_recipes/source/chapter01
Press Ctrl-C to quit.
[Sat Jan 23 16:19:52 2016] 127.0.0.1:54929 [200]: /chap_01_deep_scan_website.
php
[Sat Jan 23 16:19:52 2016] 127.0.0.1:54932 Invalid request (Unexpected EOF)
[Sat Jan 23 16:19:52 2016] 127.0.0.1:54973 [404]: /static/corp/img/book-cover
s/thousands-of-books-clean-code-a-handbook-of-agile-software-craftsmanship-97
80136083238_8.jpg - No such file or directory
[Sat Jan 23 16:19:52 2016] 127.0.0.1:54974 [404]: /static/corp/img/book-cover
s/thousands-of-books-hadoop-the-definitive-guide-9781449328917_9.jpg - No suc
h file or directory
[Sat Jan 23 16:19:52 2016] 127.0.0.1:54975 [404]: /static/corp/img/book-cover
s/thousands-of-books-big-data-revolution.jpg - No such file or directory
[Sat Jan 23 16:19:52 2016] 127.0.0.1:54976 [404]: /static/corp/img/book-cover
s/thousands-of-books-rise-of-the-robots.jpg - No such file or directory
[Sat Jan 23 16:19:52 2016] 127.0.0.1:54977 [404]: /static/corp/img/book-cover
s/thousands-of-books-don%E2%80%99t-make-me-think-9780133597271-2014-01-06.jpg
 - No such file or directory
[Sat Jan 23 16:19:52 2016] 127.0.0.1:55263 [404]: /static/corp/img/book-cover
s/thousands-of-books-your-strategy-needs-a-strategy.jpg - No such file or dir
ectory
[Sat Jan 23 16:19:52 2016] 127.0.0.1:55265 [404]: /static/corp/img/video-stil
ls/exclusive-video-content-eric-ries.jpg - No such file or directory
[Sat Jan 23 16:19:52 2016] 127.0.0.1:55264 [404]: /static/corp/img/video-stil
ls/exclusive-video-content-scott-murray.jpg - No such file or directory
[Sat Jan 23 16:19:52 2016] 127.0.0.1:55268 [404]: /static/corp/img/apps/apple
-store.png - No such file or directory
[Sat Jan 23 16:19:52 2016] 127.0.0.1:55269 [404]: /static/corp/img/apps/andro
```

Defining a test MySQL database

For test purposes, along with the source code for the book, we've provided an SQL file with sample data at `https://github.com/dbierer/php7cookbook`. The name of the database used in the recipes for this book is `php7cookbook`.

How to do it...

1. Define a MySQL database, `php7cookbook`. Also assign rights to the new database to a user called `cook` with the password `book`. The following table summarizes these settings:

Item	Notes
Database name	php7cookbook
Database user	cook
Database user password	book

2. Here is an example of SQL needed to create the database:

```
CREATE DATABASE IF NOT EXISTS dbname DEFAULT CHARACTER SET utf8
COLLATE utf8_general_ci;
CREATE USER 'user'@'%' IDENTIFIED WITH mysql_native_password;
SET PASSWORD FOR 'user'@'%' = PASSWORD('userPassword');
GRANT ALL PRIVILEGES ON dbname.* to 'user'@'%';
GRANT ALL PRIVILEGES ON dbname.* to 'user'@'localhost';
FLUSH PRIVILEGES;
```

3. Import the sample values into the new database. The import file, `php7cookbook.sql`, is located at `https://github.com/dbierer/php7cookbook/blob/master/php7cookbook.sql`.

Installing PHPUnit

Unit testing is arguably the most popular means of testing PHP code. Most developers will agree that a solid suite of tests is a requirement for any properly developed project. Few developers actually write these tests. A lucky few have an independent testing group that writes the tests for them! After months of skirmishing with the testing group, however, the remains of the lucky few tend to grumble and complain. In any event, any book on PHP would not be complete without at least a nod and a wink towards testing.

The place to find the latest version of **PHPUnit** is `https://phpunit.de/`. PHPUnit5.1 and above support PHP 7. Click on the link for the desired version, and you will download a `phpunit.phar` file. You can then execute commands using the archive, as follows:

```
php phpunit.phar <command>
```

The `phar` command stands for **PHP Archive**. The technology is based on `tar`, which itself was used in UNIX. A `phar` file is a collection of PHP files that are packed together into a single file for convenience.

Implementing class autoloading

When developing PHP using an **object-oriented programming** (**OOP**) approach, the recommendation is to place each class in its own file. The advantage of following this recommendation is the ease of long-term maintenance and improved readability. The disadvantage is that each class definition file must be included (that is, using `include` or its variants). To address this issue, there is a mechanism built into the PHP language that will *autoload* any class that has not already been specifically included.

Getting ready

The minimum requirement for PHP autoloading is to define a global `__autoload()` function. This is a *magic* function called automatically by the PHP engine when a class is requested but where said class has not been included. The name of the requested class will appear as a parameter when `__autoload()` is invoked (assuming that you have defined it!). If you are using PHP namespaces, the full namespaced name of the class will be passed. Because `__autoload()` is a *function*, it must be in the global namespace; however, there are limitations on its use. Accordingly, in this recipe, we will make use of the `spl_autoload_register()` function, which gives us more flexibility.

How to do it...

1. The class we will cover in this recipe is `Application\Autoload\Loader`. In order to take advantage of the relationship between PHP namespaces and autoloading, we name the file `Loader.php` and place it in the `/path/to/cookbook/files/Application/Autoload` folder.
2. The first method we will present simply loads a file. We use `file_exists()` to check before running `require_once()`. The reason for this is that if the file is not found, `require_once()` will generate a fatal error that cannot be caught using PHP 7's new error handling capabilities:

```
protected static function loadFile($file)
{
    if (file_exists($file)) {
        require_once $file;
        return TRUE;
    }
    return FALSE;
}
```

3. We can then test the return value of `loadFile()` in the calling program and loop through a list of alternate directories before throwing an `Exception` if it's ultimately unable to load the file.

You will notice that the methods and properties in this class are static. This gives us greater flexibility when registering the autoloading method, and also lets us treat the `Loader` class like a **Singleton**.

4. Next, we define the method that calls `loadFile()` and actually performs the logic to locate the file based on the namespaced classname. This method derives a filename by converting the PHP namespace separator \ into the directory separator appropriate for this server and appending `.php`:

```
public static function autoLoad($class)
{
    $success = FALSE;
    $fn = str_replace('\\', DIRECTORY_SEPARATOR, $class)
          . '.php';
    foreach (self::$dirs as $start) {
        $file = $start . DIRECTORY_SEPARATOR . $fn;
        if (self::loadFile($file)) {
            $success = TRUE;
            break;
        }
    }
    if (!$success) {
        if (!self::loadFile(__DIR__
            . DIRECTORY_SEPARATOR . $fn)) {
            throw new \Exception(
                self::UNABLE_TO_LOAD . ' ' . $class);
        }
    }
    return $success;
}
```

5. Next, the method loops through an array of directories we call `self::$dirs`, using each directory as a starting point for the derived filename. If not successful, as a last resort, the method attempts to load the file from the current directory. If even that is not successful, an `Exception` is thrown.

6. Next, we need a method that can add more directories to our list of directories to test. Notice that if the value provided is an array, `array_merge()` is used. Otherwise, we simply add the directory string to the `self::$dirs` array:

```
public static function addDirs($dirs)
{
    if (is_array($dirs)) {
        self::$dirs = array_merge(self::$dirs, $dirs);
    } else {
```

```
            self::$dirs[] = $dirs;
        }
    }
```

7. Then, we come to the most important part; we need to register our `autoload()` method as a **Standard PHP Library** (**SPL**) autoloader. This is accomplished using `spl_autoload_register()` with the `init()` method:

```
public static function init($dirs = array())
{
    if ($dirs) {
        self::addDirs($dirs);
    }
    if (self::$registered == 0) {
        spl_autoload_register(__CLASS__ . '::autoload');
        self::$registered++;
    }
}
```

8. At this point, we can define `__construct()`, which calls `self::init($dirs)`. This allows us to also create an instance of `Loader` if desired:

```
public function __construct($dirs = array())
{
    self::init($dirs);
}
```

How it works...

In order to use the autoloader class that we just defined, you will need to `require Loader.php`. If your namespace files are located in a directory other than the current one, you should also run `Loader::init()` and supply additional directory paths.

In order to make sure the autoloader works, we'll also need a test class. Here is a definition of `/path/to/cookbook/files/Application/Test/TestClass.php`:

```
<?php
namespace Application\Test;
class TestClass
{
    public function getTest()
    {
        return __METHOD__;
    }
}
```

Now create a sample `chap_01_autoload_test.php` code file to test the autoloader:

```
<?php
require __DIR__ . '/../Application/Autoload/Loader.php';
Application\Autoload\Loader::init(__DIR__ . '/..');
```

Next, get an instance of a class that has not already been loaded:

```
$test = new Application\Test\TestClass();
echo $test->getTest();
```

Finally, try to get a `fake` class that does not exist. Note that this will throw an error:

```
$fake = new Application\Test\FakeClass();
echo $fake->getTest();
```

Hoovering a website

Very frequently, it is of interest to scan a website and extract information from specific tags. This basic mechanism can be used to trawl the web in search of useful bits of information. At other times you need to get a list of `<IMG>` tags and the `SRC` attribute, or `<A>` tags and the corresponding `HREF` attribute. The possibilities are endless.

How to do it...

1. First of all, we need to grab the contents of the target website. At first glance it seems that we should make a cURL request, or simply use `file_get_contents()`. The problem with these approaches is that we will end up having to do a massive amount of string manipulation, most likely having to make inordinate use of the dreaded regular expression. In order to avoid all of this, we'll simply take advantage of an already existing PHP 7 class `DOMDocument`. So we create a `DOMDocument` instance, setting it to **UTF-8**. We don't care about whitespace, and use the handy `loadHTMLFile()` method to load the contents of the website into the object:

   ```
   public function getContent($url)
   {
       if (!$this->content) {
           if (stripos($url, 'http') !== 0) {
               $url = 'http://' . $url;
           }
           $this->content = new DOMDocument('1.0', 'utf-8');
           $this->content->preserveWhiteSpace = FALSE;
           // @ used to suppress warnings generated from
           // improperly configured web pages
           @$this->content->loadHTMLFile($url);
       }
   ```

```
        return $this->content;
    }
```

Note that we precede the call to the `loadHTMLFile()` method with an `@`. This is not done to obscure bad coding (`!`) as was often the case in PHP 5! Rather, the `@` suppresses notices generated when the parser encounters poorly written HTML. Presumably, we could capture the notices and log them, possibly giving our `Hoover` class a diagnostic capability as well.

2. Next, we need to extract the tags which are of interest. We use the `getElementsByTagName()` method for this purpose. If we wish to extract *all* tags, we can supply `*` as an argument:

```
public function getTags($url, $tag)
{
    $count    = 0;
    $result   = array();
    $elements = $this->getContent($url)
                ->getElementsByTagName($tag);
    foreach ($elements as $node) {
        $result[$count]['value'] = trim(
            preg_replace('/\s+/', ' ', $node->nodeValue));
        if ($node->hasAttributes()) {
            foreach ($node->attributes as $name => $attr)
            {
                $result[$count]['attributes'][$name] =
                    $attr->value;
            }
        }
        $count++;
    }
    return $result;
}
```

3. It might also be of interest to extract certain attributes rather than tags. Accordingly, we define another method for this purpose. In this case, we need to parse through all tags and use `getAttribute()`. You'll notice that there is a parameter for the DNS domain. We've added this in order to keep the scan within the same domain (if you're building a web tree, for example):

```
public function getAttribute($url, $attr, $domain = NULL)
{
    $result   = array();
    $elements = $this->getContent($url)
                ->getElementsByTagName('*');
    foreach ($elements as $node) {
```

```
                if ($node->hasAttribute($attr)) {
                    $value = $node->getAttribute($attr);
                    if ($domain) {
                        if (stripos($value, $domain) !== FALSE) {
                            $result[] = trim($value);
                        }
                    } else {
                        $result[] = trim($value);
                    }
                }
            }
            return $result;
        }
```

How it works...

In order to use the new `Hoover` class, initialize the autoloader (described previously) and create an instance of the `Hoover` class. You can then run the `Hoover::getTags()` method to produce an array of tags from the URL you specify as an argument.

Here is a block of code from `chap_01_vacuuming_website.php` that uses the `Hoover` class to scan the O'Reilly website for `<A>` tags:

```
<?php
// modify as needed
define('DEFAULT_URL', 'http://oreilly.com/');
define('DEFAULT_TAG', 'a');

require __DIR__ . '/../Application/Autoload/Loader.php';
Application\Autoload\Loader::init(__DIR__ . '/..');

// get "vacuum" class
$vac = new Application\Web\Hoover();

// NOTE: the PHP 7 null coalesce operator is used
$url = strip_tags($_GET['url'] ?? DEFAULT_URL);
$tag = strip_tags($_GET['tag'] ?? DEFAULT_TAG);

echo 'Dump of Tags: ' . PHP_EOL;
var_dump($vac->getTags($url, $tag));
```

The output will look something like this:

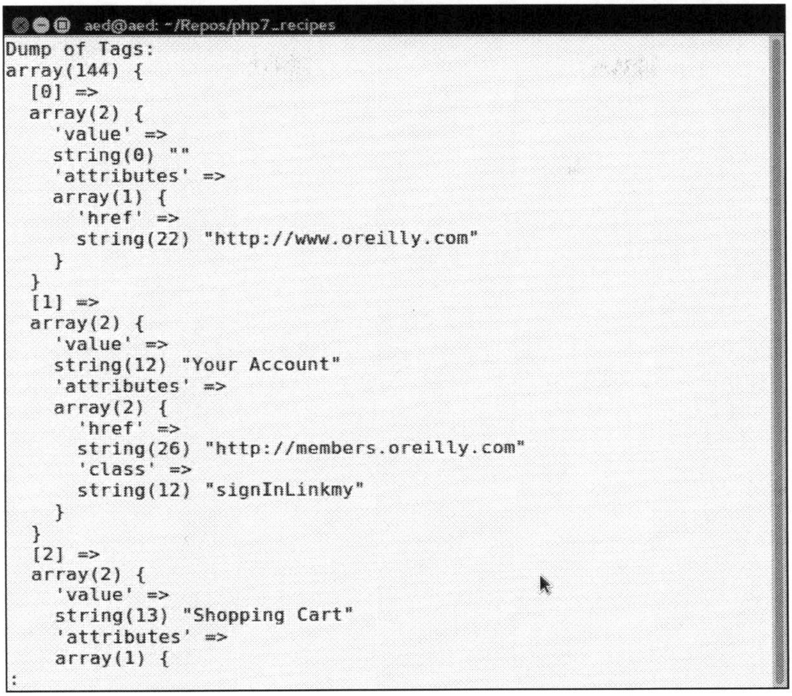

```
aed@aed: ~/Repos/php7_recipes
Dump of Tags:
array(144) {
  [0] =>
  array(2) {
    'value' =>
    string(0) ""
    'attributes' =>
    array(1) {
      'href' =>
      string(22) "http://www.oreilly.com"
    }
  }
  [1] =>
  array(2) {
    'value' =>
    string(12) "Your Account"
    'attributes' =>
    array(2) {
      'href' =>
      string(26) "http://members.oreilly.com"
      'class' =>
      string(12) "signInLinkmy"
    }
  }
  [2] =>
  array(2) {
    'value' =>
    string(13) "Shopping Cart"
    'attributes' =>
    array(1) {
:
```

See also

For more information on DOM, see the PHP reference page at `http://php.net/manual/en/class.domdocument.php`.

Building a deep web scanner

Sometimes you need to scan a website, but go one level deeper. For example, you want to build a web tree diagram of a website. This can be accomplished by looking for all `<A>` tags and following the `HREF` attributes to the next web page. Once you have acquired the child pages, you can then continue scanning in order to complete the tree.

How to do it...

1. A core component of a deep web scanner is a basic `Hoover` class, as described previously. The basic procedure presented in this recipe is to scan the target website and hoover up all the `HREF` attributes. For this purpose, we define a `Application\Web\Deep` class. We add a property that represents the DNS domain:

```
namespace Application\Web;
class Deep
{
    protected $domain;
```

2. Next, we define a method that will hoover the tags for each website represented in the scan list. In order to prevent the scanner from trawling the entire **World Wide Web** (**WWW**), we've limited the scan to the target domain. The reason why `yield from` has been added is because we need to yield the entire array produced by `Hoover::getTags()`. The `yield from` syntax allows us to treat the array as a sub-generator:

```
public function scan($url, $tag)
{
    $vac    = new Hoover();
    $scan   = $vac->getAttribute($url, 'href',
       $this->getDomain($url));
    $result = array();
    foreach ($scan as $subSite) {
        yield from $vac->getTags($subSite, $tag);
    }
    return count($scan);
}
```

The use of `yield from` turns the `scan()` method into a PHP 7 delegating generator. Normally, you would be inclined to store the results of the scan into an array. The problem, in this case, is that the amount of information retrieved could potentially be massive. Thus, it's better to immediately yield the results in order to conserve memory and to produce immediate results. Otherwise, there would be a lengthy wait, which would probably be followed by an out of memory error.

3. In order to keep within the same domain, we need a method that will return the domain from the URL. We use the convenient `parse_url()` function for this purpose:

```
public function getDomain($url)
{
    if (!$this->domain) {
```

```
            $this->domain = parse_url($url, PHP_URL_HOST);
        }
        return $this->domain;
    }
```

How it works...

First of all, go ahead and define the `Application\Web\Deep` class defined previously, as well as the `Application\Web\Hoover` class defined in the previous recipe.

Next, define a block of code from `chap_01_deep_scan_website.php` that sets up autoloading (as described earlier in this chapter):

```
<?php
// modify as needed
define('DEFAULT_URL', unlikelysource.com');
define('DEFAULT_TAG', 'img');

require __DIR__ . '/../../Application/Autoload/Loader.php';
Application\Autoload\Loader::init(__DIR__ . '/../..');
```

Next, get an instance of our new class:

```
$deep = new Application\Web\Deep();
```

At this point, you can retrieve URL and tag information from URL parameters. The PHP 7 `null coalesce` operator is useful for establishing fallback values:

```
$url = strip_tags($_GET['url'] ?? DEFAULT_URL);
$tag = strip_tags($_GET['tag'] ?? DEFAULT_TAG);
```

Some simple HTML will display results:

```
foreach ($deep->scan($url, $tag) as $item) {
    $src = $item['attributes']['src'] ?? NULL;
    if ($src && (stripos($src, 'png') || stripos($src, 'jpg'))) {
        printf('<br><img src="%s"/>', $src);
    }
}
```

See also

For more information on generators and `yield from`, please see the article at `http://php.net/manual/en/language.generators.syntax.php`.

Creating a PHP 5 to PHP 7 code converter

For the most part, PHP 5.x code can run unchanged on PHP 7. There are a few changes, however, that are classified as *backwards incompatible*. What this means is that if your PHP 5 code is written in a certain way, or uses functions that have been removed, your code will break, and you'll have a nasty error on your hands.

Getting ready

The *PHP 5 to PHP 7 Code Converter* does two things:

- Scans your code file and converts PHP 5 functionality that has been removed to its equivalent in PHP 7
- Adds comments with `// WARNING` where changes in language usage have occurred, but where a re-write is not possible

Please note that after running the converter, your code is *not* guaranteed to work in PHP 7. You will still have to review the `// WARNING` tags added. At the least, this recipe will give you a good head start converting your PHP 5 code to work in PHP 7.

The core of this recipe is the new PHP 7 `preg_replace_callback_array()` function. What this amazing function allows you to do is to present an array of regular expressions as keys, with the value representing an independent callback. You can then pass the string through a series of transformations. Not only that, the subject of the array of callbacks can *itself* be an array.

How to do it...

1. In a new class `Application\Parse\Convert`, we begin with a `scan()` method, which accepts a filename as an argument. It checks to see if the file exists. If so, it calls the PHP `file()` function, which loads the file into an array, with each array element representing one line:

```
public function scan($filename)
{
    if (!file_exists($filename)) {
        throw new Exception(
            self::EXCEPTION_FILE_NOT_EXISTS);
    }
    $contents = file($filename);
    echo 'Processing: ' . $filename . PHP_EOL;

    $result = preg_replace_callback_array( [
```

2. Next, we start passing a series of key/value pairs. The key is a regular expression, which is processed against the string. Any matches are passed to the callback, which is represented as the value part of the key/value pair. We check for opening and closing tags that have been removed from PHP 7:

```
// replace no-longer-supported opening tags
'!^\<\%(\n| )!' =>
    function ($match) {
        return '<?php' . $match[1];
    },

// replace no-longer-supported opening tags
'!^\<\%=(\n| )!' =>
    function ($match) {
        return '<?php echo ' . $match[1];
    },

// replace no-longer-supported closing tag
'!\%\>!' =>
    function ($match) {
        return '?>';
    },
```

3. Next is a series of warnings when certain operations are detected and there is a potential code-break between how they're handled in PHP 5 versus PHP 7. In all these cases, the code is not re-written. Instead, an inline comment with the word `WARNING` is added:

```
// changes in how $$xxx interpretation is handled
'!(.*?)\$\$!' =>
    function ($match) {
        return '// WARNING: variable interpolation
               . ' now occurs left-to-right' . PHP_EOL
               . '// see: http://php.net/manual/en/'
               . '// migration70.incompatible.php'
               . $match[0];
    },

// changes in how the list() operator is handled
'!(.*?)list(\s*?)?\(!' =>
    function ($match) {
        return '// WARNING: changes have been made '
               . 'in list() operator handling.'
               . 'See: http://php.net/manual/en/'
               . 'migration70.incompatible.php'
               . $match[0];
```

```
        },

    // instances of \u{
    '!(.*?)\\\u\{!' =>
        function ($match) {
        return '// WARNING: \\u{xxx} is now considered '
               . 'unicode escape syntax' . PHP_EOL
               . '// see: http://php.net/manual/en/'
               . 'migration70.new-features.php'
               . '#migration70.new-features.unicode-'
               . 'codepoint-escape-syntax' . PHP_EOL
               . $match[0];
    },

    // relying upon set_error_handler()
    '!(.*?)set_error_handler(\s*?)?.*\(!' =>
        function ($match) {
            return '// WARNING: might not '
                   . 'catch all errors'
                   . '// see: http://php.net/manual/en/'
                   . '// language.errors.php7.php'
                   . $match[0];
        },

    // session_set_save_handler(xxx)
    '!(.*?)session_set_save_handler(\s*?)?\((.*?)\)!' =>
        function ($match) {
            if (isset($match[3])) {
                return '// WARNING: a bug introduced in'
                       . 'PHP 5.4 which '
                       . 'affects the handler assigned by '
                       . 'session_set_save_handler() and '
                       . 'where ignore_user_abort() is TRUE
                       . 'has been fixed in PHP 7.'
                       . 'This could potentially break '
                       . 'your code under '
                       . 'certain circumstances.' . PHP_EOL
                       . 'See: http://php.net/manual/en/'
                       . 'migration70.incompatible.php'
                       . $match[0];
            } else {
                return $match[0];
            }
        },
```

4. Any attempts to use << or >> with a negative operator, or beyond 64, is wrapped in a `try { xxx } catch() { xxx }` block, looking for an `ArithmeticError` to be thrown:

```
// wraps bit shift operations in try / catch
'!^(.*?)(\d+\s*(\<\<|\>\>)\s*-?\d+)(.*?)$!' =>
    function ($match) {
        return '// WARNING: negative and '
               . 'out-of-range bitwise '
               . 'shift operations will now
               . 'throw an ArithmeticError' . PHP_EOL
               . 'See: http://php.net/manual/en/'
               . 'migration70.incompatible.php'
               . 'try {' . PHP_EOL
               . "\t" . $match[0] . PHP_EOL
               . '} catch (\\ArithmeticError $e) {'
               . "\t" . 'error_log("File:"
               . $e->getFile()
               . " Message:" . $e->getMessage());'
               . '}' . PHP_EOL;
    },
```

PHP 7 has changed how errors are handled. In some cases, errors are moved into a similar classification as exceptions, and can be caught! Both the `Error` and the `Exception` class implement the `Throwable` interface. If you want to catch either an `Error` or an `Exception`, catch `Throwable`.

5. Next, the converter rewrites any usage of `call_user_method*()`, which has been removed in PHP 7. These are replaced with the equivalent using `call_user_func*()`:

```
// replaces "call_user_method()" with
// "call_user_func()"
'!call_user_method\((.*?),(.*?)(,.*?)\)(\b|;)!' =>
    function ($match) {
        $params = $match[3] ?? '';
        return '// WARNING: call_user_method() has '
                  . 'been removed from PHP 7' . PHP_EOL
                  . 'call_user_func([' . trim($match[2]) . ','
                  . trim($match[1]) . ']' . $params . ');';
    },

// replaces "call_user_method_array()"
// with "call_user_func_array()"
'!call_user_method_array\((.*?),(.*?),(.*?)\)(\b|;)!' =>
```

```
            function ($match) {
                return '// WARNING: call_user_method_array()'
                       . 'has been removed from PHP 7'
                       . PHP_EOL
                       . 'call_user_func_array(['
                       . trim($match[2]) . ','
                       . trim($match[1]) . '], '
                       . $match[3] . ');';
            },
```

6. Finally, any attempt to use `preg_replace()` with the `/e` modifier is rewritten using a `preg_replace_callback()`:

```
     '!^(.*?)preg_replace.*?/e(.*?)$!' =>
    function ($match) {
        $last = strrchr($match[2], ',');
        $arg2 = substr($match[2], 2, -1 * (strlen($last)));
        $arg1 = substr($match[0],
                       strlen($match[1]) + 12,
                       -1 * (strlen($arg2) + strlen($last)));
         $arg1 = trim($arg1, '(');
         $arg1 = str_replace('/e', '/', $arg1);
         $arg3 = '// WARNING: preg_replace() "/e" modifier
                   . 'has been removed from PHP 7'
                   . PHP_EOL
                   . $match[1]
                   . 'preg_replace_callback('
                   . $arg1
                   . 'function ($m) { return '
                   .    str_replace('$1','$m', $match[1])
                   .      trim($arg2, '"\'') . '; }, '
                   .      trim($last, ',');
         return str_replace('$1', '$m', $arg3);
    },

        // end array
        ],

        // this is the target of the transformations
        $contents
    );
    // return the result as a string
    return implode('', $result);
}
```

How it works...

To use the converter, run the following code from the command line. You'll need to supply the filename of the PHP 5 code to be scanned as an argument.

This block of code, `chap_01_php5_to_php7_code_converter.php`, run from the command line, calls the converter:

```
<?php
// get filename to scan from command line
$filename = $argv[1] ?? '';

if (!$filename) {
    echo 'No filename provided' . PHP_EOL;
    echo 'Usage: ' . PHP_EOL;
    echo __FILE__ . ' <filename>' . PHP_EOL;
    exit;
}

// setup class autoloading
require __DIR__ . '/../Application/Autoload/Loader.php';

// add current directory to the path
Application\Autoload\Loader::init(__DIR__ . '/..');

// get "deep scan" class
$convert = new Application\Parse\Convert();
echo $convert->scan($filename);
echo PHP_EOL;
```

See also

For more information on backwards incompatible changes, please refer to `http://php.net/manual/en/migration70.incompatible.php`.

2

Using PHP 7 High Performance Features

In this chapter we will discuss and understand the syntax differences between PHP 5 and PHP 7, featuring the following recipes:

- Understanding the abstract syntax tree
- Understanding differences in parsing
- Understanding differences in `foreach()` handling
- Improving performance using PHP 7 enhancements
- Iterating through a massive file
- Uploading a spreadsheet into a database
- Recursive directory iterator

Introduction

In this chapter we will move directly into PHP 7, presenting recipes that take advantage of new high performance features. First, however, we will present a series of smaller recipes that serve to illustrate the differences in how PHP 7 handles parameter parsing, syntax, a `foreach()` loop, and other enhancements. Before we go into depth in this chapter, let's discuss some basic differences between PHP 5 and PHP 7.

PHP 7 introduced a new layer referred to as the **Abstract Syntax Tree** (**AST**), which effectively decouples the parsing process from the pseudo-compile process. Although the new layer has little or no impact on performance, it gives the language a new uniformity of syntax, which was not possible previously.

Another benefit of AST is the process of *dereferencing*. Dereferencing, simply put, refers to the ability to immediately acquire a property from, or run a method of, an object, immediately access an array element, and immediately execute a callback. In PHP 5 such support was inconsistent and incomplete. To execute a callback, for example, often you would first need to assign the callback or anonymous function to a variable, and then execute it. In PHP 7 you can execute it immediately.

Understanding the abstract syntax tree

As a developer, it might be of interest for you to be free from certain syntax restrictions imposed in PHP 5 and earlier. Aside from the uniformity of the syntax mentioned previously, where you'll see the most improvement in syntax is the ability to call any return value, which is **callable** by simply appending an extra set of parentheses. Also, you'll be able to directly access any array element when the return value is an array.

How to do it...

1. Any function or method that returns a callback can be immediately executed by simply appending parentheses `()` (with or without parameters). An element can be immediately dereferenced from any function or method that returns an array by simply indicating the element using square brackets `[];`. In the short (but trivial) example shown next, the function `test()` returns an array. The array contains six anonymous functions. `$a` has a value of `$t`. `$$a` is interpreted as `$test`:

```
function test()
{
    return [
        1 => function () { return [
            1 => function ($a) { return 'Level 1/1:' . ++$a; },
            2 => function ($a) { return 'Level 1/2:' . ++$a; },
        ];},
        2 => function () { return [
            1 => function ($a) { return 'Level 2/1:' . ++$a; },
            2 => function ($a) { return 'Level 2/2:' . ++$a; },
        ];}
    ];
}

$a = 't';
$t = 'test';
echo $$a()[1]()[2](100);
```

2. AST allows us to issue the `echo $$a()[1]()[2](100)` command. This is parsed left-to-right, which executes as follows:
    - `$$a()` interprets as `test()`, which returns an array
    - `[1]` dereferences array element `1`, which returns a callback
    - `()` executes this callback, which returns an array of two elements
    - `[2]` dereferences array element `2`, which returns a callback
    - `(100)` executes this callback, supplying a value of `100`, which returns `Level 1/2:101`

[Such a statement is not possible in PHP 5: a parse error would be returned.]

3. The following is a more substantive example that takes advantage of AST syntax to define a data filtering and validating class. First of all, we define the `Application\Web\Securityclass`. In the constructor, we build and define two arrays. The first array consists of filter callbacks. The second array has validation callbacks:

```
public function __construct()
  {
    $this->filter = [
      'striptags' => function ($a) { return strip_tags($a); },
      'digits'    => function ($a) { return preg_replace(
      '/[^0-9]/', '', $a); },
      'alpha'     => function ($a) { return preg_replace(
      '/[^A-Z]/i', '', $a); }
    ];
    $this->validate = [
      'alnum'  => function ($a) { return ctype_alnum($a); },
      'digits' => function ($a) { return ctype_digit($a); },
      'alpha'  => function ($a) { return ctype_alpha($a); }
    ];
  }
```

4. We want to be able to call this functionality in a *developer-friendly* manner. Thus, if we want to filter digits, then it would be ideal to run a command such as this:

```
$security->filterDigits($item));
```

5. To accomplish this we define the magic method `__call()`, which gives us access to non-existent methods:

```
public function __call($method, $params)
{
```

```
        preg_match('/^(filter|validate)(.*?)$/i', $method, $matches);
        $prefix   = $matches[1] ?? '';
        $function = strtolower($matches[2] ?? '');
        if ($prefix && $function) {
          return $this->$prefix[$function]($params[0]);
        }
        return $value;
      }
```

We use `preg_match()` to match the `$method` param against `filter` or `validate`. The second sub-match will then be converted into an array key in either `$this->filter` or `$this->validate`. If both sub-patterns produce a sub-match, we assign the first sub-match to `$prefix`, and the second sub-match `$function`. These end up as variable parameters when executing the appropriate callback.

Don't go too crazy with this stuff!

As you revel in your new found freedom of expression, made possible by AST, be sure to keep in mind that the code you end up writing could, in the long run, be extremely cryptic. This will ultimately cause long-term maintenance problems.

How it works...

First of all, we create a sample file, `chap_02_web_filtering_ast_example.php`, to take advantage of the autoloading class defined in *Chapter 1, Building the Foundation*, to obtain an instance of `Application\Web\Security`:

```
require __DIR__ . '/../Application/Autoload/Loader.php';
Application\Autoload\Loader::init(__DIR__ . '/..');
$security = new Application\Web\Security();
```

Next, we define a block of test data:

```
$data = [
    '<ul><li>Lots</li><li>of</li><li>Tags</li></ul>',
    12345,
    'This is a string',
    'String with number 12345',
];
```

Finally, we call each filter and validator for each item of test data:

```
foreach ($data as $item) {
  echo 'ORIGINAL: ' . $item . PHP_EOL;
  echo 'FILTERING' . PHP_EOL;
```

```
    printf('%12s : %s' . PHP_EOL,'Strip Tags',
      $security->filterStripTags($item));
    printf('%12s : %s' . PHP_EOL, 'Digits',
      $security->filterDigits($item));
    printf('%12s : %s' . PHP_EOL, 'Alpha',
      $security->filterAlpha($item));

    echo 'VALIDATORS' . PHP_EOL;
    printf('%12s : %s' . PHP_EOL, 'Alnum',
    ($security->validateAlnum($item))  ? 'T' : 'F');
    printf('%12s : %s' . PHP_EOL, 'Digits',
    ($security->validateDigits($item)) ? 'T' : 'F');
    printf('%12s : %s' . PHP_EOL, 'Alpha',
    ($security->validateAlpha($item))  ? 'T' : 'F');
  }
```

Here is the output of some input strings:

```
aed@aed: ~/Repos/php7_recipes/source/chapter02
ORIGINAL: <ul><li>Lots</li><li>of</li><li>Tags</li></ul>
FILTERING
  Strip Tags : LotsofTags
      Digits :
       Alpha : ulliLotsliliofliliTagsliul
VALIDATORS
       Alnum : F
      Digits : F
       Alpha : F
ORIGINAL: 12345
FILTERING
  Strip Tags : 12345
      Digits : 12345
       Alpha :
VALIDATORS
       Alnum : T
      Digits : T
       Alpha : F
ORIGINAL: This is a string
FILTERING
  Strip Tags : This is a string
      Digits :
       Alpha : Thisisastring
VALIDATORS
       Alnum : F
      Digits : F
       Alpha : F
ORIGINAL: String with number 12345
FILTERING
  Strip Tags : String with number 12345
      Digits : 12345
       Alpha : Stringwithnumber
VALIDATORS
       Alnum : F
      Digits : F
       Alpha : F
aed@aed:~/Repos/php7_recipes/source/chapter02$
```

See also

For more information on AST, please consult the RFC that addresses the **Abstract Syntax Tree**, which can be viewed at `https://wiki.php.net/rfc/abstract_syntax_tree`.

Understanding differences in parsing

In PHP 5, expressions on the right side of an assignment operation were parsed *right-to-left*. In PHP 7, parsing is consistently *left-to-right*.

How to do it...

1. A variable-variable is a way of indirectly referencing a value. In the following example, first `$$foo` is interpreted as `${$bar}`. The final return value is thus the value of `$bar` instead of the direct value of `$foo` (which would be `bar`):

   ```
   $foo = 'bar';
   $bar = 'baz';
   echo $$foo; // returns  'baz';
   ```

2. In the next example we have a variable-variable `$$foo`, which references a multi-dimensional array with a `bar key` and a `baz sub-key`:

   ```
   $foo = 'bar';
   $bar = ['bar' => ['baz' => 'bat']];
   // returns 'bat'
   echo $$foo['bar']['baz'];
   ```

3. In PHP 5, parsing occurs right-to-left, which means the PHP engine would be looking for an `$foo array`, with a `bar key` and a `baz`. sub-key The return value of the element would then be interpreted to obtain the final value `${$foo['bar']['baz']}`.
4. In PHP 7, however, parsing is consistently left-to-right, which means that `$foo` is interpreted first `($$foo)['bar']['baz']`.
5. In the next example you can see that `$foo->$bar['bada']` is interpreted quite differently in PHP 5, compared with PHP 7. In the following example, PHP 5 would first interpret `$bar['bada']`, and reference this return value against a `$foo object instance`. In PHP 7, on the other hand, parsing is consistently left-to-right, which means that `$foo->$bar` is interpreted first, and expects an array with a `bada element`. You will also note, incidentally, that this example uses the PHP 7 *anonymous class* feature:

   ```
   // PHP 5: $foo->{$bar['bada']}
   // PHP 7: ($foo->$bar)['bada']
   $bar = 'baz';
   // $foo = new class
   ```

```
{
    public $baz = ['bada' => 'boom'];
};
// returns 'boom'
echo $foo->$bar['bada'];
```

6. The last example is the same as the one immediately above, except that the return value is expected to be a callback, which is then immediately executed as follows:

```
// PHP 5: $foo->{$bar['bada']}()
// PHP 7: ($foo->$bar)['bada']()
$bar = 'baz';
// NOTE: this example uses the new PHP 7 anonymous class feature
$foo = new class
{
     public function __construct()
    {
        $this->baz = ['bada' => function () { return 'boom'; }];
    }
};
// returns 'boom'
echo $foo->$bar['bada']();
```

How it works...

Place the code examples illustrated in 1 and 2 into a single PHP file that you can call `chap_02_understanding_diffs_in_parsing.php`. Execute the script first using PHP 5, and you will notice that a series of errors will result, as follows:

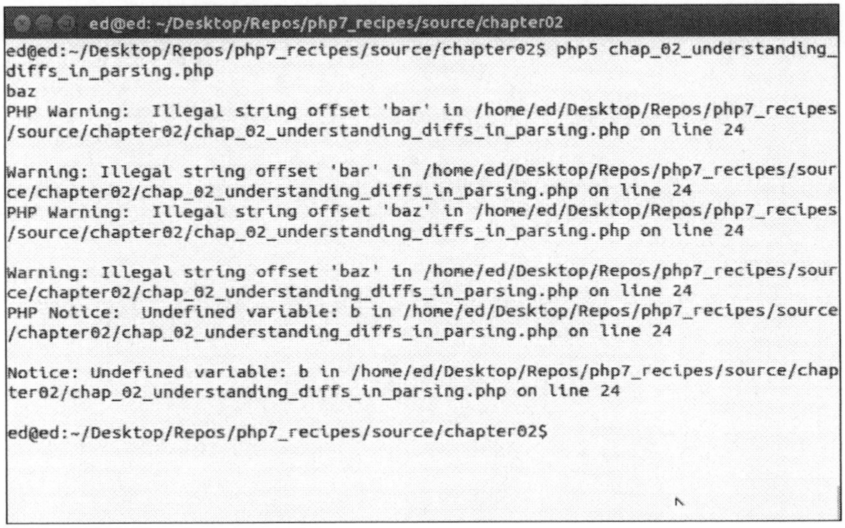

```
ed@ed: ~/Desktop/Repos/php7_recipes/source/chapter02
ed@ed:~/Desktop/Repos/php7_recipes/source/chapter02$ php5 chap_02_understanding_
diffs_in_parsing.php
baz
PHP Warning:  Illegal string offset 'bar' in /home/ed/Desktop/Repos/php7_recipes
/source/chapter02/chap_02_understanding_diffs_in_parsing.php on line 24

Warning: Illegal string offset 'bar' in /home/ed/Desktop/Repos/php7_recipes/sour
ce/chapter02/chap_02_understanding_diffs_in_parsing.php on line 24
PHP Warning:  Illegal string offset 'baz' in /home/ed/Desktop/Repos/php7_recipes
/source/chapter02/chap_02_understanding_diffs_in_parsing.php on line 24

Warning: Illegal string offset 'baz' in /home/ed/Desktop/Repos/php7_recipes/sour
ce/chapter02/chap_02_understanding_diffs_in_parsing.php on line 24
PHP Notice:  Undefined variable: b in /home/ed/Desktop/Repos/php7_recipes/source
/chapter02/chap_02_understanding_diffs_in_parsing.php on line 24

Notice: Undefined variable: b in /home/ed/Desktop/Repos/php7_recipes/source/chap
ter02/chap_02_understanding_diffs_in_parsing.php on line 24

ed@ed:~/Desktop/Repos/php7_recipes/source/chapter02$
```

The reason for the errors is that PHP 5 parses inconsistently, and arrives at the wrong conclusion regarding the state of the variable variables requested (as previously mentioned). Now you can go ahead and add the remaining examples, as shown in steps 5 and 6. If you then run this script in PHP 7, the results described will appear, as shown here:

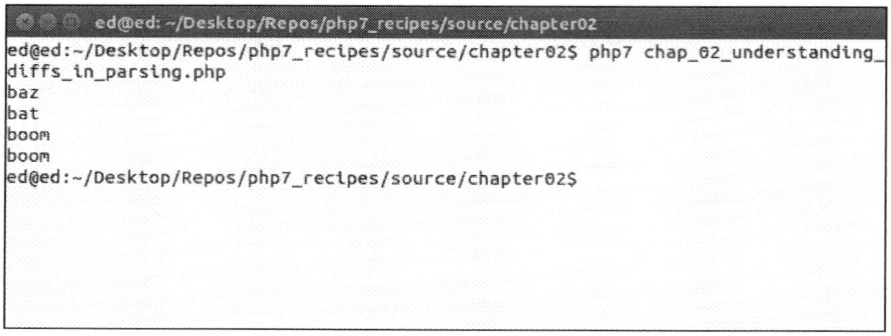

```
ed@ed: ~/Desktop/Repos/php7_recipes/source/chapter02
ed@ed:~/Desktop/Repos/php7_recipes/source/chapter02$ php7 chap_02_understanding_diffs_in_parsing.php
baz
bat
boom
boom
ed@ed:~/Desktop/Repos/php7_recipes/source/chapter02$
```

See also

For more information on parsing, please consult the RFC, which addresses **Uniform Variable Syntax**, and can be viewed at `https://wiki.php.net/rfc/uniform_variable_syntax`.

Understanding differences in foreach() handling

In certain relatively obscure circumstances, the behavior of code inside a `foreach()` loop will vary between PHP 5 and PHP 7. First of all, there have been massive internal improvements, which means that in terms of sheer speed, processing inside the `foreach()` loop will be much faster running under PHP 7, compared with PHP 5. Problems that are noticed in PHP 5 include the use of `current()`, and `unset()` on the array inside the `foreach()` loop. Other problems have to do with passing values by reference while manipulating the array itself.

How to do it...

1. Consider the following block of code:

```
$a = [1, 2, 3];
foreach ($a as $v) {
  printf("%2d\n", $v);
  unset($a[1]);
}
```

2. In both PHP 5 and 7, the output would appear as follows:

```
1
2
3
```

3. If you add an assignment before the loop, however, the behavior changes:

```
$a = [1, 2, 3];
$b = &$a;
foreach ($a as $v) {
  printf("%2d\n", $v);
  unset($a[1]);
}
```

4. Compare the output of PHP 5 and 7:

PHP 5	PHP 7
1 3	1 2 3

5. Working with functions that reference the internal array pointer also caused inconsistent behavior in PHP 5. Take the following code example:

```
$a = [1,2,3];
foreach($a as &$v) {
    printf("%2d - %2d\n", $v, current($a));
}
```

Every array has an internal pointer to its `current` element starting from `1`, `current()` returns the current element in an array.

6. Notice that the output running in PHP 7 is normalized and consistent:

PHP 5	PHP 7
1 - 2 2 - 3 3 - 0	1 - 1 2 - 1 3 - 1

7. Adding a new element inside the `foreach()` loop, once the array iteration by reference is complete, is also problematic in PHP 5. This behavior has been made consistent in PHP 7. The following code example demonstrates this:

```
$a = [1];
foreach($a as &$v) {
    printf("%2d -\n", $v);
    $a[1]=2;
}
```

8. We will observe the following output:

PHP 5	**PHP 7**
1 -	**1** - **2** -

9. Another example of bad PHP 5 behavior addressed in PHP 7, during array iteration by reference, is the use of functions that modify the array, such as `array_push()`, `array_pop()`, `array_shift()`, and `array_unshift()`.

   Have a look at this example:

```
$a=[1,2,3,4];
foreach($a as &$v) {
    echo "$v\n";
    array_pop($a);
}
```

10. You will observe the following output:

PHP 5	**PHP 7**
1 **2** **1** **1**	**1** **2**

11. Finally, we have a case where you are iterating through an array by reference, with a nested `foreach()` loop, which itself iterates on the same array by reference. In PHP 5 this construct simply did not work. In PHP 7 this has been fixed. The following block of code demonstrates this behavior:

```
$a = [0, 1, 2, 3];
foreach ($a as &$x) {
        foreach ($a as &$y) {
          echo "$x - $y\n";
          if ($x == 0 && $y == 1) {
            unset($a[1]);
```

```
                unset($a[2]);
            }
        }
    }
```

12. And here is the output:

PHP 5	PHP 7
0 - 0	0 - 0
0 - 1	0 - 1
0 - 3	0 - 3
	3 - 0
	3 -3

How it works...

Add these code examples to a single PHP file, `chap_02_foreach.php`. Run the script under PHP 5 from the command line. The expected output is as follows:

```
ed@ed: ~/Desktop/Repos/php7_recipes/source/chapter02
PHP VERSION: 5.6.22
unset() in foreach()
 1
 2
 3
unset() in foreach() after assignment by reference
 1
 3
current() in foreach()
 1 -  2
 2 -  3
 3 -  0
adding new element in foreach()
 1 -
array_pop() in foreach()
1
2
1
1
reference in foreach()
0 - 0
0 - 1
0 - 3
ed@ed:~/Desktop/Repos/php7_recipes/source/chapter02$
```

Run the same script under PHP 7 and notice the difference:

```
ed@ed: ~/Desktop/Repos/php7_recipes/source/chapter02
PHP VERSION: 7.0.7
unset() in foreach()
 1
 2
 3
unset() in foreach() after assignment by reference
 1
 2
 3
current() in foreach()
 1 -  1
 2 -  1
 3 -  1
adding new element in foreach()
 1 -
 2 -
array_pop() in foreach()
1
2
reference in foreach()
0 - 0
0 - 1
0 - 3
3 - 0
3 - 3
ed@ed:~/Desktop/Repos/php7_recipes/source/chapter02$
```

See also

For more information, consult the RFC addressing this issue, which was accepted. A write-up on this RFC can be found at: `https://wiki.php.net/rfc/php7_foreach`.

Improving performance using PHP 7 enhancements

One trend that developers are taking advantage of is the use of **anonymous functions**. One classic problem, when dealing with anonymous functions, is to write them in such a way that any object can be bound to `$this` and the function will still work. The approach used in PHP 5 code is to use `bindTo()`. In PHP 7, a new method, `call()`, was added, which offers similar functionality, but vastly improved performance.

How to do it...

To take advantage of `call()`, execute an anonymous function in a lengthy loop. In this example, we will demonstrate an anonymous function, that scans through a log file, identifying IP addresses sorted by how frequently they appear:

1. First, we define a `Application\Web\Access class`. In the constructor, we accept a filename as an argument. The log file is opened as an `SplFileObject` and assigned to `$this->log`:

```
Namespace Application\Web;

use Exception;
use SplFileObject;
class Access
{
  const ERROR_UNABLE = 'ERROR: unable to open file';
  protected $log;
  public $frequency = array();
  public function __construct($filename)
  {
    if (!file_exists($filename)) {
      $message = __METHOD__ . ' : ' . self::ERROR_UNABLE . PHP_EOL;
      $message .= strip_tags($filename) . PHP_EOL;
      throw new Exception($message);
    }
    $this->log = new SplFileObject($filename, 'r');
  }
```

2. Next, we define a generator that iterates through the file, line by line:

```
public function fileIteratorByLine()
{
  $count = 0;
  while (!$this->log->eof()) {
    yield $this->log->fgets();
    $count++;
  }
  return $count;
}
```

3. Finally, we define a method that looks for, and extracts as a sub-match, an IP address:

```
public function getIp($line)
{
  preg_match('/(\d{1,3}\.\d{1,3}\.\d{1,3}\.\d{1,3})/',
    $line, $match);
  return $match[1] ?? '';
  }
}
```

How it works...

First of all, we define a calling program, `chap_02_performance_using_php7_enchancement_call.php`, that takes advantage of the autoloading class defined in *Chapter 1 , Building a Foundation,* to obtain an instance of `Application\Web\Access`:

```
define('LOG_FILES', '/var/log/apache2/*access*.log');
require __DIR__ . '/../Application/Autoload/Loader.php';
Application\Autoload\Loader::init(__DIR__ . '/..');
```

Next we define the anonymous function, which processes one line in the log file. If an IP address is detected, it becomes a key in the `$frequency array`, and the current value for this key is incremented:

```
// define functions
$freq = function ($line) {
  $ip = $this->getIp($line);
  if ($ip) {
    echo '.';
    $this->frequency[$ip] =
    (isset($this->frequency[$ip])) ? $this->frequency[$ip] + 1 : 1;
  }
};
```

We then loop through the iteration of lines in each log file found, processing IP addresses:

```
foreach (glob(LOG_FILES) as $filename) {
  echo PHP_EOL . $filename . PHP_EOL;
  // access class
  $access = new Application\Web\Access($filename);
  foreach ($access->fileIteratorByLine() as $line) {
    $freq->call($access, $line);
  }
}
```

> You can actually do the same thing in PHP 5. Two lines of code are required, however:
>
> ```
> $func = $freq->bindTo($access);
> $func($line);
> ```
>
> Performance is 20% to 50% slower than using `call()` in PHP 7.

Finally, we reverse-sort the array, but maintain the keys. The output is produced in a simple `foreach()` loop:

```
arsort($access->frequency);
foreach ($access->frequency as $key => $value) {
  printf('%16s : %6d' . PHP_EOL, $key, $value);
}
```

The output will vary depending on which `access.log` you process. Here is a sample:

```
aed@aed: ~/Repos/php7_recipes/source/chapter02
 208.115.220.141 :    302
    207.236.68.2 :     51
   75.108.135.28 :     45
     65.170.41.5 :     45
  108.89.210.232 :     45
  208.115.113.89 :     24
 209.236.161.254 :     23
    71.72.21.154 :     16
   199.21.99.114 :     16
   66.249.74.187 :     11
    157.55.35.87 :     11
  208.115.111.73 :      9
   188.92.76.167 :      8
   184.22.188.40 :      5
     124.115.1.7 :      5
  119.147.75.140 :      5
   82.165.136.86 :      5
  183.62.115.227 :      5
  85.102.158.186 :      4
   178.77.126.55 :      4
    66.249.74.29 :      4
 178.170.123.135 :      4
   157.56.93.222 :      2
  178.255.215.78 :      2
 173.199.114.219 :      2
   41.107.33.187 :      2
    69.30.238.26 :      2
   217.69.133.67 :      2
   97.74.144.110 :      2
   64.246.161.42 :      2
:
```

There's more...

Many of the PHP 7 performance improvements have nothing to do with new features and functions. Rather, they take the form of internal improvements, which are *invisible* until you start running your programs. Here is a short list of improvements that fall into this category:

Feature	More info:	Notes
Fast parameter parsing	`https://wiki.php.net/rfc/fast_zpp`	In PHP 5, parameters provided to functions have to be parsed for every single function call. The parameters were passed in as a string, and parsed in a manner similar to the `scanf()` function. In PHP 7 this process has been optimized and made much more efficient, resulting in a significant performance improvement. The improvement is difficult to measure, but seems to be in the region of 6%.
PHP NG	`https://wiki.php.net/rfc/phpng`	The PHP **NG** (**Next Generation**) initiative represents a rewrite of most of the PHP language. It retains existing functionality, but involves any and all time-savings and efficiency measures imaginable. Data structures have been compacted, and memory is used more efficiently. Just one change, which affects array handling, for example, has resulted in a significant performance increase, while at the same time greatly reducing memory usage.

Feature	More info:	Notes
Removing dead weight	`https://wiki.php.net/rfc/removal_of_dead_sapis_and_exts`	There were approximately two dozen extensions that fell into one of these categories: deprecated, no longer maintained, unmaintained dependencies, or not ported to PHP 7. A vote by the group of core developers determined to remove about 2/3 or the extensions on the "short list". This results in reduced overhead and faster overall future development of the PHP language.

Iterating through a massive file

Functions such as `file_get_contents()` and `file()` are quick and easy to use however, owing to memory limitations, they quickly cause problems when dealing with massive files. The default setting for the `php.ini memory_limit` setting is 128 megabytes. Accordingly, any file larger than this will not be loaded.

Another consideration when parsing through massive files is how quickly does your function or class method produce output? When producing user output, for example, although it might at first glance seem better to accumulate output in an array. You would then output it all at once for improved efficiency. Unfortunately, this might have an adverse impact on the user experience. It might be better to create a **generator**, and use the `yield keyword` to produce immediate results.

How to do it...

As mentioned before, the `file*` functions (that is, `file_get_contents()`), are not suitable for large files. The simple reason is that these functions, at one point, have the entire contents of the file represented in memory. Accordingly, the focus of this recipe will be on the `f*` functions (that is, `fopen()`).

In a slight twist, however, instead of using the `f*` functions directly, instead we will use the `SplFileObject` class, which is included in the **SPL** (**Standard PHP Library**):

1. First, we define a `Application\Iterator\LargeFile` class with the appropriate properties and constants:

```
namespace Application\Iterator;

use Exception;
use InvalidArgumentException;
use SplFileObject;
use NoRewindIterator;

class LargeFile
{
  const ERROR_UNABLE = 'ERROR: Unable to open file';
  const ERROR_TYPE    = 'ERROR: Type must be "ByLength",
    "ByLine" or "Csv"';
  protected $file;
  protected $allowedTypes = ['ByLine', 'ByLength', 'Csv'];
```

2. We then define a `__construct()` method that accepts a filename as an argument and populates the `$file` property with an `SplFileObject` instance. This is also a good place to throw an exception if the file does not exist:

```
public function __construct($filename, $mode = 'r')
{
  if (!file_exists($filename)) {
    $message = __METHOD__ . ' : ' . self::ERROR_UNABLE . PHP_EOL;
    $message .= strip_tags($filename) . PHP_EOL;
    throw new Exception($message);
  }
  $this->file = new SplFileObject($filename, $mode);
}
```

3. Next we define a method `fileIteratorByLine()method` which uses `fgets()` to read one line of the file at a time. It's not a bad idea to create a complimentary `fileIteratorByLength()` method that does the same thing but uses `fread()` instead. The method that uses `fgets()` would be suitable for text files that include linefeeds. The other method could be used if parsing a large binary file:

```
protected function fileIteratorByLine()
{
  $count = 0;
  while (!$this->file->eof()) {
    yield $this->file->fgets();
    $count++;
```

```
    }
    return $count;
  }

  protected function fileIteratorByLength($numBytes = 1024)
  {
    $count = 0;
    while (!$this->file->eof()) {
      yield $this->file->fread($numBytes);
      $count++;
    }
    return $count;
  }
```

4. Finally, we define a `getIterator()` method that returns a `NoRewindIterator()` instance. This method accepts as arguments either `ByLine` or `ByLength`, which refer to the two methods defined in the previous step. This method also needs to accept `$numBytes` in case `ByLength` is called. The reason we need a `NoRewindIterator()` instance is to enforce the fact that we're reading through the file only in one direction in this example:

```
public function getIterator($type = 'ByLine', $numBytes = NULL)
{
  if(!in_array($type, $this->allowedTypes)) {
    $message = __METHOD__ . ' : ' . self::ERROR_TYPE . PHP_EOL;
    throw new InvalidArgumentException($message);
  }
  $iterator = 'fileIterator' . $type;
  return new NoRewindIterator($this->$iterator($numBytes));
}
```

How it works...

First of all, we take advantage of the autoloading class defined in *Chapter 1, Building a Foundation*, to obtain an instance of `Application\Iterator\LargeFile` in a calling program, `chap_02_iterating_through_a_massive_file.php`:

```
define('MASSIVE_FILE', '/../data/files/war_and_peace.txt');
require __DIR__ . '/../Application/Autoload/Loader.php';
Application\Autoload\Loader::init(__DIR__ . '/..');
```

Next, inside a `try {...} catch () {...}` block, we get an instance of a `ByLine` iterator:

```
try {
  $largeFile = new Application\Iterator\LargeFile(__DIR__ . MASSIVE_
FILE);
  $iterator = $largeFile->getIterator('ByLine');
```

We then provide an example of something useful to do, in this case, defining an average of words per line:

```
$words = 0;
foreach ($iterator as $line) {
  echo $line;
  $words += str_word_count($line);
}
echo str_repeat('-', 52) . PHP_EOL;
printf("%-40s : %8d\n", 'Total Words', $words);
printf("%-40s : %8d\n", 'Average Words Per Line',
($words / $iterator->getReturn()));
echo str_repeat('-', 52) . PHP_EOL;
```

We then end the `catch` block:

```
} catch (Throwable $e) {
  echo $e->getMessage();
}
```

The expected output (too large to show here!) shows us that there are 566,095 words in the project Gutenberg version of *War and Peace*. Also, we find the average number of words per line is eight.

Uploading a spreadsheet into a database

Although PHP does not have any direct capability to read a specific spreadsheet format (that is, XLSX, ODS, and so on), it does have the ability to read **(CSV Comma Separated Values)** files. Accordingly, in order to process customer spreadsheets, you will need to either ask them to furnish their files in CSV format, or you will need to perform the conversion yourself.

Getting ready...

When uploading a spreadsheet (that is, a CSV file) into a database, there are three major considerations:

- Iterating through a (potentially) massive file
- Extracting each spreadsheet row into a PHP array
- Inserting the PHP array into the database

Massive file iteration will be handled using the preceding recipe. We will use the `fgetcsv()` function to convert a CSV row into a PHP array. Finally, we will use the **(PDO PHP Data Objects**) class to make a database connection and perform the insert.

How to do it...

1. First, we define a `Application\Database\Connection` class that creates a PDO instance based on a set of parameters supplied to the constructor:

```
<?php
  namespace Application\Database;

  use Exception;
  use PDO;

  class Connection
  {
    const ERROR_UNABLE = 'ERROR: Unable to create database
      connection';
    public $pdo;

    public function __construct(array $config)
    {
      if (!isset($config['driver'])) {
        $message = __METHOD__ . ' : ' . self::ERROR_UNABLE
            . PHP_EOL;
        throw new Exception($message);
    }
    $dsn = $config['driver']
    . ':host=' . $config['host']
    . ';dbname=' . $config['dbname'];
    try {
      $this->pdo = new PDO($dsn,
      $config['user'],
      $config['password'],
      [PDO::ATTR_ERRMODE => $config['errmode']]);
    } catch (PDOException $e) {
      error_log($e->getMessage());
    }
  }

}
```

2. We then incorporate an instance of `Application\Iterator\LargeFile`. We add a new method to this class that is designed to iterate through CSV files:

```
protected function fileIteratorCsv()
{
  $count = 0;
  while (!$this->file->eof()) {
    yield $this->file->fgetcsv();
    $count++;
  }
  return $count;
}
```

3. We also need to add `Csv` to the list of allowed iterator methods:

```
  const ERROR_UNABLE = 'ERROR: Unable to open file';
  const ERROR_TYPE   = 'ERROR: Type must be "ByLength",
  "ByLine" or "Csv"';

  protected $file;
  protected $allowedTypes = ['ByLine', 'ByLength', 'Csv'];
```

How it works...

First we define a config file, `/path/to/source/config/db.config.php`, that contains database connection parameters:

```
<?php
return [
  'driver'   => 'mysql',
  'host'     => 'localhost',
  'dbname'   => 'php7cookbook',
  'user'     => 'cook',
  'password' => 'book',
  'errmode'  => PDO::ERRMODE_EXCEPTION,
];
```

Next, we take advantage of the autoloading class defined in *Chapter 1, Building a Foundation*, to obtain an instance of `Application\Database\Connection` and `Application\Iterator\LargeFile`, defining a calling program, `chap_02_uploading_csv_to_database.php`:

```
define('DB_CONFIG_FILE', '/../data/config/db.config.php');
define('CSV_FILE', '/../data/files/prospects.csv');
require __DIR__ . '/../../Application/Autoload/Loader.php';
Application\Autoload\Loader::init(__DIR__ . '/..');
```

After that, we set up a `try {...} catch () {...}` block, which catches `Throwable`. This allows us to `catch` both exceptions and errors:

```
try {
  // code goes here
} catch (Throwable $e) {
  echo $e->getMessage();
}
```

Inside the `try {...} catch () {...}` block we get an instance of the connection and large file iterator classes:

```
$connection = new Application\Database\Connection(
include __DIR__ . DB_CONFIG_FILE);
$iterator  = (new Application\Iterator\LargeFile(__DIR__ . CSV_FILE))
->getIterator('Csv');
```

We then take advantage of the PDO prepare/execute functionality. The SQL for the prepared statement uses `?` to represent values that are supplied in a loop:

```
$sql = 'INSERT INTO `prospects` '
  . '(`id`,`first_name`,`last_name`,`address`,`city`,`state_
province`,'
  . '`postal_code`,`phone`,`country`,`email`,`status`,`budget`,
     `last_updated`) '
  . ' VALUES (?,?,?,?,?,?,?,?,?,?,?,?,?)';
$statement = $connection->pdo->prepare($sql);
```

We then use `foreach()` to loop through the file iterator. Each `yield` statement produces an array of values that represents a row in the database. We can then use these values with `PDOStatement::execute()` to execute the prepared statement, inserting the row of values into the database:

```
foreach ($iterator as $row) {
  echo implode(',', $row) . PHP_EOL;
  $statement->execute($row);
}
```

You can then examine the database to verify that the data was successfully inserted.

Recursive directory iterator

Getting a list of files in a directory is extremely easy. Traditionally, developers have used the `glob()` function for this purpose. To recursively get a list of all files and directories from a specific point in a directory tree is more problematic. This recipe takes advantage of an **(SPL Standard PHP Library)** class `RecursiveDirectoryIterator`, which will serve this purpose admirably.

What this class does is to parse the directory tree, finding the first child, then it follows the branches, until there are no more children, and then it stops! Unfortunately this is not what we want. Somehow we need to get the `RecursiveDirectoryIterator` to continue parsing every tree and branch, from a given starting point, until there are no more files or directories. It so happens there is a marvelous class, `RecursiveIteratorIterator`, that does exactly that. By wrapping `RecursiveDirectoryIterator` inside `RecursiveIteratorIterator`, we accomplish a complete traversal of any directory tree.

> **Warning!**
>
> Be very careful where you start the filesystem traversal. If you start at the root directory, you could end up crashing your server as the recursion process will not stop until all files and directories have been located!

How to do it...

1. First, we define a `Application\Iterator\Directory` class that defines the appropriate properties and constants and uses external classes:

```
namespace Application\Iterator;

use Exception;
use RecursiveDirectoryIterator;
use RecursiveIteratorIterator;
use RecursiveRegexIterator;
use RegexIterator;

class Directory
{

  const ERROR_UNABLE = 'ERROR: Unable to read directory';

  protected $path;
  protected $rdi;
  // recursive directory iterator
```

2. The constructor creates a `RecursiveDirectoryIterator` instance inside `RecursiveIteratorIterator` based on a directory path:

```
public function __construct($path)
{
  try {
    $this->rdi = new RecursiveIteratorIterator(
      new RecursiveDirectoryIterator($path),
```

```
        RecursiveIteratorIterator::SELF_FIRST);
    } catch (\Throwable $e) {
      $message = __METHOD__ . ' : ' . self::ERROR_UNABLE . PHP_EOL;
      $message .= strip_tags($path) . PHP_EOL;
      echo $message;
      exit;
    }
  }
```

3. Next, we decide what to do with the iteration. One possibility is to mimic the output of the Linux `ls -l -R` command. Notice that we use the `yield` keyword, effectively making this method into a **Generator**, which can then be called from the outside. Each object produced by the directory iteration is an SPL `FileInfo` object, which can give us useful information on the file. Here is how this method might look:

```
public function ls($pattern = NULL)
{
  $outerIterator = ($pattern)
  ? $this->regex($this->rdi, $pattern)
  : $this->rdi;
  foreach($outerIterator as $obj){
    if ($obj->isDir()) {
      if ($obj->getFileName() == '..') {
        continue;
      }
      $line = $obj->getPath() . PHP_EOL;
    } else {
      $line = sprintf('%4s %1d %4s %4s %10d %12s %-40s' . PHP_EOL,
      substr(sprintf('%o', $obj->getPerms()), -4),
      ($obj->getType() == 'file') ? 1 : 2,
      $obj->getOwner(),
      $obj->getGroup(),
      $obj->getSize(),
      date('M d Y H:i', $obj->getATime()),
      $obj->getFileName());
    }
    yield $line;
  }
}
```

4. You may have noticed that the method call includes a file pattern. We need a way of filtering the recursion to only include files that match. There is another iterator available from the SPL that perfectly suits this need: the `RegexIterator` class:

```
protected function regex($iterator, $pattern)
{
  $pattern = '!^.' . str_replace('.', '\\.', $pattern) . '$!';
  return new RegexIterator($iterator, $pattern);
}
```

5. Finally, here is another method, but this time we will mimic the `dir /s` command:

```
public function dir($pattern = NULL)
{
  $outerIterator = ($pattern)
  ? $this->regex($this->rdi, $pattern)
  : $this->rdi;
  foreach($outerIterator as $name => $obj){
      yield $name . PHP_EOL;
    }
  }
}
```

How it works...

First of all, we take advantage of the autoloading class defined in *Chapter 1, Building a Foundation*, to obtain an instance of `Application\Iterator\Directory`, defining a calling program, `chap_02_recursive_directory_iterator.php`:

```
define('EXAMPLE_PATH', realpath(__DIR__ . '/../'));
require __DIR__ . '/../Application/Autoload/Loader.php';
Application\Autoload\Loader::init(__DIR__ . '/..');
$directory = new Application\Iterator\Directory(EXAMPLE_PATH);
```

Then, in a `try {...} catch () {...}` block, we make a call to our two methods, using an example directory path:

```
try {
  echo 'Mimics "ls -l -R" ' . PHP_EOL;
  foreach ($directory->ls('*.php') as $info) {
    echo $info;
  }

  echo 'Mimics "dir /s" ' . PHP_EOL;
  foreach ($directory->dir('*.php') as $info) {
    echo $info;
```

```
    }

  } catch (Throwable $e) {
    echo $e->getMessage();
  }
```

The output for `ls()` will look something like this:

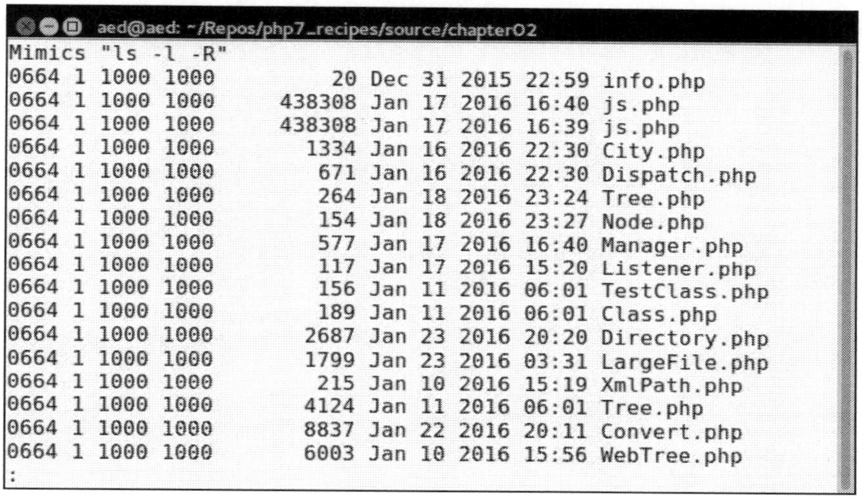

```
aed@aed: ~/Repos/php7_recipes/source/chapter02
Mimics "ls -l -R"
0664 1 1000 1000        20 Dec 31 2015 22:59 info.php
0664 1 1000 1000    438308 Jan 17 2016 16:40 js.php
0664 1 1000 1000    438308 Jan 17 2016 16:39 js.php
0664 1 1000 1000      1334 Jan 16 2016 22:30 City.php
0664 1 1000 1000       671 Jan 16 2016 22:30 Dispatch.php
0664 1 1000 1000       264 Jan 18 2016 23:24 Tree.php
0664 1 1000 1000       154 Jan 18 2016 23:27 Node.php
0664 1 1000 1000       577 Jan 17 2016 16:40 Manager.php
0664 1 1000 1000       117 Jan 17 2016 15:20 Listener.php
0664 1 1000 1000       156 Jan 11 2016 06:01 TestClass.php
0664 1 1000 1000       189 Jan 11 2016 06:01 Class.php
0664 1 1000 1000      2687 Jan 23 2016 20:20 Directory.php
0664 1 1000 1000      1799 Jan 23 2016 03:31 LargeFile.php
0664 1 1000 1000       215 Jan 10 2016 15:19 XmlPath.php
0664 1 1000 1000      4124 Jan 11 2016 06:01 Tree.php
0664 1 1000 1000      8837 Jan 22 2016 20:11 Convert.php
0664 1 1000 1000      6003 Jan 10 2016 15:56 WebTree.php
:
```

The output for `dir()` will appear as follows:

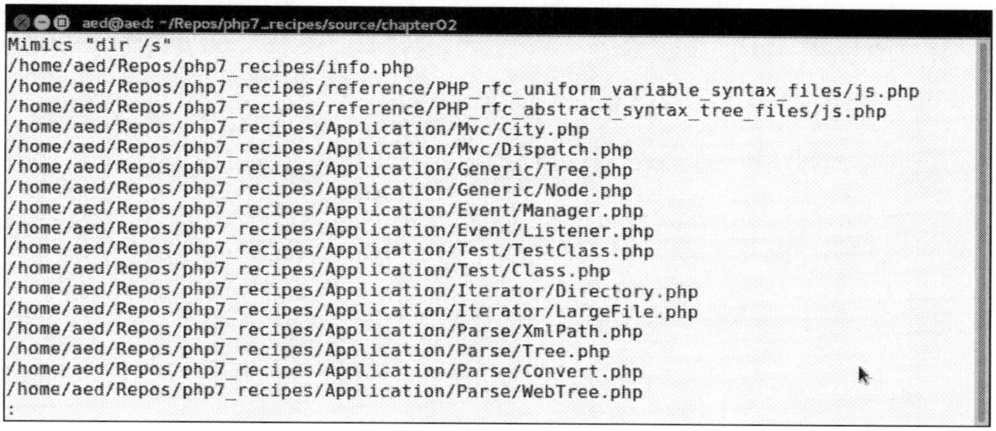

```
aed@aed: ~/Repos/php7_recipes/source/chapter02
Mimics "dir /s"
/home/aed/Repos/php7_recipes/info.php
/home/aed/Repos/php7_recipes/reference/PHP_rfc_uniform_variable_syntax_files/js.php
/home/aed/Repos/php7_recipes/reference/PHP_rfc_abstract_syntax_tree_files/js.php
/home/aed/Repos/php7_recipes/Application/Mvc/City.php
/home/aed/Repos/php7_recipes/Application/Mvc/Dispatch.php
/home/aed/Repos/php7_recipes/Application/Generic/Tree.php
/home/aed/Repos/php7_recipes/Application/Generic/Node.php
/home/aed/Repos/php7_recipes/Application/Event/Manager.php
/home/aed/Repos/php7_recipes/Application/Event/Listener.php
/home/aed/Repos/php7_recipes/Application/Test/TestClass.php
/home/aed/Repos/php7_recipes/Application/Test/Class.php
/home/aed/Repos/php7_recipes/Application/Iterator/Directory.php
/home/aed/Repos/php7_recipes/Application/Iterator/LargeFile.php
/home/aed/Repos/php7_recipes/Application/Parse/XmlPath.php
/home/aed/Repos/php7_recipes/Application/Parse/Tree.php
/home/aed/Repos/php7_recipes/Application/Parse/Convert.php
/home/aed/Repos/php7_recipes/Application/Parse/WebTree.php
:
```

3

Working with PHP Functional Programming

In this chapter we will cover the following topics:

- Developing functions
- Hinting at data types
- Using return value data typing
- Using iterators
- Writing your own iterator using generators

Introduction

In this chapter we will consider recipes that take advantage of PHP's **functional programming** capabilities. Functional, or **procedural**, programming is the traditional way PHP code was written prior to the introduction of the first implementation of **object-oriented programming** (**OOP**) in PHP version 4. Functional programming is where program logic is encapsulated into a series of discreet **functions**, which are generally stored in a separate PHP file. This file can then be included in any future scripts, allowing the functions that are defined to be called at will.

Developing functions

The most difficult aspect is deciding how to break up programming logic into functions. The mechanics of developing a function in PHP, on the other hand, are quite easy. Just use the `function` keyword, give it a name, and follow it with parentheses.

How to do it...

1. The code itself goes inside curly braces as follows:

```
function someName ($parameter)
{
  $result = 'INIT';
  // one or more statements which do something
  // to affect $result
  $result .= ' and also ' . $parameter;
  return $result;
}
```

2. You can define one or more **parameters**. To make one of them optional, simply assign a default value. If you are not sure what default value to assign, use `NULL`:

```
function someOtherName ($requiredParam, $optionalParam = NULL)
  {
    $result = 0;
    $result += $requiredParam;
    $result += $optionalParam ?? 0;
    return $result;
  }
```

You cannot redefine functions. The only exception is when duplicate functions are defined in separate namespaces. This definition would generate an error:

```
function someTest()
{
  return 'TEST';
}
function someTest($a)
{
  return 'TEST:' . $a;
}
```

3. If you don't know how many parameters will be supplied to your function, or if you want to allow for an infinite number of parameters, use `...` followed by a variable name. All parameters supplied will appear as an array in the variable:

```
function someInfinite(...$params)
{
  // any params passed go into an array $params
  return var_export($params, TRUE);
}
```

4. A function can call itself. This is referred to as **recursion**. The following function performs a recursive directory scan:

```
function someDirScan($dir)
{
  // uses "static" to retain value of $list
  static $list = array();
  // get a list of files and directories for this path
  $list = glob($dir . DIRECTORY_SEPARATOR . '*');
  // loop through
  foreach ($list as $item) {
    if (is_dir($item)) {
      $list = array_merge($list, someDirScan($item));
    }
  }
  return $list;
}
```

Usage of the `static` keyword inside functions has been in the language for more than 12 years. What `static` does is to initialize the variable once (that is, at the time `static` is declared), and then retain the value between function calls within the same request.

If you need to retain the value of a variable between HTTP requests, make sure the PHP session has been started and store the value in `$_SESSION`.

5. Functions are constrained when defined within a PHP **namespace**. This characteristic can be used to your advantage to provide additional logical separation between libraries of functions. In order to *anchor* the namespace, you need to add the `use` keyword. The following examples are placed in separate namespaces. Notice that even though the function name is the same, there is no conflict as they are not visible to each other.

6. We define `someFunction()` in namespace `Alpha`. We save this to a separate PHP file, `chap_03_developing_functions_namespace_alpha.php`:

```
<?php
namespace Alpha;

function someFunction()
{
  echo __NAMESPACE__ . ':' . __FUNCTION__ . PHP_EOL;
}
```

7. We then define `someFunction()` in namespace `Beta`. We save this to a separate PHP file, `chap_03_developing_functions_namespace_beta.php`:

```
<?php
namespace Beta;

function someFunction()
{
  echo __NAMESPACE__ . ':' . __FUNCTION__ . PHP_EOL;
}
```

8. We can then call `someFunction()` by prefixing the function name with the namespace name:

```
include (__DIR__ . DIRECTORY_SEPARATOR
         . 'chap_03_developing_functions_namespace_alpha.php');
include (__DIR__ . DIRECTORY_SEPARATOR
         . 'chap_03_developing_functions_namespace_beta.php');
      echo Alpha\someFunction();
      echo Beta\someFunction();
```

Best practice

It is considered best practice to place function libraries (and classes too!) into separate files: one file per namespace, and one class or function library per file.

It is possible to define many classes or function libraries in a single namespace. The only reason you would develop into a separate namespace is if you want to foster logical separation of functionality.

How it works...

It is considered best practice to place all logically related functions into a separate PHP file. Create a file called chap_03_developing_functions_library.php and place these functions (described previously) inside:

- someName()
- someOtherName()
- someInfinite()
- someDirScan()
- someTypeHint()

This file is then included in the code that uses these functions.

```
include (__DIR__ . DIRECTORY_SEPARATOR . 'chap_03_developing_
functions_library.php');
```

To call the someName() function, use the name and supply the parameter.

```
echo someName('TEST');   // returns "INIT and also TEST"
```

You can call the someOtherName() function using one or two parameters, as shown here:

```
echo someOtherName(1);    // returns  1
echo someOtherName(1, 1);   //  returns 2
```

The someInfinite() function accepts an infinite (or variable) number of parameters. Here are a couple of examples calling this function:

```
echo someInfinite(1, 2, 3);
echo PHP_EOL;
echo someInfinite(22.22, 'A', ['a' => 1, 'b' => 2]);
```

The output looks like this:

```
aed@aed: ~/Repos/php7_recipes/source/chapter03
-------------------------------
OUTPUT FROM: someName()
-------------------------------
INIT and also TEST

-------------------------------
OUTPUT FROM: someOtherName()
-------------------------------
1
2

-------------------------------
OUTPUT FROM: someInfinite()
-------------------------------
array (
  0 => 1,
  1 => 2,
  2 => 3,
)
array (
  0 => 22.219999999999999,
  1 => 'A',
  2 =>
  array (
    'a' => 1,
    'b' => 2,
  ),
)
:
```

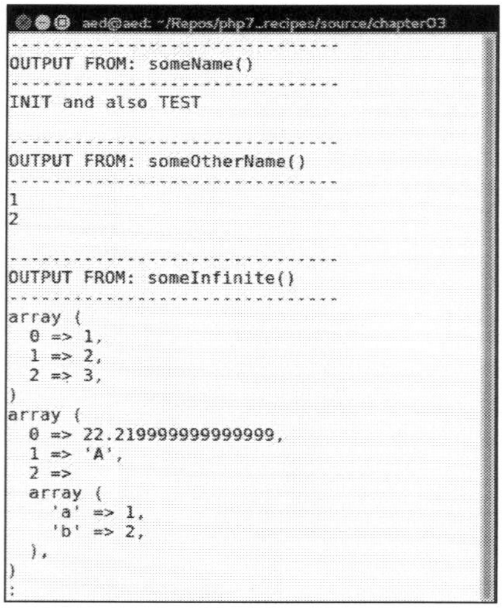

We can call `someDirScan()` as follows:

```
echo someInfinite(1, 2, 3);
echo PHP_EOL;
echo someInfinite(22.22, 'A', ['a' => 1, 'b' => 2]);
```

The output looks like this:

```
aed@aed: ~/Repos/php7_recipes/source/chapter03
-------------------------------
OUTPUT FROM: someDirScan()
-------------------------------
/home/aed/Repos/php7_recipes/source/chapter03/../Application
/home/aed/Repos/php7_recipes/source/chapter03/../Application/Autoload
/home/aed/Repos/php7_recipes/source/chapter03/../Application/Autoload/Loader.php
/home/aed/Repos/php7_recipes/source/chapter03/../Application/Database
/home/aed/Repos/php7_recipes/source/chapter03/../Application/Database/BasicOps.php
/home/aed/Repos/php7_recipes/source/chapter03/../Application/Database/Connection.php
/home/aed/Repos/php7_recipes/source/chapter03/../Application/Entity
/home/aed/Repos/php7_recipes/source/chapter03/../Application/Entity/Customer.php
/home/aed/Repos/php7_recipes/source/chapter03/../Application/Event
/home/aed/Repos/php7_recipes/source/chapter03/../Application/Event/Listener.php
/home/aed/Repos/php7_recipes/source/chapter03/../Application/Event/Manager.php
/home/aed/Repos/php7_recipes/source/chapter03/../Application/Generic
/home/aed/Repos/php7_recipes/source/chapter03/../Application/Generic/Node.php
/home/aed/Repos/php7_recipes/source/chapter03/../Application/Generic/Tree.php
/home/aed/Repos/php7_recipes/source/chapter03/../Application/Iterator
/home/aed/Repos/php7_recipes/source/chapter03/../Application/Iterator/Directory.php
/home/aed/Repos/php7_recipes/source/chapter03/../Application/Iterator/LargeFile.php
/home/aed/Repos/php7_recipes/source/chapter03/../Application/Mvc
/home/aed/Repos/php7_recipes/source/chapter03/../Application/Mvc/City.php
/home/aed/Repos/php7_recipes/source/chapter03/../Application/Mvc/Dispatch.php
/home/aed/Repos/php7_recipes/source/chapter03/../Application/Parse
/home/aed/Repos/php7_recipes/source/chapter03/../Application/Parse/Convert.php
/home/aed/Repos/php7_recipes/source/chapter03/../Application/Parse/Tree.php
/home/aed/Repos/php7_recipes/source/chapter03/../Application/Parse/WebTree.php
/home/aed/Repos/php7_recipes/source/chapter03/../Application/Parse/XmlPath.php
:
```

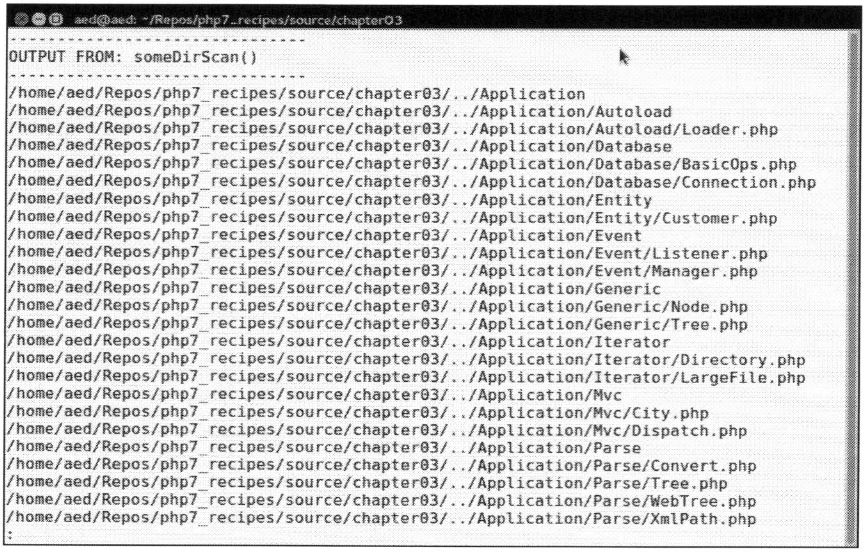

Hinting at data types

In many cases when developing functions, you might reuse the same library of functions in other projects. Also, if you work with a team, your code might be used by other developers. In order to control the use of your code, it might be appropriate to make use of a **type hint**. This involves specifying the data type your function expects for that particular parameter.

How to do it...

1. Parameters in functions can be prefixed by a type hint. The following type hints are available in both PHP 5 and PHP 7:
   - Array
   - Class
   - Callable

2. If a call to the function is made, and the wrong parameter type is passed, a `TypeError` is thrown. The following example requires an array, an instance of `DateTime`, and an anonymous function:

```
function someTypeHint(Array $a, DateTime $t, Callable $c)
{
  $message = '';
  $message .= 'Array Count: ' . count($a) . PHP_EOL;
  $message .= 'Date: ' . $t->format('Y-m-d') . PHP_EOL;
  $message .= 'Callable Return: ' . $c() . PHP_EOL;
  return $message;
}
```

> You don't have to provide a type hint for every single parameter. Use this technique only where supplying a different data type would have a negative effect on the processing of your function. As an example, if your function uses a `foreach()` loop, if you do not supply an array, or something which implements `Traversable`, an error will be generated.

3. In PHP 7, presuming the appropriate `declare()` directive is made, **scalar** (that is, integer, float, boolean, and string) type hints are allowed. Another function demonstrates how this is accomplished. At the top of the code library file which contains the function in which you wish to use scalar type hinting, add this `declare()` directive just after the opening PHP tag:

```
declare(strict_types=1);
```

4. Now you can define a function that includes scalar type hints:

```
function someScalarHint(bool $b, int $i, float $f, string $s)
{
  return sprintf("\n%20s : %5s\n%20s : %5d\n%20s " .
                 ": %5.2f\n%20s : %20s\n\n",
                 'Boolean', ($b ? 'TRUE' : 'FALSE'),
                 'Integer', $i,
                 'Float',   $f,
                 'String',  $s);
}
```

5. In PHP 7, assuming strict type hinting has been declared, boolean type hinting works a bit differently from the other three scalar types (that is, integer, float, and string). You can supply any scalar as an argument and no `TypeError` will be thrown! However, the incoming value will automatically be converted to the boolean data type once passed into the function. If you pass any data type other than scalar (that is, array or object) a `TypeError` will be thrown. Here is an example of a function that defines a `boolean` data type. Note that the return value will be automatically converted to a `boolean`:

```
function someBoolHint(bool $b)
{
  return $b;
}
```

How it works...

First of all, you can place the three functions, `someTypeHint()`, `someScalarHint()`, and `someBoolHint()`, into a separate file to be included. For this example, we will name the file `chap_03_developing_functions_type_hints_library.php`. Don't forget to add `declare(strict_types=1)` at the top!

In our calling code, you would then include the file:

```
include (__DIR__ . DIRECTORY_SEPARATOR . 'chap_03_developing_
functions_type_hints_library.php');
```

To test `someTypeHint()`, call the function twice, once with the correct data types, and the second time with incorrect types. This will throw a `TypeError`, however, so you will need to wrap the function calls in a `try { ... } catch () { ...}` block:

```
try {
    $callable = function () { return 'Callback Return'; };
    echo someTypeHint([1,2,3], new DateTime(), $callable);
    echo someTypeHint('A', 'B', 'C');
```

```
} catch (TypeError $e) {
    echo $e->getMessage();
    echo PHP_EOL;
}
```

As you can see from the output shown at the end of this sub-section, when passing the correct data types there is no problem. When passing the incorrect types, a `TypeError` is thrown.

> In PHP 7, certain errors have been converted into an `Error` class, which is processed in a somewhat similar manner to an `Exception`. This means you can catch an `Error`. `TypeError` is a specific descendant of `Error` that is thrown when incorrect data types are passed to functions.
>
> All PHP 7 `Error` classes implement the `Throwable` interface, as does the `Exception` class. If you are not sure if you need to catch an `Error` or an `Exception`, you can add a block which catches `Throwable`.

Next you can test `someScalarHint()`, calling it twice with correct and incorrect values, wrapping the calls in a `try { ... } catch () { ...}` block:

```
try {
    echo someScalarHint(TRUE, 11, 22.22, 'This is a string');
    echo someScalarHint('A', 'B', 'C', 'D');
} catch (TypeError $e) {
    echo $e->getMessage();
}
```

As expected, the first call to the function works, and the second throws a `TypeError`.

When type hinting for boolean values, any scalar value passed will *not* cause a `TypeError` to be thrown! Instead, the value will be interpreted into its boolean equivalent. If you subsequently return this value, the data type will be changed to boolean.

To test this, call the `someBoolHint()` function defined previously, and pass any scalar value in as an argument. The `var_dump()` method reveals that the data type is always boolean:

```
try {
    // positive results
    $b = someBooleanHint(TRUE);
    $i = someBooleanHint(11);
    $f = someBooleanHint(22.22);
    $s = someBooleanHint('X');
    var_dump($b, $i, $f, $s);
    // negative results
    $b = someBooleanHint(FALSE);
    $i = someBooleanHint(0);
```

```
        $f = someBooleanHint(0.0);
        $s = someBooleanHint('');
        var_dump($b, $i, $f, $s);
    } catch (TypeError $e) {
        echo $e->getMessage();
    }
```

If you now try the same function call, but pass in a non-scalar data type, a `TypeError` is thrown:

```
    try {
        $a = someBoolHint([1,2,3]);
        var_dump($a);
    } catch (TypeError $e) {
        echo $e->getMessage();
    }
    try {
        $o = someBoolHint(new stdClass());
        var_dump($o);
    } catch (TypeError $e) {
        echo $e->getMessage();
    }
```

Here is the overall output:

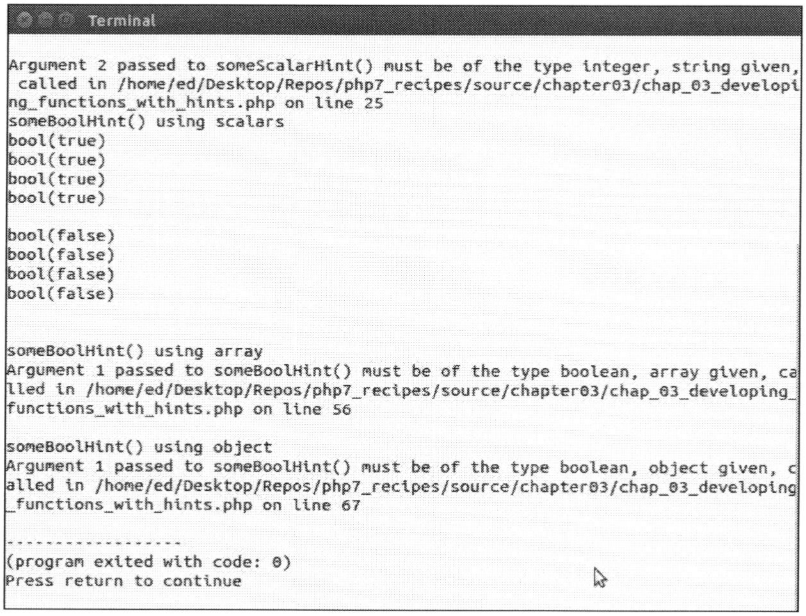

```
Terminal
Argument 2 passed to someScalarHint() must be of the type integer, string given,
 called in /home/ed/Desktop/Repos/php7_recipes/source/chapter03/chap_03_developi
ng_functions_with_hints.php on line 25
someBoolHint() using scalars
bool(true)
bool(true)
bool(true)
bool(true)

bool(false)
bool(false)
bool(false)
bool(false)


someBoolHint() using array
Argument 1 passed to someBoolHint() must be of the type boolean, array given, ca
lled in /home/ed/Desktop/Repos/php7_recipes/source/chapter03/chap_03_developing_
functions_with_hints.php on line 56

someBoolHint() using object
Argument 1 passed to someBoolHint() must be of the type boolean, object given, c
alled in /home/ed/Desktop/Repos/php7_recipes/source/chapter03/chap_03_developing
_functions_with_hints.php on line 67

------------------
(program exited with code: 0)
Press return to continue
```

See also

PHP 7.1 introduced a new type hint `iterable` which allows arrays, `Iterators` or `Generators` as arguments. See this for more information:

- `https://wiki.php.net/rfc/iterable`

For a background discussion on the rationale behind the implementation of scalar type hinting, have a look at this article:

- `https://wiki.php.net/rfc/scalar_type_hints_v5`

Using return value data typing

PHP 7 allows you to specify a data type for the return value of a function. Unlike scalar type hinting, however, you don't need to add any special declarations.

How to do it...

1. This example shows you how to assign a data type to a function return value. To assign a return data type, first define the function as you would normally. After the closing parenthesis, add a space, followed by the data type and a colon:

```
function returnsString(DateTime $date, $format) : string
{
  return $date->format($format);
}
```

PHP 7.1 introduced a variation on return data typing called **nullable types**. All you need to do is to change `string` to `?string`. This allows the function to return either `string` or `NULL`.

2. Anything returned by the function, regardless of its data type inside the function, will be converted to the declared data type as a return value. Notice, in this example, the values of `$a`, `$b`, and `$c` are added together to produce a single sum, which is returned. Normally you would expect the return value to be a numeric data type. In this case, however, the return data type is declared as `string`, which overrides PHP's type-juggling process:

```
function convertsToString($a, $b, $c) : string

  return $a + $b + $c;
}
```

3. You can also assign classes as a return data type. In this example, we assign a return type of `DateTime`, part of the PHP `DateTime` extension:

```
function makesDateTime($year, $month, $day) : DateTime
{
  $date = new DateTime();
  $date->setDate($year, $month, $day);
  return $date;
}
```

The `makesDateTime()` function would be a potential candidate for scalar type hinting. If `$year`, `$month`, or `$day` are not integers, a `Warning` is generated when `setDate()` is called. If you use scalar type hinting, and the wrong data types are passed, a `TypeError` is thrown. Although it really doesn't matter whether a warning is generated or a `TypeError` is thrown, at least the `TypeError` will cause the errant developer who is misusing your code to sit up and take notice!

4. If a function has a return data type, and you return the wrong data type in your function code, a `TypeError` will be thrown at runtime. This function assigns a return type of `DateTime`, but returns a string instead. A `TypeError` will be thrown, but not until runtime, when the PHP engine detects the discrepancy:

```
function wrongDateTime($year, $month, $day) : DateTime
{
  return date($year . '-' . $month . '-' . $day);
}
```

If the return data type class is not one of the built-in PHP classes (that is, a class that is part of the SPL), you will need to make sure the class has been auto-loaded, or included.

How it works...

First, place the functions mentioned previously into a library file called `chap_03_developing_functions_return_types_library.php`. This file needs to be included in the `chap_03_developing_functions_return_types.php` script that calls these functions:

```
include (__DIR__ . '/chap_03_developing_functions_return_types_
library.php');
```

Now you can call `returnsString()`, supplying a `DateTime` instance and a format string:

```
$date   = new DateTime();
$format = 'l, d M Y';
$now    = returnsString($date, $format);
echo $now . PHP_EOL;
var_dump($now);
```

As expected, the output is a string:

```
aed@aed: ~/Repos/php7_recipes/source/chapter03
aed@aed:~/Repos/php7_recipes/source/chapter03$ php chap_03_developing_functions_with_hints.php

returnsString()
Sunday, 31 Jan 2016
string(19) "Sunday, 31 Jan 2016"
aed@aed:~/Repos/php7_recipes/source/chapter03$
```

Now you can call `convertsToString()` and supply three integers as arguments. Notice that the return type is string:

```
echo "\nconvertsToString()\n";
var_dump(convertsToString(2, 3, 4));
```

```
aed@aed: ~/Repos/php7_recipes/source/chapter03
aed@aed:~/Repos/php7_recipes/source/chapter03$ php chap_03_developing_functions_with_hints.php

convertsToString()
string(1) "9"
aed@aed:~/Repos/php7_recipes/source/chapter03$
```

To demonstrate that, you can assign a class as a return value, call `makesDateTime()` with three integer parameters:

```
echo "\nmakesDateTime()\n";
$d = makesDateTime(2015, 11, 21);
var_dump($d);
```

```
aed@aed: ~/Repos/php7_recipes/source/chapter03
aed@aed:~/Repos/php7_recipes/source/chapter03$ php chap_03_developing_functions_with_hints.php

makesDateTime()
class DateTime#1 (3) {
  public $date =>
  string(26) "2015-11-21 18:32:25.000000"
  public $timezone_type =>
  int(3)
  public $timezone =>
  string(13) "Europe/London"
}
aed@aed:~/Repos/php7_recipes/source/chapter03$
```

Finally, call `wrongDateTime()` with three integer parameters:

```
try {
    $e = wrongDateTime(2015, 11, 21);
    var_dump($e);
} catch (TypeError $e) {
    echo $e->getMessage();
}
```

Notice that a `TypeError` is thrown at runtime:

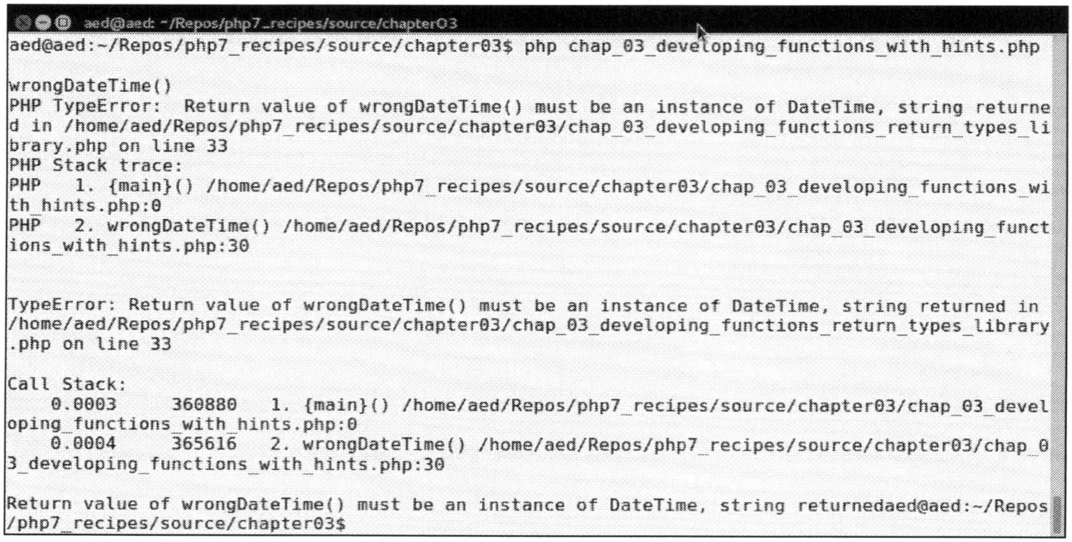

```
aed@aed: ~/Repos/php7_recipes/source/chapter03
aed@aed:~/Repos/php7_recipes/source/chapter03$ php chap_03_developing_functions_with_hints.php

wrongDateTime()
PHP TypeError:  Return value of wrongDateTime() must be an instance of DateTime, string returne
d in /home/aed/Repos/php7_recipes/source/chapter03/chap_03_developing_functions_return_types_li
brary.php on line 33
PHP Stack trace:
PHP   1. {main}() /home/aed/Repos/php7_recipes/source/chapter03/chap_03_developing_functions_wi
th_hints.php:0
PHP   2. wrongDateTime() /home/aed/Repos/php7_recipes/source/chapter03/chap_03_developing_funct
ions_with_hints.php:30


TypeError: Return value of wrongDateTime() must be an instance of DateTime, string returned in
/home/aed/Repos/php7_recipes/source/chapter03/chap_03_developing_functions_return_types_library
.php on line 33

Call Stack:
    0.0003     360880   1. {main}() /home/aed/Repos/php7_recipes/source/chapter03/chap_03_devel
oping_functions_with_hints.php:0
    0.0004     365616   2. wrongDateTime() /home/aed/Repos/php7_recipes/source/chapter03/chap_0
3_developing_functions_with_hints.php:30

Return value of wrongDateTime() must be an instance of DateTime, string returnedaed@aed:~/Repos
/php7_recipes/source/chapter03$
```

There's more...

PHP 7.1 adds a new return value type, `void`. This is used when you do not wish to return any value from the function. For more information, please refer to `https://wiki.php.net/rfc/void_return_type`.

See also

For more information on return type declarations, see the following articles:

- `http://php.net/manual/en/functions.arguments.php#functions.arguments.type-declaration.strict`
- `https://wiki.php.net/rfc/return_types`

For information on nullable types, please refer to this article:

- https://wiki.php.net/rfc/nullable_types

Using iterators

An **iterator** is a special type of class that allows you to **traverse** a *container* or list. The keyword here is *traverse*. What this means is that the iterator provides the means to go through a list, but it does not perform the traversal itself.

The SPL provides a rich assortment of generic and specialized iterators designed for different contexts. The `ArrayIterator`, for example, is designed to allow object-oriented traversal of arrays. The `DirectoryIterator` is designed for filesystem scanning.

Certain SPL iterators are designed to work with others, and add value. Examples include `FilterIterator` and `LimitIterator`. The former gives you the ability to remove unwanted values from the parent iterator. The latter provides a pagination capability whereby you can designate how many items to traverse along with an offset that determines where to start.

Finally, there are a series of *recursive* iterators, which allow you to repeatedly call the parent iterator. An example would be `RecursiveDirectoryIterator` which scans a directory tree all the way from a starting point to the last possible subdirectory.

How to do it...

1. We first examine the `ArrayIterator` class. It's extremely easy to use. All you need to do is to supply an array as an argument to the constructor. After that you can use any of the methods that are standard to all SPL-based iterators, such as `current()`, `next()`, and so on.

```
$iterator = new ArrayIterator($array);
```

Using `ArrayIterator` converts a standard PHP array into an iterator. In a certain sense, this provides a bridge between procedural programming and OOP.

2. As an example of a practical use for the iterator, have a look at this example. It takes an iterator and produces a series of HTML `<ul>` and `<li>` tags:

```
function htmlList($iterator)
{
  $output = '<ul>';
  while ($value = $iterator->current()) {
    $output .= '<li>' . $value . '</li>';
    $iterator->next();
```

```
    }
    $output .= '</ul>';
    return $output;
}
```

3. Alternatively, you can simply wrap the `ArrayIterator` instance into a simple `foreach()` loop:

```
function htmlList($iterator)
{
  $output = '<ul>';
  foreach($iterator as $value) {
    $output .= '<li>' . $value . '</li>';
  }
  $output .= '</ul>';
  return $output;
}
```

4. `CallbackFilterIterator` is a great way to add value to any existing iterator you might be using. It allows you to wrap any existing iterator and screen the output. In this example we'll define `fetchCountryName()`, which iterates through a database query which produces a list of country names. First, we define an `ArrayIterator` instance from a query that uses the `Application\Database\Connection` class defined in *Chapter 1, Building a Foundation*:

```
function fetchCountryName($sql, $connection)
{
  $iterator = new ArrayIterator();
  $stmt = $connection->pdo->query($sql);
  while($row = $stmt->fetch(PDO::FETCH_ASSOC)) {
    $iterator->append($row['name']);
  }
  return $iterator;
}
```

5. Next, we define a filter method, `nameFilterIterator()`, which accepts a partial country name as an argument along with the `ArrayIterator` instance:

```
function nameFilterIterator($innerIterator, $name)
{
  if (!$name) return $innerIterator;
  $name = trim($name);
  $iterator = new CallbackFilterIterator($innerIterator,
    function($current, $key, $iterator) use ($name) {
      $pattern = '/' . $name . '/i';
```

```
      return (bool) preg_match($pattern, $current);
    }
  );
  return $iterator;
}
```

6. `LimitIterator` adds a basic pagination aspect to your applications. To use this iterator, you only need to supply the parent iterator, an offset, and a limit. `LimitIterator` will then only produce a subset of the entire data set starting at the offset. Taking the same example mentioned in step 2, we'll paginate the results coming from our database query. We can do this quite simply by wrapping the iterator produced by the `fetchCountryName()` method inside a `LimitIterator` instance:

```
$pagination = new LimitIterator(fetchCountryName(
$sql, $connection), $offset, $limit);
```

> Be careful when using `LimitIterator`. It needs to have the *entire* data set in memory in order to effect a limit. Accordingly, this would not be a good tool to use when iterating through large data sets.

7. Iterators can be *stacked*. In this simple example, an `ArrayIterator` is processed by a `FilterIterator`, which in turn is limited by a `LimitIterator`. First we set up an instance of `ArrayIterator`:

```
$i = new ArrayIterator($a);
```

8. Next, we plug the `ArrayIterator` into a `FilterIterator` instance. Note that we are using the new PHP 7 anonymous class feature. In this case the anonymous class extends `FilterIterator` and overrides the `accept()` method, allowing only letters with even-numbered ASCII codes:

```
$f = new class ($i) extends FilterIterator {
  public function accept()
  {
    $current = $this->current();
    return !(ord($current) & 1);
  }
};
```

9. Finally, we supply the `FilterIterator` instance as an argument to `LimitIterator`, and provide an offset (`2` in this example) and a limit (`6` in this example):

```
$l = new LimitIterator($f, 2, 6);
```

10. We could then define a simple function to display output, and call each iterator in turn to see the results on a simple array produced by `range('A', 'Z')`:

```
function showElements($iterator)
{
  foreach($iterator as $item)  echo $item . ' ';
  echo PHP_EOL;
}

$a = range('A', 'Z');
$i = new ArrayIterator($a);
showElements($i);
```

11. Here is a variation that produces every other letter by stacking a `FilterIterator` on top of an `ArrayIterator`:

```
$f = new class ($i) extends FilterIterator {
public function accept()
  {
    $current = $this->current();
    return !(ord($current) & 1);
  }
};
showElements($f);
```

12. And here's yet another variation that only produces `F H J L N P`, which demonstrates a `LimitIterator` that consumes a `FilterIterator`, which in turn consumes an `ArrayIterator`. The output of these three examples is as follows:

```
$l = new LimitIterator($f, 2, 6);
showElements($l);
```

```
ArrayIterator
A B C D E F G H I J K L M N O P Q R S T U V W X Y Z

ArrayIterator + FilterIterator
B D F H J L N P R T V X Z

ArrayIterator + FilterIterator + LimitIterator
F H J L N P


------------------
(program exited with code: 0)
Press return to continue
```

13. Returning to our example that produces a list of country names, suppose, instead of only the country name, we wished to iterate through a multi-dimensional array consisting of country names and ISO codes. The simple iterators mentioned so far would not be sufficient. Instead, we will use what are known as **recursive** iterators.

14. First of all, we need to define a method that uses the database connection class mentioned previously to pull all columns from the database. As before, we return an `ArrayIterator` instance populated with data from the query:

    ```
    function fetchAllAssoc($sql, $connection)
    {
      $iterator = new ArrayIterator();
      $stmt = $connection->pdo->query($sql);
      while($row = $stmt->fetch(PDO::FETCH_ASSOC)) {
        $iterator->append($row);
      }
      return $iterator;
    }
    ```

15. At first glance one would be tempted to simply wrap a standard `ArrayIterator` instance inside `RecursiveArrayIterator`. Unfortunately, this approach only performs a **shallow** iteration, and doesn't give us what we want: an iteration through all elements of the multi-dimensional array that is returned from a database query:

    ```
    $iterator = fetchAllAssoc($sql, $connection);
    $shallow  = new RecursiveArrayIterator($iterator);
    ```

16. Although this returns an iteration where each item represents a row from the database query, in this case we wish to provide an iteration that will iterate through all columns of all rows returned by the query. In order to accomplish this, we'll need to roll out the big brass by way of a `RecursiveIteratorIterator`.

17. Monty Python fans will revel in the rich irony of this class name as it brings back fond memories of the *The Department of Redundancy Department*. Fittingly, this class causes our old friend the `RecursiveArrayIterator` class to work overtime and perform a **deep** iteration through all levels of the array:

    ```
    $deep     = new RecursiveIteratorIterator($shallow);
    ```

How it works...

As a practical example, you can develop a test script which implements filtering and pagination using iterators. For this illustration, you could call the `chap_03_developing_functions_filtered_and_paginated.php` test code file.

First of all, following best practices, place the functions described above into an include file called `chap_03_developing_functions_iterators_library.php`. In the test script, be sure to include this file.

The data source is a table called `iso_country_codes`, which contains ISO2, ISO3, and country names. The database connection could be in a `config/db.config.php` file. You could also include the `Application\Database\Connection` class discussed in the previous chapter:

```
define('DB_CONFIG_FILE', '/../config/db.config.php');
define('ITEMS_PER_PAGE', [5, 10, 15, 20]);
include (__DIR__ . '/chap_03_developing_functions_iterators_library.
php');
include (__DIR__ . '/../Application/Database/Connection.php');
```

In PHP 7 you can define constants as arrays. In this example, `ITEMS_PER_PAGE` was defined as an array, and used to generate an HTML `SELECT` element.

Next, you can process input parameters for the country name and the number of items per page. The current page number will start at `0` and can be incremented (next page) or decremented (previous page):

```
$name = strip_tags($_GET['name'] ?? '');
$limit  = (int) ($_GET['limit'] ?? 10);
$page   = (int) ($_GET['page']  ?? 0);
$offset = $page * $limit;
$prev   = ($page > 0) ? $page - 1 : 0;
$next   = $page + 1;
```

Now you're ready to fire up the database connection and run a simple `SELECT` query. This should be placed in a `try {} catch {}` block. You can then place the iterators to be stacked inside the `try {}` block:

```
try {
    $connection = new Application\Database\Connection(
      include __DIR__ . DB_CONFIG_FILE);
    $sql    = 'SELECT * FROM iso_country_codes';
    $arrayIterator    = fetchCountryName($sql, $connection);
    $filteredIterator = nameFilterIterator($arrayIterator, $name);
    $limitIterator    = pagination(
    $filteredIterator, $offset, $limit);
} catch (Throwable $e) {
    echo $e->getMessage();
}
```

Now we're ready for the HTML. In this simple example we present a form that lets the user select the number of items per page and the country name:

```
<form>
  Country Name:
```

```
    <input type="text" name="name"
          value="<?= htmlspecialchars($name) ?>">
    Items Per Page:
    <select name="limit">
      <?php foreach (ITEMS_PER_PAGE as $item) : ?>
        <option<?= ($item == $limit) ? ' selected' : '' ?>>
        <?= $item ?></option>
      <?php endforeach; ?>
    </select>
    <input type="submit" />
  </form>
    <a href="?name=<?= $name ?>&limit=<?= $limit ?>
      &page=<?= $prev ?>">
    << PREV</a>
    <a href="?name=<?= $name ?>&limit=<?= $limit ?>
      &page=<?= $next ?>">
    NEXT >></a>
  <?= htmlList($limitIterator); ?>
```

The output will look something like this:

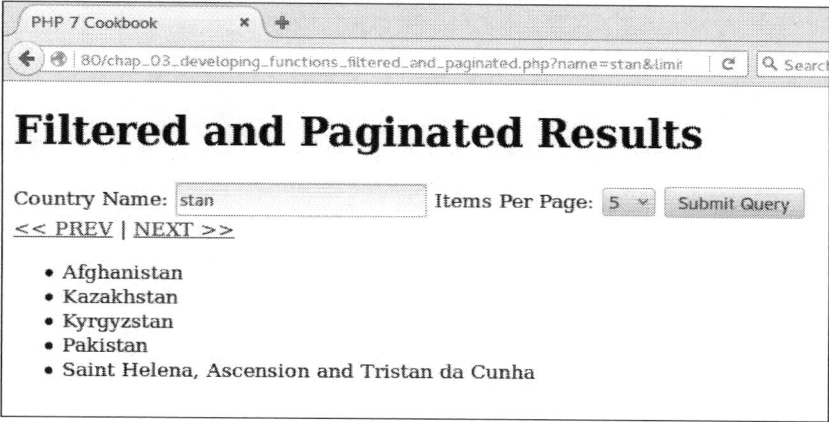

Finally, in order to test the recursive iteration of the country database lookup, you will need to include the iterator's library file, as well as the `Application\Database\Connection` class:

```
define('DB_CONFIG_FILE', '/../config/db.config.php');
include (__DIR__ . '/chap_03_developing_functions_iterators_library.
php');
include (__DIR__ . '/../Application/Database/Connection.php');
```

As before, you should wrap your database query in a `try {} catch {}` block. You can then place the code to test the recursive iteration inside the `try {}` block:

```
try {
    $connection = new Application\Database\Connection(
    include __DIR__ . DB_CONFIG_FILE);
    $sql      = 'SELECT * FROM iso_country_codes';
    $iterator = fetchAllAssoc($sql, $connection);
    $shallow  = new RecursiveArrayIterator($iterator);
    foreach ($shallow as $item) var_dump($item);
    $deep     = new RecursiveIteratorIterator($shallow);
    foreach ($deep as $item) var_dump($item);
} catch (Throwable $e) {
    echo $e->getMessage();
}
```

Here is what you can expect to see in terms of output from `RecursiveArrayIterator`:

```
aed@aed: ~/Repos/php7_recipes/source/chapter03

RecursiveArrayIterator
array(5) {
  'name' =>
  string(11) "Afghanistan"
  'iso2' =>
  string(2) "AF"
  'iso3' =>
  string(3) "AFG"
  'iso_numeric' =>
  string(1) "4"
  'iso_3166' =>
  string(13) "ISO 3166-2:AF"
}
array(5) {
  'name' =>
  string(7) "Albania"
  'iso2' =>
  string(2) "AL"
  'iso3' =>
  string(3) "ALB"
  'iso_numeric' =>
  string(1) "8"
  'iso_3166' =>
  string(13) "ISO 3166-2:AL"
}
:
```

Here is the output after using `RecursiveIteratorIterator`:

```
aed@aed: ~/Repos/php7_recipes/source/chapter03

RecursiveIteratorIterator
string(11) "Afghanistan"
string(2) "AF"
string(3) "AFG"
string(1) "4"
string(13) "ISO 3166-2:AF"
string(7) "Albania"
string(2) "AL"
string(3) "ALB"
string(1) "8"
string(13) "ISO 3166-2:AL"
string(10) "Antarctica"
string(2) "AQ"
string(3) "ATA"
string(2) "10"
string(13) "ISO 3166-2:AQ"
string(7) "Algeria"
string(2) "DZ"
string(3) "DZA"
string(2) "12"
string(13) "ISO 3166-2:DZ"
string(14) "American Samoa"
string(2) "AS"
string(3) "ASM"
string(2) "16"
:
```

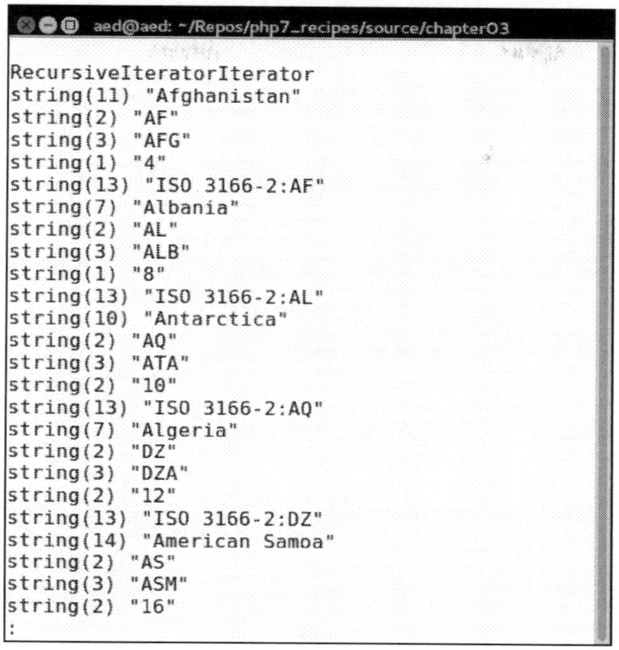

Writing your own iterator using generators

In the preceding set of recipes we demonstrated the use of iterators provided in the PHP 7 SPL. But what if this set doesn't provide you with what is needed for a given project? One solution would be to develop a function that, instead of building an array that is then returned, uses the `yield` keyword to return values progressively by way of iteration. Such a function is referred to as a **generator**. In fact, in the background, the PHP engine will automatically convert your function into a special built-in class called `Generator`.

There are several advantages to this approach. The main benefit is seen when you have a large container to traverse (that is, parsing a massive file). The traditional approach has been to build up an array, and then return that array. The problem with this is that you are effectively doubling the amount of memory required! Also, performance is affected in that results are only achieved once the final array has been returned.

How to do it...

1. In this example we build on the library of iterator-based functions, adding a generator of our own design. In this case we will duplicate the functionality described in the section above on iterators where we stacked an `ArrayIterator`, `FilterIterator`, and `LimitIterator`.
2. Because we need access to the source array, the desired filter, page number, and number of items per page, we include the appropriate parameters into a single `filteredResultsGenerator()` function. We then calculate the offset based on the page number and limit (that is, number of items per page). Next, we loop through the array, apply the filter, and continue the loop if the offset has not yet been reached, or break if the limit has been reached:

```
function filteredResultsGenerator(array $array, $filter,
                                  $limit = 10, $page = 0)
  {
    $max    = count($array);
    $offset = $page * $limit;
    foreach ($array as $key => $value) {
      if (!stripos($value, $filter) !== FALSE) continue;
      if (--$offset >= 0) continue;
      if (--$limit <= 0) break;
      yield $value;
    }
  }
```

3. You'll notice the primary difference between this function and others is the `yield` keyword. The effect of this keyword is to signal the PHP engine to produce a `Generator` instance and encapsulate the code.

How it works...

To demonstrate the use of the `filteredResultsGenerator()` function we'll have you implement a web application that scans a web page and produces a filtered and paginated list of URLs hoovered from `HREF` attributes.

First you need to add the code for the `filteredResultsGenerator()` function to the library file used in the previous recipe, then place the functions described previously into an include file, `chap_03_developing_functions_iterators_library.php`.

Next, define a test script, `chap_03_developing_functions_using_generator.php`, that includes both the function library as well as the file that defines `Application\Web\Hoover`, described in *Chapter 1, Building a Foundation*:

```
include (__DIR__ . DIRECTORY_SEPARATOR . 'chap_03_developing_
functions_iterators_library.php');
include (__DIR__ . '/../Application/Web/Hoover.php');
```

You will then need to gather input from the user regarding which URL to scan, what string to use as a filter, how many items per page, and the current page number.

The **null coalesce** operator (`??`) is ideal for getting input from the Web. It does not generate any notices if not defined. If the parameter is not received from user input, you can supply a default.

```
$url    = trim(strip_tags($_GET['url'] ?? ''));
$filter = trim(strip_tags($_GET['filter'] ?? ''));
$limit  = (int) ($_GET['limit'] ?? 10);
$page   = (int) ($_GET['page']  ?? 0);
```

Best practice

Web security should always be a priority consideration. In this example you can use `strip_tags()` and also force the data type to integer `(int)` as measures to sanitize user input.

You are then in a position to define variables used in links for previous and next pages in the paginated list. Note that you could also apply a *sanity check* to make sure the next page doesn't go off the end of the result set. For the sake of brevity, such a sanity check was not applied in this example:

```
$next   = $page + 1;
$prev   = $page - 1;
$base   = '?url=' . htmlspecialchars($url)
        . '&filter=' . htmlspecialchars($filter)
        . '&limit=' . $limit
        . '&page=';
```

We then need to create an `Application\Web\Hoover` instance and grab `HREF` attributes from the target URL:

```
$vac    = new Application\Web\Hoover();
$list   = $vac->getAttribute($url, 'href');
```

Finally, we define HTML output that renders an input form and runs our generator through the `htmlList()` function described previously:

```
<form>
<table>
<tr>
<th>URL</th>
<td>
<input type="text" name="url"
  value="<?= htmlspecialchars($url) ?>"/>
</td>
</tr>
<tr>
<th>Filter</th>
<td>
<input type="text" name="filter"
  value="<?= htmlspecialchars($filter) ?>"/></td>
</tr>
<tr>
<th>Limit</th>
<td><input type="text" name="limit" value="<?= $limit ?>"/></td>
</tr>
<tr>
<th> </th><td><input type="submit" /></td>
</tr>
<tr>
<td> </td>
<td>
<a href="<?= $base . $prev ?>"><-- PREV |
<a href="<?= $base . $next ?>">NEXT --></td>
</tr>
</table>
</form>
<hr>
<?= htmlList(filteredResultsGenerator(
$list, $filter, $limit, $page)); ?>
```

Here is an example of the output:

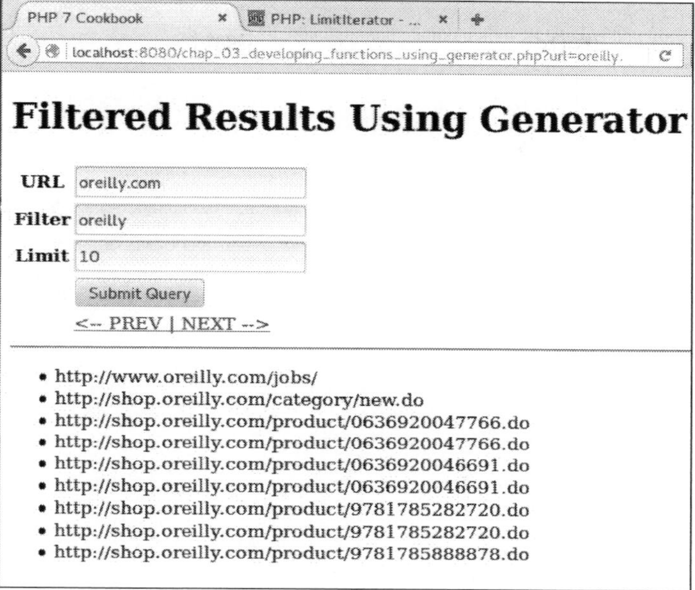

4
Working with PHP Object-Oriented Programming

In this chapter we will cover:

- Developing classes
- Extending classes
- Using static properties and methods
- Using namespaces
- Defining visibility
- Using interfaces
- Using traits
- Implementing anonymous classes

Introduction

In this chapter, we will consider recipes that take advantage of the **object-oriented programming** (**OOP**) capabilities available in PHP 7.0, 7.1, and above. Most of the OOP functionality available in PHP 7.x is also available in PHP 5.6. A new feature introduced in PHP 7 is support for **anonymous classes**. In PHP 7.1, you can modify the visibility of class constants.

Another radically new feature is the ability to **catch** certain types of error. This is discussed in greater detail in *Chapter 13, Best Practices, Testing, and Debugging*.

Developing classes

The traditional development approach is to place the class into its own file. Typically, classes contain logic that implements a single purpose. Classes are further broken down into self-contained functions which are referred to as **methods**. Variables defined inside classes are referred to as **properties**. It is recommended to develop a test class at the same time, a topic discussed in more detail in *Chapter 13, Best Practices, Testing, and Debugging*.

How to do it...

1. Create a file to contain the class definition. For the purposes of autoloading it is recommended that the filename match the classname. At the top of the file, before the keyword `class`, add a **DocBlock**. You can then define properties and methods. In this example, we define a class `Test`. It has a property `$test`, and a method `getTest()`:

```
<?php
declare(strict_types=1);
/**
 * This is a demonstration class.
 *
 * The purpose of this class is to get and set
 * a protected property $test
 *
 */
class Test
{

  protected $test = 'TEST';

  /**
   * This method returns the current value of $test
   *
   * @return string $test
   */
  public function getTest() : string
  {
    return $this->test;
  }
```

```
    /**
     * This method sets the value of $test
     *
     * @param string $test
     * @return Test $this
     */
    public function setTest(string $test)
    {
      $this->test = $test;
      return $this;
    }
}
```

Best practice

It is considered best practice to name the file after the class. Although class names in PHP are not case sensitive, it is further considered best practice to use an uppercase letter for the first name of a class. You should not put executable code in a class definition file.

Each class should contain a **DocBlock** before the keyword `class`. In the DocBlock you should include a short description of the purpose of the class. Skip a line, and then include a more detailed description. You can also include @ tags such as `@author`, `@license` and so on. Each method should likewise be preceded by a DocBlock that identifies the purpose of the method, as well as its incoming parameters and return value.

2. It's possible to define more than one class per file, but is not considered best practice. In this example we create a file, `NameAddress.php`, which defines two classes, `Name` and `Address`:

```
<?php
declare(strict_types=1);
class Name
{

  protected $name = '';

  public function getName() : string
  {
    return $this->name;
  }

  public function setName(string $name)
  {
```

```
        $this->name = $name;

        return $this;
    }
}

class Address
{

    protected $address = '';

    public function getAddress() : string
    {
        return $this->address;
    }

    public function setAddress(string $address)
    {
        $this->address = $address;
        return $this;
    }
}
```

Although you can define more than one class in a single file, as shown in the preceding code snippet, it is not considered best practice. Not only does this negate the logical purity of the file, but it makes autoloading more difficult.

3. Class names are case-insensitive. Duplications will be flagged as errors. In this example, in a file `TwoClass.php`, we define two classes, `TwoClass` and `twoclass`:

```
<?php
class TwoClass
{
  public function showOne()
  {
    return 'ONE';
  }
}

// a fatal error will occur when the second class definition is
parsed
class twoclass
{
```

```
    public function showTwo()
    {
      return 'TWO';
    }
  }
```

4. PHP 7.1 has addressed inconsistent behavior in the use of the keyword `$this`. Although permitted in PHP 7.0 and PHP 5.x, any of the following uses of `$this` will now generate an error as of PHP 7.1, if `$this` is used as:
   - A parameter
   - A `static` variable
   - A `global` variable
   - A variable used in `try...catch` blocks
   - A variable used in `foreach()`
   - As an argument to `unset()`
   - As a variable (that is, `$a = 'this'; echo $$a`)
   - Indirectly via reference
5. If you need to create an object instance but don't care to define a discreet class, you can use the generic `stdClass` which is built into PHP. `stdClass` allows you to define properties *on the fly* without having to define a discreet class that extends `stdClass`:

   ```
   $obj = new stdClass();
   ```

6. This facility is used in a number of different places in PHP. As an example, when you use **PHP Data Objects** (**PDO**) to do a database query, one of the fetch modes is `PDO::FETCH_OBJ`. This mode returns instances of `stdClass` where the properties represent database table columns:

   ```
   $stmt = $connection->pdo->query($sql);
   $row  = $stmt->fetch(PDO::FETCH_OBJ);
   ```

How it works...

Take the example for the `Test` class shown in the preceding code snippet, and place the code in a file named `Test.php`. Create another file called `chap_04_oop_defining_class_test.php`. Add the following code:

```
require __DIR__ . '/Test.php';

$test = new Test();
echo $test->getTest();
echo PHP_EOL;
```

```
$test->setTest('ABC');
echo $test->getTest();
echo PHP_EOL;
```

The output will show the initial value of the `$test` property, followed by the new value modified by calling `setTest()`:

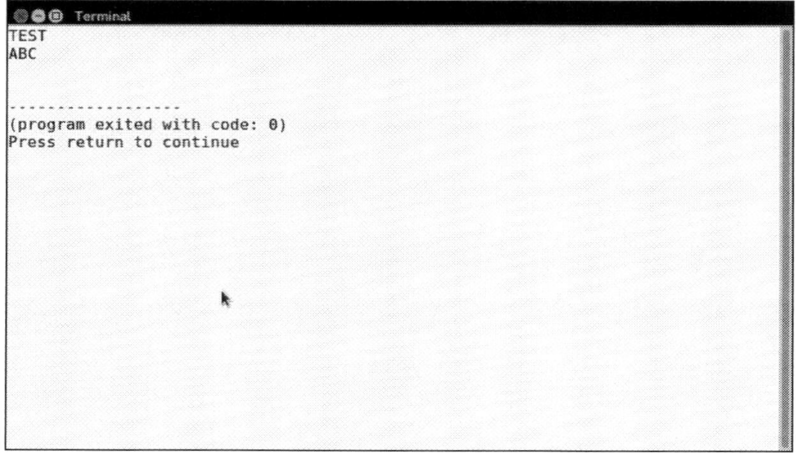

The next example has you define two classes, `Name` and `Address` in a single file `NameAddress.php`. You can call and use these two classes with the following code:

```
require __DIR__ . '/NameAddress.php';

$name = new Name();
$name->setName('TEST');
$addr = new Address();
$addr->setAddress('123 Main Street');

echo $name->getName() . ' lives at ' . $addr->getAddress();
```

Although no errors are generated by the PHP interpreter, by defining multiple classes, the logical purity of the file is compromised. Also, the filename doesn't match the classname, which could impact the ability to autoload.

The output from this example is shown next:

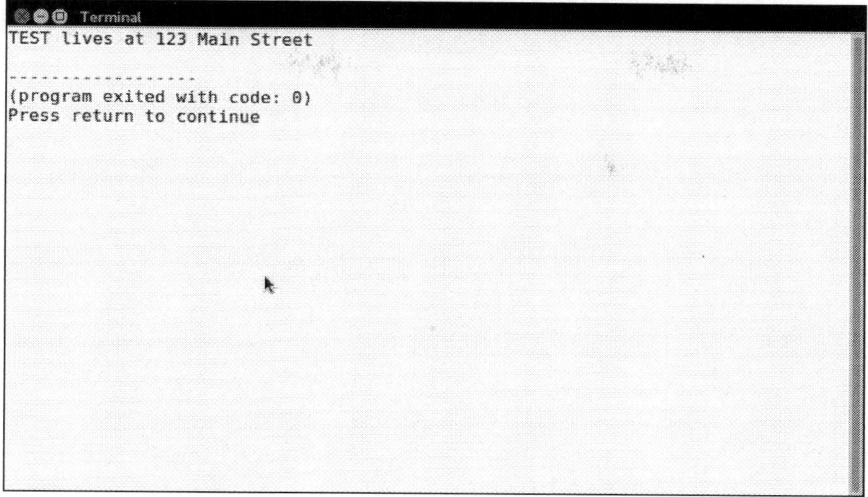
Terminal
TEST lives at 123 Main Street

(program exited with code: 0)
Press return to continue

Step 3 also shows two class definitions in one file. In this case, however, the objective is to demonstrate that classnames in PHP are case-insensitive. Place the code into a file, `TwoClass.php`. When you try to include the file, an error is generated:

```
PHP Fatal error:  Cannot declare class twoclass, because the name is already in
use in /home/aed/Repos/php7_recipes/source/chapter04/TwoClass.php on line 25
PHP Stack trace:
PHP   1. {main}() /home/aed/Repos/php7_recipes/source/chapter04/chap_04_oop_clas
ses_case_insensitive.php:0
PHP   2. require() /home/aed/Repos/php7_recipes/source/chapter04/chap_04_oop_cla
sses_case_insensitive.php:6

Fatal error: Cannot declare class twoclass, because the name is already in use i
n /home/aed/Repos/php7_recipes/source/chapter04/TwoClass.php on line 25

Call Stack:
    0.0002     357952   1. {main}() /home/aed/Repos/php7_recipes/source/chapter0
4/chap_04_oop_classes_case_insensitive.php:0
    0.0003     360752   2. require('/home/aed/Repos/php7_recipes/source/chapter0
4/TwoClass.php') /home/aed/Repos/php7_recipes/source/chapter04/chap_04_oop_class
es_case_insensitive.php:6

------------------
(program exited with code: 255)
Press return to continue
```

To demonstrate the direct use of `stdClass`, create an instance, assign a value to a property, and use `var_dump()` to display the results. To see how `stdClass` is used internally, use `var_dump()` to display the results of a `PDO` query where the fetch mode is set to `FETCH_OBJ`.

Enter the following code:

```
$obj = new stdClass();
$obj->test = 'TEST';
echo $obj->test;
echo PHP_EOL;

include (__DIR__ . '/../Application/Database/Connection.php');
$connection = new Application\Database\Connection(
  include __DIR__ . DB_CONFIG_FILE);

$sql  = 'SELECT * FROM iso_country_codes';
$stmt = $connection->pdo->query($sql);
$row  = $stmt->fetch(PDO::FETCH_OBJ);
var_dump($row);
```

Here is the output:

```
TEST
class stdClass#5 (5) {
  public $name =>
  string(11) "Afghanistan"
  public $iso2 =>
  string(2) "AF"
  public $iso3 =>
  string(3) "AFG"
  public $iso_numeric =>
  string(1) "4"
  public $iso_3166 =>
  string(13) "ISO 3166-2:AF"
}


-----------------
(program exited with code: 0)
Press return to continue
```

See also...

For more information on refinements in PHP 7.1 on the keyword `$this`, please see `https://wiki.php.net/rfc/this_var`.

Extending classes

One of the primary reasons developers use OOP is because of its ability to re-use existing code, yet, at the same time, add or override functionality. In PHP, the keyword `extends` is used to establish a parent/child relationship between classes.

How to do it...

1. In the `child` class, use the keyword `extends` to set up inheritance. In the example that follows, the `Customer` class extends the `Base` class. Any instance of `Customer` will inherit visible methods and properties, in this case, `$id`, `getId()` and `setId()`:

```
class Base
{
  protected $id;
  public function getId()
  {
    return $this->id;
  }
  public function setId($id)
  {
    $this->id = $id;
  }
}

class Customer extends Base
{
  protected $name;
  public function getName()
  {
    return $this->name;
  }
  public function setName($name)
  {
    $this->name = $name;
  }
}
```

2. You can force any developer using your class to define a method by marking it `abstract`. In this example, the `Base` class defines as `abstract` the `validate()` method. The reason why it must be abstract is because it would be impossible to determine exactly how a child class would be validated from the perspective of the parent `Base` class:

```
abstract class Base
{
  protected $id;
  public function getId()
  {
    return $this->id;
  }
```

```
    public function setId($id)
    {
      $this->id = $id;
    }
    public function validate();
  }
```

If a class contains an **abstract method**, the class itself must be declared as `abstract`.

3. PHP only supports a single line of inheritance. The next example shows a class, `Member`, which inherits from `Customer`. `Customer`, in turn, inherits from `Base`:

```
class Base
{
  protected $id;
  public function getId()
  {
    return $this->id;
  }
  public function setId($id)
  {
    $this->id = $id;
  }
}

class Customer extends Base
{
  protected $name;
  public function getName()
  {
    return $this->name;
  }
  public function setName($name)
  {
    $this->name = $name;
  }
}

class Member extends Customer
{
  protected $membership;
  public function getMembership()
  {
```

```
        return $this->membership;
    }
    public function setMembership($memberId)
    {
        $this->membership = $memberId;
    }
}
```

4. To satisfy a type-hint, any child of the target class can be used. The `test()` function, shown in the following code snippet, requires an instance of the `Base` class as an argument. Any class within the line of inheritance can be accepted as an argument. Anything else passed to `test()` throws a `TypeError`:

```
function test(Base $object)
{
  return $object->getId();
}
```

How it works...

In the first bullet point, a `Base` class and a `Customer` class were defined. For the sake of demonstration, place these two class definitions in a single file, `chap_04_oop_extends.php`, and add the following code:

```
$customer = new Customer();
$customer->setId(100);
$customer->setName('Fred');
var_dump($customer);
```

Note that the `$id` property and the `getId()` and `setId()` methods are inherited from the parent `Base` class into the child `Customer` class:

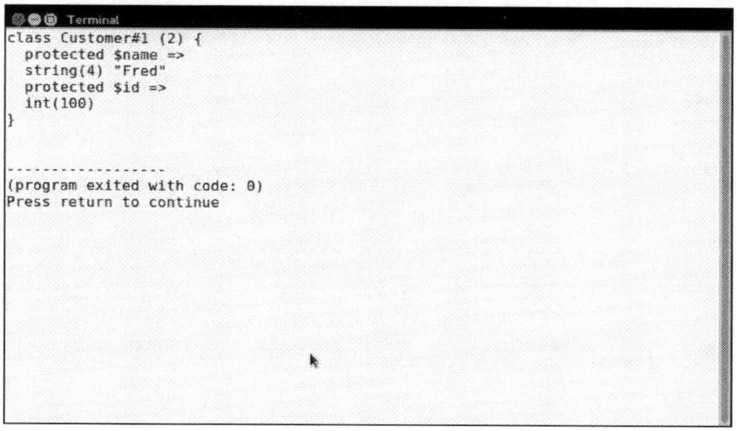

```
class Customer#1 (2) {
  protected $name =>
  string(4) "Fred"
  protected $id =>
  int(100)
}


------------------
(program exited with code: 0)
Press return to continue
```

To illustrate the use of an `abstract` method, imagine that you wish to add some sort of validation capability to any class that extends `Base`. The problem is that there is no way to know what might be validated in the inherited classes. The only thing that is certain is that you must have a validation capability.

Take the same `Base` class mentioned in the preceding explanation and add a new method, `validate()`. Label the method as `abstract`, and do not define any code. Notice what happens when the child `Customer` class extends `Base`.

```
Terminal
PHP Fatal error:  Class Base contains 1 abstract method and must therefore be de
clared abstract or implement the remaining methods (Base::validate) in /home/aed
/Repos/php7_recipes/source/chapter04/chap_04_oop_abstract.php on line 16

Fatal error: Class Base contains 1 abstract method and must therefore be declare
d abstract or implement the remaining methods (Base::validate) in /home/aed/Repo
s/php7_recipes/source/chapter04/chap_04_oop_abstract.php on line 16



------------------
(program exited with code: 255)
Press return to continue
```

If you then label the `Base` class as `abstract`, but fail to define a `validate()` method in the child class, the *same error* will be generated. Finally, go ahead and implement the `validate()` method in a child `Customer` class:

```
class Customer extends Base
{
  protected $name;
  public function getName()
  {
    return $this->name;
  }
  public function setName($name)
  {
    $this->name = $name;
  }
  public function validate()
  {
    $valid = 0;
    $count = count(get_object_vars($this));
```

```
        if (!empty($this->id) &&is_int($this->id)) $valid++;
        if (!empty($this->name)
        &&preg_match('/[a-z0-9 ]/i', $this->name)) $valid++;
        return ($valid == $count);
      }
    }
```

You can then add the following procedural code to test the results:

```
    $customer = new Customer();

    $customer->setId(100);
    $customer->setName('Fred');
    echo "Customer [id]: {$customer->getName()}" .
         . "[{$customer->getId()}]\n";
    echo ($customer->validate()) ? 'VALID' : 'NOT VALID';
    $customer->setId('XXX');
    $customer->setName('$%£&*()');
    echo "Customer [id]: {$customer->getName()}"
      . "[{$customer->getId()}]\n";
    echo ($customer->validate()) ? 'VALID' : 'NOT VALID';
```

Here is the output:

```
Terminal
Customer [id]: Fred [100]
VALID
Customer [id]: $%£&*() [XXX]
NOT VALID


------------------
(program exited with code: 0)
Press return to continue
```

To show a single line of inheritance, add a new `Member` class to the first example of `Base` and `Customer` shown in the preceding step 1:

```
    class Member extends Customer
    {
      protected $membership;
      public function getMembership()
```

```
    {
      return $this->membership;
    }
    public function setMembership($memberId)
    {
      $this->membership = $memberId;
    }
}
```

Create an instance of `Member`, and notice, in the following code, that all properties and methods are available from every inherited class, even if not directly inherited:

```
$member = new Member();
$member->setId(100);
$member->setName('Fred');
$member->setMembership('A299F322');
var_dump($member);
```

Here is the output:

```
class Member#1 (3) {
  protected $membership =>
  string(8) "A299F322"
  protected $name =>
  string(4) "Fred"
  protected $id =>
  int(100)
}


-----------------
(program exited with code: 0)
Press return to continue
```

Now define a function, `test()`, which takes an instance of `Base` as an argument:

```
function test(Base $object)
{
  return $object->getId();
}
```

Notice that instances of `Base`, `Customer`, and `Member` are all acceptable as arguments:

```
$base = new Base();
$base->setId(100);
```

```
$customer = new Customer();
$customer->setId(101);

$member = new Member();
$member->setId(102);

// all 3 classes work in test()
echo test($base)      . PHP_EOL;
echo test($customer) . PHP_EOL;
echo test($member)    . PHP_EOL;
```

Here is the output:

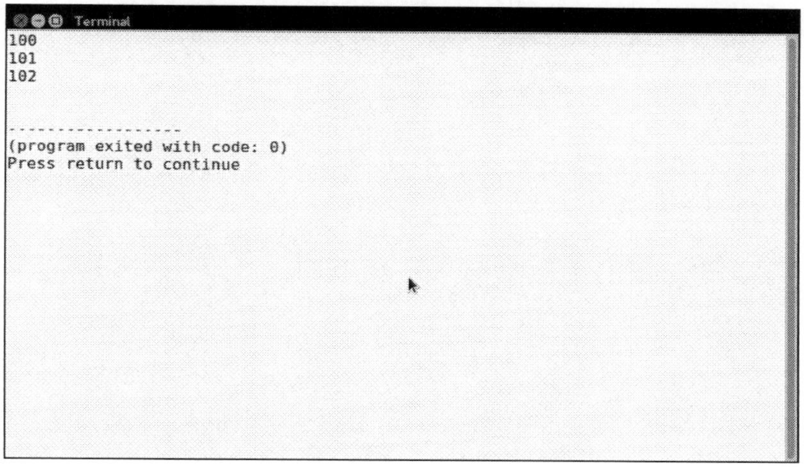

```
100
101
102


------------------
(program exited with code: 0)
Press return to continue
```

However, if you try to run `test()` with an object instance that is not in the line of inheritance, a `TypeError` is thrown:

```
class Orphan
{
  protected $id;
  public function getId()
  {
    return $this->id;
  }
  public function setId($id)
  {
    $this->id = $id;
  }
}
try {
```

```
    $orphan = new Orphan();
    $orphan->setId(103);
    echo test($orphan) . PHP_EOL;
} catch (TypeError $e) {
    echo 'Does not work!' . PHP_EOL;
    echo $e->getMessage();
}
```

We can observe this in the following image:

```
Terminal
100
101
102

PHP TypeError:  Argument 1 passed to test() must be an instance of Base, instanc
e of Orphan given, called in /home/aed/Repos/php7_recipes/source/chapter04/chap_
04_oop_type_hint.php on line 80 in /home/aed/Repos/php7_recipes/source/chapter04
/chap_04_oop_type_hint.php on line 56
PHP Stack trace:
PHP   1. {main}() /home/aed/Repos/php7_recipes/source/chapter04/chap_04_oop_type
_hint.php:0
PHP   2. test() /home/aed/Repos/php7_recipes/source/chapter04/chap_04_oop_type_h
int.php:80


TypeError: Argument 1 passed to test() must be an instance of Base, instance of
Orphan given, called in /home/aed/Repos/php7_recipes/source/chapter04/chap_04_oo
p_type_hint.php on line 80 in /home/aed/Repos/php7_recipes/source/chapter04/chap
_04_oop_type_hint.php on line 56

Call Stack:
    0.0012     370176   1. {main}() /home/aed/Repos/php7_recipes/source/chapter0
4/chap_04_oop_type_hint.php:0
    0.0015     370496   2. test() /home/aed/Repos/php7_recipes/source/chapter04/
```

Using static properties and methods

PHP lets you access properties or methods without having to create an instance of the class. The keyword used for this purpose is **static**.

How to do it...

1. At its simplest, simply add the `static` keyword after stating the visibility level when declaring an ordinary property or method. Use the `self` keyword to reference the property internally:

```
class Test
{
  public static $test = 'TEST';
  public static function getTest()
  {
```

```
        return self::$test;
    }
}
```

2. The `self` keyword will bind early, which will cause problems when accessing static information in child classes. If you absolutely need to access information from the child class, use the `static` keyword in place of `self`. This process is referred to as **Late Static Binding**.
3. In the following example, if you echo `Child::getEarlyTest()`, the output will be **TEST**. If, on the other hand, you run `Child::getLateTest()`, the output will be **CHILD**. The reason is that PHP will bind to the *earliest* definition when using `self`, whereas the *latest* binding is used for the `static` keyword:

```
class Test2
{
  public static $test = 'TEST2';
  public static function getEarlyTest()
  {
    return self::$test;
  }
  public static function getLateTest()
  {
    return static::$test;
  }
}

class Child extends Test2
{
  public static $test = 'CHILD';
}
```

4. In many cases, the **Factory** design pattern is used in conjunction with static methods to produce instances of objects given different parameters. In this example, a static method `factory()` is defined which returns a PDO connection:

```
public static function factory(
  $driver,$dbname,$host,$user,$pwd,array $options = [])
  {
    $dsn = sprintf('%s:dbname=%s;host=%s',
    $driver, $dbname, $host);
    try {
        return new PDO($dsn, $user, $pwd, $options);
    } catch (PDOException $e) {
        error_log($e->getMessage);
    }
  }
```

How it works...

You can reference static properties and methods using the **class resolution operator** "::". Given the `Test` class shown previously, if you run this code:

```
echo Test::$test;
echo PHP_EOL;
echo Test::getTest();
echo PHP_EOL;
```

You will see this output:

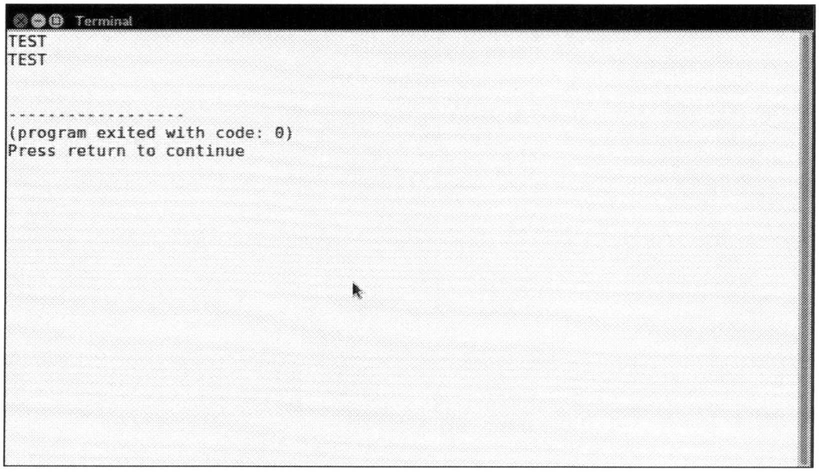

```
TEST
TEST


------------------
(program exited with code: 0)
Press return to continue
```

To illustrate Late Static Binding, based on the classes `Test2` and `Child` shown previously, try this code:

```
echo Test2::$test;
echo Child::$test;
echo Child::getEarlyTest();
echo Child::getLateTest();
```

The output illustrates the difference between `self` and `static`:

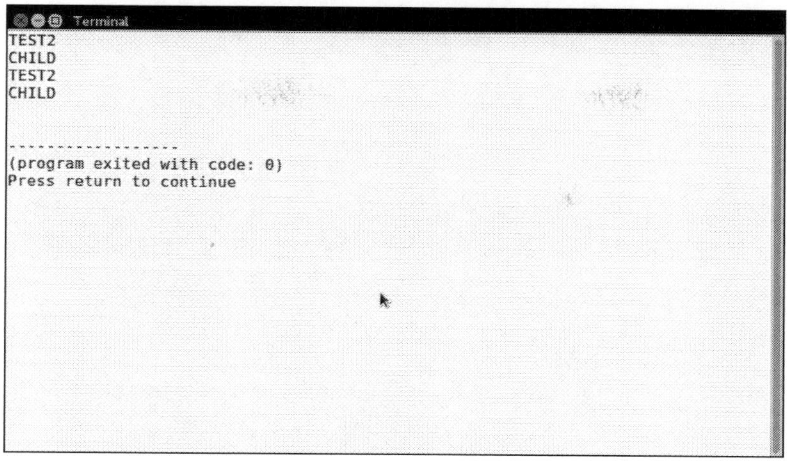

```
TEST2
CHILD
TEST2
CHILD


------------------
(program exited with code: 0)
Press return to continue
```

Finally, to test the `factory()` method shown previously, save the code into the `Application\Database\Connection` class in a `Connection.php` file in the `Application\Database` folder. You can then try this:

```
include __DIR__ . '/../Application/Database/Connection.php';
use Application\Database\Connection;
$connection = Connection::factory(
'mysql', 'php7cookbook', 'localhost', 'test', 'password');
$stmt = $connection->query('SELECT name FROM iso_country_codes');
while ($country = $stmt->fetch(PDO::FETCH_COLUMN))
echo $country . '';
```

You will see a list of countries pulled from the sample database:

```
Afghanistan Albania Antarctica Algeria American Samoa Andorra Angola Antigua and
 Barbuda Azerbaijan Argentina Australia Austria Bahamas Bahrain Bangladesh Armen
ia Barbados Belgium Bermuda Bhutan Bolivia, Plurinational State of Bosnia and He
rzegovina Botswana Bouvet Island Brazil Belize British Indian Ocean Territory So
lomon Islands Virgin Islands, British Brunei Darussalam Bulgaria Myanmar Burundi
 Belarus Cambodia Cameroon Canada Cape Verde Cayman Islands Central African Repu
blic Sri Lanka Chad Chile China Taiwan, Province of China Christmas Island Cocos
 (Keeling) Islands Colombia Comoros Mayotte Congo Congo, the Democratic Republic
 of the Cook Islands Costa Rica Croatia Cuba Cyprus Czech Republic Benin Denmark
 Dominica Dominican Republic Ecuador El Salvador Equatorial Guinea Ethiopia Erit
rea Estonia Faroe Islands Falkland Islands (Malvinas) South Georgia and the Sout
h Sandwich Islands Fiji Finland Åland Islands France French Guiana French Polyne
sia French Southern Territories Djibouti Gabon Georgia Gambia Palestine, State o
f Germany Ghana Gibraltar Kiribati Greece Greenland Grenada Guadeloupe Guam Guat
emala Guinea Guyana Haiti Heard Island and McDonald Islands Holy See (Vatican Ci
ty State) Honduras Hong Kong Hungary Iceland India Indonesia Iran, Islamic Repub
lic of Iraq Ireland Israel Italy Côte d'Ivoire Jamaica Japan Kazakhstan Jordan K
enya Korea, Democratic People's Republic of Korea, Republic of Kuwait Kyrgyzstan
 Lao People's Democratic Republic Lebanon Lesotho Latvia Liberia Libya Liechtens
tein Lithuania Luxembourg Macao Madagascar Malawi Malaysia Maldives Mali Malta M
artinique Mauritania Mauritius Mexico Monaco Mongolia Moldova, Republic of Monte
negro Montserrat Morocco Mozambique Oman Namibia Nauru Nepal Netherlands Curaçao
 Aruba Sint Maarten (Dutch part) Bonaire, Sint Eustatius and Saba New Caledonia
Vanuatu New Zealand Nicaragua Niger Nigeria Niue Norfolk Island Norway Northern
```

See also

For more information on Late Static Binding, see this explanation in the PHP documentation:

http://php.net/manual/en/language.oop5.late-static-bindings.php

Using namespaces

An aspect that is critical to advanced PHP development is the use of namespaces. The arbitrarily defined namespace becomes a prefix to the class name, thereby avoiding the problem of accidental class duplication, and allowing you extraordinary freedom of development. Another benefit to the use of a namespace, assuming it matches the directory structure, is that it facilitates autoloading, as discussed in *Chapter 1, Building a Foundation*.

How to do it...

1. To define a class within a namespace, simply add the keyword `namespace` at the top of the code file:

   ```
   namespace Application\Entity;
   ```

Best practice

As with the recommendation to have only one class per file, likewise you should have only one namespace per file.

2. The only PHP code that should precede the keyword `namespace` would be a comment and/or the keyword `declare`:

   ```
   <?php
   declare(strict_types=1);
   namespace Application\Entity;
   /**
    * Address
    *
    */
   class Address
   {
     // some code
   }
   ```

3. In PHP 5, if you needed to access a class in an external namespace you could prepend a `use` statement containing only the namespace. You would need to then prefix any class reference within this namespace with the last component of the namespace:

```
use Application\Entity;
$name = new Entity\Name();
$addr = new Entity\Address();
$prof = new Entity\Profile();
```

4. Alternatively, you could distinctly specify all three classes:

```
use Application\Entity\Name;
use Application\Entity\Address;
use Application\Entity\Profile;
$name = new Name();
$addr = new Address();
$prof = new Profile();
```

5. PHP 7 has introduced a syntactical improvement referred to as **group use** which greatly improves code readability:

```
use Application\Entity\ {
  Name,
  Address,
  Profile
};
$name = new Name();
$addr = new Address();
$prof = new Profile();
```

6. As mentioned in *Chapter 1, Building a Foundation*, namespaces form an integral part of the **autoloading** process. This example shows a demonstration autoloader which echoes the argument passed, and then attempts to include a file based on the namespace and class name. This assumes that the directory structure matches the namespace:

```
function __autoload($class)
{
  echo "Argument Passed to Autoloader = $class\n";
  include __DIR__ . '/../' . str_replace(
                    '\\', DIRECTORY_SEPARATOR, $class) . '.php';
}
```

How it works...

For illustration purposes, define a directory structure that matches the `Application\*` namespace. Create a base folder `Application`, and a sub-folder `Entity`. You can also include any sub-folders as desired, such as `Database` and `Generic`, used in other chapters:

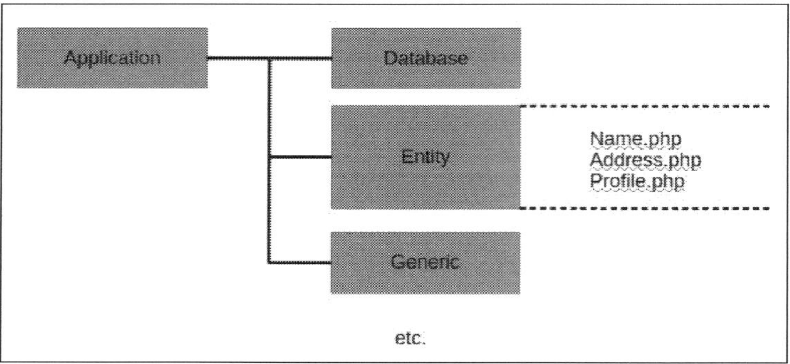

Next, create three `entity` classes, each in their own file, under the `Application/Entity` folder: `Name.php`, `Address.php`, and `Profile.php`. We only show `Application\Entity\Name` here. `Application\Entity\Address` and `Application\Entity\Profile` will be the same, except that `Address` has an `$address` property, and `Profile` has a `$profile` property, each with an appropriate `get` and `set` method:

```
<?php
declare(strict_types=1);
namespace Application\Entity;
/**
 * Name
 *
 */
class Name
{

  protected $name = '';

  /**
   * This method returns the current value of $name
   *
   * @return string $name
   */
  public function getName() : string
  {
    return $this->name;
  }

  /**
```

```
     * This method sets the value of $name
     *
     * @param string $name
     * @return name $this
     */
    public function setName(string $name)
    {
      $this->name = $name;
      return $this;
    }
}
```

You can then either use the autoloader defined in *Chapter 1, Building a Foundation*, or use the simple autoloader mentioned previously. Place the commands to set up autoloading in a file, `chap_04_oop_namespace_example_1.php`. In this file, you can then specify a use statement which only references the namespace, not the class names. Create instances of the three entity classes `Name`, `Address` and `Profile`, by prefixing the class name with the last part of the namespace, `Entity`:

```
use Application\Entity;
$name = new Entity\Name();
$addr = new Entity\Address();
$prof = new Entity\Profile();

var_dump($name);
var_dump($addr);
var_dump($prof);
```

Here is the output:

```
Terminal
Argument Passed to Autoloader = Application\Entity\Name
Argument Passed to Autoloader = Application\Entity\Address
Argument Passed to Autoloader = Application\Entity\Profile
class Application\Entity\Name#1 (1) {
  protected $name =>
  string(0) ""
}
class Application\Entity\Address#2 (1) {
  protected $address =>
  string(0) ""
}
class Application\Entity\Profile#3 (1) {
  protected $profile =>
  string(0) ""
}


------------------
(program exited with code: 0)
Press return to continue
```

Next, use **Save as** to copy the file to a new one named `chap_04_oop_namespace_example_2.php`. Change the `use` statement to the following:

```
use Application\Entity\Name;
use Application\Entity\Address;
use Application\Entity\Profile;
```

You can now create class instances using only the class name:

```
$name = new Name();
$addr = new Address();
$prof = new Profile();
```

When you run this script, here is the output:

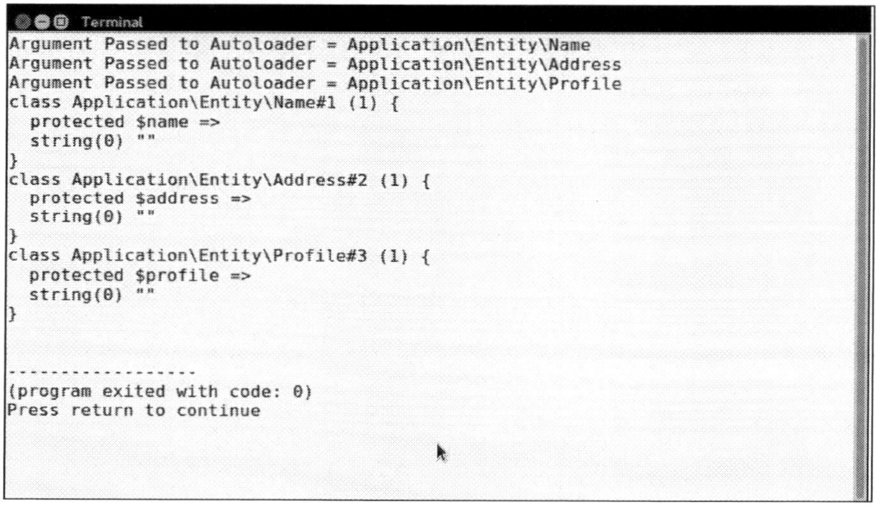

```
Terminal
Argument Passed to Autoloader = Application\Entity\Name
Argument Passed to Autoloader = Application\Entity\Address
Argument Passed to Autoloader = Application\Entity\Profile
class Application\Entity\Name#1 (1) {
  protected $name =>
  string(0) ""
}
class Application\Entity\Address#2 (1) {
  protected $address =>
  string(0) ""
}
class Application\Entity\Profile#3 (1) {
  protected $profile =>
  string(0) ""
}


------------------
(program exited with code: 0)
Press return to continue
```

Finally, again run **Save as** and create a new file, `chap_04_oop_namespace_example_3.php`. You can now test the **group use** feature introduced in PHP 7:

```
use Application\Entity\ {
  Name,
  Address,
  Profile
};
$name = new Name();
$addr = new Address();
$prof = new Profile();
```

Again, when you run this block of code, the output will be the same as the preceding output:

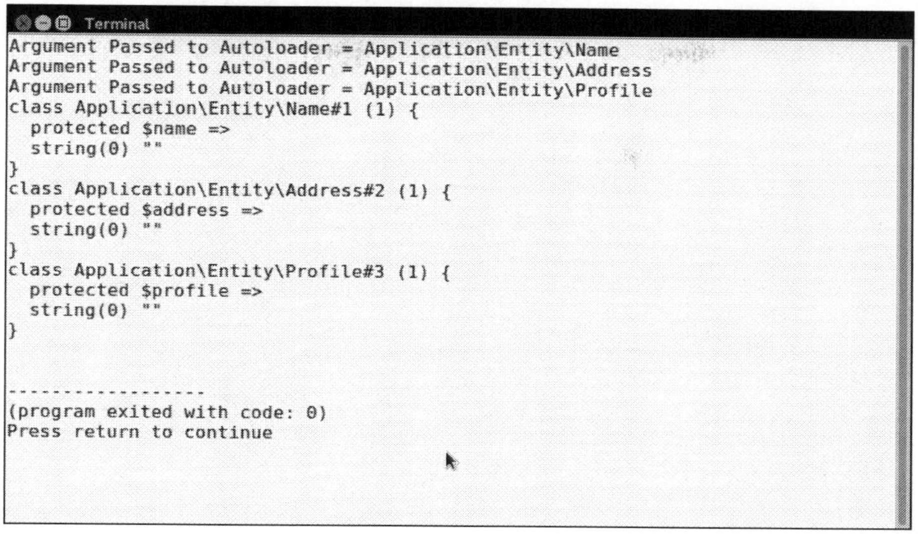

```
Terminal
Argument Passed to Autoloader = Application\Entity\Name
Argument Passed to Autoloader = Application\Entity\Address
Argument Passed to Autoloader = Application\Entity\Profile
class Application\Entity\Name#1 (1) {
  protected $name =>
  string(0) ""
}
class Application\Entity\Address#2 (1) {
  protected $address =>
  string(0) ""
}
class Application\Entity\Profile#3 (1) {
  protected $profile =>
  string(0) ""
}


------------------
(program exited with code: 0)
Press return to continue
```

Defining visibility

Deceptively, the word *visibility* has nothing to do with application security! Instead it is simply a mechanism to control the use of your code. It can be used to steer an inexperienced developer away from the *public* use of methods that should only be called inside the class definition.

How to do it...

1. Indicate the visibility level by prepending the `public`, `protected`, or `private` keyword in front of any property or method definition. You can label properties as `protected` or `private` to enforce access only through public `getters` and `setters`.
2. In this example, a `Base` class is defined with a protected property `$id`. In order to access this property, the `getId()` and `setId()` public methods are defined. The protected method `generateRandId()` can be used internally, and is inherited in the `Customer` child class. This method cannot be called directly outside of class definitions. Note the use of the new PHP 7 `random_bytes()` function to create a random ID.

```
class Base
{
  protected $id;
  private $key = 12345;
```

```
    public function getId()
    {
      return $this->id;
    }
    public function setId()
    {
      $this->id = $this->generateRandId();
    }
    protected function generateRandId()
    {
      return unpack('H*', random_bytes(8))[1];
    }
  }

  class Customer extends Base
  {
    protected $name;
    public function getName()
    {
      return $this->name;
    }
    public function setName($name)
    {
      $this->name = $name;
    }
  }
```

Best practice

Mark properties as `protected`, and define the `publicgetNameOfProperty()` and `setNameOfProperty()` methods to control access to the property. Such methods are referred to as `getters` and `setters`.

3. Mark a property or method as `private` to prevent it from being inherited or visible from *outside* the class definition. This is a good way to create a class as a **singleton**.
4. The next code example shows a class `Registry`, of which there can only be one instance. Because the constructor is marked as `private`, the only way an instance can be created is through the static method `getInstance()`:

```
class Registry
{
  protected static $instance = NULL;
  protected $registry = array();
  private function __construct()
```

```
    {
      // nobody can create an instance of this class
    }
    public static function getInstance()
    {
      if (!self::$instance) {
        self::$instance = new self();
      }
      return self::$instance;
    }
    public function __get($key)
    {
      return $this->registry[$key] ?? NULL;
    }
    public function __set($key, $value)
    {
      $this->registry[$key] = $value;
    }
  }
```

You can mark a method as `final` to prevent it from being overridden. Mark a class as `final` to prevent it from being extended.

5. Normally, class constants are considered to have a visibility level of `public`. As of PHP 7.1, you can declare class constants to be `protected` or `private`. In the following example, the `TEST_WHOLE_WORLD` class constant behaves exactly as in PHP 5. The next two constants, `TEST_INHERITED` and `TEST_LOCAL`, follow the same rules as any `protected` or `private` property or method:

```
class Test
{

  public const TEST_WHOLE_WORLD  = 'visible.everywhere';

  // NOTE: only works in PHP 7.1 and above
  protected const TEST_INHERITED = 'visible.in.child.classes';

  // NOTE: only works in PHP 7.1 and above
  private const TEST_LOCAL= 'local.to.class.Test.only';

  public static function getTestInherited()
  {
    return static::TEST_INHERITED;
```

```
    }

    public static function getTestLocal()
    {
      return static::TEST_LOCAL;
    }

  }
```

How it works...

Create a file `chap_04_basic_visibility.php` and define two classes: `Base` and `Customer`. Next, write code to create instances of each:

```
$base     = new Base();
$customer = new Customer();
```

Notice that the following code works OK, and is in fact considered the best practice:

```
$customer->setId();
$customer->setName('Test');
echo 'Welcome ' . $customer->getName() . PHP_EOL;
echo 'Your new ID number is: ' . $customer->getId() . PHP_EOL;
```

Even though `$id` is `protected`, the corresponding methods, `getId()` and `setId()`, are both `public`, and therefore accessible from outside the class definition. Here is the output:

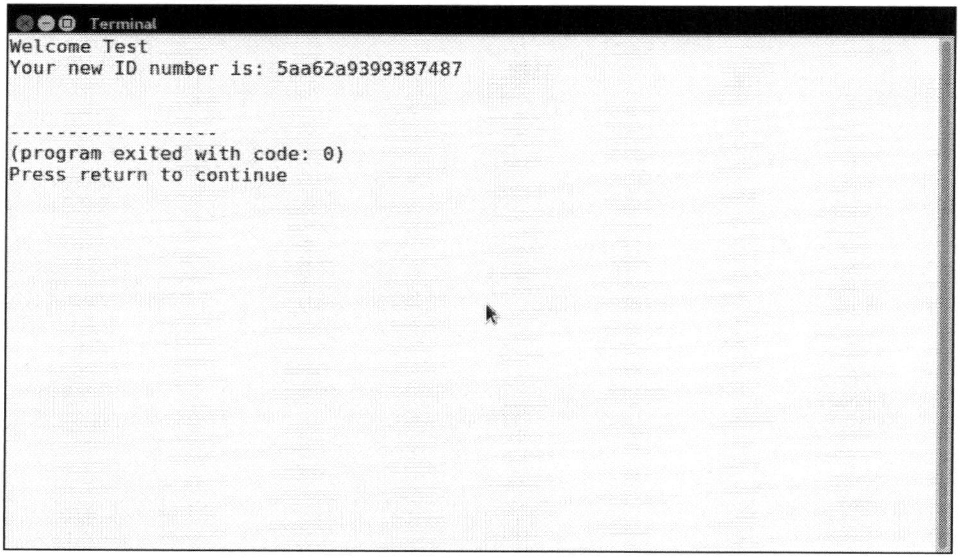

```
Terminal
Welcome Test
Your new ID number is: 5aa62a9399387487


------------------
(program exited with code: 0)
Press return to continue
```

The following lines of code will not work, however, as `private` and `protected` properties are not accessible from outside the class definition:

```
echo 'Key (does not work): ' . $base->key;
echo 'Key (does not work): ' . $customer->key;
echo 'Name (does not work): ' . $customer->name;
echo 'Random ID (does not work): ' . $customer->generateRandId();
```

The following output shows the expected errors:

```
Terminal
Welcome Test
Your new ID number is: 38d038476157732d

PHP Error:  Cannot access private property Base::$key in /home/aed/Repos/php7_re
cipes/source/chapter04/chap_04_oop_basic_visibility.php on line 52
PHP Stack trace:
PHP   1. {main}() /home/aed/Repos/php7_recipes/source/chapter04/chap_04_oop_basi
c_visibility.php:0
PHP Fatal error:  Uncaught Error: Cannot access private property Base::$key in /
home/aed/Repos/php7_recipes/source/chapter04/chap_04_oop_basic_visibility.php:52
Stack trace:
#0 {main}
  thrown in /home/aed/Repos/php7_recipes/source/chapter04/chap_04_oop_basic_visi
bility.php on line 52


------------------
(program exited with code: 255)
Press return to continue
```

See also

For more information on `getters` and `setters`, see the recipe in this chapter entitled *Using getters and setters*. For more information on PHP 7.1 class constant visibility settings, please see `https://wiki.php.net/rfc/class_const_visibility`.

Using interfaces

Interfaces are useful tools for systems architects and are often used to prototype an **Application Programming Interface** (**API**). Interfaces don't contain actual code, but can contain names of methods as well as method signatures.

All methods identified in the `Interface` have a visibility level of `public`.

How to do it...

1. Methods identified by the interface cannot contain actual code implementations. You can, however, specify the data types of method arguments.
2. In this example, `ConnectionAwareInterface` identifies a method, `setConnection()`, which requires an instance of `Connection` as an argument:

```
interface ConnectionAwareInterface
{
  public function setConnection(Connection $connection);
}
```

3. To use the interface, add the keyword `implements` after the open line that defines the class. We have defined two classes, `CountryList` and `CustomerList`, both of which require access to the `Connection` class via a method, `setConnection()`. In order to identify this dependency, both classes implement `ConnectionAwareInterface`:

```
class CountryList implements ConnectionAwareInterface
{
  protected $connection;
  public function setConnection(Connection $connection)
  {
    $this->connection = $connection;
  }
  public function list()
  {
    $list = [];
    $stmt = $this->connection->pdo->query(
      'SELECT iso3, name FROM iso_country_codes');
    while ($country = $stmt->fetch(PDO::FETCH_ASSOC)) {
      $list[$country['iso3']] =  $country['name'];
    }
    return $list;
  }

}
class CustomerList implements ConnectionAwareInterface
{
  protected $connection;
  public function setConnection(Connection $connection)
  {
    $this->connection = $connection;
  }
  public function list()
  {
```

```
    $list = [];
    $stmt = $this->connection->pdo->query(
      'SELECT id, name FROM customer');
    while ($customer = $stmt->fetch(PDO::FETCH_ASSOC)) {
      $list[$customer['id']] =  $customer['name'];
    }
    return $list;
  }

}
```

4. Interfaces can be used to satisfy a type hint. The following class, `ListFactory`, contains a `factory()` method, which initializes any class that implements `ConnectionAwareInterface`. The interface is a guarantee that the `setConnection()` method is defined. Setting the type hint to the interface instead of a specific class instance makes the `factory` method more generically useful:

```
namespace Application\Generic;

use PDO;
use Exception;
use Application\Database\Connection;
use Application\Database\ConnectionAwareInterface;

class ListFactory
{
  const ERROR_AWARE = 'Class must be Connection Aware';
  public static function factory(
    ConnectionAwareInterface $class, $dbParams)
  {
    if ($class instanceofConnectionAwareInterface) {
        $class->setConnection(new Connection($dbParams));
        return $class;
    } else {
        throw new Exception(self::ERROR_AWARE);
    }
    return FALSE;
  }
}
```

5. If a class implements multiple interfaces, a **naming collision** occurs if method signatures do not match. In this example, there are two interfaces, `DateAware` and `TimeAware`. In addition to defining the `setDate()` and `setTime()` methods, they both define `setBoth()`. Having duplicate method names is not an issue, although it is not considered best practice. The problem lies in the fact that the method signatures differ:

```
interface DateAware
{
  public function setDate($date);
  public function setBoth(DateTime $dateTime);
}

interface TimeAware
{
  public function setTime($time);
  public function setBoth($date, $time);
}

class DateTimeHandler implements DateAware, TimeAware
{
  protected $date;
  protected $time;
  public function setDate($date)
  {
    $this->date = $date;
  }
  public function setTime($time)
  {
    $this->time = $time;
  }
  public function setBoth(DateTime $dateTime)
  {
    $this->date = $date;
  }
}
```

6. As the code block stands, a fatal error will be generated (which cannot be caught!). To resolve the problem, the preferred approach would be to remove the definition of `setBoth()` from one or the other interface. Alternatively, you could adjust the method signatures to match.

Best practice

Do not define interfaces with duplicate or overlapping method definitions.

How it works...

In the `Application/Database` folder, create a file, `ConnectionAwareInterface.php`. Insert the code discussed in the preceding step 2.

Next, in the `Application/Generic` folder, create two files, `CountryList.php` and `CustomerList.php`. Insert the code discussed in step 3.

Next, in a directory parallel to the `Application` directory, create a source code file, `chap_04_oop_simple_interfaces_example.php`, which initializes the autoloader and includes the database parameters:

```
<?php
define('DB_CONFIG_FILE', '/../config/db.config.php');
require __DIR__ . '/../Application/Autoload/Loader.php';
Application\Autoload\Loader::init(__DIR__ . '/..');
$params = include __DIR__ . DB_CONFIG_FILE;
```

The database parameters in this example are assumed to be in a database configuration file indicated by the `DB_CONFIG_FILE` constant.

You are now in a position to use `ListFactory::factory()` to generate `CountryList` and `CustomerList` objects. Note that if these classes did not implement `ConnectionAwareInterface`, an error would be thrown:

```
$list = Application\Generic\ListFactory::factory(
  new Application\Generic\CountryList(), $params);
foreach ($list->list() as $item) echo $item . '';
```

Here is the output for country list:

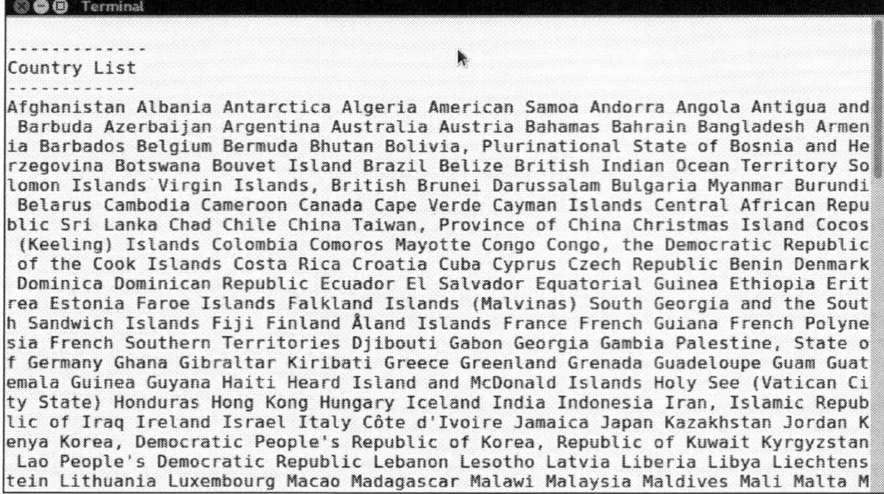

You can also use the `factory` method to generate a `CustomerList` object and use it:

```
$list = Application\Generic\ListFactory::factory(
  new Application\Generic\CustomerList(), $params);
foreach ($list->list() as $item) echo $item . '';
```

Here is the output for `CustomerList`:

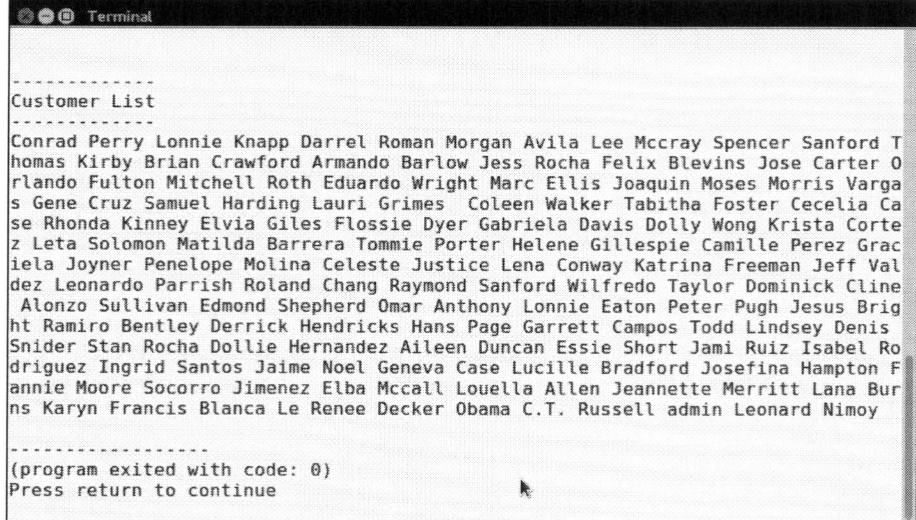

If you want to examine what happens when multiple interfaces are implemented, but where the method signature differs, enter the code shown in the preceding step 4 into a file, `chap_04_oop_interfaces_collisions.php`. When you try to run the file, an error is generated, as shown here:

```
Terminal
PHP Fatal error:  Declaration of DateTimeHandler::setBoth($dateTime) must be com
patible with DateAware::setBoth(DateTime $dateTime) in /home/aed/Repos/php7_reci
pes/source/chapter04/chap_04_oop_interfaces_collisions.php on line 19
PHP Stack trace:
PHP   1. {main}() /home/aed/Repos/php7_recipes/source/chapter04/chap_04_oop_inte
rfaces_collisions.php:0

Fatal error: Declaration of DateTimeHandler::setBoth($dateTime) must be compatib
le with DateAware::setBoth(DateTime $dateTime) in /home/aed/Repos/php7_recipes/s
ource/chapter04/chap_04_oop_interfaces_collisions.php on line 19

Call Stack:
    0.0002     363024   1. {main}() /home/aed/Repos/php7_recipes/source/chapter0
4/chap_04_oop_interfaces_collisions.php:0



------------------
(program exited with code: 255)
Press return to continue
```

If you make the following adjustment in the `TimeAware` interface, no errors will result:

```
interface TimeAware
{
  public function setTime($time);
  // this will cause a problem
  public function setBoth(DateTime $dateTime);
}
```

Using traits

If you have ever done any C programming, you are perhaps familiar with macros. A macro is a predefined block of code that *expands* at the line indicated. In a similar manner, traits can contain blocks of code that are copied and pasted into a class at the line indicated by the PHP interpreter.

How to do it...

1. Traits are identified with the keyword `trait`, and can contain properties and/or methods. You may have noticed duplication of code when examining the previous recipe featuring the `CountryList` and `CustomerList` classes. In this example, we will re-factor the two classes, and move the functionality of the `list()` method into a `Trait`. Notice that the `list()` method is the same in both classes.
2. Traits are used in situations where there is duplication of code between classes. Please note, however, that the conventional approach to creating an abstract class and extending it might have certain advantages over using traits. Traits cannot be used to identify a line of inheritance, whereas abstract parent classes can be used for this purpose.
3. We will now copy `list()` into a trait called `ListTrait`:

```
trait ListTrait
{
  public function list()
  {
    $list = [];
    $sql  = sprintf('SELECT %s, %s FROM %s',
      $this->key, $this->value, $this->table);
    $stmt = $this->connection->pdo->query($sql);
    while ($item = $stmt->fetch(PDO::FETCH_ASSOC)) {
      $list[$item[$this->key]] =
      $item[$this->value];
    }
    return $list;
  }
}
```

4. We can then insert the code from `ListTrait` into a new class, `CountryListUsingTrait`, as shown in the following code snippet. The entire `list()` method can now be removed from this class:

```
class CountryListUsingTrait implements ConnectionAwareInterface
{

  use ListTrait;

  protected $connection;
  protected $key   = 'iso3';
  protected $value = 'name';
  protected $table = 'iso_country_codes';

  public function setConnection(Connection $connection)
```

```
    {
      $this->connection = $connection;
    }

  }
```

> Any time you have duplication of code, a potential problem arises when you need to make a change. You might find yourself having to do too many global search and replace operations, or cutting and pasting of code, often with disastrous results. Traits are a great way to avoid this maintenance nightmare.

5. Traits are affected by namespaces. In the example shown in step 1, if our new `CountryListUsingTrait` class is placed into a namespace, `Application\Generic`, we will also need to move `ListTrait` into that namespace as well:

```
namespace Application\Generic;

use PDO;

trait ListTrait
{
  public function list()
  {
    // code as shown above
  }
}
```

6. Methods in traits override inherited methods.
7. In the following example, you will notice that the return value for the `setId()` method differs between the `Base` parent class and the `Test` trait. The `Customer` class inherits from `Base`, but also uses `Test`. In this case, the method defined in the trait will override the method defined in the `Base` parent class:

```
trait Test
{
  public function setId($id)
  {
    $obj = new stdClass();
    $obj->id = $id;
    $this->id = $obj;
  }
}

class Base
```

```
{
  protected $id;
  public function getId()
  {
    return $this->id;
  }
  public function setId($id)
  {
    $this->id = $id;
  }
}

class Customer extends Base
{
  use Test;
  protected $name;
  public function getName()
  {
    return $this->name;
  }
  public function setName($name)
  {
    $this->name = $name;
  }
}
```

In PHP 5, traits could also override properties. In PHP 7, if the property in a trait is initialized to a different value than in the parent class, a fatal error is generated.

8. Methods directly defined in the class that use the trait override duplicate methods defined in the trait.
9. In this example, the `Test` trait defines a property `$id` along with the `getId()` methods and `setId()`. The trait also defines `setName()`, which conflicts with the same method defined in the `Customer` class. In this case, the directly defined `setName()` method from `Customer` will override the `setName()` defined in the trait:

```
trait Test
{
  protected $id;
  public function getId()
  {
    return $this->id;
  }
```

```
    public function setId($id)
    {
      $this->id = $id;
    }
    public function setName($name)
    {
      $obj = new stdClass();
      $obj->name = $name;
      $this->name = $obj;
    }
}

class Customer
{
    use Test;
    protected $name;
    public function getName()
    {
      return $this->name;
    }
    public function setName($name)
    {
      $this->name = $name;
    }
}
```

10. Use the `insteadof` keywords to resolve method name conflicts when using multiple traits. In conjunction, use the `as` keyword to alias method names.
11. In this example, there are two traits, `IdTrait` and `NameTrait`. Both traits define a `setKey()` method, but express the key in different ways. The `Test` class uses both traits. Note the `insteadof` keyword, which allows us to distinguish between the conflicting methods. Thus, when `setKey()` is called from the `Test` class, the source will be drawn from `NameTrait`. In addition, `setKey()` from `IdTrait` will still be available, but under an alias, `setKeyDate()`:

```
trait IdTrait
{
    protected $id;
    public $key;
    public function setId($id)
    {
      $this->id = $id;
    }
    public function setKey()
    {
```

```
        $this->key = date('YmdHis')
        . sprintf('%04d', rand(0,9999));
    }
}

trait NameTrait
{
    protected $name;
    public $key;
    public function setName($name)
    {
        $this->name = $name;
    }
    public function setKey()
    {
        $this->key = unpack('H*', random_bytes(18))[1];
    }
}

class Test
{
    use IdTrait, NameTrait {
        NameTrait::setKeyinsteadofIdTrait;
        IdTrait::setKey as setKeyDate;
    }
}
```

How it works...

From step 1, you learned that traits are used in situations where there is duplication of code. You need to gauge whether or not you could simply define a base class and extend it, or whether using a trait better serves your purposes. Traits are especially useful where the duplication of code is seen in logically unrelated classes.

To illustrate how trait methods override inherited methods, copy the block of code mentioned in step 7 into a separate file, `chap_04_oop_traits_override_inherited.php`. Add these lines of code:

```
$customer = new Customer();
$customer->setId(100);
$customer->setName('Fred');
var_dump($customer);
```

As you can see from the output (shown next), the property `$id` is stored as an instance of `stdClass()`, which is the behavior defined in the trait:

```
class Customer#1 (2) {
  protected $name =>
  string(4) "Fred"
  protected $id =>
  class stdClass#2 (1) {
    public $id =>
    int(100)
  }
}


-----------------
(program exited with code: 0)
Press return to continue
```

To illustrate how directly defined class methods override trait methods, copy the block of code mentioned in step 9 into a separate file, `chap_04_oop_trait_methods_do_not_override_class_methods.php`. Add these lines of code:

```
$customer = new Customer();
$customer->setId(100);
$customer->setName('Fred');
var_dump($customer);
```

As you can see from the following output, the `$id` property is stored as an integer, as defined in the `Customer` class, whereas the trait defines `$id` as an instance of `stdClass`:

```
class Customer#1 (2) {
  protected $name =>
  string(4) "Fred"
  public $id =>
  int(100)
}


-----------------
(program exited with code: 0)
Press return to continue
```

In step 10, you learned how to resolve duplicate method name conflicts when using multiple traits. Copy the block of code shown in step 11 into a separate file, `chap_04_oop_trait_multiple.php`. Add the following code:

```
$a = new Test();
$a->setId(100);
$a->setName('Fred');
$a->setKey();
var_dump($a);

$a->setKeyDate();
var_dump($a);
```

Notice in the following output that `setKey()` yields the output produced from the new PHP 7 function, `random_bytes()` (defined in `NameTrait`), whereas `setKeyDate()` produces a key using the `date()` and `rand()` functions (defined in `IdTrait`):

```
Terminal
class Test#1 (3) {
  protected $id =>
  int(100)
  public $key =>
  string(36) "823b46fb10071c64baa373a4cdb8181c6d9c"
  protected $name =>
  string(4) "Fred"
}
class Test#1 (3) {
  protected $id =>
  int(100)
  public $key =>
  string(18) "201602180643172034"
  protected $name =>
  string(4) "Fred"
}


------------------
(program exited with code: 0)
Press return to continue
```

Implementing anonymous classes

PHP 7 introduced a new feature, **anonymous classes**. Much like anonymous functions, anonymous classes can be defined as part of an expression, creating a class that has no name. Anonymous classes are used in situations where you need to create an object *on the fly*, which is used and then discarded.

How to do it...

1. An alternative to `stdClass` is to define an anonymous class.

   In the definition, you can define any properties and methods (including magic methods). In this example, we define an anonymous class with two properties and a magic method, `__construct()`:

```
$a = new class (123.45, 'TEST') {
  public $total = 0;
  public $test  = '';
  public function __construct($total, $test)
  {
    $this->total = $total;
    $this->test  = $test;
  }
};
```

2. An anonymous class can extend any class.

   In this example, an anonymous class extends `FilterIterator`, and overrides both the `__construct()` and `accept()` methods. As an argument, it accepts `ArrayIterator $b`, which represents an array of 10 to 100 in increments of 10. The second argument serves as a limit on the output:

```
$b = new ArrayIterator(range(10,100,10));
$f = new class ($b, 50) extends FilterIterator {
  public $limit = 0;
  public function __construct($iterator, $limit)
  {
    $this->limit = $limit;
    parent::__construct($iterator);
  }
  public function accept()
  {
    return ($this->current() <= $this->limit);
  }
};
```

3. An anonymous class can implement an interface.

   In this example, an anonymous class is used to generate an HTML color code chart. The class implements the built-in PHP `Countable` interface. A `count()` method is defined, which is called when this class is used with a method or function that requires `Countable`:

```
define('MAX_COLORS', 256 ** 3);

$d = new class () implements Countable {
```

```
    public $current = 0;
    public $maxRows = 16;
    public $maxCols = 64;
    public function cycle()
    {
      $row = '';
      $max = $this->maxRows * $this->maxCols;
      for ($x = 0; $x < $this->maxRows; $x++) {
        $row .= '<tr>';
        for ($y = 0; $y < $this->maxCols; $y++) {
          $row .= sprintf(
            '<td style="background-color: #%06X;"',
            $this->current);
          $row .= sprintf(
            'title="#%06X"> </td>',
            $this->current);
          $this->current++;
          $this->current = ($this->current >MAX_COLORS) ? 0
               : $this->current;
        }
        $row .= '</tr>';
      }
      return $row;
    }
    public function count()
    {
      return MAX_COLORS;
    }
  };
```

4. Anonymous classes can use traits.
5. This last example is a modification from the preceding one defined immediately. Instead of defining a class `Test`, we define an anonymous class instead:

```
$a = new class() {
  use IdTrait, NameTrait {
    NameTrait::setKeyinsteadofIdTrait;
    IdTrait::setKey as setKeyDate;
  }
};
```

How it works...

In an anonymous class you can define any properties or methods. Using the preceding example, you could define an anonymous class that accepts constructor arguments, and where you can access properties. Place the code described in step 2 into a test script `chap_04_oop_anonymous_class.php`. Add these `echo` statements:

```
echo "\nAnonymous Class\n";
echo $a->total .PHP_EOL;
echo $a->test . PHP_EOL;
```

Here is the output from the anonymous class:

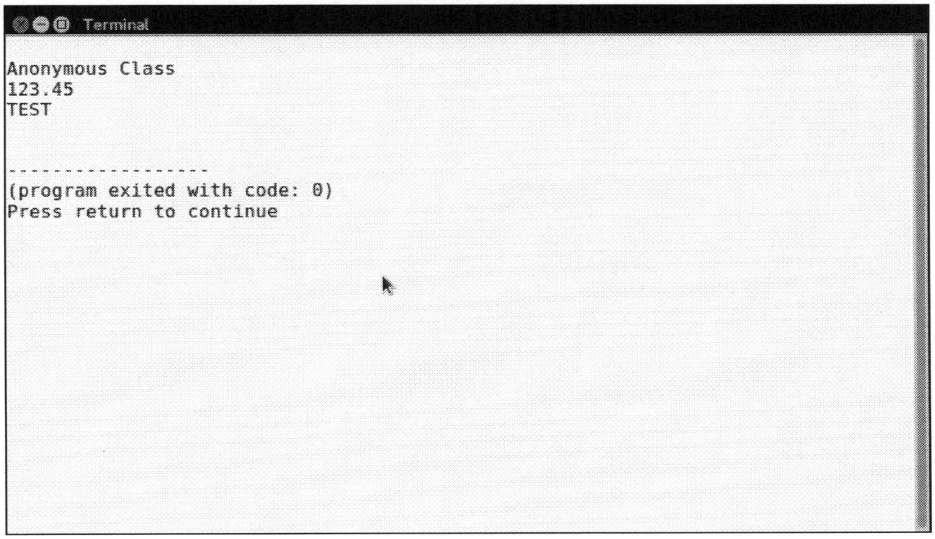

```
Terminal

Anonymous Class
123.45
TEST


------------------
(program exited with code: 0)
Press return to continue
```

In order to use `FilterIterator` you *must* override the `accept()` method. In this method, you define criteria for which elements of the iteration are to be included as output. Go ahead now and add the code shown in step 4 to the test script. You can then add these `echo` statements to test the anonymous class:

```
echo "\nAnonymous Class Extends FilterIterator\n";
foreach ($f as $item) echo $item . '';
echo PHP_EOL;
```

In this example, a limit of 50 is established. The original `ArrayIterator` contains an array of values, 10 to 100, in increments of 10, as seen in the following output:

```
Terminal
Anonymous Class Extends FilterIterator
10 20 30 40 50


------------------
(program exited with code: 0)
Press return to continue
```

To have a look at an anonymous class that implements an interface, consider the example shown in steps 5 and 6. Place this code in a file, `chap_04_oop_anonymous_class_interfaces.php`.

Next, add code that lets you paginate through the HTML color chart:

```
$d->current = $_GET['current'] ?? 0;
$d->current = hexdec($d->current);
$factor = ($d->maxRows * $d->maxCols);
$next = $d->current + $factor;
$prev = $d->current - $factor;
$next = ($next <MAX_COLORS) ? $next : MAX_COLORS - $factor;
$prev = ($prev>= 0) ? $prev : 0;
$next = sprintf('%06X', $next);
$prev = sprintf('%06X', $prev);
?>
```

Finally, go ahead and present the HTML color chart as a web page:

```
<h1>Total Possible Color Combinations: <?= count($d); ?></h1>
<hr>
<table>
<?= $d->cycle(); ?>
</table>
<a href="?current=<?= $prev ?>"><<PREV</a>
<a href="?current=<?= $next ?>">NEXT >></a>
```

Notice that you can take advantage of the `Countable` interface by passing the instance of the anonymous class into the `count()` function (shown between `<H1>` tags). Here is the output shown in a browser window:

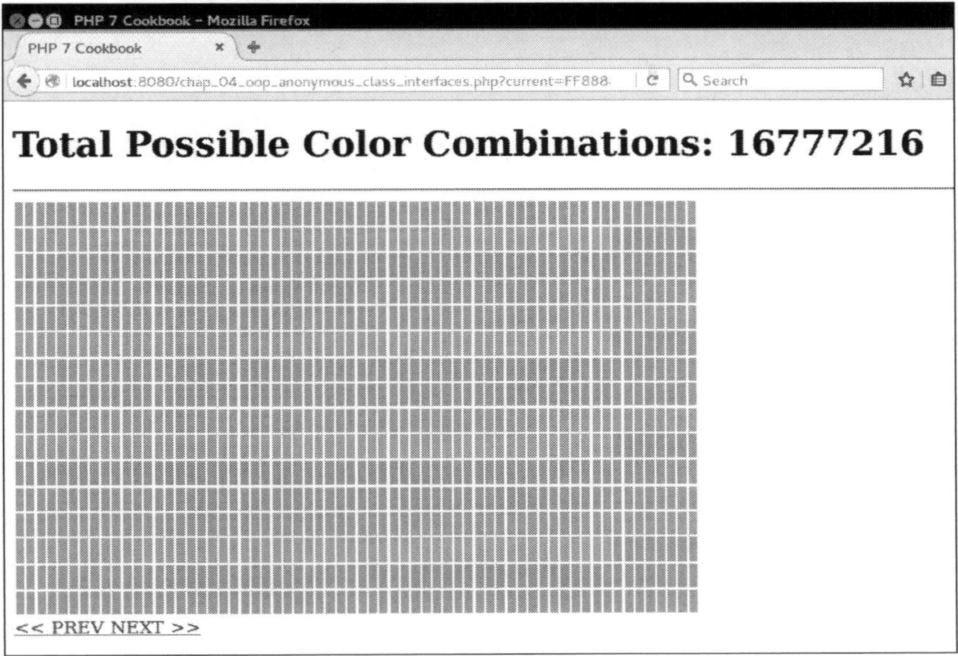

Lastly, to illustrate the use of traits in anonymous classes, copy the `chap_04_oop_trait_multiple.php` file mentioned in the previous recipe to a new file, `chap_04_oop_trait_anonymous_class.php`. Remove the definition of the `Test` class, and replace it with an anonymous class:

```
$a = new class() {
  use IdTrait, NameTrait {
    NameTrait::setKeyinsteadofIdTrait;
    IdTrait::setKey as setKeyDate;
  }
};
```

Remove this line:

```
$a = new Test();
```

When you run the code, you will see exactly the same output as shown in the preceding screenshot, except that the class reference will be anonymous:

```
Terminal
class class@anonymous#1 (3) {
  protected $id =>
  int(100)
  public $key =>
  string(36) "6d809645b8a7d904620f88f7a9757a20b821"
  protected $name =>
  string(4) "Fred"
}
class class@anonymous#1 (3) {
  protected $id =>
  int(100)
  public $key =>
  string(18) "201602180650100429"
  protected $name =>
  string(4) "Fred"
}


------------------
(program exited with code: 0)
Press return to continue
```

5
Interacting with a Database

In this chapter, we will cover the following topics:

- Using PDO to connect to a database
- Building an OOP SQL query builder
- Handling pagination
- Defining entities to match database tables
- Tying entity classes to RDBMS queries
- Embedding secondary lookups into query results
- Implementing jQuery DataTables PHP lookups

Introduction

In this chapter, we will cover a series of database connectivity recipes that take advantage of the **PHP Data Objects** (**PDO**) extension. Common programming problems such as **Structured Query Language** (**SQL**) generation, pagination, and tying objects to database tables, will be addressed. Finally, at the end, we will present code that processes secondary lookups in the form of embedded anonymous functions, and using jQuery DataTables to make AJAX requests.

Using PDO to connect to a database

PDO is a highly performant and actively maintained database extension that has a unique advantage over vendor-specific extensions. It has a common **Application Programming Interface** (**API**) that is compatible with almost a dozen different **Relational Database Management Systems** (**RDBMS**). Learning how to use this extension will save you hours of time trying to master the command subsets of the equivalent individual vendor-specific database extensions.

PDO is subdivided into four main classes, as summarized in the following table:

Class	Functionality
`PDO`	Maintains the actual connection to the database, and also handles low-level functionality such as transaction support
`PDOStatement`	Processes results
`PDOException`	Database-specific exceptions
`PDODriver`	Communicates with the actual vendor-specific database

How to do it...

1. Set up the database connection by creating a `PDO` instance.
2. You need to construct a **Data Source Name** (**DSN**). The information contained in the DSN varies according to the database driver used. As an example, here is a DSN used to connect to a **MySQL** database:

```
$params = [
  'host' => 'localhost',
  'user' => 'test',
  'pwd'  => 'password',
  'db'   => 'php7cookbook'
];

try {
  $dsn  = sprintf('mysql:host=%s;dbname=%s',
  $params['host'], $params['db']);
  $pdo  = new PDO($dsn, $params['user'], $params['pwd']);
} catch (PDOException $e) {
  echo $e->getMessage();
} catch (Throwable $e) {
  echo $e->getMessage();
}
```

3. On the other hand, **SQlite**, a simpler extension, only requires the following command:

```
$params = [
  'db'    => __DIR__ . '/../data/db/php7cookbook.db.sqlite'
];
$dsn   = sprintf('sqlite:' . $params['db']);
```

4. **PostgreSQL**, on the other hand, includes the username and password directly in the DSN:

```
$params = [
  'host' => 'localhost',
  'user' => 'test',
  'pwd'  => 'password',
  'db'   => 'php7cookbook'
];
$dsn   = sprintf('pgsql:host=%s;dbname=%s;user=%s;password=%s',
                 $params['host'],
                 $params['db'],
                 $params['user'],
                 $params['pwd']);
```

5. The DSN could also include server-specific directives, such as `unix_socket`, as shown in the following example:

```
$params = [
  'host' => 'localhost',
  'user' => 'test',
  'pwd'  => 'password',
  'db'   => 'php7cookbook',
  'sock' => '/var/run/mysqld/mysqld.sock'
];

try {
  $dsn  = sprintf('mysql:host=%s;dbname=%s;unix_socket=%s',
                  $params['host'], $params['db'], $params['sock']);
  $opts = [PDO::ATTR_ERRMODE => PDO::ERRMODE_EXCEPTION];
  $pdo  = new PDO($dsn, $params['user'], $params['pwd'], $opts);
} catch (PDOException $e) {
  echo $e->getMessage();
} catch (Throwable $e) {
  echo $e->getMessage();
}
```

Best practice

Wrap the statement that creates the PDO instance in a `try {} catch {}` block. Catch a `PDOException` for database-specific information in case of failure. Catch `Throwable` for errors or any other exceptions. Set the PDO error mode to `PDO::ERRMODE_EXCEPTION` for best results. See step 8 for more details about error modes.

In PHP 5, if the PDO object cannot be constructed (for example, when invalid parameters are used), the instance is assigned a value of `NULL`. In PHP 7, an `Exception` is thrown. If you wrap the construction of the PDO object in a `try {} catch {}` block, and the `PDO::ATTR_ERRMODE` is set to `PDO::ERRMODE_EXCEPTION`, you can catch and log such errors without having to test for `NULL`.

6. Send an SQL command using `PDO::query()`. A `PDOStatement` instance is returned, against which you can fetch results. In this example, we are looking for the first 20 customers sorted by ID:

```
$stmt = $pdo->query(
'SELECT * FROM customer ORDER BY id LIMIT 20');
```

PDO also provides a convenience method, `PDO::exec()`, which does not return a result iteration, just the number of rows affected. This method is best used for administrative operations such as `ALTER TABLE`, `DROP TABLE`, and so on.

7. Iterate through the `PDOStatement` instance to process results. Set the **fetch mode** to either `PDO::FETCH_NUM` or `PDO::FETCH_ASSOC` to return results in the form of a numeric or associative array. In this example we use a `while()` loop to process results. When the last result has been fetched, the result is a boolean `FALSE`, ending the loop:

```
while ($row = $stmt->fetch(PDO::FETCH_ASSOC)) {
  printf('%4d | %20s | %5s' . PHP_EOL, $row['id'],
  $row['name'], $row['level']);
}
```

PDO fetch operations involve a **cursor** that defines the direction (that is, forward or reverse) of the iteration. The second argument to `PDOStatement::fetch()` can be any of the `PDO::FETCH_ORI_*` constants. Cursor orientations include prior, first, last, absolute, and relative. The default cursor orientation is `PDO::FETCH_ORI_NEXT`.

8. Set the fetch mode to `PDO::FETCH_OBJ` to return results as a `stdClass` instance. Here you will note that the `while()` loop takes advantage of the fetch mode, `PDO::FETCH_OBJ`. Notice that the `printf()` statement refers to object properties, in contrast with the preceding example, which references array elements:

```
while ($row = $stmt->fetch(PDO::FETCH_OBJ)) {
  printf('%4d | %20s | %5s' . PHP_EOL,
  $row->id, $row->name, $row->level);
}
```

9. If you want to create an instance of a specific class while processing a query, set the fetch mode to `PDO::FETCH_CLASS`. You must also have the class definition available, and `PDO::query()` should set the class name. As you can see in the following code snippet, we have defined a class called `Customer`, with public properties `$id`, `$name`, and `$level`. Properties need to be `public` for the fetch injection to work properly:

```
class Customer
{
  public $id;
  public $name;
  public $level;
}

$stmt = $pdo->query($sql, PDO::FETCH_CLASS, 'Customer');
```

10. When fetching objects, a simpler alternative to the technique shown in step 5 is to use `PDOStatement::fetchObject()`:

```
while ($row = $stmt->fetchObject('Customer')) {
  printf('%4d | %20s | %5s' . PHP_EOL,
  $row->id, $row->name, $row->level);
}
```

11. You could also use `PDO::FETCH_INTO`, which is essentially the same as `PDO::FETCH_CLASS`, but you need an active object instance instead of a class reference. Each iteration through the loop re-populates the same object instance with the current information set. This example assumes the same class `Customer` as in step 5, with the same database parameters and PDO connections as defined in step 1:

```
$cust = new Customer();
while ($stmt->fetch(PDO::FETCH_INTO)) {
  printf('%4d | %20s | %5s' . PHP_EOL,
  $cust->id, $cust->name, $cust->level);
}
```

12. If you do not specify an error mode, the default PDO error mode is `PDO::ERRMODE_SILENT`. You can set the error mode using the `PDO::ATTR_ERRMODE` key, and either the `PDO::ERRMODE_WARNING` or the `PDO::ERRMODE_EXCEPTION` value. The error mode can be specified as the fourth argument to the PDO constructor in the form of an associative array. Alternatively, you can use `PDO::setAttribute()` on an existing instance.

13. Let us assume you have the following DSN and SQL (before you start thinking that this is a new form of SQL, please be assured: this SQL statement will not work!):

    ```
    $params = [
      'host' => 'localhost',
      'user' => 'test',
      'pwd'  => 'password',
      'db'   => 'php7cookbook'
    ];
    $dsn  = sprintf('mysql:host=%s;dbname=%s', $params['host'],
    $params['db']);
    $sql  = 'THIS SQL STATEMENT WILL NOT WORK';
    ```

14. If you then formulate your PDO connection using the default error mode, the only clue that something is wrong is that instead of producing a `PDOStatement` instance, the `PDO::query()` will return a boolean `FALSE`:

    ```
    $pdo1  = new PDO($dsn, $params['user'], $params['pwd']);
    $stmt = $pdo1->query($sql);
    $row = ($stmt) ? $stmt->fetch(PDO::FETCH_ASSOC) : 'No Good';
    ```

15. The next example shows setting the error mode to `WARNING` using the constructor approach:

    ```
    $pdo2 = new PDO(
      $dsn,
      $params['user'],
      $params['pwd'],
      [PDO::ATTR_ERRMODE => PDO::ERRMODE_WARNING]);
    ```

16. If you need full separation of the prepare and execute phases, use `PDO::prepare()` and `PDOStatement::execute()` instead. The statement is then sent to the database server to be pre-compiled. You can then execute the statement as many times as is warranted, most likely in a loop.

17. The first argument to `PDO::prepare()` can be an SQL statement with placeholders in place of actual values. An array of values can then be supplied to `PDOStatement::execute()`. PDO automatically provides database quoting, which helps safeguard against **SQL Injection**.

Best practice

Any application in which external input (that is, from a form posting) is combined with an SQL statement is subject to an SQL injection attack. All external input must first be properly filtered, validated, and otherwise sanitized. Do not put external input directly into the SQL statement. Instead, use placeholders, and provide the actual (sanitized) values during the execution phase.

18. To iterate through the results in reverse, you can change the orientation of the **scrollable cursor**. Alternatively, and probably more easily, just reverse the `ORDER BY` from `ASC` to `DESC`. This line of code sets up a `PDOStatement` object requesting a scrollable cursor:

```
$dsn  = sprintf('pgsql:charset=UTF8;host=%s;dbname=%s',
$params['host'], $params['db']);
$opts = [PDO::ATTR_ERRMODE => PDO::ERRMODE_EXCEPTION];
$pdo  = new PDO($dsn, $params['user'], $params['pwd'], $opts);
$sql  = 'SELECT * FROM customer '
    . 'WHERE balance > :min AND balance < :max '
    . 'ORDER BY id LIMIT 20';
$stmt = $pdo->prepare($sql, [PDO::ATTR_CURSOR  =>
  PDO::CURSOR_SCROLL]);
```

19. You also need to specify cursor instructions during the fetch operation. This example gets the last row in the result set, and then scrolls backwards:

```
$stmt->execute(['min' => $min, 'max' => $max]);
$row = $stmt->fetch(PDO::FETCH_ASSOC, PDO::FETCH_ORI_LAST);
do {
  printf('%4d | %20s | %5s | %8.2f' . PHP_EOL,
       $row['id'],
       $row['name'],
       $row['level'],
       $row['balance']);
} while ($row = $stmt->fetch(PDO::FETCH_ASSOC,
  PDO::FETCH_ORI_PRIOR));
```

20. Neither MySQL nor SQLite support scrollable cursors! To achieve the same results, try the following modifications to the preceding code:

```
$dsn  = sprintf('mysql:charset=UTF8;host=%s;dbname=%s',
$params['host'], $params['db']);
$opts = [PDO::ATTR_ERRMODE => PDO::ERRMODE_EXCEPTION];
$pdo  = new PDO($dsn, $params['user'], $params['pwd'], $opts);
$sql  = 'SELECT * FROM customer '
    . 'WHERE balance > :min AND balance < :max '
```

```
    . 'ORDER BY id DESC
       . 'LIMIT 20';
$stmt = $pdo->prepare($sql);
while ($row = $stmt->fetch(PDO::FETCH_ASSOC));
printf('%4d | %20s | %5s | %8.2f' . PHP_EOL,
       $row['id'],
       $row['name'],
       $row['level'],
       $row['balance']);
}
```

21. PDO provides support for transactions. Borrowing the code from step 9, we can wrap the `INSERT` series of commands into a transactional block:

```
try {
    $pdo->beginTransaction();
    $sql  = "INSERT INTO customer ('"
    . implode("','", $fields) . "') VALUES (?,?,?,?,?,?)";
    $stmt = $pdo->prepare($sql);
    foreach ($data as $row) $stmt->execute($row);
    $pdo->commit();
} catch (PDOException $e) {
    error_log($e->getMessage());
    $pdo->rollBack();
}
```

22. Finally, to keep everything modular and re-usable, we can wrap the PDO connection into a separate class `Application\Database\Connection`. Here, we build a connection through the constructor. Alternatively, there is a static `factory()` method that lets us generate a series of PDO instances:

```
namespace Application\Database;
use Exception;
use PDO;
class Connection
{
    const ERROR_UNABLE = 'ERROR: no database connection';
    public $pdo;
    public function __construct(array $config)
    {
        if (!isset($config['driver'])) {
            $message = __METHOD__ . ' : '
            . self::ERROR_UNABLE . PHP_EOL;
            throw new Exception($message);
        }
        $dsn = $this->makeDsn($config);
```

```
        try {
            $this->pdo = new PDO(
                $dsn,
                $config['user'],
                $config['password'],
                [PDO::ATTR_ERRMODE => $config['errmode']]);
            return TRUE;
        } catch (PDOException $e) {
            error_log($e->getMessage());
            return FALSE;
        }
    }

    public static function factory(
      $driver, $dbname, $host, $user,
      $pwd, array $options = array())
    {
        $dsn = $this->makeDsn($config);

        try {
            return new PDO($dsn, $user, $pwd, $options);
        } catch (PDOException $e) {
            error_log($e->getMessage);
        }
    }
```

23. An important component of this `Connection` class is a generic method that can be used to construct a DSN. All we need for this to work is to establish the `PDODriver` as a prefix, followed by ":". After that, we simply append key/value pairs from our configuration array. Each key/value pair is separated by a semi-colon. We also need to strip off the trailing semi-colon, using `substr()` with a negative limit for that purpose:

```
  public function makeDsn($config)
  {
    $dsn = $config['driver'] . ':';
    unset($config['driver']);
    foreach ($config as $key => $value) {
      $dsn .= $key . '=' . $value . ';';
    }
    return substr($dsn, 0, -1);
  }
}
```

How it works...

First of all, you can copy the initial connection code from step 1 into a `chap_05_pdo_connect_mysql.php` file. For the purposes of this illustration, we will assume you have created a MySQL database called `php7cookbook`, with a username of cook and a password of book. Next, we send a simple SQL statement to the database using the `PDO::query()` method. Finally, we use the resulting statement object to fetch results in the form of an associative array. Don't forget to wrap your code in a `try {} catch {}` block:

```
<?php
$params = [
  'host' => 'localhost',
  'user' => 'test',
  'pwd'  => 'password',
  'db'   => 'php7cookbook'
];
try {
  $dsn  = sprintf('mysql:charset=UTF8;host=%s;dbname=%s',
    $params['host'], $params['db']);
  $pdo  = new PDO($dsn, $params['user'], $params['pwd']);
  $stmt = $pdo->query(
    'SELECT * FROM customer ORDER BY id LIMIT 20');
  printf('%4s | %20s | %5s | %7s' . PHP_EOL,
    'ID', 'NAME', 'LEVEL', 'BALANCE');
  printf('%4s | %20s | %5s | %7s' . PHP_EOL,
    '----', str_repeat('-', 20), '-----', '-------');
  while ($row = $stmt->fetch(PDO::FETCH_ASSOC)) {
    printf('%4d | %20s | %5s | %7.2f' . PHP_EOL,
    $row['id'], $row['name'], $row['level'], $row['balance']);
  }
} catch (PDOException $e) {
  error_log($e->getMessage());
} catch (Throwable $e) {
  error_log($e->getMessage());
}
```

Here is the resulting output:

```
ID |                 NAME | LEVEL | BALANCE
---- | -------------------- | ----- | -------
 1 |         Conrad Perry |  INT |  440.00
 2 |         Lonnie Knapp |      |  555.55
 3 |         Darrel Roman |  INT |  444.44
 4 |         Morgan Avila |  ADV |  888.88
 5 |           Lee Mccray |      |  539.35
 6 |      Spencer Sanford |  INT |   99.99
 7 |         Thomas Kirby |      |  412.45
 8 |       Brian Crawford |  ADV |  125.58
 9 |       Armando Barlow |  BEG | 6524.00
10 |           Jess Rocha |  ADV | 6405.00
11 |         Felix Blevins |  BEG |  130.57
12 |           Jose Carter |  INT |   56.22
13 |       Orlando Fulton |      |  222.22
14 |        Mitchell Roth |  INT |  591.07
15 |       Eduardo Wright |  BEG |  156.36
16 |           Marc Ellis |  ADV |   69.04
17 |        Joaquin Moses |  INT |  936.64
18 |        Morris Vargas |      |  486.60
19 |            Gene Cruz |  ADV |  683.55
20 |       Samuel Harding |  ADV |  -11.56
```

Add the option to the PDO constructor, which sets the error mode to `EXCEPTION`. Now alter the SQL statement and observe the resulting error message:

```
$opts = [PDO::ATTR_ERRMODE => PDO::ERRMODE_EXCEPTION];
$pdo  = new PDO($dsn, $params['user'], $params['pwd'], $opts);
$stmt = $pdo->query('THIS SQL STATEMENT WILL NOT WORK');
```

You will observe something like this:

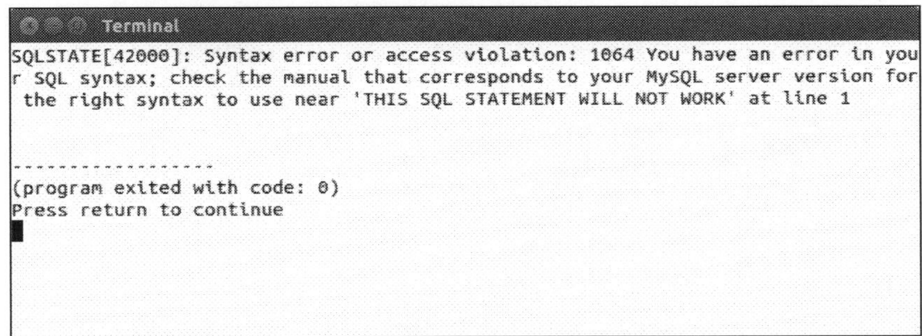

```
SQLSTATE[42000]: Syntax error or access violation: 1064 You have an error in you
r SQL syntax; check the manual that corresponds to your MySQL server version for
 the right syntax to use near 'THIS SQL STATEMENT WILL NOT WORK' at line 1


------------------
(program exited with code: 0)
Press return to continue
```

Placeholders can be named or positional. **Named placeholders** are preceded by a colon (`:`) in the prepared SQL statement, and are references as keys in an associative array provided to `execute()`. **Positional placeholders** are represented as question marks (`?`) in the prepared SQL statement.

In the following example, named placeholders are used to represent values in a WHERE clause:

```
try {
  $dsn  = sprintf('mysql:host=%s;dbname=%s',
                  $params['host'], $params['db']);
  $pdo  = new PDO($dsn,
                  $params['user'],
                  $params['pwd'],
                  [PDO::ATTR_ERRMODE => PDO::ERRMODE_EXCEPTION]);
  $sql  = 'SELECT * FROM customer '
      . 'WHERE balance < :val AND level = :level '
      . 'ORDER BY id LIMIT 20'; echo $sql . PHP_EOL;
  $stmt = $pdo->prepare($sql);
  $stmt->execute(['val' => 100, 'level' => 'BEG']);
  while ($row = $stmt->fetch(PDO::FETCH_ASSOC)) {
    printf('%4d | %20s | %5s | %5.2f' . PHP_EOL,
          $row['id'], $row['name'], $row['level'], $row['balance']);
  }
} catch (PDOException $e) {
  echo $e->getMessage();
} catch (Throwable $e) {
  echo $e->getMessage();
}
```

This example shows using positional placeholders in an INSERT operation. Notice that the data to be inserted as the fourth customer includes a potential SQL injection attack. You will also notice that some awareness of the SQL syntax for the database being used is required. In this case, MySQL column names are quoted using back-ticks ('):

```
$fields = ['name', 'balance', 'email',
           'password', 'status', 'level'];
$data = [
  ['Saleen',0,'saleen@test.com', 'password',0,'BEG'],
  ['Lada',55.55,'lada@test.com',   'password',0,'INT'],
  ['Tonsoi',999.99,'tongsoi@test.com','password',1,'ADV'],
  ['SQL Injection',0.00,'bad','bad',1,
   'BEG\';DELETE FROM customer;--'],
];

try {
  $dsn  = sprintf('mysql:host=%s;dbname=%s',
    $params['host'], $params['db']);
  $pdo  = new PDO($dsn,
                  $params['user'],
```

```
                    $params['pwd'],
                    [PDO::ATTR_ERRMODE => PDO::ERRMODE_EXCEPTION]);
  $sql  = "INSERT INTO customer ('"
   . implode("','", $fields)
   . "') VALUES (?,?,?,?,?,?)";
  $stmt = $pdo->prepare($sql);
  foreach ($data as $row) $stmt->execute($row);
} catch (PDOException $e) {
  echo $e->getMessage();
} catch (Throwable $e) {
  echo $e->getMessage();
}
```

To test the use of a prepared statement with named parameters, modify the SQL statement to add a `WHERE` clause that checks for customers with a balance less than a certain amount, and a level equal to either `BEG`, `INT`, or `ADV` (that is, beginning, intermediate, or advanced). Instead of using `PDO::query()`, use `PDO::prepare()`. Before fetching results, you must then perform `PDOStatement::execute()`, supplying the values for balance and level:

```
$sql  = 'SELECT * FROM customer '
     . 'WHERE balance < :val AND level = :level '
     . 'ORDER BY id LIMIT 20';
$stmt = $pdo->prepare($sql);
$stmt->execute(['val' => 100, 'level' => 'BEG']);
```

Here is the resulting output:

```
Terminal
 ID |                NAME | LEVEL | BALANCE
----|---------------------|-------|--------
 25 |       Rhonda Kinney |   BEG |   46.61
 45 |     Wilfredo Taylor |   BEG |   25.11
 57 |      Garrett Campos |   BEG |    9.47
 88 |               Obama |   BEG |    0.00
 92 |         C.T. Russell |   BEG |    0.00


------------------
(program exited with code: 0)
Press return to continue
```

Instead of providing parameters when calling `PDOStatement::execute()`, you could alternatively bind parameters. This allows you to assign variables to placeholders. At the time of execution, the current value of the variable is used.

In this example, we bind the variables `$min`, `$max`, and `$level` to the prepared statement:

```
$min   = 0;
$max   = 0;
$level = '';

try {
  $dsn  = sprintf('mysql:host=%s;dbname=%s', $params['host'],
    $params['db']);
  $opts = [PDO::ATTR_ERRMODE => PDO::ERRMODE_EXCEPTION];
  $pdo  = new PDO($dsn, $params['user'], $params['pwd'], $opts);
  $sql  = 'SELECT * FROM customer '
      . 'WHERE balance > :min '
      . 'AND balance < :max AND level = :level '
      . 'ORDER BY id LIMIT 20';
  $stmt = $pdo->prepare($sql);
  $stmt->bindParam('min',   $min);
  $stmt->bindParam('max',   $max);
  $stmt->bindParam('level', $level);

  $min   =  5000;
  $max   = 10000;
  $level = 'ADV';
  $stmt->execute();
  showResults($stmt, $min, $max, $level);

  $min   = 0;
  $max   = 100;
  $level = 'BEG';
  $stmt->execute();
  showResults($stmt, $min, $max, $level);

} catch (PDOException $e) {
  echo $e->getMessage();
} catch (Throwable $e) {
  echo $e->getMessage();
}
```

When the values of these variables change, the next execution will reflect the modified criteria.

Best practice

Use `PDO::query()` for one-time database commands. Use `PDO::prepare()` and `PDOStatement::execute()` when you need to process the same statement multiple times but using different values.

See also

For information on the syntax and unique behavior associated with different vendor-specific PDO drivers, have a look this article:

- `http://php.net/manual/en/pdo.drivers.php`

For a summary of PDO predefined constants, including fetch modes, cursor orientation, and attributes, see the following article:

- `http://php.net/manual/en/pdo.constants.php`

Building an OOP SQL query builder

PHP 7 implements something called a **context sensitive lexer**. What this means is that words that are normally reserved can be used if the context allows. Thus, when building an object-oriented SQL builder, we can get away with using methods named `and`, `or`, `not`, and so on.

How to do it...

1. We define a `Application\Database\Finder` class. In the class, we define methods that match our favorite SQL operations:

```
namespace Application\Database;
class Finder
{
  public static $sql      = '';
  public static $instance = NULL;
  public static $prefix   = '';
  public static $where    = array();
  public static $control  = ['', ''];

    // $a == name of table
    // $cols = column names
    public static function select($a, $cols = NULL)
    {
      self::$instance  = new Finder();
      if ($cols) {
           self::$prefix = 'SELECT ' . $cols . ' FROM ' . $a;
      } else {
        self::$prefix = 'SELECT * FROM ' . $a;
      }
      return self::$instance;
    }
```

```
public static function where($a = NULL)
{
    self::$where[0] = ' WHERE ' . $a;
    return self::$instance;
}

public static function like($a, $b)
{
    self::$where[] = trim($a . ' LIKE ' . $b);
    return self::$instance;
}

public static function and($a = NULL)
{
    self::$where[] = trim('AND ' . $a);
    return self::$instance;
}

public static function or($a = NULL)
{
    self::$where[] = trim('OR ' . $a);
    return self::$instance;
}

public static function in(array $a)
{
    self::$where[] = 'IN ( ' . implode(',', $a) . ' )';
    return self::$instance;
}

public static function not($a = NULL)
{
    self::$where[] = trim('NOT ' . $a);
    return self::$instance;
}

public static function limit($limit)
{
    self::$control[0] = 'LIMIT ' . $limit;
    return self::$instance;
}

public static function offset($offset)
{
```

```
            self::$control[1] = 'OFFSET ' . $offset;
            return self::$instance;
        }

    public static function getSql()
    {
      self::$sql = self::$prefix
         . implode(' ', self::$where)
                 . ' '
                 . self::$control[0]
                 . ' '
                 . self::$control[1];
      preg_replace('/  /', ' ', self::$sql);
      return trim(self::$sql);
    }
  }
```

2. Each function used to generate an SQL fragment returns the same property, `$instance`. This allows us to represent the code using a fluent interface, such as this:

```
$sql = Finder::select('project')->where('priority > 9') … etc.
```

How it works...

Copy the code defined precedingly into a `Finder.php` file in the `Application\Database` folder. You can then create a `chap_05_oop_query_builder.php` calling program, which initializes the autoloader defined in *Chapter 1, Building a Foundation*. You can then run `Finder::select()` to generate an object from which the SQL string can be rendered:

```
<?php
require __DIR__ . '/../Application/Autoload/Loader.php';
Application\Autoload\Loader::init(__DIR__ . '/..');
use Application\Database\Finder;

$sql = Finder::select('project')
  ->where()
  ->like('name', '%secret%')
  ->and('priority > 9')
  ->or('code')->in(['4', '5', '7'])
  ->and()->not('created_at')
  ->limit(10)
  ->offset(20);

echo Finder::getSql();
```

Here is the result of the precding code:

```
SELECT * FROM project WHERE  name LIKE %secret% AND priority > 9 OR code IN ( 4,
5,7 ) AND NOT created_at LIMIT 10 OFFSET 20

------------------
(program exited with code: 0)
Press return to continue
```

See also

For more information on the context-sensitive lexer, have a look at this article:

`https://wiki.php.net/rfc/context_sensitive_lexer`

Handling pagination

Pagination involves providing a limited subset of the results of a database query. This is usually done for display purposes, but could easily apply to other situations. At first glance, it would seem the `LimitIterator` class is ideally suited for the purposes of pagination. In cases where the potential result set could be massive; however, `LimitIterator` is not such an ideal candidate, as you would need to supply the entire result set as an inner iterator, which would most likely exceed memory limitations. The second and third arguments to the `LimitIterator` class constructor are offset and count. This suggests the pagination solution we will adopt, which is native to SQL: adding `LIMIT` and `OFFSET` clauses to a given SQL statement.

How to do it...

1. First, we create a class called `Application\Database\Paginate` to hold the pagination logic. We add properties to represent values associated with pagination, `$sql`, `$page`, and `$linesPerPage`:

```
namespace Application\Database;

class Paginate
{

  const DEFAULT_LIMIT  = 20;
  const DEFAULT_OFFSET = 0;
```

```
  protected $sql;
  protected $page;
  protected $linesPerPage;

}
```

2. Next, we define a `__construct()` method that accepts a base SQL statement, the current page number, and the number of lines per page as arguments. We then need to refactor the SQL string modifying or adding the `LIMIT` and `OFFSET` clauses.
3. In the constructor, we need to calculate the offset using the current page number and the number of lines per page. We also need to check to see if `LIMIT` and `OFFSET` are already present in the SQL statement. Finally, we need to revise the statement using lines per page as our `LIMIT` with the recalculated `OFFSET`:

```
public function __construct($sql, $page, $linesPerPage)
{
  $offset = $page * $linesPerPage;
  switch (TRUE) {
    case (stripos($sql, 'LIMIT') && strpos($sql, 'OFFSET')) :
      // no action needed
      break;
    case (stripos($sql, 'LIMIT')) :
      $sql .= ' LIMIT ' . self::DEFAULT_LIMIT;
      break;
    case (stripos($sql, 'OFFSET')) :
      $sql .= ' OFFSET ' . self::DEFAULT_OFFSET;
      break;
    default :
      $sql .= ' LIMIT ' . self::DEFAULT_LIMIT;
      $sql .= ' OFFSET ' . self::DEFAULT_OFFSET;
      break;
  }
  $this->sql = preg_replace('/LIMIT \d+.*OFFSET \d+/Ui',
     'LIMIT ' . $linesPerPage . ' OFFSET ' . $offset,
     $sql);
}
```

4. We are now ready to execute the query using the `Application\Database\Connection` class discussed in the first recipe.
5. In our new pagination class, we add a `paginate()` method, which takes a `Connection` instance as an argument. We also need the PDO fetch mode, and optional prepared statement parameters:

```
use PDOException;
public function paginate(
  Connection $connection,
```

```
    $fetchMode,
    $params = array())
    {
    try {
      $stmt = $connection->pdo->prepare($this->sql);
      if (!$stmt) return FALSE;
      if ($params) {
        $stmt->execute($params);
      } else {
        $stmt->execute();
      }
      while ($result = $stmt->fetch($fetchMode)) yield $result;
    } catch (PDOException $e) {
      error_log($e->getMessage());
      return FALSE;
    } catch (Throwable $e) {
      error_log($e->getMessage());
      return FALSE;
    }
  }
```

6. It might not be a bad idea to provide support for the query builder class mentioned in the previous recipe. This will make updating `LIMIT` and `OFFSET` much easier. All we need to do to provide support for `Application\Database\Finder` is to use the class and modify the `__construct()` method to check to see if the incoming SQL is an instance of this class:

```
if ($sql instanceof Finder) {
  $sql->limit($linesPerPage);
  $sql->offset($offset);
  $this->sql = $sql::getSql();
} elseif (is_string($sql)) {
  switch (TRUE) {
    case (stripos($sql, 'LIMIT')
    && strpos($sql, 'OFFSET')) :
        // remaining code as shown in bullet #3 above
    }
 }
```

7. Now all that remains to be done is to add a `getSql()` method in case we need to confirm that the SQL statement was correctly formed:

```
public function getSql()
{
  return $this->sql;
}
```

How it works...

Copy the preceding code into a `Paginate.php` file in the `Application/Database` folder. You can then create a `chap_05_pagination.php` calling program, which initializes the autoloader defined in *Chapter 1, Building a Foundation*:

```
<?php
define('DB_CONFIG_FILE', '/../config/db.config.php');
define('LINES_PER_PAGE', 10);
define('DEFAULT_BALANCE', 1000);
require __DIR__ . '/../Application/Autoload/Loader.php';
Application\Autoload\Loader::init(__DIR__ . '/..');
```

Next, use the `Application\Database\Finder`, `Connection`, and `Paginate` classes, create an instance of `Application\Database\Connection`, and use `Finder` to generate SQL:

```
use Application\Database\ { Finder, Connection, Paginate};
$conn = new Connection(include __DIR__ . DB_CONFIG_FILE);
$sql = Finder::select('customer')->where('balance < :bal');
```

We can now get the page number and balance from `$_GET` parameters, and create the `Paginate` object, ending the PHP block:

```
$page = (int) ($_GET['page'] ?? 0);
$bal  = (float) ($_GET['balance'] ?? DEFAULT_BALANCE);
$paginate = new Paginate($sql::getSql(), $page, LINES_PER_PAGE);
?>
```

In the output portion of the script, we simply iterate through the pagination using a simple `foreach()` loop:

```
<h3><?= $paginate->getSql(); ?></h3>
<hr>
<pre>
<?php
printf('%4s | %20s | %5s | %7s' . PHP_EOL,
  'ID', 'NAME', 'LEVEL', 'BALANCE');
printf('%4s | %20s | %5s | %7s' . PHP_EOL,
  '----', str_repeat('-', 20), '-----', '-------');
foreach ($paginate->paginate($conn, PDO::FETCH_ASSOC,
  ['bal' => $bal]) as $row) {
  printf('%4d | %20s | %5s | %7.2f' . PHP_EOL,
      $row['id'],$row['name'],$row['level'],$row['balance']);
}
printf('%4s | %20s | %5s | %7s' . PHP_EOL,
```

```
    '----', str_repeat('-', 20), '-----', '-------');
?>
<a href="?page=<?= $page - 1; ?>&balance=<?= $bal ?>">
<< Prev </a>  
<a href="?page=<?= $page + 1; ?>&balance=<?= $bal ?>">
Next >></a>
</pre>
```

Here is page 3 of the output, where the balance is less than 1,000:

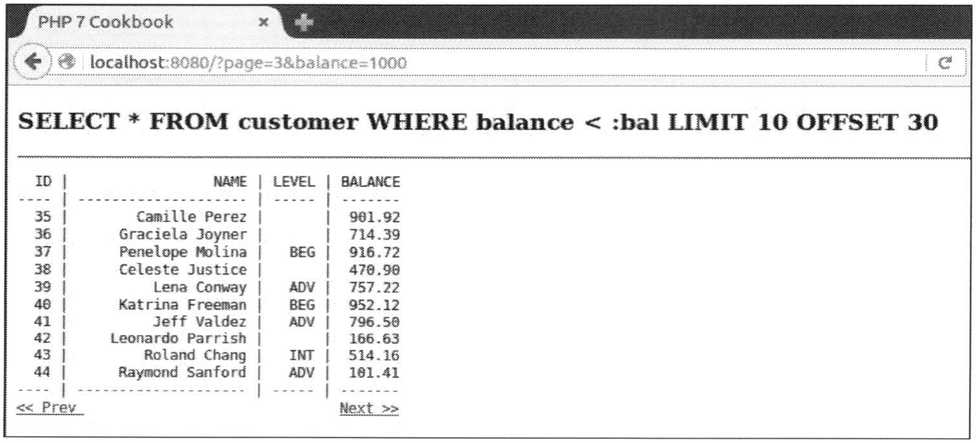

PHP 7 Cookbook

localhost:8080/?page=3&balance=1000

SELECT * FROM customer WHERE balance < :bal LIMIT 10 OFFSET 30

```
  ID |                 NAME | LEVEL | BALANCE
---- | -------------------- | ----- | -------
  35 |        Camille Perez |       |  901.92
  36 |      Graciela Joyner |       |  714.39
  37 |     Penelope Molina |   BEG |  916.72
  38 |      Celeste Justice |       |  470.90
  39 |          Lena Conway |   ADV |  757.22
  40 |      Katrina Freeman |   BEG |  952.12
  41 |          Jeff Valdez |   ADV |  796.50
  42 |    Leonardo Parrish |       |  166.63
  43 |         Roland Chang |   INT |  514.16
  44 |      Raymond Sanford |   ADV |  101.41
---- | -------------------- | ----- | -------
<< Prev                              Next >>
```

See also

For more information on the `LimitIterator` class, refer to this article:

- `http://php.net/manual/en/class.limititerator.php`

Defining entities to match database tables

A very common practice among PHP developers is to create classes that represent database tables. Such classes are often referred to as **entity** classes, and form the core of the **domain model** software design pattern.

How to do it...

1. First of all, we will establish some common features of a series of entity classes. These might include common properties and common methods. We will put these into a `Application\Entity\Base` class. All future entity classes will then extend `Base`.

2. For the purposes of this illustration, let's assume all entities will have two properties in common: `$mapping` (discussed later), and `$id` (with its corresponding getter and setter):

```
namespace Application\Entity;

class Base
{

  protected $id = 0;
  protected $mapping = ['id' => 'id'];

  public function getId() : int
  {
    return $this->id;
  }

  public function setId($id)
  {
    $this->id = (int) $id;
  }
}
```

3. It's not a bad idea to define a `arrayToEntity()` method, which converts an array to an instance of the entity class, and vice versa (`entityToArray()`). These methods implement a process often referred to as **hydration**. As these methods should be generic, they are best placed in the `Base` class.

4. In the following methods, the `$mapping` property is used to translate between database column names and object property names. `arrayToEntity()` populates values of this object instance from an array. We can define this method as static in case we need to call it outside of an active instance:

```
public static function arrayToEntity($data, Base $instance)
{
  if ($data && is_array($data)) {
    foreach ($instance->mapping as $dbColumn => $propertyName) {
      $method = 'set' . ucfirst($propertyName);
      $instance->$method($data[$dbColumn]);
    }
    return $instance;
  }
  return FALSE;
}
```

5. The `entityToArray()` produces an array from current instance property values:

```
public function entityToArray()
{
  $data = array();
  foreach ($this->mapping as $dbColumn => $propertyName) {
    $method = 'get' . ucfirst($propertyName);
    $data[$dbColumn] = $this->$method() ?? NULL;
  }
  return $data;
}
```

6. To build the specific entity, you need to have the structure of the database table you plan to model at hand. Create properties that map to the database columns. The initial values assigned should reflect the ultimate data-type of the database column.
7. In this example we'll use the `customer` table. Here is the `CREATE` statement from a MySQL data dump, which illustrates its data structure:

```
CREATE TABLE 'customer' (
  'id' int(11) NOT NULL AUTO_INCREMENT,
  'name' varchar(256) CHARACTER SET latin1 COLLATE
    latin1_general_cs NOT NULL,
  'balance' decimal(10,2) NOT NULL,
  'email' varchar(250) NOT NULL,
  'password' char(16) NOT NULL,
  'status' int(10) unsigned NOT NULL DEFAULT '0',
  'security_question' varchar(250) DEFAULT NULL,
  'confirm_code' varchar(32) DEFAULT NULL,
  'profile_id' int(11) DEFAULT NULL,
  'level' char(3) NOT NULL,
  PRIMARY KEY ('id'),
  UNIQUE KEY 'UNIQ_81398E09E7927C74' ('email')
);
```

8. We are now in a position to flesh out the class properties. This is also a good place to identify the corresponding table. In this case, we will use a `TABLE_NAME` class constant:

```
namespace Application\Entity;

class Customer extends Base
{
  const TABLE_NAME = 'customer';
  protected $name = '';
  protected $balance = 0.0;
  protected $email = '';
  protected $password = '';
```

```
    protected $status = '';
    protected $securityQuestion = '';
    protected $confirmCode = '';
    protected $profileId = 0;
    protected $level = '';
  }
```

9. It is considered a best practice to define the properties as `protected`. In order to access these properties, you will need to design `public` methods that `get` and `set` the properties. Here is a good place to put to use the PHP 7 ability to data-type to the return value.

10. In the following block of code, we have defined getters and setters for `$name` and `$balance`. You can imagine how the remainder of these methods will be defined:

```
    public function getName() : string
    {
      return $this->name;
    }
    public function setName($name)
    {
      $this->name = $name;
    }
    public function getBalance() : float
    {
      return $this->balance;
    }
    public function setBalance($balance)
    {
      $this->balance = (float) $balance;
    }
  }
```

It is not a good idea to data type check the incoming values on the setters. The reason is that the return values from a RDBMS database query will all be a `string` data type.

11. If the property names do not exactly match the corresponding database column, you should consider creating a `mapping` property, an array of key/value pairs where the key represents the database column name and the value the property name.

12. You will note that three properties, `$securityQuestion`, `$confirmCode`, and `$profileId`, do not correspond to their equivalent column names, `security_question`, `confirm_code`, and `profile_id`. The `$mapping` property will ensure that the appropriate translation takes place:

    ```
    protected $mapping = [
      'id'                => 'id',
      'name'              => 'name',
      'balance'           => 'balance',
      'email'             => 'email',
      'password'          => 'password',
      'status'            => 'status',
      'security_question' => 'securityQuestion',
      'confirm_code'      => 'confirmCode',
      'profile_id'        => 'profileId',
      'level'             => 'level'
    ];
    ```

How it works...

Copy the code from steps 2, 4, and 5 into a `Base.php` file in the `Application/Entity` folder. Copy the code from steps 8 through 12 into a `Customer.php` file, also in the `Application/Entity` folder. You will then need to create getters and setters for the remaining properties not shown in step 10: `email`, `password`, `status`, `securityQuestion`, `confirmCode`, `profileId`, and `level`.

You can then create a `chap_05_matching_entity_to_table.php` calling program, which initializes the autoloader defined in *Chapter 1*, *Building a Foundation*, uses the `Application\Database\Connection`, and the newly created `Application\Entity\Customer` classes:

```
<?php
define('DB_CONFIG_FILE', '/../config/db.config.php');
require __DIR__ . '/../Application/Autoload/Loader.php';
Application\Autoload\Loader::init(__DIR__ . '/..');
use Application\Database\Connection;
use Application\Entity\Customer;
```

Next, get a database connection, and use the connection to acquire an associative array of data for one customer at random:

```
$conn = new Connection(include __DIR__ . DB_CONFIG_FILE);
$id = rand(1,79);
$stmt = $conn->pdo->prepare(
  'SELECT * FROM customer WHERE id = :id');
$stmt->execute(['id' => $id]);
$result = $stmt->fetch(PDO::FETCH_ASSOC);
```

Finally, you can create a new `Customer` entity instance from the array and use `var_dump()` to view the result:

```
$cust = Customer::arrayToEntity($result, new Customer());
var_dump($cust);
```

Here is the output of the preceding code:

```
Terminal
object(Application\Entity\Customer)#4 (12) {
  ["name":protected]=>
  string(15) "Edmond Shepherd"
  ["balance":protected]=>
  float(135.29)
  ["email":protected]=>
  string(30) "edmond.shepherd@southmedia.com"
  ["password":protected]=>
  string(13) "tobacco6334he"
  ["status":protected]=>
  int(1)
  ["securityQuestion":protected]=>
  string(0) ""
  ["confirmCode":protected]=>
  string(0) ""
  ["profileId":protected]=>
  int(48)
  ["level":protected]=>
  string(3) "ADV"
  ["purchases":protected]=>
  array(0) {
  }
  ["mapping":protected]=>
  array(10) {
```

See also

There are many good works that describe the domain model. Probably the most influential is *Patterns of Enterprise Application Architecture* by Martin Fowler (see `http://martinfowler.com/books/eaa.html`). There is also a nice study, also available as a free download, entitled *Domain Driven Design Quickly* by InfoQ (see `http://www.infoq.com/minibooks/domain-driven-design-quickly`).

Tying entity classes to RDBMS queries

Most commercially viable RDBMS systems evolved at a time when procedural programming was at the fore. Imagine the RDBMS world as two dimensional, square, and procedurally oriented. In contrast, entities could be thought of as round, three dimensional, and object oriented. This gives you a picture of what we want to accomplish by tying the results of an RDBMS query into an iteration of entity instances.

The **relational model**, upon which modern RDBMS systems are based, was first described by the mathematician Edgar F. Codd in 1969. The first commercially viable systems evolved in the mid-to-late 1970s. So, in other words, RDBMS technology is over 40 years old!

How to do it...

1. First of all, we need to design a class which will house our query logic. If you are following the Domain Model, this class might be called a **repository**. Alternatively, to keep things simple and generic, we could simply call the new class `Application\Database\CustomerService`. The class will accept an `Application\Database\Connection` instance as an argument:

```
namespace Application\Database;

use Application\Entity\Customer;

class CustomerService
{

    protected $connection;

    public function __construct(Connection $connection)
    {
      $this->connection = $connection;
    }

}
```

2. Now we will define a `fetchById()` method, which takes a customer ID as an argument, and returns a single `Application\Entity\Customer` instance or boolean `FALSE` on failure. At first glance, it would seem a no-brainer to simply use `PDOStatement::fetchObject()` and specify the entity class as an argument:

```
public function fetchById($id)
{
  $stmt = $this->connection->pdo
               ->prepare(Finder::select('customer')
               ->where('id = :id')::getSql());
  $stmt->execute(['id' => (int) $id]);
  return $stmt->fetchObject('Application\Entity\Customer');
}
```

The danger here, however, is that `fetchObject()` actually populates the properties (even if they are protected) before the constructor is called! Accordingly, there is a danger that the constructor could accidentally overwrite values. If you don't define a constructor, or if you can live with this danger, we're done. Otherwise, it starts to get tougher to properly implement the tie between RDBMS query and OOP results.

3. Another approach for the `fetchById()` method is to create the object instance first, thereby running its constructor, and setting the fetch mode to `PDO::FETCH_INTO`, as shown in the following example:

```
public function fetchById($id)
{
  $stmt = $this->connection->pdo
              ->prepare(Finder::select('customer')
              ->where('id = :id')::getSql());
  $stmt->execute(['id' => (int) $id]);
  $stmt->setFetchMode(PDO::FETCH_INTO, new Customer());
  return $stmt->fetch();
}
```

4. Here again, however, we encounter a problem: `fetch()`, unlike `fetchObject()`, is not able to overwrite protected properties; the following error message is generated if it tries. This means we will either have to define all properties as `public`, or consider another approach.

```
Terminal

Fatal error: Uncaught Error: Cannot access protected property Application\Entity
\Customer::$id in /home/ed/Desktop/Repos/php7_recipes/source/Application/Databas
e/CustomerService.php:28
Stack trace:
#0 /home/ed/Desktop/Repos/php7_recipes/source/Application/Database/CustomerServi
ce.php(28): PDOStatement->fetch()
#1 /home/ed/Desktop/Repos/php7_recipes/source/chapter05/chap_05_entity_to_query_
fetch_by_id.php(19): Application\Database\CustomerService->fetchById(19)
#2 {main}

Next Error: Cannot access protected property Application\Entity\Customer::$name
in /home/ed/Desktop/Repos/php7_recipes/source/Application/Database/CustomerServi
ce.php:28
Stack trace:
#0 /home/ed/Desktop/Repos/php7_recipes/source/Application/Database/CustomerServi
ce.php(28): PDOStatement->fetch()
#1 /home/ed/Desktop/Repos/php7_recipes/source/chapter05/chap_05_entity_to_query_
fetch_by_id.php(19): Application\Database\CustomerService->fetchById(19)
#2 {main}

Next Error: Cannot access protected property Application\Entity\Customer::$balan
ce in /home/ed/Deskt in /home/ed/Desktop/Repos/php7_recipes/source/Application/D
atabase/CustomerService.php on line 28
```

5. The last approach we will consider will be to fetch the results in the form of an array, and manually *hydrate* the entity. Even though this approach is slightly more costly in terms of performance, it allows any potential entity constructor to run properly, and keeps properties safely defined as `private` or `protected`:

```
public function fetchById($id)
{
  $stmt = $this->connection->pdo
              ->prepare(Finder::select('customer')
              ->where('id = :id')::getSql());
  $stmt->execute(['id' => (int) $id]);
  return Customer::arrayToEntity(
    $stmt->fetch(PDO::FETCH_ASSOC));
}
```

6. To process a query that produces multiple results, all we need to do is to produce an iteration of populated entity objects. In this example, we implement a `fetchByLevel()` method that returns all customers for a given level, in the form of `Application\Entity\Customer` instances:

```
public function fetchByLevel($level)
{
  $stmt = $this->connection->pdo->prepare(
          Finder::select('customer')
          ->where('level = :level')::getSql());
  $stmt->execute(['level' => $level]);
  while ($row = $stmt->fetch(PDO::FETCH_ASSOC)) {
    yield Customer::arrayToEntity($row, new Customer());
  }
}
```

7. The next method we wish to implement is `save()`. Before we can proceed, however, some thought must be given to what value will be returned if an `INSERT` takes place.

8. Normally, we would return the newly completed entity class after an `INSERT`. There is a convenient `PDO::lastInsertId()` method which, at first glance, would seem to do the trick. Further reading of the documentation reveals, however, that not all database extensions support this feature, and the ones that do are not consistent in their implementation. Accordingly, it would be a good idea to have a unique column other than `$id` that can be used to uniquely identify the new customer.

9. In this example we have chosen the `email` column, and thus need to implement a `fetchByEmail()` service method:

```
public function fetchByEmail($email)
{
  $stmt = $this->connection->pdo->prepare(
    Finder::select('customer')
```

```
    ->where('email = :email')::getSql());
  $stmt->execute(['email' => $email]);
  return Customer::arrayToEntity(
    $stmt->fetch(PDO::FETCH_ASSOC), new Customer());
}
```

10. Now we are ready to define the `save()` method. Rather than distinguish between `INSERT` and `UPDATE`, we will architect this method to update if the ID already exists, and otherwise do an insert.
11. First, we define a basic `save()` method, which accepts a `Customer` entity as an argument, and uses `fetchById()` to determine if this entry already exists. If it exists, we call an `doUpdate()` update method; otherwise, we call a `doInsert()` insert method:

```
public function save(Customer $cust)
{
  // check to see if customer ID > 0 and exists
  if ($cust->getId() && $this->fetchById($cust->getId())) {
    return $this->doUpdate($cust);
  } else {
    return $this->doInsert($cust);
  }
}
```

12. Next, we define `doUpdate()`, which pulls `Customer` entity object properties into an array, builds an initial SQL statement, and calls a `flush()` method, which pushes data to the database. We do not want the ID field updated, as it's the primary key. Also we need to specify which row to update, which means appending a `WHERE` clause:

```
protected function doUpdate($cust)
{
  // get properties in the form of an array
  $values = $cust->entityToArray();
  // build the SQL statement
  $update = 'UPDATE ' . $cust::TABLE_NAME;
  $where = ' WHERE id = ' . $cust->getId();
  // unset ID as we want do not want this to be updated
  unset($values['id']);
  return $this->flush($update, $values, $where);
}
```

13. The `doInsert()` method is similar, except that the initial SQL needs to start with `INSERT INTO ...` and the `id` array element needs to be unset. The reason for the latter is that we want this property to be auto-generated by the database. If this is successful, we use our newly defined `fetchByEmail()` method to look up the new customer and return a completed instance:

```
protected function doInsert($cust)
{
  $values = $cust->entityToArray();
  $email  = $cust->getEmail();
  unset($values['id']);
  $insert = 'INSERT INTO ' . $cust::TABLE_NAME . ' ';
  if ($this->flush($insert, $values)) {
    return $this->fetchByEmail($email);
  } else {
    return FALSE;
  }
}
```

14. Finally, we are in a position to define `flush()`, which does the actual preparation and execution:

```
protected function flush($sql, $values, $where = '')
{
  $sql .=  ' SET ';
  foreach ($values as $column => $value) {
    $sql .= $column . ' = :' . $column . ',';
  }
  // get rid of trailing ','
  $sql     = substr($sql, 0, -1) . $where;
  $success = FALSE;
  try {
    $stmt = $this->connection->pdo->prepare($sql);
    $stmt->execute($values);
    $success = TRUE;
  } catch (PDOException $e) {
    error_log(__METHOD__ . ':' . __LINE__ . ':'
    . $e->getMessage());
    $success = FALSE;
  } catch (Throwable $e) {
    error_log(__METHOD__ . ':' . __LINE__ . ':'
    . $e->getMessage());
    $success = FALSE;
  }
  return $success;
}
```

15. To round off the discussion, we need to define a `remove()` method, which deletes a customer from the database. Again, as with the `save()` method defined previously, we use `fetchById()` to ensure the operation was successful:

```
public function remove(Customer $cust)
{
  $sql = 'DELETE FROM ' . $cust::TABLE_NAME . ' WHERE id = :id';
  $stmt = $this->connection->pdo->prepare($sql);
  $stmt->execute(['id' => $cust->getId()]);
  return ($this->fetchById($cust->getId())) ? FALSE : TRUE;
}
```

How it works...

Copy the code described in steps 1 to 5 into a `CustomerService.php` file in the `Application/Database` folder. Define a `chap_05_entity_to_query.php` calling program. Have the calling program initialize the autoloader, using the appropriate classes:

```
<?php
define('DB_CONFIG_FILE', '/../config/db.config.php');
require __DIR__ . '/../Application/Autoload/Loader.php';
Application\Autoload\Loader::init(__DIR__ . '/..');
use Application\Database\Connection;
use Application\Database\CustomerService;
```

You can now create an instance of the service, and fetch a single customer at random. The service will then return a customer entity as a result:

```
// get service instance
$service = new CustomerService(new Connection(
                                include __DIR__ . DB_CONFIG_FILE));

echo "\nSingle Result\n";
var_dump($service->fetchById(rand(1,79)));
```

Here is the output:

```
Terminal

Single Result
object(Application\Entity\Customer)#6 (12) {
  ["name":protected]=>
  string(16) "Leonardo Parrish"
  ["balance":protected]=>
  float(166.63)
  ["email":protected]=>
  string(28) "leonardo.parrish@eastnet.net"
  ["password":protected]=>
  string(9) "I9898bend"
  ["status":protected]=>
  int(1)
  ["securityQuestion":protected]=>
  string(0) ""
  ["confirmCode":protected]=>
  string(0) ""
  ["profileId":protected]=>
  int(42)
  ["level":protected]=>
  string(0) ""
  ["purchases":protected]=>
  array(0) {
  }
```

Now copy the code shown in steps 6 to 15 into the service class. Add the data to insert to the `chap_05_entity_to_query.php` calling program. We then generate a `Customer` entity instance using this data:

```
// sample data
$data = [
  'name'              => 'Doug Bierer',
  'balance'           => 326.33,
  'email'             => 'doug' . rand(0,999) . '@test.com',
  'password'          => 'password',
  'status'            => 1,
  'security_question' => 'Who\'s on first?',
  'confirm_code'      => 12345,
  'level'             => 'ADV'
];

// create new Customer
$cust = Customer::arrayToEntity($data, new Customer());
```

We can then examine the ID before and after the call to `save()`:

```
echo "\nCustomer ID BEFORE Insert: {$cust->getId()}\n";
$cust = $service->save($cust);
echo "Customer ID AFTER Insert: {$cust->getId()}\n";
```

Finally, we modify the balance, and again call `save()`, viewing the results:

```
echo "Customer Balance BEFORE Update: {$cust->getBalance()}\n";
$cust->setBalance(999.99);
$service->save($cust);
echo "Customer Balance AFTER Update: {$cust->getBalance()}\n";
var_dump($cust);
```

Here is the output from the calling program:

```
Terminal
Customer ID BEFORE Insert: 0
Customer ID AFTER Insert: 111
Customer Balance BEFORE Update: 326.33
Customer Balance AFTER Update: 999.99
object(Application\Entity\Customer)#7 (12) {
  ["name":protected]=>
  string(11) "Doug Bierer"
  ["balance":protected]=>
  float(999.99)
  ["email":protected]=>
  string(26) "doug176@unlikelysource.com"
  ["password":protected]=>
  string(8) "password"
  ["status":protected]=>
  int(1)
  ["securityQuestion":protected]=>
  string(15) "Who's on first?"
  ["confirmCode":protected]=>
  string(5) "12345"
  ["profileId":protected]=>
  int(0)
  ["level":protected]=>
  string(3) "ADV"
```

There's more...

For more information on the relational model, please refer to `https://en.wikipedia.org/wiki/Relational_model`. For more information on RDBMS, please refer to `https://en.wikipedia.org/wiki/Relational_database_management_system`. For information on how `PDOStatement::fetchObject()` inserts property values even before the constructor, have a look at the comment by "rasmus at mindplay dot dk" in the php.net documentation reference on `fetchObject()` (`http://php.net/manual/en/pdostatement.fetchobject.php`).

Embedding secondary lookups into query results

On the road towards implementing relationships between entity classes, let us first take a look at how we can embed the code needed to perform a secondary lookup. An example of such a lookup is when displaying information on a customer, have the view logic perform a second lookup that gets a list of purchases for that customer.

> The advantage of this approach is that processing is deferred until the actual view logic is executed. This will ultimately smooth the performance curve, with the workload distributed more evenly between the initial query for customer information, and the later query for purchase information. Another benefit is that a massive `JOIN` is avoided with its inherent redundant data.

How to do it...

1. First of all, define a function that finds a customer based on their ID. For the purposes of this illustration, we will simply fetch an array using the fetch mode `PDO::FETCH_ASSOC`. We will also continue to use the `Application\Database\Connection` class discussed in *Chapter 1, Building a Foundation*:

```
function findCustomerById($id, Connection $conn)
{
  $stmt = $conn->pdo->query(
    'SELECT * FROM customer WHERE id = ' . (int) $id);
  $results = $stmt->fetch(PDO::FETCH_ASSOC);
  return $results;
}
```

2. Next, we analyze the purchases table to see how the `customer` and `product` tables are linked. As you can see from the `CREATE` statement for this table, the `customer_id` and `product_id` foreign keys form the relationships:

```
CREATE TABLE 'purchases' (
  'id' int(11) NOT NULL AUTO_INCREMENT,
  'transaction' varchar(8) NOT NULL,
  'date' datetime NOT NULL,
  'quantity' int(10) unsigned NOT NULL,
  'sale_price' decimal(8,2) NOT NULL,
  'customer_id' int(11) DEFAULT NULL,
  'product_id' int(11) DEFAULT NULL,
  PRIMARY KEY ('id'),
```

```
    KEY 'IDX_C3F3' ('customer_id'),
    KEY 'IDX_665A' ('product_id'),
    CONSTRAINT 'FK_665A' FOREIGN KEY ('product_id')
    REFERENCES 'products' ('id'),
    CONSTRAINT 'FK_C3F3' FOREIGN KEY ('customer_id')
    REFERENCES 'customer' ('id')
);
```

3. We now expand the original `findCustomerById()` function, defining the secondary lookup in the form of an anonymous function, which can then be executed in a view script. The anonymous function is assigned to the `$results['purchases']` element:

```
function findCustomerById($id, Connection $conn)
{
  $stmt = $conn->pdo->query(
       'SELECT * FROM customer WHERE id = ' . (int) $id);
  $results = $stmt->fetch(PDO::FETCH_ASSOC);
  if ($results) {
    $results['purchases'] =
      // define secondary lookup
      function ($id, $conn) {
        $sql = 'SELECT * FROM purchases AS u '
           . 'JOIN products AS r '
           . 'ON u.product_id = r.id '
           . 'WHERE u.customer_id = :id '
           . 'ORDER BY u.date';
          $stmt = $conn->pdo->prepare($sql);
          $stmt->execute(['id' => $id]);
          while ($row = $stmt->fetch(PDO::FETCH_ASSOC)) {
            yield $row;
          }
      };
  }
  return $results;
}
```

4. Assuming we have successfully retrieved customer information into a `$results` array, in the view logic, all we need to do is to loop through the return value of the anonymous function. In this example, we retrieve customer information at random:

```
$result = findCustomerById(rand(1,79), $conn);
```

5. In the view logic, we loop through the results returned by the secondary lookup. The call to the embedded anonymous function is highlighted in the following code:

```
<table>
  <tr>
<th>Transaction</th><th>Date</th><th>Qty</th>
<th>Price</th><th>Product</th>
  </tr>
<?php
foreach ($result['purchases']($result['id'], $conn) as $purchase)
: ?>
  <tr>
    <td><?= $purchase['transaction'] ?></td>
    <td><?= $purchase['date'] ?></td>
    <td><?= $purchase['quantity'] ?></td>
    <td><?= $purchase['sale_price'] ?></td>
    <td><?= $purchase['title'] ?></td>
  </tr>
<?php endforeach; ?>
</table>
```

How it works...

Create a `chap_05_secondary_lookups.php` calling program and insert the code needed to create an instance of `Application\Database\Connection`:

```
<?php
define('DB_CONFIG_FILE', '/../config/db.config.php');
include __DIR__ . '/../Application/Database/Connection.php';
use Application\Database\Connection;
$conn = new Connection(include __DIR__ . DB_CONFIG_FILE);
```

Next, add the `findCustomerById()` function shown in step 3. You can then pull information for a random customer, ending the PHP part of the calling program:

```
function findCustomerById($id, Connection $conn)
{
  // code shown in bullet #3 above
}
$result = findCustomerById(rand(1,79), $conn);
?>
```

For the view logic, you can display core customer information as shown in several of the preceding recipes:

```
<h1><?= $result['name'] ?></h1>
<div class="row">
<div class="left">Balance</div>
<div class="right"><?= $result['balance']; ?></div>
</div>
<!-- etc.l -->
```

You can display information on purchases like so:

```
<table>
<tr><th>Transaction</th><th>Date</th><th>Qty</th>
<th>Price</th><th>Product</th></tr>
  <?php
  foreach ($result['purchases']($result['id'], $conn)
           as $purchase) : ?>
  <tr>
    <td><?= $purchase['transaction'] ?></td>
    <td><?= $purchase['date'] ?></td>
    <td><?= $purchase['quantity'] ?></td>
    <td><?= $purchase['sale_price'] ?></td>
    <td><?= $purchase['title'] ?></td>
  </tr>
<?php endforeach; ?>
</table>
```

The critical piece is that the secondary lookup is performed as part of the view logic by calling the embedded anonymous function, `$result['purchases']($result['id'], $conn)`. Here is the output:

PHP 7 Cookbook

localhost:8080

Leonardo Parrish

Balance 166.63
Email leonardo.parrish@eastnet.net
Status 1
Level

Transaction	Date	Qty	Price	Product
LHN0514	1994-10-22 16:43:14	16	68.80	Pop Tarts
WMN2186	1995-01-02 12:59:19	5	28.50	Napoleon
XAW8061	1995-01-25 19:23:36	13	48.10	Coconut Custard Pie
ZKK3941	1995-05-24 09:42:32	9	48.60	Banana Bread
PUL9552	1995-08-29 02:10:16	12	75.60	Chocolate Soufflé
UZX7716	1995-09-26 00:53:59	16	22.40	Napoleon
ODZ9892	1996-05-07 11:11:48	18	61.20	Chocolate Toaster Tarts
JZD3542	1996-07-14 14:58:59	13	15.60	Chocolate Toaster Tarts
NOC8370	1996-08-04 09:20:02	4	11.20	Mint Chocolate Milk Shake
IUQ0690	1997-01-04 12:33:24	12	57.60	Chocolate Fondue
EAJ5532	1997-01-18 04:57:20	5	32.00	Oreo Cookies
HTR6003	1997-01-18 06:08:03	11	59.40	Pecan Praline Ice Cream
HTR6003	1997-01-18 06:08:03	11	5.50	Devils Food Cake

Implementing jQuery DataTables PHP lookups

Another approach to secondary lookups is to have the frontend generate the request. In this recipe, we will make a slight modification to the secondary lookup code presented in the preceding recipe, Embedding secondary lookups into QueryResults. In the previous recipe, even though the view logic is performing the lookup, all processing is still done on the server. When using **jQuery DataTables**, however, the secondary lookup is actually performed directly by the client, in the form of an **Asynchronous JavaScript and XML** (**AJAX**) request issued by the browser.

How to do it...

1. First we need to spin-off the secondary lookup logic (discussed in the recipe above) into a separate PHP file. The purpose of this new script is to perform the secondary lookup and return a JSON array.
2. The new script we will call `chap_05_jquery_datatables_php_lookups_ajax.php`. It looks for a `$_GET` parameter, `id`. Notice that the `SELECT` statement is very specific as to which columns are delivered. You will also note that the fetch mode has been changed to `PDO::FETCH_NUM`. You might also notice that the last line takes the results and assigns it to a `data` key in a JSON-encoded array.

It is *extremely* important when dealing with zero configuration jQuery DataTables to only return the exact number of columns matching the header.

```
$id  = $_GET['id'] ?? 0;
sql = 'SELECT u.transaction,u.date,
  u.quantity,u.sale_price,r.title '
    . 'FROM purchases AS u '
    . 'JOIN products AS r '
    . 'ON u.product_id = r.id '
    . 'WHERE u.customer_id = :id';
$stmt = $conn->pdo->prepare($sql);
$stmt->execute(['id' => (int) $id]);
$results = array();
while ($row = $stmt->fetch(PDO::FETCH_NUM)) {
  $results[] = $row;
}
echo json_encode(['data' => $results]);
```

3. Next, we need to modify the function that retrieves customer information by ID, removing the secondary lookup embedded in the previous recipe:

```
function findCustomerById($id, Connection $conn)
{
  $stmt = $conn->pdo->query(
    'SELECT * FROM customer WHERE id = ' . (int) $id);
  $results = $stmt->fetch(PDO::FETCH_ASSOC);
  return $results;
}
```

4. After that, in the view logic, we import the minimum jQuery, DataTables, and stylesheets for a zero configuration implementation. At a minimum, you will need jQuery itself (in this example `jquery-1.12.0.min.js`) and DataTables (`jquery.dataTables.js`). We've also added a convenient stylesheet associated with DataTables, `jquery.dataTables.css`:

```
<!DOCTYPE html>
<head>
  <script src="https://code.jquery.com/jquery-1.12.0.min.js">
  </script>
    <script type="text/javascript"
      charset="utf8"
      src="//cdn.datatables.net/1.10.11/js/jquery.dataTables.js">
    </script>
  <link rel="stylesheet"
    type="text/css"
    href="//cdn.datatables.net/1.10.11/css/jquery.dataTables.css">
</head>
```

5. We then define a jQuery document `ready` function, which associates a table with DataTables. In this case, we assign an id attribute of `customerTable` to the table element that will be assigned to DataTables. You'll also notice that we specify the AJAX data source as the script defined in step 1, `chap_05_jquery_datatables_php_lookups_ajax.php`. As we have the `$id` available, this is appended to the data source URL:

```
<script>
$(document).ready(function() {
  $('#customerTable').DataTable(
    { "ajax": '/chap_05_jquery_datatables_php_lookups_ajax.
       php?id=<?= $id ?>'
  });
} );
</script>
```

6. In the body of the view logic, we define the table, making sure the `id` attribute matches the one specified in the preceding code. We also need to define headers that will match the data presented in response to the AJAX request:

```
<table id="customerTable" class="display" cellspacing="0"
width="100%">
  <thead>
    <tr>
      <th>Transaction</th>
      <th>Date</th>
      <th>Qty</th>
      <th>Price</th>
      <th>Product</th>
    </tr>
  </thead>
</table>
```

7. Now, all that remains to do is to load the page, choose the customer ID (in this case, at random), and let jQuery make the request for the secondary lookup.

How it works...

Create a `chap_05_jquery_datatables_php_lookups_ajax.php` script, which will respond to an AJAX request. Inside, place the code to initialize auto-loading and create a `Connection` instance. You can then append the code shown in step 2 of the preceding recipe:

```
<?php
define('DB_CONFIG_FILE', '/../config/db.config.php');
include __DIR__ . '/../Application/Database/Connection.php';
use Application\Database\Connection;
$conn = new Connection(include __DIR__ . DB_CONFIG_FILE);
```

Next, create a `chap_05_jquery_datatables_php_lookups.php` calling program that will pull information on a random customer. Add the function described in step 3 of the preceding code:

```
<?php
define('DB_CONFIG_FILE', '/../config/db.config.php');
include __DIR__ . '/../Application/Database/Connection.php';
use Application\Database\Connection;
$conn = new Connection(include __DIR__ . DB_CONFIG_FILE);
// add function findCustomerById() here
$id     = random_int(1,79);
$result = findCustomerById($id, $conn);
?>
```

The calling program will also contain the view logic that imports the minimum JavaScript to implement jQuery DataTables. You can add the code shown in step 3 of the preceding code. Then, add the document `ready` function and the display logic shown in steps 5 and 6. Here is the output:

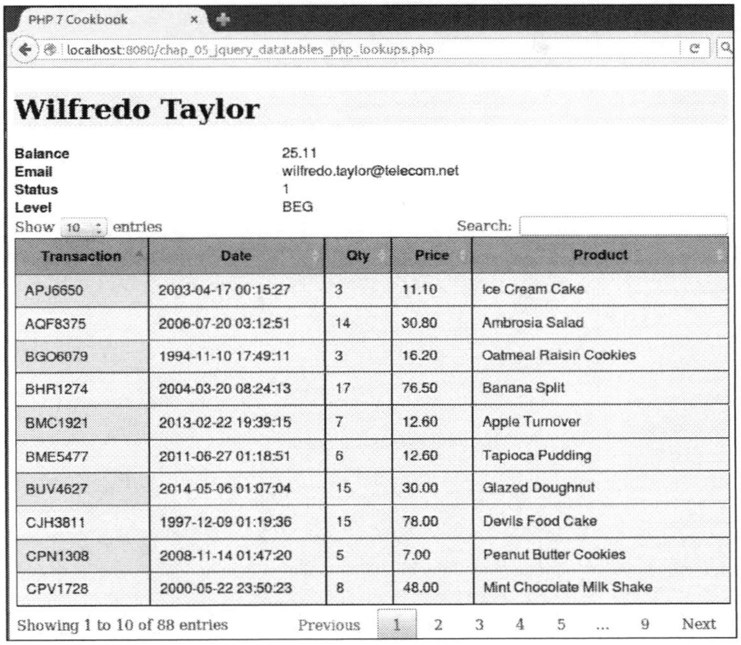

PHP 7 Cookbook

localhost:8080/chap_05_jquery_datatables_php_lookups.php

Wilfredo Taylor

Balance 25.11
Email wilfredo.taylor@telecom.net
Status 1
Level BEG

Show 10 entries Search:

Transaction	Date	Qty	Price	Product
APJ6650	2003-04-17 00:15:27	3	11.10	Ice Cream Cake
AQF8375	2006-07-20 03:12:51	14	30.80	Ambrosia Salad
BGO6079	1994-11-10 17:49:11	3	16.20	Oatmeal Raisin Cookies
BHR1274	2004-03-20 08:24:13	17	76.50	Banana Split
BMC1921	2013-02-22 19:39:15	7	12.60	Apple Turnover
BME5477	2011-06-27 01:18:51	6	12.60	Tapioca Pudding
BUV4627	2014-05-06 01:07:04	15	30.00	Glazed Doughnut
CJH3811	1997-12-09 01:19:36	15	78.00	Devils Food Cake
CPN1308	2008-11-14 01:47:20	5	7.00	Peanut Butter Cookies
CPV1728	2000-05-22 23:50:23	8	48.00	Mint Chocolate Milk Shake

Showing 1 to 10 of 88 entries Previous 1 2 3 4 5 ... 9 Next

There's more...

For more information on jQuery, please visit their website at `https://jquery.com/`. To read about the DataTables plugin to jQuery, refer to this article at `https://www.datatables.net/`. Zero configuration data tables are discussed at `https://datatables.net/examples/basic_init/zero_configuration.html`. For more information on AJAX sourced data, have a look at `https://datatables.net/examples/data_sources/ajax.html`.

6
Building Scalable Websites

In this chapter, we will cover the following topics:

- Creating a generic form element generator
- Creating an HTML radio element generator
- Creating an HTML select element generator
- Implementing a form factory
- Chaining `$_POST` filters
- Chaining `$_POST` validators
- Tying validation to a form

Introduction

In this chapter, we will show you how to build classes that generate HTML form elements. The generic element generator can be used for text, text areas, passwords, and similar HTML input types. After that, we will show variations that allow you to pre-configure the element with an array of values. The form factory recipe will bring all these generators together, allowing you to render an entire form using a single configuration array. Finally, we introduce recipes that allow filtering and the validation of incoming `$_POST` data.

Creating a generic form element generator

It's pretty easy to create a function that simply outputs a form input tag such as `<input type="text" name="whatever" >`. In order to make a form generator generically useful, however, we need to think about the bigger picture. Here are some other considerations over and above the basic input tag:

- The form `input` tag and its associated HTML attributes
- A label that tells the user what information they are entering
- The ability to display entry errors following validation (more on that later!)
- Some sort of wrapper, such as a `<div>` tag, or an HTML table `<td>` tag

How to do it...

1. First, we define a `Application\Form\Generic` class. This will also later serve as a base class for specialized form elements:

   ```
   namespace Application\Form;

   class Generic
   {
     // some code ...
   }
   ```

2. Next, we define some class constants, which will be generally useful in form element generation.
3. The first three will become keys associated with the major components of a single form element. We then define supported input types and defaults:

   ```
   const ROW = 'row';
   const FORM = 'form';
   const INPUT = 'input';
   const LABEL = 'label';
   const ERRORS = 'errors';
   const TYPE_FORM = 'form';
   const TYPE_TEXT = 'text';
   const TYPE_EMAIL = 'email';
   const TYPE_RADIO = 'radio';
   const TYPE_SUBMIT = 'submit';
   const TYPE_SELECT = 'select';
   const TYPE_PASSWORD = 'password';
   const TYPE_CHECKBOX = 'checkbox';
   const DEFAULT_TYPE = self::TYPE_TEXT;
   const DEFAULT_WRAPPER = 'div';
   ```

4. Next, we can define properties and a constructor that sets them.
5. In this example, we require two properties, `$name` and `$type`, as we cannot effectively use the element without these attributes. The other constructor arguments are optional. Furthermore, in order to base one form element on another, we include a provision whereby the second argument, `$type`, can alternatively be an instance of `Application\Form\Generic`, in which case we simply run the *getters* (discussed later) to populate properties:

```
protected $name;
protected $type     = self::DEFAULT_TYPE;
protected $label    = '';
protected $errors   = array();
protected $wrappers;
protected $attributes;    // HTML form attributes
protected $pattern =  '<input type="%s" name="%s" %s>';

public function __construct($name,
                $type,
                $label = '',
                array $wrappers = array(),
                array $attributes = array(),
                array $errors = array())
{
  $this->name = $name;
  if ($type instanceof Generic) {
      $this->type       = $type->getType();
      $this->label      = $type->getLabelValue();
      $this->errors     = $type->getErrorsArray();
      $this->wrappers   = $type->getWrappers();
      $this->attributes = $type->getAttributes();
  } else {
      $this->type       = $type ?? self::DEFAULT_TYPE;
      $this->label      = $label;
      $this->errors     = $errors;
      $this->attributes = $attributes;
      if ($wrappers) {
          $this->wrappers = $wrappers;
      } else {
          $this->wrappers[self::INPUT]['type'] =
            self::DEFAULT_WRAPPER;
          $this->wrappers[self::LABEL]['type'] =
            self::DEFAULT_WRAPPER;
          $this->wrappers[self::ERRORS]['type'] =
            self::DEFAULT_WRAPPER;
    }
```

```
    }
    $this->attributes['id'] = $name;
  }
```

Note that `$wrappers` has three primary subkeys: `INPUT`, `LABEL`, and `ERRORS`. This allows us to define separate wrappers for labels, the input tag, and errors.

6. Before defining the core methods that will produce HTML for the label, input tag, and errors, we should define a `getWrapperPattern()` method, which will produce the appropriate *wrapping* tags for the label, input, and error display.
7. If, for example, the wrapper is defined as `<div>`, and its attributes include `['class' => 'label']`, this method will return a `sprintf()` format pattern that looks like this: `<div class="label">%s</div>`. The final HTML produced for the label, for example, would then replace `%s`.
8. Here is how the `getWrapperPattern()` method might look:

```
public function getWrapperPattern($type)
{
  $pattern = '<' . $this->wrappers[$type]['type'];
  foreach ($this->wrappers[$type] as $key => $value) {
    if ($key != 'type') {
      $pattern .= ' ' . $key . '="' . $value . '"';
    }
  }
  $pattern .= '>%s</' . $this->wrappers[$type]['type'] . '>';
  return $pattern;
}
```

9. We are now ready to define the `getLabel()` method. All this method needs to do is to plug the label into the wrapper using `sprintf()`:

```
public function getLabel()
{
  return sprintf($this->getWrapperPattern(self::LABEL),
                 $this->label);
}
```

10. In order to produce the core `input` tag, we need a way to assemble the attributes. Fortunately, this is easily accomplished as long as they are supplied to the constructor in the form of an associative array. All we need to do, in this case, is to define a `getAttribs()` method that produces a string of key-value pairs separated by a space. We return the final value using `trim()` to remove excess spaces.

11. If the element includes either the `value` or `href` attribute, for security reasons we should escape the values on the assumption that they are, or could be, user-supplied (and therefore suspect). Accordingly, we need to add an `if` statement that checks and then uses `htmlspecialchars()` or `urlencode()`:

```
public function getAttribs()
{
  foreach ($this->attributes as $key => $value) {
    $key = strtolower($key);
    if ($value) {
      if ($key == 'value') {
        if (is_array($value)) {
            foreach ($value as $k => $i)
              $value[$k] = htmlspecialchars($i);
        } else {
            $value = htmlspecialchars($value);
        }
      } elseif ($key == 'href') {
          $value = urlencode($value);
      }
      $attribs .= $key . '="' . $value . '" ';
    } else {
        $attribs .= $key . ' ';
    }
  }
  return trim($attribs);
}
```

12. For the core input tag, we split the logic into two separate methods. The primary method, `getInputOnly()`, produces *only* the HTML input tag. The second method, `getInputWithWrapper()`, produces the input embedded in a wrapper. The reason for the split is that when creating spin-off classes, such as a class to generate radio buttons, we will not need the wrapper:

```
public function getInputOnly()
{
  return sprintf($this->pattern, $this->type, $this->name,
                 $this->getAttribs());
}

public function getInputWithWrapper()
{
  return sprintf($this->getWrapperPattern(self::INPUT),
                 $this->getInputOnly());
}
```

13. We now define a method that displays element validation errors. We will assume that the errors will be supplied in the form of an array. If there are no errors, we return an empty string. Otherwise, errors are rendered as `<ul><li>error 1</li><li>error 2</li></ul>` and so on:

```
public function getErrors()
{
  if (!$this->errors || count($this->errors == 0)) return '';
  $html = '';
  $pattern = '<li>%s</li>';
  $html .= '<ul>';
  foreach ($this->errors as $error)
  $html .= sprintf($pattern, $error);
  $html .= '</ul>';
  return sprintf($this->getWrapperPattern(self::ERRORS), $html);
}
```

14. For certain attributes, we might need more finite control over various aspects of the property. As an example, we might need to add a single error to the already existing array of errors. Also, it might be useful to set a single attribute:

```
public function setSingleAttribute($key, $value)
{
  $this->attributes[$key] = $value;
}
public function addSingleError($error)
{
  $this->errors[] = $error;
}
```

15. Finally, we define getters and setters that allow us to retrieve or set the values of properties. For example, you might have noticed that the default value for `$pattern` is `<input type="%s" name="%s" %s>`. For certain tags (for example, `select` and `form` tags), we will need to set this property to a different value:

```
public function setPattern($pattern)
{
  $this->pattern = $pattern;
}
public function setType($type)
{
  $this->type = $type;
}
public function getType()
{
```

```
  return $this->type;
}
public function addSingleError($error)
{
  $this->errors[] = $error;
}
// define similar get and set methods
// for name, label, wrappers, errors and attributes
```

16. We also need to add methods that will give the label value (not the HTML), as well as the errors array:

```
public function getLabelValue()
{
  return $this->label;
}
public function getErrorsArray()
{
  return $this->errors;
}
```

How it works...

Be sure to copy all the preceding code into a single `Application\Form\Generic` class. You can then define a `chap_06_form_element_generator.php` calling script that sets up autoloading and anchors the new class:

```
<?php
require __DIR__ . '/../Application/Autoload/Loader.php';
Application\Autoload\Loader::init(__DIR__ . '/..');
use Application\Form\Generic;
```

Next, define the wrappers. For illustration, we'll use HTML table data and header tags. Note that the label uses `TH`, whereas input and errors use `TD`:

```
$wrappers = [
  Generic::INPUT => ['type' => 'td', 'class' => 'content'],
  Generic::LABEL => ['type' => 'th', 'class' => 'label'],
  Generic::ERRORS => ['type' => 'td', 'class' => 'error']
];
```

You can now define an email element by passing parameters to the constructor:

```
$email = new Generic('email', Generic::TYPE_EMAIL, 'Email', $wrappers,
                    ['id' => 'email',
                     'maxLength' => 128,
                     'title' => 'Enter address',
                     'required' => '']);
```

Alternatively, define the password element using setters:

```
$password = new Generic('password', $email);
$password->setType(Generic::TYPE_PASSWORD);
$password->setLabel('Password');
$password->setAttributes(['id' => 'password',
                          'title' => 'Enter your password',
                          'required' => '']);
```

Lastly, be sure to define a submit button:

```
$submit = new Generic('submit',
  Generic::TYPE_SUBMIT,
  'Login',
  $wrappers,
  ['id' => 'submit','title' => 'Click to login','value' =>
   'Click Here']);
```

The actual display logic might look like this:

```
<div class="container">
  <!-- Login Form -->
  <h1>Login</h1>
  <form name="login" method="post">
  <table id="login" class="display"
    cellspacing="0" width="100%">
    <tr><?= $email->render(); ?></tr>
    <tr><?= $password->render(); ?></tr>
    <tr><?= $submit->render(); ?></tr>
    <tr>
      <td colspan=2>
        <br>
        <?php var_dump($_POST); ?>
      </td>
    </tr>
  </table>
  </form>
</div>
```

Here is the actual output:

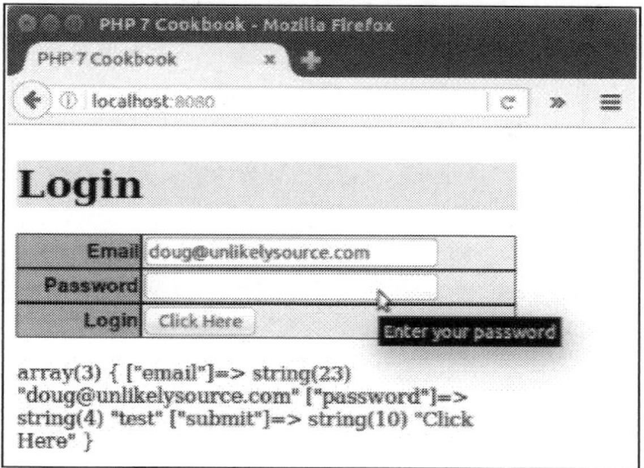

Creating an HTML radio element generator

A radio button element generator will share similarities with the generic HTML form element generator. As with any generic element, a set of radio buttons needs the ability to display an overall label and errors. There are two major differences, however:

- Typically, you will want two or more radio buttons
- Each button needs to have its own label

How to do it...

1. First of all, create a new `Application\Form\Element\Radio` class that extends `Application\Form\Generic`:

```
namespace Application\Form\Element;
use Application\Form\Generic;
class Radio extends Generic
{
  // code
}
```

2. Next, we define class constants and properties that pertain to the special needs of a set of radio buttons.

3. In this illustration, we will need a `spacer`, which will be placed between the radio button and its label. We also need to decide whether to place the radio button label before or after the actual button, thus, we use the `$after` flag. If we need a default, or if we are re-displaying existing form data, we need a way of designating the selected key. Finally, we need an array of options from which we will populate the list of buttons:

   ```
   const DEFAULT_AFTER = TRUE;
   const DEFAULT_SPACER = '&nbps;';
   const DEFAULT_OPTION_KEY = 0;
   const DEFAULT_OPTION_VALUE = 'Choose';

   protected $after = self::DEFAULT_AFTER;
   protected $spacer = self::DEFAULT_SPACER;
   protected $options = array();
   protected $selectedKey = DEFAULT_OPTION_KEY;
   ```

4. Given that we are extending `Application\Form\Generic`, we have the option of expanding the `__construct()` method, or, alternatively, simply defining a method that can be used to set specific options. For this illustration, we have chosen the latter course.

5. To ensure the property `$this->options` is populated, the first parameter (`$options`) is defined as mandatory (without a default). All other parameters are optional.

   ```
   public function setOptions(array $options,
     $selectedKey = self::DEFAULT_OPTION_KEY,
     $spacer = self::DEFAULT_SPACER,
     $after  = TRUE)
   {
     $this->after = $after;
     $this->spacer = $spacer;
     $this->options = $options;
     $this->selectedKey = $selectedKey;
   }
   ```

6. Finally, we are ready to override the core `getInputOnly()` method.

7. We save the `id` attribute into an independent variable, `$baseId`, and later combine it with `$count` so that each `id` attribute is unique. If the option associated with the selected key is defined, it is assigned as the value; otherwise, we use the default:

   ```
   public function getInputOnly()
   {
     $count  = 1;
     $baseId = $this->attributes['id'];
   ```

8. Inside the `foreach()` loop we check to see if the key is the one selected. If so, the `checked` attribute is added for that radio button. We then call the parent class `getInputOnly()` method to return the HTML for each button. Note that the `value` attribute of the input element is the options array key. The button label is the options array element value:

```
foreach ($this->options as $key => $value) {
  $this->attributes['id'] = $baseId . $count++;
  $this->attributes['value'] = $key;
  if ($key == $this->selectedKey) {
      $this->attributes['checked'] = '';
  } elseif (isset($this->attributes['checked'])) {
            unset($this->attributes['checked']);
  }
  if ($this->after) {
      $html = parent::getInputOnly() . $value;
  } else {
      $html = $value . parent::getInputOnly();
  }
  $output .= $this->spacer . $html;
  }
  return $output;
}
```

How it works...

Copy the preceding code into a new `Radio.php` file in the `Application/Form/Element` folder. You can then define a `chap_06_form_element_radio.php` calling script that sets up autoloading and anchors the new class:

```
<?php
require __DIR__ . '/../Application/Autoload/Loader.php';
Application\Autoload\Loader::init(__DIR__ . '/..');
use Application\Form\Generic;
use Application\Form\Element\Radio;
```

Next, define the wrappers using the `$wrappers` array defined in the previous recipe.

Then you can define a `$status` array and create an element instance by passing parameters to the constructor:

```
$statusList = [
  'U' => 'Unconfirmed',
  'P' => 'Pending',
  'T' => 'Temporary Approval',
  'A' => 'Approved'
```

```
];

$status = new Radio('status',
          Generic::TYPE_RADIO,
          'Status',
          $wrappers,
          ['id' => 'status']);
```

Now you can see if there is any status input from `$_GET` and set the options. Any input will become the selected key. Otherwise, the selected key is the default:

```
$checked = $_GET['status'] ?? 'U';
$status->setOptions($statusList, $checked, '<br>', TRUE);
```

Lastly, don't forget to define a submit button:

```
$submit = new Generic('submit',
          Generic::TYPE_SUBMIT,
          'Process',
          $wrappers,
          ['id' => 'submit','title' =>

          'Click to process','value' => 'Click Here']);
```

The display logic might look like this:

```
<form name="status" method="get">
<table id="status" class="display" cellspacing="0" width="100%">
  <tr><?= $status->render(); ?></tr>
  <tr><?= $submit->render(); ?></tr>
  <tr>
    <td colspan=2>
      <br>
      <pre><?php var_dump($_GET); ?></pre>
    </td>
  </tr>
</table>
</form>
```

Here is the actual output:

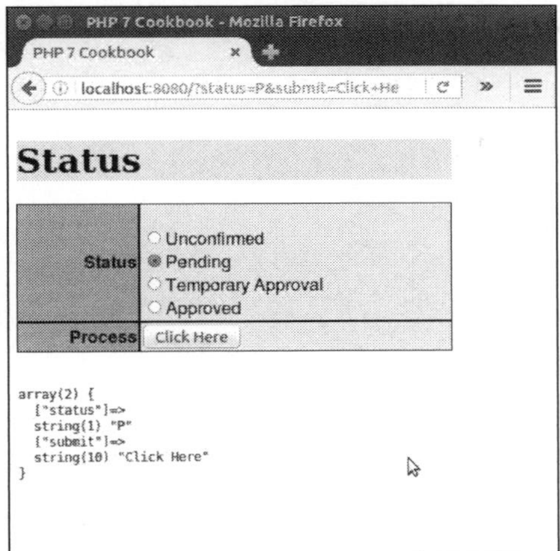

There's more...

A checkbox element generator would be almost identical to the HTML radio button generator. The main difference is that a set of checkboxes can have more than one value checked. Accordingly, you would use PHP array notation for the element names. The element type should be `Generic::TYPE_CHECKBOX`.

Creating an HTML select element generator

Generating an HTML single select element is similar to the process of generating radio buttons. The tags are structured differently, however, in that both a `SELECT` tag and a series of `OPTION` tags need to be generated.

How to do it...

1. First of all, create a new `Application\Form\Element\Select` class that extends `Application\Form\Generic`.
2. The reason why we extend `Generic` rather than `Radio` is because the structuring of the element is entirely different:

```
namespace Application\Form\Element;

use Application\Form\Generic;

class Select extends Generic
```

```
{
  // code
}
```

3. The class constants and properties will only need to add slightly to `Application\Form\Generic`. Unlike radio buttons or checkboxes, there is no need to account for *spacers* or the placement of the selected text:

```
const DEFAULT_OPTION_KEY = 0;
const DEFAULT_OPTION_VALUE = 'Choose';

protected $options;
protected $selectedKey = DEFAULT_OPTION_KEY;
```

4. Now we turn our attention to setting options. As an HTML select element can select single or multiple values, the `$selectedKey` property could be either a string or an array. Accordingly, we do not add a **type hint** for this property. It is important, however, that we identify whether or not the `multiple` attribute has been set. This can be obtained from a `$this->attributes` property via inheritance from the parent class.
5. If the `multiple` attribute has been set, it's important to formulate the `name` attribute as an array. Accordingly, we would append `[]` to the name if this were the case:

```
public function setOptions(array $options, $selectedKey =
                           self::DEFAULT_OPTION_KEY)
{
  $this->options = $options;
  $this->selectedKey = $selectedKey;
  if (isset($this->attributes['multiple'])) {
    $this->name .= '[]';
  }
}
```

In PHP, if the HTML select `multiple` attribute has been set, and the `name` attribute is not specified as an array, only a single value will be returned!

6. Before we can define the core `getInputOnly()` method, we need to define a method to generate the `select` tag. We then return the final HTML using `sprintf()`, using `$pattern`, `$name`, and the return value of `getAttribs()` as arguments.

7. We replace the default value for `$pattern` with `<select name="%s" %s>`. We then loop through the attributes, adding them as key-value pairs with spaces in between:

   ```
   protected function getSelect()
   {
     $this->pattern = '<select name="%s" %s> ' . PHP_EOL;
     return sprintf($this->pattern, $this->name,
     $this->getAttribs());
   }
   ```

8. Next, we define a method to obtain the `option` tags that will be associated with the `select` tag.
9. As you will recall, the *key* from the `$this->options` array represents the return value, whereas the *value* part of the array represents the text that will appear on screen. If `$this->selectedKey` is in array form, we check to see if the value is in the array. Otherwise, we assume `$this-> selectedKey` is a string and we simply determine if it is equal to the key. If the selected key matches, we add the `selected` attribute:

   ```
   protected function getOptions()
   {
     $output = '';
     foreach ($this->options as $key => $value) {
       if (is_array($this->selectedKey)) {
           $selected = (in_array($key, $this->selectedKey))
           ? ' selected' : '';
       } else {
           $selected = ($key == $this->selectedKey)
           ? ' selected' : '';
       }
           $output .= '<option value="' . $key . '"'
           . $selected  . '>'
           . $value
           . '</option>';
     }
     return $output;
   }
   ```

10. Finally we are ready to override the core `getInputOnly()` method.
11. You will note that the logic for this method only needs to capture the return values from the `getSelect()` and `getOptions()` methods described in the preceding code. We also need to add the closing `</select>` tag:

    ```
    public function getInputOnly()
    {
      $output = $this->getSelect();
      $output .= $this->getOptions();
    ```

```
        $output .= '</' . $this->getType() . '>';
        return $output;
    }
```

How it works...

Copy the code described above into a new `Select.php` file in the `Application/Form/Element` folder. Then define a `chap_06_form_element_select.php` calling script that sets up autoloading and anchors the new class:

```
<?php
require __DIR__ . '/../Application/Autoload/Loader.php';
Application\Autoload\Loader::init(__DIR__ . '/..');
use Application\Form\Generic;
use Application\Form\Element\Select;
```

Next, define the wrappers using the array `$wrappers` defined in the first recipe. You can also use the `$statusList` array defined in the *Creating an HTML radio element generator* recipe. You can then create instances of `SELECT` elements. The first instance is single select, and the second is multiple:

```
$status1 = new Select('status1',
           Generic::TYPE_SELECT,
           'Status 1',
           $wrappers,
           ['id' => 'status1']);
$status2 = new Select('status2',
           Generic::TYPE_SELECT,
           'Status 2',
           $wrappers,
           ['id' => 'status2',
            'multiple' => '',
            'size' => '4']);
```

See if there is any status input from `$_GET` and set the options. Any input will become the selected key. Otherwise, the selected key is the default. As you will recall, the second instance is multiple select, so the value obtained from `$_GET` and the default setting should both be in the form of an array:

```
$checked1 = $_GET['status1'] ?? 'U';
$checked2 = $_GET['status2'] ?? ['U'];
$status1->setOptions($statusList, $checked1);
$status2->setOptions($statusList, $checked2);
```

Lastly, be sure to define a submit button (as shown in the *Creating a generic form element generator* recipe of this chapter).

The actual display logic is identical to the radio button recipe, except that we need to render two separate HTML select instances:

```
<form name="status" method="get">
<table id="status" class="display" cellspacing="0" width="100%">
  <tr><?= $status1->render(); ?></tr>
  <tr><?= $status2->render(); ?></tr>
  <tr><?= $submit->render(); ?></tr>
  <tr>
    <td colspan=2>
      <br>
      <pre>
        <?php var_dump($_GET); ?>
      </pre>
    </td>
  </tr>
</table>
</form>
```

Here is the actual output:

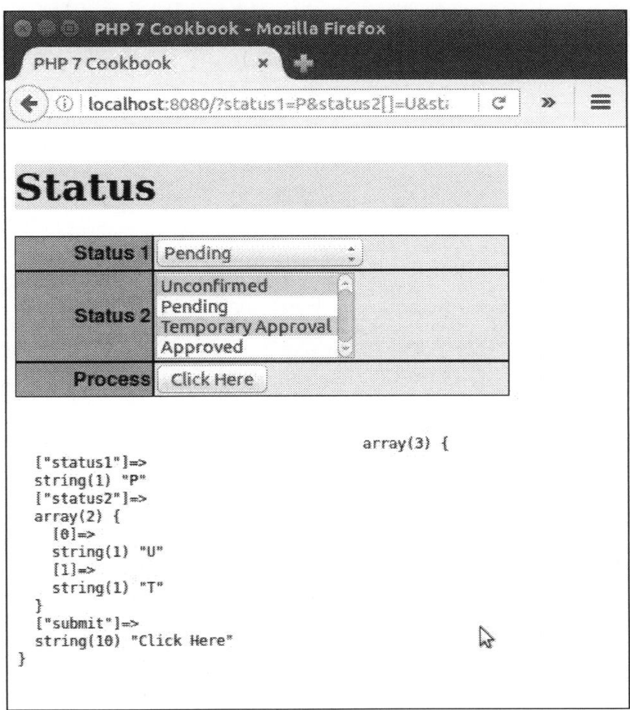

Also, you can see how the elements appear in the *view source* page:

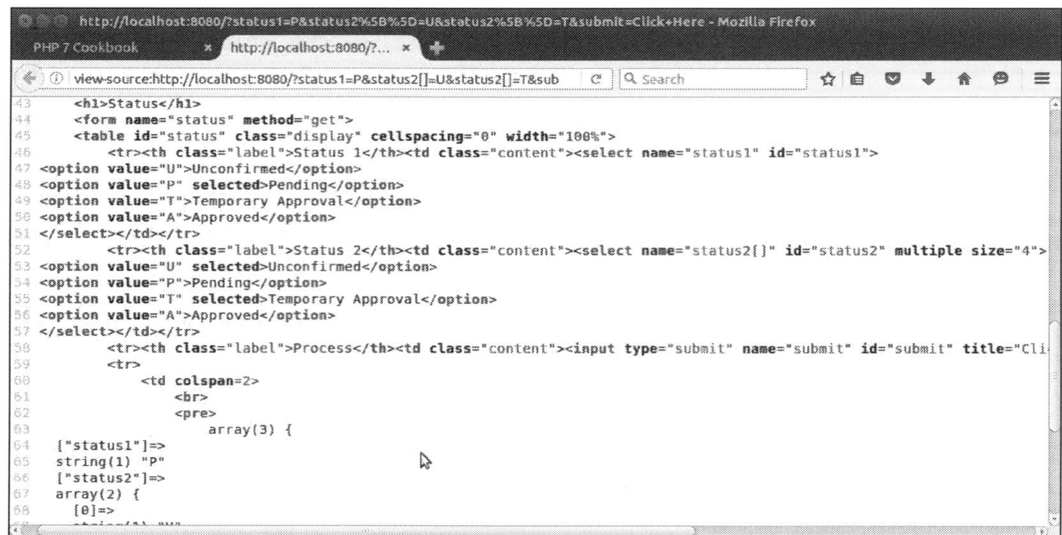

Implementing a form factory

The purpose of a form factory is to generate a usable form object from a single configuration array. The form object should have the ability to retrieve the individual elements it contains so that output can be generated.

How to do it...

1. First, let's create a class called `Application\Form\Factory` to contain the factory code. It will have only one property, `$elements`, with a getter:

```
namespace Application\Form;

class Factory
{
  protected $elements;
  public function getElements()
  {
    return $this->elements;
  }
  // remaining code
}
```

2. Before we define the primary form generation method, it's important to consider what configuration format we plan to receive, and what exactly the form generation will produce. For this illustration, we will assume that the generation will produce a `Factory` instance, with an `$elements` property. This property would be an array of `Application\Form\Generic` or `Application\Form\Element` classes.

3. We are now ready to tackle the `generate()` method. This will cycle through the configuration array, creating the appropriate `Application\Form\Generic` or `Application\Form\Element\*` objects, which in turn will be stored in the `$elements` array. The new method will accept the configuration array as an argument. It is convenient to define this method as static so that we can generate as many instances as are needed using different blocks of configuration.

4. We create an instance of `Application\Form\Factory`, and then we start looping through the configuration array:

```
public static function generate(array $config)
{
  $form = new self();
  foreach ($config as $key => $p) {
```

5. Next, we check for parameters that are optional in the constructor for the `Application\Form\Generic` class:

```
  $p['errors'] = $p['errors'] ?? array();
  $p['wrappers'] = $p['wrappers'] ?? array();
  $p['attributes'] = $p['attributes'] ?? array();
```

6. Now that all the constructor parameters are in place, we can create the form element instance, which is then stored in `$elements`:

```
  $form->elements[$key] = new $p['class']
  (
    $key,
    $p['type'],
    $p['label'],
    $p['wrappers'],
    $p['attributes'],
    $p['errors']
  );
```

7. Next, we turn our attention to options. If the `options` parameter is set, we extract the array values into variables using `list()`. We then test the element type using `switch()` and run `setOptions()` with the appropriate number of parameters:

```
    if (isset($p['options'])) {
      list($a,$b,$c,$d) = $p['options'];
      switch ($p['type']) {
        case Generic::TYPE_RADIO    :
        case Generic::TYPE_CHECKBOX :
```

```
            $form->elements[$key]->setOptions($a,$b,$c,$d);
            break;
          case Generic::TYPE_SELECT    :
            $form->elements[$key]->setOptions($a,$b);
            break;
          default                      :
            $form->elements[$key]->setOptions($a,$b);
            break;
        }
      }
    }
```

8. Finally, we return the form object and close out the method:

```
  return $form;
}
```

9. Theoretically, at this point, we could easily render the form in our view logic by simply iterating through the array of elements and running the `render()` method. The view logic might look like this:

```
<form name="status" method="get">
  <table id="status" class="display" cellspacing="0" width="100%">
    <?php foreach ($form->getElements() as $element) : ?>
      <?php echo $element->render(); ?>
    <?php endforeach; ?>
  </table>
</form>
```

10. Finally, we return the form object and close out the method.

11. Next, we need to define a discrete `Form` class under `Application\Form\Element`:

```
namespace Application\Form\Element;
class Form extends Generic
{
  public function getInputOnly()
  {
    $this->pattern = '<form name="%s" %s> ' . PHP_EOL;
    return sprintf($this->pattern, $this->name,
                   $this->getAttribs());
  }
  public function closeTag()
  {
    return '</' . $this->type . '>';
  }
}
```

12. Returning to the `Application\Form\Factory` class, we now need to define a simple method that returns a `sprintf()` wrapper pattern that will serve as an envelope for input. As an example, if the wrapper is `div` with an attribute `class="test"` we would produce this pattern: `<div class="test">%s</div>`. Our content would then be substituted in place of `%s` by the `sprintf()` function:

```
protected function getWrapperPattern($wrapper)
{
  $type = $wrapper['type'];
  unset($wrapper['type']);
  $pattern = '<' . $type;
  foreach ($wrapper as $key => $value) {
    $pattern .= ' ' . $key . '="' . $value . '"';
  }
  $pattern .= '>%s</' . $type . '>';
  return $pattern;
}
```

13. Finally, we are ready to define a method that does overall form rendering. We obtain wrapper `sprintf()` patterns for each form row. We then loop through the elements, render each one, and wrap the output in the row pattern. Next, we generate an `Application\Form\Element\Form` instance. We then retrieve the form wrapper `sprintf()` pattern and check the `form_tag_inside_wrapper` flag, which tells us whether we need to place the form tag inside or outside the form wrapper:

```
public static function render($form, $formConfig)
{
  $rowPattern = $form->getWrapperPattern(
  $formConfig['row_wrapper']);
  $contents   = '';
  foreach ($form->getElements() as $element) {
    $contents .= sprintf($rowPattern, $element->render());
  }
  $formTag = new Form($formConfig['name'],
                  Generic::TYPE_FORM,
                  '',
                  array(),
                  $formConfig['attributes']);

  $formPattern = $form->getWrapperPattern(
  $formConfig['form_wrapper']);
  if (isset($formConfig['form_tag_inside_wrapper'])
      && !$formConfig['form_tag_inside_wrapper']) {
        $formPattern = '%s' . $formPattern . '%s';
        return sprintf($formPattern, $formTag->getInputOnly(),
        $contents, $formTag->closeTag());
```

```
        } else {
              return sprintf($formPattern, $formTag->getInputOnly()
              . $contents . $formTag->closeTag());
        }
      }
```

How it works...

Referring to the preceding code, create the `Application\Form\Factory` and `Application\Form\Element\Form` classes.

Next, you can define a `chap_06_form_factor.php` calling script that sets up autoloading and anchors the new class:

```
<?php
require __DIR__ . '/../Application/Autoload/Loader.php';
Application\Autoload\Loader::init(__DIR__ . '/..');
use Application\Form\Generic;
use Application\Form\Factory;
```

Next, define the wrappers using the `$wrappers` array defined in the first recipe. You can also use the `$statusList` array defined in the second recipe.

See if there is any status input from `$_POST`. Any input will become the selected key. Otherwise, the selected key is the default.

```
$email    = $_POST['email']   ?? '';
$checked0 = $_POST['status0'] ?? 'U';
$checked1 = $_POST['status1'] ?? 'U';
$checked2 = $_POST['status2'] ?? ['U'];
$checked3 = $_POST['status3'] ?? ['U'];
```

Now you can define the overall form configuration. The `name` and `attributes` parameters are used to configure the `form` tag itself. The other two parameters represent form-level and row-level wrappers. Lastly, we provide a `form_tag_inside_wrapper` flag to indicate that the form tag should *not* appear inside the wrapper (that is, `<table>`). If the wrapper was `<div>`, we would set this flag to `TRUE`:

```
$formConfig = [
  'name'          => 'status_form',
  'attributes'    => ['id'=>'statusForm','method'=>'post',
                      'action'=>'chap_06_form_factory.php'],
  'row_wrapper'   => ['type' => 'tr', 'class' => 'row'],
  'form_wrapper'  => ['type'=>'table','class'=>'table',
                      'id'=>'statusTable',
```

```
                        'class'=>'display','cellspacing'=>'0'],
                        'form_tag_inside_wrapper' => FALSE,
];
```

Next, define an array that holds parameters for each form element to be created by the factory. The array key becomes the name of the form element, and must be unique:

```
$config = [
  'email' => [
    'class'      => 'Application\Form\Generic',
    'type'       => Generic::TYPE_EMAIL,
    'label'      => 'Email',
    'wrappers'   => $wrappers,
    'attributes'=> ['id'=>'email','maxLength'=>128,
                     'title'=>'Enter address',
                     'required'=>'','value'=>strip_tags($email)]
  ],
  'password' => [
    'class'       => 'Application\Form\Generic',
    'type'        => Generic::TYPE_PASSWORD,
    'label'       => 'Password',
    'wrappers'    => $wrappers,
    'attributes' => ['id'=>'password',
    'title'       => 'Enter your password',
    'required'    => '']
  ],
  // etc.
];
```

Lastly, be sure to generate the form:

```
$form = Factory::generate($config);
```

The actual display logic is extremely simple, as we simply call the form level `render()` method:

```
<?= $form->render($form, $formConfig); ?>
```

Here is the actual output:

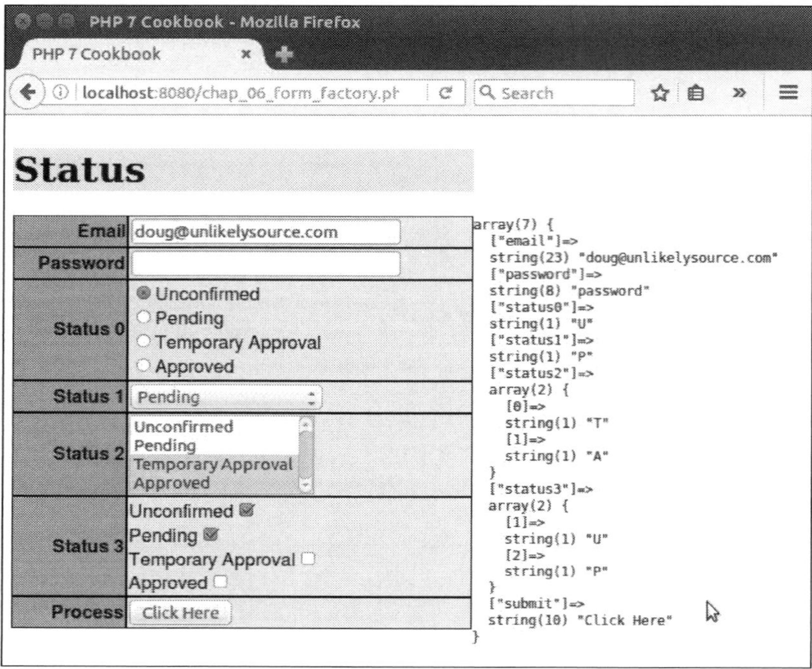

Chaining $_POST filters

Proper filtering and validation is a common problem when processing data submitted by users from an online form. It is arguably also the number one security vulnerability for a website. Furthermore, it can be quite awkward to have the filters and validators scattered all over the application. A chaining mechanism would resolve these issues neatly, and would also allow you to exert control over the order in which the filters and validators are processed.

How to do it...

1. There is a little-known PHP function, `filter_input_array()`, that, at first glance, seems well suited for this task. Looking more deeply into its functionality, however, it soon becomes apparent that this function was designed in the early days, and is not up to modern requirements for protection against attack and flexibility. Accordingly, we will instead present a much more flexible mechanism based on an array of callbacks performing filtering and validation.

The difference between *filtering* and *validation* is that filtering can potentially remove or transform values. Validation, on the other hand, tests data using criteria appropriate to the nature of the data, and returns a boolean result.

2. In order to increase flexibility, we will make our base filter and validation classes relatively light. By this, we mean *not* defining any specific filters or validation methods. Instead, we will operate entirely on the basis of a configuration array of callbacks. In order to ensure compatibility in filtering and validation results, we will also define a specific result object, `Application\Filter\Result`.
3. The primary function of the `Result` class will be to hold a `$item` value, which would be the filtered value or a boolean result of validation. Another property, `$messages`, will hold an array of messages populated during the filtering or validation operation. In the constructor, the value supplied for `$messages` is formulated as an array. You might observe that both properties are defined `public`. This is to facilitate ease of access:

```
namespace Application\Filter;

class Result
{

  public $item;  // (mixed) filtered data | (bool) result
                    of validation
  public $messages = array();  // [(string) message,
                                   (string) message ]

  public function __construct($item, $messages)
  {
    $this->item = $item;
    if (is_array($messages)) {
        $this->messages = $messages;
    } else {
        $this->messages = [$messages];
    }
  }
```

4. We also define a method that allows us to merge this `Result` instance with another. This is important as at some point we will be processing the same value through a chain of filters. In such a case, we want the newly filtered value to overwrite the existing one, but we want the messages to be merged:

```
public function mergeResults(Result $result)
{
  $this->item = $result->item;
  $this->mergeMessages($result);
```

```
    }

    public function mergeMessages(Result $result)
    {
      if (isset($result->messages) && is_array($result->messages)) {
        $this->messages = array_merge($this->messages,
                                      $result->messages);
      }
    }
```

5. Finally, to finish the methods for this class, we add a method that merges validation results. The important consideration here is that *any* value of `FALSE`, up or down the validation chain, must cause the *entire* result to be `FALSE`:

```
    public function mergeValidationResults(Result $result)
    {
      if ($this->item === TRUE) {
        $this->item = (bool) $result->item;
      }
      $this->mergeMessages($result);
      }

    }
```

6. Next, to make sure that the callbacks produce compatible results, we will define an `Application\Filter\CallbackInterface` interface. You will note that we are taking advantage of the PHP 7 ability to data type the return value to ensure that we are getting a `Result` instance in return:

```
namespace Application\Filter;
interface CallbackInterface
{
  public function __invoke ($item, $params) : Result;
}
```

7. Each callback should reference the same set of messages. Accordingly, we define a `Application\Filter\Messages` class with a series of static properties. We provide methods to set all messages, or just one message. The `$messages` property has been made `public` for easier access:

```
namespace Application\Filter;
class Messages
{
  const MESSAGE_UNKNOWN = 'Unknown';
  public static $messages;
  public static function setMessages(array $messages)
  {
```

```
    self::$messages = $messages;
  }
  public static function setMessage($key, $message)
  {
    self::$messages[$key] = $message;
  }
  public static function getMessage($key)
  {
    return self::$messages[$key] ?? self::MESSAGE_UNKNOWN;
  }
}
```

8. We are now in a position to define a `Application\Web\AbstractFilter` class that implements core functionality. As mentioned previously, this class will be relatively *lightweight* and we do not need to worry about specific filters or validators as they will be supplied through configuration. We use the `UnexpectedValueException` class, provided as part of the PHP 7 **Standard PHP Library** (**SPL**), in order to throw a descriptive exception in case one of the callbacks does not implement `CallbackInterface`:

```
namespace Application\Filter;
use UnexpectedValueException;
abstract class AbstractFilter
{
  // code described in the next several bullets
```

9. First, we define useful class constants that hold various *housekeeping* values. The last four shown here control the format of messages to be displayed, and how to describe *missing* data:

```
const BAD_CALLBACK = 'Must implement CallbackInterface';
const DEFAULT_SEPARATOR = '<br>' . PHP_EOL;
const MISSING_MESSAGE_KEY = 'item.missing';
const DEFAULT_MESSAGE_FORMAT = '%20s : %60s';
const DEFAULT_MISSING_MESSAGE = 'Item Missing';
```

10. Next, we define core properties. `$separator` is used in conjunction with filtering and validation messages. `$callbacks` represents the array of callbacks that perform filtering and validation. `$assignments` map data fields to filters and/or validators. `$missingMessage` is represented as a property so that it can be overwritten (that is, for multi-language websites). Finally, `$results` is an array of `Application\Filter\Result` objects and is populated by the filtering or validation operation:

```
protected $separator;    // used for message display
protected $callbacks;
protected $assignments;
protected $missingMessage;
protected $results = array();
```

11. At this point, we can build the `__construct()` method. Its main function is to set the array of callbacks and assignments. It also either sets values or accepts defaults for the separator (used in message display), and the *missing* message:

```
public function __construct(array $callbacks, array $assignments,
                            $separator = NULL, $message = NULL)
{
  $this->setCallbacks($callbacks);
  $this->setAssignments($assignments);
  $this->setSeparator($separator ?? self::DEFAULT_SEPARATOR);
  $this->setMissingMessage($message
                           ?? self::DEFAULT_MISSING_MESSAGE);
}
```

12. Next, we define a series of methods that allow us to set or remove callbacks. Notice that we allow the getting and setting of a single callback. This is useful if you have a generic set of callbacks, and need to modify just one. You will also note that `setOneCall()` checks to see if the callback implements `CallbackInterface`. If it does not, an `UnexpectedValueException` is thrown:

```
public function getCallbacks()
{
  return $this->callbacks;
}

public function getOneCallback($key)
{
  return $this->callbacks[$key] ?? NULL;
}

public function setCallbacks(array $callbacks)
{
  foreach ($callbacks as $key => $item) {
    $this->setOneCallback($key, $item);
  }
}

public function setOneCallback($key, $item)
{
  if ($item instanceof CallbackInterface) {
      $this->callbacks[$key] = $item;
  } else {
      throw new UnexpectedValueException(self::BAD_CALLBACK);
  }
```

```
}

public function removeOneCallback($key)
{
  if (isset($this->callbacks[$key]))
  unset($this->callbacks[$key]);
}
```

13. Methods for results processing are quite simple. For convenience, we added `getItemsAsArray()`, otherwise `getResults()` will return an array of `Result` objects:

```
public function getResults()
{
  return $this->results;
}

public function getItemsAsArray()
{
  $return = array();
  if ($this->results) {
    foreach ($this->results as $key => $item)
    $return[$key] = $item->item;
  }
  return $return;
}
```

14. Retrieving messages is just a matter of looping through the array of `$this->results` and extracting the `$messages` property. For convenience, we also added `getMessageString()` with some formatting options. To easily produce an array of messages, we use the PHP 7 `yield from` syntax. This has the effect of turning `getMessages()` into a **delegating generator**. The array of messages becomes a **sub-generator**:

```
public function getMessages()
{
  if ($this->results) {
      foreach ($this->results as $key => $item)
      if ($item->messages) yield from $item->messages;
  } else {
      return array();
  }
}

public function getMessageString($width = 80, $format = NULL)
{
```

```
    if (!$format)
    $format = self::DEFAULT_MESSAGE_FORMAT . $this->separator;
    $output = '';
    if ($this->results) {
      foreach ($this->results as $key => $value) {
        if ($value->messages) {
          foreach ($value->messages as $message) {
            $output .= sprintf(
              $format, $key, trim($message));
          }
        }
      }
    }
    return $output;
  }
```

15. Lastly, we define a mixed group of useful getters and setters:

```
    public function setMissingMessage($message)
    {
      $this->missingMessage = $message;
    }
    public function setSeparator($separator)
    {
      $this->separator = $separator;
    }
    public function getSeparator()
    {
      return $this->separator;
    }
    public function getAssignments()
    {
      return $this->assignments;
    }
    public function setAssignments(array $assignments)
    {
      $this->assignments = $assignments;
    }
    // closing bracket for class AbstractFilter
  }
```

16. Filtering and validation, although often performed together, are just as often performed separately. Accordingly, we define discrete classes for each. We'll start with `Application\Filter\Filter`. We make this class extend `AbstractFilter` in order to provide the core functionality described previously:

```
namespace Application\Filter;
class Filter extends AbstractFilter
{
  // code
}
```

17. Within this class we define a core `process()` method that scans an array of data and applies filters as per the array of assignments. If there are no assigned filters for this data set, we simply return `NULL`:

```
public function process(array $data)
{
  if (!(isset($this->assignments)
      && count($this->assignments))) {
        return NULL;
  }
```

18. Otherwise, we initialize `$this->results` to an array of `Result` objects where the `$item` property is the original value from `$data`, and the `$messages` property is an empty array:

```
foreach ($data as $key => $value) {
  $this->results[$key] = new Result($value, array());
}
```

19. We then make a copy of `$this->assignments` and check to see if there are any *global* filters (identified by the '*' key. If so, we run `processGlobal()` and then unset the '*' key:

```
$toDo = $this->assignments;
if (isset($toDo['*'])) {
  $this->processGlobalAssignment($toDo['*'], $data);
  unset($toDo['*']);
}
```

20. Finally, we loop through any remaining assignments, calling `processAssignment()`:

```
foreach ($toDo as $key => $assignment) {
  $this->processAssignment($assignment, $key);
}
```

21. As you will recall, each *assignment* is keyed to the data field, and represents an array of callbacks for that field. Thus, in `processGlobalAssignment()` we need to loop through the array of callbacks. In this case, however, because these assignments are *global*, we also need to loop through the *entire* data set, and apply each global filter in turn:

```
protected function processGlobalAssignment($assignment, $data)
{
  foreach ($assignment as $callback) {
```

```
        if ($callback === NULL) continue;
        foreach ($data as $k => $value) {
          $result = $this->callbacks[$callback['key']]
                                   ($this->results[$k]->item,
          $callback['params']);
          $this->results[$k]->mergeResults($result);
        }
      }
    }
```

The tricky bit is this line of code:

```
$result = $this->callbacks[$callback['key']]($this
->results[$k]->item, $callback['params']);
```

Remember, each callback is actually an anonymous class that defines the PHP magic `__invoke()` method. The arguments supplied are the actual data item to be filtered, and an array of parameters. By running `$this->callbacks[$callback['key']]()` we are in fact magically calling `__invoke()`.

22. When we define `processAssignment()`, in a manner akin to `processGlobalAssignment()`, we need to execute each remaining callback assigned to each data key:

```
      protected function processAssignment($assignment, $key)
      {
        foreach ($assignment as $callback) {
          if ($callback === NULL) continue;
          $result = $this->callbacks[$callback['key']]
                                   ($this->results[$key]->item,
                                    $callback['params']);
          $this->results[$key]->mergeResults($result);
        }
      }
    }  // closing brace for Application\Filter\Filter
```

It is important that any filtering operation that alters the original user-supplied data should display a message indicating that a change was made. This can become part of an audit trail to safeguard you against potential legal liability when a change is made without user knowledge or consent.

How it works...

Create an `Application\Filter` folder. In this folder, create the following class files, using code from the preceding steps:

Application\Filter* class file	Code described in these steps
`Result.php`	3 - 5
`CallbackInterface.php`	6
`Messages.php`	7
`AbstractFilter.php`	8 – 15
`Filter.php`	16 - 22

Next, take the code discussed in step 5, and use it to configure an array of messages in a `chap_06_post_data_config_messages.php` file. Each callback references the `Messages::$messages` property. Here is a sample configuration:

```
<?php
use Application\Filter\Messages;
Messages::setMessages(
  [
    'length_too_short' => 'Length must be at least %d',
    'length_too_long'  => 'Length must be no more than %d',
    'required'         => 'Please be sure to enter a value',
    'alnum'            => 'Only letters and numbers allowed',
    'float'            => 'Only numbers or decimal point',
    'email'            => 'Invalid email address',
    'in_array'         => 'Not found in the list',
    'trim'             => 'Item was trimmed',
    'strip_tags'       => 'Tags were removed from this item',
    'filter_float'     => 'Converted to a decimal number',
    'phone'            => 'Phone number is [+n] nnn-nnn-nnnn',
    'test'             => 'TEST',
    'filter_length'    => 'Reduced to specified length',
  ]
);
```

Next, create a `chap_06_post_data_config_callbacks.php` callback configuration file that contains configuration for filtering callbacks, as described in step 4. Each callback should follow this generic template:

```
'callback_key' => new class () implements CallbackInterface
{
  public function __invoke($item, $params) : Result
```

```
    {
      $changed  = array();
      $filtered = /* perform filtering operation on $item */
      if ($filtered !== $item)
          $changed = Messages::$messages['callback_key'];
      return new Result($filtered, $changed);
    }
  }
```

The callbacks themselves must implement the interface and return a `Result` instance. We can take advantage of the PHP 7 **anonymous class** capability by having our callbacks return an anonymous class that implements `CallbackInterface`. Here is how an array of filtering callbacks might look:

```
use Application\Filter\ { Result, Messages, CallbackInterface };
$config = [ 'filters' => [
  'trim' => new class () implements CallbackInterface
  {
    public function __invoke($item, $params) : Result
    {
      $changed  = array();
      $filtered = trim($item);
      if ($filtered !== $item)
      $changed = Messages::$messages['trim'];
      return new Result($filtered, $changed);
    }
  },
  'strip_tags' => new class ()
  implements CallbackInterface
  {
    public function __invoke($item, $params) : Result
    {
      $changed  = array();
      $filtered = strip_tags($item);
      if ($filtered !== $item)
      $changed = Messages::$messages['strip_tags'];
      return new Result($filtered, $changed);
    }
  },
  // etc.
]
];
```

For test purposes, we will use the prospects table as a target. Instead of providing data from `$_POST`, we will construct an array of *good* and *bad* data:

Field name	Type	Allow nulls?
id	int(11)	No
first_name	varchar(128)	No
last_name	varchar(128)	No
address	varchar(256)	Yes
city	varchar(64)	Yes
state_province	varchar(32)	Yes
postal_code	char(16)	No
phone	varchar(16)	No
country	char(2)	No
email	varchar(250)	No
status	char(8)	Yes
budget	decimal(10,2)	Yes
last_updated	datetime	Yes

You can now create a `chap_06_post_data_filtering.php` script that sets up autoloading, includes the messages and callbacks configuration files:

```
<?php
require __DIR__ . '/../Application/Autoload/Loader.php';
Application\Autoload\Loader::init(__DIR__ . '/..');
include __DIR__ . '/chap_06_post_data_config_messages.php';
include __DIR__ . '/chap_06_post_data_config_callbacks.php';
```

You then need to define *assignments* that represent a mapping between the data fields and filter callbacks. Use the `*` key to define a *global* filter that applies to all data:

```
$assignments = [
  '*'    => [ ['key' => 'trim', 'params' => []],
            ['key' => 'strip_tags', 'params' => []] ],
  'first_name'  => [ ['key' => 'length',
   'params' => ['length' => 128]] ],
  'last_name'  => [ ['key' => 'length',
   'params' => ['length' => 128]] ],
  'city'          => [ ['key' => 'length',
   'params' => ['length' => 64]] ],
  'budget'     => [ ['key' => 'filter_float', 'params' => []] ],
];
```

Next, define *good* and *bad* test data:

```
$goodData = [
  'first_name'      => 'Your Full',
  'last_name'       => 'Name',
  'address'         => '123 Main Street',
  'city'            => 'San Francisco',
  'state_province'  => 'California',
  'postal_code'     => '94101',
  'phone'           => '+1 415-555-1212',
  'country'         => 'US',
  'email'           => 'your@email.address.com',
  'budget'          => '123.45',
];
$badData = [
  'first_name'      => 'This+Name<script>bad tag</script>Valid!',
  'last_name'       => 'ThisLastNameIsWayTooLong
                       Abcdefghijklmnopqrstuvwxyz0123456789
                       Abcdefghijklmnopqrstuvwxyz0123456789
                       Abcdefghijklmnopqrstuvwxyz0123456789
                       Abcdefghijklmnopqrstuvwxyz0123456789',
  //'address'       => '',    // missing
  'city'            => '
ThisCityNameIsTooLong0123456789012345678901234
56789012345678901234567890123456789  ',
  //'state_province'=> '',    // missing
  'postal_code'     => '!"£$%^Non Alpha Chars',
  'phone'           => ' 12345 ',
  'country'         => 'XX',
  'email'           => 'this.is@not@an.email',
  'budget'          => 'XXX',
];
```

Finally, you can create an `Application\Filter\Filter` instance, and test the data:

```
$filter = new Application\Filter\Filter(
$config['filters'], $assignments);
$filter->setSeparator(PHP_EOL);
  $filter->process($goodData);
echo $filter->getMessageString();
  var_dump($filter->getItemsAsArray());

$filter->process($badData);
echo $filter->getMessageString();
var_dump($filter->getItemsAsArray());
```

Processing *good* data produces no messages other than one indicating that the value for the *float* field was converted from string to `float`. The *bad* data, on the other hand, produces the following output:

```
Terminal

Bad Data:
    first_name : Tags were removed from this item
     last_name : Item was reduced to specified length
          city : Item was trimmed
          city : Item was reduced to specified length
         phone : Item was trimmed
        budget : Item was converted to a decimal number

array(10) {
  ["first_name"]=>
  string(22) "This+Namebad tagValid!"
  ["last_name"]=>
  string(128) "ThisLastNameIsWayTooLongAbcdefghijklmnopqrstuvwxyz0123456789Abcde
fghijklmnopqrstuvwxyz0123456789Abcdefghijklmnopqrstuvwxyz012345"
  ["address"]=>
  string(15) "123 Main Street"
  ["city"]=>
  string(64) "ThisCityNameIsTooLong0123456789012345678901234567890123456789012"
  ["state_province"]=>
  string(10) "California"
  ["postal_code"]=>
  string(22) "!"£$%^Non Alpha Chars"
  ["phone"]=>
```

You will also notice that tags were removed from `first_name`, and that both `last_name` and `city` were truncated.

There's more...

The `filter_input_array()` function takes two arguments: the input source (in the form of a pre-defined constant used to indicate one of the `$_*` PHP super-globals, that is, `$_POST`), and an array of matching field definitions as keys and filters or validators as values. This function performs not only filtering operations, but validation as well. The flags labeled *sanitize* are actually filters.

See also

Documentation and examples of `filter_input_array()` can be found at `http://php.net/manual/en/function.filter-input-array.php`. You might also have a look at the different types of *filters* that are available on `http://php.net/manual/en/filter.filters.php`.

Chaining $_POST validators

The *heavy lifting* for this recipe has already been accomplished in the preceding recipe. Core functionality is defined by `Application\Filter\AbstractFilter`. The actual validation is performed by an array of validating callbacks.

How to do it...

1. Look over the preceding recipe, *Chaining $_POST filters*. We will be using all of the classes and configuration files in this recipe, except where noted here.
2. To begin, we define a configuration array of validation callbacks. As with the preceding recipe, each callback should implement `Application\Filter\CallbackInterface`, and should return an instance of `Application\Filter\Result`. Validators would take this generic form:

```
use Application\Filter\ { Result, Messages, CallbackInterface };
$config = [
  // validator callbacks
  'validators' => [
    'key' => new class () implements CallbackInterface
    {
      public function __invoke($item, $params) : Result
      {
        // validation logic goes here
        return new Result($valid, $error);
      }
    },
    // etc.
```

3. Next, we define a `Application\Filter\Validator` class, which loops through the array of assignments, testing each data item against its assigned validator callbacks. We make this class extend `AbstractFilter` in order to provide the core functionality described previously:

```
namespace Application\Filter;
class Validator extends AbstractFilter
{
  // code
}
```

4. Within this class, we define a core `process()` method that scans an array of data and applies validators as per the array of assignments. If there are no assigned validators for this data set, we simply return the current status of `$valid` (which is `TRUE`):

   ```
   public function process(array $data)
   {
     $valid = TRUE;
     if (!(isset($this->assignments)
         && count($this->assignments))) {
           return $valid;
     }
   ```

5. Otherwise, we initialize `$this->results` to an array of `Result` objects where the `$item` property is set to `TRUE`, and the `$messages` property is an empty array:

   ```
   foreach ($data as $key => $value) {
     $this->results[$key] = new Result(TRUE, array());
   }
   ```

6. We then make a copy of `$this->assignments` and check to see if there are any *global* filters (identified by the '*' key). If so, we run `processGlobal()` and then unset the '*' key:

   ```
   $toDo = $this->assignments;
   if (isset($toDo['*'])) {
     $this->processGlobalAssignment($toDo['*'], $data);
     unset($toDo['*']);
   }
   ```

7. Finally, we loop through any remaining assignments, calling `processAssignment()`. This is an ideal place to check to see if any fields present in the assignments array is missing from the data. Note that we set `$valid` to `FALSE` if any validation callback returns `FALSE`:

   ```
   foreach ($toDo as $key => $assignment) {
     if (!isset($data[$key])) {
         $this->results[$key] =
         new Result(FALSE, $this->missingMessage);
     } else {
         $this->processAssignment(
           $assignment, $key, $data[$key]);
     }
     if (!$this->results[$key]->item) $valid = FALSE;
     }
     return $valid;
   }
   ```

8. As you will recall, each *assignment* is keyed to the data field, and represents an array of callbacks for that field. Thus, in `processGlobalAssignment()`, we need to loop through the array of callbacks. In this case, however, because these assignments are *global*, we also need to loop through the *entire* data set, and apply each global filter in turn.

9. In contrast to the equivalent `Application\Filter\Fiter::processGlobalAssignment()` method, we need to call `mergeValidationResults()`. The reason for this is that if the value of `$result->item` is already `FALSE`, we need to ensure that it does not subsequently get overwritten by a value of `TRUE`. Any validator in the chain that returns `FALSE` must overwrite any other validation result:

    ```
    protected function processGlobalAssignment($assignment, $data)
    {
      foreach ($assignment as $callback) {
        if ($callback === NULL) continue;
        foreach ($data as $k => $value) {
          $result = $this->callbacks[$callback['key']]
          ($value, $callback['params']);
          $this->results[$k]->mergeValidationResults($result);
        }
      }
    }
    ```

10. When we define `processAssignment()`, in a manner akin to `processGlobalAssignment()`, we need to execute each remaining callback assigned to each data key, again calling `mergeValidationResults()`:

    ```
    protected function processAssignment($assignment, $key, $value)
    {
      foreach ($assignment as $callback) {
        if ($callback === NULL) continue;
            $result = $this->callbacks[$callback['key']]
           ($value, $callback['params']);
            $this->results[$key]->mergeValidationResults($result);
        }
      }
    ```

How it works...

As with the preceding recipe, be sure to define the following classes:

- `Application\Filter\Result`
- `Application\Filter\CallbackInterface`

- `Application\Filter\Messages`
- `Application\Filter\AbstractFilter`

You can use the `chap_06_post_data_config_messages.php` file, also described in the previous recipe.

Next, create a `Validator.php` file in the `Application\Filter` folder. Place the code described in step 3 to 10.

Next, create a `chap_06_post_data_config_callbacks.php` callback configuration file that contains configurations for validation callbacks, as described in step 2. Each callback should follow this generic template:

```
'validation_key' => new class () implements CallbackInterface
{
  public function __invoke($item, $params) : Result
  {
    $error = array();
    $valid = /* perform validation operation on $item */
    if (!$valid)
    $error[] = Messages::$messages['validation_key'];
    return new Result($valid, $error);
  }
}
```

Now you can create a `chap_06_post_data_validation.php` calling script that initializes autoloading and includes the configuration scripts:

```
<?php
require __DIR__ . '/../Application/Autoload/Loader.php';
Application\Autoload\Loader::init(__DIR__ . '/..');
include __DIR__ . '/chap_06_post_data_config_messages.php';
include __DIR__ . '/chap_06_post_data_config_callbacks.php';
```

Next, define an array of assignments, mapping data fields to validator callback keys:

```
$assignments = [
  'first_name'       => [ ['key' => 'length',
  'params'    => ['min' => 1, 'max' => 128]],
                 ['key' => 'alnum',
  'params'    => ['allowWhiteSpace' => TRUE]],
                 ['key'    => 'required','params' => []] ],
  'last_name'=> [ ['key' => 'length',
  'params'    => ['min'    => 1, 'max' => 128]],
                 ['key'    => 'alnum',
  'params'    => ['allowWhiteSpace' => TRUE]],
                 ['key'    => 'required','params' => []] ],
```

```
    'address'          => [ ['key' => 'length',
    'params'           => ['max' => 256]] ],
    'city'             => [ ['key' => 'length',
    'params'           => ['min' => 1, 'max' => 64]] ],
    'state_province'=> [ ['key' => 'length',
    'params'           => ['min' => 1, 'max' => 32]] ],
    'postal_code'      => [ ['key' => 'length',
    'params'           => ['min' => 1, 'max' => 16] ],
                          ['key' => 'alnum',
    'params'           => ['allowWhiteSpace' => TRUE]],
                          ['key' => 'required','params' => []] ],
    'phone'            => [ ['key' => 'phone', 'params' => []] ],
    'country'          => [ ['key' => 'in_array',
    'params'           => $countries ],
                          ['key' => 'required','params' => []] ],
    'email'            => [ ['key' => 'email', 'params' => [] ],
                          ['key' => 'length',
    'params'           => ['max' => 250] ],
                          ['key' => 'required','params' => [] ] ],
    'budget'           => [ ['key' => 'float', 'params' => []] ]
];
```

For test data, use the same *good* and *bad* data defined in the `chap_06_post_data_filtering.php` file described in the previous recipe. After that, you are in a position to create an `Application\Filter\Validator` instance, and test the data:

```
$validator = new Application\Filter\Validator($config['validators'],
$assignments);
$validator->setSeparator(PHP_EOL);
$validator->process($badData);
echo $validator->getMessageString(40, '%14s : %-26s' . PHP_EOL);
var_dump($validator->getItemsAsArray());
$validator->process($goodData);
echo $validator->getMessageString(40, '%14s : %-26s' . PHP_EOL);
var_dump($validator->getItemsAsArray());
```

As expected, the *good* data does not produce any validation errors. The *bad* data, on the other hand, generates the following output:

```
Bad Data:
     first_name : Item must contain only letters and numbers
      last_name : Length must be no more than 128
           city : Length must be no more than 64
    postal_code : Length must be no more than 16
    postal_code : Item must contain only letters and numbers
          phone : Phone number must be in a format [+n] nnn-nnn-nnnn
        country : Item was not found in the list of valid values
          email : Invalid email address
        address : Item Missing
state_province : Item Missing

array(10) {
  ["first_name"]=>
  bool(false)
  ["last_name"]=>
  bool(false)
  ["city"]=>
  bool(false)
  ["postal_code"]=>
  bool(false)
  ["phone"]=>
  bool(false)
  ["country"]=>
  bool(false)
  ["email"]=>
  bool(false)
  ["budget"]=>
  bool(true)
  ["address"]=>
  bool(false)
  ["state_province"]=>
  bool(false)
}
```

Notice that the *missing* fields, `address` and `state_province` validate `FALSE`, and return the missing item message.

Tying validation to a form

When a form is first rendered, there is little value in having a form class (such as `Application\Form\Factory`, described in the previous recipe) tied to a class that can perform filtering or validation (such as the `Application\Filter\*` described in the previous recipe). Once the form data has been submitted, however, interest grows. If the form data fails validation, the values can be filtered, and then re-displayed. Validation error messages can be tied to form elements, and rendered next to form fields.

How to do it...

1. First of all, be sure to implement the classes defined in the *Implementing a Form Factory*, *Chaining $_POST Filters*, and *Chaining $_POST Validators* recipes.
2. We will now turn our attention to the `Application\Form\Factory` class, and add properties and setters that allow us to attach instances of `Application\Filter\Filter` and `Application\Filter\Validator`. We also need define `$data`, which will be used to retain the filtered and/or validated data:

```
const DATA_NOT_FOUND = 'Data not found. Run setData()';
const FILTER_NOT_FOUND = 'Filter not found. Run setFilter()';
```

```
const VALIDATOR_NOT_FOUND = 'Validator not found.
  Run setValidator()';

protected $filter;
protected $validator;
protected $data;

public function setFilter(Filter $filter)
{
  $this->filter = $filter;
}

public function setValidator(Validator $validator)
{
  $this->validator = $validator;
}

public function setData($data)
{
  $this->data = $data;
}
```

3. Next, we define a `validate()` method that calls the `process()` method of the embedded `Application\Filter\Validator` instance. We check to see if `$data` and `$validator` exist. If not, the appropriate exceptions are thrown with instructions on which method needs to be run first:

```
public function validate()
{
  if (!$this->data)
  throw new RuntimeException(self::DATA_NOT_FOUND);

  if (!$this->validator)
  throw new RuntimeException(self::VALIDATOR_NOT_FOUND);
```

4. After calling the `process()` method, we associate validation result messages with form element messages. Note that the `process()` method returns a boolean value that represents the overall validation status of the data set. When the form is re-displayed following failed validation, error messages will appear next to each element:

```
$valid = $this->validator->process($this->data);

foreach ($this->elements as $element) {
  if (isset($this->validator->getResults()
      [$element->getName()])) {
        $element->setErrors($this->validator->getResults()
```

```
        [$element->getName()]->messages);
      }
    }
    return $valid;
  }
```

5. In a similar manner, we define a `filter()` method that calls the `process()` method of the embedded `Application\Filter\Filter` instance. As with the `validate()` method described in step 3, we need to check for the existence of `$data` and `$filter`. If either is missing, we throw a `RuntimeException` with the appropriate message:

```
public function filter()
{
  if (!$this->data)
  throw new RuntimeException(self::DATA_NOT_FOUND);

  if (!$this->filter)
  throw new RuntimeException(self::FILTER_NOT_FOUND);
```

6. We then run the `process()` method, which produces an array of `Result` objects where the `$item` property represents the end result of the filter chain. We then loop through the results, and, if the corresponding `$element` key matches, set the `value` attribute to the filtered value. We also add any messages resulting from the filtering process. When the form is then re-displayed, all value attributes will display filtered results:

```
$this->filter->process($this->data);
foreach ($this->filter->getResults() as $key => $result) {
  if (isset($this->elements[$key])) {
    $this->elements[$key]
    ->setSingleAttribute('value', $result->item);
    if (isset($result->messages)
        && count($result->messages)) {
      foreach ($result->messages as $message) {
        $this->elements[$key]->addSingleError($message);
      }
    }
  }
}
}
```

How it works...

You can start by making the changes to `Application\Form\Factory` as described above. For a test target you can use the prospects database table shown in the *How it works...* section of the *Chaining $_POST filters* recipe. The various column settings should give you an idea of which form elements, filters, and validators to define.

As an example, you can define a `chap_06_tying_filters_to_form_definitions.php` file, which will contain definitions for form wrappers, elements, and filter assignments. Here are some examples:

```
<?php
use Application\Form\Generic;

define('VALIDATE_SUCCESS', 'SUCCESS: form submitted ok!');
define('VALIDATE_FAILURE', 'ERROR: validation errors detected');

$wrappers = [
  Generic::INPUT  => ['type' => 'td', 'class' => 'content'],
  Generic::LABEL  => ['type' => 'th', 'class' => 'label'],
  Generic::ERRORS => ['type' => 'td', 'class' => 'error']
];

$elements = [
  'first_name' => [
     'class'      => 'Application\Form\Generic',
     'type'       => Generic::TYPE_TEXT,
     'label'      => 'First Name',
     'wrappers'   => $wrappers,
     'attributes'=> ['maxLength'=>128,'required'=>'']
  ],
  'last_name'   => [
    'class'      => 'Application\Form\Generic',
    'type'       => Generic::TYPE_TEXT,
    'label'      => 'Last Name',
    'wrappers'   => $wrappers,
    'attributes'=> ['maxLength'=>128,'required'=>'']
  ],
    // etc.
];

// overall form config
$formConfig = [
  'name'        => 'prospectsForm',
  'attributes' => [
```

```
'method'=>'post',
'action'=>'chap_06_tying_filters_to_form.php'
],
  'row_wrapper'  => ['type' => 'tr', 'class' => 'row'],
  'form_wrapper' => [
    'type'=>'table',
    'class'=>'table',
    'id'=>'prospectsTable',
    'class'=>'display','cellspacing'=>'0'
  ],
  'form_tag_inside_wrapper' => FALSE,
];

$assignments = [
  'first_name'     => [ ['key' => 'length',
  'params'         => ['min' => 1, 'max' => 128]],
                      ['key' => 'alnum',
  'params'         => ['allowWhiteSpace' => TRUE]],
                      ['key' => 'required','params' => []] ],
  'last_name'      => [ ['key' => 'length',
  'params'         => ['min' => 1, 'max' => 128]],
                      ['key' => 'alnum',
  'params'         => ['allowWhiteSpace' => TRUE]],
                      ['key' => 'required','params' => []] ],
  'address'        => [ ['key' => 'length',
  'params'         => ['max' => 256]] ],
  'city'           => [ ['key' => 'length',
  'params'         => ['min' => 1, 'max' => 64]] ],
  'state_province'=> [ ['key' => 'length',
  'params'         => ['min' => 1, 'max' => 32]] ],
  'postal_code'    => [ ['key' => 'length',
  'params'         => ['min' => 1, 'max' => 16] ],
                      ['key' => 'alnum',
  'params'         => ['allowWhiteSpace' => TRUE]],
                      ['key' => 'required','params' => []] ],
  'phone'          => [ ['key' => 'phone',   'params' => []] ],
  'country'        => [ ['key' => 'in_array',
  'params'         => $countries ],
                      ['key' => 'required','params' => []] ],
  'email'          => [ ['key' => 'email',   'params' => [] ],
                      ['key' => 'length',
  'params'         => ['max' => 250] ],
                      ['key' => 'required','params' => [] ] ],
  'budget'         => [ ['key' => 'float',   'params' => []] ]
];
```

You can use the already existing `chap_06_post_data_config_callbacks.php` and `chap_06_post_data_config_messages.php` files described in the previous recipes. Finally, define a `chap_06_tying_filters_to_form.php` file that sets up autoloading and includes these three configuration files:

```
<?php
require __DIR__ . '/../Application/Autoload/Loader.php';
Application\Autoload\Loader::init(__DIR__ . '/..');
include __DIR__ . '/chap_06_post_data_config_messages.php';
include __DIR__ . '/chap_06_post_data_config_callbacks.php';
include __DIR__ . '/chap_06_tying_filters_to_form_definitions.php';
```

Next, you can create instances of the form factory, filter, and validator classes:

```
use Application\Form\Factory;
use Application\Filter\ { Validator, Filter };
$form = Factory::generate($elements);
$form->setFilter(new Filter($callbacks['filters'],
$assignments['filters']));
$form->setValidator(new Validator($callbacks['validators'],
$assignments['validators']));
```

You can then check to see if there is any `$_POST` data. If so, perform validation and filtering:

```
$message = '';
if (isset($_POST['submit'])) {
  $form->setData($_POST);
  if ($form->validate()) {
    $message = VALIDATE_SUCCESS;
  } else {
    $message = VALIDATE_FAILURE;
  }
  $form->filter();
}
?>
```

The view logic is extremely simple: just render the form. Any validation messages and values for the various elements will be assigned as part of validation and filtering:

```
<?= $form->render($form, $formConfig); ?>
```

Here is an example using bad form data:

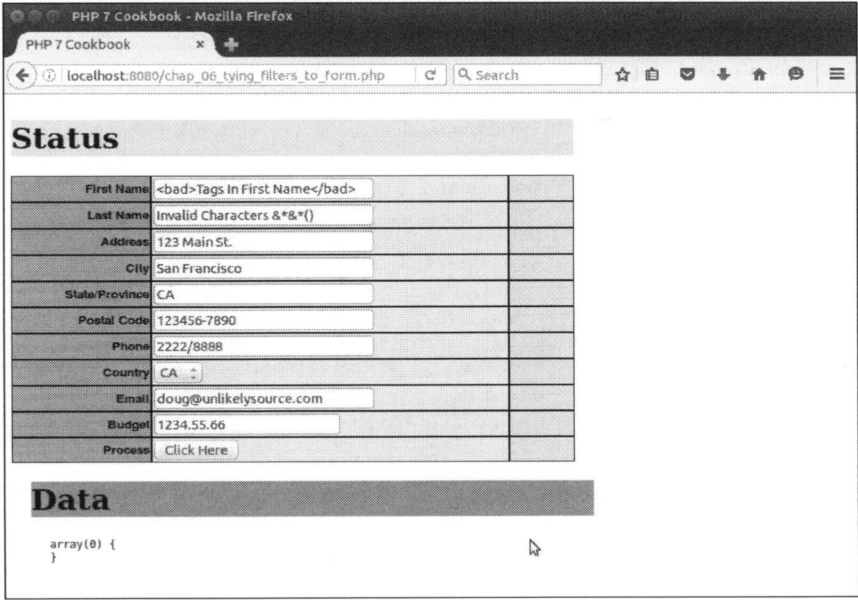

Notice the filtering and validation messages. Also notice the bad tags:

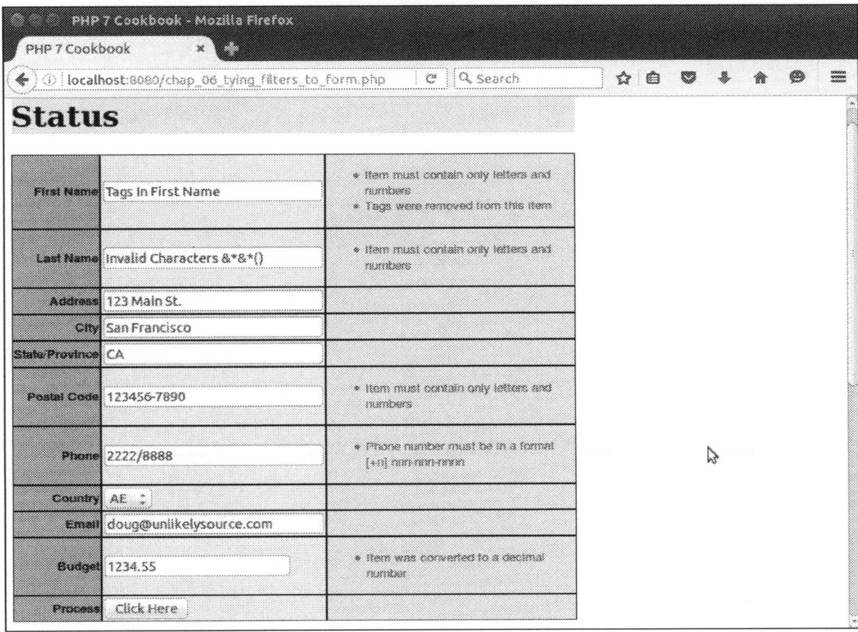

7
Accessing Web Services

In this chapter, we will cover the following topics:

- Converting between PHP and XML
- Creating a simple REST client
- Creating a simple REST server
- Creating a simple SOAP client
- Creating a simple SOAP server

Introduction

Making background queries to external web services is becoming an ever-increasing part of any PHP web practice. The ability to provide appropriate, timely, and plentiful data means more business for your customers and the websites you develop. We start with a couple of recipes aimed at data conversion between **eXtensible Markup Language** (**XML**) and native PHP. Next, we show you how to implement a simple **Representational State Transfer** (**REST**) client and server. After that, we turn our attention to **SOAP** clients and servers.

Converting between PHP and XML

When considering a conversion between PHP native data types and XML, we would normally consider an array as the primary target. With this in mind, the process of converting from a PHP array to XML differs radically from the approach needed to do the reverse.

Objects could also be considered for conversion; however, it is difficult to render object methods in XML. Properties can be represented, however, by using the `get_object_vars()` function, which reads object properties into an array.

How to do it...

1. First, we define an `Application\Parse\ConvertXml` class. This class will hold the methods that will convert from XML to a PHP array, and vice versa. We will need both the `SimpleXMLElement` and `SimpleXMLIterator` classes from the SPL:

```
namespace Application\Parse;
use SimpleXMLIterator;
use SimpleXMLElement;
class ConvertXml
{
}
```

2. Next, we define a `xmlToArray()` method that will accept a `SimpleXMLIterator` instance as an argument. It will be called recursively and will produce a PHP array from an XML document. We take advantage of the `SimpleXMLIterator` ability to advance through the XML document, using the `key()`, `current()`, `next()`, and `rewind()` methods to navigate:

```
public function xmlToArray(SimpleXMLIterator $xml) : array
{
  $a = array();
  for( $xml->rewind(); $xml->valid(); $xml->next() ) {
    if(!array_key_exists($xml->key(), $a)) {
      $a[$xml->key()] = array();
    }
    if($xml->hasChildren()){
      $a[$xml->key()][] = $this->xmlToArray($xml->current());
    }
    else{
      $a[$xml->key()] = (array) $xml->current()->attributes();
      $a[$xml->key()]['value'] = strval($xml->current());
    }
  }
  return $a;
}
```

3. For the reverse process, also called recursively, we define two methods. The first method, `arrayToXml()`, sets up an initial `SimpleXMLElement` instance, and then calls the second method, `phpToXml()`:

```
public function arrayToXml(array $a)
{
  $xml = new SimpleXMLElement(
  '<?xml version="1.0" standalone="yes"?><root></root>');
  $this->phpToXml($a, $xml);
  return $xml->asXML();
}
```

4. Note that in the second method, we use `get_object_vars()` in case one of the array elements is an object. You'll also note that numbers alone are not allowed as XML tags, which means adding some text in front of the number:

```
protected function phpToXml($value, &$xml)
{
  $node = $value;
  if (is_object($node)) {
    $node = get_object_vars($node);
  }
  if (is_array($node)) {
    foreach ($node as $k => $v) {
      if (is_numeric($k)) {
        $k = 'number' . $k;
      }
      if (is_array($v)) {
          $newNode = $xml->addChild($k);
          $this->phpToXml($v, $newNode);
      } elseif (is_object($v)) {
          $newNode = $xml->addChild($k);
          $this->phpToXml($v, $newNode);
      } else {
          $xml->addChild($k, $v);
      }
    }
  } else  {
      $xml->addChild(self::UNKNOWN_KEY, $node);
  }
}
```

How it works...

As a sample XML document, you can use the **Web Services Definition Language** (**WSDL**) for the United States National Weather Service. This is an XML document that describes a SOAP service, and can be found at `http://graphical.weather.gov/xml/SOAP_server/ndfdXMLserver.php?wsdl`.

We will use the `SimpleXMLIterator` class to provide an iteration mechanism. You can then configure autoloading, and get an instance of `Application\Parse\ConvertXml`, using `xmlToArray()` to convert the WSDL to a PHP array:

```
require __DIR__ . '/../Application/Autoload/Loader.php';
Application\Autoload\Loader::init(__DIR__ . '/..');
use Application\Parse\ConvertXml;
$wsdl = 'http://graphical.weather.gov/xml/'
. 'SOAP_server/ndfdXMLserver.php?wsdl';
$xml = new SimpleXMLIterator($wsdl, 0, TRUE);
$convert = new ConvertXml();
var_dump($convert->xmlToArray($xml));
```

The resulting array is shown here:

```
ed@ed: ~/Desktop/Repos/php7_recipes/source/chapter07
array(5) {
  ["types"]=>
  array(1) {
    [0]=>
    array(0) {
    }
  }
  ["message"]=>
  array(24) {
    [0]=>
    array(1) {
      ["part"]=>
      array(2) {
        ["@attributes"]=>
        array(2) {
          ["name"]=>
          string(17) "weatherParameters"
          ["type"]=>
          string(25) "tns:weatherParametersType"
        }
        ["value"]=>
        string(0) ""
      }
    }
    [1]=>
    array(1) {
:
```

To do the reverse, use the `arrayToXml()` method described in this recipe. As a source document, you can use a `source/data/mongo.db.global.php` file that contains an outline for a training video on MongoDB available through O'Reilly Media (disclaimer: by this author!). Using the same autoloader configuration and instance of `Application\Parse\ConvertXml`, here is the sample code you could use:

```
$convert = new ConvertXml();
header('Content-Type: text/xml');
echo $convert->arrayToXml(include CONFIG_FILE);
```

Here is the output in a browser:

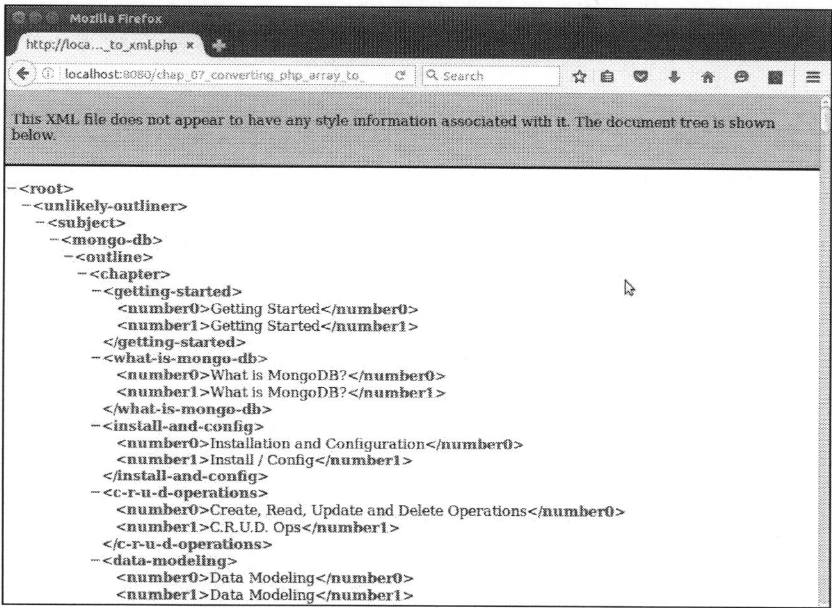

Creating a simple REST client

REST clients use **HyperText Transfer Protocol** (**HTTP**) to generate requests to external web services. By changing the HTTP method, we can cause the external service to perform different operations. Although there are quite a few methods (or verbs) available, we will only focus on `GET` and `POST`. In this recipe, we will use the **Adapter** software design pattern to present two different ways of implementing a REST client.

How to do it...

1. Before we can define REST client adapters, we need to define common classes to represent request and response information. First, we will start with an abstract class that has methods and properties needed for either a request or response:

```
namespace Application\Web;

class AbstractHttp
{
```

2. Next, we define class constants that represent HTTP information:

```
const METHOD_GET = 'GET';
const METHOD_POST = 'POST';
const METHOD_PUT = 'PUT';
const METHOD_DELETE = 'DELETE';
const CONTENT_TYPE_HTML = 'text/html';
const CONTENT_TYPE_JSON = 'application/json';
const CONTENT_TYPE_FORM_URL_ENCODED =
  'application/x-www-form-urlencoded';
const HEADER_CONTENT_TYPE = 'Content-Type';
const TRANSPORT_HTTP = 'http';
const TRANSPORT_HTTPS = 'https';
const STATUS_200 = '200';
const STATUS_401 = '401';
const STATUS_500 = '500';
```

3. We then define properties that are needed for either a request or a response:

```
protected $uri;      // i.e. http://xxx.com/yyy
protected $method;    // i.e. GET, PUT, POST, DELETE
protected $headers;  // HTTP headers
protected $cookies;  // cookies
protected $metaData;  // information about the transmission
protected $transport;  // i.e. http or https
protected $data = array();
```

4. It logically follows to define getters and setters for these properties:

```
public function setMethod($method)
{
  $this->method = $method;
}
public function getMethod()
{
  return $this->method ?? self::METHOD_GET;
}
// etc.
```

5. Some properties require access by key. For this purpose, we define `getXxxByKey()` and `setXxxByKey()` methods:

```
public function setHeaderByKey($key, $value)
{
  $this->headers[$key] = $value;
}
public function getHeaderByKey($key)
{
```

```
    return $this->headers[$key] ?? NULL;
  }
  public function getDataByKey($key)
  {
    return $this->data[$key] ?? NULL;
  }
  public function getMetaDataByKey($key)
  {
    return $this->metaData[$key] ?? NULL;
  }
```

6. In some cases, the request will require parameters. We will assume that the parameters will be in the form of a PHP array stored in the `$data` property. We can then build the request URL using the `http_build_query()` function:

```
public function setUri($uri, array $params = NULL)
{
  $this->uri = $uri;
  $first = TRUE;
  if ($params) {
    $this->uri .= '?' . http_build_query($params);
  }
}
public function getDataEncoded()
{
  return http_build_query($this->getData());
}
```

7. Finally, we set `$transport` based on the original request:

```
public function setTransport($transport = NULL)
{
  if ($transport) {
      $this->transport = $transport;
  } else {
      if (substr($this->uri, 0, 5) == self::TRANSPORT_HTTPS) {
          $this->transport = self::TRANSPORT_HTTPS;
      } else {
          $this->transport = self::TRANSPORT_HTTP;
      }
    }
  }
```

8. In this recipe, we will define a `Application\Web\Request` class that can accept parameters when we wish to generate a request, or, alternatively, populate properties with incoming request information when implementing a server that accepts requests:

```
namespace Application\Web;
class Request extends AbstractHttp
{
  public function __construct(
    $uri = NULL, $method = NULL, array $headers = NULL,
    array $data = NULL, array $cookies = NULL)
    {
      if (!$headers) $this->headers = $_SERVER ?? array();
      else $this->headers = $headers;
      if (!$uri) $this->uri = $this->headers['PHP_SELF'] ?? '';
      else $this->uri = $uri;
      if (!$method) $this->method =
        $this->headers['REQUEST_METHOD'] ?? self::METHOD_GET;
      else $this->method = $method;
      if (!$data) $this->data = $_REQUEST ?? array();
      else $this->data = $data;
      if (!$cookies) $this->cookies = $_COOKIE ?? array();
      else $this->cookies = $cookies;
      $this->setTransport();
    }
}
```

9. Now we can turn our attention to a response class. In this case, we will define an `Application\Web\Received` class. The name reflects the fact that we are re-packaging data received from the external web service:

```
namespace Application\Web;
class Received extends AbstractHttp
{
  public function __construct(
    $uri = NULL, $method = NULL, array $headers = NULL,
    array $data = NULL, array $cookies = NULL)
  {
    $this->uri = $uri;
    $this->method = $method;
    $this->headers = $headers;
    $this->data = $data;
    $this->cookies = $cookies;
    $this->setTransport();
  }
}
```

Creating a streams-based REST client

We are now ready to consider two different ways to implement a REST client. The first approach is to use an underlying PHP I/O layer referred to as **Streams**. This layer provides a series of wrappers that provide access to external streaming resources. By default, any of the PHP file commands will use the file wrapper, which gives access to the local filesystem. We will use the `http://` or `https://` wrappers to implement the `Application\Web\Client\Streams` adapter:

1. First, we define a `Application\Web\Client\Streams` class:

```
namespace Application\Web\Client;
use Application\Web\ { Request, Received };
class Streams
{
  const BYTES_TO_READ = 4096;
```

2. Next, we define a method to send the request to the external web service. In the case of `GET`, we add the parameters to the URI. In the case of `POST`, we create a stream context that contains metadata instructing the remote service that we are supplying data. Using PHP Streams, making a request is just a matter of composing the URI, and, in the case of `POST`, setting the stream context. We then use a simple `fopen()`:

```
public static function send(Request $request)
{
  $data = $request->getDataEncoded();
  $received = new Received();
  switch ($request->getMethod()) {
    case Request::METHOD_GET :
      if ($data) {
        $request->setUri($request->getUri() . '?' . $data);
      }
      $resource = fopen($request->getUri(), 'r');
      break;
    case Request::METHOD_POST :
      $opts = [
        $request->getTransport() =>
        [
          'method'  => Request::METHOD_POST,
          'header'  => Request::HEADER_CONTENT_TYPE
          . ': ' . Request::CONTENT_TYPE_FORM_URL_ENCODED,
          'content' => $data
        ]
      ];
      $resource = fopen($request->getUri(), 'w',
      stream_context_create($opts));
      break;
```

```
    }
    return self::getResults($received, $resource);
}
```

3. Finally, we have a look at retrieving and packaging results into a `Received` object. You will notice that we added a provision to decode data received in JSON format:

```
protected static function getResults(Received $received, $resource)
{
  $received->setMetaData(stream_get_meta_data($resource));
  $data = $received->getMetaDataByKey('wrapper_data');
  if (!empty($data) && is_array($data)) {
    foreach($data as $item) {
      if (preg_match('!^HTTP/\d\.\d (\d+?) .*?$!',
          $item, $matches)) {
          $received->setHeaderByKey('status', $matches[1]);
      } else {
          list($key, $value) = explode(':', $item);
          $received->setHeaderByKey($key, trim($value));
      }
    }
  }
  $payload = '';
  while (!feof($resource)) {
    $payload .= fread($resource, self::BYTES_TO_READ);
  }
  if ($received->getHeaderByKey(Received::HEADER_CONTENT_TYPE)) {
    switch (TRUE) {
      case stripos($received->getHeaderByKey(
                   Received::HEADER_CONTENT_TYPE),
                   Received::CONTENT_TYPE_JSON) !== FALSE:
        $received->setData(json_decode($payload));
        break;
      default :
        $received->setData($payload);
        break;
          }
    }
    return $received;
}
```

Defining a cURL-based REST client

We will now have a look at our second approach for a REST client, one of which is based on the cURL extension:

1. For this approach, we will assume the same request and response classes. The initial class definition is much the same as for the Streams client discussed previously:

```
namespace Application\Web\Client;
use Application\Web\ { Request, Received };
class Curl
{
```

2. The `send()` method is quite a bit simpler than when using Streams. All we need to do is to define an array of options, and let cURL do the rest:

```
public static function send(Request $request)
{
  $data = $request->getDataEncoded();
  $received = new Received();
  switch ($request->getMethod()) {
    case Request::METHOD_GET :
      $uri = ($data)
        ? $request->getUri() . '?' . $data
        : $request->getUri();
          $options = [
            CURLOPT_URL => $uri,
            CURLOPT_HEADER => 0,
            CURLOPT_RETURNTRANSFER => TRUE,
            CURLOPT_TIMEOUT => 4
          ];
          break;
```

3. `POST` requires slightly different cURL parameters:

```
case Request::METHOD_POST :
  $options = [
    CURLOPT_POST => 1,
    CURLOPT_HEADER => 0,
    CURLOPT_URL => $request->getUri(),
    CURLOPT_FRESH_CONNECT => 1,
    CURLOPT_RETURNTRANSFER => 1,
    CURLOPT_FORBID_REUSE => 1,
    CURLOPT_TIMEOUT => 4,
    CURLOPT_POSTFIELDS => $data
  ];
  break;
}
```

4. We then execute a series of cURL functions and run the results through `getResults()`:

    ```
    $ch = curl_init();
    curl_setopt_array($ch, ($options));
    if( ! $result = curl_exec($ch))
    {
      trigger_error(curl_error($ch));
    }
    $received->setMetaData(curl_getinfo($ch));
    curl_close($ch);
    return self::getResults($received, $result);
    }
    ```

5. The `getResults()` method packages results into a `Received` object:

    ```
    protected static function getResults(Received $received, $payload)
    {
      $type = $received->getMetaDataByKey('content_type');
      if ($type) {
        switch (TRUE) {
          case stripos($type,
              Received::CONTENT_TYPE_JSON) !== FALSE):
              $received->setData(json_decode($payload));
              break;
          default :
              $received->setData($payload);
              break;
        }
      }
      return $received;
    }
    ```

How it works...

Be sure to copy all the preceding code into these classes:

- `Application\Web\AbstractHttp`
- `Application\Web\Request`
- `Application\Web\Received`
- `Application\Web\Client\Streams`
- `Application\Web\Client\Curl`

For this illustration, you can make a REST request to the Google Maps API to obtain driving directions between two points. You also need to create an API key for this purpose by following the directions given at `https://developers.google.com/maps/documentation/directions/get-api-key`.

You can then define a `chap_07_simple_rest_client_google_maps_curl.php` calling script that issues a request using the `Curl` client. You might also consider define a `chap_07_simple_rest_client_google_maps_streams.php` calling script that issues a request using the `Streams` client:

```
<?php
define('DEFAULT_ORIGIN', 'New York City');
define('DEFAULT_DESTINATION', 'Redondo Beach');
define('DEFAULT_FORMAT', 'json');
$apiKey = include __DIR__ . '/google_api_key.php';
require __DIR__ . '/../Application/Autoload/Loader.php';
Application\Autoload\Loader::init(__DIR__ . '/..');
use Application\Web\Request;
use Application\Web\Client\Curl;
```

You can then get the origin and destination:

```
$start = $_GET['start'] ?? DEFAULT_ORIGIN;
$end   = $_GET['end'] ?? DEFAULT_DESTINATION;
$start = strip_tags($start);
$end   = strip_tags($end);
```

You are now in a position to populate the `Request` object, and use it to generate the request:

```
$request = new Request(
  'https://maps.googleapis.com/maps/api/directions/json',
  Request::METHOD_GET,
  NULL,
  ['origin' => $start, 'destination' => $end, 'key' => $apiKey],
  NULL
);

$received = Curl::send($request);
$routes   = $received->getData()->routes[0];
include __DIR__ . '/chap_07_simple_rest_client_google_maps_template.
php';
```

For the purposes of illustration, you could also define a template that represents view logic to display the results of the request:

```
<?php foreach ($routes->legs as $item) : ?>
  <!-- Trip Info -->
```

```
    <br>Distance: <?= $item->distance->text; ?>
    <br>Duration: <?= $item->duration->text; ?>
    <!-- Driving Directions -->
    <table>
      <tr>
      <th>Distance</th><th>Duration</th><th>Directions</th>
      </tr>
      <?php foreach ($item->steps as $step) : ?>
      <?php $class = ($count++ & 01) ? 'color1' : 'color2'; ?>
      <tr>
      <td class="<?= $class ?>"><?= $step->distance->text ?></td>
      <td class="<?= $class ?>"><?= $step->duration->text ?></td>
      <td class="<?= $class ?>">
      <?= $step->html_instructions ?></td>
      </tr>
      <?php endforeach; ?>
    </table>
  <?php endforeach; ?>
```

Here are the results of the request as seen in a browser:

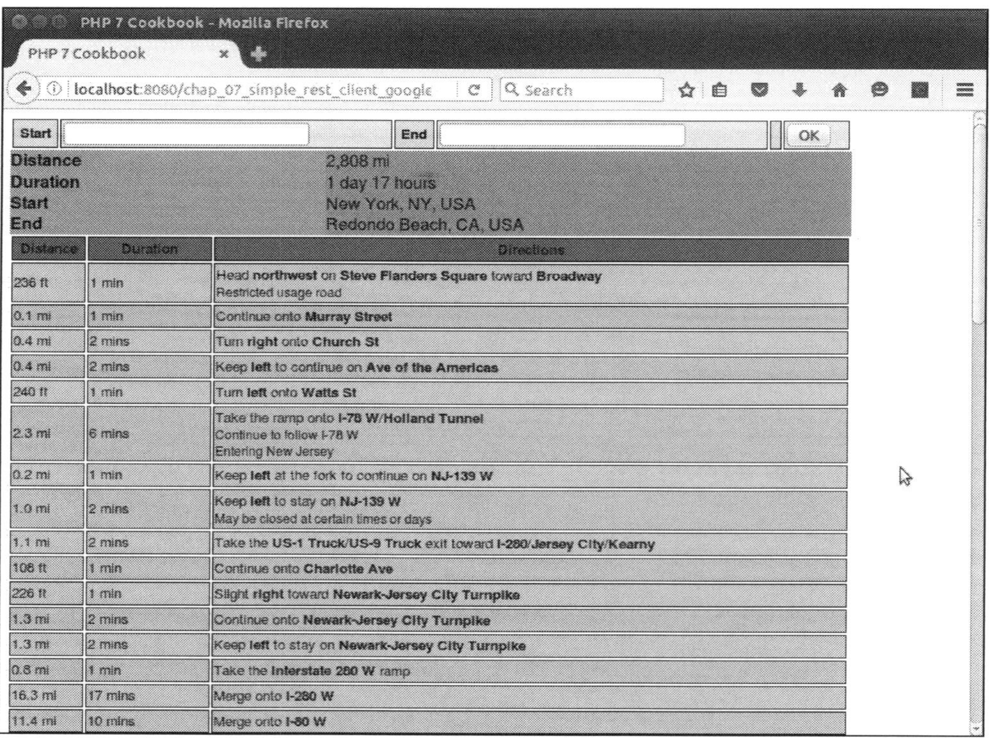

There's more...

PHP Standards Recommendations (**PSR-7**) precisely defines request and response objects to be used when making requests between PHP applications. This is covered extensively in *Appendix, Defining PSR-7 Classes.*

See also

For more information on `Streams`, see this PHP documentation page `http://php.net/manual/en/book.stream.php`. An often asked question is "what is the difference between HTTP PUT and POST?" for an excellent discussion on this topic please refer to `http://stackoverflow.com/questions/107390/whats-the-difference-between-a-post-and-a-put-http-request`. For more information on obtaining an API key from Google, please refer to these web pages:

`https://developers.google.com/maps/documentation/directions/get-api-key`

`https://developers.google.com/maps/documentation/directions/intro#Introduction`

Creating a simple REST server

There are several considerations when implementing a REST server. The answers to these three questions will then let you define your REST service:

- How is the raw request captured?
- What **Application Programming Interface** (**API**) do you want to publish?
- How do you plan to map HTTP verbs (for example, `GET`, `PUT`, `POST`, and `DELETE`) to API methods?

How to do it...

1. We will implement our REST server by building onto the request and response classes defined in the previous recipe, *Creating a simple REST client*. Review the classes discussed in the previous recipe, including the following:
    - `Application\Web\AbstractHttp`
    - `Application\Web\Request`
    - `Application\Web\Received`

2. We will also need to define a formal `Application\Web\Response` response class, based on `AbstractHttp`. The primary difference between this class and the others is that it accepts an instance of `Application\Web\Request` as an argument. The primary work is accomplished in the `__construct()` method. It's also important to set the `Content-Type` header and status:

```
namespace Application\Web;
class Response extends AbstractHttp
{

  public function __construct(Request $request = NULL,
                              $status = NULL, $contentType = NULL)
  {
    if ($request) {
      $this->uri = $request->getUri();
      $this->data = $request->getData();
      $this->method = $request->getMethod();
      $this->cookies = $request->getCookies();
      $this->setTransport();
    }
    $this->processHeaders($contentType);
    if ($status) {
      $this->setStatus($status);
    }
  }
  protected function processHeaders($contentType)
  {
    if (!$contentType) {
      $this->setHeaderByKey(self::HEADER_CONTENT_TYPE,
        self::CONTENT_TYPE_JSON);
    } else {
      $this->setHeaderByKey(self::HEADER_CONTENT_TYPE,
        $contentType);
    }
  }
  public function setStatus($status)
  {
    $this->status = $status;
  }
  public function getStatus()
  {
    return $this->status;
  }
}
```

3. We are now in a position to define the `Application\Web\Rest\Server` class. You may be surprised at how simple it is. The real work is done in the associated API class:

[Note the use of the PHP 7 group use syntax:

```
use Application\Web\ { Request,Response,Received }
```
]

```
namespace Application\Web\Rest;
use Application\Web\ { Request, Response, Received };
class Server
{
  protected $api;
  public function __construct(ApiInterface $api)
  {
    $this->api = $api;
  }
```

4. Next, we define a `listen()` method that serves as a target for the request. The heart of the server implementation is this line of code:

```
$jsonData = json_decode(file_get_contents('php://input'),true);
```

5. This captures raw input, which is assumed to be in JSON format:

```
public function listen()
{
  $request  = new Request();
  $response = new Response($request);
  $getPost  = $_REQUEST ?? array();
  $jsonData = json_decode(
    file_get_contents('php://input'),true);
  $jsonData = $jsonData ?? array();
  $request->setData(array_merge($getPost,$jsonData));
```

[We have also added a provision for authentication. Otherwise, anybody could make requests and obtain potentially sensitive data. You will note that we do not have the server class performing authentication; rather, we leave it to the API class:

```
if (!$this->api->authenticate($request)) {
    $response->setStatus(Request::STATUS_401);
    echo $this->api::ERROR;
    exit;
}
```
]

6. We then map API methods to the primary HTTP methods `GET`, `PUT`, `POST`, and `DELETE`:

```
$id = $request->getData()[$this->api::ID_FIELD] ?? NULL;
switch (strtoupper($request->getMethod())) {
  case Request::METHOD_POST :
    $this->api->post($request, $response);
    break;
  case Request::METHOD_PUT :
    $this->api->put($request, $response);
    break;
  case Request::METHOD_DELETE :
    $this->api->delete($request, $response);
    break;
  case Request::METHOD_GET :
  default :
    // return all if no params
  $this->api->get($request, $response);
}
```

7. Finally, we package the response and send it out, JSON-encoded:

```
  $this->processResponse($response);
  echo json_encode($response->getData());
}
```

8. The `processResponse()` method sets headers and makes sure the result is packaged as an `Application\Web\Response` object:

```
protected function processResponse($response)
{
  if ($response->getHeaders()) {
    foreach ($response->getHeaders() as $key => $value) {
      header($key . ': ' . $value, TRUE,
             $response->getStatus());
    }
  }
  header(Request::HEADER_CONTENT_TYPE
  . ': ' . Request::CONTENT_TYPE_JSON, TRUE);
  if ($response->getCookies()) {
    foreach ($response->getCookies() as $key => $value) {
      setcookie($key, $value);
    }
  }
}
```

9. As mentioned earlier, the real work is done by the API class. We start by defining an abstract class that ensures the primary methods `get()`, `put()`, and so on are represented, and that all such methods accept request and response objects as arguments. You might notice that we have added a `generateToken()` method that uses the PHP 7 `random_bytes()` function to generate a truly random series of 16 bytes:

```
namespace Application\Web\Rest;
use Application\Web\ { Request, Response };
abstract class AbstractApi implements ApiInterface
{
  const TOKEN_BYTE_SIZE  = 16;
  protected $registeredKeys;
  abstract public function get(Request $request,
                               Response $response);
  abstract public function put(Request $request,
                               Response $response);
  abstract public function post(Request $request,
                                Response $response);
  abstract public function delete(Request $request,
                                  Response $response);
  abstract public function authenticate(Request $request);
  public function __construct($registeredKeys, $tokenField)
  {
    $this->registeredKeys = $registeredKeys;
  }
  public static function generateToken()
  {
    return bin2hex(random_bytes(self::TOKEN_BYTE_SIZE));
  }
}
```

10. We also define a corresponding interface that can be used for architectural and design purposes, as well as code development control:

```
namespace Application\Web\Rest;
use Application\Web\ { Request, Response };
interface ApiInterface
{
  public function get(Request $request, Response $response);
  public function put(Request $request, Response $response);
  public function post(Request $request, Response $response);
  public function delete(Request $request, Response $response);
  public function authenticate(Request $request);
}
```

11. Here, we present a sample API based on `AbstractApi`. This class leverages database classes defined in *Chapter 5, Interacting with a Database*:

```
namespace Application\Web\Rest;
use Application\Web\ { Request, Response, Received };
use Application\Entity\Customer;
use Application\Database\ { Connection, CustomerService };

class CustomerApi extends AbstractApi
{
  const ERROR = 'ERROR';
  const ERROR_NOT_FOUND = 'ERROR: Not Found';
  const SUCCESS_UPDATE = 'SUCCESS: update succeeded';
  const SUCCESS_DELETE = 'SUCCESS: delete succeeded';
  const ID_FIELD = 'id';       // field name of primary key
  const TOKEN_FIELD = 'token';  // field used for authentication
  const LIMIT_FIELD = 'limit';
  const OFFSET_FIELD = 'offset';
  const DEFAULT_LIMIT = 20;
  const DEFAULT_OFFSET = 0;

  protected $service;

  public function __construct($registeredKeys,
                              $dbparams, $tokenField = NULL)
  {
    parent::__construct($registeredKeys, $tokenField);
    $this->service = new CustomerService(
      new Connection($dbparams));
  }
```

12. All methods receive request and response as arguments. You will notice the use of `getDataByKey()` to retrieve data items. The actual database interaction is performed by the service class. You might also notice that in all cases, we set an HTTP status code to inform the client of success or failure. In the case of `get()`, we look for an ID parameter. If received, we deliver information on a single customer only. Otherwise, we deliver a list of all customers using limit and offset:

```
public function get(Request $request, Response $response)
{
  $result = array();
  $id = $request->getDataByKey(self::ID_FIELD) ?? 0;
  if ($id > 0) {
      $result = $this->service->
        fetchById($id)->entityToArray();
  } else {
```

```
        $limit  = $request->getDataByKey(self::LIMIT_FIELD)
          ?? self::DEFAULT_LIMIT;
        $offset = $request->getDataByKey(self::OFFSET_FIELD)
          ?? self::DEFAULT_OFFSET;
        $result = [];
        $fetch = $this->service->fetchAll($limit, $offset);
        foreach ($fetch as $row) {
          $result[] = $row;
        }
      }
      if ($result) {
          $response->setData($result);
          $response->setStatus(Request::STATUS_200);
      } else {
          $response->setData([self::ERROR_NOT_FOUND]);
          $response->setStatus(Request::STATUS_500);
      }
    }
```

13. The `put()` method is used to insert customer data:

```
    public function put(Request $request, Response $response)
    {
      $cust = Customer::arrayToEntity($request->getData(),
                                      new Customer());
      if ($newCust = $this->service->save($cust)) {
          $response->setData(['success' => self::SUCCESS_UPDATE,
                              'id' => $newCust->getId()]);
          $response->setStatus(Request::STATUS_200);
      } else {
          $response->setData([self::ERROR]);
          $response->setStatus(Request::STATUS_500);
      }
    }
```

14. The `post()` method is used to update existing customer entries:

```
    public function post(Request $request, Response $response)
    {
      $id = $request->getDataByKey(self::ID_FIELD) ?? 0;
      $reqData = $request->getData();
      $custData = $this->service->
        fetchById($id)->entityToArray();
      $updateData = array_merge($custData, $reqData);
      $updateCust = Customer::arrayToEntity($updateData,
```

```
    new Customer());
    if ($this->service->save($updateCust)) {
        $response->setData(['success' => self::SUCCESS_UPDATE,
                            'id' => $updateCust->getId()]);
        $response->setStatus(Request::STATUS_200);
    } else {
        $response->setData([self::ERROR]);
        $response->setStatus(Request::STATUS_500);
    }
  }
```

15. As the name implies, `delete()` removes a customer entry:

```
public function delete(Request $request, Response $response)
{
  $id = $request->getDataByKey(self::ID_FIELD) ?? 0;
  $cust = $this->service->fetchById($id);
  if ($cust && $this->service->remove($cust)) {
      $response->setData(['success' => self::SUCCESS_DELETE,
                          'id' => $id]);
      $response->setStatus(Request::STATUS_200);
  } else {
      $response->setData([self::ERROR_NOT_FOUND]);
      $response->setStatus(Request::STATUS_500);
  }
}
```

16. Finally, we define `authenticate()` to provide, in this example, a low-level mechanism to protect API usage:

```
public function authenticate(Request $request)
{
  $authToken = $request->getDataByKey(self::TOKEN_FIELD)
    ?? FALSE;
  if (in_array($authToken, $this->registeredKeys, TRUE)) {
      return TRUE;
  } else {
      return FALSE;
  }
}
}
```

How it works...

Define the following classes, which were discussed in the previous recipe:

- `Application\Web\AbstractHttp`
- `Application\Web\Request`
- `Application\Web\Received`

You can then define the following classes, described in this recipe, summarized in this table:

Class Application\Web*	Discussed in these steps
`Response`	2
`Rest\Server`	3 - 8
`Rest\AbstractApi`	9
`Rest\ApiInterface`	10
`Rest\CustomerApi`	11 - 16

You are now free to develop your own API class. If you choose to follow the illustration `Application\Web\Rest\CustomerApi`, however, you will need to also be sure to implement these classes, covered in *Chapter 5, Interacting with a Database*:

- `Application\Entity\Customer`
- `Application\Database\Connection`
- `Application\Database\CustomerService`

You can now define a `chap_07_simple_rest_server.php` script that invokes the REST server:

```
<?php
$dbParams = include __DIR__ . '/../../config/db.config.php';
require __DIR__ . '/../Application/Autoload/Loader.php';
Application\Autoload\Loader::init(__DIR__ . '/..');
use Application\Web\Rest\Server;
use Application\Web\Rest\CustomerApi;
$apiKey = include __DIR__ . '/api_key.php';
$server = new Server(new CustomerApi([$apiKey], $dbParams, 'id'));
$server->listen();
```

You can then use the built-in PHP 7 development server to listen on port `8080` for REST requests:

```
php -S localhost:8080 chap_07_simple_rest_server.php
```

To test your API, use the `Application\Web\Rest\AbstractApi::generateToken()` method to generate an authentication token that you can place in an `api_key.php` file, something like this:

```
<?php return '79e9b5211bbf2458a4085707ea378129';
```

You can then use a generic API client (such as the one described in the previous recipe), or a browser plugin such as RESTClient by Chao Zhou (see `http://restclient.net/` for more information) to generate sample requests. Make sure you include the token for your request, otherwise the API as defined will reject the request.

Here is an example of a `POST` request for `ID 1`, which sets the `balance` field to a value of `888888`:

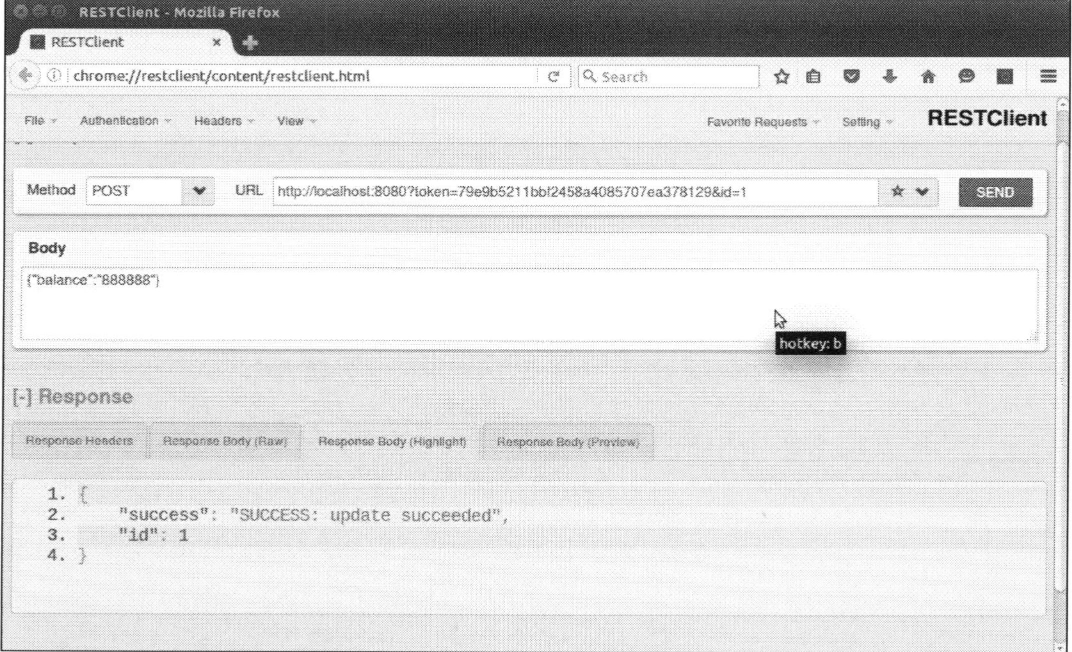

There's more...

There are a number of libraries that help you implement a REST server. One of my favorites is an example implementing a REST server in a single file: `https://www.leaseweb.com/labs/2015/10/creating-a-simple-rest-api-in-php/`

Various frameworks, such as CodeIgniter and Zend Framework, also have REST server implementations.

Creating a simple SOAP client

Using SOAP, in contrast to the process of implementing a REST client or server, is quite easy as there is a PHP SOAP extension that provides both capabilities.

> A frequently asked question is "what is the difference between SOAP and REST?" SOAP uses XML internally as its data format. SOAP uses HTTP but only for transport, and otherwise has no awareness of other HTTP methods. REST directly operates HTTP, and can use anything for data formats, but JSON is preferred. Another key difference is that SOAP can operate in conjunction with a WSDL, which makes the service self-describing, thus more publicly available. Thus, SOAP services are often offered by public institutions such as national health organizations.

How to do it...

For this example, we will make a SOAP request for an existing SOAP service offered by the United States National Weather service:

1. The first consideration is to identify the **WSDL** document. The WSDL is an XML document that describes the service:

```
$wsdl = 'http://graphical.weather.gov/xml/SOAP_server/'
   . 'ndfdXMLserver.php?wsdl';
```

2. Next, we create a `soap client` instance using the WSDL:

```
$soap = new SoapClient($wsdl, array('trace' => TRUE));
```

3. We are then free to initialize some variables in anticipation of a weather forecast request:

```
$units = 'm';
$params = '';
$numDays = 7;
$weather = '';
$format = '24 hourly';
$startTime = new DateTime();
```

4. We can then make a `LatLonListCityNames()` SOAP request, identified as an operation in the WSDL, for a list of cities supported by the service. The request is returned in XML format, which suggests creating a `SimpleXLMElement` instance:

```
$xml = new SimpleXMLElement($soap->LatLonListCityNames(1));
```

5. Unfortunately, the list of cities and their corresponding latitude and longitude are in separate XML nodes. Accordingly, we use the `array_combine()` PHP function to create an associative array where latitude/longitude is the key, and the city name is the value. We can then later use this to present an HTML `SELECT` drop-down list, using `asort()` to alphabetize the list:

```
$cityNames = explode('|', $xml->cityNameList);
$latLonCity = explode(' ', $xml->latLonList);
$cityLatLon = array_combine($latLonCity, $cityNames);
asort($cityLatLon);
```

6. We can then get city data from a web request as follows:

```
$currentLatLon = (isset($_GET['city'])) ? strip_tags(
                   urldecode($_GET['city'])) : '';
```

7. The SOAP call we wish to make is `NDFDgenByDay()`. We can determine the nature of the parameters supplied to the SOAP server by examining the WSDL:

```
<message name="NDFDgenByDayRequest">
<part name="latitude" type="xsd:decimal"/>
<part name="longitude" type="xsd:decimal"/>
<part name="startDate" type="xsd:date"/>
<part name="numDays" type="xsd:integer"/>
<part name="Unit" type="xsd:string"/>
<part name="format" type="xsd:string"/>
</message>
```

8. If the value of `$currentLatLon` is set, we can process the request. We wrap the request in a `try {} catch {}` block in case any exceptions are thrown:

```
if ($currentLatLon) {
  list($lat, $lon) = explode(',', $currentLatLon);
  try {
      $weather = $soap->NDFDgenByDay($lat,$lon,
        $startTime->format('Y-m-d'),$numDays,$unit,$format);
  } catch (Exception $e) {
      $weather .= PHP_EOL;
      $weather .= 'Latitude: ' . $lat . ' | Longitude: ' . $lon;
      $weather .= 'ERROR' . PHP_EOL;
      $weather .= $e->getMessage() . PHP_EOL;
      $weather .= $soap->__getLastResponse() . PHP_EOL;
  }
}
?>
```

How it works...

Copy all the preceding code into a `chap_07_simple_soap_client_weather_service.php` file. You can then add view logic that displays a form with the list of cities, as well as the results:

```
<form method="get" name="forecast">
<br> City List:
<select name="city">
<?php foreach ($cityLatLon as $latLon => $city) : ?>
<?php $select = ($currentLatLon == $latLon) ? ' selected' : ''; ?>
<option value="<?= urlencode($latLon) ?>" <?= $select ?>>
<?= $city ?></option>
<?php endforeach; ?>
</select>
<br><input type="submit" value="OK"></td>
</form>
<pre>
<?php var_dump($weather); ?>
</pre>
```

Here is the result, in a browser, of requesting the weather forecast for Cleveland, Ohio:

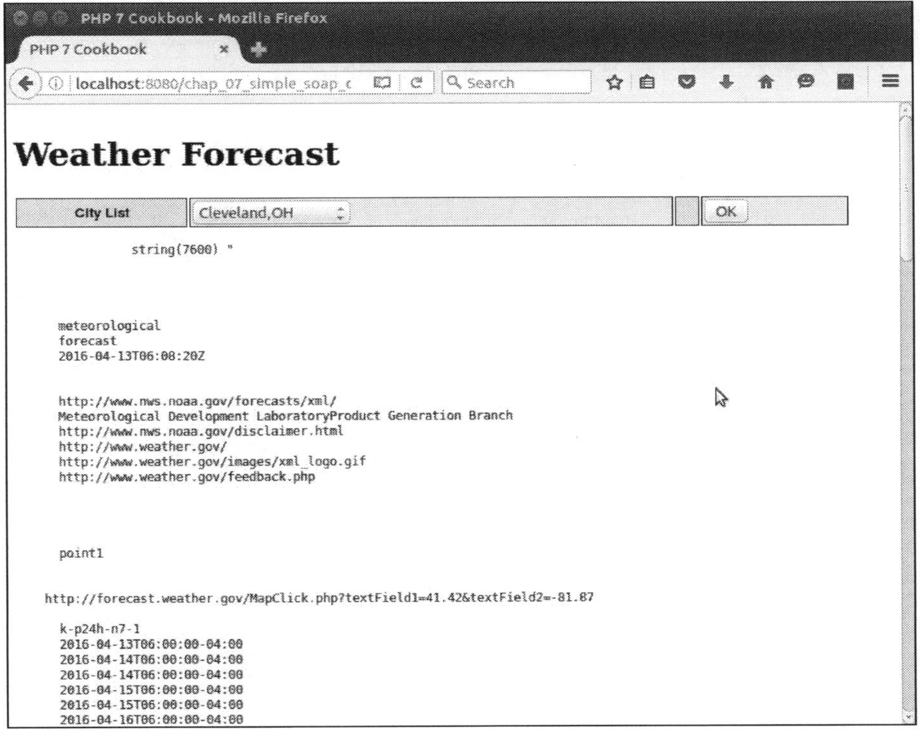

See also

For a good discussion on the difference between SOAP and REST, refer to the article present at `http://stackoverflow.com/questions/209905/representational-state-transfer-rest-and-simple-object-access-protocol-soap?lq=1`.

Creating a simple SOAP server

As with the SOAP client, we can use the PHP SOAP extension to implement a SOAP server. The most difficult part of the implementation will be generating the WSDL from the API class. We do not cover that process here as there are a number of good WSDL generators available.

How to do it...

1. First, you need an API that will be handled by the SOAP server. For this example, we define an `Application\Web\Soap\ProspectsApi` class that allows us to create, read, update, and delete the `prospects` table:

```
namespace Application\Web\Soap;
use PDO;
class ProspectsApi
{
  protected $registerKeys;
  protected $pdo;

  public function __construct($pdo, $registeredKeys)
  {
    $this->pdo = $pdo;
    $this->registeredKeys = $registeredKeys;
  }
}
```

2. We then define methods that correspond to create, read, update, and delete. In this example, the methods are named `put()`, `get()`, `post()`, and `delete()`. These, in turn, call methods that generate SQL requests that are executed from a PDO instance. An example for `get()` is as follows:

```
public function get(array $request, array $response)
{
  if (!$this->authenticate($request)) return FALSE;
  $result = array();
  $id = $request[self::ID_FIELD] ?? 0;
  $email = $request[self::EMAIL_FIELD] ?? 0;
  if ($id > 0) {
      $result = $this->fetchById($id);
```

```
        $response[self::ID_FIELD] = $id;
    } elseif ($email) {
        $result = $this->fetchByEmail($email);
        $response[self::ID_FIELD] = $result[self::ID_FIELD] ?? 0;
    } else {
        $limit = $request[self::LIMIT_FIELD]
          ?? self::DEFAULT_LIMIT;
        $offset = $request[self::OFFSET_FIELD]
          ?? self::DEFAULT_OFFSET;
        $result = [];
        foreach ($this->fetchAll($limit, $offset) as $row) {
          $result[] = $row;
        }
    }
    $response = $this->processResponse(
      $result, $response, self::SUCCESS, self::ERROR);
      return $response;
    }

    protected function processResponse($result, $response,
                                       $success_code, $error_code)
    {
      if ($result) {
          $response['data'] = $result;
          $response['code'] = $success_code;
          $response['status'] = self::STATUS_200;
      } else {
          $response['data'] = FALSE;
          $response['code'] = self::ERROR_NOT_FOUND;
          $response['status'] = self::STATUS_500;
      }
      return $response;
    }
```

3. You can then generate a WSDL from your API. There are quite a few PHP-based WSDL generators available (see the *There's more...* section). Most require that you add `phpDocumentor` tags before the methods that will be published. In our example, the two arguments are both arrays. Here is the full WSDL for the API discussed earlier:

```
<?xml version="1.0" encoding="UTF-8"?>
  <wsdl:definitions xmlns:tns="php7cookbook"
    targetNamespace="php7cookbook"
    xmlns:soap="http://schemas.xmlsoap.org/wsdl/soap/"
    xmlns:s="http://www.w3.org/2001/XMLSchema"
    xmlns:wsdl="http://schemas.xmlsoap.org/wsdl/"
    xmlns:soapenc="http://schemas.xmlsoap.org/soap/encoding/">
```

```
<wsdl:message name="getSoapIn">
  <wsdl:part name="request" type="tns:array" />
  <wsdl:part name="response" type="tns:array" />
</wsdl:message>
<wsdl:message name="getSoapOut">
  <wsdl:part name="return" type="tns:array" />
</wsdl:message>
<!—some nodes removed to conserve space -->
<wsdl:portType name="CustomerApiSoap">
<!—some nodes removed to conserve space -->
<wsdl:binding name="CustomerApiSoap" type="tns:CustomerApiSoap">
<soap:binding transport="http://schemas.xmlsoap.org/soap/http"
  style="rpc" />
  <wsdl:operation name="get">
    <soap:operation soapAction="php7cookbook#get" />
      <wsdl:input>
        <soap:body use="encoded" encodingStyle=
          "http://schemas.xmlsoap.org/soap/encoding/"
          namespace="php7cookbook" parts="request response" />
      </wsdl:input>
      <wsdl:output>
        <soap:body use="encoded" encodingStyle=
          "http://schemas.xmlsoap.org/soap/encoding/"
          namespace="php7cookbook" parts="return" />
      </wsdl:output>
  </wsdl:operation>
<!—some nodes removed to conserve space -->
</wsdl:binding>
<wsdl:service name="CustomerApi">
  <wsdl:port name="CustomerApiSoap"
    binding="tns:CustomerApiSoap">
  <soap:address location="http://localhost:8080/" />
  </wsdl:port>
</wsdl:service>
</wsdl:definitions>
```

4. Next, create a `chap_07_simple_soap_server.php` file, which will execute the SOAP server. Start by defining the location of the WSDL and any other necessary files (in this case, one for database configuration). If the `wsdl` parameter is set, deliver the WSDL rather than attempting to process the request. In this example, we use a simple API key to authenticate requests. We then create a SOAP server instance, assign an instance of our API class, and run `handle()`:

```
<?php
define('DB_CONFIG_FILE', '/../config/db.config.php');
```

```
define('WSDL_FILENAME', __DIR__ . '/chap_07_wsdl.xml');

if (isset($_GET['wsdl'])) {
    readfile(WSDL_FILENAME);
    exit;
}
$apiKey = include __DIR__ . '/api_key.php';
require __DIR__ . '/../Application/Web/Soap/ProspectsApi.php';
require __DIR__ . '/../Application/Database/Connection.php';
use Application\Database\Connection;
use Application\Web\Soap\ProspectsApi;
$connection = new Application\Database\Connection(
  include __DIR__ . DB_CONFIG_FILE);
$api = new Application\Web\Soap\ProspectsApi(
  $connection->pdo, [$apiKey]);
$server = new SoapServer(WSDL_FILENAME);
$server->setObject($api);
echo $server->handle();
```

Depending on the settings for your `php.ini` file, you may need to disable the WSDL cache, as follows:

```
ini_set('soap.wsdl_cache_enabled', 0);
```

If you have problems with incoming `POST` data, you can adjust this parameter as follows:

```
ini_set('always_populate_raw_post_data', -1);
```

How it works...

You can easily test this recipe by first creating your target API class, and then generating a WSDL. You can then use the built-in PHP webserver to deliver the SOAP service with this command:

php -S localhost:8080 chap_07_simple_soap_server.php

You can then use the SOAP client discussed in the previous recipe to make a call to test the SOAP service:

```
<?php
define('WSDL_URL', 'http://localhost:8080?wsdl=1');
$clientKey = include __DIR__ . '/api_key.php';
try {
  $client = new SoapClient(WSDL_URL);
  $response = [];
```

```
    $email = some_email_generated_by_test;
    $email = 'test5393@unlikelysource.com';
    echo "\nGet Prospect Info for Email: " . $email . "\n";
    $request = ['token' => $clientKey, 'email' => $email];
    $result = $client->get($request,$response);
    var_dump($result);

  } catch (SoapFault $e) {
    echo 'ERROR' . PHP_EOL;
    echo $e->getMessage() . PHP_EOL;
  } catch (Throwable $e) {
    echo 'ERROR' . PHP_EOL;
    echo $e->getMessage() . PHP_EOL;
  } finally {
    echo $client->__getLastResponse() . PHP_EOL;
  }
```

Here is the output for email address `test5393@unlikelysource.com`:

```
Terminal

Get Prospect Info for Email: test5393@unlikelysource.com
array(4) {
  ["id"]=>
  string(2) "50"
  ["data"]=>
  array(13) {
    ["id"]=>
    string(2) "50"
    ["first_name"]=>
    string(4) "Test"
    ["last_name"]=>
    string(8) "Test5393"
    ["address"]=>
    string(16) "5393 Main Street"
    ["city"]=>
    string(9) "City 5393"
    ["state_province"]=>
    string(2) "YS"
    ["postal_code"]=>
    string(6) "065F92"
    ["phone"]=>
    string(16) "+17 961-402-2978"
    ["country"]=>
```

See also

A simple Google search for WSDL generators for PHP came back with easily a dozen results. The one used to generate the WSDL for the `ProspectsApi` class was based on `https://code.google.com/archive/p/php-wsdl-creator/`. For more information on `phpDocumentor`, refer to the page at `https://www.phpdoc.org/`.

8
Working with Date/Time and International Aspects

In this chapter, we will cover the following topics:

- Using emoticons or emoji in a view script
- Converting complex characters
- Getting the locale from browser data
- Formatting numbers by locale
- Handling currency by locale
- Formatting date/time by locale
- Creating an HTML international calendar generator
- Building a recurring events generator
- Handling translation without gettext

Introduction

We will start this chapter with two recipes that take advantage of a new **Unicode** escape syntax introduced with **PHP 7**. After that, we will cover how to determine a web visitor's **locale** from browser data. The next few recipes will cover the creation of a locale class, which will allow you to represent numbers, currency, dates, and time in a format specific to a locale. Finally, we will cover recipes that demonstrate how to generate an internationalized calendar, handle recurring events, and perform translation without having to use `gettext`.

Using emoticons or emoji in a view script

The word **emoticons** is a composite of *emotion* and *icon*. **Emoji**, originating from Japan, is another, larger, widely used set of icons. These icons are the little smiley faces, tiny ninjas, and rolling-on-the-floor-laughing icons that are so popular on any website that has a social networking aspect. Prior to PHP 7, however, producing these little beasties was an exercise in frustration.

How to do it...

1. First and foremost, you need to know the Unicode for the icon you wish to present. A quick search on the Internet will direct you to any one of several excellent charts. Here are the codes for the three *hear-no-evil*, *see-no-evil*, and *speak-no-evil* monkey icons:

   `U+1F648`, `U+1F649`, and `U+1F64A`

2. Any Unicode output to the browser must be properly identified. This is most often done by way of a `meta` tag. You should set the character set to UTF-8. Here is an example:

```
<head>
  <title>PHP 7 Cookbook</title>
  <meta http-equiv="content-type"
    content="text/html;charset=utf-8" />
</head>
```

3. The traditional approach was to simply use HTML to display the icons. Thus, you could do something like this:

```
<table>
  <tr>
    <td>&#x1F648;</td>
    <td>&#x1F649;</td>
    <td>&#x1F64A;</td>
  </tr>
</table>
```

4. As of PHP 7, you can now construct full Unicode characters using this syntax: `"\u{xxx}"`. Here is an example with the same three icons as in the preceding bullet:

```
<table>
  <tr>
    <td><?php echo "\u{1F648}"; ?></td>
    <td><?php echo "\u{1F649}"; ?></td>
    <td><?php echo "\u{1F64A}"; ?></td>
  </tr>
</table>
```

Your operating system and browser must both support Unicode and must also have the right set of fonts. In Ubuntu Linux, for example, you would need to install the `ttf-ancient-fonts` package to see emoji in your browser.

How it works...

In PHP 7, a new syntax was introduced that lets you render any Unicode character. Unlike other languages, the new PHP syntax allows for a variable number of hex digits. The basic format is this:

```
\u{xxxx}
```

The entire construct must be double quoted (or use **heredoc**). `xxxx` could be any combination of hex digits, 2, 4, 6, and above.

Create a file called `chap_08_emoji_using_html.php`. Be sure to include the `meta` tag that signals the browser that UTF-8 character encoding is being used:

```
<!DOCTYPE html>
<html>
  <head>
    <title>PHP 7 Cookbook</title>
    <meta http-equiv="content-type"
      content="text/html;charset=utf-8" />
  </head>
```

Next, set up a basic HTML table, and display a row of emoticons/emoji:

```
  <body>
    <table>
      <tr>
        <td>&#x1F648;</td>
        <td>&#x1F649;</td>
        <td>&#x1F64A;</td>
```

```
        </tr>
      </table>
    </body>
  </html>
```

Now add a row using PHP to emit emoticons/emoji:

```
<tr>
  <td><?php echo "\u{1F648}"; ?></td>
  <td><?php echo "\u{1F649}"; ?></td>
  <td><?php echo "\u{1F64A}"; ?></td>
</tr>
```

Here is the output seen from Firefox:

See also

- For a list of emoji codes, see `http://unicode.org/emoji/charts/full-emoji-list.html`

Converting complex characters

The ability to access the entire Unicode character set opens up many new possibilities for rendering complex characters, especially characters in alphabets other than Latin-1.

How to do it...

1. Some languages are read right-to-left instead of left-to-right. Examples include Hebrew and Arabic. In this example, we show you how to present *reverse* text using the `U+202E` Unicode character for right-to-left override. The following line of code prints `txet desreveR`:

   ```
   echo "\u{202E}Reversed text";
   echo "\u{202D}";    // returns output to left-to-right
   ```

Don't forget to invoke the left-to-right override character, `U+202D`, when finished!

2. Another consideration is the use of composed characters. One such example is `ñ` (the letter `n` with a tilde ~ floating above). This is used in words such as *mañana* (the Spanish word for morning or tomorrow, depending on the context). There is a *composed character* available, represented by Unicode code `U+00F1`. Here is an example of its use, which echoes `mañana`:

   ```
   echo "ma\u{00F1}ana"; // shows mañana
   ```

3. This could potentially impact search possibilities, however. Imagine that your customers do not have a keyboard with this composed character. If they start to type `man` in an attempt to search for `mañana`, they will be unsuccessful.
4. Having access to the *full* Unicode set offers other possibilities. Instead of using the *composed* character, you can use a combination of the original letter `n` along with the Unicode *combining* code, which places a floating tilde on top of the letter. In this `echo` command, the output is the same as previously. Only the way the word is formed differs:

   ```
   echo "man\u{0303}ana"; // also shows mañana
   ```

5. A similar application could be made for accents. Consider the French word `élève` (student). You could render it using composed characters, or by using combining codes to float the accents above the letter. Consider the two following examples. Both examples produce the same output, but are rendered differently:

   ```
   echo "\u{00E9}l\u{00E8}ve";
   echo "e\u{0301}le\u{0300}ve";
   ```

How it works...

Create a file called `chap_08_control_and_combining_unicode.php`. Be sure to include the `meta` tag that signals the browser that UTF-8 character encoding is being used:

```
<!DOCTYPE html>
<html>
  <head>
    <title>PHP 7 Cookbook</title>
    <meta http-equiv="content-type"
      content="text/html;charset=utf-8" />
  </head>
```

Next, set up basic PHP and HTML to display the examples discussed previously:

```
  <body>
    <pre>
      <?php
        echo "\u{202E}Reversed text"; // reversed
        //echo "\u{202D}"; // stops reverse
        echo "mañana";  // using pre-composed characters
        echo "ma\u{00F1}ana"; // pre-composed character
        echo "man\u{0303}ana"; // "n" with combining ~ character
                                  (U+0303)
        echo "élève";
        echo "\u{00E9}l\u{00E8}ve"; // pre-composed characters
        echo "e\u{0301}le\u{0300}ve"; // e + combining characters
      ?>
    </pre>
</body>
</html>
```

Here is the output from a browser:

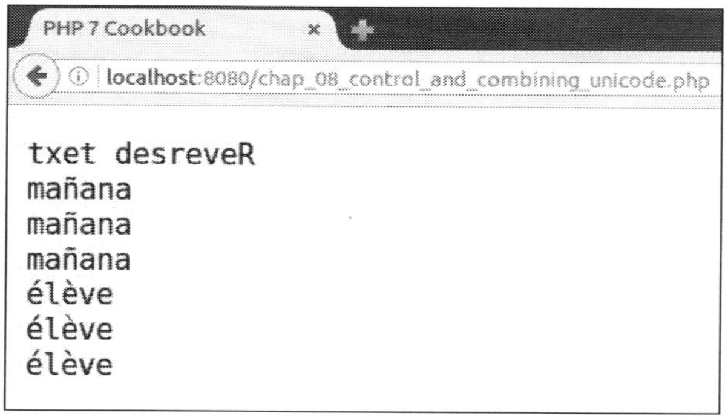

PHP 7 Cookbook
localhost:8080/chap_08_control_and_combining_unicode.php

```
txet desreveR
mañana
mañana
mañana
élève
élève
élève
```

Getting the locale from browser data

In order to improve the user experience on a website, it's important to display information in a format that is acceptable in the user's locale. **Locale** is a generic term used to indicate an area of the world. An effort in the I.T. community has been made to codify locales using a two-part designation consisting of codes for both language and country. But when a person visits your website, how do you know their locale? Probably the most useful technique involves examining the HTTP language header.

How to do it...

1. In order to encapsulate locale functionality, we will assume a class, `Application\I18n\Locale`. We will have this class extend an existing class, `Locale`, which is part of the PHP `Intl` extension.

I18n is a common abbreviation for **Internationalization**. (Count the number of letters!)

```
namespace Application\I18n;
use Locale as PhpLocale;
class Locale extends PhpLocale
{
  const FALLBACK_LOCALE = 'en';
  // some code
}
```

2. To get an idea of what an incoming request looks like, use `phpinfo(INFO_VARIABLES)`. Be sure to disable this function immediately after testing as it gives away too much information to potential attackers:

```
<?php phpinfo(INFO_VARIABLES); ?>
```

3. Locale information is stored in `$_SERVER['HTTP_ACCEPT_LANGUAGE']`. The value will take this general form: `ll-CC,rl;q=0.n, ll-CC,rl;q=0.n`, as defined in this table:

Abbreviation	Meaning
`ll`	Two-character lowercase code representing the language.
`-`	Separates language from country in the locale code `ll-CC`.
`CC`	Two-character uppercase code representing the country.
`,`	Separates locale code from fallback **root locale** code (usually the same as the language code).
`rl`	Two-character lowercase code representing the suggested root locale.
`;`	Separates locale information from quality. If quality is missing, default is `q=1` (100%) probability; this is preferred.
`q`	Quality.
`0.n`	Some value between 0.00 and 1.0. Multiply this value by 100 to get the percentage of probability that this is the actual language preferred by this visitor.

4. There can easily be more than one locale listed. For example, the website visitor could have multiple languages installed on their computer. It so happens that the PHP `Locale` class has a method, `acceptFromHttp()`, which reads the `Accept-language` header string and gives us the desired setting:

```
protected $localeCode;
public function setLocaleCode($acceptLangHeader)
{
  $this->localeCode =
    $this->acceptFromHttp($acceptLangHeader);
}
```

5. We can then define the appropriate getters. The `get AcceptLanguage()` method returns the value from `$_SERVER['HTTP_ACCEPT_LANGUAGE']`:

```
public function getAcceptLanguage()
{
  return $_SERVER['HTTP_ACCEPT_LANGUAGE'] ??
    self::FALLBACK_LOCALE;
}
public function getLocaleCode()
{
  return $this->localeCode;
}
```

6. Next we define a constructor that allows us to "manually" set the locale. Otherwise, the locale information is drawn from the browser:

```
public function __construct($localeString = NULL)
{
  if ($localeString) {
    $this->setLocaleCode($localeString);
  } else {
    $this->setLocaleCode($this->getAcceptLanguage());
  }
}
```

7. Now comes the big decision: what to do with this information! This is covered in the next few recipes.

Even though a visitor appears to accept one or more languages, that visitor does not necessarily want contents in the language/locale indicated by their browser. Accordingly, although you can certainly set the locale given this information, you should also provide them with a static list of alternative languages.

How it works...

In this illustration, let's take three examples:

- information derived from the browser
- a preset locale `fr-FR`
- a string taken from RFC 2616: `da, en-gb;q=0.8, en;q=0.7`

Place the code from steps 1 to 6 into a file, `Locale.php`, which is in the `Application\I18n` folder.

Next, create a file, `chap_08_getting_locale_from_browser.php`, which sets up autoloading and uses the new class:

```
<?php
  require __DIR__ . '/../Application/Autoload/Loader.php';
  Application\Autoload\Loader::init(__DIR__ . '/..');
  use Application\I18n\Locale;
```

Now you can define an array with the three test locale strings:

```
$locale = [NULL, 'fr-FR', 'da, en-gb;q=0.8, en;q=0.7'];
```

Finally, loop through the three locale strings, creating instances of the new class. Echo the value returned from `getLocaleCode()` to see what choice was made:

```
echo '<table>';
foreach ($locale as $code) {
  $locale = new Locale($code);
  echo '<tr>
    <td>' . htmlspecialchars($code) . '</td>
    <td>' . $locale->getLocaleCode() . '</td>
  </tr>';
}
echo '</table>';
```

Here is the result (with a little bit of styling):

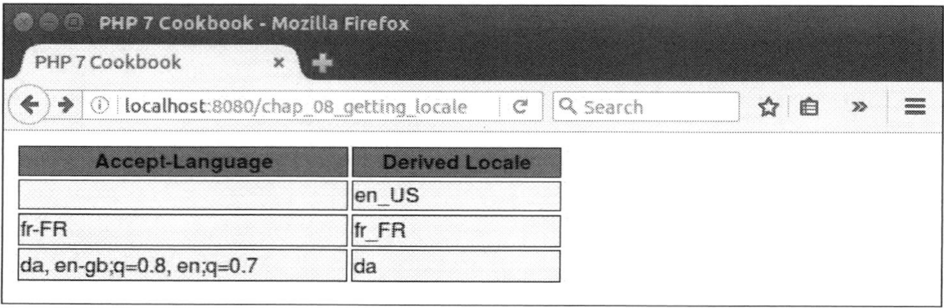

See also

- For information on the PHP `Locale` class, see `http://php.net/manual/en/class.locale.php`
- For more information on the `Accept-Language` header, see section 14.4 of RFC 2616: `https://www.w3.org/Protocols/rfc2616/rfc2616-sec14.html`

Formatting numbers by locale

Numeric representations can vary by locale. As a simple example, in the UK one would see the number three million, eighty thousand, five hundred and twelve, and ninety-two one hundredths as follows:

```
3,080,512.92.
```

In France, however, the same number might appear like so:

```
3 080 512,92
```

How to do it...

Before you can represent a number in a locale-specific manner, you need to determine the locale. This can be accomplished using the `Application\I18n\Locale` class discussed in the previous recipe. The locale can be set manually or from header information.

1. Next, we will make use of the `format()` method of the `NumberFormatter` class, to both output and parse numbers in a locale-specific format. First we add a property that will contain an instance of the `NumberFormatter` class:

```
use NumberFormatter;
protected $numberFormatter;
```

Our initial thought would be to consider using the PHP function `setlocale()` to produce numbers formatted according to locale. The problem with this legacy approach, however, is that *everything* will be considered based on this locale. This could introduce problems dealing with data that is stored according to database specifications. Another issue with `setlocale()` is that it is based on outdated standards, including RFC 1766 and ISO 639. Finally, `setlocale()` is highly dependent on operating system locale support, which will make our code non-portable.

2. Normally, the next step would be to set `$numberFormatter` in the constructor. The problem with this approach, in the case of our `Application\I18n\Locale` class, is that we would end up with a top-heavy class, as we will also need to perform currency and date formatting as well. Accordingly, we add a `getter` that first checks to see whether an instance of `NumberFormatter` has already been created. If not, an instance is created and returned. The first argument in the new `NumberFormatter` is the locale code. The second argument, `NumberFormatter::DECIMAL`, represents what type of formatting we need:

```
public function getNumberFormatter()
{
  if (!$this->numberFormatter) {
    $this->numberFormatter =
      new NumberFormatter($this->getLocaleCode(),
      NumberFormatter::DECIMAL);
  }
  return $this->numberFormatter;
}
```

3. We then add a method that, given any number, will produce a string that represents that number formatted according to the locale:

```
public function formatNumber($number)
{
  return $this->getNumberFormatter()->format($number);
}
```

4. Next we add a method that can be used to parse numbers according to the locale, producing a native PHP numeric value. Please note that the result might not return `FALSE` on parse failure depending on the server's ICU version:

```
public function parseNumber($string)
{
  $result = $this->getNumberFormatter()->parse($string);
  return ($result) ? $result : self::ERROR_UNABLE_TO_PARSE;
}
```

How it works...

Make the additions to the `Application\I18n\Locale` class as discussed in the preceding bullet points. You can then create a `chap_08_formatting_numbers.php` file, which sets up autoloading and uses this class:

```
<?php
  require __DIR__ . '/../Application/Autoload/Loader.php';
  Application\Autoload\Loader::init(__DIR__ . '/..');
  use Application\I18n\Locale;
```

For this illustration, create two `Locale` instances, one for the UK, the other for France. You can also designate a large number to be used for testing:

```
  $localeFr = new Locale('fr_FR');
  $localeUk = new Locale('en_GB');
  $number   = 1234567.89;
?>
```

Finally, you can wrap the `formatNumber()` and `parseNumber()` methods in the appropriate HTML display logic and view the results:

```
<!DOCTYPE html>
<html>
  <head>
    <title>PHP 7 Cookbook</title>
    <meta http-equiv="content-type"
      content="text/html;charset=utf-8" />
    <link rel="stylesheet" type="text/css"
      href="php7cookbook_html_table.css">
  </head>
  <body>
    <table>
      <tr>
```

```
          <th>Number</th>
          <td>1234567.89</td>
        </tr>
        <tr>
          <th>French Format</th>
          <td><?= $localeFr->formatNumber($number); ?></td>
        </tr>
        <tr>
          <th>UK Format</th>
          <td><?= $localeUk->formatNumber($number); ?></td>
        </tr>
        <tr>
          <th>UK Parse French Number:
            <?= $localeFr->formatNumber($number) ?></th>
          <td><?= $localeUk->
            parseNumber($localeFr->formatNumber($number)); ?></td>
        </tr>
        <tr>
          <th>UK Parse UK Number:
            <?= $localeUk->formatNumber($number) ?></th>
          <td><?= $localeUk->
            parseNumber($localeUk->formatNumber($number)); ?></td>
        </tr>
        <tr>
          <th>FR Parse FR Number:
            <?= $localeFr->formatNumber($number) ?></th>
          <td><?= $localeFr->
            parseNumber($localeFr->formatNumber($number)); ?></td>
        </tr>
        <tr>
          <th>FR Parse UK Number:
            <?= $localeUk->formatNumber($number) ?></th>
          <td><?= $localeFr->
            parseNumber($localeUk->formatNumber($number)); ?></td>
        </tr>
      </table>
    </body>
  </html>
```

Here is the result as seen from a browser:

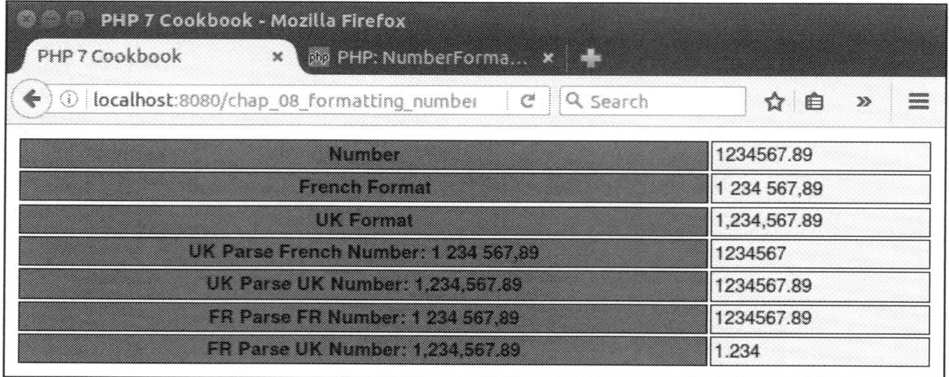

Note that if the locale is set to `fr_FR`, a UK formatted number, when parsed, does not return the correct value. Likewise, when the locale is set to `en_GB`, a French formatted number does not return the correct value upon parsing. Accordingly, you might want to consider adding a validation check before attempting to parse the number.

See also

- For more information on the use and abuse of `setlocale()` please refer to this page: `http://php.net/manual/en/function.setlocale.php`.
- For a brief note on why number formatting will produce an error on some servers, but not others, check the **ICU** (**International Components for Unicode**) version. See the comments on this page: `http://php.net/manual/en/numberformatter.parse.php`. For more info on ICU formatting, see `http://userguide.icu-project.org/formatparse`.

Handling currency by locale

The technique for handling currency is similar to that for numbers. We will even use the same `NumberFormatter` class! There is one major difference, however, and it is a *show stopper*: in order to properly format currency, you will need to have on hand the currency code.

How to do it...

1. The first order of business is to have the currency codes available in some format. One possibility is to simply add the currency code as an `Application\I18n\Locale` class constructor argument:

```
const FALLBACK_CURRENCY = 'GBP';
protected $currencyCode;
public function __construct($localeString = NULL,
  $currencyCode = NULL)
{
  // add this to the existing code:
  $this->currencyCode = $currencyCode ??
    self::FALLBACK_CURRENCY;
}
```

> This approach, although obviously solid and workable, tends to fall into the category called *halfway measures* or *the easy way out*! This approach would also tend to eliminate full automation as the currency code is not available from the HTTP header. As you have probably gathered from other recipes in this book, we do not shy away from a more complex solution so, as the saying goes, *strap on your seat belts*!

2. We will first need to establish some sort of lookup mechanism, where, given a country code, we can obtain its predominant currency code. For this illustration, we will use the Adapter software design pattern. According to this pattern, we should be able to create different classes, which could potentially operate in entirely different ways, but which produce the same result. Accordingly, we need to define the desired result. For this purpose, we introduce a class, `Application\I18n\IsoCodes`. As you can see, this class has all the pertinent properties, along with a sort-of universal constructor:

```
namespace Application\I18n;
class IsoCodes
{
  public $name;
  public $iso2;
  public $iso3;
  public $iso_numeric;
  public $iso_3166;
  public $currency_name;
  public $currency_code;
  public $currency_number;
  public function __construct(array $data)
  {
```

```
      $vars = get_object_vars($this);
      foreach ($vars as $key => $value) {
        $this->$key = $data[$key] ?? NULL;
      }
    }
  }
```

3. Next we define an interface that has the method we require to perform the *country-code-to-currency-code* lookup. In this case, we introduce `Application\I18n\IsoCodesInterface`:

```
namespace Application\I18n;

interface IsoCodesInterface
{
  public function getCurrencyCodeFromIso2CountryCode($iso2)
    : IsoCodes;
}
```

4. Now we are ready to build a lookup adapter class, which we will call `Application\I18n\IsoCodesDb`. It implements the abovementioned interface, and accepts an `Application\Database\Connection` instance (see *Chapter 1, Building a Foundation*), which is used to perform the lookup. The constructor sets up the required information, including the connection, the lookup table name, and the column that represents the ISO2 code. The lookup method required by the interface then issues an SQL statement and returns an array, which is then used to build an `IsoCodes` instance:

```
namespace Application\I18n;

use PDO;
use Application\Database\Connection;

class IsoCodesDb implements IsoCodesInterface
{
  protected $isoTableName;
  protected $iso2FieldName;
  protected $connection;
  public function __construct(Connection $connection,
    $isoTableName, $iso2FieldName)
  {
    $this->connection = $connection;
    $this->isoTableName = $isoTableName;
    $this->iso2FieldName = $iso2FieldName;
  }
  public function getCurrencyCodeFromIso2CountryCode($iso2)
    : IsoCodes
```

```
  {
    $sql = sprintf('SELECT * FROM %s WHERE %s = ?',
      $this->isoTableName,
      $this->iso2FieldName);
    $stmt = $this->connection->pdo->prepare($sql);
    $stmt->execute([$iso2]);
    return new IsoCodes($stmt->fetch(PDO::FETCH_ASSOC);
  }
}
```

5. Now we turn our attention back to the `Application\I18n\Locale` class. We first add a couple of new properties and class constants:

```
const ERROR_UNABLE_TO_PARSE = 'ERROR: Unable to parse';
const FALLBACK_CURRENCY = 'GBP';

protected $currencyFormatter;
protected $currencyLookup;
protected $currencyCode;
```

6. We add new method that retrieves the country code from the locale string. We can leverage the `getRegion()` method, which comes from the PHP `Locale` class (which we extend). Just in case it's needed, we also add a method, `getCurrencyCode()`:

```
public function getCountryCode()
{
  return $this->getRegion($this->getLocaleCode());
}
public function getCurrencyCode()
{
  return $this->currencyCode;
}
```

7. As with formatting numbers, we define a `getCurrencyFormatter(I)`, much as we did `getNumberFormatter()` (shown previously). Notice that `$currencyFormatter` is defined using `NumberFormatter`, but with a different second parameter:

```
public function getCurrencyFormatter()
{
  if (!$this->currencyFormatter) {
    $this->currencyFormatter =
      new NumberFormatter($this->getLocaleCode(),
      NumberFormatter::CURRENCY);
  }
  return $this->currencyFormatter;
}
```

8. We then add a currency code lookup to the class constructor if the lookup class has been defined:

```
public function __construct($localeString = NULL,
  IsoCodesInterface $currencyLookup = NULL)
{
  // add this to the existing code:
  $this->currencyLookup = $currencyLookup;
  if ($this->currencyLookup) {
    $this->currencyCode =
      $this->currencyLookup
      ->getCurrencyCodeFromIso2CountryCode($this
      ->getCountryCode())
      ->currency_code;
  } else {
    $this->currencyCode = self::FALLBACK_CURRENCY;
  }
}
```

9. Then add the appropriate currency format and parse methods. Note that parsing currency, unlike parsing numbers, will return `FALSE` if the parsing operation is not successful:

```
public function formatCurrency($currency)
{
  return $this->getCurrencyFormatter()
    ->formatCurrency($currency, $this->currencyCode);
}
public function parseCurrency($string)
{
  $result = $this->getCurrencyFormatter()
    ->parseCurrency($string, $this->currencyCode);
  return ($result) ? $result : self::ERROR_UNABLE_TO_PARSE;
}
```

How it works...

Create the following classes, as covered in the first several bullet points:

Class	**Bullet point discussed**
`Application\I18n\IsoCodes`	3
`Application\I18n\IsoCodesInterface`	4
`Application\I18n\IsoCodesDb`	5

We will assume, for the purposes of this illustration, that we have a populated MySQL database table, `iso_country_codes`, which has this structure:

```
CREATE TABLE `iso_country_codes` (
  `name` varchar(128) NOT NULL,
  `iso2` varchar(2) NOT NULL,
  `iso3` varchar(3) NOT NULL,
  `iso_numeric` int(11) NOT NULL AUTO_INCREMENT,
  `iso_3166` varchar(32) NOT NULL,
  `currency_name` varchar(32) DEFAULT NULL,
  `currency_code` char(3) DEFAULT NULL,
  `currency_number` int(4) DEFAULT NULL,
  PRIMARY KEY (`iso_numeric`)
) ENGINE=InnoDB AUTO_INCREMENT=895 DEFAULT CHARSET=utf8;
```

Make the additions to the `Application\I18n\Locale` class, as discussed in bullet points 6 to 9 previously. You can then create a `chap_08_formatting_currency.php` file, which sets up autoloading and uses the appropriate classes:

```
<?php
define('DB_CONFIG_FILE', __DIR__ . '/../config/db.config.php');
require __DIR__ . '/../Application/Autoload/Loader.php';
Application\Autoload\Loader::init(__DIR__ . '/..');
use Application\I18n\Locale;
use Application\I18n\IsoCodesDb;
use Application\Database\Connection;
use Application\I18n\Locale;
```

Next, we create instances of the `Connection` and `IsoCodesDb` classes:

```
$connection = new Connection(include DB_CONFIG_FILE);
$isoLookup = new IsoCodesDb($connection,
  'iso_country_codes', 'iso2');
```

For this illustration, create two `Locale` instances, one for the UK, the other for France. You can also designate a large number to be used for testing:

```
$localeFr = new Locale('fr-FR', $isoLookup);
$localeUk = new Locale('en_GB', $isoLookup);
$number   = 1234567.89;
?>
```

Finally, you can wrap the `formatCurrency()` and `parseCurrency()` methods in the appropriate HTML display logic and view the results. Base your view logic on that presented in the *How it works...* section of the previous recipe (not repeated here to save trees!). Here is the final output:

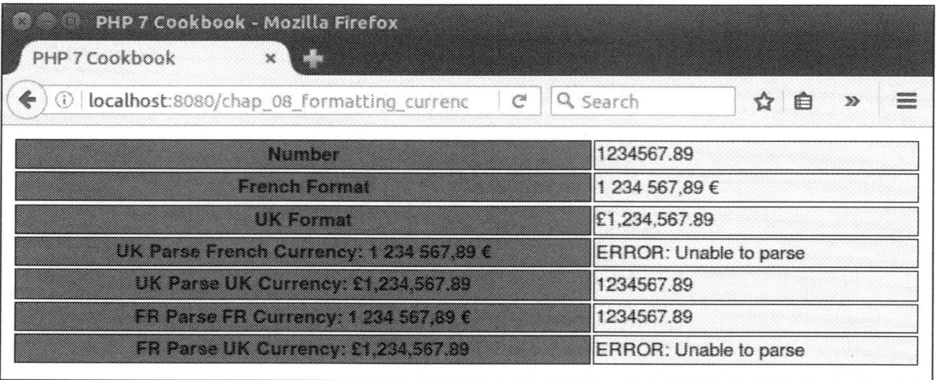

See also

- The most up-to-date list of currency codes is maintained by **ISO** (**International Standards Organization**). You can obtain this list in either **XML** or **XLS** (that is, **Microsoft Excel** spreadsheet format). Here is the page where these lists can be found: `http://www.currency-iso.org/en/home/tables/table-a1.html`.

Formatting date/time by locale

The formatting of date and time varies region to region. As a classic example, consider the year 2016, month April, day 15 and a time in the evening. The format preferred by denizens of the United States would be 7:23 PM, 4/15/2016, whereas in China you would most likely see 2016-04-15 19:23. As mentioned with number and currency formatting, it would also be important to display (and parse) dates in a format acceptable to your web visitors.

How to do it...

1. First of all, we need to modify `Application\I18n\Locale`, adding statements to use date formatting classes:

```
use IntlCalendar;
use IntlDateFormatter;
```

2. Next, we add a property to represent an `IntlDateFormatter` instance, as well as a series of predefined constants:

```
const DATE_TYPE_FULL   = IntlDateFormatter::FULL;
const DATE_TYPE_LONG   = IntlDateFormatter::LONG;
const DATE_TYPE_MEDIUM = IntlDateFormatter::MEDIUM;
const DATE_TYPE_SHORT  = IntlDateFormatter::SHORT;

const ERROR_UNABLE_TO_PARSE = 'ERROR: Unable to parse';
const ERROR_UNABLE_TO_FORMAT = 'ERROR: Unable to format date';
const ERROR_ARGS_STRING_ARRAY =
  'ERROR: Date must be string YYYY-mm-dd HH:ii:ss
  or array(y,m,d,h,i,s)';
const ERROR_CREATE_INTL_DATE_FMT =
  'ERROR: Unable to create international date formatter';

protected $dateFormatter;
```

3. After that, we are in a position to define a method, `getDateFormatter()`, which returns an `IntlDateFormatter` instance. The value of `$type` matches one of the `DATE_TYPE_*` constants defined previously:

```
public function getDateFormatter($type)
{
  switch ($type) {
    case self::DATE_TYPE_SHORT :
      $formatter = new IntlDateFormatter($this
        ->getLocaleCode(),
        IntlDateFormatter::SHORT,
        IntlDateFormatter::SHORT);
      break;
    case self::DATE_TYPE_MEDIUM :
      $formatter = new IntlDateFormatter($this
        ->getLocaleCode(),
        IntlDateFormatter::MEDIUM,
        IntlDateFormatter::MEDIUM);
      break;
    case self::DATE_TYPE_LONG :
      $formatter = new IntlDateFormatter($this
        ->getLocaleCode(),
        IntlDateFormatter::LONG,
        IntlDateFormatter::LONG);
      break;
    case self::DATE_TYPE_FULL :
      $formatter = new IntlDateFormatter($this
        ->getLocaleCode(),
        IntlDateFormatter::FULL,
        IntlDateFormatter::FULL);
```

```
        break;
      default :
        throw new
InvalidArgumentException(self::ERROR_CREATE_INTL_DATE_FMT);
    }
    $this->dateFormatter = $formatter;
    return $this->dateFormatter;
  }
```

4. Next we define a method that produces a locale formatted date. Defining the format of the incoming `$date` is a bit tricky. It cannot be locale-specific, otherwise we will need to parse it according to locale rules, with unpredictable results. A better strategy would be to accept an array of values that represent year, month, day, and so on as integers. As a fallback, we will accept a string but only in this format: `YYYY-mm-dd HH:ii:ss`. Time zone is optional, and can be set separately. First we initialize variables:

```
public function formatDate($date, $type, $timeZone = NULL)
{
  $result    = NULL;
  $year      = date('Y');
  $month     = date('m');
  $day       = date('d');
  $hour      = 0;
  $minutes   = 0;
  $seconds   = 0;
```

5. After that we produce a breakdown of values that represent year, month, day, and so on:

```
if (is_string($date)) {
  list($dateParts, $timeParts) = explode(' ', $date);
  list($year,$month,$day) = explode('-',$dateParts);
  list($hour,$minutes,$seconds) = explode(':',$timeParts);
} elseif (is_array($date)) {
  list($year,$month,$day,$hour,$minutes,$seconds) = $date;
} else {
  throw new InvalidArgumentException(self::ERROR_ARGS_STRING_
ARRAY);
}
```

6. Next we create an `IntlCalendar` instance, which will serve as an argument when running `format()`. We set the date using the discreet integer values:

```
$intlDate = IntlCalendar::createInstance($timeZone,
  $this->getLocaleCode());
$intlDate->set($year,$month,$day,$hour,$minutes,$seconds);
```

7. Finally, we obtain the date formatter instance, and produce the result:

```
    $formatter = $this->getDateFormatter($type);
    if ($timeZone) {
      $formatter->setTimeZone($timeZone);
    }
    $result = $formatter->format($intlDate);
    return $result ?? self::ERROR_UNABLE_TO_FORMAT;
  }
```

8. The `parseDate()` method is actually simpler than formatting. The only complication is what to do if the type is not specified (which will be the most likely case). All we need to do is to loop through all possible types (of which there are only four) until a result is produced:

```
public function parseDate($string, $type = NULL)
{
  if ($type) {
   $result = $this->getDateFormatter($type)->parse($string);
  } else {
   $tryThese = [self::DATE_TYPE_FULL,
     self::DATE_TYPE_LONG,
     self::DATE_TYPE_MEDIUM,
     self::DATE_TYPE_SHORT];
   foreach ($tryThese as $type) {
   $result = $this->getDateFormatter($type)->parse($string);
     if ($result) {
       break;
     }
   }
  }
  return ($result) ? $result : self::ERROR_UNABLE_TO_PARSE;
 }
```

How it works...

Code the changes to `Application\I18n\Locale`, discussed previously. You can then create a test file, `chap_08_formatting_date.php`, which sets up autoloading, and creates two instances of the `Locale` class, one for the USA, the other for France:

```
<?php
require __DIR__ . '/../Application/Autoload/Loader.php';
Application\Autoload\Loader::init(__DIR__ . '/..');
use Application\I18n\Locale;

$localeFr = new Locale('fr-FR');
$localeUs = new Locale('en_US');
$date     = '2016-02-29 17:23:58';
?>
```

Next, with suitable styling, run a test of `formatDate()` and `parseDate()`:

```
echo $localeFr->formatDate($date, Locale::DATE_TYPE_FULL);
echo $localeUs->formatDate($date, Locale::DATE_TYPE_MEDIUM);
$localeUs->parseDate($localeFr->formatDate($date, Locale::DATE_TYPE_
MEDIUM));
// etc.
```

An example of the output is shown here:

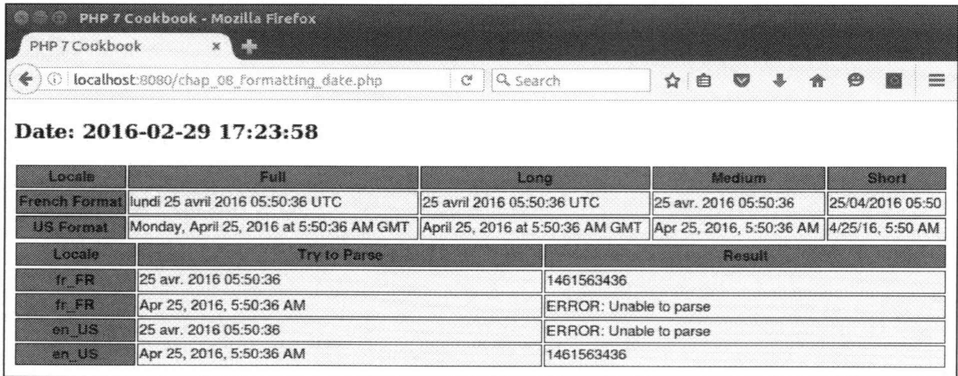

Date: 2016-02-29 17:23:58

Locale	Full	Long	Medium	Short
French Format	lundi 25 avril 2016 05:50:36 UTC	25 avril 2016 05:50:36 UTC	25 avr. 2016 05:50:36	25/04/2016 05:50
US Format	Monday, April 25, 2016 at 5:50:36 AM GMT	April 25, 2016 at 5:50:36 AM GMT	Apr 25, 2016, 5:50:36 AM	4/25/16, 5:50 AM

Locale	Try to Parse	Result
fr_FR	25 avr. 2016 05:50:36	1461563436
fr_FR	Apr 25, 2016, 5:50:36 AM	ERROR: Unable to parse
en_US	25 avr. 2016 05:50:36	ERROR: Unable to parse
en_US	Apr 25, 2016, 5:50:36 AM	1461563436

See also

- ISO 8601 gives precise definitions for all aspects of date and time. There is also an RFC that discusses the impact of ISO 8601 on the Internet. For reference, see `https://tools.ietf.org/html/rfc3339`. For a good overview of date formats by country, see `https://en.wikipedia.org/wiki/Date_format_by_country`.

Creating an HTML international calendar generator

Creating a program to display a calendar is something you would most likely do as a student at secondary school. A nested `for()` loop, where the inside loop generates a list of seven days, will generally suffice. Even the problem of how many days there are in the month is easily solved in the form of a simple array. Where it starts to get tricky is when you need to figure out, for any given year, on what day of the week does the 1st of January fall. Also, what if you want to represent the months and days of the week in a language and format acceptable to a specific locale? As you have probably guessed, we will build a solution using the previously discussed `Application\I18n\Locale` class.

How to do it...

1. First we need to create a generic class that will hold information for a single day. Initially it will only hold an integer value, `$dayOfMonth`. Later, in the next recipe, we'll expand it to include events. As the primary purpose of this class will be to yield `$dayOfMonth`, we'll incorporate this value into its constructor, and define `__invoke()` to return this value as well:

```
namespace Application\I18n;

class Day
{
  public $dayOfMonth;
  public function __construct($dayOfMonth)
  {
    $this->dayOfMonth = $dayOfMonth;
  }
  public function __invoke()
  {
    return $this->dayOfMonth ?? '';
  }
}
```

2. Create a new class that will hold the appropriate calendar-generation methods. It will accept an instance of `Application\I18n\Locale`, and will define a couple of class constants and properties. The format codes, such as `EEEEE` and `MMMM`, are drawn from ICU date formats:

```
namespace Application\I18n;

use IntlCalendar;

class Calendar
{

  const DAY_1 = 'EEEEE';  // T
  const DAY_2 = 'EEEEEE'; // Tu
  const DAY_3 = 'EEE';   // Tue
  const DAY_FULL = 'EEEE'; // Tuesday
  const MONTH_1 = 'MMMMM'; // M
  const MONTH_3 = 'MMM';  // Mar
  const MONTH_FULL = 'MMMM';  // March
  const DEFAULT_ACROSS = 3;
  const HEIGHT_FULL = '150px';
  const HEIGHT_SMALL = '60px';
```

```
    protected $locale;
    protected $dateFormatter;
    protected $yearArray;
    protected $height;

    public function __construct(Locale $locale)
    {
      $this->locale = $locale;
    }

      // other methods are discussed in the following bullets

  }
```

3. Then we define a method that returns an `IntlDateFormatter` instance from our `locale` class. This is stored in a class property, as it will be used frequently:

```
protected function getDateFormatter()
{
 if (!$this->dateFormatter) {
  $this->dateFormatter =
   $this->locale->getDateFormatter(Locale::DATE_TYPE_FULL);
 }
 return $this->dateFormatter;
}
```

4. Next we define a core method, `buildMonthArray()`, which creates a multi-dimensional array where the outer key is the week of the year, and the inner array is seven elements representing the days of the week. We accept the year, month, and optional time zone as arguments. Note, as part of variable initialization, we subtract 1 from the month. This is because the `IntlCalendar::set()` method expects a 0-based value for the month, where 0 represents January, 1 is February, and so on:

```
public function buildMonthArray($year, $month, $timeZone =
  NULL)
{
$month -= 1;
//IntlCalendar months are 0 based; Jan==0, Feb==1 and so on
  $day = 1;
  $first = TRUE;
  $value = 0;
  $monthArray = array();
```

5. We then create an `IntlCalendar` instance, and use it to determine how many days are in this month:

```
$cal = IntlCalendar::createInstance(
  $timeZone, $this->locale->getLocaleCode());
$cal->set($year, $month, $day);
$maxDaysInMonth = $cal
  ->getActualMaximum(IntlCalendar::FIELD_DAY_OF_MONTH);
```

6. After that we use our `IntlDateFormatter` instance to determine what day of the week equates to the 1st of this month. After that, we set the pattern to `w`, which will subsequently give us the week number:

```
$formatter = $this->getDateFormatter();
$formatter->setPattern('e');
$firstDayIsWhatDow = $formatter->format($cal);
```

7. We are now ready to loop through all days in the month with nested loops. An outer `while()` loop ensures we don't go past the end of the month. The inner loop represents the days of the week. You will note that we take advantage of `IntlCalendar::get()`, which allows us to retrieve values from a wide range of predefined fields. We also adjust the week of the year value to 0 if it exceeds 52:

```
while ($day <= $maxDaysInMonth) {
  for ($dow = 1; $dow <= 7; $dow++) {
    $cal->set($year, $month, $day);
    $weekOfYear = $cal
      ->get(IntlCalendar::FIELD_WEEK_OF_YEAR);
    if ($weekOfYear > 52) $weekOfYear = 0;
```

8. We then check to see whether `$first` is still set `TRUE`. If so, we start adding day numbers to the array. Otherwise, the array value is set to `NULL`. We then close all open statements and return the array. Note that we also need to make sure the inner loop doesn't go past the number of days in the month, hence the extra `if()` statement in the outer `else` clause.

Note that instead of just storing the value for the day of the month, we use the newly defined `Application\I18n\Day` class.

```
      if ($first) {
        if ($dow == $firstDayIsWhatDow) {
          $first = FALSE;
          $value = $day++;
        } else {
          $value = NULL;
        }
      } else {
```

```
            if ($day <= $maxDaysInMonth) {
              $value = $day++;
            } else {
              $value = NULL;
            }
          }
          $monthArray[$weekOfYear][$dow] = new Day($value);
        }
      }
      return $monthArray;
    }
```

Refining internationalized output

1. First, a series of small methods, starting with one that extracts the internationally formatted day based on type. The type determines whether we deliver the full name of the day, an abbreviation, or just a single letter, all appropriate for that locale:

   ```
   protected function getDay($type, $cal)
   {
     $formatter = $this->getDateFormatter();
     $formatter->setPattern($type);
     return $formatter->format($cal);
   }
   ```

2. Next we need a method that returns an HTML row of day names, calling the newly defined `getDay()` method. As mentioned previous, the type dictates the appearance of the days:

   ```
   protected function getWeekHeaderRow($type, $cal, $year, $month,
   $week)
   {
     $output = '<tr>';
     $width  = (int) (100/7);
     foreach ($week as $day) {
       $cal->set($year, $month, $day());
       $output .= '<th style="vertical-align:top;"
         width="' . $width . '%">'
         . $this->getDay($type, $cal) . '</th>';
     }
     $output .= '</tr>' . PHP_EOL;
     return $output;
   }
   ```

3. After that, we define a very simple method to return a row of week dates. Note that we take advantage of `Day::__invoke()` using: `$day()`:

```
protected function getWeekDaysRow($week)
{
  $output = '<tr style="height:' . $this->height . ';">';
  $width  = (int) (100/7);
  foreach ($week as $day) {
    $output .= '<td style="vertical-align:top;"
      width="' . $width . '%">'
      . $day() .  '</td>';
  }
  $output .= '</tr>' . PHP_EOL;
  return $output;
}
```

4. And finally, a method that puts the smaller methods together to generate a calendar for a single month. First we build the month array, but only if `$yearArray` is not already available:

```
public function calendarForMonth($year,
    $month,
    $timeZone = NULL,
    $dayType = self::DAY_3,
    $monthType = self::MONTH_FULL,
    $monthArray = NULL)
{
  $first = 0;
  if (!$monthArray)
    $monthArray = $this->yearArray[$year][$month]
    ?? $this->buildMonthArray($year, $month, $timeZone);
```

5. The month needs to be decremented by `1` as `IntlCalendar` months are 0-based: Jan = 0, Feb = 1, and so on. We then build an `IntlCalendar` instance using the time zone (if any), and the locale. We next create a `IntlDateFormatter` instance to retrieve the month name and other information according to locale:

```
  $month--;
  $cal = IntlCalendar::createInstance(
    $timeZone, $this->locale->getLocaleCode());
  $cal->set($year, $month, 1);
  $formatter = $this->getDateFormatter();
  $formatter->setPattern($monthType);
```

6. We then loop through the month array, and call the smaller methods just mentioned to build the final output:

   ```
   $this->height = ($dayType == self::DAY_FULL)
      ? self::HEIGHT_FULL : self::HEIGHT_SMALL;
   $html = '<h1>' . $formatter->format($cal) . '</h1>';
   $header = '';
   $body   = '';
   foreach ($monthArray as $weekNum => $week) {
     if ($first++ == 1) {
       $header .= $this->getWeekHeaderRow(
         $dayType, $cal, $year, $month, $week);
     }
     $body .= $this->getWeekDaysRow($dayType, $week);
   }
   $html .= '<table>' . $header . $body .
     '</table>' . PHP_EOL;
   return $html;
   }
   ```

7. In order to generate a calendar for the entire year, it's a simple matter of looping through months 1 to 12. To facilitate outside access, we first define a method that builds a year array:

   ```
   public function buildYearArray($year, $timeZone = NULL)
   {
     $this->yearArray = array();
     for ($month = 1; $month <= 12; $month++) {
       $this->yearArray[$year][$month] =
         $this->buildMonthArray($year, $month, $timeZone);
     }
     return $this->yearArray;
   }

   public function getYearArray()
   {
     return $this->yearArray;
   }
   ```

8. To generate a calendar for a year, we define a method, `calendarForYear()`. If the year array has not been build, we call `buildYearArray()`. We take into account how many monthly calendars we wish to display across and then call `calendarForMonth()`:

   ```
   public function calendarForYear($year,
     $timeZone = NULL,
     $dayType = self::DAY_1,
   ```

```
    $monthType = self::MONTH_3,
    $across = self::DEFAULT_ACROSS)
  {
    if (!$this->yearArray) $this->buildYearArray($year,
      $timeZone);
    $yMax = (int) (12 / $across);
    $width = (int) (100 / $across);
    $output = '<table>' . PHP_EOL;
    $month = 1;
    for ($y = 1; $y <= $yMax; $y++) {
      $output .= '<tr>';
      for ($x = 1; $x <= $across; $x++) {
        $output .= '<td style="vertical-align:top;"
          width="' . $width . '%">'
          . $this->calendarForMonth($year, $month,
          $timeZone, $dayType, $monthType,
          $this->yearArray[$year][$month++]) . '</td>';
      }
      $output .= '</tr>' . PHP_EOL;
    }
    $output .= '</table>';
    return $output;
  }
```

How it works...

First of all, make sure you build the `Application\I18n\Locale` class as defined in the previous recipe. After that, create a new file, `Calendar.php`, in the `Application\I18n` folder, with all the methods described in this recipe.

Next, define a calling program, `chap_08_html_calendar.php`, which sets up autoloading and creates `Locale` and `Calendar` instances. Also be sure to define the year and month:

```
<?php
require __DIR__ . '/../Application/Autoload/Loader.php';
Application\Autoload\Loader::init(__DIR__ . '/..');
use Application\I18n\Locale;
use Application\I18n\Calendar;

$localeFr = new Locale('fr-FR');
$localeUs = new Locale('en_US');
$localeTh = new Locale('th_TH');
$calendarFr = new Calendar($localeFr);
$calendarUs = new Calendar($localeUs);
$calendarTh = new Calendar($localeTh);
$year = 2016;
$month = 1;
?>
```

You can then develop appropriate view logic to display the different calendars. For example, you can include parameters to display the full month and day names:

```
<!DOCTYPE html>
<html>
  <head>
  <title>PHP 7 Cookbook</title>
  <meta http-equiv="content-type"
    content="text/html;charset=utf-8" />
  <link rel="stylesheet" type="text/css"
    href="php7cookbook_html_table.css">
  </head>
  <body>
    <h3>Year: <?= $year ?></h3>
    <?= $calendarFr->calendarForMonth($year, $month, NULL,
      Calendar::DAY_FULL); ?>
    <?= $calendarUs->calendarForMonth($year, $month, NULL,
      Calendar::DAY_FULL); ?>
    <?= $calendarTh->calendarForMonth($year, $month, NULL,
      Calendar::DAY_FULL); ?>
  </body>
</html>
```

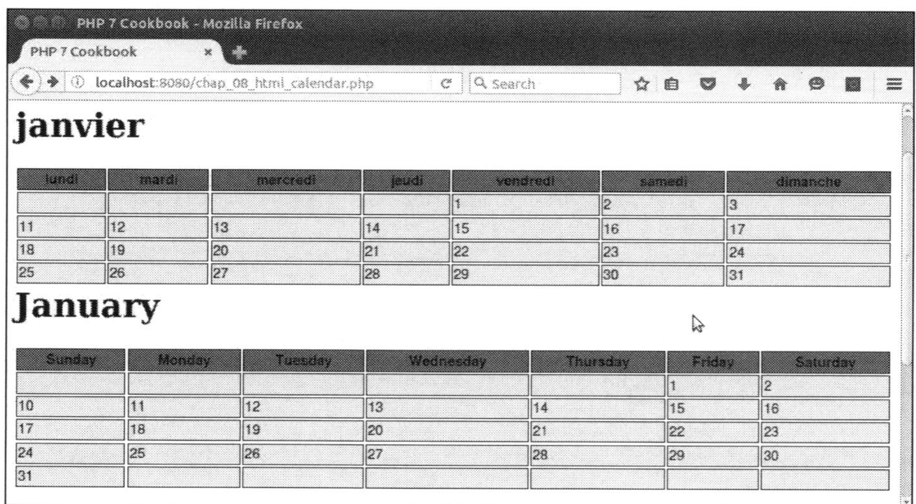

With a couple of modifications, you can also display a calendar for the entire year:

```
$localeTh = new Locale('th_TH');
$localeEs = new Locale('es_ES');
$calendarTh = new Calendar($localeTh);
```

```
$calendarEs = new Calendar($localeEs);
$year = 2016;
echo $calendarTh->calendarForYear($year);
echo $calendarEs->calendarForYear($year);
```

Here is the browser output showing a full year calendar in Spanish:

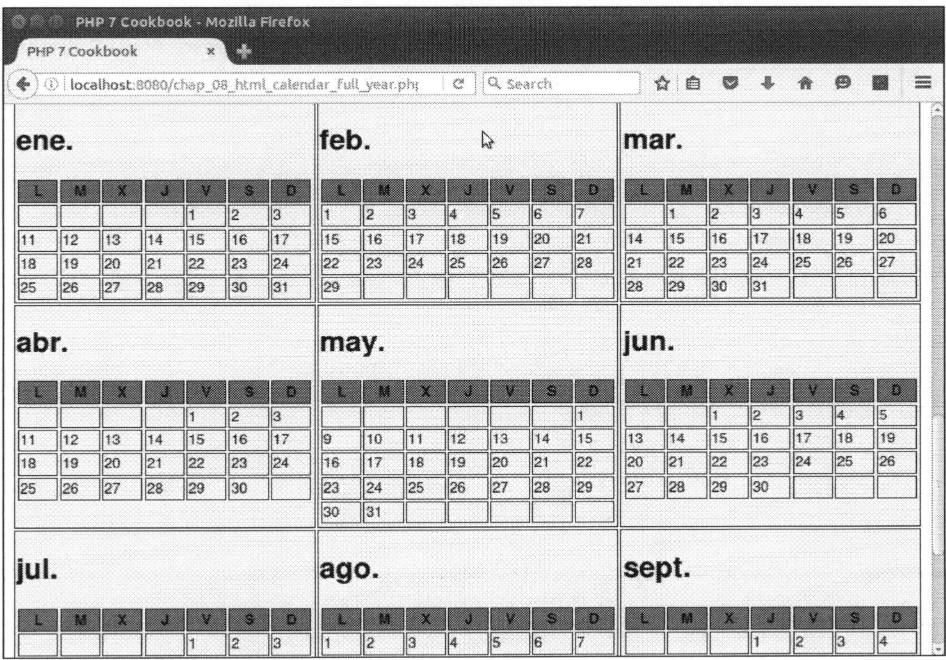

See also

- For more information on codes used by `IntlDateFormatter::setPattern()`, see this article: `http://userguide.icu-project.org/formatparse/datetime`

Building a recurring events generator

A very common need related to generating a calendar is the scheduling of events. Events can be in the form of *one-off* events, which take place on one day, or on a weekend. There is a much greater need, however, to track events that are *recurring*. We need to account for the start date, the recurring interval (daily, weekly, monthly), and the number of occurrences or a specific end date.

How to do it...

1. Before anything else, it would be an excellent idea to create a class that represents an event. Ultimately you'll probably end up storing the data in such a class in a database. For this illustration, however, we will simply define the class, and leave the database aspect to your imagination. You will notice that we will use a number of classes included in the `DateTime` extension admirably suited to event generation:

```
namespace Application\I18n;

use DateTime;
use DatePeriod;
use DateInterval;
use InvalidArgumentException;

class Event
{
  // code
}
```

2. Next, we define a series of useful class constants and properties. You will notice that we defined most of the properties `public` in order to economize on the number of getters and setters needed. The intervals are defined as `sprintf()` format strings; `%d` will be substituted for a value:

```
const INTERVAL_DAY = 'P%dD';
const INTERVAL_WEEK = 'P%dW';
const INTERVAL_MONTH = 'P%dM';
const FLAG_FIRST = 'FIRST';     // 1st of the month
const ERROR_INVALID_END  = 'Need to supply either # occurrences or
an end date';
const ERROR_INVALID_DATE = 'String i.e. YYYY-mm-dd or DateTime
instance only';
const ERROR_INVALID_INTERVAL = 'Interval must take the form "P\
d+(D | W | M)"';

public $id;
public $flag;
public $value;
public $title;
public $locale;
public $interval;
public $description;
public $occurrences;
public $nextDate;
protected $endDate;
protected $startDate;
```

3. Next we turn our attention to the constructor. We need to collect and set all information pertinent to an event. The variable names are self-explanatory.

> `$value` is not quite so clear. This parameter will ultimately be substituted for the value in the interval format string. So, for example, if the user selects `$interval` as `INTERVAL_DAY`, and `$value` as `2`, the resulting interval string will be `P2D`, which means every other day (or every 2nd day).

```
public function __construct($title,
    $description,
    $startDate,
    $interval,
    $value,
    $occurrences = NULL,
    $endDate = NULL,
    $flag = NULL)
{
```

4. We then initialize variables. Note that the ID is pseudo-randomly generated, but might ultimately end up being the primary key in a database `events` table. Here we use `md5()` not for security purposes, but rather to quickly generate a hash so that IDs have a consistent appearance:

```
$this->id = md5($title . $interval . $value) . sprintf('%04d',
rand(0,9999));
$this->flag = $flag;
$this->value = $value;
$this->title = $title;
$this->description = $description;
$this->occurrences = $occurrences;
```

5. As mentioned previously, the interval parameter is a `sprintf()` pattern used to construct a proper `DateInterval` instance:

```
try {
  $this->interval = new DateInterval(sprintf($interval, $value));
  } catch (Exception $e) {
  error_log($e->getMessage());
  throw new InvalidArgumentException(self::ERROR_INVALID_
INTERVAL);
}
```

6. To initialize `$startDate`, we call `stringOrDate()`. We then attempt to generate a value for `$endDate` by calling either `stringOrDate()` or `calcEndDateFromOccurrences()`. If we have neither an end date nor a number of occurrences, an exception is thrown:

   ```
     $this->startDate = $this->stringOrDate($startDate);
     if ($endDate) {
       $this->endDate = $this->stringOrDate($endDate);
     } elseif ($occurrences) {
       $this->endDate = $this->calcEndDateFromOccurrences();
     } else {
     throw new InvalidArgumentException(self::ERROR_INVALID_END);
     }
     $this->nextDate = $this->startDate;
   }
   ```

7. The `stringOrDate()` method consists of a few lines of code that check the data type of the date variable, and return a `DateTime` instance or `NULL`:

   ```
   protected function stringOrDate($date)
   {
     if ($date === NULL) {
       $newDate = NULL;
     } elseif ($date instanceof DateTime) {
       $newDate = $date;
     } elseif (is_string($date)) {
       $newDate = new DateTime($date);
     } else {
       throw new InvalidArgumentException(self::ERROR_INVALID_END);
     }
     return $newDate;
   }
   ```

8. We call the `calcEndDateFromOccurrences()` method from the constructor if `$occurrences` is set so that we'll know the end date for this event. We take advantage of the `DatePeriod` class, which provides an iteration based on a start date, `DateInterval`, and number of occurrences:

   ```
   protected function calcEndDateFromOccurrences()
   {
     $endDate = new DateTime('now');
     $period = new DatePeriod(
   $this->startDate, $this->interval, $this->occurrences);
     foreach ($period as $date) {
       $endDate = $date;
     }
     return $endDate;
   }
   ```

9. Next we throw in a `__toString()` magic method, which simple echoes the title of the event:

```
public function __toString()
{
  return $this->title;
}
```

10. The last method we need to define for our `Event` class is `getNextDate()`, which is used when generating a calendar:

```
public function  getNextDate(DateTime $today)
{
  if ($today > $this->endDate) {
    return FALSE;
  }
  $next = clone $today;
  $next->add($this->interval);
  return $next;
}
```

11. Next we turn our attention to the `Application\I18n\Calendar` class described in the previous recipe. With a bit of minor surgery, we are ready to tie our newly defined `Event` class into the calendar. First we add a new property, `$events`, and a method to add events in the form of an array. We use the `Event::$id` property to make sure events are merged and not overwritten:

```
protected $events = array();
public function addEvent(Event $event)
{
  $this->events[$event->id] = $event;
}
```

12. Next we add a method, `processEvents()`, which adds an `Event` instance to a `Day` object when building the year calendar. First we check to see whether there are any events, and whether or not the `Day` object is `NULL`. As you may recall, it's likely that the first day of the month doesn't fall on the first day of the week, and thus the need to set the value of a `Day` object to `NULL`. We certainly do not want to add events to a non-operative day! We then call `Event::getNextDate()` and see whether the dates match. If so, we store the `Event` into `Day::$events[]` and set the next date on the `Event` object:

```
protected function processEvents($dayObj, $cal)
{
  if ($this->events && $dayObj()) {
    $calDateTime = $cal->toDateTime();
    foreach ($this->events as $id => $eventObj) {
      $next = $eventObj->getNextDate($eventObj->nextDate);
```

```
          if ($next) {
            if ($calDateTime->format('Y-m-d') ==
                $eventObj->nextDate->format('Y-m-d')) {
              $dayObj->events[$eventObj->id] = $eventObj;
              $eventObj->nextDate = $next;
            }
          }
        }
      }
      return $dayObj;
    }
```

> Note that we do not do a direct comparison of the two objects. Two reasons for this: first of all, one is a `DateTime` instance, the other is an `IntlCalendar` instance. The other, more compelling reason, is that it's possible that hours:minutes:seconds were included when the `DateTime` instance was obtained, resulting in actual value differences between the two objects.

13. Now we need to add a call to `processEvents()` in the `buildMonthArray()` method so that it looks like this:

```
    while ($day <= $maxDaysInMonth) {
      for ($dow = 1; $dow <= 7; $dow++) {
        // add this to the existing code:
        $dayObj = $this->processEvents(new Day($value), $cal);
        $monthArray[$weekOfYear][$dow] = $dayObj;
      }
    }
```

14. Finally, we need to modify `getWeekDaysRow()`, adding the necessary code to output event information inside the box along with the date:

```
protected function getWeekDaysRow($type, $week)
{
  $output = '<tr style="height:' . $this->height . ';">';
  $width  = (int) (100/7);
  foreach ($week as $day) {
    $events = '';
    if ($day->events) {
      foreach ($day->events as $single) {
        $events .= '<br>' . $single->title;
        if ($type == self::DAY_FULL) {
          $events .= '<br><i>' . $single->description . '</i>';
        }
```

```
          }
        }
        $output .= '<td style="vertical-align:top;"
          width="' . $width . '%">'
      . $day() . $events . '</td>';
      }
      $output .= '</tr>' . PHP_EOL;
      return $output;
    }
```

How it works...

To tie events to the calendar, first code the `Application\I18n\Event` class described in steps 1 to 10. Next, modify `Application\I18n\Calendar` as described in steps 11 to 14. You can then create a test script, `chap_08_recurring_events.php`, which sets up autoloading and creates `Locale` and `Calendar` instances. For the purposes of illustration, go ahead and use '`es_ES`' as a locale:

```
<?php
require __DIR__ . '/../Application/Autoload/Loader.php';
Application\Autoload\Loader::init(__DIR__ . '/..');
use Application\I18n\ { Locale, Calendar, Event };

try {
  $year = 2016;
  $localeEs = new Locale('es_ES');
  $calendarEs = new Calendar($localeEs);
```

Now we can start defining and adding events to the calendar. The first example adds an event that lasts 3 days and starts on 8 January 2016:

```
  // add event: 3 days
  $title = 'Conf';
  $description = 'Special 3 day symposium on eco-waste';
  $startDate = '2016-01-08';
  $event = new Event($title, $description, $startDate,
                     Event::INTERVAL_DAY, 1, 2);
  $calendarEs->addEvent($event);
```

Here is another example, an event that occurs on the first of every month until September 2017:

```
$title = 'Pay Rent';
$description = 'Sent rent check to landlord';
$startDate = new DateTime('2016-02-01');
$event = new Event($title, $description, $startDate,
  Event::INTERVAL_MONTH, 1, '2017-09-01', NULL, Event::FLAG_FIRST);
$calendarEs->addEvent($event);
```

You can then add sample weekly, bi-weekly, monthly, and so on events as desired. You can then close the `try...catch` block, and produce suitable display logic:

```
} catch (Throwable $e) {
  $message = $e->getMessage();
}
?>
<!DOCTYPE html>
<head>
  <title>PHP 7 Cookbook</title>
  <meta http-equiv="content-type" content="text/html;charset=utf-8" />
  <link rel="stylesheet" type="text/css" href="php7cookbook_html_
table.css">
</head>
<body>
<h3>Year: <?= $year ?></h3>
<?= $calendarEs->calendarForYear($year, 'Europe/Berlin',
    Calendar::DAY_3, Calendar::MONTH_FULL, 2); ?>
<?= $calendarEs->calendarForMonth($year, 1  , 'Europe/Berlin',
    Calendar::DAY_FULL); ?>
</body>
</html>
```

Here is the output showing the first few months of the year:

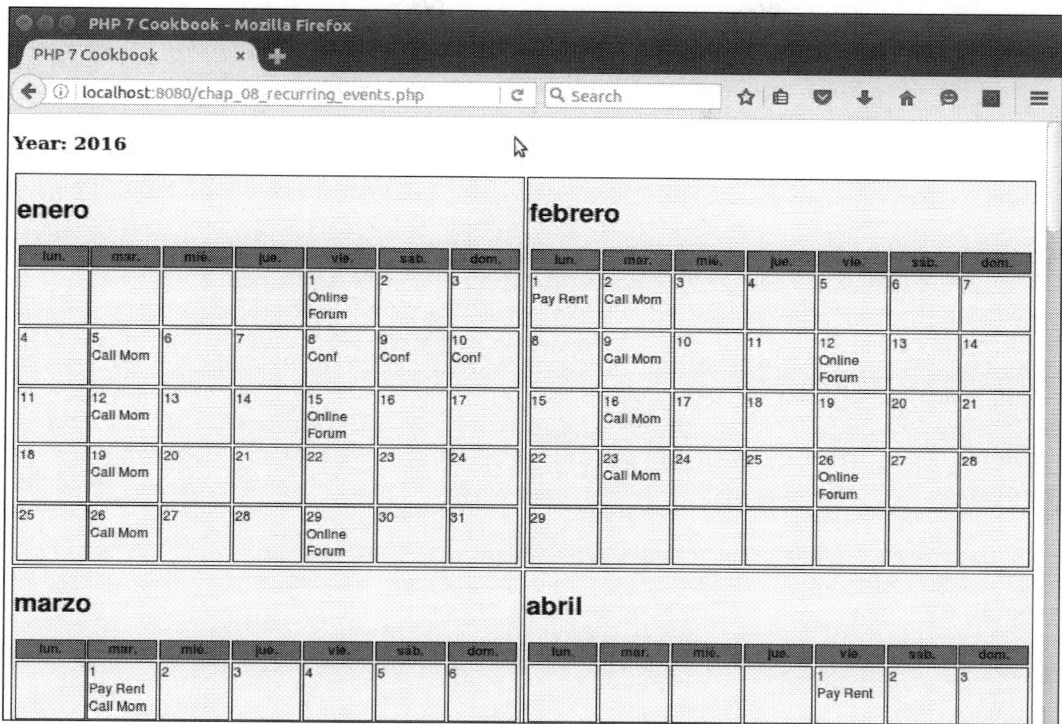

See also

- For more information on `IntlCalendar` field constants that can be used with `get()`, please refer to this page: `http://php.net/manual/en/class.intlcalendar.php#intlcalendar.constants`

Handling translation without gettext

Translation is an important part of making your website accessible to an international customer base. One way this is accomplished it to use the PHP `gettext` functions, which are based on the **GNU** `gettext` operating system tools installed on the local server. `gettext` is well documented and well supported, but uses a legacy approach and has distinct disadvantages. Accordingly, in this recipe, we present an alternative approach to translation where you can build your own *adapter*.

Something important to recognize is that the programmatic translation tools available to PHP are primarily designed to provide limited translation of a word or phrase, referred to as the **msgid** (**message ID**). The translated equivalent is referred to as the **msgstr** (**message string**). Accordingly, incorporating translation typically only involves relatively unchanging items such as menus, forms, error or success messages, and so on. For the purposes of this recipe, we will assume that you have the actual web page translations stored as blocks of text.

If you need to translate entire pages of content, you might consider using the *Google Translate API*. This is, however, a paid service. Alternatively, you could outsource the translation to individuals with multi-lingual skills cheaply using *Amazon Mechanical Turk*. See the *See Also* section at the end of this recipe for the URLs.

How to do it...

1. We will once again use the Adapter software design pattern, in this case to provide alternatives to the translation source. In this recipe, we will demonstrate adapters for `.ini` files, `.csv` files, and databases.
2. To begin, we will define an interface that will later be used to identify a translation adapter. The requirements for a translation adapter are quite simple, we only need to return a message string for a given message ID:

```
namespace Application\I18n\Translate\Adapter;
interface TranslateAdapterInterface
{
  public function translate($msgid);
}
```

3. Next we define a trait that matches the interface. The trait will contain the actual code required. Note that if we fail to find the message string, we simply return the message ID:

```
namespace Application\I18n\Translate\Adapter;

trait TranslateAdapterTrait
{
  protected $translation;
  public function translate($msgid)
  {
    return $this->translation[$msgid] ?? $msgid;
  }
}
```

4. Now we're ready to define our first adapter. In this recipe, we'll start with an adapter that uses an `.ini` file as the source of translations. The first thing you'll notice is that we use the trait defined previously. The constructor method will vary between adapters. In this case, we use `parse_ini_file()` to produce an array of key/value pairs where the key is the message ID. Notice that we use the `$filePattern` parameter to substitute the locale, which then allows us to load the appropriate translation file:

```
namespace Application\I18n\Translate\Adapter;

use Exception;
use Application\I18n\Locale;

class Ini implements TranslateAdapterInterface
{
  use TranslateAdapterTrait;
  const ERROR_NOT_FOUND = 'Translation file not found';
  public function __construct(Locale $locale, $filePattern)
  {
    $translateFileName = sprintf($filePattern,
                                 $locale->getLocaleCode());
    if (!file_exists($translateFileName)) {
      error_log(self::ERROR_NOT_FOUND . ':' . $translateFileName);
      throw new Exception(self::ERROR_NOT_FOUND);
    } else {
      $this->translation = parse_ini_file($translateFileName);
    }
  }
}
```

5. The next adapter, `Application\I18n\Translate\Adapter\Csv`, is identical, except that we open the translation file and loop through using `fgetcsv()` to retrieve the message ID / message string key pairs. Here we show only the difference in the constructor:

```
public function __construct(Locale $locale, $filePattern)
{
  $translateFileName = sprintf($filePattern,
    $locale->getLocaleCode());
  if (!file_exists($translateFileName)) {
    error_log(self::ERROR_NOT_FOUND . ':' . $translateFileName);
    throw new Exception(self::ERROR_NOT_FOUND);
  } else {
    $fileObj = new SplFileObject($translateFileName, 'r');
    while ($row = $fileObj->fgetcsv()) {
      $this->translation[$row[0]] = $row[1];
```

```
        }
    }
}
```

The big disadvantage of both of these adapters is that we need to preload the entire translation set, which puts a strain on memory if there is a large number of translations. Also, the translation file needs to be opened and parsed, which drags down performance.

6. We now present the third adapter, which performs a database lookup and avoids the problems of the other two adapters. We use a `PDO` prepared statement which is sent to the database in the beginning, and only one time. We then execute as many times as needed, supplying the message ID as an argument. You will also notice that we needed to override the `translate()` method defined in the trait. Finally, you might have noticed the use of `PDOStatement::fetchColumn()` as we only need the one value:

```
namespace Application\I18n\Translate\Adapter;

use Exception;
use Application\Database\Connection;
use Application\I18n\Locale;

class Database implements TranslateAdapterInterface
{
  use TranslateAdapterTrait;
  protected $connection;
  protected $statement;
  protected $defaultLocaleCode;
  public function __construct(Locale $locale,
                              Connection $connection,
                              $tableName)
  {
    $this->defaultLocaleCode = $locale->getLocaleCode();
    $this->connection = $connection;
    $sql = 'SELECT msgstr FROM ' . $tableName
        . ' WHERE localeCode = ? AND msgid = ?';
    $this->statement = $this->connection->pdo->prepare($sql);
  }
  public function translate($msgid, $localeCode = NULL)
  {
    if (!$localeCode) $localeCode = $this->defaultLocaleCode;
    $this->statement->execute([$localeCode, $msgid]);
    return $this->statement->fetchColumn();
  }
}
```

7. We are now ready to define the core `Translation` class, which is tied to one (or more) adapters. We assign a class constant to represent the default locale, and properties for the locale, adapter, and text file pattern (explained later):

```
namespace Application\I18n\Translate;

use Application\I18n\Locale;
use Application\I18n\Translate\Adapter\TranslateAdapterInterface;

class Translation
{
  const DEFAULT_LOCALE_CODE = 'en_GB';
  protected $defaultLocaleCode;
  protected $adapter = array();
  protected $textFilePattern = array();
```

8. In the constructor, we determine the locale, and set the initial adapter to this locale. In this manner, we are able to host multiple adapters:

```
public function __construct(TranslateAdapterInterface $adapter,
              $defaultLocaleCode = NULL,
              $textFilePattern = NULL)
{
  if (!$defaultLocaleCode) {
    $this->defaultLocaleCode = self::DEFAULT_LOCALE_CODE;
  } else {
    $this->defaultLocaleCode = $defaultLocaleCode;
  }
  $this->adapter[$this->defaultLocaleCode] = $adapter;
  $this->textFilePattern[$this->defaultLocaleCode] =
$textFilePattern;
}
```

9. Next we define a series of setters, which gives us more flexibility:

```
public function setAdapter($localeCode, TranslateAdapterInterface
$adapter)
{
  $this->adapter[$localeCode] = $adapter;
}
public function setDefaultLocaleCode($localeCode)
{
  $this->defaultLocaleCode = $localeCode;
}
public function setTextFilePattern($localeCode, $pattern)
{
  $this->textFilePattern[$localeCode] = $pattern;
}
```

10. We then define the PHP magic method `__invoke()`, which lets us make a direct call to the translator instance, returning the message string given the message ID:

```
public function __invoke($msgid, $locale = NULL)
{
  if ($locale === NULL) $locale = $this->defaultLocaleCode;
  return $this->adapter[$locale]->translate($msgid);
}
```

11. Finally, we also add a method that can return translated blocks of text from text files. Bear in mind that this could be modified to use a database instead. We did not include this functionality in the adapter, as its purpose is completely different; we just want to return large blocks of code given a key, which could conceivably be the filename of the translated text file:

```
public function text($key, $localeCode = NULL)
{
  if ($localeCode === NULL) $localeCode =
      $this->defaultLocaleCode;
  $contents = $key;
  if (isset($this->textFilePattern[$localeCode])) {
    $fn = sprintf($this->textFilePattern[$localeCode],
                  $localeCode, $key);
    if (file_exists($fn)) {
      $contents = file_get_contents($fn);
    }
  }
  return $contents;
}
```

How it works...

First you will need to define a directory structure to house the translation files. For the purposes of this illustration, you can make a directory ,`/path/to/project/files/data/languages`. Under this directory structure, create sub-directories that represent different locales. For this illustration, you could use these: `de_DE`, `fr_FR`, `en_GB`, and `es_ES`, representing German, French, English, and Spanish.

Next you will need to create the different translation files. As an example, here is a representative `data/languages/es_ES/translation.ini` file in Spanish:

```
Welcome=Bienvenido
About Us=Sobre Nosotros
Contact Us=Contáctenos
Find Us=Encontrarnos
click=clic para más información
```

Likewise, to demonstrate the CSV adapter, create the same thing as a CSV file, `data/languages/es_ES/translation.csv`:

```
"Welcome","Bienvenido"
"About Us","Sobre Nosotros"
"Contact Us","Contáctenos"
"Find Us","Encontrarnos"
"click","clic para más información"
```

Finally, create a database table, `translation`, and populate it with the same data. The main difference is that the database table will have three fields: `msgid`, `msgstr`, and `locale_code`:

```
CREATE TABLE `translation` (
  `msgid` varchar(255) NOT NULL,
  `msgstr` varchar(255) NOT NULL,
  `locale_code` char(6) NOT NULL DEFAULT '',
  PRIMARY KEY (`msgid`,`locale_code`)
) ENGINE=InnoDB DEFAULT CHARSET=latin1;
```

Next, define the classes mentioned previously, using the code shown in this recipe:

- `Application\I18n\Translate\Adapter\TranslateAdapterInterface`
- `Application\I18n\Translate\Adapter\TranslateAdapterTrait`
- `Application\I18n\Translate\Adapter\Ini`
- `Application\I18n\Translate\Adapter\Csv`
- `Application\I18n\Translate\Adapter\Database`
- `Application\I18n\Translate\Translation`

Now you can create a test file, `chap_08_translation_database.php`, to test the database translation adapter. It should implement autoloading, use the appropriate classes, and create a `Locale` and `Connection` instance. Note that the `TEXT_FILE_PATTERN` constant is a `sprintf()` pattern in which the locale code and filename are substituted:

```
<?php
define('DB_CONFIG_FILE', '/../config/db.config.php');
define('TEXT_FILE_PATTERN', __DIR__ . '/../data/languages/%s/%s.txt');
require __DIR__ . '/../Application/Autoload/Loader.php';
Application\Autoload\Loader::init(__DIR__ . '/..');
use Application\I18n\Locale;
use Application\I18n\Translate\ { Translation, Adapter\Database };
use Application\Database\Connection;

$conn = new Connection(include __DIR__ . DB_CONFIG_FILE);
$locale = new Locale('fr_FR');
```

Next, create a translation adapter instance and use that to create a `Translation` instance:

```
$adapter = new Database($locale, $conn, 'translation');
$translate = new Translation($adapter, $locale->getLocaleCode(), TEXT_
FILE_PATTERN);
?>
```

Finally, create display logic that uses the `$translate` instance:

```
<!DOCTYPE html>
<head>
  <title>PHP 7 Cookbook</title>
  <meta http-equiv="content-type" content="text/html;charset=utf-8" />
  <link rel="stylesheet" type="text/css" href="php7cookbook_html_
table.css">
</head>
<body>
<table>
<tr>
  <th><h1 style="color:white;"><?= $translate('Welcome') ?></h1></th>
  <td>
    <div style="float:left;width:50%;vertical-align:middle;">
    <h3 style="font-size:24pt;"><i>Some Company, Inc.</i></h3>
    </div>
    <div style="float:right;width:50%;">
    <img src="jcartier-city.png" width="300px"/>
    </div>
  </td>
</tr>
<tr>
  <th>
    <ul>
      <li><?= $translate('About Us') ?></li>
      <li><?= $translate('Contact Us') ?></li>
      <li><?= $translate('Find Us') ?></li>
    </ul>
  </th>
  <td>
    <p>
    <?= $translate->text('main_page'); ?>
    </p>
    <p>
    <a href="#"><?= $translate('click') ?></a>
    </p>
  </td>
</tr>
</table>
</body>
</html>
```

You can then perform additional similar tests, substituting a new locale to get a different language, or using another adapter to test a different data source. Here is an example of output using a locale of `fr_FR` and the database translation adapter:

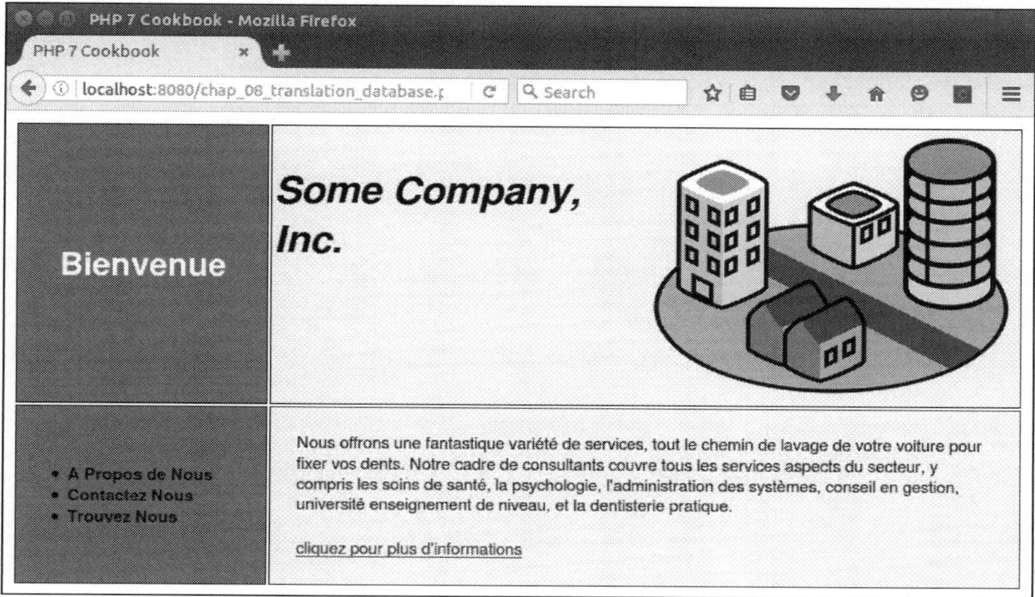

See also

- For more information on the Google Translation API, see `https://cloud.google.com/translate/v2/translating-text-with-rest`.
- For more information on Amazon Mechanical Turk, see `https://www.mturk.com/mturk/welcome`. For more information on `gettext`, see `http://www.gnu.org/software/gettext/manual/gettext.html`.

9
Developing Middleware

In this chapter, we will cover the following topics:

- Authenticating with middleware
- Using middleware to implement access control
- Improving performance using the cache
- Implementing routing
- Making inter-framework system calls
- Using middleware to cross languages

Introduction

As often happens in the IT industry, terms get invented, and then used and abused. The term **middleware** is no exception. Arguably the first use of the term came out of the **Internet Engineering Task Force** (**IETF**) in the year 2000. Originally, the term was applied to any software which operates between the transport (that is, TCP/IP) and the application layer. More recently, especially with the acceptance of **PHP Standard Recommendation number 7** (**PSR-7**), middleware, specifically in the PHP world, has been applied to the web client-server environment.

The recipes in this section will make use of the concrete classes defined in *Appendix, Defining PSR-7 Classes*.

Authenticating with middleware

One very important usage of middleware is to provide authentication. Most web-based applications need the ability to verify a visitor via username and password. By incorporating PSR-7 standards into an authentication class, you will make it generically useful across the board, so to speak, being secure enough that it can be used in any framework that provides PSR-7-compliant request and response objects.

How to do it...

1. We begin by defining an `Application\Acl\AuthenticateInterface` class. We use this interface to support the Adapter software design pattern, making our `Authenticate` class more generically useful by allowing a variety of adapters, each of which can draw authentication from a different source (for example, from a file, using OAuth2, and so on). Note the use of the PHP 7 ability to define the return value data type:

```
namespace Application\Acl;
use Psr\Http\Message\ { RequestInterface, ResponseInterface };
interface AuthenticateInterface
{
  public function login(RequestInterface $request) :
    ResponseInterface;
}
```

Note that by defining a method that requires a PSR-7-compliant request, and produces a PSR-7-compliant response, we have made this interface universally applicable.

2. Next, we define the adapter that implements the `login()` method required by the interface. We make sure to use the appropriate classes, and define fitting constants and properties. The constructor makes use of `Application\Database\Connection`, defined in *Chapter 5, Interacting with a Database*:

```
namespace Application\Acl;
use PDO;
use Application\Database\Connection;
use Psr\Http\Message\ { RequestInterface, ResponseInterface };
use Application\MiddleWare\ { Response, TextStream };
class DbTable  implements AuthenticateInterface
```

```
{
  const ERROR_AUTH = 'ERROR: authentication error';
  protected $conn;
  protected $table;
  public function __construct(Connection $conn, $tableName)
  {
    $this->conn = $conn;
    $this->table = $tableName;
  }
```

3. The core `login()` method extracts the username and password from the request object. We then do a straightforward database lookup. If there is a match, we store user information in the response body, JSON-encoded:

```
public function login(RequestInterface $request) :
  ResponseInterface
{
  $code = 401;
  $info = FALSE;
  $body = new TextStream(self::ERROR_AUTH);
  $params = json_decode($request->getBody()->getContents());
  $response = new Response();
  $username = $params->username ?? FALSE;
  if ($username) {
      $sql = 'SELECT * FROM ' . $this->table
         . ' WHERE email = ?';
      $stmt = $this->conn->pdo->prepare($sql);
      $stmt->execute([$username]);
      $row = $stmt->fetch(PDO::FETCH_ASSOC);
      if ($row) {
          if (password_verify($params->password,
              $row['password'])) {
                unset($row['password']);
                $body =
                new TextStream(json_encode($row));
                $response->withBody($body);
                $code = 202;
                $info = $row;
              }
          }
        }
        return $response->withBody($body)->withStatus($code);
      }
    }
```

Best practice

Never store passwords in clear text. When you need to do a password match, use `password_verify()`, which negates the need to reproduce the password hash.

4. The `Authenticate` class is a wrapper for an adapter class that implements `AuthenticationInterface`. Accordingly, the constructor takes an adapter class as an argument, as well as a string that serves as the key, in which authentication information is stored in `$_SESSION`:

```
namespace Application\Acl;
use Application\MiddleWare\ { Response, TextStream };
use Psr\Http\Message\ { RequestInterface, ResponseInterface };
class Authenticate
{
  const ERROR_AUTH = 'ERROR: invalid token';
  const DEFAULT_KEY = 'auth';
  protected $adapter;
  protected $token;
  public function __construct(
  AuthenticateInterface $adapter, $key)
  {
    $this->key = $key;
    $this->adapter = $adapter;
  }
```

5. In addition, we provide a login form with a security token, which helps prevent **Cross Site Request Forgery** (**CSRF**) attacks:

```
public function getToken()
{
  $this->token = bin2hex(random_bytes(16));
  $_SESSION['token'] = $this->token;
  return $this->token;
}
public function matchToken($token)
{
  $sessToken = $_SESSION['token'] ?? date('Ymd');
  return ($token == $sessToken);
}
public function getLoginForm($action = NULL)
{
  $action = ($action) ? 'action="' . $action . '" ' : '';
```

```
    $output = '<form method="post" ' . $action . '>';
    $output .= '<table><tr><th>Username</th><td>';
    $output .= '<input type="text" name="username" /></td>';
    $output .= '</tr><tr><th>Password</th><td>';
    $output .= '<input type="password" name="password" />';
    $output .= '</td></tr><tr><th> </th>';
    $output .= '<td><input type="submit" /></td>';
    $output .= '</tr></table>';
    $output .= '<input type="hidden" name="token" value="';
    $output .= $this->getToken() . '" />';
    $output .= '</form>';
    return $output;
  }
```

6. Finally, the `login()` method in this class checks whether the token is valid. If not, a 400 response is returned. Otherwise, the `login()` method of the adapter is called:

```
public function login(
RequestInterface $request) : ResponseInterface
{
  $params = json_decode($request->getBody()->getContents());
  $token = $params->token ?? FALSE;
  if (!($token && $this->matchToken($token))) {
      $code = 400;
      $body = new TextStream(self::ERROR_AUTH);
      $response = new Response($code, $body);
  } else {
      $response = $this->adapter->login($request);
  }
  if ($response->getStatusCode() >= 200
      && $response->getStatusCode() < 300) {
      $_SESSION[$this->key] =
        json_decode($response->getBody()->getContents());
  } else {
      $_SESSION[$this->key] = NULL;
  }
  return $response;
}

}
```

How it works...

First of all, be sure to follow the recipes defined in *Appendix*, *Defining PSR-7 Classes*. Next, go ahead and define the classes presented in this recipe, summarized in the following table:

Class	Discussed in these steps
`Application\Acl\AuthenticateInterface`	1
`Application\Acl\DbTable`	2-3
`Application\Acl\Authenticate`	4-6

You can then define a `chap_09_middleware_authenticate.php` calling program that sets up autoloading and uses the appropriate classes:

```
<?php
session_start();
define('DB_CONFIG_FILE', __DIR__ . '/../config/db.config.php');
define('DB_TABLE', 'customer_09');
define('SESSION_KEY', 'auth');
require __DIR__ . '/../Application/Autoload/Loader.php';
Application\Autoload\Loader::init(__DIR__ . '/..');

use Application\Database\Connection;
use Application\Acl\ { DbTable, Authenticate };
use Application\MiddleWare\ { ServerRequest, Request, Constants,
TextStream };
```

You are now in a position to set up the authentication adapter and core class:

```
$conn   = new Connection(include DB_CONFIG_FILE);
$dbAuth = new DbTable($conn, DB_TABLE);
$auth   = new Authenticate($dbAuth, SESSION_KEY);
```

Be sure to initialize the incoming request, and set up the request to be made to the authentication class:

```
$incoming = new ServerRequest();
$incoming->initialize();
$outbound = new Request();
```

Check the incoming class method to see if it is `POST`. If so, pass a request to the authentication class:

```
if ($incoming->getMethod() == Constants::METHOD_POST) {
  $body = new TextStream(json_encode(
```

```
    $incoming->getParsedBody()));
    $response = $auth->login($outbound->withBody($body));
}
$action = $incoming->getServerParams()['PHP_SELF'];
?>
```

The display logic looks like this:

```
<?= $auth->getLoginForm($action) ?>
```

Here is the output from an invalid authentication attempt. Notice the `401` status code on the right. In this illustration, you could add a `var_dump()` of the response object:

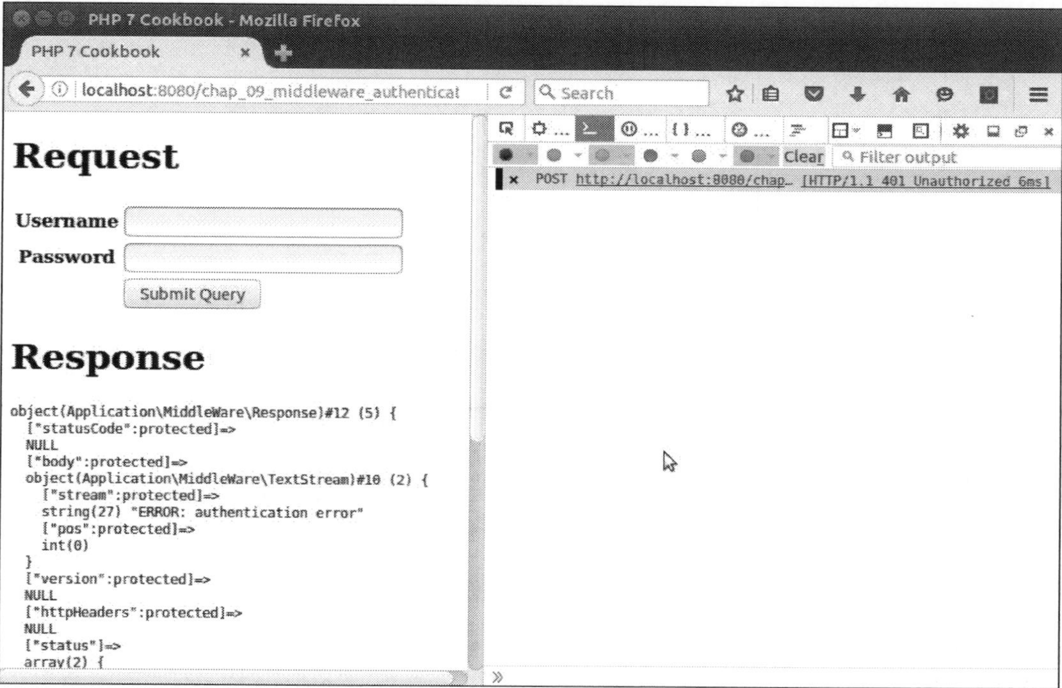

Here is a successful authentication:

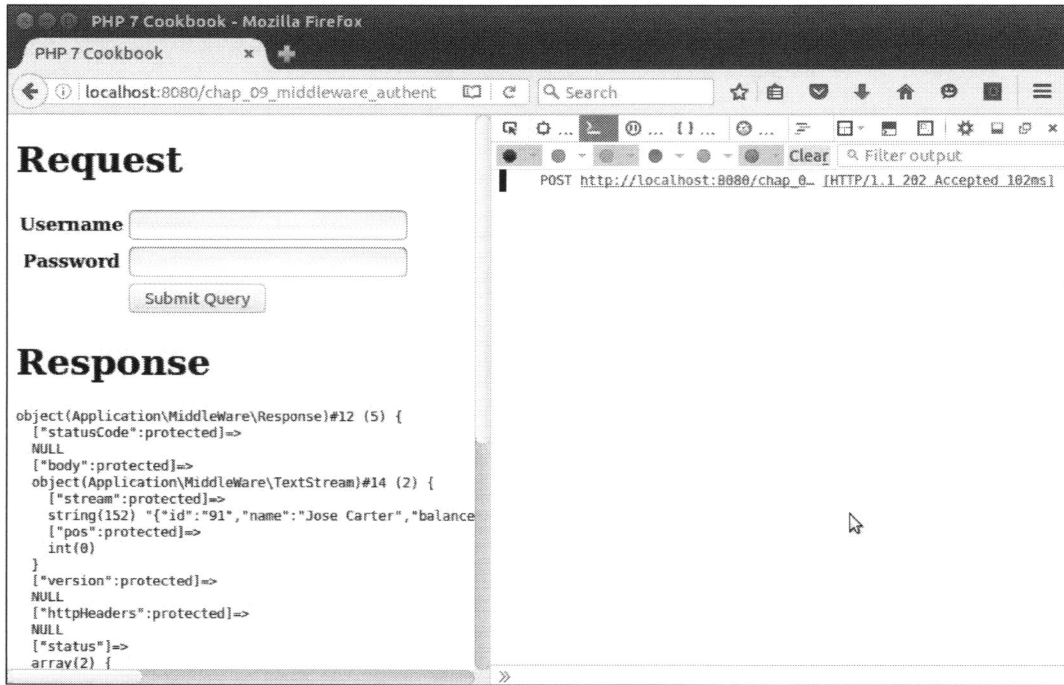

See also

For guidance on how to avoid CSRF and other attacks, please see *Chapter 12, Improving Web Security*.

Using middleware to implement access control

As the name implies, middleware sits in the middle of a sequence of function or method calls. Accordingly, middleware is well suited for the task of "gate keeper". You can easily implement an **Access Control List** (**ACL**) mechanism with a middleware class that reads the ACL, and allows or denies access to the next function or method call in the sequence.

How to do it...

1. Probably the most difficult part of the process is determining which factors to include in the ACL. For the purposes of illustration, let's say that our users are all assigned a `level` and a `status`. In this illustration, the level is defined as follows:

```
'levels' => [0, 'BEG', 'INT', 'ADV']
```

2. The status could indicate how far they are in the membership signup process. For example, a status of `0` could indicate they've initiated the membership signup process, but have not yet been confirmed. A status of `1` could indicate their e-mail address is confirmed, but they have not paid the monthly fee, and so on.
3. Next, we need to define the resources we plan to control. In this case, we will assume there is a need to control access to a series of web pages on the site. Accordingly, we need to define an array of such resources. In the ACL, we can then refer to the key:

```
'pages'   => [0 => 'sorry', 'logout' => 'logout',
              'login'  => 'auth',
              1 => 'page1', 2 => 'page2', 3 => 'page3',
              4 => 'page4', 5 => 'page5', 6 => 'page6',
              7 => 'page7', 8 => 'page8', 9 => 'page9']
```

4. Finally, the most important piece of configuration is to make assignments to pages according to `level` and `status`. The generic template used in the configuration array might look like this:

```
status => ['inherits' => <key>, 'pages' => [level =>
           [pages allowed], etc.]]
```

5. Now we are in a position to define the `Acl` class. As before, we use a few classes, and define constants and properties appropriate for access control:

```
namespace Application\Acl;

use InvalidArgumentException;
use Psr\Http\Message\RequestInterface;
use Application\MiddleWare\ { Constants, Response, TextStream };

class Acl
{
  const DEFAULT_STATUS = '';
  const DEFAULT_LEVEL  = 0;
  const DEFAULT_PAGE   = 0;
  const ERROR_ACL = 'ERROR: authorization error';
  const ERROR_APP = 'ERROR: requested page not listed';
```

```
  const ERROR_DEF =
    'ERROR: must assign keys "levels", "pages" and "allowed"';
  protected $default;
  protected $levels;
  protected $pages;
  protected $allowed;
```

6. In the `__construct()` method, we break up the assignments array into `$pages`, the resources to be controlled, `$levels`, and `$allowed`, which are the actual assignments. If the array does not include one of these three sub-components, an exception is thrown:

```
public function __construct(array $assignments)
{
  $this->default = $assignments['default']
    ?? self::DEFAULT_PAGE;
  $this->pages   = $assignments['pages'] ?? FALSE;
  $this->levels  = $assignments['levels'] ?? FALSE;
  $this->allowed = $assignments['allowed'] ?? FALSE;
  if (!($this->pages && $this->levels && $this->allowed)) {
      throw new InvalidArgumentException(self::ERROR_DEF);
  }
}
```

7. You may have noticed that we allow inheritance. In `$allowed`, the `inherits` key can be set to another key within the array. If so, we need to merge its values with the values currently under examination. We iterate through `$allowed` in reverse, merging any inherited values each time through the loop. This method, incidentally, also only isolates rules that apply to a certain `status` and `level`:

```
protected function mergeInherited($status, $level)
{
  $allowed = $this->allowed[$status]['pages'][$level]
    ?? array();
  for ($x = $status; $x > 0; $x--) {
    $inherits = $this->allowed[$x]['inherits'];
    if ($inherits) {
        $subArray =
          $this->allowed[$inherits]['pages'][$level]
          ?? array();
        $allowed = array_merge($allowed, $subArray);
    }
  }
  return $allowed;
}
```

8. When processing authorization, we initialize a few variables, and then extract the page requested from the original request URI. If the page parameter doesn't exist, we set a `400` code:

```
public function isAuthorized(RequestInterface $request)
{
  $code = 401;    // unauthorized
  $text['page'] = $this->pages[$this->default];
  $text['authorized'] = FALSE;
  $page = $request->getUri()->getQueryParams()['page']
    ?? FALSE;
  if ($page === FALSE) {
      $code = 400;    // bad request
```

9. Otherwise, we decode the request body contents, and acquire the `status` and `level`. We are then in a position to call `mergeInherited()`, which returns an array of pages accessible to this `status` and `level`:

```
} else {
    $params = json_decode(
      $request->getBody()->getContents());
    $status = $params->status ?? self::DEFAULT_LEVEL;
    $level  = $params->level  ?? '*';
    $allowed = $this->mergeInherited($status, $level);
```

10. If the requested page is in the `$allowed` array, we set the status code to a happy `200`, and return an authorized setting along with the web page that corresponds to the page code requested:

```
if (in_array($page, $allowed)) {
    $code = 200;    // OK
    $text['authorized'] = TRUE;
    $text['page'] = $this->pages[$page];
} else {
    $code = 401;            }
}
```

11. We then return the response, JSON-encoded, and we are done:

```
$body = new TextStream(json_encode($text));
return (new Response())->withStatus($code)
->withBody($body);
}

}
```

How it works...

After that, you will need to define `Application\Acl\Acl`, which is discussed in this recipe. Now move to the `/path/to/source/for/this/chapter` folder and create two directories: `public` and `pages`. In `pages`, create a series of PHP files, such as `page1.php`, `page2.php`, and so on. Here is an example of how one of these pages might look:

```
<?php // page 1 ?>
<h1>Page 1</h1>
<hr>
<p>Lorem ipsum dolor sit amet, consectetur adipiscing elit. etc.</p>
```

You can also define a `menu.php` page, which could be included in the output:

```
<?php // menu ?>
<a href="?page=1">Page 1</a>
<a href="?page=2">Page 2</a>
<a href="?page=3">Page 3</a>
// etc.
```

The `logout.php` page should destroy the session:

```
<?php
  $_SESSION['info'] = FALSE;
  session_destroy();
?>
<a href="/">BACK</a>
```

The `auth.php` page will display a login screen (as described in the previous recipe):

```
<?= $auth->getLoginForm($action) ?>
```

You can then create a configuration file that allows access to web pages depending on level and status. For the sake of illustration, call it `chap_09_middleware_acl_config.php` and return an array that might look like this:

```
<?php
$min = [0, 'logout'];
return [
  'default' => 0,     // default page
  'levels' => [0, 'BEG', 'INT', 'ADV'],
  'pages'  => [0 => 'sorry',
  'logout' => 'logout',
  'login' => 'auth',
             1 => 'page1', 2 => 'page2', 3 => 'page3',
             4 => 'page4', 5 => 'page5', 6 => 'page6',
```

```
                7 => 'page7', 8 => 'page8', 9 => 'page9'],
    'allowed' => [
                0 => ['inherits' => FALSE,
                      'pages' => [ '*' => $min, 'BEG' => $min,
                      'INT' => $min,'ADV' => $min]],
                1 => ['inherits' => FALSE,
                      'pages' => ['*' => ['logout'],
                     'BEG' => [1, 'logout'],
                     'INT' => [1,2, 'logout'],
                     'ADV' => [1,2,3, 'logout']]],
                2 => ['inherits' => 1,
                      'pages' => ['BEG' => [4],
                      'INT' => [4,5],
                      'ADV' => [4,5,6]]],
                3 => ['inherits' => 2,
                      'pages' => ['BEG' => [7],
                      'INT' => [7,8],
                      'ADV' => [7,8,9]]]
    ]
];
```

Finally, in the `public` folder, define `index.php`, which sets up autoloading, and ultimately calls up both the `Authenticate` and `Acl` classes. As with other recipes, define configuration files, set up autoloading, and use certain classes. Also, don't forget to start the session:

```
<?php
session_start();
session_regenerate_id();
define('DB_CONFIG_FILE', __DIR__ . '/../../config/db.config.php');
define('DB_TABLE', 'customer_09');
define('PAGE_DIR', __DIR__ . '/../pages');
define('SESSION_KEY', 'auth');
require __DIR__ . '/../../Application/Autoload/Loader.php';
Application\Autoload\Loader::init(__DIR__ . '/../..');

use Application\Database\Connection;
use Application\Acl\ { Authenticate, Acl };
use Application\MiddleWare\ { ServerRequest, Request, Constants,
  TextStream };
```

Best practice

It is a best practice to protect your sessions. An easy way to help protect a session is to use `session_regenerate_id()`, which invalidates the existing PHP session identifier and generates a new one. Thus, if an attacker were to obtain the session identifier through illegal means, the window of time in which any given session identifier is valid is kept to a minimum.

You can now pull in the ACL configuration, and create instances for `Authenticate` as well as `Acl`:

```
$config = require __DIR__ . '/../chap_09_middleware_acl_config.php';
$acl    = new Acl($config);
$conn   = new Connection(include DB_CONFIG_FILE);
$dbAuth = new DbTable($conn, DB_TABLE);
$auth   = new Authenticate($dbAuth, SESSION_KEY);
```

Next, define incoming and outbound request instances:

```
$incoming = new ServerRequest();
$incoming->initialize();
$outbound = new Request();
```

If the incoming request method was `post`, process the authentication calling the `login()` method:

```
if (strtolower($incoming->getMethod()) == Constants::METHOD_POST) {
    $body = new TextStream(json_encode(
    $incoming->getParsedBody()));
    $response = $auth->login($outbound->withBody($body));
}
```

If the session key defined for authentication is populated, that means the user has been successfully authenticated. If not, we program an anonymous function, called **later**, which includes the authentication login page:

```
$info = $_SESSION[SESSION_KEY] ?? FALSE;
if (!$info) {
    $execute = function () use ($auth) {
      include PAGE_DIR . '/auth.php';
    };
```

Otherwise, you can proceed with the ACL check. You first need to find, from the original query, which web page the user wants to visit, however:

```
} else {
    $query = $incoming->getServerParams()['QUERY_STRING'] ?? '';
```

You can then reprogram the `$outbound` request to include this information:

```
$outbound->withBody(new TextStream(json_encode($info)));
$outbound->getUri()->withQuery($query);
```

Next, you'll be in a position to check authorization, supplying the outbound request as an argument:

```
$response = $acl->isAuthorized($outbound);
```

You can then examine the return response for the `authorized` parameter, and program an anonymous function to include the return `page` parameter if OK, and the `sorry` page otherwise:

```
$params    = json_decode($response->getBody()->getContents());
$isAllowed = $params->authorized ?? FALSE;
if ($isAllowed) {
    $execute = function () use ($response, $params) {
      include PAGE_DIR .'/' . $params->page . '.php';
      echo '<pre>', var_dump($response), '</pre>';
      echo '<pre>', var_dump($_SESSION[SESSION_KEY]);
      echo '</pre>';
    };
} else {
    $execute = function () use ($response) {
      include PAGE_DIR .'/sorry.php';
      echo '<pre>', var_dump($response), '</pre>';
      echo '<pre>', var_dump($_SESSION[SESSION_KEY]);
      echo '</pre>';
    };
}
}
```

Now all you need to do is to set the form action and wrap the anonymous function in HTML:

```
$action = $incoming->getServerParams()['PHP_SELF'];
?>
<!DOCTYPE html>
<head>
  <title>PHP 7 Cookbook</title>
  <meta http-equiv="content-type" content="text/html;charset=utf-8" />
</head>
<body>
  <?php $execute(); ?>
</body>
</html>
```

To test it, you can use the built-in PHP web server, but you will need to use the `-t` flag to indicate that the document root is `public`:

```
cd /path/to/source/for/this/chapter
php -S localhost:8080 -t public
```

From a browser, you can access the `http://localhost:8080/` URL.

If you try to access any page, you will simply be redirected back to the login page. As per the configuration, a user with status = `1`, and level = `BEG` can only access page `1` and log out. If, when logged in as this user, you try to access page 2, here is the output:

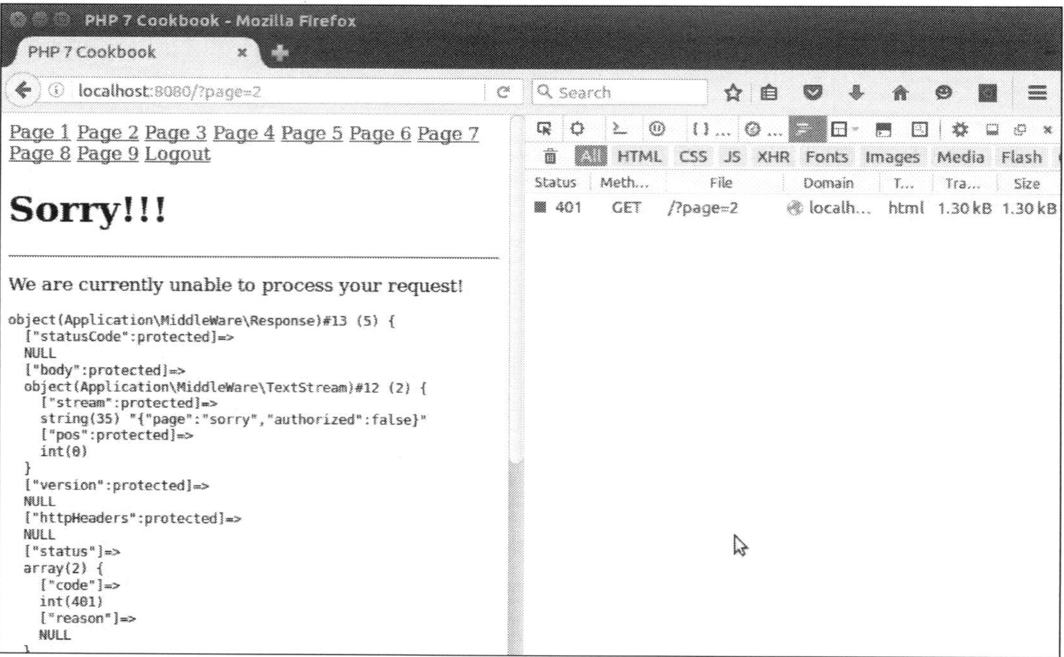

See also

This example relies on `$_SESSION` as the sole means of user authentication once they have logged in. For good examples of how you can protect PHP sessions, please see *Chapter 12, Improving Web Security*, specifically the recipe entitled *Safeguarding the PHP session*.

Improving performance using the cache

The cache software design pattern is where you store a result that takes a long time to generate. This could take the form of a lengthy view script or a complex database query. The storage destination needs to be highly performant, of course, if you wish to improve the user experience of website visitors. As different installations will have different potential storage targets, the cache mechanism lends itself to the adapter pattern as well. Examples of potential storage destinations include memory, a database, and the filesystem.

How to do it...

1. As with a couple of other recipes in this chapter, as there are shared constants, we define a discreet `Application\Cache\Constants` class:

```
<?php
namespace Application\Cache;

class Constants
{
  const DEFAULT_GROUP  = 'default';
  const DEFAULT_PREFIX = 'CACHE_';
  const DEFAULT_SUFFIX = '.cache';
  const ERROR_GET      = 'ERROR: unable to retrieve from cache';
  // not all constants are shown to conserve space
}
```

2. Seeing as we are following the adapter design pattern, we define an interface next:

```
namespace Application\Cache;
interface  CacheAdapterInterface
{
  public function hasKey($key);
  public function getFromCache($key, $group);
  public function saveToCache($key, $data, $group);
  public function removeByKey($key);
  public function removeByGroup($group);
}
```

3. Now we are ready to define our first cache adapter, in this illustration, by using a MySQL database. We need to define properties that will hold column names as well as prepared statements:

```
namespace Application\Cache;
use PDO;
use Application\Database\Connection;
```

```
class Database implements CacheAdapterInterface
{
  protected $sql;
  protected $connection;
  protected $table;
  protected $dataColumnName;
  protected $keyColumnName;
  protected $groupColumnName;
  protected $statementHasKey       = NULL;
  protected $statementGetFromCache = NULL;
  protected $statementSaveToCache  = NULL;
  protected $statementRemoveByKey  = NULL;
  protected $statementRemoveByGroup= NULL;
```

4. The constructor allows us to provide key column names as well as an `Application\Database\Connection` instance and the name of the table used for the cache:

```
public function __construct(Connection $connection,
  $table,
  $idColumnName,
  $keyColumnName,
  $dataColumnName,
  $groupColumnName = Constants::DEFAULT_GROUP)
  {
    $this->connection  = $connection;
    $this->setTable($table);
    $this->setIdColumnName($idColumnName);
    $this->setDataColumnName($dataColumnName);
    $this->setKeyColumnName($keyColumnName);
    $this->setGroupColumnName($groupColumnName);
  }
```

5. The next few methods prepare statements, and are called when we access the database. We do not show all the methods, but present enough to give you the idea:

```
public function prepareHasKey()
{
  $sql = 'SELECT `' . $this->idColumnName . '` '
  . 'FROM `'    . $this->table . '` '
  . 'WHERE `'   . $this->keyColumnName . '` = :key ';
  $this->sql[__METHOD__] = $sql;
  $this->statementHasKey =
  $this->connection->pdo->prepare($sql);
}
public function prepareGetFromCache()
```

```
{
  $sql = 'SELECT `' . $this->dataColumnName . '` '
  . 'FROM `'    . $this->table . '` '
  . 'WHERE `'   . $this->keyColumnName . '` = :key '
  . 'AND `'     . $this->groupColumnName . '` = :group';
  $this->sql[__METHOD__] = $sql;
  $this->statementGetFromCache =
  $this->connection->pdo->prepare($sql);
}
```

6. Now we define a method that determines whether data for a given key exists:

```
public function hasKey($key)
{
  $result = 0;
  try {
      if (!$this->statementHasKey) $this->prepareHasKey();
          $this->statementHasKey->execute(['key' => $key]);
  } catch (Throwable $e) {
      error_log(__METHOD__ . ':' . $e->getMessage());
      throw new Exception(Constants::ERROR_REMOVE_KEY);
  }
  return (int) $this->statementHasKey
  ->fetch(PDO::FETCH_ASSOC)[$this->idColumnName];
}
```

7. The core methods are ones that read from and write to the cache. Here is the method that retrieves from the cache. All we need to do is to execute the prepared statement, which performs a `SELECT`, with a `WHERE` clause, which incorporates the key and group:

```
public function getFromCache(
$key, $group = Constants::DEFAULT_GROUP)
{
  try {
      if (!$this->statementGetFromCache)
          $this->prepareGetFromCache();
          $this->statementGetFromCache->execute(
            ['key' => $key, 'group' => $group]);
          while ($row = $this->statementGetFromCache
            ->fetch(PDO::FETCH_ASSOC)) {
            if ($row && count($row)) {
                yield unserialize($row[$this->dataColumnName]);
            }
          }
```

```
        } catch (Throwable $e) {
            error_log(__METHOD__ . ':' . $e->getMessage());
            throw new Exception(Constants::ERROR_GET);
        }
    }
```

8. When writing to the cache, we first determine whether an entry for this cache key exists. If so, we perform an `UPDATE`; otherwise, we perform an `INSERT`:

```
public function saveToCache($key, $data,
                            $group = Constants::DEFAULT_GROUP)
{
  $id = $this->hasKey($key);
  $result = 0;
  try {
      if ($id) {
          if (!$this->statementUpdateCache)
              $this->prepareUpdateCache();
              $result = $this->statementUpdateCache
              ->execute(['key' => $key,
              'data' => serialize($data),
              'group' => $group,
              'id' => $id]);
          } else {
              if (!$this->statementSaveToCache)
              $this->prepareSaveToCache();
              $result = $this->statementSaveToCache
              ->execute(['key' => $key,
              'data' => serialize($data),
              'group' => $group]);
          }
      } catch (Throwable $e) {
          error_log(__METHOD__ . ':' . $e->getMessage());
          throw new Exception(Constants::ERROR_SAVE);
      }
      return $result;
  }
```

9. We then define two methods that remove the cache either by key or by group. Removal by group provides a convenient mechanism if there are a large number of items that need to be deleted:

```
public function removeByKey($key)
{
  $result = 0;
  try {
```

```
        if (!$this->statementRemoveByKey)
        $this->prepareRemoveByKey();
        $result = $this->statementRemoveByKey->execute(
          ['key' => $key]);
    } catch (Throwable $e) {
        error_log(__METHOD__ . ':' . $e->getMessage());
        throw new Exception(Constants::ERROR_REMOVE_KEY);
    }
    return $result;
  }

  public function removeByGroup($group)
  {
    $result = 0;
    try {
        if (!$this->statementRemoveByGroup)
            $this->prepareRemoveByGroup();
            $result = $this->statementRemoveByGroup->execute(
              ['group' => $group]);
        } catch (Throwable $e) {
            error_log(__METHOD__ . ':' . $e->getMessage());
            throw new Exception(Constants::ERROR_REMOVE_GROUP);
        }
        return $result;
    }
```

10. Lastly, we define getters and setters for each of the properties. Not all are shown here to conserve space:

```
public function setTable($name)
{
  $this->table = $name;
}
public function getTable()
{
  return $this->table;
}
// etc.
}
```

11. The filesystem cache adapter defines the same methods as defined earlier. Note the use of `md5()`, not for security, but as a way of quickly generating a text string from the key:

```
namespace Application\Cache;
use RecursiveIteratorIterator;
```

```
use RecursiveDirectoryIterator;
class File implements CacheAdapterInterface
{
  protected $dir;
  protected $prefix;
  protected $suffix;
  public function __construct(
    $dir, $prefix = NULL, $suffix = NULL)
  {
    if (!file_exists($dir)) {
        error_log(__METHOD__ . ':' . Constants::ERROR_DIR_NOT);
        throw new Exception(Constants::ERROR_DIR_NOT);
    }
    $this->dir = $dir;
    $this->prefix = $prefix ?? Constants::DEFAULT_PREFIX;
    $this->suffix = $suffix ?? Constants::DEFAULT_SUFFIX;
  }

  public function hasKey($key)
  {
    $action = function ($name, $md5Key, &$item) {
      if (strpos($name, $md5Key) !== FALSE) {
        $item ++;
      }
    };

    return $this->findKey($key, $action);
  }

  public function getFromCache($key,
                              $group = Constants::DEFAULT_GROUP)
  {
    $fn = $this->dir . '/' . $group . '/'
    . $this->prefix . md5($key) . $this->suffix;
    if (file_exists($fn)) {
        foreach (file($fn) as $line) { yield $line; }
    } else {
        return array();
    }
  }

  public function saveToCache(
    $key, $data, $group = Constants::DEFAULT_GROUP)
  {
```

```
    $baseDir = $this->dir . '/' . $group;
    if (!file_exists($baseDir)) mkdir($baseDir);
    $fn = $baseDir . '/' . $this->prefix . md5($key)
    . $this->suffix;
    return file_put_contents($fn, json_encode($data));
  }

  protected function findKey($key, callable $action)
  {
    $md5Key = md5($key);
    $iterator = new RecursiveIteratorIterator(
      new RecursiveDirectoryIterator($this->dir),
      RecursiveIteratorIterator::SELF_FIRST);
      $item = 0;
    foreach ($iterator as $name => $obj) {
      $action($name, $md5Key, $item);
    }
    return $item;
  }

  public function removeByKey($key)
  {
    $action = function ($name, $md5Key, &$item) {
      if (strpos($name, $md5Key) !== FALSE) {
        unlink($name);
        $item++;
      }
    };
    return $this->findKey($key, $action);
  }

  public function removeByGroup($group)
  {
    $removed = 0;
    $baseDir = $this->dir . '/' . $group;
    $pattern = $baseDir . '/' . $this->prefix . '*'
    . $this->suffix;
    foreach (glob($pattern) as $file) {
      unlink($file);
      $removed++;
    }
    return $removed;
  }
}
```

12. Now we are ready to present the core cache mechanism. In the constructor, we accept a class that implements `CacheAdapterInterface` as an argument:

    ```
    namespace Application\Cache;
    use Psr\Http\Message\RequestInterface;
    use Application\MiddleWare\ { Request, Response, TextStream };
    class Core
    {
      public function __construct(CacheAdapterInterface $adapter)
      {
        $this->adapter = $adapter;
      }
    ```

13. Next are a series of wrapper methods that call methods of the same name from the adapter, but accept a `Psr\Http\Message\RequestInterface` class an an argument, and return a `Psr\Http\Message\ResponseInterface` as a response. We start with a simple one: `hasKey()`. Note how we extract the `key` from the request parameters:

    ```
    public function hasKey(RequestInterface $request)
    {
      $key = $request->getUri()->getQueryParams()['key'] ?? '';
      $result = $this->adapter->hasKey($key);
    }
    ```

14. To retrieve information from the cache, we need to pull the key and group parameters from the request object, and then call the same method from the adapter. If no results are obtained, we set a `204` code, which indicates the request was a success, but no content was produced. Otherwise, we set a `200` (success) code, and iterate through the results. Everything is then stuffed into a response object, which is returned:

    ```
    public function getFromCache(RequestInterface $request)
    {
      $text = array();
      $key = $request->getUri()->getQueryParams()['key'] ?? '';
      $group = $request->getUri()->getQueryParams()['group']
        ?? Constants::DEFAULT_GROUP;
      $results = $this->adapter->getFromCache($key, $group);
      if (!$results) {
          $code = 204;
      } else {
          $code = 200;
          foreach ($results as $line) $text[] = $line;
      }
    ```

```
    if (!$text || count($text) == 0) $code = 204;
    $body = new TextStream(json_encode($text));
    return (new Response())->withStatus($code)
                           ->withBody($body);
}
```

15. Strangely, writing to the cache is almost identical, except that the results are expected to be either a number (that is, the number of rows affected), or a Boolean result:

```
public function saveToCache(RequestInterface $request)
{
  $text = array();
  $key = $request->getUri()->getQueryParams()['key'] ?? '';
  $group = $request->getUri()->getQueryParams()['group']
    ?? Constants::DEFAULT_GROUP;
  $data = $request->getBody()->getContents();
  $results = $this->adapter->saveToCache($key, $data, $group);
  if (!$results) {
      $code = 204;
  } else {
      $code = 200;
      $text[] = $results;
  }
      $body = new TextStream(json_encode($text));
      return (new Response())->withStatus($code)
                             ->withBody($body);
  }
```

16. The remove methods are, as expected, quite similar to each other:

```
public function removeByKey(RequestInterface $request)
{
  $text = array();
  $key = $request->getUri()->getQueryParams()['key'] ?? '';
  $results = $this->adapter->removeByKey($key);
  if (!$results) {
      $code = 204;
  } else {
      $code = 200;
      $text[] = $results;
  }
  $body = new TextStream(json_encode($text));
  return (new Response())->withStatus($code)
```

```
                                    ->withBody($body);
    }

    public function removeByGroup(RequestInterface $request)
    {
      $text = array();
      $group = $request->getUri()->getQueryParams()['group']
        ?? Constants::DEFAULT_GROUP;
      $results = $this->adapter->removeByGroup($group);
      if (!$results) {
          $code = 204;
      } else {
          $code = 200;
          $text[] = $results;
      }
      $body = new TextStream(json_encode($text));
      return (new Response())->withStatus($code)
                                    ->withBody($body);
      }
    } // closing brace for class Core
```

How it works...

In order to demonstrate the use of the `Acl` class, you will need to define the classes described in this recipe, summarized here:

Class	Discussed in these steps
`Application\Cache\Constants`	1
`Application\Cache\CacheAdapterInterface`	2
`Application\Cache\Database`	3 - 10
`Application\Cache\File`	11
`Application\Cache\Core`	12 - 16

Next, define a test program, which you could call `chap_09_middleware_cache_db.php`. In this program, as usual, define constants for necessary files, set up autoloading, use the appropriate classes, oh... and write a function that produces prime numbers (you're probably re-reading that last little bit at this point. Not to worry, we can help you with that!):

```
<?php
define('DB_CONFIG_FILE', __DIR__ . '/../config/db.config.php');
define('DB_TABLE', 'cache');
define('CACHE_DIR', __DIR__ . '/cache');
define('MAX_NUM', 100000);
```

```
require __DIR__ . '/../Application/Autoload/Loader.php';
Application\Autoload\Loader::init(__DIR__ . '/..');
use Application\Database\Connection;
use Application\Cache\{ Constants, Core, Database, File };
use Application\MiddleWare\ { Request, TextStream };
```

Well, a function that takes a long time to run is needed, so prime number generator, here we go! The numbers 1, 2, and 3 are given as primes. We use the PHP 7 `yield from` syntax to produce these first three. then, we skip right to 5, and proceed up to the maximum value requested:

```
function generatePrimes($max)
{
  yield from [1,2,3];
  for ($x = 5; $x < $max; $x++)
  {
    if($x & 1) {
        $prime = TRUE;
        for($i = 3; $i < $x; $i++) {
            if(($x % $i) === 0) {
                $prime = FALSE;
                break;
            }
        }
        if ($prime) yield $x;
    }
  }
}
```

You can then set up a database cache adapter instance, which serves as an argument for the core:

```
$conn    = new Connection(include DB_CONFIG_FILE);
$dbCache = new Database(
  $conn, DB_TABLE, 'id', 'key', 'data', 'group');
$core    = new Core($dbCache);
```

Alternatively, if you wish to use the file cache adapter instead, here is the appropriate code:

```
$fileCache = new File(CACHE_DIR);
$core      = new Core($fileCache);
```

If you wanted to clear the cache, here is how it might be done:

```
$uriString = '/?group=' . Constants::DEFAULT_GROUP;
$cacheRequest = new Request($uriString, 'get');
$response = $core->removeByGroup($cacheRequest);
```

You can use `time()` and `microtime()` to see how long this script runs with and without the cache:

```
$start = time() + microtime(TRUE);
echo "\nTime: " . $start;
```

Next, generate a cache request. A status code of `200` indicates you were able to obtain a list of primes from the cache:

```
$uriString = '/?key=Test1';
$cacheRequest = new Request($uriString, 'get');
$response = $core->getFromCache($cacheRequest);
$status   = $response->getStatusCode();
if ($status == 200) {
    $primes = json_decode($response->getBody()->getContents());
```

Otherwise, you can assume nothing was obtained from the cache, which means you need to generate prime numbers, and save the results to the cache:

```
} else {
    $primes = array();
    foreach (generatePrimes(MAX_NUM) as $num) {
        $primes[] = $num;
    }
    $body = new TextStream(json_encode($primes));
    $response = $core->saveToCache(
    $cacheRequest->withBody($body));
}
```

You can then check the stop time, calculate the difference, and have a look at your new list of primes:

```
$time = time() + microtime(TRUE);
$diff = $time - $start;
echo "\nTime: $time";
echo "\nDifference: $diff";
var_dump($primes);
```

Here is the expected output before values were stored in the cache:

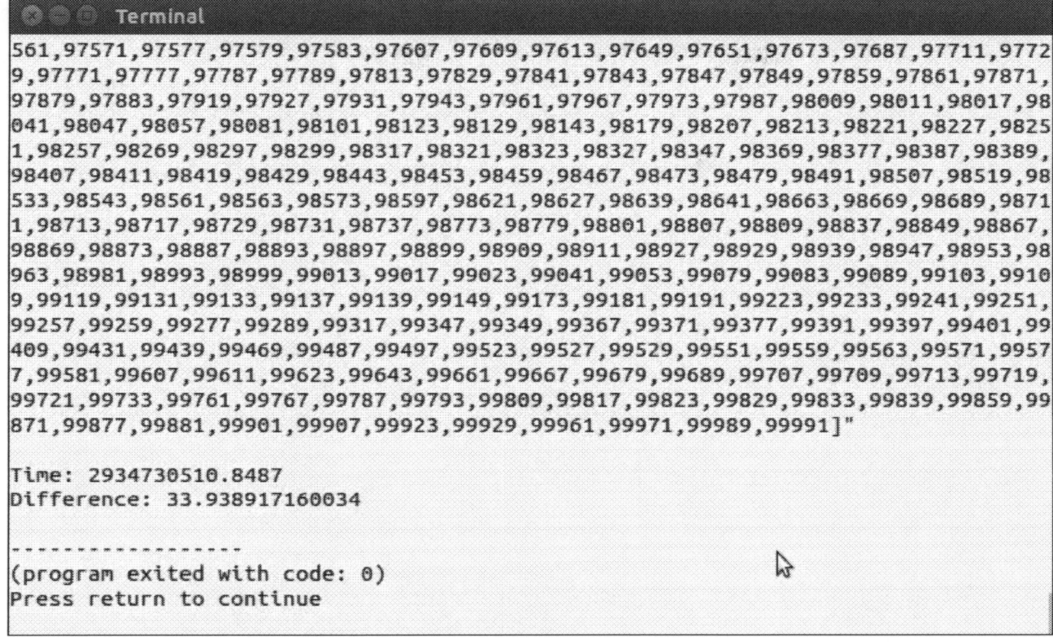

You can now run the same program again, this time retrieving from the cache:

```
Terminal
729,97771,97777,97787,97789,97813,97829,97841,97843,97847,97849,97859,97861,9787
1,97879,97883,97919,97927,97931,97943,97961,97967,97973,97987,98009,98011,98017,
98041,98047,98057,98081,98101,98123,98129,98143,98179,98207,98213,98221,98227,98
251,98257,98269,98297,98299,98317,98321,98323,98327,98347,98369,98377,98387,9838
9,98407,98411,98419,98429,98443,98453,98459,98467,98473,98479,98491,98507,98519,
98533,98543,98561,98563,98573,98597,98621,98627,98639,98641,98663,98669,98689,98
711,98713,98717,98729,98731,98737,98773,98779,98801,98807,98809,98837,98849,9886
7,98869,98873,98887,98893,98897,98899,98909,98911,98927,98929,98939,98947,98953,
98963,98981,98993,98999,99013,99017,99023,99041,99053,99079,99083,99089,99103,99
109,99119,99131,99133,99137,99139,99149,99173,99181,99191,99223,99233,99241,9925
1,99257,99259,99277,99289,99317,99347,99349,99367,99371,99377,99391,99397,99401,
99409,99431,99439,99469,99487,99497,99523,99527,99529,99551,99559,99563,99571,99
577,99581,99607,99611,99623,99643,99661,99667,99679,99689,99707,99709,99713,9971
9,99721,99733,99761,99767,99787,99793,99809,99817,99823,99829,99833,99839,99859,
99871,99877,99881,99901,99907,99923,99929,99961,99971,99989,99991]"
}

Time: 2934730718.9282
Difference: 0.0031728744506836

------------------
(program exited with code: 0)
Press return to continue
```

Allowing for the fact that our little prime number generator is not the world's most efficient, and also that the demonstration was run on a laptop, the time went from over 30 seconds down to milliseconds.

There's more...

Another possible cache adapter could be built around commands that are part of the **Alternate PHP Cache** (**APC**) extension. This extension includes such functions as `apc_exists()`, `apc_store()`, `apc_fetch()`, and `apc_clear_cache()`. These functions are perfect for our `hasKey()`, `saveToCache()`, `getFromCache()`, and `removeBy*()` functions.

See also

You might consider making slight changes to the cache adapter classes described previously following PSR-6, which is a standards recommendation directed towards the cache. There is not the same level of acceptance of this standard as with PSR-7, however, so we decided to not follow this standard exactly in the recipe presented here. For more information on PSR-6, please refer to `http://www.php-fig.org/psr/psr-6/`.

Implementing routing

Routing refers to the process of accepting user-friendly URLs, dissecting the URL into its component parts, and then making a determination as to which class and method should be dispatched. The advantage of such an implementation is that not only can you make your URLs **Search Engine Optimization** (**SEO**)-friendly, but you can also create rules, incorporating regular expression patterns, which can extract values of parameters.

How to do it...

1. Probably the most popular approach is to take advantage of a web server that supports **URL rewriting**. An example of this is an Apache web server configured to use `mod_rewrite`. You then define rewriting rules that allow graphic file requests and requests for CSS and JavaScript to pass untouched. Otherwise, the request would be funneled through a routing method.
2. Another potential approach is to simply have your web server virtual host definition point to a specific routing script, which then invokes the routing class, make routing decisions, and redirect appropriately.

3. The first code to consider is how to define routing configuration. The obvious answer is to construct an array, where each key would point to a regular expression against which the URI path would match, and some form of action. An example of such configuration is shown in the following code snippet. In this example, we have three routes defined: `home`, `page`, and the default. The default should be last as it will match anything not matched previously. The action is in the form of an anonymous function that will be executed if a route match occurs:

```
$config = [
  'home' => [
    'uri' => '!^/$!',
    'exec' => function ($matches) {
      include PAGE_DIR . '/page0.php'; }
  ],
  'page' => [
    'uri' => '!^/(page)/(\d+)$!',
      'exec' => function ($matches) {
        include PAGE_DIR . '/page' . $matches[2] . '.php'; }
  ],
  Router::DEFAULT_MATCH => [
    'uri' => '!.*!',
    'exec' => function ($matches) {
      include PAGE_DIR . '/sorry.php'; }
  ],
];
```

4. Next, we define our `Router` class. We first define constants and properties that will be of use during the process of examining and matching a route:

```
namespace Application\Routing;
use InvalidArgumentException;
use Psr\Http\Message\ServerRequestInterface;
class Router
{
  const DEFAULT_MATCH = 'default';
  const ERROR_NO_DEF  = 'ERROR: must supply a default match';
  protected $request;
  protected $requestUri;
  protected $uriParts;
  protected $docRoot;
  protected $config;
  protected $routeMatch;
```

5. The constructor accepts a `ServerRequestInterface` compliant class, the path to the document root, and the configuration file mentioned earlier. Note that we throw an exception if the default configuration is not supplied:

```
public function __construct(ServerRequestInterface $request,
  $docRoot, $config)
{
  $this->config = $config;
  $this->docRoot = $docRoot;
  $this->request = $request;
  $this->requestUri =
    $request->getServerParams()['REQUEST_URI'];
  $this->uriParts = explode('/', $this->requestUri);
  if (!isset($config[self::DEFAULT_MATCH])) {
      throw new InvalidArgumentException(
        self::ERROR_NO_DEF);
  }
}
```

6. Next, we have a series of getters that allow us to retrieve the original request, document root, and final route match:

```
public function getRequest()
{
  return $this->request;
}
public function getDocRoot()
{
  return $this->docRoot;
}
public function getRouteMatch()
{
  return $this->routeMatch;
}
```

7. The `isFileOrDir()` method is used to determine whether we are trying to match against a CSS, JavaScript, or graphic request (among other possibilities):

```
public function isFileOrDir()
{
  $fn = $this->docRoot . '/' . $this->requestUri;
  $fn = str_replace('//', '/', $fn);
  if (file_exists($fn)) {
      return $fn;
  } else {
      return '';
  }
}
```

8. Finally we define `match()`, which iterates through the configuration array and runs the `uri` parameter through `preg_match()`. If positive, the configuration key and `$matches` array populated by `preg_match()` are stored in `$routeMatch`, and the callback is returned. If there is no match, the default callback is returned:

```
public function match()
{
  foreach ($this->config as $key => $route) {
    if (preg_match($route['uri'],
        $this->requestUri, $matches)) {
        $this->routeMatch['key'] = $key;
        $this->routeMatch['match'] = $matches;
        return $route['exec'];
    }
  }
  return $this->config[self::DEFAULT_MATCH]['exec'];
}
}
```

How it works...

First, change to `/path/to/source/for/this/chapter` and create a directory called `routing`. Next, define a file, `index.php`, which sets up autoloading and uses the right classes. You can define a constant `PAGE_DIR` that points to the `pages` directory created in the previous recipe:

```
<?php
define('DOC_ROOT', __DIR__);
define('PAGE_DIR', DOC_ROOT . '/../pages');

require_once __DIR__ . '/../../Application/Autoload/Loader.php';
Application\Autoload\Loader::init(__DIR__ . '/../..');
use Application\MiddleWare\ServerRequest;
use Application\Routing\Router;
```

Next, add the configuration array discussed in step 3 of this recipe. Note that you could add `(/)?` at the end of the pattern to account for an optional trailing slash. Also, for the `home` route, you could offer two options: either / or `/home`:

```
$config = [
  'home' => [
    'uri' => '!^(/|/home)$!',
    'exec' => function ($matches) {
      include PAGE_DIR . '/page0.php'; }
```

```
    ],
    'page' => [
      'uri' => '!^/(page)/(\d+)(/)?$!',
      'exec' => function ($matches) {
        include PAGE_DIR . '/page' . $matches[2] . '.php'; }
    ],
    Router::DEFAULT_MATCH => [
      'uri' => '!.*!',
      'exec' => function ($matches) {
        include PAGE_DIR . '/sorry.php'; }
    ],
  ];
```

You can then define a router instance, supplying an initialized `ServerRequest` instance as the first argument:

```
$router = new Router((new ServerRequest())
  ->initialize(), DOC_ROOT, $config);
$execute = $router->match();
$params  = $router->getRouteMatch()['match'];
```

You then need to check to see whether the request is a file or directory, and also whether the route match is /:

```
if ($fn = $router->isFileOrDir()
    && $router->getRequest()->getUri()->getPath() != '/') {
    return FALSE;
} else {
    include DOC_ROOT . '/main.php';
}
```

Next, define `main.php`, something like this:

```
<?php // demo using middleware for routing ?>
<!DOCTYPE html>
<head>
  <title>PHP 7 Cookbook</title>
  <meta http-equiv="content-type"
  content="text/html;charset=utf-8" />
</head>
<body>
    <?php include PAGE_DIR . '/route_menu.php'; ?>
    <?php $execute($params); ?>
</body>
</html>
```

And finally, a revised menu that uses user-friendly routing is required:

```
<?php // menu for routing ?>
<a href="/home">Home</a>
<a href="/page/1">Page 1</a>
<a href="/page/2">Page 2</a>
<a href="/page/3">Page 3</a>
<!-- etc. -->
```

To test the configuration using Apache, define a virtual host definition that points to `/path/to/source/for/this/chapter/routing`. In addition, define a `.htaccess` file that directs any request that is not a file, directory, or link to `index.php`. Alternatively, you could just use the built-in PHP webserver. In a terminal window or command prompt, type this command:

```
cd /path/to/source/for/this/chapter/routing
php -S localhost:8080
```

In a browser, the output when requesting `http://localhost:8080/home` is something like this:

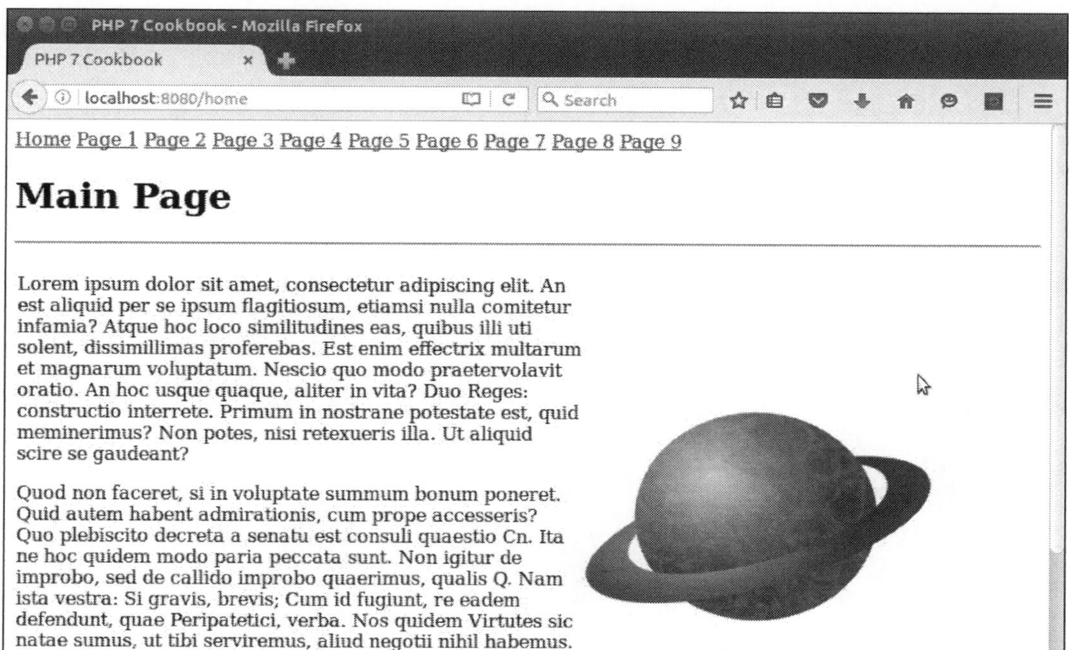

See also

For information on rewriting using the **NGINX** web server, have a look at this article: `http://nginx.org/en/docs/http/ngx_http_rewrite_module.html`. There are plenty of sophisticated PHP routing libraries available that introduce far greater functionality than the simple router presented here. These include Altorouter (`http://altorouter.com/`), TreeRoute (`https://github.com/baryshev/TreeRoute`), FastRoute (`https://github.com/nikic/FastRoute`), and Aura.Router. (`https://github.com/auraphp/Aura.Router`). In addition, most frameworks (for example, Zend Framework 2 or CodeIgniter) have their own routing capabilities.

Making inter-framework system calls

One of the primary reasons for the development of PSR-7 (and middleware) was a growing need to make calls between frameworks. It is of interest to note that the main documentation for PSR-7 is hosted by **PHP Framework Interop Group** (**PHP-FIG**).

How to do it...

1. The primary mechanism used in middleware inter-framework calls is to create a driver program that executes framework calls in succession, maintaining a common request and response object. The request and response objects are expected to represent `Psr\Http\Message\ServerRequestInterface` and `Psr\Http\Message\ResponseInterface`, respectively.
2. For the purposes of this illustration, we define a middleware session validator. The constants and properties reflect the session `thumbprint`, which is a term we use to incorporate factors such as the website visitor's IP address, browser, and language settings:

```
namespace Application\MiddleWare\Session;
use InvalidArgumentException;
use Psr\Http\Message\ {
  ServerRequestInterface, ResponseInterface };
use Application\MiddleWare\ { Constants, Response, TextStream };
class Validator
{
  const KEY_TEXT = 'text';
  const KEY_SESSION = 'thumbprint';
  const KEY_STATUS_CODE = 'code';
  const KEY_STATUS_REASON = 'reason';
```

```
const KEY_STOP_TIME = 'stop_time';
const ERROR_TIME = 'ERROR: session has exceeded stop time';
const ERROR_SESSION = 'ERROR: thumbprint does not match';
const SUCCESS_SESSION = 'SUCCESS: session validates OK';
protected $sessionKey;
protected $currentPrint;
protected $storedPrint;
protected $currentTime;
protected $storedTime;
```

3. The constructor takes a `ServerRequestInterface` instance and the session as arguments. If the session is an array (such as `$_SESSION`), we wrap it in a class. The reason why we do this is in case we are passed a session object, such as `JSession` used in Joomla. We then create the thumbprint using the previously mentioned factors. If the stored thumbprint is not available, we assume this is the first time, and store the current print as well as stop time, if this parameter is set. We used `md5()` because it's a fast hash, is not exposed externally, and is therefore useful to this application:

```
public function __construct(
  ServerRequestInterface $request, $stopTime = NULL)
{
  $this->currentTime  = time();
  $this->storedTime   = $_SESSION[self::KEY_STOP_TIME] ?? 0;
  $this->currentPrint =
    md5($request->getServerParams()['REMOTE_ADDR']
      . $request->getServerParams()['HTTP_USER_AGENT']
      . $request->getServerParams()['HTTP_ACCEPT_LANGUAGE']);
        $this->storedPrint  = $_SESSION[self::KEY_SESSION]
      ?? NULL;
  if (empty($this->storedPrint)) {
      $this->storedPrint = $this->currentPrint;
      $_SESSION[self::KEY_SESSION] = $this->storedPrint;
      if ($stopTime) {
          $this->storedTime = $stopTime;
          $_SESSION[self::KEY_STOP_TIME] = $stopTime;
      }
  }
}
```

4. It's not required to define `__invoke()`, but this magic method is quite convenient for standalone middleware classes. As is the convention, we accept `ServerRequestInterface` and `ResponseInterface` instances as arguments. In this method, we simply check to see whether the current thumbprint matches the one stored. The first time, of course, they will match. But on subsequent requests, the chances are an attacker intent on session hijacking will be caught out. In addition, if the session time exceeds the stop time (if set), likewise, a `401` code will be sent:

```
public function __invoke(
  ServerRequestInterface $request, Response $response)
{
  $code = 401;  // unauthorized
  if ($this->currentPrint != $this->storedPrint) {
      $text[self::KEY_TEXT] = self::ERROR_SESSION;
      $text[self::KEY_STATUS_REASON] =
        Constants::STATUS_CODES[401];
  } elseif ($this->storedTime) {
      if ($this->currentTime > $this->storedTime) {
          $text[self::KEY_TEXT] = self::ERROR_TIME;
          $text[self::KEY_STATUS_REASON] =
            Constants::STATUS_CODES[401];
      } else {
          $code = 200; // success
      }
  }
  if ($code == 200) {
      $text[self::KEY_TEXT] = self::SUCCESS_SESSION;
      $text[self::KEY_STATUS_REASON] =
        Constants::STATUS_CODES[200];
  }
  $text[self::KEY_STATUS_CODE] = $code;
  $body = new TextStream(json_encode($text));
  return $response->withStatus($code)->withBody($body);
}
```

5. We can now put our new middleware class to use. The main problems with inter-framework calls, at least at this point, are summarized here. Accordingly, how we implement middleware depends heavily on the last point:
   - Not all PHP frameworks are PSR-7-compliant
   - Existing PSR-7 implementations are not complete
   - All frameworks want to be the "boss"

6. As an example, have a look at the configuration files for **Zend Expressive**, which is a self-proclaimed *PSR7 Middleware Microframework*. Here is the file, `middleware-pipeline.global.php`, which is located in the `config/autoload` folder in a standard Expressive application. The dependencies key is used to identify the middleware wrapper classes that will be activated in the pipeline:

```
<?php
use Zend\Expressive\Container\ApplicationFactory;
use Zend\Expressive\Helper;
return [
  'dependencies' => [
     'factories' => [
        Helper\ServerUrlMiddleware::class =>
        Helper\ServerUrlMiddlewareFactory::class,
        Helper\UrlHelperMiddleware::class =>
        Helper\UrlHelperMiddlewareFactory::class,
        // insert your own class here
     ],
  ],
```

7. Under the `middleware_pipline` key, you can identify classes that will be executed before or after the routing process occurs. Optional parameters include `path`, `error`, and `priority`:

```
'middleware_pipeline' => [
   'always' => [
      'middleware' => [
         Helper\ServerUrlMiddleware::class,
      ],
      'priority' => 10000,
   ],
   'routing' => [
      'middleware' => [
         ApplicationFactory::ROUTING_MIDDLEWARE,
         Helper\UrlHelperMiddleware::class,
         // insert reference to middleware here
         ApplicationFactory::DISPATCH_MIDDLEWARE,
      ],
      'priority' => 1,
   ],
   'error' => [
      'middleware' => [
         // Add error middleware here.
      ],
      'error'    => true,
```

```
            'priority' => -10000,
        ],
    ],
];
```

8. Another technique is to modify the source code of an existing framework module, and make a request to a PSR-7-compliant middleware application. Here is an example modifying a **Joomla!** installation to include a middleware session validator.
9. Next, add this code the end of the `index.php` file in the `/path/to/joomla` folder. Since Joomla! uses Composer, we can leverage the Composer autoloader:

```
session_start();     // to support use of $_SESSION
$loader = include __DIR__ . '/libraries/vendor/autoload.php';
$loader->add('Application', __DIR__ . '/libraries/vendor');
$loader->add('Psr', __DIR__ . '/libraries/vendor');
```

10. We can then create an instance of our middleware session validator, and make a validation request just before `$app = JFactory::getApplication('site');`:

```
$session = JFactory::getSession();
$request =
  (new Application\MiddleWare\ServerRequest())->initialize();
$response = new Application\MiddleWare\Response();
$validator = new Application\Security\Session\Validator(
  $request, $session);
$response = $validator($request, $response);
if ($response->getStatusCode() != 200) {
  // take some action
}
```

How it works...

First, create the `Application\MiddleWare\Session\Validator` test middleware class described in steps 2-5. Then you will need to go to `https://getcomposer.org/` and follow the directions to obtain Composer. Download it to the `/path/to/source/for/this/chapter` folder. Next, build a basic Zend Expressive application, as shown next. Be sure to select `No` when prompted for minimal skeleton:

```
cd /path/to/source/for/this/chapter
php composer.phar create-project zendframework/zend-expressive-skeleton expressive
```

This will create a folder `/path/to/source/for/this/chapter/expressive`. Change to this directory. Modify `public/index.php` as follows:

```
<?php
if (php_sapi_name() === 'cli-server'
    && is_file(__DIR__ . parse_url(
$_SERVER['REQUEST_URI'], PHP_URL_PATH))
) {
    return false;
}
chdir(dirname(__DIR__));
session_start();
$_SESSION['time'] = time();
$appDir = realpath(__DIR__ . '/../../..');
$loader = require 'vendor/autoload.php';
$loader->add('Application', $appDir);
$container = require 'config/container.php';
$app = $container->get(\Zend\Expressive\Application::class);
$app->run();
```

You will then need to create a wrapper class that invokes our session validator middleware. Create a `SessionValidateAction.php` file that needs to go in the `/path/to/source/for/this/chapter/expressive/src/App/Action` folder. For the purposes of this illustration, set the stop time parameter to a short duration. In this case, `time() + 10` gives you 10 seconds:

```
namespace App\Action;
use Application\MiddleWare\Session\Validator;
use Zend\Diactoros\ { Request, Response };
use Psr\Http\Message\ResponseInterface;
use Psr\Http\Message\ServerRequestInterface;
class SessionValidateAction
{
  public function __invoke(ServerRequestInterface $request,
  ResponseInterface $response, callable $next = null)
  {
    $inbound   = new Response();
    $validator = new Validator($request, time()+10);
    $inbound   = $validator($request, $response);
    if ($inbound->getStatusCode() != 200) {
        session_destroy();
        setcookie('PHPSESSID', 0, time()-300);
        $params = json_decode(
          $inbound->getBody()->getContents(), TRUE);
```

```
            echo '<h1>',$params[Validator::KEY_TEXT],'</h1>';
            echo '<pre>',var_dump($inbound),'</pre>';
            exit;
        }
        return $next($request,$response);
    }
}
```

You will now need to add the new class to the middleware pipeline. Modify `config/autoload/middleware-pipeline.global.php` as follows. Modifications are shown in **bold**:

```
<?php
use Zend\Expressive\Container\ApplicationFactory;
use Zend\Expressive\Helper;
return [
  'dependencies' => [
     'invokables' => [
        App\Action\SessionValidateAction::class =>
        App\Action\SessionValidateAction::class,
     ],
   'factories' => [
      Helper\ServerUrlMiddleware::class =>
      Helper\ServerUrlMiddlewareFactory::class,
      Helper\UrlHelperMiddleware::class =>
      Helper\UrlHelperMiddlewareFactory::class,
    ],
  ],
  'middleware_pipeline' => [
      'always' => [
         'middleware' => [
            Helper\ServerUrlMiddleware::class,
         ],
         'priority' => 10000,
      ],
      'routing' => [
         'middleware' => [
            ApplicationFactory::ROUTING_MIDDLEWARE,
            Helper\UrlHelperMiddleware::class,
            App\Action\SessionValidateAction::class,
            ApplicationFactory::DISPATCH_MIDDLEWARE,
         ],
         'priority' => 1,
      ],
```

```
        'error' => [
            'middleware' => [
                // Add error middleware here.
            ],
            'error'    => true,
            'priority' => -10000,
        ],
    ],
];
```

You might also consider modifying the home page template to show the status of `$_SESSION`. The file in question is `/path/to/source/for/this/chapter/expressive/templates/app/home-page.phtml`. Simply adding `var_dump($_SESSION)` should suffice.

Initially, you should see something like this:

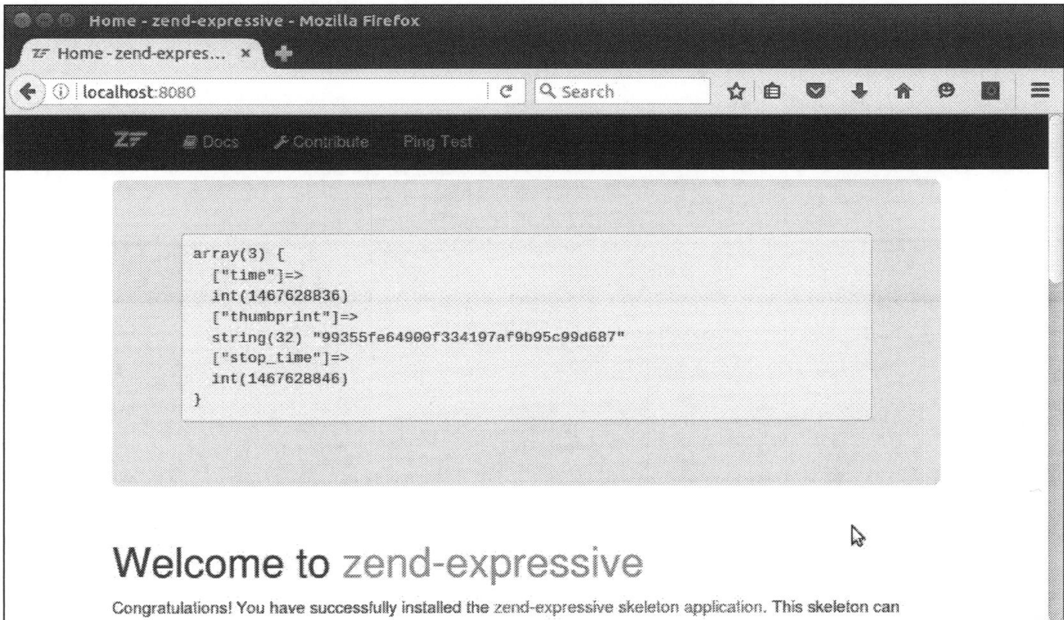

After 10 seconds, refresh the browser. You should now see this:

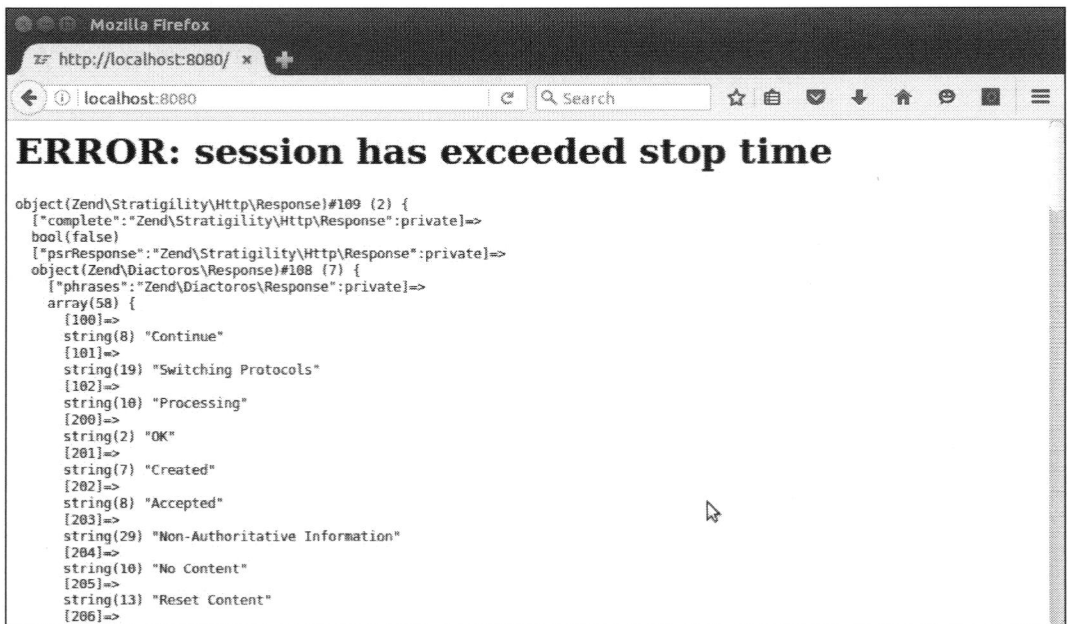

Using middleware to cross languages

Except in cases where you are trying to communicate between different versions of PHP, PSR-7 middleware will be of minimal use. Recall what the acronym stands for: **PHP Standards Recommendations**. Accordingly, if you need to make a request to an application written in another language, treat it as you would any other web service HTTP request.

How to do it...

1. In the case of PHP 4, you actually have a chance in that there is limited support for object-oriented programming. Accordingly, the best approach would be to downgrade the basic PSR-7 classes described in the first three recipes. There is not enough space to cover all the changes, but we present a potential PHP 4 version of `Application\MiddleWare\ServerRequest`. The first thing to note is that there are no namespaces! Accordingly, we use a classname with underscores, _, in place of namespace separators:

```
class Application_MiddleWare_ServerRequest
extends Application_MiddleWare_Request
implements Psr_Http_Message_ServerRequestInterface
{
```

2. All properties are identified in PHP 4 using the key word `var`:

```
var $serverParams;
var $cookies;
var $queryParams;
// not all properties are shown
```

3. The `initialize()` method is almost the same, except that syntax such as `$this->getServerParams()['REQUEST_URI']` was not allowed in PHP 4. Accordingly, we need to split this out into a separate variable:

```
function initialize()
{
  $params = $this->getServerParams();
  $this->getCookieParams();
  $this->getQueryParams();
  $this->getUploadedFiles;
  $this->getRequestMethod();
  $this->getContentType();
  $this->getParsedBody();
  return $this->withRequestTarget($params['REQUEST_URI']);
}
```

4. All of the `$_XXX` super-globals were present in later versions of PHP 4:

```
function getServerParams()
{
  if (!$this->serverParams) {
      $this->serverParams = $_SERVER;
  }
  return $this->serverParams;
}
// not all getXXX() methods are shown to conserve space
```

5. The null coalesce operator was only introduced in PHP 7. We need to use `isset(XXX) ? XXX : '';` instead:

```
function getRequestMethod()
{
  $params = $this->getServerParams();
  $method = isset($params['REQUEST_METHOD'])
    ? $params['REQUEST_METHOD'] : '';
  $this->method = strtolower($method);
  return $this->method;
}
```

6. The JSON extension was not introduced until PHP 5. Accordingly, we need to be satisfied with raw input. We could also possibly use `serialize()` or `unserialize()` in place of `json_encode()` and `json_decode()`:

```
function getParsedBody()
{
  if (!$this->parsedBody) {
      if (($this->getContentType() ==
           Constants::CONTENT_TYPE_FORM_ENCODED
           || $this->getContentType() ==
           Constants::CONTENT_TYPE_MULTI_FORM)
           && $this->getRequestMethod() ==
           Constants::METHOD_POST)
      {
          $this->parsedBody = $_POST;
      } elseif ($this->getContentType() ==
                Constants::CONTENT_TYPE_JSON
                || $this->getContentType() ==
                Constants::CONTENT_TYPE_HAL_JSON)
      {
          ini_set("allow_url_fopen", true);
          $this->parsedBody =
            file_get_contents('php://stdin');
      } elseif (!empty($_REQUEST)) {
          $this->parsedBody = $_REQUEST;
      } else {
          ini_set("allow_url_fopen", true);
          $this->parsedBody =
            file_get_contents('php://stdin');
      }
  }
  return $this->parsedBody;
}
```

7. The `withXXX()` methods work pretty much the same in PHP 4:

```
function withParsedBody($data)
{
  $this->parsedBody = $data;
  return $this;
}
```

8. Likewise, the `withoutXXX()` methods work the same as well:

```
function withoutAttribute($name)
{
  if (isset($this->attributes[$name])) {
      unset($this->attributes[$name]);
  }
  return $this;
}

}
```

9. For websites using other languages, we could use the PSR-7 classes to formulate requests and responses, but would then need to use an HTTP client to communicate with the other website. As an example, recall the demonstration of a `Request` discussed in the recipe *Developing a PSR-7 request class* from this chapter. Here is the example from the *How it works...* section:

```
$request = new Request(
  TARGET_WEBSITE_URL,
  Constants::METHOD_POST,
  new TextStream($contents),
  [Constants::HEADER_CONTENT_TYPE =>
  Constants::CONTENT_TYPE_FORM_ENCODED,
  Constants::HEADER_CONTENT_LENGTH => $body->getSize()]
);

$data = http_build_query(['data' =>
$request->getBody()->getContents()]);

$defaults = array(
  CURLOPT_URL => $request->getUri()->getUriString(),
  CURLOPT_POST => true,
  CURLOPT_POSTFIELDS => $data,
);
$ch = curl_init();
curl_setopt_array($ch, $defaults);
$response = curl_exec($ch);
curl_close($ch);
```

10
Looking at Advanced Algorithms

In this chapter, we will cover:

- Using getters and setters
- Implementing a linked list
- Building a bubble sort
- Implementing a stack
- Building a binary search class
- Implementing a search engine
- Displaying a multi-dimensional array and accumulating totals

Introduction

In this chapter, we cover recipes that implement various advanced algorithms such as linked list, bubble sort, stacks, and binary search. In addition, we cover getters and setters, as well as implementing a search engine and displaying values from a multi-dimensional array with accumulated totals.

Using getters and setters

At first glance, it would seemingly make sense to define classes with `public` properties, which can then be directly read or written. It is considered a best practice, however, to make properties `protected`, and to then define a **getter** and **setter** for each. As the name implies, a *getter* retrieves the value of a property. A *setter* is used to set the value.

Best practice

Define properties as `protected` to prevent accidental *outside* access. Use `public` get* and set* methods to provide access to these properties. In this manner, not only can you more precisely control access, but you can also make formatting and data type changes to the properties while getting and setting them.

How to do it...

1. Getters and setters provide additional flexibility when getting or setting values. You are able to add an additional layer of logic if needed, something which would not be possible if you were to directly read or write a public property. All you need to do is to create a public method with a prefix of either `get` or `set`. The name of the property becomes the suffix. It is a convention to make the first letter of the variable uppercase. Thus, if the property is `$testValue`, the getter would be `getTestValue()`.
2. In this example, we define a class with a protected property, `$date`. Notice that the `get` and `set` methods allow for treatment as either a `DateTime` object or as a string. The value is actually stored in any event as a `DateTime` instance:

```
$a = new class() {
  protected $date;
  public function setDate($date)
  {
    if (is_string($date)) {
        $this->date = new DateTime($date);
    } else {
        $this->date = $date;
    }
  }
  public function getDate($asString = FALSE)
  {
    if ($asString) {
        return $this->date->format('Y-m-d H:i:s');
    } else {
        return $this->date;
```

```
        }
    }
};
```

3. Getters and setters allow you to filter or sanitize the data coming in or going out. In the following example, there are two properties, `$intVal` and `$arrVal`, which are set to a default initial value of `NULL`. Notice that not only are the return values for the getters data-typed, but they also provide defaults. The setters also either enforce the incoming data-type, or type-cast the incoming value to a certain data-type:

```
<?php
class GetSet
{
  protected $intVal = NULL;
  protected $arrVal = NULL;
  // note the use of the null coalesce operator to return a
    default value
  public function getIntVal() : int
  {
    return $this->intVal ?? 0;
  }
  public function getArrVal() : array
  {
    return $this->arrVal ?? array();
  }
  public function setIntVal($val)
  {
    $this->intVal = (int) $val ?? 0;
  }
  public function setArrVal(array $val)
  {
    $this->arrVal = $val ?? array();
  }
}
```

4. If you have a class with lots and lots of properties, it might become tedious to define a distinct getter and setter for each property. In this case, you can define a kind of *fallback* using the magic method `__call()`. The following class defines nine different properties. Instead of having to define nine getters and nine setters, we define a single method, `__call()`, which makes a determination whether or not the usage is `get` or `set`. If `get`, it retrieves the key from an internal array. If `set`, it stores the value in the internal array.

The `__call()` method is a magic method which is executed if an application makes a call to a non-existent method.

```
<?php
class LotsProps
{
  protected $firstName  = NULL;
  protected $lastName   = NULL;
  protected $addr1      = NULL;
  protected $addr2      = NULL;
  protected $city       = NULL;
  protected $state      = NULL;
  protected $province   = NULL;
  protected $postalCode = NULL;
  protected $country    = NULL;
  protected $values     = array();

  public function __call($method, $params)
  {
    preg_match('/^(get|set)(.*?)$/i', $method, $matches);
    $prefix = $matches[1] ?? '';
    $key    = $matches[2] ?? '';
    $key    = strtolower($key);
    if ($prefix == 'get') {
        return $this->values[$key] ?? '---';
    } else {
        $this->values[$key] = $params[0];
    }
  }
}
```

How it works...

Copy the code mentioned in step 1 into a new file, `chap_10_oop_using_getters_and_setters.php`. To test the class, add the following:

```
// set date using a string
$a->setDate('2015-01-01');
var_dump($a->getDate());

// retrieves the DateTime instance
var_dump($a->getDate(TRUE));
```

```
// set date using a DateTime instance
$a->setDate(new DateTime('now'));
var_dump($a->getDate());

// retrieves the DateTime instance
var_dump($a->getDate(TRUE));
```

In the output (shown next), you can see that the `$date` property can be set using either a `string` or an actual `DateTime` instance. When `getDate()` is executed, you can return either a `string` or a `DateTime` instance, depending on the value of the `$asString` flag:

```
Terminal
class DateTime#2 (3) {
  public $date =>
  string(26) "2015-01-01 00:00:00.000000"
  public $timezone_type =>
  int(3)
  public $timezone =>
  string(13) "Europe/London"
}
string(19) "2015-01-01 00:00:00"
class DateTime#3 (3) {
  public $date =>
  string(26) "2016-02-18 07:04:39.000000"
  public $timezone_type =>
  int(3)
  public $timezone =>
  string(13) "Europe/London"
}
string(19) "2016-02-18 07:04:39"


------------------
(program exited with code: 0)
Press return to continue
```

Next, have a look at the code defined in step 2. Copy this code into a file, `chap_10_oop_using_getters_and_setters_defaults.php`, and add the following:

```
// create the instance
$a = new GetSet();

// set a "proper" value
$a->setIntVal(1234);
echo $a->getIntVal();
echo PHP_EOL;

// set a bogus value
$a->setIntVal('some bogus value');
```

```
echo $a->getIntVal();
echo PHP_EOL;

// NOTE: boolean TRUE == 1
$a->setIntVal(TRUE);
echo $a->getIntVal();
echo PHP_EOL;

// returns array() even though no value was set
var_dump($a->getArrVal());
echo PHP_EOL;

// sets a "proper" value
$a->setArrVal(['A','B','C']);
var_dump($a->getArrVal());
echo PHP_EOL;

try {
    $a->setArrVal('this is not an array');
    var_dump($a->getArrVal());
    echo PHP_EOL;
} catch (TypeError $e) {
    echo $e->getMessage();
}

echo PHP_EOL;
```

As you can see from the following output, setting a *proper* integer value works as expected. A non-numeric value defaults to `0`. Interestingly, if you supply a Boolean `TRUE` as an argument to `setIntVal()`, it is interpolated to `1`.

If you call `getArrVal()` without setting a value, the default is an empty array. Setting an array value works as expected. However, if you supply a non-array value as an argument, the type hint of the array causes a `TypeError` to be thrown, which can be caught as shown here:

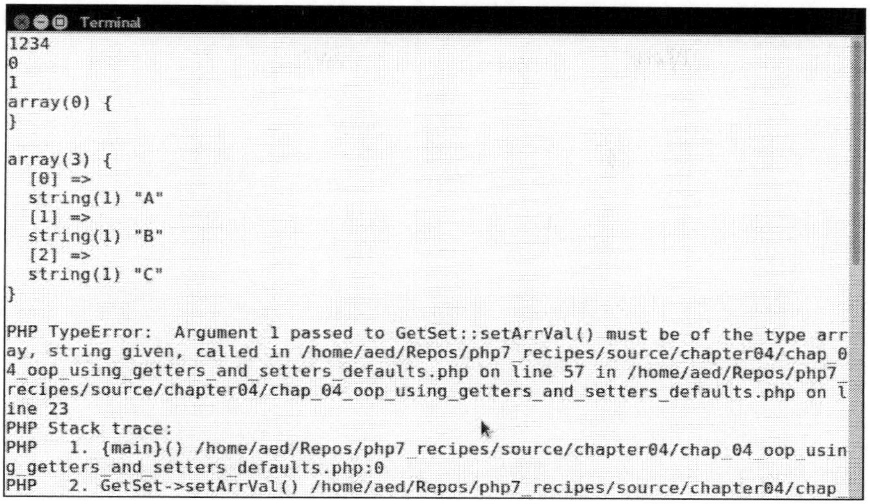

```
Terminal
1234
0
1
array(0) {
}

array(3) {
  [0] =>
  string(1) "A"
  [1] =>
  string(1) "B"
  [2] =>
  string(1) "C"
}

PHP TypeError:  Argument 1 passed to GetSet::setArrVal() must be of the type arr
ay, string given, called in /home/aed/Repos/php7_recipes/source/chapter04/chap_0
4_oop_using_getters_and_setters_defaults.php on line 57 in /home/aed/Repos/php7_
recipes/source/chapter04/chap_04_oop_using_getters_and_setters_defaults.php on l
ine 23
PHP Stack trace:
PHP   1. {main}() /home/aed/Repos/php7_recipes/source/chapter04/chap_04_oop_usin
g_getters_and_setters_defaults.php:0
PHP   2. GetSet->setArrVal() /home/aed/Repos/php7_recipes/source/chapter04/chap_
```

Finally, take the `LotsProps` class defined in step 3 and place it in a separate file, `chap_10_oop_using_getters_and_setters_magic_call.php`. Now add code to set values. What will happen, of course, is that the magic method `__call()` is invoked. After running `preg_match()`, the remainder of the non-existent property, after the letters `set`, will become a key in the internal array `$values`:

```
$a = new LotsProps();
$a->setFirstName('Li\'l Abner');
$a->setLastName('Yokum');
$a->setAddr1('1 Dirt Street');
$a->setCity('Dogpatch');
$a->setState('Kentucky');
$a->setPostalCode('12345');
$a->setCountry('USA');
?>
```

You can then define HTML that displays the values using the corresponding `get` methods. These will in turn return keys from the internal array:

```
<div class="container">
<div class="left blue1">Name</div>
<div class="right yellow1">
<?= $a->getFirstName() . ' ' . $a->getLastName() ?></div>
</div>
<div class="left blue2">Address</div>
<div class="right yellow2">
    <?= $a->getAddr1() ?>
    <br><?= $a->getAddr2() ?>
```

```
        <br><?= $a->getCity() ?>
        <br><?= $a->getState() ?>
        <br><?= $a->getProvince() ?>
        <br><?= $a->getPostalCode() ?>
        <br><?= $a->getCountry() ?>
    </div>
    </div>
```

Here is the final output:

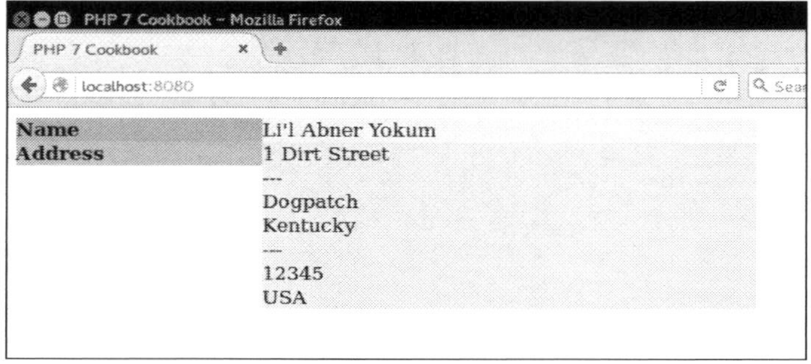

Implementing a linked list

A linked list is where one list contains keys that point to keys in another list. An analogy, in database terms, would be where you have a table that contains data, and a separate index that points to the data. One index might produce a list of items by ID. Another index might yield a list according to title and so on. The salient feature of the linked list is that you do not have to touch the original list of items.

For example, in the diagram shown next, the primary list contains ID numbers and the names of fruits. If you were to directly output the primary list, the fruit names would display in this order: **Apple**, **Grape**, **Banana**, **Orange**, **Cherry**. If you were to use the linked list as an index, on the other hand, the resulting output of fruit names would be **Apple**, **Banana**, **Cherry**, **Grape**, and **Orange**:

Linked List	Primary List	
101	101	Apple
102	105	Grape
103	102	Banana
105	104	Orange
104	103	Cherry

How to do it...

1. One of the primary uses of a linked list is to produce a display of items in a different order. One approach would be to create an iteration of key value pairs, where the key represents the new order, and the value contains the value of the key in the primary list. Such a function might look like this:

   ```
   function buildLinkedList(array $primary,
                            callable $makeLink)
   {
     $linked = new ArrayIterator();
     foreach ($primary as $key => $row) {
       $linked->offsetSet($makeLink($row), $key);
     }
     $linked->ksort();
     return $linked;
   }
   ```

2. We use an anonymous function to generate the new key in order to provide extra flexibility. You will also notice that we do a sort by key (`ksort()`) so that the linked list iterates in key order.

3. All we need to do to use the linked list is to iterate through it, but produce results from the primary list, `$customer` in this example:

   ```
   foreach ($linked as $key => $link) {
     $output .= printRow($customer[$link]);
   }
   ```

4. Note that in no way do we touch the primary list. This allows us to generate multiple linked lists, each representing a different order, while retaining our original set of data.

5. Another important use of a linked list is for the purposes of filtering. The technique is similar to that shown previously. The only difference is that we expand the `buildLinkedList()` function, adding a filter column and filter value:

   ```
   function buildLinkedList(array $primary,
                            callable $makeLink,
                            $filterCol = NULL,
                            $filterVal = NULL)
   {
     $linked = new ArrayIterator();
     $filterVal = trim($filterVal);
     foreach ($primary as $key => $row) {
       if ($filterCol) {
         if (trim($row[$filterCol]) == $filterVal) {
           $linked->offsetSet($makeLink($row), $key);
   ```

```
            }
        } else {
            $linked->offsetSet($makeLink($row), $key);
        }
    }
    $linked->ksort();
    return $linked;
}
```

6. We only include items in the linked list where the value represented by `$filterCol` in the primary list matches `$filterVal`. The iteration logic is the same as that shown in step 2.
7. Finally, another form of linked list is the *doubly* linked list. In this case, the list is constructed in such a manner that the iteration can occur in either a forward or reverse direction. In the case of PHP, we are fortunate to have an SPL class, `SplDoublyLinkedList`, which neatly does the trick. Here is a function that builds a doubly linked list:

```
function buildDoublyLinkedList(ArrayIterator $linked)
{
  $double = new SplDoublyLinkedList();
  foreach ($linked as $key => $value) {
    $double->push($value);
  }
  return $double;
}
```

The terminology for `SplDoublyLinkedList` can be misleading. `SplDoublyLinkedList::top()` actually points to the *end* of the list, whereas `SplDoublyLinkedList::bottom()` points to the *beginning*!

How it works...

Copy the code shown in the first bullet into a file, `chap_10_linked_list_include.php`. In order to demonstrate the use of a linked list, you will need a source of data. For this illustration, you can make use of the `customer.csv` file that was mentioned in earlier recipes. It is a CSV file with the following columns:

```
"id","name","balance","email","password","status","security_question",
"confirm_code","profile_id","level"
```

You can add the following functions to the include file mentioned previously to generate a primary list of customers, and to display information about them. Note that we use the first column, id as the primary key:

```
function readCsv($fn, &$headers)
{
  if (!file_exists($fn)) {
    throw new Error('File Not Found');
  }
  $fileObj = new SplFileObject($fn, 'r');
  $result = array();
  $headers = array();
  $firstRow = TRUE;
  while ($row = $fileObj->fgetcsv()) {
    // store 1st row as headers
    if ($firstRow) {
      $firstRow = FALSE;
      $headers = $row;
    } else {
      if ($row && $row[0] !== NULL && $row[0] !== 0) {
        $result[$row[0]] = $row;
      }
    }
  }
  return $result;
}

function printHeaders($headers)
{
  return sprintf('%4s : %18s : %8s : %32s : %4s' . PHP_EOL,
                 ucfirst($headers[0]),
                 ucfirst($headers[1]),
                 ucfirst($headers[2]),
                 ucfirst($headers[3]),
                 ucfirst($headers[9]));
}

function printRow($row)
{
  return sprintf('%4d : %18s : %8.2f : %32s : %4s' . PHP_EOL,
                 $row[0], $row[1], $row[2], $row[3], $row[9]);
}
```

```
function printCustomer($headers, $linked, $customer)
{
  $output = '';
  $output .= printHeaders($headers);
  foreach ($linked as $key => $link) {
    $output .= printRow($customer[$link]);
  }
  return $output;
}
```

You can then define a calling program, `chap_10_linked_list_in_order.php`, which includes the file defined previously, and reads `customer.csv`:

```
<?php
define('CUSTOMER_FILE', __DIR__ . '/../data/files/customer.csv');
include __DIR__ . '/chap_10_linked_list_include.php';
$headers = array();
$customer = readCsv(CUSTOMER_FILE, $headers);
```

You can then define an anonymous function that will produce a key in the linked list. In this illustration, define a function that breaks down column 1 (name) into first and last names:

```
$makeLink = function ($row) {
  list($first, $last) = explode(' ', $row[1]);
  return trim($last) . trim($first);
};
```

You can then call the function to build the linked list, and use `printCustomer()` to display the results:

```
$linked = buildLinkedList($customer, $makeLink);
echo printCustomer($headers, $linked, $customer);
```

Here is how the output might appear:

```
Terminal
Id :                Name :  Balance :                         Email : Level
74 :       Louella Allen :   847.65 :      louella.allen@telecom.net :  ADV
49 :        Omar Anthony :  3733.00 :     omar.anthony@fastmedia.com :  INT
 4 :        Morgan Avila :   888.88 :     morgan.avila@northmedia.com :  ADV
 9 :      Armando Barlow :  6524.00 :    armando.barlow@cablecom.com :  BEG
32 :     Matilda Barrera :   470.32 :   matilda.barrera@northcom.com :  INT
54 :      Ramiro Bentley :   565.81 :    ramiro.bentley@westmedia.com :  BEG
11 :       Felix Blevins :   130.57 :     felix.blevins@southcom.net :  BEG
69 :    Lucille Bradford :   677.58 : lucille.bradford@westmedia.com :  ADV
52 :        Jesus Bright :   869.09 :        jesus.bright@cablenet.net :  BEG
76 :          Lana Burns :   261.98 :          lana.burns@westcom.com :  ADV
57 :      Garrett Campos :     9.47 :     garrett.campos@fastcom.net :  BEG
12 :         Jose Carter :    56.22 :          jose.carter@westcom.net :  INT
24 :        Cecelia Case :   592.19 :     cecelia.case@southmedia.net :  INT
68 :         Geneva Case :   268.75 :       geneva.case@westmedia.com :  BEG
43 :        Roland Chang :   514.16 :    roland.chang@southmedia.com :  INT
46 :      Dominick Cline :   881.77 :     dominick.cline@telecom.com :  INT
22 :        Coleen Walker :  6595.20 :    coleen.walker@fastmedia.com :  INT
39 :         Lena Conway :   757.22 :         lena.conway@eastnet.net :  ADV
30 :       Krista Cortez :   414.66 :       krista.cortez@eastcom.com :  BEG
 8 :      Brian Crawford :   125.58 :      brian.crawford@fastcom.net :  ADV
19 :           Gene Cruz :   683.55 :            gene.cruz@eastcom.com :  ADV
28 :      Gabriela Davis :    88.07 :  gabriela.davis@southmedia.net :
79 :        Renee Decker :   447.83 :         renee.decker@westcom.net :
```

To produce a filtered result, modify `buildLinkedList()` as discussed in step 4. You can then add logic that checks to see whether the value of the filter column matches the value in the filter:

```
define('LEVEL_FILTER', 'INT');

$filterCol = 9;
$filterVal = LEVEL_FILTER;
$linked = buildLinkedList($customer, $makeLink, $filterCol,
$filterVal);
```

There's more...

PHP 7.1 introduced the use of `[ ]` as an alternative to `list()`. If you look at the anonymous function mentioned previously, you could rewrite this in PHP 7.1 as follows:

```
$makeLink = function ($row) {
  [$first, $last] = explode(' ', $row[1]);
  return trim($last) . trim($first);
};
```

For more information, see `https://wiki.php.net/rfc/short_list_syntax`.

Building a bubble sort

The classic **bubble sort** is an exercise often assigned to university students. Nonetheless, it's important to master this algorithm as there are many occasions where built-in PHP sorting functions do not apply. An example would be sorting a multi-dimensional array where the sort key is not the first column.

The way the bubble sort works is to recursively iterate through the list and swap the current value with the next value. If you want items to be in ascending order, the swap occurs if the next item is less than the current item. For descending order, the swap occurs if the reverse is true. The sort is concluded when no more swaps occur.

In the following diagram, after the first pass, **Grape** and **Banana** are swapped, as are **Orange** and **Cherry**. After the 2nd pass, **Grape** and **Cherry** are swapped. No more swaps occur on the last pass, and the bubble sort ends:

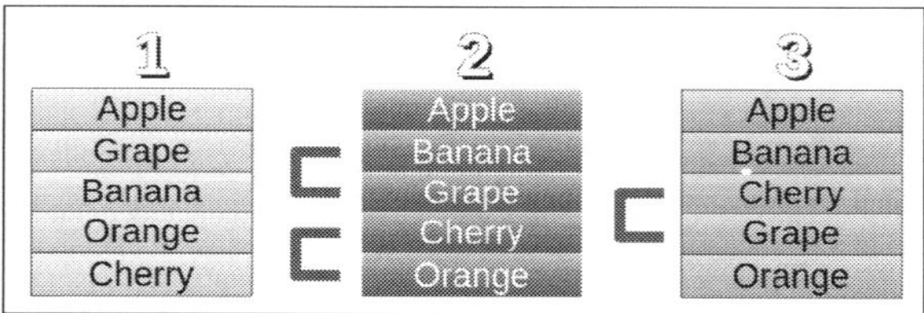

How to do it...

1. We do not want to actually *move* the values around in the array; that would be horribly expensive in terms of resource usage. Instead, we will use a **linked list**, discussed in the previous recipe.
2. First we build a linked list using the `buildLinkedList()` function discussed in the previous recipe.
3. We then define a new function, `bubbleSort()`, which accepts the linked list by reference, the primary list, a sort field, and a parameter that represents sort order (ascending or descending):

```
function bubbleSort(&$linked, $primary, $sortField, $order = 'A')
{
```

4. The variables needed include one that represents the number of iterations, the number of swaps, and an iterator based upon the linked list:

```
  static $iterations = 0;
  $swaps = 0;
  $iterator = new ArrayIterator($linked);
```

5. In the `while()` loop, we only proceed if the iteration is still `valid`, which is to say still in progress. We then obtain the current key and value, and the next key and value. Note the extra `if()` statement to ensure the iteration is still valid (that is, to make sure we don't drop off the end of the list!):

```
while ($iterator->valid()) {
  $currentLink = $iterator->current();
  $currentKey  = $iterator->key();
  if (!$iterator->valid()) break;
  $iterator->next();
  $nextLink = $iterator->current();
  $nextKey  = $iterator->key();
```

6. Next we check to see whether the sort is to be ascending or descending. Depending on the direction, we check to see whether the next value is greater than, or less than, the current value. The result of the comparison is stored in `$expr`:

```
if ($order == 'A') {
    $expr = $primary[$linked->offsetGet
            ($currentKey)][$sortField] >
            $primary[$linked->offsetGet($nextKey)][$sortField];
} else {
    $expr = $primary[$linked->offsetGet
            ($currentKey)][$sortField] <
            $primary[$linked->offsetGet($nextKey)][$sortField];
}
```

7. If the value of `$expr` is `TRUE`, and we have valid current and next keys, the values are swapped in the linked list. We also increment `$swaps`:

```
if ($expr && $currentKey && $nextKey
    && $linked->offsetExists($currentKey)
    && $linked->offsetExists($nextKey)) {
    $tmp = $linked->offsetGet($currentKey);
    $linked->offsetSet($currentKey,
    $linked->offsetGet($nextKey));
    $linked->offsetSet($nextKey, $tmp);
    $swaps++;
  }
}
```

8. Finally, if any swaps have occurred, we need to run through the iteration again, until there are no more swaps. Accordingly, we make a recursive call to the same method:

```
if ($swaps) bubbleSort($linked, $primary, $sortField, $order);
```

9. The *real* return value is the re-organized linked list. We also return the number of iterations just for reference:

```
  return ++$iterations;
}
```

How it works...

Add the `bubbleSort()` function discussed previously to the include file created in the previous recipe. You can use the same logic discussed in the previous recipe to read the `customer.csv` file, producing a primary list:

```
<?php
define('CUSTOMER_FILE', __DIR__ . '/../data/files/customer.csv');
include __DIR__ . '/chap_10_linked_list_include.php';
$headers = array();
$customer = readCsv(CUSTOMER_FILE, $headers);
```

You can then produce a linked list using the first column as a sort key:

```
$makeLink = function ($row) {
  return $row[0];
};
$linked = buildLinkedList($customer, $makeLink);
```

Finally, call the `bubbleSort()` function, providing the linked list and customer list as arguments. You can also provide a sort column, in this illustration column 2, that represents the account balance, using the letter `'A'` to indicate ascending order. The `printCustomer()` function can be used to display output:

```
echo 'Iterations: ' . bubbleSort($linked,
                                   $customer, 2, 'A') . PHP_EOL;
echo printCustomer($headers, $linked, $customer);
```

Here is an example of the output:

```
Terminal
Iterations: 82
 Id :               Name :  Balance :                              Email : Level
101 :     Leonard Nimoy :   -99.99 :        mrspock788843@starfleet.gov :  ADV
 21 :       Lauri Grimes :   -37.95 :          lauri.grimes@cablecom.com :  ADV
 20 :     Samuel Harding :   -11.56 :     samuel.harding@southmedia.net :  ADV
 88 :              Obama :     0.00 :             obama@president.gov :  BEG
 92 :       C.T. Russell :     0.00 :                  ctrussell@jw.org :  BEG
 99 :              admin :     0.00 :         admin@sweetscomplete.com :  ADV
 57 :     Garrett Campos :     9.47 :         garrett.campos@fastcom.net :  BEG
 45 :    Wilfredo Taylor :    25.11 :        wilfredo.taylor@telecom.net :  BEG
 25 :      Rhonda Kinney :    46.61 :        rhonda.kinney@fastmedia.com :  BEG
 58 :       Todd Lindsey :    48.91 :           todd.lindsey@fastnet.net :  ADV
 12 :        Jose Carter :    56.22 :            jose.carter@westcom.net :  INT
 71 :       Fannie Moore :    68.48 :        fannie.moore@cablemedia.net :  ADV
 16 :        Marc Ellis :    69.04 :              marc.ellis@westnet.com :  ADV
 28 :     Gabriela Davis :    88.07 :     gabriela.davis@southmedia.net :
  6 :    Spencer Sanford :    99.99 :       spencer.sanford@cablenet.net :  INT
 44 :    Raymond Sanford :   101.41 :       raymond.sanford@cablenet.net :  ADV
  8 :     Brian Crawford :   125.58 :          brian.crawford@fastcom.net :  ADV
 11 :      Felix Blevins :   130.57 :         felix.blevins@southcom.net :  BEG
 48 :    Edmond Shepherd :   135.29 :     edmond.shepherd@southmedia.com :  ADV
 50 :       Lonnie Eaton :   139.07 :          lonnie.eaton@southcom.net :  ADV
 65 :   Isabel Rodriguez :   142.87 :       isabel.rodriguez@fastcom.net :  BEG
 75 :  Jeannette Merritt :   146.89 : jeannette.merritt@northmedia.com :  BEG
```

Implementing a stack

A **stack** is a simple algorithm normally implemented as **Last In First Out** (**LIFO**). Think of a stack of books sitting on a library table. When the librarian goes to restore the books to their place, the topmost book is processed first, and so on in order, until the book at the bottom of the stack has been replaced. The topmost book was the last one to be placed on the stack, thus last in first out.

In programming terms, a stack is used to temporarily store information. The retrieval order facilitates retrieving the most recent item first.

How to do it...

1. First we define a class, `Application\Generic\Stack`. The core logic is encapsulated in an SPL class, `SplStack`:

```
namespace Application\Generic;
use SplStack;
class Stack
{
  // code
}
```

2. Next we define a property to represent the stack, and set up an `SplStack` instance:

```
protected $stack;
public function __construct()
{
  $this->stack = new SplStack();
}
```

3. After that we define methods to add and remove from the stack, the classic `push()` and `pop()` methods:

```
public function push($message)
{
  $this->stack->push($message);
}
public function pop()
{
  return $this->stack->pop();
}
```

4. We also throw in an implementation of `__invoke()` that returns an instance of the `stack` property. This allows us to use the object in a direct function call:

```
public function __invoke()
{
  return $this->stack;
}
```

How it works...

One possible use for a stack is to store messages. In the case of messages, it is usually desirable to retrieve the latest first, thus it is a perfect use case for a stack. Define the `Application\Generic\Stack` class as discussed in this recipe. Next, define a calling program that sets up autoloading and creates an instance of the `stack`:

```
<?php
// setup class autoloading
require __DIR__ . '/../Application/Autoload/Loader.php';
Application\Autoload\Loader::init(__DIR__ . '/..');
use Application\Generic\Stack;
$stack = new Stack();
```

To do something with the stack, store a series of messages. As you would most likely store messages at different points in your application, you can use `sleep()` to simulate other code running:

```
echo 'Do Something ... ' . PHP_EOL;
$stack->push('1st Message: ' . date('H:i:s'));
sleep(3);

echo 'Do Something Else ... ' . PHP_EOL;
$stack->push('2nd Message: ' . date('H:i:s'));
sleep(3);

echo 'Do Something Else Again ... ' . PHP_EOL;
$stack->push('3rd Message: ' . date('H:i:s'));
sleep(3);
```

Finally, simply iterate through the stack to retrieve messages. Note that you can call the stack object as if it were a function, which returns the `SplStack` instance:

```
echo 'What Time Is It?' . PHP_EOL;
foreach ($stack() as $item) {
  echo $item . PHP_EOL;
}
```

Here is the expected output:

```
Do Something ...
Do Something Else ...
Do Something Else Again ...
What Time Is It?
3rd Message: 03:10:08
2nd Message: 03:10:05
1st Message: 03:10:02


-----------------
(program exited with code: 0)
Press return to continue
```

Building a binary search class

Conventional searches often proceed through the list of items in a sequential manner. This means that the maximum possible number of items to be searched could be the same as the length of the list! This is not very efficient. If you need to expedite a search, consider implementing a *binary* search.

The technique is quite simple: you find the midpoint in the list, and determine whether the search item is less than, equal to, or greater than the midpoint item. If less, you set the upper limit to the midpoint, and search only the first half of the list. If greater, set the lower limit to the midpoint, and search only the last half of the list. You would then proceed to divide the list into 1/4, 1/8, 1/16, and so on, until the search item is found (or not).

It's important to note that although the maximum number of comparisons is considerably smaller than a sequential search (*log n + 1* where *n* is the number of elements in the list, and *log* is the binary logarithm), the list involved in the search must first be sorted, which of course downgrades performance.

How to do it...

1. We first construct a search class, `Application\Generic\Search`, which accepts the primary list as an argument. As a control, we also define a property, `$iterations`:

```
namespace Application\Generic;
class Search
{
```

```
  protected $primary;
  protected $iterations;
  public function __construct($primary)
  {
    $this->primary = $primary;
  }
```

2. Next we define a method, `binarySearch()`, which sets up the search infrastructure. The first order of business is to build a separate array, `$search`, where the key is a composite of the columns included in the search. We then sort by key:

```
public function binarySearch(array $keys, $item)
{
  $search = array();
  foreach ($this->primary as $primaryKey => $data) {
    $searchKey = function ($keys, $data) {
      $key = '';
      foreach ($keys as $k) $key .= $data[$k];

      return $key;
    };
    $search[$searchKey($keys, $data)] = $primaryKey;
  }
  ksort($search);
```

3. We then pull out the keys into another array, `$binary`, so that we can perform the binary sort based on numeric keys. We then call `doBinarySearch()`, which results in a key from our intermediary array `$search`, or a Boolean, `FALSE`:

```
  $binary = array_keys($search);
  $result = $this->doBinarySearch($binary, $item);
  return $this->primary[$search[$result]] ?? FALSE;
}
```

4. The first `doBinarySearch()` initializes a series of parameters. `$iterations`, `$found`, `$loop`, `$done`, and `$max` are all used to prevent an endless loop. `$upper` and `$lower` represent the slice of the list to be examined:

```
public function doBinarySearch($binary, $item)
{
  $iterations = 0;
  $found = FALSE;
  $loop  = TRUE;
  $done  = -1;
  $max   = count($binary);
  $lower = 0;
  $upper = $max - 1;
```

5. We then implement a `while()` loop and set the midpoint:

```
while ($loop && !$found) {
  $mid = (int) (($upper - $lower) / 2) + $lower;
```

6. We now get to use the new PHP 7 **spaceship operator**, which gives us, in a single comparison, less than, equal to, or greater than. If less, we set the upper limit to the midpoint. If greater, the lower limit is adjusted to the midpoint. If equal, we're done and home free:

```
switch ($item <=> $binary[$mid]) {
  // $item < $binary[$mid]
  case -1 :
  $upper = $mid;
  break;
  // $item == $binary[$mid]
  case 0 :
  $found = $binary[$mid];
  break;
  // $item > $binary[$mid]
  case 1 :
  default :
  $lower = $mid;
}
```

7. Now for a bit of loop control. We increment the number of iterations and make sure it does not exceed the size of the list. If so, something is definitely wrong and we need to bail out. Otherwise, we check to see whether the upper and lower limits are the same more than twice in a row, in which case the search item has not been found. Then we store the number of iterations and return whatever was found (or not):

```
    $loop = (($iterations++ < $max) && ($done < 1));
    $done += ($upper == $lower) ? 1 : 0;
  }
  $this->iterations = $iterations;
  return $found;
}
```

How it works...

First, implement the `Application\Generic\Search` class defining the methods described in this recipe. Next, define a calling program, `chap_10_binary_search.php`, which sets up autoloading and reads the `customer.csv` file as a search target (as discussed in the previous recipe):

```
<?php
define('CUSTOMER_FILE', __DIR__ . '/../data/files/customer.csv');
include __DIR__ . '/chap_10_linked_list_include.php';
require __DIR__ . '/../Application/Autoload/Loader.php';
Application\Autoload\Loader::init(__DIR__ . '/..');
use Application\Generic\Search;
$headers = array();
$customer = readCsv(CUSTOMER_FILE, $headers);
```

You can then create a new `Search` instance, and specify an item somewhere in the middle of the list. In this illustration, the search is based on column 1, customer name, and the item is `Todd Lindsey`:

```
$search = new Search($customer);
$item = 'Todd Lindsey';
$cols = [1];
echo "Searching For: $item\n";
var_dump($search->binarySearch($cols, $item));
```

For illustration, add this line just before `switch()` in `Application\Generic\Search::doBinarySearch()`:

```
echo 'Upper:Mid:Lower:<=> | ' . $upper . ':' . $mid . ':' .
  $lower . ':' . ($item <=> $binary[$mid]);
```

The output is shown here. Notice how the upper, middle, and lower limits adjust until the item is found:

```
Terminal
Searching For: Todd Lindsey
Upper:Mid:Lower:<=> | 81:40:0:1
Upper:Mid:Lower:<=> | 81:60:40:1
Upper:Mid:Lower:<=> | 81:70:60:1
Upper:Mid:Lower:<=> | 81:75:70:1
Upper:Mid:Lower:<=> | 81:78:75:0
array(10) {
  [0]=>
  string(2) "58"
  [1]=>
  string(12) "Todd Lindsey"
  [2]=>
  string(5) "48.91"
  [3]=>
  string(24) "todd.lindsey@fastnet.net"
  [4]=>
  string(16) "an2073Conscience"
  [5]=>
  string(1) "1"
  [6]=>
  string(0) ""
  [7]=>
  string(0) ""
  [8]=>
```

See also

For more information on binary search, there is an excellent article on Wikipedia that goes through the basic math at `https://en.wikipedia.org/wiki/Binary_search_algorithm`.

Implementing a search engine

In order to implement a search engine, we need to make provision for multiple columns to be included in the search. In addition, it's important to recognize that the search item might be found in the middle of the field, and that very rarely will users provide enough information for an exact match. Accordingly, we will rely heavily on the SQL `LIKE %value%` clause.

How to do it...

1. First, we define a basic class to hold search criteria. The object contains three properties: the key, which ultimately represents a database column; the operator (`LIKE`, `<`, `>`, and so on); and optionally an item. The reason why an item is optional is that some operators, such as `IS NOT NULL`, do not require specific data:

```
namespace Application\Database\Search;
class Criteria
{
  public $key;
  public $item;
```

```
  public $operator;
  public function __construct($key, $operator, $item = NULL)
  {
    $this->key  = $key;
    $this->operator = $operator;
    $this->item = $item;
  }
}
```

2. Next we need to define a class, `Application\Database\Search\Engine`, and provide the necessary class constants and properties. The difference between `$columns` and `$mapping` is that `$columns` holds information that will ultimately appear in an HTML `SELECT` field (or the equivalent). For security reasons, we do not want to expose the actual names of the database columns, thus the need for another array `$mapping`:

```
namespace Application\Database\Search;
use PDO;
use Application\Database\Connection;
class Engine
{
  const ERROR_PREPARE = 'ERROR: unable to prepare statement';
  const ERROR_EXECUTE = 'ERROR: unable to execute statement';
  const ERROR_COLUMN  = 'ERROR: column name not on list';
  const ERROR_OPERATOR= 'ERROR: operator not on list';
  const ERROR_INVALID = 'ERROR: invalid search criteria';

  protected $connection;
  protected $table;
  protected $columns;
  protected $mapping;
  protected $statement;
  protected $sql = '';
```

3. Next, we define a set of operators we are willing to support. The key represents actual SQL. The value is what will appear in the form:

```
  protected $operators = [
      'LIKE'     => 'Equals',
      '<'        => 'Less Than',
      '>'        => 'Greater Than',
      '<>'       => 'Not Equals',
      'NOT NULL' => 'Exists',
  ];
```

4. The constructor accepts a database connection instance as an argument. For our purposes, we will use `Application\Database\Connection`, defined in *Chapter 5, Interacting with a Database*. We also need to provide the name of the database table, as well as `$columns`, an array of arbitrary column keys and labels, which will appear in the HTML form. This will reference `$mapping`, where the key matches `$columns`, but where the value represents actual database column names:

```
public function __construct(Connection $connection,
                            $table, array $columns, array $mapping)
{
  $this->connection  = $connection;
  $this->setTable($table);
  $this->setColumns($columns);
  $this->setMapping($mapping);
}
```

5. After the constructor, we provide a series of useful getters and setters:

```
public function setColumns($columns)
{
  $this->columns = $columns;
}
public function getColumns()
{
  return $this->columns;
}
// etc.
```

6. Probably the most critical method is the one that builds the SQL statement to be prepared. After the initial `SELECT` setup, we add a `WHERE` clause, using `$mapping` to add the actual database column name. We then add the operator and implement `switch()` which, based on the operator, may or may not add a named placeholder that will represent the search item:

```
public function prepareStatement(Criteria $criteria)
{
  $this->sql = 'SELECT * FROM ' . $this->table . ' WHERE ';
  $this->sql .= $this->mapping[$criteria->key] . ' ';
  switch ($criteria->operator) {
    case 'NOT NULL' :
      $this->sql .= ' IS NOT NULL OR ';
      break;
    default :
      $this->sql .= $criteria->operator . ' :'
      . $this->mapping[$criteria->key] . ' OR ';
  }
```

7. Now that the core SELECT has been defined, we remove any trailing OR keywords, and add a clause that causes the result to be sorted according to the search column. The statement is then sent to the database to be prepared:

```
  $this->sql = substr($this->sql, 0, -4)
    . ' ORDER BY ' . $this->mapping[$criteria->key];
  $statement = $this->connection->pdo->prepare($this->sql);
  return $statement;
}
```

8. We are now ready to move on to the main show, the search() method. We accept an Application\Database\Search\Criteria object as an argument. This ensures that we have an item key and operator at a minimum. To be on the safe side, we add an if() statement to check these properties:

```
public function search(Criteria $criteria)
{
  if (empty($criteria->key) || empty($criteria->operator)) {
    yield ['error' => self::ERROR_INVALID];
    return FALSE;
  }
```

9. We then call prepareStatement() using try / catch to trap errors:

```
try {
    if (!$statement = $this->prepareStatement($criteria)) {
      yield ['error' => self::ERROR_PREPARE];
      return FALSE;
}
```

10. Next we build an array of parameters that will be supplied to execute(). The key represents the database column name that was used as a placeholder in the prepared statement. Note that instead of using =, we use the LIKE %value% construct:

```
$params = array();
switch ($criteria->operator) {
  case 'NOT NULL' :
    // do nothing: already in statement
    break;
    case 'LIKE' :
    $params[$this->mapping[$criteria->key]] =
    '%' . $criteria->item . '%';
    break;
    default :
    $params[$this->mapping[$criteria->key]] =
    $criteria->item;
}
```

11. The statement is executed, and the results returned using the `yield` keywords, which effectively turns this method into a generator:

```
        $statement->execute($params);
        while ($row = $statement->fetch(PDO::FETCH_ASSOC)) {
          yield $row;
        }
      } catch (Throwable $e) {
        error_log(__METHOD__ . ':' . $e->getMessage());
        throw new Exception(self::ERROR_EXECUTE);
      }
      return TRUE;
    }
```

How it works...

Place the code discussed in this recipe in the files `Criteria.php` and `Engine.php` under `Application\Database\Search`. You can then define a calling script, `chap_10_search_engine.php`, which sets up autoloading. You can take advantage of the `Application\Database\Connection` class discussed in *Chapter 5, Interacting with a Database*, and the form element classes covered in *Chapter 6, Building Scalable Websites*:

```
<?php
define('DB_CONFIG_FILE', '/../config/db.config.php');
require __DIR__ . '/../Application/Autoload/Loader.php';
Application\Autoload\Loader::init(__DIR__ . '/..');

use Application\Database\Connection;
use Application\Database\Search\ { Engine, Criteria };
use Application\Form\Generic;
use Application\Form\Element\Select;
```

You can now define which database columns will appear in the form, and a matching mapping file:

```
$dbCols = [
  'cname' => 'Customer Name',
  'cbal' => 'Account Balance',
  'cmail' => 'Email Address',
  'clevel' => 'Level'
];

$mapping = [
  'cname' => 'name',
  'cbal' => 'balance',
  'cmail' => 'email',
  'clevel' => 'level'
];
```

You can now set up the database connection and create the search engine instance:

```
$conn = new Connection(include __DIR__ . DB_CONFIG_FILE);
$engine = new Engine($conn, 'customer', $dbCols, $mapping);
```

In order to display the appropriate drop-down `SELECT` elements, we define wrappers and elements based on `Application\Form\*` classes:

```
$wrappers = [
  Generic::INPUT => ['type' => 'td', 'class' => 'content'],
  Generic::LABEL => ['type' => 'th', 'class' => 'label'],
  Generic::ERRORS => ['type' => 'td', 'class' => 'error']
];

// define elements
$fieldElement = new Select('field',
                Generic::TYPE_SELECT,
                'Field',
                $wrappers,
                ['id' => 'field']);
                $opsElement = new Select('ops',
                Generic::TYPE_SELECT,
                'Operators',
                $wrappers,
                ['id' => 'ops']);
                $itemElement = new Generic('item',
                Generic::TYPE_TEXT,
                'Searching For ...',
                $wrappers,
                ['id' => 'item','title' => 'If more than one item,
                separate with commas']);
                $submitElement = new Generic('submit',
                Generic::TYPE_SUBMIT,
                'Search',
                $wrappers,
                ['id' => 'submit','title' => 'Click to Search',
                'value' => 'Search']);
```

We then get input parameters (if defined), set form element options, create search criteria, and run the search:

```
$key  = (isset($_GET['field']))
? strip_tags($_GET['field']) : NULL;
$op   = (isset($_GET['ops'])) ? $_GET['ops'] : NULL;
$item = (isset($_GET['item'])) ? strip_tags($_GET['item']) : NULL;
$fieldElement->setOptions($dbCols, $key);
$itemElement->setSingleAttribute('value', $item);
$opsElement->setOptions($engine->getOperators(), $op);
$criteria = new Criteria($key, $op, $item);
$results = $engine->search($criteria);
?>
```

The display logic mainly orients towards rendering the form. A more thorough presentation is discussed in *Chapter 6, Building Scalable Websites*, but we show the core logic here:

```
<form name="search" method="get">
<table class="display" cellspacing="0" width="100%">
  <tr><?= $fieldElement->render(); ?></tr>
  <tr><?= $opsElement->render(); ?></tr>
  <tr><?= $itemElement->render(); ?></tr>
  <tr><?= $submitElement->render(); ?></tr>
  <tr>
  <th class="label">Results</th>
    <td class="content" colspan=2>
    <span style="font-size: 10pt;font-family:monospace;">
    <table>
    <?php foreach ($results as $row) : ?>
      <tr>
        <td><?= $row['id'] ?></td>
        <td><?= $row['name'] ?></td>
        <td><?= $row['balance'] ?></td>
        <td><?= $row['email'] ?></td>
        <td><?= $row['level'] ?></td>
      </tr>
    <?php endforeach; ?>
    </table>
    </span>
    </td>
  </tr>
</table>
</form>
```

Here is sample output from a browser:

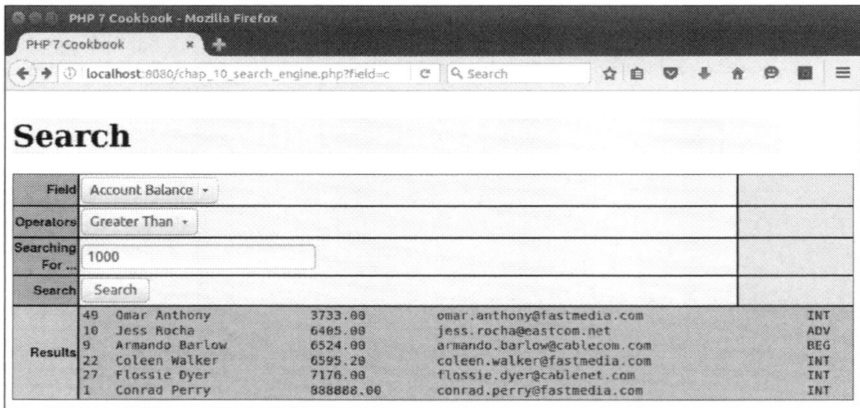

Displaying a multi-dimensional array and accumulating totals

How to properly display data from a multi-dimensional array has been a classic problem for any web developer. For illustration, assume you wish to display a list of customers and their purchases. For each customer, you wish to show their name, phone number, account balance, and so on. This already represents a two dimensional array where the *x* axis represents customers and the *y* axis represents data for that customer. Now add in purchases and you have a third axis! How can you represent a 3D model on a 2D screen? One possible solution would be to incorporate "hidden" division tags with a simple JavaScript visibility toggle.

How to do it...

1. First we need to generate a 3D array from a SQL statement that uses a number of `JOIN` clauses. We will use the `Application/Database/Connection` class introduced in *Chapter 1, Building a Foundation,* to formulate an appropriate SQL query. We leave two parameters open, `min` and `max`, in order to support pagination. Unfortunately, we cannot use a simple `LIMIT` and `OFFSET` in this case, as the number of rows will vary depending on the number of purchases for any given customer. Accordingly, we can restrict the number of rows by placing restrictions on the customer ID that presumably (hopefully) is incremental. To make this work properly, we also need to set the primary `ORDER` to customer ID:

```
define('ITEMS_PER_PAGE', 6);
define('SUBROWS_PER_PAGE', 6);
define('DB_CONFIG_FILE', '/../config/db.config.php');
include __DIR__ . '/../Application/Database/Connection.php';
```

```
use Application\Database\Connection;
$conn = new Connection(include __DIR__ . DB_CONFIG_FILE);
$sql  = 'SELECT c.id,c.name,c.balance,c.email,f.phone, '
  . 'u.transaction,u.date,u.quantity,u.sale_price,r.title '
  . 'FROM customer AS c '
  . 'JOIN profile AS f '
  . 'ON f.id = c.id '
  . 'JOIN purchases AS u '
  . 'ON u.customer_id = c.id '
  . 'JOIN products AS r '
  . 'ON u.product_id = r.id '
  . 'WHERE c.id >= :min AND c.id < :max '
  . 'ORDER BY c.id ASC, u.date DESC ';
```

2. Next we can implement a form of pagination, based on restrictions on the customer ID, using simple `$_GET` parameters. Note that we add an extra check to make sure the value of `$prev` does not go below zero. You might consider adding another control that ensures the value of `$next` does not go beyond the last customer ID. In this illustration, we just allow it to increment:

```
$page = $_GET['page'] ?? 1;
$page = (int) $page;
$next = $page + 1;
$prev = $page - 1;
$prev = ($prev >= 0) ? $prev : 0;
```

3. We then calculate the values for `$min` and `$max`, and prepare and execute the SQL statement:

```
$min  = $prev * ITEMS_PER_PAGE;
$max  = $page * ITEMS_PER_PAGE;
$stmt = $conn->pdo->prepare($sql);
$stmt->execute(['min' => $min, 'max' => $max]);
```

4. A `while()` loop can be used to fetch results. We use a simple fetch mode of `PDO::FETCH_ASSOC` for the purpose of this example. Using the customer ID as a key, we store basic customer information as array parameters. We then store an array of purchase information in a sub-array, `$results[$key]['purchases'][]`. When the customer ID changes, it's a signal to store the same information for the next customer. Note that we accumulate totals per customer in an array key total:

```
$custId = 0;
$result = array();
$grandTotal = 0.0;
while ($row = $stmt->fetch(PDO::FETCH_ASSOC)) {
  if ($row['id'] != $custId) {
    $custId = $row['id'];
    $result[$custId] = [
```

```
        'name'    => $row['name'],
        'balance' => $row['balance'],
        'email'   => $row['email'],
        'phone'   => $row['phone'],
      ];
      $result[$custId]['total'] = 0;
    }
    $result[$custId]['purchases'][] = [
      'transaction' => $row['transaction'],
      'date'        => $row['date'],
      'quantity'    => $row['quantity'],
      'sale_price'  => $row['sale_price'],
      'title'       => $row['title'],
    ];
    $result[$custId]['total'] += $row['sale_price'];
    $grandTotal += $row['sale_price'];
  }
  ?>
```

5. Next we implement the view logic. First, we start with a block that displays primary customer information:

```
<div class="container">
<?php foreach ($result as $key => $data) : ?>
<div class="mainLeft color0">
    <?= $data['name'] ?> [<?= $key ?>]
</div>
<div class="mainRight">
  <div class="row">
    <div class="left">Balance</div>
           <div class="right"><?= $data['balance']; ?></div>
  </div>
  <div class="row">
    <div class="left color2">Email</div>
           <div class="right"><?= $data['email']; ?></div>
  </div>
  <div class="row">
    <div class="left">Phone</div>
           <div class="right"><?= $data['phone']; ?></div>
    </div>
  <div class="row">
        <div class="left color2">Total Purchases</div>
    <div class="right">
<?= number_format($data['total'],2); ?>
</div>
  </div>
```

6. Next comes the logic to display a list of purchases for this customer:

```
<!-- Purchases Info -->
<table>
  <tr>
  <th>Transaction</th><th>Date</th><th>Qty</th>
   <th>Price</th><th>Product</th>
  </tr>
  <?php $count  = 0; ?>
  <?php foreach ($data['purchases'] as $purchase) : ?>
  <?php $class = ($count++ & 01) ? 'color1' : 'color2'; ?>
  <tr>
  <td class="<?= $class ?>"><?= $purchase['transaction'] ?></td>
  <td class="<?= $class ?>"><?= $purchase['date'] ?></td>
  <td class="<?= $class ?>"><?= $purchase['quantity'] ?></td>
  <td class="<?= $class ?>"><?= $purchase['sale_price'] ?></td>
  <td class="<?= $class ?>"><?= $purchase['title'] ?></td>
  </tr>
  <?php endforeach; ?>
</table>
```

7. For the purposes of pagination, we then add buttons to represent *previous* and *next*:

```
<?php endforeach; ?>
<div class="container">
  <a href="?page=<?= $prev ?>">
        <input type="button" value="Previous"></a>
  <a href="?page=<?= $next ?>">
        <input type="button" value="Next" class="buttonRight"></a>
</div>
<div class="clearRow"></div>
</div>
```

8. The result so far, unfortunately, is nowhere near neat and tidy! Accordingly we add a simple JavaScript function to toggle the visibility of a `<div>` tag based on its `id` attribute:

```
<script type="text/javascript">
function showOrHide(id) {
  var div = document.getElementById(id);
  div.style.display = div.style.display == "none" ?
    "block" : "none";
}
</script>
```

9. Next we wrap the purchases table inside an initially invisible `<div>` tag. Then, we can place a limit of how many sub-rows are initially visible, and add a link that *reveals* the remaining purchase data:

```
<div class="row" id="<?= 'purchase' . $key ?>"
style="display:none;">
  <table>
    <tr>
      <th>Transaction</th><th>Date</th><th>Qty</th>
                 <th>Price</th><th>Product</th>
    </tr>
  <?php $count  = 0; ?>
  <?php $first  = TRUE; ?>
  <?php foreach ($data['purchases'] as $purchase) : ?>
    <?php if ($count > SUBROWS_PER_PAGE && $first) : ?>
    <?php     $first = FALSE; ?>
    <?php     $subId = 'subrow' . $key; ?>
    </table>
    <a href="#" onClick="showOrHide('<?= $subId ?>')">More</a>
    <div id="<?= $subId ?>" style="display:none;">
    <table>
    <?php endif; ?>
  <?php $class = ($count++ & 01) ? 'color1' : 'color2'; ?>
  <tr>
  <td class="<?= $class ?>"><?= $purchase['transaction'] ?></td>
  <td class="<?= $class ?>"><?= $purchase['date'] ?></td>
  <td class="<?= $class ?>"><?= $purchase['quantity'] ?></td>
  <td class="<?= $class ?>"><?= $purchase['sale_price'] ?></td>
  <td class="<?= $class ?>"><?= $purchase['title'] ?></td>
  </tr>
  <?php endforeach; ?>
  </table>
  <?php if (!$first) : ?></div><?php endif; ?>
</div>
```

10. We then add a button that, when clicked, reveals the hidden `<div>` tag:

```
<input type="button" value="Purchases" class="buttonRight"
    onClick="showOrHide('<?= 'purchase' . $key ?>')">
```

How it works...

Place the code described in steps 1 to 5 into a file, `chap_10_html_table_multi_array_hidden.php`.

Just inside the `while()` loop, add the following:

```
printf('%6s : %20s : %8s : %20s' . PHP_EOL,
    $row['id'], $row['name'], $row['transaction'], $row['title']);
```

Just after the `while()` loop, add an `exit` command. Here is the output:

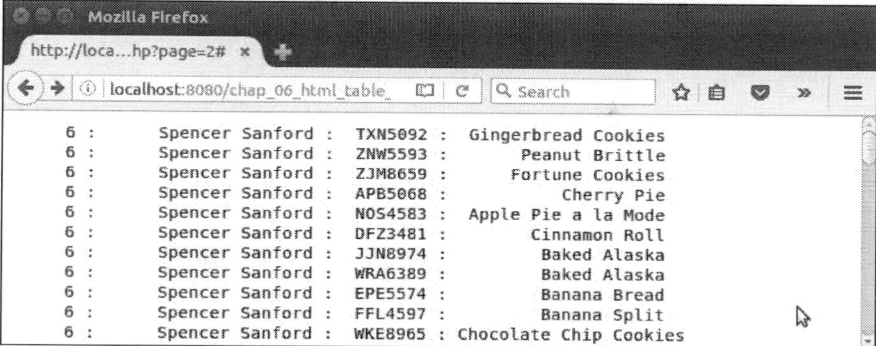

You will notice that the basic customer information, such as the ID and name, repeats for each result row, but purchase information, such as transaction and product title, varies. Go ahead and remove the `printf()` statement.

Replace the `exit` command with the following:

```
echo '<pre>', var_dump($result), '</pre>'; exit;
```

Here is how the newly composed 3D array looks:

```
array(6) {
  [6]=>
  array(5) {
    ["name"]=>
    string(15) "Spencer Sanford"
    ["balance"]=>
    string(5) "99.99"
    ["email"]=>
    string(28) "spencer.sanford@cablenet.net"
    ["phone"]=>
    string(12) "451-815-7386"
    ["purchases"]=>
    array(92) {
      [0]=>
      array(5) {
        ["transaction"]=>
        string(7) "TXN5092"
        ["date"]=>
        string(19) "2016-09-12 05:46:16"
        ["quantity"]=>
        string(2) "44"
        ["sale_price"]=>
        string(5) "10.50"
        ["title"]=>
        string(19) "Gingerbread Cookies"
      }
      [1]=>
      array(5) {
        ["transaction"]=>
        string(7) "ZNW5593"
        ["date"]=>
        string(19) "2015-09-18 03:58:26"
```

You can now add the display logic shown in steps 5 to 7. As mentioned, although you are now showing all data, the visual display is not helpful. Now go ahead and add the refinements mentioned in the remaining steps. Here is how the initial output might appear:

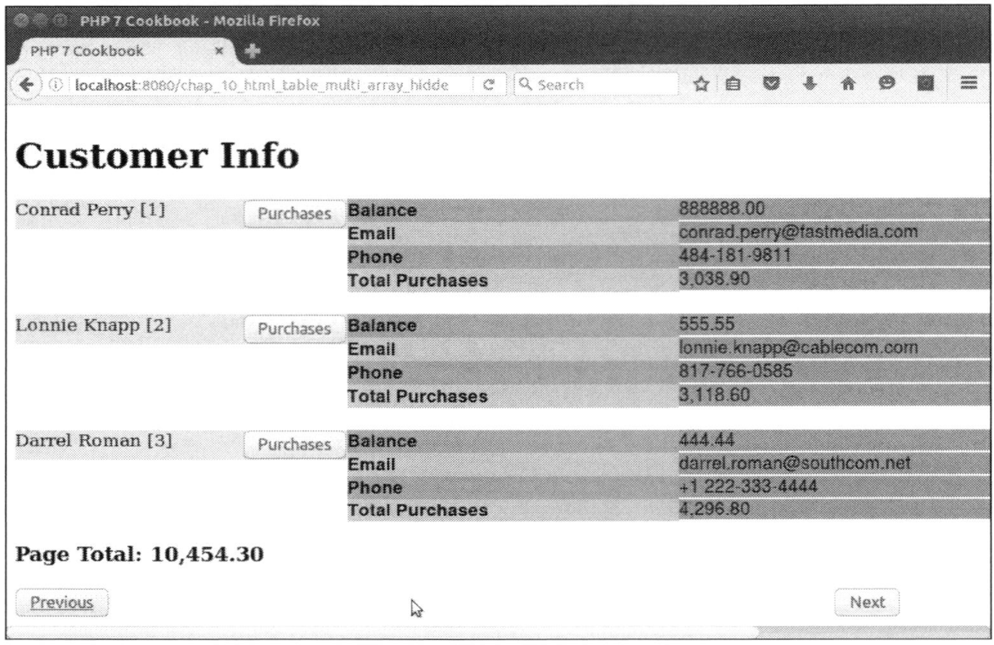

When the **Purchases** button is clicked, initial purchase info appears. If the link to **More** is clicked, the remaining purchase information shows:

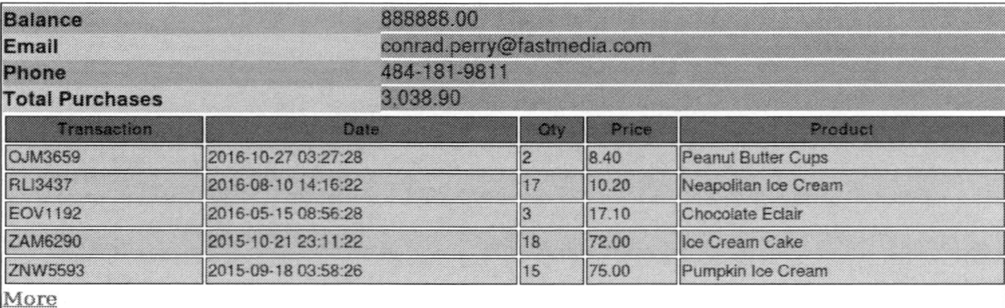

Balance	888888.00
Email	conrad.perry@fastmedia.com
Phone	484-181-9811
Total Purchases	3,038.90

Transaction	Date	Qty	Price	Product
OJM3659	2016-10-27 03:27:28	2	8.40	Peanut Butter Cups
RLI3437	2016-08-10 14:16:22	17	10.20	Neapolitan Ice Cream
EOV1192	2016-05-15 08:56:28	3	17.10	Chocolate Eclair
ZAM6290	2015-10-21 23:11:22	18	72.00	Ice Cream Cake
ZNW5593	2015-09-18 03:58:26	15	75.00	Pumpkin Ice Cream

More

11

Implementing Software Design Patterns

In this chapter, we will cover the following topics:

- Creating an array to object hydrator
- Building an object to array hydrator
- Implementing a strategy pattern
- Defining a mapper
- Implementing object-relational mapping
- Implementing the Pub/Sub design pattern

Introduction

The idea of incorporating **software design patterns** into **object-oriented programming** (**OOP**) code was first discussed in a seminal work entitled *Design Patterns: Elements of Reusable Object-Oriented Software*, authored by the famous Gang of Four (E. Gamma, R. Helm, R. Johnson, and J. Vlissides) in 1994. Defining neither standards nor protocols, this work identified common generic software designs that have proven useful over the years. The patterns discussed in this book are generally thought to fall into three categories: creational, structural, and behavioral.

Examples of many of these patterns have already been presented in this book. Here is a brief summary:

Design pattern	**Chapter**	**Recipe**
Singleton	2	Defining visibility
Factory	6	Implementing a form factory
Adapter	8	Handling translation without `gettext()`
Proxy	7	Creating a simple REST client Creating a simple SOAP client
Iterator	2 3	Recursive directory iterator Using iterators

In this chapter, we will examine a number of additional design patterns, focusing primarily on Concurrency and Architectural patterns.

Creating an array to object hydrator

The **Hydrator** pattern is a variation of the **Data Transfer Object** design pattern. Its design principle is quite simple: moving data from one place to another. In this illustration, we will define classes to move data from an array to an object.

How to do it...

1. First, we define a `Hydrator` class that is able to use getters and setters. For this illustration we will use `Application\Generic\Hydrator\GetSet`:

```
namespace Application\Generic\Hydrator;
class GetSet
{
  // code
}
```

2. Next, we define a `hydrate()` method, which takes both an array and an object as arguments. It then calls the `setXXX()` methods on the object to populate it with values from the array. We use `get_class()` to determine the object's class, and then `get_class_methods()` to get a list of all methods. `preg_match()` is used to match the method prefix and its suffix, which is subsequently assumed to be the array key:

```
public static function hydrate(array $array, $object)
{
  $class = get_class($object);
  $methodList = get_class_methods($class);
```

```
        foreach ($methodList as $method) {
          preg_match('/^(set)(.*?)$/i', $method, $matches);
          $prefix = $matches[1] ?? '';
          $key    = $matches[2] ?? '';
          $key    = strtolower(substr($key, 0, 1)) . substr($key, 1);
          if ($prefix == 'set' && !empty($array[$key])) {
              $object->$method($array[$key]);
          }
        }
        return $object;
      }
```

How it works...

To demonstrate how the array to hydrator object is used, first define the `Application\Generic\Hydrator\GetSet` class as described in the *How to do it...* section. Next, define an entity class that can be used to test the concept. For the purposes of this illustration, create a `Application\Entity\Person` class, with the appropriate properties and methods. Be sure to define getters and setters for all properties. Not all such methods are shown here:

```
namespace Application\Entity;
class Person
{
  protected $firstName  = '';
  protected $lastName   = '';
  protected $address    = '';
  protected $city       = '';
  protected $stateProv  = '';
  protected $postalCode = '';
  protected $country    = '';

  public function getFirstName()
  {
    return $this->firstName;
  }

  public function setFirstName($firstName)
  {
    $this->firstName = $firstName;
  }

  // etc.
}
```

You can now create a calling program called `chap_11_array_to_object.php`, which sets up autoloading, and uses the appropriate classes:

```
<?php
require __DIR__ . '/../Application/Autoload/Loader.php';
Application\Autoload\Loader::init(__DIR__ . '/..');
use Application\Entity\Person;
use Application\Generic\Hydrator\GetSet;
```

Next, you can define a test array with values that will be added to a new `Person` instance:

```
$a['firstName'] = 'Li\'l Abner';
$a['lastName']  = 'Yokum';
$a['address']   = '1 Dirt Street';
$a['city']      = 'Dogpatch';
$a['stateProv'] = 'Kentucky';
$a['postalCode']= '12345';
$a['country']   = 'USA';
```

You can now call `hydrate()` and `extract()` in a static manner:

```
$b = GetSet::hydrate($a, new Person());
var_dump($b);
```

The results are shown in the following screenshot:

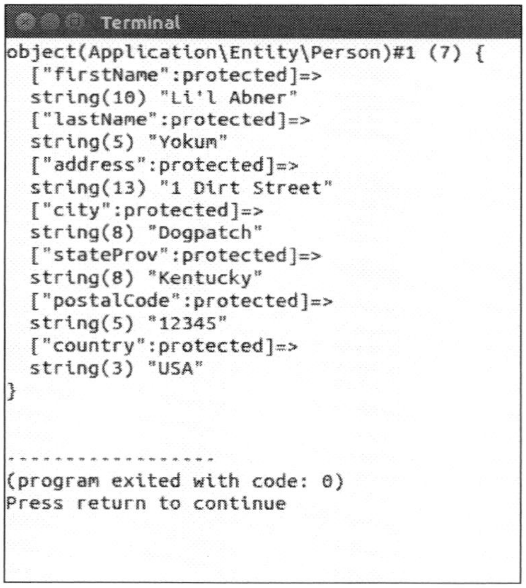

```
Terminal
object(Application\Entity\Person)#1 (7) {
  ["firstName":protected]=>
  string(10) "Li'l Abner"
  ["lastName":protected]=>
  string(5) "Yokum"
  ["address":protected]=>
  string(13) "1 Dirt Street"
  ["city":protected]=>
  string(8) "Dogpatch"
  ["stateProv":protected]=>
  string(8) "Kentucky"
  ["postalCode":protected]=>
  string(5) "12345"
  ["country":protected]=>
  string(3) "USA"
}


------------------
(program exited with code: 0)
Press return to continue
```

Building an object to array hydrator

This recipe is the converse of the *Creating an array to object hydrator* recipe. In this case, we need to pull values from object properties and return an associative array where the key will be the column name.

How to do it...

1. For this illustration we will build upon the `Application\Generic\Hydrator\GetSet` class defined in the previous recipe:

   ```
   namespace Application\Generic\Hydrator;
   class GetSet
   {
     // code
   }
   ```

2. After the `hydrate()` method defined in the previous recipe, we define an `extract()` method, which takes an object as an argument. The logic is similar to that used with `hydrate()`, except this time we're searching for `getXXX()` methods. Again, `preg_match()` is used to match the method prefix and its suffix, which is subsequently assumed to be the array key:

   ```
   public static function extract($object)
   {
     $array = array();
     $class = get_class($object);
     $methodList = get_class_methods($class);
     foreach ($methodList as $method) {
       preg_match('/^(get)(.*?)$/i', $method, $matches);
       $prefix = $matches[1] ?? '';
       $key    = $matches[2] ?? '';
       $key    = strtolower(substr($key, 0, 1)) . substr($key, 1);
       if ($prefix == 'get') {
         $array[$key] = $object->$method();
       }
     }
     return $array;
   }
   }
   ```

Note that we have defined `hydrate()` and `extract()` as static methods for convenience.

How it works...

Define a calling program called `chap_11_object_to_array.php`, which sets up autoloading, and uses the appropriate classes:

```
<?php
require __DIR__ . '/../Application/Autoload/Loader.php';
Application\Autoload\Loader::init(__DIR__ . '/..');
use Application\Entity\Person;
use Application\Generic\Hydrator\GetSet;
```

Next, define an instance of `Person`, setting values for its properties:

```
$obj = new Person();
$obj->setFirstName('Li\'lAbner');
$obj->setLastName('Yokum');
$obj->setAddress('1DirtStreet');
$obj->setCity('Dogpatch');
$obj->setStateProv('Kentucky');
$obj->setPostalCode('12345');
$obj->setCountry('USA');
```

Finally, call the new `extract()` method in a static manner:

```
$a = GetSet::extract($obj);
var_dump($a);
```

The output is shown in the following screenshot:

```
Terminal
array(7) {
  ["firstName"]=>
  string(9) "Li'lAbner"
  ["lastName"]=>
  string(5) "Yokum"
  ["address"]=>
  string(11) "1DirtStreet"
  ["city"]=>
  string(8) "Dogpatch"
  ["stateProv"]=>
  string(8) "Kentucky"
  ["postalCode"]=>
  string(5) "12345"
  ["country"]=>
  string(3) "USA"
}


------------------
(program exited with code: 0)
Press return to continue
```

Implementing a strategy pattern

It is often the case that runtime conditions force the developer to define several ways of doing the same thing. Traditionally, this involved a massive `if/elseif/else` block of commands. You would then either have to define large blocks of logic inside the `if` statement, or create a series of functions or methods to enable the different approaches. The strategy pattern attempts to formalize this process by having the primary class encapsulate a series of sub-classes that represent different approaches to solve the same problem.

How to do it...

1. In this illustration, we will use the `GetSet` hydrator class defined previously as a strategy. We will define a primary `Application\Generic\Hydrator\Any` class, which will then consume strategy classes in the `Application\Generic\Hydrator\Strategy` namespace, including `GetSet`, `PublicProps`, and `Extending`.
2. We first define class constants that reflect the built-in strategies that are available:

```
namespace Application\Generic\Hydrator;
use InvalidArgumentException;
use Application\Generic\Hydrator\Strategy\ {
GetSet, PublicProps, Extending };
class Any
{
  const STRATEGY_PUBLIC  = 'PublicProps';
  const STRATEGY_GET_SET = 'GetSet';
  const STRATEGY_EXTEND  = 'Extending';
  protected $strategies;
  public $chosen;
```

3. We then define a constructor that adds all built-in strategies to the `$strategies` property:

```
public function __construct()
{
  $this->strategies[self::STRATEGY_GET_SET] = new GetSet();
  $this->strategies[self::STRATEGY_PUBLIC] = new PublicProps();
  $this->strategies[self::STRATEGY_EXTEND] = new Extending();
}
```

4. We also add an `addStrategy()` method that allows us to overwrite or add new strategies without having to recode the class:

```
public function addStrategy($key, HydratorInterface $strategy)
{
  $this->strategies[$key] = $strategy;
}
```

5. The `hydrate()` and `extract()` methods simply call those of the chosen strategy:

```
public function hydrate(array $array, $object)
{
  $strategy = $this->chooseStrategy($object);
  $this->chosen = get_class($strategy);
  return $strategy::hydrate($array, $object);
}

public function extract($object)
{
  $strategy = $this->chooseStrategy($object);
  $this->chosen = get_class($strategy);
  return $strategy::extract($object);
}
```

6. The tricky bit is figuring out which hydration strategy to choose. For this purpose we define `chooseStrategy()`, which takes an object as an argument. We first perform some detective work by way of getting a list of class methods. We then scan through the list to see if we have any `getXXX()` or `setXXX()` methods. If so, we choose the `GetSet` hydrator as our chosen strategy:

```
public function chooseStrategy($object)
{
  $strategy = NULL;
  $methodList = get_class_methods(get_class($object));
  if (!empty($methodList) && is_array($methodList)) {
      $getSet = FALSE;
      foreach ($methodList as $method) {
        if (preg_match('/^get|set.*$/i', $method)) {
            $strategy = $this->strategies[self::STRATEGY_GET_SET];
      break;
    }
  }
}
```

7. Still within our `chooseStrategy()` method, if there are no getters or setters, we next use `get_class_vars()` to determine if there are any available properties. If so, we choose `PublicProps` as our hydrator:

```
if (!$strategy) {
    $vars = get_class_vars(get_class($object));
    if (!empty($vars) && count($vars)) {
        $strategy = $this->strategies[self::STRATEGY_PUBLIC];
    }
}
```

8. If all else fails, we fall back to the `Extending` hydrator, which returns a new class that simply extends the object class, thus making any `public` or `protected` properties available:

```
if (!$strategy) {
    $strategy = $this->strategies[self::STRATEGY_EXTEND];
}
return $strategy;
}
}
```

9. Now we turn our attention to the strategies themselves. First, we define a new `Application\Generic\Hydrator\Strategy` namespace.
10. In the new namespace, we define an interface that allows us to identify any strategies that can be consumed by `Application\Generic\Hydrator\Any`:

```
namespace Application\Generic\Hydrator\Strategy;
interface HydratorInterface
{
  public static function hydrate(array $array, $object);
  public static function extract($object);
}
```

11. The `GetSet` hydrator is exactly as defined in the previous two recipes, with the only addition being that it will implement the new interface:

```
namespace Application\Generic\Hydrator\Strategy;
class GetSet implements HydratorInterface
{

  public static function hydrate(array $array, $object)
  {
    // defined in the recipe:
    // "Creating an Array to Object Hydrator"
  }

  public static function extract($object)
```

```
    {
      // defined in the recipe:
      // "Building an Object to Array Hydrator"
    }
  }
```

12. The next hydrator simply reads and writes public properties:

```
namespace Application\Generic\Hydrator\Strategy;
class PublicProps implements HydratorInterface
{
  public static function hydrate(array $array, $object)
  {
    $propertyList= array_keys(
      get_class_vars(get_class($object)));
    foreach ($propertyList as $property) {
      $object->$property = $array[$property] ?? NULL;
    }
    return $object;
  }

  public static function extract($object)
  {
    $array = array();
    $propertyList = array_keys(
      get_class_vars(get_class($object)));
    foreach ($propertyList as $property) {
      $array[$property] = $object->$property;
    }
    return $array;
  }
}
```

13. Finally, `Extending`, the Swiss Army knife of hydrators, extends the object class, thus providing direct access to properties. We further define magic getters and setters to provide access to properties.

14. The `hydrate()` method is the most difficult as we are assuming no getters or setters are defined, nor are the properties defined with a visibility level of `public`. Accordingly, we need to define a class that extends the class of the object to be hydrated. We do this by first defining a string that will be used as a template to build the new class:

```
namespace Application\Generic\Hydrator\Strategy;
class Extending implements HydratorInterface
{
  const UNDEFINED_PREFIX = 'undefined';
```

```
    const TEMP_PREFIX = 'TEMP_';
    const ERROR_EVAL = 'ERROR: unable to evaluate object';
    public static function hydrate(array $array, $object)
    {
      $className = get_class($object);
      $components = explode('\\', $className);
      $realClass  = array_pop($components);
      $nameSpace  = implode('\\', $components);
      $tempClass = $realClass . self::TEMP_SUFFIX;
      $template = 'namespace '
        . $nameSpace . '{'
        . 'class ' . $tempClass
        . ' extends ' . $realClass . ' '
```

15. Continuing in the `hydrate()` method, we define a `$values` property, and a constructor that assigns the array to be hydrated into the object as an argument. We loop through the array of values, assigning values to properties. We also define a useful `getArrayCopy()` method, which returns these values if needed, as well as a magic `__get()` method to simulate direct property access:

```
. '{ '
. '  protected $values; '
. '  public function __construct($array) '
. '  { $this->values = $array; '
. '    foreach ($array as $key => $value) '
. '       $this->$key = $value; '
. '  } '
. '  public function getArrayCopy() '
. '  { return $this->values; } '
```

16. For convenience we define a magic `__get()` method, which simulates direct variable access as if they were public:

```
. '  public function __get($key) '
. '  { return $this->values[$key] ?? NULL; } '
```

17. Still in the template for the new class, we define also a magic `__call()` method, which simulates getters and setters:

```
. '  public function __call($method, $params) '
. '  { '
. '    preg_match("/^(get|set)(.*?)$/i", '
. '        $method, $matches); '
. '    $prefix = $matches[1] ?? ""; '
. '    $key    = $matches[2] ?? ""; '
. '    $key    = strtolower(substr($key, 0, 1)) '
. '              substr($key, 1); '
```

```
. '     if ($prefix == "get") { '
. '         return $this->values[$key] ?? NULL; '
. '      } else { '
. '         $this->values[$key] = $params[0]; '
. '      } '
. '   } '
. '} '
. '} // ends namespace ' . PHP_EOL
```

18. Finally, still in the template for the new class, we add a function, in the global namespace, that builds and returns the class instance:

```
. 'namespace { '
. 'function build($array) '
. '{ return new ' . $nameSpace . '\\'
.    $tempClass . '($array); } '
. '} // ends global namespace '
. PHP_EOL;
```

19. Still in the `hydrate()` method, we execute the completed template using `eval()`. We then run the `build()` method defined just at the end of the template. Note that as we are unsure of the namespace of the class to be populated, we define and call `build()` from the global namespace:

```
try {
    eval($template);
} catch (ParseError $e) {
    error_log(__METHOD__ . ':' . $e->getMessage());
    throw new Exception(self::ERROR_EVAL);
}
return \build($array);
}
```

20. The `extract()` method is much easier to define as our choices are extremely limited. Extending a class and populating it from an array using magic methods is easily accomplished. The reverse is not the case. If we were to extend the class, we would lose all the property values, as we are extending the class, not the object instance. Accordingly, our only option is to use a combination of getters and public properties:

```
public static function extract($object)
{
  $array = array();
  $class = get_class($object);
  $methodList = get_class_methods($class);
  foreach ($methodList as $method) {
    preg_match('/^(get)(.*?)$/i', $method, $matches);
```

```
        $prefix = $matches[1] ?? '';
        $key    = $matches[2] ?? '';
        $key    = strtolower(substr($key, 0, 1))
        . substr($key, 1);
        if ($prefix == 'get') {
            $array[$key] = $object->$method();
        }
      }
      $propertyList= array_keys(get_class_vars($class));
      foreach ($propertyList as $property) {
        $array[$property] = $object->$property;
      }
      return $array;
      }
    }
```

How it works...

You can begin by defining three test classes with identical properties: `firstName`, `lastName`, and so on. The first, `Person`, should have protected properties along with getters and setters. The second, `PublicPerson`, will have public properties. The third, `ProtectedPerson`, has protected properties but no getters nor setters:

```
<?php
namespace Application\Entity;
class Person
{
  protected $firstName  = '';
  protected $lastName   = '';
  protected $address    = '';
  protected $city       = '';
  protected $stateProv  = '';
  protected $postalCode = '';
  protected $country    = '';

    public function getFirstName()
    {
      return $this->firstName;
    }

    public function setFirstName($firstName)
    {
      $this->firstName = $firstName;
```

```
    }

  // be sure to define remaining getters and setters

}
```

```
<?php
namespace Application\Entity;
class PublicPerson
{
  private $id = NULL;
  public $firstName  = '';
  public $lastName   = '';
  public $address    = '';
  public $city       = '';
  public $stateProv  = '';
  public $postalCode = '';
  public $country    = '';
}
```

```
<?php
namespace Application\Entity;

class ProtectedPerson
{
  private $id = NULL;
  protected $firstName  = '';
  protected $lastName   = '';
  protected $address    = '';
  protected $city       = '';
  protected $stateProv  = '';
  protected $postalCode = '';
  protected $country    = '';
}
```

You can now define a calling program called `chap_11_strategy_pattern.php`, which sets up autoloading and uses the appropriate classes:

```
<?php
require __DIR__ . '/../Application/Autoload/Loader.php';
Application\Autoload\Loader::init(__DIR__ . '/..');
use Application\Entity\ { Person, PublicPerson, ProtectedPerson };
use Application\Generic\Hydrator\Any;
use Application\Generic\Hydrator\Strategy\ { GetSet, Extending,
  PublicProps };
```

Next, create an instance of `Person` and run the setters to define values for properties:

```
$obj = new Person();
$obj->setFirstName('Li\'lAbner');
$obj->setLastName('Yokum');
$obj->setAddress('1 Dirt Street');
$obj->setCity('Dogpatch');
$obj->setStateProv('Kentucky');
$obj->setPostalCode('12345');
$obj->setCountry('USA');
```

Next, create an instance of the `Any` hydrator, call `extract()`, and use `var_dump()` to view the results:

```
$hydrator = new Any();
$b = $hydrator->extract($obj);
echo "\nChosen Strategy: " . $hydrator->chosen . "\n";
var_dump($b);
```

Observe, in the following output, that the `GetSet` strategy was chosen:

```
Terminal

Chosen Strategy: Application\Generic\Hydrator\Strategy\GetSet
array(7) {
  ["firstName"]=>
  string(9) "Li'lAbner"
  ["lastName"]=>
  string(5) "Yokum"
  ["address"]=>
  string(13) "1 Dirt Street"
  ["city"]=>
  string(8) "Dogpatch"
  ["stateProv"]=>
  string(8) "Kentucky"
  ["postalCode"]=>
  string(5) "12345"
  ["country"]=>
  string(3) "USA"
}
```

Note that the `id` property is not set as its visibility level is `private`.

Next, you can define an array with the same values. Call `hydrate()` on the `Any` instance, and supply a new `PublicPerson` instance as an argument:

```
$a = [
  'firstName'  => 'Li\'lAbner',
  'lastName'   => 'Yokum',
```

```
    'address'    => '1 Dirt Street',
    'city'       => 'Dogpatch',
    'stateProv'  => 'Kentucky',
    'postalCode' => '12345',
    'country'    => 'USA'
];

$p = $hydrator->hydrate($a, new PublicPerson());
echo "\nChosen Strategy: " . $hydrator->chosen . "\n";
var_dump($p);
```

Here is the result. Note that the `PublicProps` strategy was chosen in this case:

```
Terminal

Chosen Strategy: Application\Generic\Hydrator\Strategy\PublicProps
object(Application\Entity\PublicPerson)#6 (8) {
  ["id":"Application\Entity\PublicPerson":private]=>
  NULL
  ["firstName"]=>
  string(9) "Li'lAbner"
  ["lastName"]=>
  string(5) "Yokum"
  ["address"]=>
  string(13) "1 Dirt Street"
  ["city"]=>
  string(8) "Dogpatch"
  ["stateProv"]=>
  string(8) "Kentucky"
  ["postalCode"]=>
  string(5) "12345"
  ["country"]=>
  string(3) "USA"
}
```

Finally, call `hydrate()` again, but this time supply an instance of `ProtectedPerson` as the object argument. We then call `getFirstName()` and `getLastName()` to test the magic getters. We also access first and last names as direct variable access:

```
$q = $hydrator->hydrate($a, new ProtectedPerson());
echo "\nChosen Strategy: " . $hydrator->chosen . "\n";
echo "Name: {$q->getFirstName()} {$q->getLastName()}\n";
echo "Name: {$q->firstName} {$q->lastName}\n";
var_dump($q);
```

Here is the last output, showing that the `Extending` strategy was chosen. You'll also note that the instance is a new `ProtectedPerson_TEMP` class, and that the protected properties are fully populated:

```
Terminal
Chosen Strategy: Application\Generic\Hydrator\Strategy\Extending
Name: Li'lAbner Yokum
Name: Li'lAbner Yokum
object(Application\Entity\ProtectedPerson_TEMP)#8 (9) {
  ["values":protected]=>
  array(7) {
    ["firstName"]=>
    string(9) "Li'lAbner"
    ["lastName"]=>
    string(5) "Yokum"
    ["address"]=>
    string(13) "1 Dirt Street"
    ["city"]=>
    string(8) "Dogpatch"
    ["stateProv"]=>
    string(8) "Kentucky"
    ["postalCode"]=>
    string(5) "12345"
    ["country"]=>
    string(3) "USA"
  }
  ["id":"Application\Entity\ProtectedPerson":private]=>
  NULL
  ["firstName":protected]=>
  string(9) "Li'lAbner"
  ["lastName":protected]=>
  string(5) "Yokum"
  ["address":protected]=>
  string(13) "1 Dirt Street"
```

Defining a mapper

A **mapper** or **data mapper** works in much the same manner as a hydrator: converting data from one model, be it array or object, into another. A critical difference is that the hydrator is generic and does not need to have object property names pre-programmed, whereas the mapper is the opposite: it needs precise information on property names for both models. In this recipe we will demonstrate the use of a mapper to convert data from one database table into another.

How to do it...

1. We first define a `Application\Database\Mapper\FieldConfig` class, which contains mapping instructions for individual fields. We also define appropriate class constants:

```
namespace Application\Database\Mapper;
use InvalidArgumentException;
class FieldConfig
{
  const ERROR_SOURCE =
    'ERROR: need to specify destTable and/or source';
  const ERROR_DEST   = 'ERROR: need to specify either '
    . 'both destTable and destCol or neither';
```

2. Key properties are defined along with the appropriate class constants. `$key` is used to identify the object. `$source` represents the column from the source database table. `$destTable` and `$destCol` represent the target database table and column. `$default`, if defined, contains a default value or a callback that produces the appropriate value:

```
public $key;
public $source;
public $destTable;
public $destCol;
public $default;
```

3. We now turn our attention to the constructor, which assigns default values, builds the key, and checks to see that either or both `$source` or `$destTable` and `$destCol` are defined:

```
public function __construct($source = NULL,
                            $destTable = NULL,
                            $destCol   = NULL,
                            $default   = NULL)
{
  // generate key from source + destTable + destCol
  $this->key = $source . '.' . $destTable . '.' . $destCol;
  $this->source = $source;
  $this->destTable = $destTable;
  $this->destCol = $destCol;
  $this->default = $default;
  if (($destTable && !$destCol) ||
      (!$destTable && $destCol)) {
      throw new InvalidArgumentException(self::ERROR_DEST);
  }
  if (!$destTable && !$source) {
      throw new InvalidArgumentException(
        self::ERROR_SOURCE);
  }
}
```

Note that we allow source and destination columns to be `NULL`. The reason for this is that we might have a source column that has no place in the destination table. Likewise, there might be mandatory columns in the destination table that are not represented in the source table.

4. In the case of defaults, we need to check to see if the value is a callback. If so, we run the callback; otherwise, we return the direct value. Note that the callbacks should be defined so that they accept a database table row as an argument:

```
public function getDefault()
{
  if (is_callable($this->default)) {
      return call_user_func($this->default, $row);
  } else {
      return $this->default;
  }
}
```

5. Finally, to wrap up this class, we define getters and setters for each of the five properties:

```
public function getKey()
{
  return $this->key;
}

public function setKey($key)
{
  $this->key = $key;
}

// etc.
```

6. Next, we define a `Application\Database\Mapper\Mapping` mapping class, which accepts the name of the source and destination tables as well as an array of `FieldConfig` objects as an argument. You will see later that we allow the destination table property to be an array, as the mapping might be to two or more destination tables:

```
namespace Application\Database\Mapper;
class Mapping
{
  protected $sourceTable;
  protected $destTable;
  protected $fields;
  protected $sourceCols;
  protected $destCols;

  public function __construct(
    $sourceTable, $destTable, $fields = NULL)
  {
    $this->sourceTable = $sourceTable;
```

```
        $this->destTable = $destTable;
        $this->fields = $fields;
    }
```

7. We then define getters and setters for these properties:

```
public function getSourceTable()
{
  return $this->sourceTable;
}
public function setSourceTable($sourceTable)
{
  $this->sourceTable = $sourceTable;
}
// etc.
```

8. For field configuration, we also need to provide the ability to add an individual field. There is no need to supply the key as a separate argument as this can be obtained from the `FieldConfig` instance:

```
public function addField(FieldConfig $field)
{
  $this->fields[$field->getKey()] = $field;
  return $this;
}
```

9. It is extremely important to obtain an array of source column names. The problem is that the source column name is a property buried in a `FieldConfig` object. Accordingly, when this method is called, we loop through the array of `FieldConfig` objects and invoke `getSource()` on each one to obtain the source column name:

```
public function getSourceColumns()
{
  if (!$this->sourceCols) {
      $this->sourceCols = array();
      foreach ($this->getFields() as $field) {
        if (!empty($field->getSource())) {
            $this->sourceCols[$field->getKey()] =
              $field->getSource();
        }
      }
  }
  return $this->sourceCols;
}
```

10. We use a similar approach for `getDestColumns()`. The big difference compared to getting a list of source columns is that we only want the columns for one specific destination table, which is critical if there's more than one such table is defined. We do not need to check to see if `$destCol` is set as this is already taken care of in the constructor for `FieldConfig`:

    ```
    public function getDestColumns($table)
    {
      if (empty($this->destCols[$table])) {
          foreach ($this->getFields() as $field) {
            if ($field->getDestTable()) {
              if ($field->getDestTable() == $table) {
                  $this->destCols[$table][$field->getKey()] =
                    $field->getDestCol();
              }
            }
          }
      }
      return $this->destCols[$table];
    }
    ```

11. Finally, we define a method that accepts as a first argument an array representing one row of data from the source table. The second argument is the name of the destination table. The method produces an array of data ready to be inserted into the destination table.

12. We had to make a decision as to which would take precedence: the default value (which could be provided by a callback), or data from the source table. We decided to test for a default value first. If the default comes back `NULL`, data from the source is used. Note that if further processing is required, the default should be defined as a callback.

    ```
    public function mapData($sourceData, $destTable)
    {
      $dest = array();
      foreach ($this->fields as $field) {
        if ($field->getDestTable() == $destTable) {
            $dest[$field->getDestCol()] = NULL;
            $default = $field->getDefault($sourceData);
            if ($default) {
                $dest[$field->getDestCol()] = $default;
            } else {
                $dest[$field->getDestCol()] =
                      $sourceData[$field->getSource()];
            }
        }
      }
    ```

```
        return $dest;
    }
    }
```

Note that some columns will appear in the destination insert that are not present in the source row. In this case, the `$source` property of the `FieldConfig` object is left as `NULL`, and a default value is supplied, either as a scalar value or as a callback.

13. We are now ready to define two methods that will generate SQL. The first such method will generate an SQL statement to read from the source table. The statement will include placeholders to be prepared (for example, using `PDO::prepare()`):

```
public function getSourceSelect($where = NULL)
{
  $sql = 'SELECT '
  . implode(',', $this->getSourceColumns()) . ' ';
  $sql .= 'FROM ' . $this->getSourceTable() . ' ';
  if ($where) {
    $where = trim($where);
    if (stripos($where, 'WHERE') !== FALSE) {
        $sql .= $where;
    } else {
        $sql .= 'WHERE ' . $where;
    }
  }
  return trim($sql);
}
```

14. The other SQL generation method produces a statement to be prepared for a specific destination table. Notice that the placeholders are the same as the column names preceded by "`:`":

```
public function getDestInsert($table)
{
  $sql = 'INSERT INTO ' . $table . ' ';
  $sql .= '( '
  . implode(',', $this->getDestColumns($table))
  . ' ) ';
  $sql .= ' VALUES ';
  $sql .= '( :'
  . implode(',:', $this->getDestColumns($table))
  . ' ) ';
  return trim($sql);
}
```

How it works...

Use the code shown in steps 1 to 5 to produce an `Application\Database\Mapper\FieldConfig` class. Place the code shown in steps 6 to 14 into a second `Application\Database\Mapper\Mapping` class.

Before defining a calling program that performs mapping, it's important to consider the source and destination database tables. The definition for the source table, `prospects_11`, is as follows:

```
CREATE TABLE `prospects_11` (
  `id` int(11) NOT NULL AUTO_INCREMENT,
  `first_name` varchar(128) NOT NULL,
  `last_name` varchar(128) NOT NULL,
  `address` varchar(256) DEFAULT NULL,
  `city` varchar(64) DEFAULT NULL,
  `state_province` varchar(32) DEFAULT NULL,
  `postal_code` char(16) NOT NULL,
  `phone` varchar(16) NOT NULL,
  `country` char(2) NOT NULL,
  `email` varchar(250) NOT NULL,
  `status` char(8) DEFAULT NULL,
  `budget` decimal(10,2) DEFAULT NULL,
  `last_updated` datetime DEFAULT NULL,
  PRIMARY KEY (`id`),
  UNIQUE KEY `UNIQ_35730C06E7927C74` (`email`)
) ENGINE=InnoDB DEFAULT CHARSET=utf8;
```

In this example, you can use two destination tables, `customer_11` and `profile_11`, between which there is a 1:1 relationship:

```
CREATE TABLE `customer_11` (
  `id` int(11) NOT NULL AUTO_INCREMENT,
  `name` varchar(256) CHARACTER SET latin1
     COLLATE latin1_general_cs NOT NULL,
  `balance` decimal(10,2) NOT NULL,
  `email` varchar(250) NOT NULL,
  `password` char(16) NOT NULL,
  `status` int(10) unsigned NOT NULL DEFAULT '0',
  `security_question` varchar(250) DEFAULT NULL,
  `confirm_code` varchar(32) DEFAULT NULL,
  `profile_id` int(11) DEFAULT NULL,
  `level` char(3) NOT NULL,
  PRIMARY KEY (`id`),
  UNIQUE KEY `UNIQ_81398E09E7927C74` (`email`)
```

```
) ENGINE=InnoDB AUTO_INCREMENT=80 DEFAULT CHARSET=utf8
COMMENT='Customers';

CREATE TABLE `profile_11` (
  `id` int(11) NOT NULL AUTO_INCREMENT,
  `address` varchar(256) NOT NULL,
  `city` varchar(64) NOT NULL,
  `state_province` varchar(32) NOT NULL,
  `postal_code` varchar(10) NOT NULL,
  `country` varchar(3) NOT NULL,
  `phone` varchar(16) NOT NULL,
  `photo` varchar(128) NOT NULL,
  `dob` datetime NOT NULL,
  PRIMARY KEY (`id`)
) ENGINE=InnoDB AUTO_INCREMENT=80 DEFAULT CHARSET=utf8
COMMENT='Customers';
```

You can now define a calling program called `chap_11_mapper.php`, which sets up autoloading and uses the two classes mentioned previously. You can also use the `Connection` class defined in *Chapter 5, Interacting with a Database*:

```
<?php
define('DB_CONFIG_FILE', '/../config/db.config.php');
define('DEFAULT_PHOTO', 'person.gif');
require __DIR__ . '/../Application/Autoload/Loader.php';
Application\Autoload\Loader::init(__DIR__ . '/..');
use Application\Database\Mapper\ { FieldConfig, Mapping };
use Application\Database\Connection;
$conn = new Connection(include __DIR__ . DB_CONFIG_FILE);
```

For demonstration purposes, after having made sure the two destination tables exist, you can truncate both tables so that any data that appears is clean:

```
$conn->pdo->query('DELETE FROM customer_11');
$conn->pdo->query('DELETE FROM profile_11');
```

You are now ready to build the `Mapping` instance and populate it with `FieldConfig` objects. Each `FieldConfig` object represents a mapping between source and destination. In the constructor, supply the name of the source table and the two destination tables in the form of an array:

```
$mapper = new Mapping('prospects_11', ['customer_11','profile_11']);
```

You can start simply by mapping fields between `prospects_11` and `customer_11` where there are no defaults:

```
$mapper>addField(new FieldConfig('email','customer_11','email'))
```

Note that `addField()` returns the current mapping instance so there is no need to keep specifying `$mapper->addField()`. This technique is referred to as the **fluent interface**.

The name field is tricky, as in the `prospects_11` table it's represented by two columns, but only one column in the `customer_11` table. Accordingly, you can add a callback as default for `first_name` to combine the two fields into one. You will also need to define an entry for `last_name` but where there is no destination mapping:

```
->addField(new FieldConfig('first_name','customer_11','name',
  function ($row) { return trim(($row['first_name'] ?? '')
. ' ' .  ($row['last_name'] ?? ''));}))
->addField(new FieldConfig('last_name'))
```

The `customer_11::status` field can use the null coalesce operator (`??`) to determine if it's set or not:

```
->addField(new FieldConfig('status','customer_11','status',
  function ($row) { return $row['status'] ?? 'Unknown'; }))
```

The `customer_11::level` field is not represented in the source table, thus you can make a `NULL` entry for the source field, but make sure the destination table and column are set. Likewise, `customer_11::password` is not present in the source table. In this case, the callback uses the phone number as a temporary password:

```
->addField(new FieldConfig(NULL,'customer_11','level','BEG'))
->addField(new FieldConfig(NULL,'customer_11','password',
  function ($row) { return $row['phone']; }))
```

You can also set mappings from `prospects_11` to `profile_11` as follows. Note that as the source photo and date of birth columns are not present in `prospects_11`, you can set any appropriate default:

```
->addField(new FieldConfig('address','profile_11','address'))
->addField(new FieldConfig('city','profile_11','city'))
->addField(new FieldConfig('state_province','profile_11',
'state_province', function ($row) {
  return $row['state_province'] ?? 'Unknown'; }))
->addField(new FieldConfig('postal_code','profile_11',
'postal_code'))
->addField(new FieldConfig('phone','profile_11','phone'))
->addField(new FieldConfig('country','profile_11','country'))
->addField(new FieldConfig(NULL,'profile_11','photo',
DEFAULT_PHOTO))
->addField(new FieldConfig(NULL,'profile_11','dob',
date('Y-m-d')));
```

In order to establish the 1:1 relationship between the `profile_11` and `customer_11` tables, we set the values of `customer_11::id`, `customer_11::profile_id` and `profile_11::id` to the value of `$row['id']` using a callback:

```
$idCallback = function ($row) { return $row['id']; };
$mapper->addField(new FieldConfig('id','customer_11','id',
$idCallback))
->addField(new FieldConfig(NULL,'customer_11','profile_id',
$idCallback))
->addField(new FieldConfig('id','profile_11','id',$idCallback));
```

You can now call the appropriate methods to generate three SQL statements, one to read from the source table, and two to insert into the two destination tables:

```
$sourceSelect  = $mapper->getSourceSelect();
$custInsert    = $mapper->getDestInsert('customer_11');
$profileInsert = $mapper->getDestInsert('profile_11');
```

These three statements can immediately be prepared for later execution:

```
$sourceStmt  = $conn->pdo->prepare($sourceSelect);
$custStmt    = $conn->pdo->prepare($custInsert);
$profileStmt = $conn->pdo->prepare($profileInsert);
```

We then execute the `SELECT` statement, which produces rows from the source table. In a loop we then generate `INSERT` data for each destination table, and execute the appropriate prepared statements:

```
$sourceStmt->execute();
while ($row = $sourceStmt->fetch(PDO::FETCH_ASSOC)) {
  $custData = $mapper->mapData($row, 'customer_11');
  $custStmt->execute($custData);
  $profileData = $mapper->mapData($row, 'profile_11');
  $profileStmt->execute($profileData);
  echo "Processing: {$custData['name']}\n";
}
```

Here are the three SQL statements produced:

```
ed@ed: ~/Desktop/Repos/php7_recipes/source/chapter11
SQL Statements:
SELECT email,first_name,last_name,status,address,city,state_province,postal_code,phone,
country,id,id FROM prospects_11
INSERT INTO customer_11 ( email,name,status,level,password,id,profile_id )  VALUES ( :e
mail,:name,:status,:level,:password,:id,:profile_id )
INSERT INTO profile_11 ( address,city,state_province,postal_code,phone,country,photo,do
b,id )  VALUES ( :address,:city,:state_province,:postal_code,:phone,:country,:photo,:do
b,:id )

Processing: WILFREDO RICHARDS
Processing: WILLARD ATKINSON
Processing: MANUEL WHITE
Processing: EDGAR SLOAN
Processing: AARON ALSTON
Processing: JEFF CASTRO
Processing: NEAL CHAVEZ
Processing: LEONARD LOVE
Processing: ROLANDO LANDRY
Processing: FREDRICK BEASLEY
Processing: RANDAL STUART
Processing: DARRYL LAWSON
Processing: SEAN DOMINGUEZ
Processing: CARLTON MCCLAIN
:
```

We can then view the data directly from the database using SQL `JOIN` to ensure the relationship has been maintained:

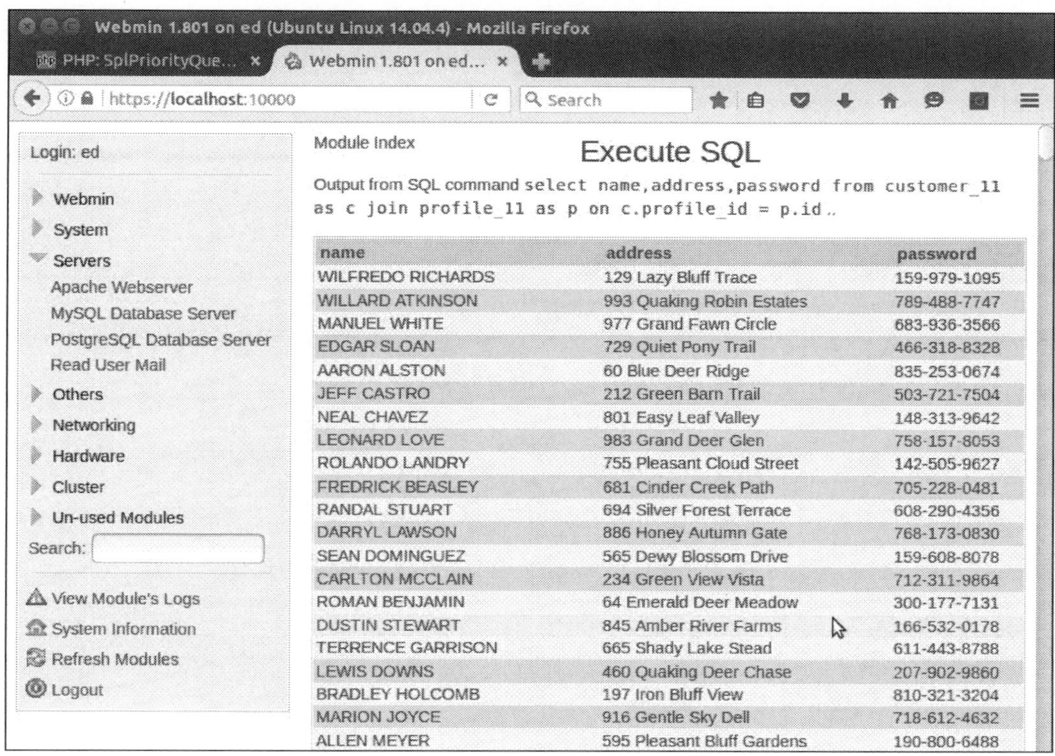

name	address	password
WILFREDO RICHARDS	129 Lazy Bluff Trace	159-979-1095
WILLARD ATKINSON	993 Quaking Robin Estates	789-488-7747
MANUEL WHITE	977 Grand Fawn Circle	683-936-3566
EDGAR SLOAN	729 Quiet Pony Trail	466-318-8328
AARON ALSTON	60 Blue Deer Ridge	835-253-0674
JEFF CASTRO	212 Green Barn Trail	503-721-7504
NEAL CHAVEZ	801 Easy Leaf Valley	148-313-9642
LEONARD LOVE	983 Grand Deer Glen	758-157-8053
ROLANDO LANDRY	755 Pleasant Cloud Street	142-505-9627
FREDRICK BEASLEY	681 Cinder Creek Path	705-228-0481
RANDAL STUART	694 Silver Forest Terrace	608-290-4356
DARRYL LAWSON	886 Honey Autumn Gate	768-173-0830
SEAN DOMINGUEZ	565 Dewy Blossom Drive	159-608-8078
CARLTON MCCLAIN	234 Green View Vista	712-311-9864
ROMAN BENJAMIN	64 Emerald Deer Meadow	300-177-7131
DUSTIN STEWART	845 Amber River Farms	166-532-0178
TERRENCE GARRISON	665 Shady Lake Stead	611-443-8788
LEWIS DOWNS	460 Quaking Deer Chase	207-902-9860
BRADLEY HOLCOMB	197 Iron Bluff View	810-321-3204
MARION JOYCE	916 Gentle Sky Dell	718-612-4632
ALLEN MEYER	595 Pleasant Bluff Gardens	190-800-6488

Implementing object-relational mapping

There are two primary techniques to achieve a relational mapping between objects. The first technique involves pre-loading the related child objects into the parent object. The advantage to this approach is that it is easy to implement, and all parent-child information is immediately available. The disadvantage is that large amounts of memory are potentially consumed, and the performance curve is skewed.

The second technique is to embed a secondary lookup into the parent object. In this latter approach, when you need to access the child objects, you would run a getter that would perform the secondary lookup. The advantage of this approach is that performance demands are spread out throughout the request cycle, and memory usage is (or can be) more easily managed. The disadvantage of this approach is that there are more queries generated, which means more work for the database server.

Please note, however, that we will show how the use of **prepared statements** can be used to greatly offset this disadvantage.

How to do it...

Let's have a look at two techniques to implement object-relational mapping.

Technique #1 – pre-loading all child information

First, we will discuss how to implement object relational mapping by pre-loading all child information into the parent class. For this illustration, we will use three related database tables, `customer`, `purchases`, and `products`:

1. We will use the existing `Application\Entity\Customer` class (defined in *Chapter 5, Interacting with a Database*, in the *Defining entity classes to match database tables recipe*) as a model to develop an `Application\Entity\Purchase` class. As before, we will use the database definition as the basis of the entity class definition. Here is the database definition for the `purchases` table:

```
CREATE TABLE `purchases` (
  `id` int(11) NOT NULL AUTO_INCREMENT,
  `transaction` varchar(8) NOT NULL,
  `date` datetime NOT NULL,
  `quantity` int(10) unsigned NOT NULL,
  `sale_price` decimal(8,2) NOT NULL,
  `customer_id` int(11) DEFAULT NULL,
  `product_id` int(11) DEFAULT NULL,
  PRIMARY KEY (`id`),
  KEY `IDX_C3F3` (`customer_id`),
```

```
    KEY `IDX_665A` (`product_id`),
    CONSTRAINT `FK_665A` FOREIGN KEY (`product_id`) REFERENCES
      `products` (`id`),
    CONSTRAINT `FK_C3F3` FOREIGN KEY (`customer_id`) REFERENCES
      `customer` (`id`)
);
```

2. Based on the customer entity class, here is how `Application\Entity\Purchase` might look. Note that not all getters and setters are shown:

```
namespace Application\Entity;

class Purchase extends Base
{

  const TABLE_NAME = 'purchases';
  protected $transaction = '';
  protected $date = NULL;
  protected $quantity = 0;
  protected $salePrice = 0.0;
  protected $customerId = 0;
  protected $productId = 0;

  protected $mapping = [
    'id'            => 'id',
    'transaction'   => 'transaction',
    'date'          => 'date',
    'quantity'      => 'quantity',
    'sale_price'    => 'salePrice',
    'customer_id'   => 'customerId',
    'product_id'    => 'productId',
  ];

  public function getTransaction() : string
  {
    return $this->transaction;
  }
  public function setTransaction($transaction)
  {
    $this->transaction = $transaction;
  }
  // NOTE: other getters / setters are not shown here
}
```

3. We are now ready to define `Application\Entity\Product`. Here is the database definition for the `products` table:

```
CREATE TABLE `products` (
  `id` int(11) NOT NULL AUTO_INCREMENT,
  `sku` varchar(16) DEFAULT NULL,
  `title` varchar(255) NOT NULL,
  `description` varchar(4096) DEFAULT NULL,
  `price` decimal(10,2) NOT NULL,
  `special` int(11) NOT NULL,
  `link` varchar(128) NOT NULL,
  PRIMARY KEY (`id`),
  UNIQUE KEY `UNIQ_38C4` (`sku`)
);
```

4. Based on the customer entity class, here is how `Application\Entity\Product` might look:

```
namespace Application\Entity;

class Product extends Base
{

  const TABLE_NAME = 'products';
  protected $sku = '';
  protected $title = '';
  protected $description = '';
  protected $price = 0.0;
  protected $special = 0;
  protected $link = '';

  protected $mapping = [
    'id'          => 'id',
    'sku'         => 'sku',
    'title'       => 'title',
    'description' => 'description',
    'price'       => 'price',
    'special'     => 'special',
    'link'        => 'link',
  ];

  public function getSku() : string
  {
    return $this->sku;
  }
  public function setSku($sku)
```

```
    {
      $this->sku = $sku;
    }
    // NOTE: other getters / setters are not shown here
}
```

5. Next, we need to implement a way to embed related objects. We will start with the `Application\Entity\Customer` parent class. For this section, we will assume the following relationships, illustrated in the following diagram:
    - One customer, many purchases
    - One purchase, one product

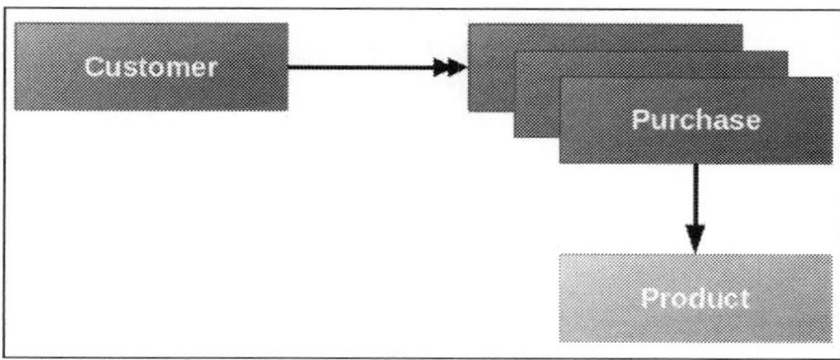

6. Accordingly, we define a getter and setter that process purchases in the form of an array of objects:

```
protected $purchases = array();
public function addPurchase($purchase)
{
  $this->purchases[] = $purchase;
}
public function getPurchases()
{
  return $this->purchases;
}
```

7. Now we turn our attention to `Application\Entity\Purchase`. In this case, there is a 1:1 relationship between a purchase and a product, so there's no need to process an array:

```
protected $product = NULL;
public function getProduct()
{
  return $this->product;
}
public function setProduct(Product $product)
{
  $this->product = $product;
}
```

Notice that in both entity classes, we do not alter the `$mapping` array. This is because implementing object relational mapping has no bearing on the mapping between entity property names and database column names.

8. Since the core functionality of obtaining basic customer information is still needed, all we need to do is to extend the `Application\Database\CustomerService` class described in *Chapter 5, Interacting with a Database*, in the *Tying entity classes to RDBMS queries* recipe. We can create a new `Application\Database\CustomerOrmService_1` class, which extends `Application\Database\CustomerService`:

```
namespace Application\Database;
use PDO;
use PDOException;
use Application\Entity\Customer;
use Application\Entity\Product;
use Application\Entity\Purchase;
class CustomerOrmService_1 extends CustomerService
{
  // add methods here
}
```

9. We then add a method to the new service class that performs a lookup and embeds the results, in the form of `Product` and `Purchase` entities, into the core customer entity. This method performs a lookup in the form of a `JOIN`. This is possible because there is a 1:1 relationship between purchase and product. Because the `id` column has the same name in both tables, we need to add the purchase ID column as an alias. We then loop through the results, creating `Product` and `Purchase` entities. After overriding the ID, we can then embed the `Product` entity into the `Purchase` entity, and then add the `Purchase` entity to the array in the `Customer` entity:

```
protected function fetchPurchasesForCustomer(Customer $cust)
{
  $sql = 'SELECT u.*,r.*,u.id AS purch_id '
    . 'FROM purchases AS u '
    . 'JOIN products AS r '
    . 'ON r.id = u.product_id '
    . 'WHERE u.customer_id = :id '
    . 'ORDER BY u.date';
  $stmt = $this->connection->pdo->prepare($sql);
  $stmt->execute(['id' => $cust->getId()]);
  while ($result = $stmt->fetch(PDO::FETCH_ASSOC)) {
    $product = Product::arrayToEntity($result, new Product());
    $product->setId($result['product_id']);
```

```
        $purch = Purchase::arrayToEntity($result, new Purchase());
        $purch->setId($result['purch_id']);
        $purch->setProduct($product);
        $cust->addPurchase($purch);
      }
      return $cust;
    }
```

10. Next, we provide a wrapper for the original `fetchById()` method. This block of code needs to not only get the original `Customer` entity, but needs to look up and embed `Product and Purchase` entities. We can call the new `fetchByIdAndEmbedPurchases()` method and accept a customer ID as an argument:

    ```
    public function fetchByIdAndEmbedPurchases($id)
    {
      return $this->fetchPurchasesForCustomer(
        $this->fetchById($id));
    }
    ```

Technique #2 – embedding secondary lookups

Now we will cover embedding secondary lookups into the related entity classes. We will continue to use the same illustration as above, using the entity classes defined that correspond to three related database tables, `customer`, `purchases`, and `products`:

1. The mechanics of this approach are quite similar to those described in the preceding section. The main difference is that instead of doing the database lookup, and producing entity classes right away, we will embed a series of anonymous functions that will do the same thing, but called from the view logic.
2. We need to add a new method to the `Application\Entity\Customer` class that adds a single entry to the `purchases` property. Instead of an array of `Purchase` entities, we will be supplying an anonymous function:

    ```
    public function setPurchases(Closure $purchaseLookup)
    {
      $this->purchases = $purchaseLookup;
    }
    ```

3. Next, we will make a copy of the `Application\Database\CustomerOrmService_1` class, and call it `Application\Database\CustomerOrmService_2`:

    ```
    namespace Application\Database;
    use PDO;
    use PDOException;
    ```

```
use Application\Entity\Customer;
use Application\Entity\Product;
use Application\Entity\Purchase;
class CustomerOrmService_2 extends CustomerService
{
  // code
}
```

4. We then define a `fetchPurchaseById()` method, which looks up a single purchase based on its ID and produces a `Purchase` entity. Because we will ultimately be making a series of repetitive requests for single purchases in this approach, we can regain database efficiency by working off the same prepared statement, in this case, a property called `$purchPreparedStmt`:

```
public function fetchPurchaseById($purchId)
{
  if (!$this->purchPreparedStmt) {
      $sql = 'SELECT * FROM purchases WHERE id = :id';
      $this->purchPreparedStmt =
      $this->connection->pdo->prepare($sql);
  }
  $this->purchPreparedStmt->execute(['id' => $purchId]);
  $result = $this->purchPreparedStmt->fetch(PDO::FETCH_ASSOC);
  return Purchase::arrayToEntity($result, new Purchase());
}
```

5. After that, we need a `fetchProductById()` method that looks up a single product based on its ID and produces a `Product` entity. Given that a customer may have purchased the same product several times, we can introduce an additional level of efficiency by storing acquired product entities in a `$products` array. In addition, as with purchases, we can perform lookups on the same prepared statement:

```
public function fetchProductById($prodId)
{
  if (!isset($this->products[$prodId])) {
      if (!$this->prodPreparedStmt) {
          $sql = 'SELECT * FROM products WHERE id = :id';
          $this->prodPreparedStmt =
          $this->connection->pdo->prepare($sql);
      }
      $this->prodPreparedStmt->execute(['id' => $prodId]);
      $result = $this->prodPreparedStmt
      ->fetch(PDO::FETCH_ASSOC);
      $this->products[$prodId] =
        Product::arrayToEntity($result, new Product());
  }
  return $this->products[$prodId];
}
```

6. We can now rework the `fetchPurchasesForCustomer()` method to have it embed an anonymous function that makes calls to both `fetchPurchaseById()` and `fetchProductById()`, and then assigns the resulting product entity to the newly found purchase entity. In this example, we do an initial lookup that just returns the IDs of all purchases for this customer. We then embed a sequence of anonymous functions in the `Customer::$purchases` property, storing the purchase ID as the array key, and the anonymous function as its value:

```
public function fetchPurchasesForCustomer(Customer $cust)
{
  $sql = 'SELECT id '
    . 'FROM purchases AS u '
    . 'WHERE u.customer_id = :id '
    . 'ORDER BY u.date';
  $stmt = $this->connection->pdo->prepare($sql);
  $stmt->execute(['id' => $cust->getId()]);
  while ($result = $stmt->fetch(PDO::FETCH_ASSOC)) {
    $cust->addPurchaseLookup(
    $result['id'],
    function ($purchId, $service) {
      $purchase = $service->fetchPurchaseById($purchId);
      $product  = $service->fetchProductById(
                  $purchase->getProductId());
      $purchase->setProduct($product);
      return $purchase; }
    );
  }
  return $cust;
}
```

How it works...

Define the following classes based on the steps from this recipe as follows:

Class	**Technique #1 steps**
`Application\Entity\Purchase`	1 - 2, 7
`Application\Entity\Product`	3 - 4
`Application\Entity\Customer`	6, 16, + described in *Chapter 5, Interacting with a Database*.
`Application\Database\CustomerOrmService_1`	8 - 10

The second approach to this would be as follows:

Class	Technique #2 steps
`Application\Entity\Customer`	2
`Application\Database\CustomerOrmService_2`	3 - 6

In order to implement approach #1, where entities are embedded, define a calling program called `chap_11_orm_embedded.php`, which sets up autoloading and uses the appropriate classes:

```
<?php
define('DB_CONFIG_FILE', '/../config/db.config.php');
require __DIR__ . '/../Application/Autoload/Loader.php';
Application\Autoload\Loader::init(__DIR__ . '/..');
use Application\Database\Connection;
use Application\Database\CustomerOrmService_1;
```

Next, create an instance of the service, and look up a customer using a random ID:

```
$service = new CustomerOrmService_1(
           new Connection(include __DIR__ . DB_CONFIG_FILE));
$id    = rand(1,79);
$cust = $service->fetchByIdAndEmbedPurchases($id);
```

In the view logic, you will have acquired a fully populated `Customer` entity by way of the `fetchByIdAndEmbedPurchases()` method. Now all you need to do is to call the right getters to display information:

```
<!-- Customer Info -->
<h1><?= $cust->getname() ?></h1>
<div class="row">
  <div class="left">Balance</div><div class="right">
    <?= $cust->getBalance(); ?></div>
</div>
  <!-- etc. -->
```

The logic needed to display purchase information would then look something like the following HTML. Notice that `Customer::getPurchases()` returns an array of `Purchase` entities. To get product information from the `Purchase` entity, inside the loop, call `Purchase::getProduct()`, which produces a `Product` entity. You can then call any of the `Product` getters, in this example, `Product::getTitle()`:

```
<!-- Purchases Info -->
<table>
<?php foreach ($cust->getPurchases() as $purchase) : ?>
```

```
    <tr>
    <td><?= $purchase->getTransaction() ?></td>
    <td><?= $purchase->getDate() ?></td>
    <td><?= $purchase->getQuantity() ?></td>
    <td><?= $purchase->getSalePrice() ?></td>
    <td><?= $purchase->getProduct()->getTitle() ?></td>
    </tr>
    <?php endforeach; ?>
  </table>
```

Turning your attention to the second approach, which uses secondary lookups, define a calling program called `chap_11_orm_secondary_lookups.php`, which sets up autoloading and uses the appropriate classes:

```
<?php
define('DB_CONFIG_FILE', '/../config/db.config.php');
require __DIR__ . '/../Application/Autoload/Loader.php';
Application\Autoload\Loader::init(__DIR__ . '/..');
use Application\Database\Connection;
use Application\Database\CustomerOrmService_2;
```

Next, create an instance of the service, and look up a customer using a random ID:

```
$service = new CustomerOrmService_2(new Connection(include __DIR__ .
DB_CONFIG_FILE));
$id    = rand(1,79);
```

You can now retrieve an `Application\Entity\Customer` instance and call `fetchPurchasesForCustomer()` for this customer, which embeds the sequence of anonymous functions:

```
$cust = $service->fetchById($id);
$cust = $service->fetchPurchasesForCustomer($cust);
```

The view logic for displaying core customer information remains the same as described previously. The logic needed to display purchase information would then look something like the following HTML code snippet. Notice that `Customer::getPurchases()` returns an array of anonymous functions. Each function call returns one specific purchase and related products:

```
<table>
  <?php foreach($cust->getPurchases() as $purchId => $function) : ?>
  <tr>
  <?php $purchase = $function($purchId, $service); ?>
  <td><?= $purchase->getTransaction() ?></td>
  <td><?= $purchase->getDate() ?></td>
  <td><?= $purchase->getQuantity() ?></td>
  <td><?= $purchase->getSalePrice() ?></td>
```

```
    <td><?= $purchase->getProduct()->getTitle() ?></td>
    </tr>
    <?php endforeach; ?>
  </table>
```

Here is an example of the output:

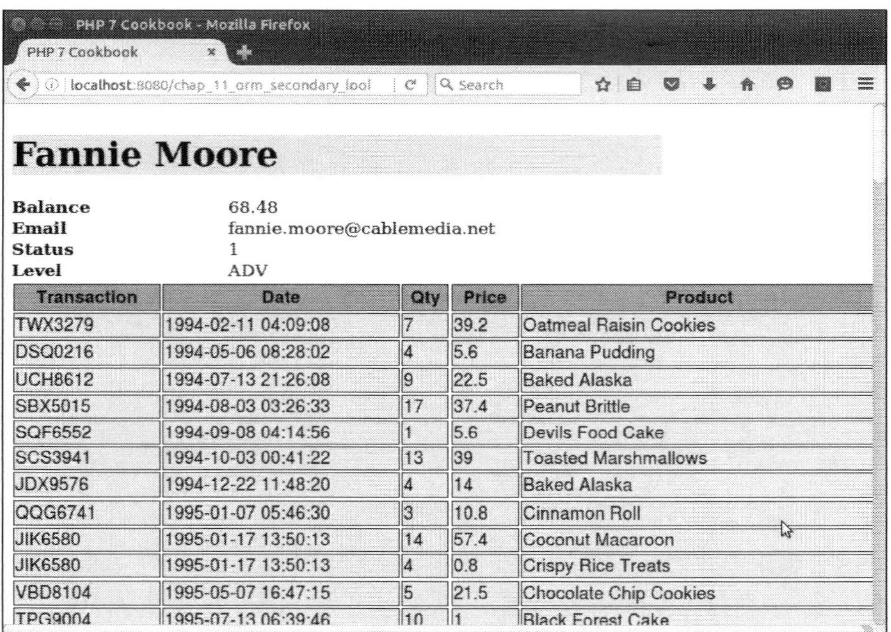

Fannie Moore

Balance	68.48
Email	fannie.moore@cablemedia.net
Status	1
Level	ADV

Transaction	Date	Qty	Price	Product
TWX3279	1994-02-11 04:09:08	7	39.2	Oatmeal Raisin Cookies
DSQ0216	1994-05-06 08:28:02	4	5.6	Banana Pudding
UCH8612	1994-07-13 21:26:08	9	22.5	Baked Alaska
SBX5015	1994-08-03 03:26:33	17	37.4	Peanut Brittle
SQF6552	1994-09-08 04:14:56	1	5.6	Devils Food Cake
SCS3941	1994-10-03 00:41:22	13	39	Toasted Marshmallows
JDX9576	1994-12-22 11:48:20	4	14	Baked Alaska
QQG6741	1995-01-07 05:46:30	3	10.8	Cinnamon Roll
JIK6580	1995-01-17 13:50:13	14	57.4	Coconut Macaroon
JIK6580	1995-01-17 13:50:13	4	0.8	Crispy Rice Treats
VBD8104	1995-05-07 16:47:15	5	21.5	Chocolate Chip Cookies
TPG9004	1995-07-13 06:39:46	10	1	Black Forest Cake

Best practice

Although each iteration of the loop represents two independent database queries (one for purchase, one for product), efficiency is retained by the use of *prepared statements*. Two statements are prepared in advance: one that looks up a specific purchase, and one that looks up a specific product. These prepared statements are then executed multiple times. Also, each product retrieval is independently stored in an array, resulting in even greater efficiency.

See also

Probably the best example of a library that implements object-relational mapping is Doctrine. Doctrine uses an embedded approach that its documentation refers to as a proxy. For more information, please refer to `http://www.doctrine-project.org/projects/orm.html`.

You might also consider reviewing a training video on *Learning Doctrine*, available from O'Reilly Media at `http://shop.oreilly.com/product/0636920041382.do`. (Disclaimer: this is a shameless plug by the author of both this book and this video!)

Implementing the Pub/Sub design pattern

The **Publish/Subscribe** (**Pub/Sub**) design pattern often forms the basis of software event-driven programming. This methodology allows **asynchronous** communications between different software applications, or different software modules within a single application. The purpose of the pattern is to allow a method or function to publish a signal when an action of significance has taken place. One or more classes would then subscribe and take action if a certain signal has been published.

Example of such actions are when the database is modified, or when a user has logged in. Another common use for this design pattern is when an application delivers news feeds. If an urgent news item has been posted, the application would publish this fact, allowing client subscribers to refresh their news listings.

How to do it...

1. First, we define our publisher class, `Application\PubSub\Publisher`. You'll notice that we are making use of two useful **Standard PHP Library** (**SPL**) interfaces, `SplSubject` and `SplObserver`:

```
namespace Application\PubSub;
use SplSubject;
use SplObserver;
class Publisher implements SplSubject
{
  // code
}
```

2. Next, we add properties to represent the publisher name, data to be passed to subscribers, and an array of subscribers (also referred to as listeners). You will also note that we will use a linked list (described in *Chapter 10, Looking at Advanced Algorithms*) to allow for priority:

```
protected $name;
protected $data;
protected $linked;
protected $subscribers;
```

3. The constructor initializes these properties. We also throw in `__toString()` in case we need quick access to the name of this publisher:

```
public function __construct($name)
{
  $this->name = $name;
  $this->data = array();
  $this->subscribers = array();
  $this->linked = array();
}

public function __toString()
{
  return $this->name;
}
```

4. In order to associate a subscriber with this publisher, we define `attach()`, which is specified in the `SplSubject` interface. We accept an `SplObserver` instance as an argument. Note that we need to add entries to both the `$subscribers` and `$linked` properties. `$linked` is then sorted by value, represented by the priority, using `arsort()`, which sorts in reverse and maintains the key:

```
public function attach(SplObserver $subscriber)
{
  $this->subscribers[$subscriber->getKey()] = $subscriber;
  $this->linked[$subscriber->getKey()] =
    $subscriber->getPriority();
  arsort($this->linked);
}
```

5. The interface also requires us to define `detach()`, which removes the subscriber from the list:

```
public function detach(SplObserver $subscriber)
{
  unset($this->subscribers[$subscriber->getKey()]);
  unset($this->linked[$subscriber->getKey()]);
}
```

6. Also required by the interface, we define `notify()`, which calls `update()` on all the subscribers. Note that we loop through the linked list to ensure the subscribers are called in order of priority:

```
public function notify()
{
  foreach ($this->linked as $key => $value)
  {
    $this->subscribers[$key]->update($this);
  }
}
```

7. Next, we define the appropriate getters and setters. We don't show them all here to conserve space:

```
public function getName()
{
  return $this->name;
}

public function setName($name)
{
  $this->name = $name;
}
```

8. Finally, we need to provide a means of setting data items by key, which will then be available to subscribers when `notify()` is invoked:

```
public function setDataByKey($key, $value)
{
  $this->data[$key] = $value;
}
```

9. Now we can have a look at `Application\PubSub\Subscriber`. Typically, we would define multiple subscribers for each publisher. In this case, we implement the `SplObserver` interface:

```
namespace Application\PubSub;
use SplSubject;
use SplObserver;
class Subscriber implements SplObserver
{
  // code
}
```

10. Each subscriber needs a unique identifier. In this case, we create the key using `md5()` and date/time information, combined with a random number. The constructor initializes the properties as follows. The actual logical functionality performed by the subscriber is in the form of a callback:

```
protected $key;
protected $name;
protected $priority;
protected $callback;
public function __construct(
  string $name, callable $callback, $priority = 0)
{
  $this->key = md5(date('YmdHis') . rand(0,9999));
  $this->name = $name;
  $this->callback = $callback;
  $this->priority = $priority;
}
```

11. The `update()` function is called when `notifiy()` on the publisher is invoked. We pass a publisher instance as an argument, and call the callback defined for this subscriber:

    ```
    public function update(SplSubject $publisher)
    {
      call_user_func($this->callback, $publisher);
    }
    ```

12. We also need to define getters and setters for convenience. Not all are shown here:

    ```
    public function getKey()
    {
      return $this->key;
    }

    public function setKey($key)
    {
      $this->key = $key;
    }

    // other getters and setters not shown
    ```

How it works...

For the purposes of this illustration, define a calling program called `chap_11_pub_sub_simple_example.php`, which sets up autoloading and uses the appropriate classes:

```
<?php
require __DIR__ . '/../Application/Autoload/Loader.php';
Application\Autoload\Loader::init(__DIR__ . '/..');
use Application\PubSub\ { Publisher, Subscriber };
```

Next, create a publisher instance and assign data:

```
$pub = new Publisher('test');
$pub->setDataByKey('1', 'AAA');
$pub->setDataByKey('2', 'BBB');
$pub->setDataByKey('3', 'CCC');
$pub->setDataByKey('4', 'DDD');
```

Now you can create test subscribers that read data from the publisher and echo the results. The first parameter is the name, the second the callback, and the last is the priority:

```
$sub1 = new Subscriber(
  '1',
  function ($pub) {
```

```
    echo '1:' . $pub->getData()[1] . PHP_EOL;
  },
  10
);
$sub2 = new Subscriber(
  '2',
  function ($pub) {
    echo '2:' . $pub->getData()[2] . PHP_EOL;
  },
  20
);
$sub3 = new Subscriber(
  '3',
  function ($pub) {
    echo '3:' . $pub->getData()[3] . PHP_EOL;
  },
  99
);
```

For test purposes, attach the subscribers out of order, and call `notify()` twice:

```
$pub->attach($sub2);
$pub->attach($sub1);
$pub->attach($sub3);
$pub->notify();
$pub->notify();
```

Next, define and attach another subscriber that looks at the data for subscriber 1 and exits if it's not empty:

```
$sub4 = new Subscriber(
  '4',
  function ($pub) {
    echo '4:' . $pub->getData()[4] . PHP_EOL;
    if (!empty($pub->getData()[1]))
      die('1 is set ... halting execution');
  },
  25
);
$pub->attach($sub4);
$pub->notify();
```

Here is the output. Note that the output is in order of priority (where higher priority goes first), and that the second block of output is interrupted:

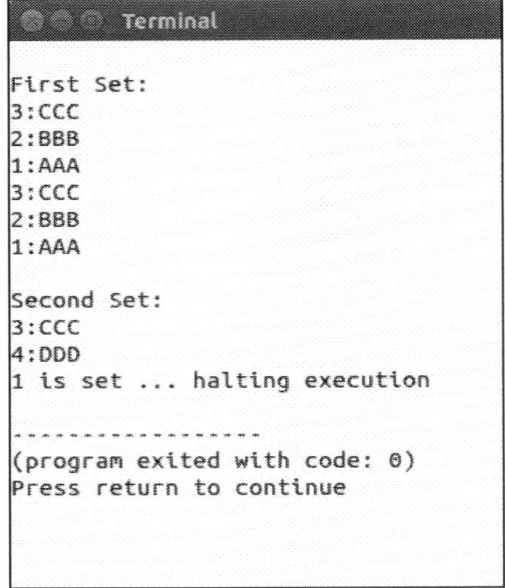

Terminal
First Set:
3:CCC
2:BBB
1:AAA
3:CCC
2:BBB
1:AAA
Second Set:
3:CCC
4:DDD
1 is set ... halting execution

(program exited with code: 0)
Press return to continue

There's more...

A closely related software design pattern is **Observer**. The mechanism is similar but the generally agreed difference is that Observer operates in a synchronous manner, where all observer methods are called when a signal (often also referred to as message or event) is received. The Pub/Sub pattern, in contrast, operates asynchronously, typically using a message queue. Another difference is that in the Pub/Sub pattern, publishers do not need to be aware of subscribers.

See also

For a good discussion on the difference between the Observer and Pub/Sub patterns, refer to the article at `http://stackoverflow.com/questions/15594905/difference-between-observer-pub-sub-and-data-binding`.

12
Improving Web Security

In this chapter, we will cover the following topics:

- Filtering `$_POST` data
- Validating `$_POST` data
- Safeguarding the PHP session
- Securing forms with a token
- Building a secure password generator
- Safeguarding forms with a CAPTCHA
- Encrypting/decrypting without `mcrypt`

Introduction

In this chapter, we will show you how to set up a simple yet effective mechanism for filtering and validating a block of post data. Then, we will cover how to protect your PHP sessions from potential session hijacking and other forms of attack. The next recipe shows how to protect forms from **Cross Site Request Forgery** (**CSRF**) attacks using a randomly generated token. The recipe on password generation shows you how to incorporate PHP 7 true randomization to generate secure passwords. We then show you two forms of **CAPTCHA**: one that is text based, the other using a distorted image. Finally, there is a recipe that covers strong encryption without using the discredited and soon-to-be-deprecated `mcrypt` extension.

Filtering $_POST data

The process of filtering data can encompass any or all of the following:

- Removing unwanted characters (that is, removing `<script>` tags)
- Performing transformations on the data (that is, converting a quote to `"`)
- Encrypting or decrypting the data

Encryption is covered in the last recipe of this chapter. Otherwise, we will present a basic mechanism that can be used to filter `$_POST` data arriving following form submission.

How to do it...

1. First of all, you need to have an awareness of the data that will be present in `$_POST`. Also, perhaps more importantly, you will need to be aware of the restrictions imposed by the database table in which the form data will presumably be stored. As an example, have a look at the database structure for the `prospects` table:

```
COLUMN          TYPE             NULL   DEFAULT
first_name      varchar(128)     No     None      NULL
last_name       varchar(128)     No     None      NULL
address         varchar(256)     Yes    None      NULL
city            varchar(64)      Yes    None      NULL
state_province  varchar(32)      Yes    None      NULL
postal_code     char(16)         No     None      NULL
phone           varchar(16)      No     None      NULL
country         char(2)          No     None      NULL
email           varchar(250)     No     None      NULL
status          char(8)          Yes    None      NULL
budget          decimal(10,2)    Yes    None      NULL
last_updated    datetime         Yes    None      NULL
```

2. Once you have completed an analysis of the data to be posted and stored, you can determine what type of filtering is to occur, and which PHP functions will serve this purpose.

3. As an example, if you need to get rid of leading and trailing white space, which is completely possible from user supplied form data, you can use the PHP `trim()` function. All of the character data has length limits according to the database structure. Accordingly, you might consider using `substr()` to ensure the length is not exceeded. If you wanted to remove non-alphabetical characters, you might consider using `preg_replace()` with the appropriate pattern.

4. We can now group the set of desired PHP functions into a single array of callbacks. Here is an example based on the filtering needs for the form data that will eventually be stored in the `prospects` table:

```
$filter = [
  'trim' => function ($item) { return trim($item); },
  'float' => function ($item) { return (float) $item; },
  'upper' => function ($item) { return strtoupper($item); },
  'email' => function ($item) {
     return filter_var($item, FILTER_SANITIZE_EMAIL); },
  'alpha' => function ($item) {
     return preg_replace('/[^A-Za-z]/', '', $item); },
  'alnum' => function ($item) {
     return preg_replace('/[^0-9A-Za-z ]/', '', $item); },
  'length' => function ($item, $length) {
     return substr($item, 0, $length); },
  'stripTags' => function ($item) { return strip_tags($item); },
];
```

5. Next, we define an array that matches the field names expected in `$_POST`. In this array, we specify the key in the `$filter` array, along with any parameters. Note the first key, `*`. We will use that as a wildcard to be applied to all fields:

```
$assignments = [
  '*'              => ['trim' => NULL, 'stripTags' => NULL],
  'first_name'     => ['length' => 32, 'alnum' => NULL],
  'last_name'      => ['length' => 32, 'alnum' => NULL],
  'address'        => ['length' => 64, 'alnum' => NULL],
  'city'           => ['length' => 32],
  'state_province'=> ['length' => 20],
  'postal_code'    => ['length' => 12, 'alnum' => NULL],
  'phone'          => ['length' => 12],
  'country'        => ['length' => 2, 'alpha' => NULL,
                       'upper' => NULL],
  'email'          => ['length' => 128, 'email' => NULL],
  'budget'         => ['float' => NULL],
];
```

6. We then loop through the data set (that is, coming from `$_POST`) and apply the callbacks in turn. We first run all callbacks assigned to the wildcard (`*`) key.

> It is important to implement a wildcard filter to avoid redundant settings. In the preceding example, we wish to apply filters that represent the PHP functions `strip_tags()` and `trim()` for every item.

7. Next, we run through all callbacks assigned to a particular data field. When we're done, all values in `$data` will be filtered:

```
foreach ($data as $field => $item) {
  foreach ($assignments['*'] as $key => $option) {
    $item = $filter[$key]($item, $option);
  }
  foreach ($assignments[$field] as $key => $option) {
    $item = $filter[$key]($item, $option);
  }
}
```

How it works...

Place the code shown in steps 4 through 6 into a file called `chap_12_post_data_filtering_basic.php`. You will also need to define an array to simulate data that would be present in `$_POST`. In this case, you could define two arrays, one with *good* data, and one with *bad* data:

```
$testData = [
  'goodData'    => [
    'first_name'      => 'Doug',
    'last_name'       => 'Bierer',
    'address'         => '123 Main Street',
    'city'            => 'San Francisco',
    'state_province'=> 'California',
    'postal_code'     => '94101',
    'phone'           => '+1 415-555-1212',
    'country'         => 'US',
    'email'           => 'doug@unlikelysource.com',
    'budget'          => '123.45',
  ],
  'badData' => [
    'first_name' => 'This+Name<script>bad tag</script>Valid!',
    'last_name'  =>
      'ThisLastNameIsWayTooLongAbcdefghijklmnopqrstuvwxyz0123456789
      Abcdefghijklmnopqrstuvwxyz0123456789Abcdefghijklmnopqrstuvwxyz
      0123456789Abcdefghijklmnopqrstuvwxyz0123456789',
    //'address'  => '',     // missing
    'city'       => 'ThisCityNameIsTooLong01234567890123456
      7890123456789012345678901234567890123456789  ',
    //'state_province'=> '',     // missing
    'postal_code'      => '!"£$%^Non Alpha Chars',
    'phone'            => ' 12345 ',
    'country'          => '12345',
```

```
      'email'           => 'this.is@not@an.email',
      'budget'          => 'XXX',
    ]
  ];
```

Finally, you will need to loop through the filter assignments, presenting the good and bad data:

```
foreach ($testData as $data) {
  foreach ($data as $field => $item) {
    foreach ($assignments['*'] as $key => $option) {
      $item = $filter[$key]($item, $option);
    }
    foreach ($assignments[$field] as $key => $option) {
      $item = $filter[$key]($item, $option);
    }
    printf("%16s : %s\n", $field, $item);
  }
}
```

Here's how the output might appear for this example:

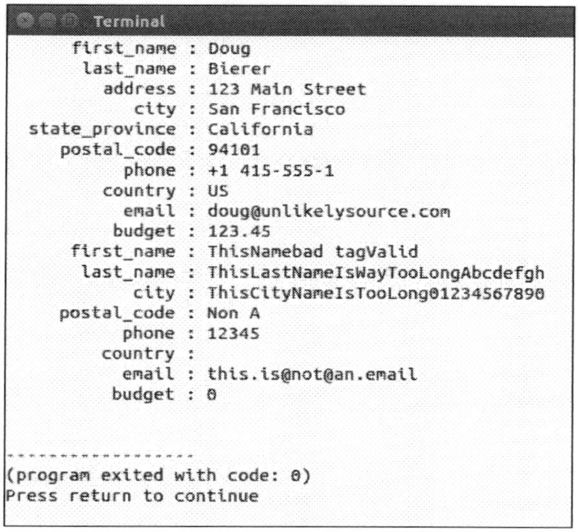

```
      first_name : Doug
       last_name : Bierer
         address : 123 Main Street
            city : San Francisco
  state_province : California
     postal_code : 94101
           phone : +1 415-555-1
         country : US
           email : doug@unlikelysource.com
          budget : 123.45
      first_name : ThisNamebad tagValid
       last_name : ThisLastNameIsWayTooLongAbcdefgh
            city : ThisCityNameIsTooLong01234567890
     postal_code : Non A
           phone : 12345
         country :
           email : this.is@not@an.email
          budget : 0


------------------
(program exited with code: 0)
Press return to continue
```

Note that the names were truncated and tags were removed. You will also note that although the e-mail address was filtered, it is still not a valid address. It's important to note that for proper treatment of data, it might be necessary to *validate* as well as to filter.

See also

In *Chapter 6, Building Scalable Websites*, the recipe entitled *Chaining $_POST filters*, discusses how to incorporate the basic filtering concepts covered here into a comprehensive filter chaining mechanism.

Validating $_POST data

The primary difference between filtering and validation is that the latter does not alter the original data. Another difference is in intent. The purpose of validation is to confirm that the data matches certain criteria established according to the needs of your customer.

How to do it...

1. The basic validation mechanism we will present here is identical to that shown in the preceding recipe. As with filtering, it is vital to have an idea of the nature of the data to be validated, how it fits your customer's requirements, and also whether it matches the criteria enforced by the database. For example, if in the database, the maximum width of the column is 128, the validation callback could use `strlen()` to confirm that the length of the data submitted is less than or equal to 128 characters. Likewise, you could use `ctype_alnum()` to confirm that the data only contains letters and numbers, as appropriate.
2. Another consideration for validation is to present an appropriate validation failure message. The validation process, in a certain sense, is also a *confirmation* process, where somebody presumably will review the validation to confirm success or failure. If the validation fails, that person will need to know the reason why.
3. For this illustration, we will again focus on the `prospects` table. We can now group the set of desired PHP functions into a single array of callbacks. Here is an example based on the validation needs for the form data, which will eventually be stored in the `prospects` table:

```
$validator = [
  'email' => [
    'callback' => function ($item) {
      return filter_var($item, FILTER_VALIDATE_EMAIL); },
    'message'  => 'Invalid email address'],
  'alpha' => [
    'callback' => function ($item) {
      return ctype_alpha(str_replace(' ', '', $item)); },
    'message'  => 'Data contains non-alpha characters'],
  'alnum' => [
    'callback' => function ($item) {
      return ctype_alnum(str_replace(' ', '', $item)); },
```

```
      'message'  => 'Data contains characters which are '
         . 'not letters or numbers'],
    'digits' => [
      'callback' => function ($item) {
        return preg_match('/[^0-9.]/', $item); },
      'message'  => 'Data contains characters which '
        . 'are not numbers'],
    'length' => [
      'callback' => function ($item, $length) {
        return strlen($item) <= $length; },
      'message'  => 'Item has too many characters'],
    'upper' => [
      'callback' => function ($item) {
        return $item == strtoupper($item); },
      'message'  => 'Item is not upper case'],
    'phone' => [
      'callback' => function ($item) {
        return preg_match('/[^0-9() -+]/', $item); },
      'message'  => 'Item is not a valid phone number'],
];
```

Notice, for the alpha and alnum callbacks, we allow for whitespace by first removing it using `str_replace()`. We can then call `ctype_alpha()` or `ctype_alnum()`, which will determine whether any disallowed characters are present.

4. Next, we define an array of assignments that matches the field names expected in `$_POST`. In this array, we specify the key in the `$validator` array, along with any parameters:

```
$assignments = [
  'first_name'     => ['length' => 32, 'alpha' => NULL],
  'last_name'      => ['length' => 32, 'alpha' => NULL],
  'address'        => ['length' => 64, 'alnum' => NULL],
  'city'           => ['length' => 32, 'alnum' => NULL],
  'state_province'=> ['length' => 20, 'alpha' => NULL],
  'postal_code'    => ['length' => 12, 'alnum' => NULL],
  'phone'          => ['length' => 12, 'phone' => NULL],
  'country'        => ['length' => 2, 'alpha' => NULL,
                       'upper' => NULL],
  'email'          => ['length' => 128, 'email' => NULL],
  'budget'         => ['digits' => NULL],
];
```

5. We then use nested `foreach()` loops to iterate through the block of data one field at a time. For each field, we loop through the callbacks assigned to that field:

```
foreach ($data as $field => $item) {
  echo 'Processing: ' . $field . PHP_EOL;
  foreach ($assignments[$field] as $key => $option) {
    if ($validator[$key]['callback']($item, $option)) {
        $message = 'OK';
    } else {
        $message = $validator[$key]['message'];
    }
    printf('%8s : %s' . PHP_EOL, $key, $message);
  }
}
```

Instead of echoing the output directly, as shown, you might log the validation success/failure to be presented to the reviewer at a later time. Also, as shown in *Chapter 6, Building Scalable Websites*, you can work the validation mechanism into the form, displaying validation messages next to their matching form elements.

How it works...

Place the code shown in steps 3 through 5 into a file called `chap_12_post_data_validation_basic.php`. You will also need to define an array of data that simulates data that would be present in `$_POST`. In this case, you use the two arrays mentioned in the preceding recipe, one with *good* data, and one with *bad* data. The final output should look something like this:

```
Processing: postal_code
-----------------------------------
  length : Item has too many characters
   alnum : Data contains characters which are not letters or numbers
-----------------------------------
Processing: phone
-----------------------------------
  length : Item has too many characters
   phone : OK
-----------------------------------
Processing: country
-----------------------------------
  length : Item has too many characters
   alpha : Data contains non-alpha characters
   upper : OK
-----------------------------------
Processing: email
-----------------------------------
  length : OK
   email : Invalid email address
-----------------------------------
Processing: budget
-----------------------------------
  digits : OK
```

See also

- In *Chapter 6, Building Scalable Websites*, the recipe entitled *Chaining $_POST validators* discusses how to incorporate the basic validation concepts covered here into a comprehensive filter chaining mechanism.

Safeguarding the PHP session

The PHP session mechanism is quite simple. Once the session is started using `session_start()` or the `php.ini session.autostart` setting, the PHP engine generates a unique token that is, by default, conveyed to the user by way of a cookie. On subsequent requests, while the session is still considered active, the user's browser (or equivalent) presents the session identifier, again usually by way of a cookie, for inspection. The PHP engine then uses this identifier to locate the appropriate file on the server, populating `$_SESSION` with the stored information. There are tremendous security concerns when the session identifier is the sole means of identifying a returning website visitor. In this recipe, we will present several techniques that will help you to safeguard your sessions, which, in turn, will vastly improve the overall security of the website.

How to do it...

1. First of all, it's important to recognize how using the session as the sole means of authentication can be dangerous. Imagine for a moment that when a valid user logs in to your website, that you set a `loggedIn` flag in `$_SESSION`:

```
session_start();
$loggedIn = $_SESSION['isLoggedIn'] ?? FALSE;
if (isset($_POST['login'])) {
  if ($_POST['username'] == // username lookup
      && $_POST['password'] == // password lookup) {
      $loggedIn = TRUE;
      $_SESSION['isLoggedIn'] = TRUE;
  }
}
```

2. In your program logic, you allow the user to see sensitive information if `$_SESSION['isLoggedIn']` is set to `TRUE`:

```
<br>Secret Info
<br><?php if ($loggedIn) echo // secret information; ?>
```

3. If an attacker were to obtain the session identifier, for example, by means of a successfully executed **Cross-site scripting** (**XSS**) attack, all he/she would need to do would be to set the value of the `PHPSESSID` cookie to the illegally obtained one, and they are now viewed by your application as a valid user.

4. One quick and easy way to narrow the window of time during which the `PHPSESSID` is valid is to use `session_regenerate_id()`. This very simple command generates a new session identifier, invalidates the old one, maintains session data intact, and has a minimal impact on performance. This command can only be executed after the session has started:

```
session_start();
session_regenerate_id();
```

5. Another often overlooked technique is to ensure that web visitors have a logout option. It is important, however, to not only destroy the session using `session_destroy()`, but also to unset `$_SESSION` data and to expire the session cookie:

```
session_unset();
session_destroy();
setcookie('PHPSESSID', 0, time() - 3600);
```

6. Another easy technique that can be used to prevent session hijacking is to develop a finger-print or thumb-print of the website visitor. One way to implement this technique is to collect information unique to the website visitor over and above the session identifier. Such information includes the user agent (that is, the browser), languages accepted, and remote IP address. You can derive a simple hash from this information, and store the hash on the server in a separate file. The next time the user visits the website, if you have determined they are logged in based on session information, you can then perform a secondary verification by matching finger-prints:

```
$remotePrint = md5($_SERVER['REMOTE_ADDR']
                   . $_SERVER['HTTP_USER_AGENT']
                   . $_SERVER['HTTP_ACCEPT_LANGUAGE']);
$printsMatch = file_exists(THUMB_PRINT_DIR . $remotePrint);
if ($loggedIn && !$printsMatch) {
    $info = 'SESSION INVALID!!!';
    error_log('Session Invalid: ' . date('Y-m-d H:i:s'), 0);
    // take appropriate action
}
```

We are using `md5()` as it's a fast hashing algorithm and is well suited for internal usage. It is *not recommended* to use `md5()` for any external use as it is subject to brute-force attacks.

How it works...

To demonstrate how a session is vulnerable, code a simple login script that sets a `$_SESSION['isLoggedIn'] flag` upon successful login. You could call the file `chap_12_session_hijack.php`:

```
session_start();
$loggedUser = $_SESSION['loggedUser'] ?? '';
$loggedIn = $_SESSION['isLoggedIn'] ?? FALSE;
$username = 'test';
$password = 'password';
$info = 'You Can Now See Super Secret Information!!!';

if (isset($_POST['login'])) {
  if ($_POST['username'] == $username
      && $_POST['password'] == $password) {
        $loggedIn = TRUE;
        $_SESSION['isLoggedIn'] = TRUE;
        $_SESSION['loggedUser'] = $username;
        $loggedUser = $username;
  }
} elseif (isset($_POST['logout'])) {
  session_destroy();
}
```

You can then add code that displays a simple login form. To test for session vulnerability, follow this procedure using the `chap_12_session_hijack.php` file we just created:

1. Change to the directory containing the file.
2. Run the `php -S localhost:8080` command.
3. Using one browser, open the URL `http://localhost:8080/<filename>`.
4. Login as user `test` with a password as `password`.
5. You should be able to see **You Can Now See Super Secret Information!!!**.
6. Refresh the page: each time, you should see a new session identifier.
7. Copy the value of the `PHPSESSID` cookie.
8. Open another browser to the same web page.
9. Modify the cookie sent by the browser by copying the value of `PHPSESSID`.

For illustration, we are also showing the value of `$_COOKIE` and `$_SESSION`, shown in the following screenshot using the Vivaldi browser:

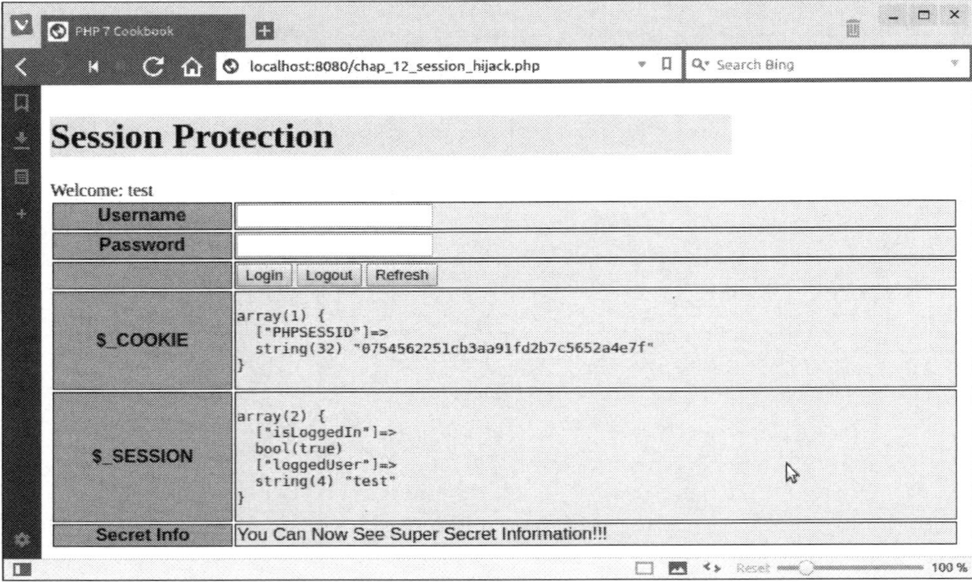

We then copy the value of `PHPSESSID`, open a Firefox browser, and use a tool called Tamper Data to modify the value of the cookie:

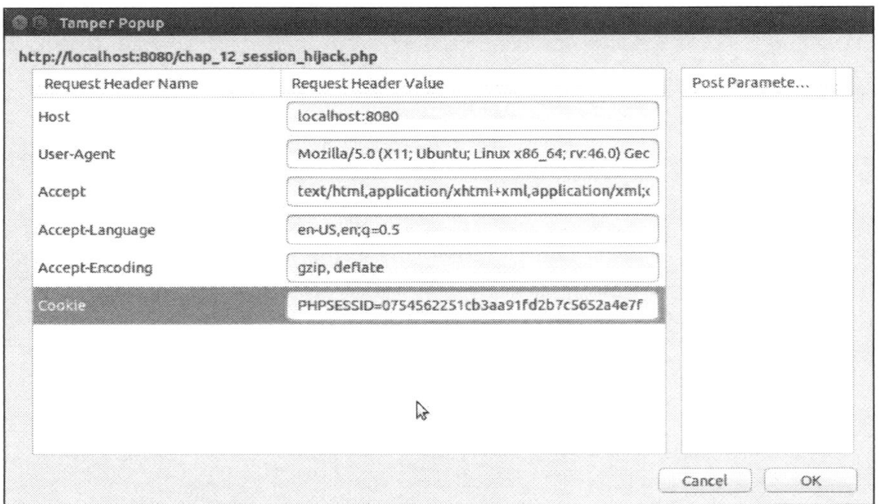

You can see in the next screenshot that we are now an authenticated user without entering the username or password:

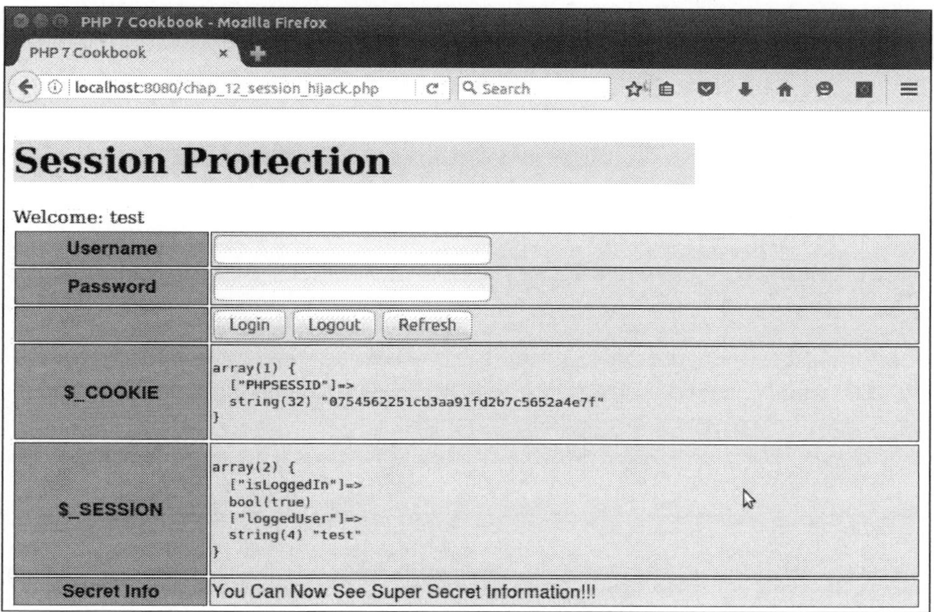

You can now implement the changes discussed in the preceding steps. Copy the file created previously to `chap_12_session_protected.php`. Now go ahead and regenerate the session ID:

```
<?php
define('THUMB_PRINT_DIR', __DIR__ . '/../data/');
session_start();
session_regenerate_id();
```

Next, initialize variables and determine the logged in status (as before):

```
$username = 'test';
$password = 'password';
$info = 'You Can Now See Super Secret Information!!!';
$loggedIn = $_SESSION['isLoggedIn'] ?? FALSE;
$loggedUser = $_SESSION['user'] ?? 'guest';
```

You can add a session thumb-print using the remote address, user agent, and language settings:

```
$remotePrint = md5($_SERVER['REMOTE_ADDR']
  . $_SERVER['HTTP_USER_AGENT']
```

```
    . $_SERVER['HTTP_ACCEPT_LANGUAGE']);
$printsMatch = file_exists(THUMB_PRINT_DIR . $remotePrint);
```

If the login is successful, we store thumb-print info and login status in the session:

```
if (isset($_POST['login'])) {
  if ($_POST['username'] == $username
      && $_POST['password'] == $password) {
        $loggedIn = TRUE;
        $_SESSION['user'] = strip_tags($username);
        $_SESSION['isLoggedIn'] = TRUE;
        file_put_contents(
          THUMB_PRINT_DIR . $remotePrint, $remotePrint);
  }
```

You can also check for the logout option and implement a proper logout procedure: unset `$_SESSION` variables, invalidate the session, and expire the cookie. You can also remove the thumb-print file and implement a redirect:

```
} elseif (isset($_POST['logout'])) {
  session_unset();
  session_destroy();
  setcookie('PHPSESSID', 0, time() - 3600);
  if (file_exists(THUMB_PRINT_DIR . $remotePrint))
    unlink(THUMB_PRINT_DIR . $remotePrint);
    header('Location: ' . $_SERVER['REQUEST_URI'] );
  exit;
```

Otherwise, if the operation is not login or logout, you can check to see whether the user is considered logged in, and if the thumb-print doesn't match, the session is considered invalid, and the appropriate action is taken:

```
} elseif ($loggedIn && !$printsMatch) {
    $info = 'SESSION INVALID!!!';
    error_log('Session Invalid: ' . date('Y-m-d H:i:s'), 0);
    // take appropriate action
}
```

You can now run the same procedure as mentioned previously using the new `chap_12_session_protected.php` file. The first thing you will notice is that the session is now considered invalid. The output will look something like this:

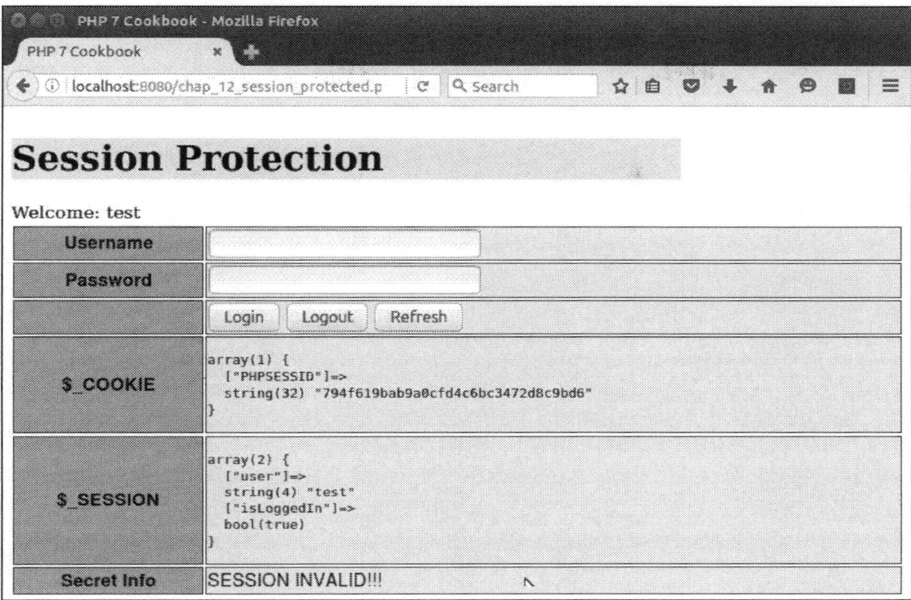

The reason for this is that the thumb-print does not match as you are now using a different browser. Likewise, if you refresh the page of the first browser, the session identifier is regenerated, making any previously copied identifier obsolete. Finally, the logout button will completely clear session information.

See also

For an excellent overview of website vulnerabilities, please refer to the article present at `https://www.owasp.org/index.php/Category:Vulnerability`. For information on session hijacking, refer to `https://www.owasp.org/index.php/Session_hijacking_attack`.

Securing forms with a token

This recipe presents another very simple technique that will safeguard your forms against **Cross Site Request Forgery** (**CSRF**) attacks. Simply put, a CSRF attack is possible when, possibly using other techniques, an attacker is able to infect a web page on your website. In most cases, the infected page will then start issuing requests (that is, using JavaScript to purchase items, or make settings changes) using the credentials of a valid, logged-in user. It's extremely difficult for your application to detect such activity. One measure that can easily be taken is to generate a random token that is included in every form to be submitted. Since the infected page will not have access to the token, nor have the ability to generate one that matches, form validation will fail.

How to do it...

1. First, to demonstrate the problem, we create a web page that simulates an infected page that generates a request to post an entry to the database. For this illustration, we will call the file `chap_12_form_csrf_test_unprotected.html`:

   ```
   <!DOCTYPE html>
     <body onload="load()">
     <form action="/chap_12_form_unprotected.php"
       method="post" id="csrf_test" name="csrf_test">
       <input name="name" type="hidden" value="No Goodnick" />
       <input name="email" type="hidden" value="malicious@owasp.org" />
       <input name="comments" type="hidden"
          value="Form is vulnerable to CSRF attacks!" />
       <input name="process" type="hidden" value="1" />
     </form>
     <script>
       function load() { document.forms['csrf_test'].submit(); }
     </script>
   </body>
   </html>
   ```

2. Next, we create a script called `chap_12_form_unprotected.php` that responds to the form posting. As with other calling programs in this book, we set up autoloading and use the `Application\Database\Connection` class covered in *Chapter 5, Interacting with a Database*:

   ```
   <?php
   define('DB_CONFIG_FILE', '/../config/db.config.php');
   require __DIR__ . '/../Application/Autoload/Loader.php';
   Application\Autoload\Loader::init(__DIR__ . '/..');
   use Application\Database\Connection;
   $conn = new Connection(include __DIR__ . DB_CONFIG_FILE);
   ```

3. We then check to see the process button has been pressed, and even implement a filtering mechanism, as covered in the *Filtering $_POST data* recipe in this chapter. This is to prove that a CSRF attack is easily able to bypass filters:

   ```
   if ($_POST['process']) {
       $filter = [
         'trim' => function ($item) { return trim($item); },
         'email' => function ($item) {
           return filter_var($item, FILTER_SANITIZE_EMAIL); },
         'length' => function ($item, $length) {
           return substr($item, 0, $length); },
         'stripTags' => function ($item) {
   ```

```
        return strip_tags($item); },
    ];

    $assignments = [
      '*'          => ['trim' => NULL, 'stripTags' => NULL],
      'email'    => ['length' => 249, 'email' => NULL],
      'name'     => ['length' => 128],
      'comments'=> ['length' => 249],
    ];

    $data = $_POST;
    foreach ($data as $field => $item) {
      foreach ($assignments['*'] as $key => $option) {
        $item = $filter[$key]($item, $option);
      }
      if (isset($assignments[$field])) {
        foreach ($assignments[$field] as $key => $option) {
          $item = $filter[$key]($item, $option);
        }
        $filteredData[$field] = $item;
      }
    }
```

4. Finally, we insert the filtered data into the database using a prepared statement. We then redirect to another script, called `chap_12_form_view_results.php`, which simply dumps the contents of the `visitors` table:

```
try {
    $filteredData['visit_date'] = date('Y-m-d H:i:s');
    $sql = 'INSERT INTO visitors '
        . ' (email,name,comments,visit_date) '
        . 'VALUES (:email,:name,:comments,:visit_date)';
    $insertStmt = $conn->pdo->prepare($sql);
    $insertStmt->execute($filteredData);
} catch (PDOException $e) {
    echo $e->getMessage();
}
}
header('Location: /chap_12_form_view_results.php');
exit;
```

5. The result, of course, is that the attack is allowed, despite filtering and the use of prepared statements.

6. Implementing the form protection token is actually quite easy! First of all, you need to generate the token and store it in the session. We take advantage of the new `random_bytes()` PHP 7 function to generate a truly random token, one which will be difficult, if not impossible, for an attacker to match:

   ```
   session_start();
   $token = urlencode(base64_encode((random_bytes(32))));
   $_SESSION['token'] = $token;
   ```

> The output of `random_bytes()` is binary. We use `base64_encode()` to convert it into a usable string. We then further process it using `urlencode()` so that it is properly rendered in an HTML form.

7. When we render the form, we then present the token as a hidden field:

   ```
   <input type="hidden" name="token" value="<?= $token ?>" />
   ```

8. We then copy and alter the `chap_12_form_unprotected.php` script mentioned previously, adding logic to first check to see whether the token matches the one stored in the session. Note that we unset the current token to make it invalid for future use. We call the new script `chap_12_form_protected_with_token.php`:

   ```
   if ($_POST['process']) {
       $sessToken = $_SESSION['token'] ?? 1;
       $postToken = $_POST['token'] ?? 2;
       unset($_SESSION['token']);
       if ($sessToken != $postToken) {
           $_SESSION['message'] = 'ERROR: token mismatch';
       } else {
           $_SESSION['message'] = 'SUCCESS: form processed';
           // continue with form processing
       }
   }
   ```

How it works...

To test how an infected web page might launch a CSRF attack, create the following files, as shown earlier in the recipe:

- `chap_12_form_csrf_test_unprotected.html`
- `chap_12_form_unprotected.php`

You can then define a file called `chap_12_form_view_results.php`, which dumps the `visitors` table:

```
<?php
session_start();
define('DB_CONFIG_FILE', '/../config/db.config.php');
require __DIR__ . '/../Application/Autoload/Loader.php';
Application\Autoload\Loader::init(__DIR__ . '/..');
use Application\Database\Connection;
$conn = new Connection(include __DIR__ . DB_CONFIG_FILE);
$message = $_SESSION['message'] ?? '';
unset($_SESSION['message']);
$stmt = $conn->pdo->query('SELECT * FROM visitors');
?>
<!DOCTYPE html>
<body>
<div class="container">
  <h1>CSRF Protection</h1>
  <h3>Visitors Table</h3>
  <?php while ($row = $stmt->fetch(PDO::FETCH_ASSOC)) : ?>
  <pre><?php echo implode(':', $row); ?></pre>
  <?php endwhile; ?>
  <?php if ($message) : ?>
  <b><?= $message; ?></b>
  <?php endif; ?>
</div>
</body>
</html>
```

From a browser, launch `chap_12_form_csrf_test_unprotected.html`. Here is how the output might appear:

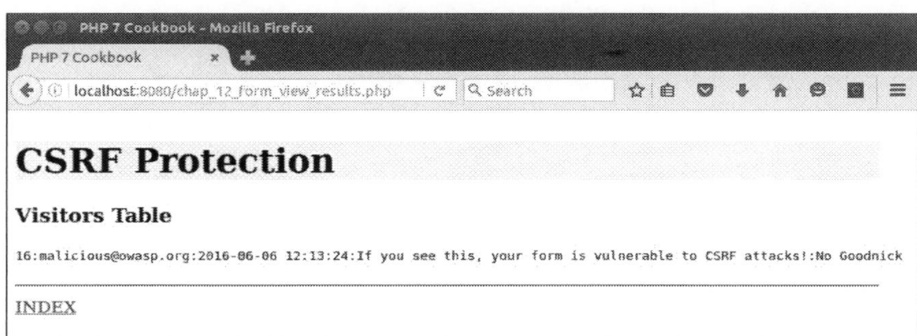

As you can see, the attack was successful despite filtering and the use of prepared statements!

Next, copy the `chap_12_form_unprotected.php` file to `chap_12_form_protected.php`. Make the change indicated in step 8 in the recipe. You will also need to alter the test HTML file, copying `chap_12_form_csrf_test_unprotected.html` to `chap_12_form_csrf_test_protected.html`. Change the value for the action parameter in the `FORM` tag as follows:

```
<form action="/chap_12_form_protected_with_token.php"
  method="post" id="csrf_test" name="csrf_test">
```

When you run the new HTML file from a browser, it calls `chap_12_form_protected.php`, which looks for a token that does not exist. Here is the expected output:

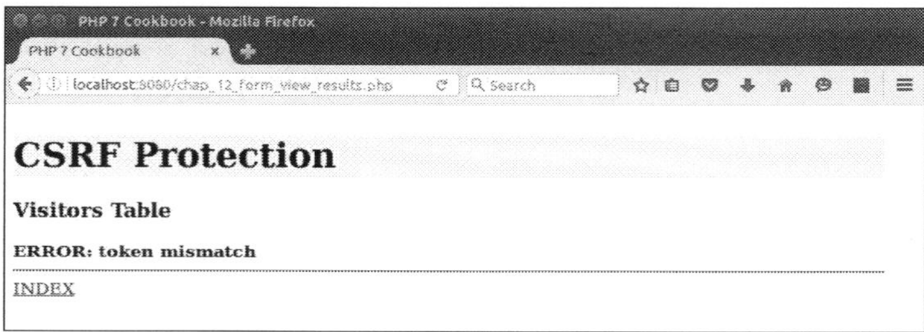

Finally, go ahead and define a file called `chap_12_form_protected.php` that generates a token and displays it as a hidden element:

```
<?php
session_start();
$token = urlencode(base64_encode((random_bytes(32))));
$_SESSION['token'] = $token;
?>
<!DOCTYPE html>
<body onload="load()">
<div class="container">
<h1>CSRF Protected Form</h1>
<form action="/chap_12_form_protected_with_token.php"
     method="post" id="csrf_test" name="csrf_test">
<table>
<tr><th>Name</th><td><input name="name" type="text" /></td></tr>
<tr><th>Email</th><td><input name="email" type="text" /></td></tr>
<tr><th>Comments</th><td>
<input name="comments" type="textarea" rows=4 cols=80 />
</td></tr>
<tr><th> </th><td>
```

```
<input name="process" type="submit" value="Process" />
</td></tr>
</table>
<input type="hidden" name="token" value="<?= $token ?>" />
</form>
<a href="/chap_12_form_view_results.php">
    CLICK HERE</a> to view results
</div>
</body>
</html>
```

When we display and submit data from the form, the token is validated and the data insertion is allowed to continue, as shown here:

See also

For more information on CSFR attacks, please refer to `https://www.owasp.org/index.php/Cross-Site_Request_Forgery_(CSRF)`.

Building a secure password generator

A common misconception is that the only way attackers crack hashed passwords is by using **brute force attacks** and **rainbow tables**. Although this is often the first pass in an attack sequence, attackers will use much more sophisticated attacks on a second, third, or fourth pass. Other attacks include *combination*, *dictionary*, *mask*, and rules-based. Dictionary attacks use a database of words literally from the dictionary to guess passwords. Combination is where dictionary words are combined. Mask attacks are similar to brute force, but more selective, thus cutting down the time to crack. Rules-based attacks will detect things such as substituting the number 0 for the letter o.

The good news is that by simply increasing the length of the password beyond the magic length of six characters exponentially increases the time to crack the hashed password. Other factors, such as interspersing uppercase with lowercase letters randomly, random digits, and special characters, will also have an exponential impact on the time to crack. At the end of the day, we need to bear in mind that a human being will eventually need to enter the passwords created, which means that need to be at least marginally memorable.

Best practice

Passwords should be stored as a hash, and never as plain text. MD5 and SHA* are no longer considered secure (although SHA* is much better than MD5). Using a utility such as `oclHashcat`, an attacker can generate an average of 55 billion attempts per second on a password hashed using MD5 that has been made available through an exploit (that is, a successful SQL injection attack).

How to do it...

1. First, we define a `Application\Security\PassGen` class that will hold the methods needed for password generation. We also define certain class constants and properties that will be used as part of the process:

```
namespace Application\Security;
class PassGen
{
  const SOURCE_SUFFIX = 'src';
  const SPECIAL_CHARS =
    '\`¬|!"£$%^&*()_-+={}[]:@~;\'#<>?,./|\\';
  protected $algorithm;
  protected $sourceList;
  protected $word;
  protected $list;
```

2. We then define low-level methods that will be used for password generation. As the names suggest, `digits()` produces random digits, and `special()` produces a single character from the `SPECIAL_CHARS` class constant:

```
public function digits($max = 999)
{
  return random_int(1, $max);
}

public function special()
{
  $maxSpecial = strlen(self::SPECIAL_CHARS) - 1;
  return self::SPECIAL_CHARS[random_int(0, $maxSpecial)];
}
```

Notice that we are frequently using the new PHP 7 function `random_int()` in this example. Although marginally slower, this method offers true **Cryptographically Secure Pseudo Random Number Generator** (**CSPRNG**) capabilities compared to the more dated `rand()` function.

3. Now comes the tricky part: generating a hard-to-guess word. This is where the `$wordSource` constructor parameter comes into play. It is an array of websites from which our word base will be derived. Accordingly, we need a method that will pull a unique list of words from the sources indicated, and store the results in a file. We accept the `$wordSource` array as an argument, and loop through each URL. We use `md5()` to produce a hash of the website name, which is then built into a filename. The newly produced filename is then stored in `$sourceList`:

```
public function processSource(
$wordSource, $minWordLength, $cacheDir)
{
  foreach ($wordSource as $html) {
    $hashKey = md5($html);
    $sourceFile = $cacheDir . '/' . $hashKey . '.'
    . self::SOURCE_SUFFIX;
    $this->sourceList[] = $sourceFile;
```

4. If the file doesn't exist, or is zero-byte, we process the contents. If the source is HTML, we only accept content inside the <body> tag. We then use `str_word_count()` to pull a list of words out of the string, also employing `strip_tags()` to remove any markup:

```
if (!file_exists($sourceFile) || filesize($sourceFile) == 0) {
    echo 'Processing: ' . $html . PHP_EOL;
    $contents = file_get_contents($html);
    if (preg_match('/<body>(.*)<\/body>/i',
        $contents, $matches)) {
        $contents = $matches[1];
    }
    $list = str_word_count(strip_tags($contents), 1);
```

5. We then remove any words that are too short, and use `array_unique()` to get rid of duplicates. The final result is stored in a file:

```
     foreach ($list as $key => $value) {
       if (strlen($value) < $minWordLength) {
         $list[$key] = 'xxxxxx';
       } else {
         $list[$key] = trim($value);
       }
     }
```

```
            $list = array_unique($list);
            file_put_contents($sourceFile, implode("\n",$list));
          }
        }
        return TRUE;
      }
```

6. Next, we define a method that *flips* random letters in the word to uppercase:

```
public function flipUpper($word)
{
  $maxLen   = strlen($word);
  $numFlips = random_int(1, $maxLen - 1);
  $flipped  = strtolower($word);
  for ($x = 0; $x < $numFlips; $x++) {
       $pos = random_int(0, $maxLen - 1);
       $word[$pos] = strtoupper($word[$pos]);
  }
  return $word;
}
```

7. Finally, we are ready to define a method that chooses a word from our source. We choose a word source at random, and use the `file()` function to read from the appropriate cached file:

```
public function word()
{
  $wsKey    = random_int(0, count($this->sourceList) - 1);
  $list     = file($this->sourceList[$wsKey]);
  $maxList  = count($list) - 1;
  $key      = random_int(0, $maxList);
  $word     = $list[$key];
  return $this->flipUpper($word);
}
```

8. So that we do not always produce passwords of the same pattern, we define a method that allows us to place the various components of a password in different positions in the final password string. The algorithms are defined as an array of method calls available within this class. So, for example, an algorithm of `['word', 'digits', 'word', 'special']` might end up looking like `hElLo123aUTo!`:

```
public function initAlgorithm()
{
  $this->algorithm = [
    ['word', 'digits', 'word', 'special'],
    ['digits', 'word', 'special', 'word'],
    ['word', 'word', 'special', 'digits'],
```

```
        ['special', 'word', 'special', 'digits'],
        ['word', 'special', 'digits', 'word', 'special'],
        ['special', 'word', 'special', 'digits',
        'special', 'word', 'special'],
      ];
    }
```

9. The constructor accepts the word source array, minimum word length, and location of the cache directory. It then processes the source files and initializes the algorithms:

```
public function __construct(
  array $wordSource, $minWordLength, $cacheDir)
{
  $this->processSource($wordSource, $minWordLength, $cacheDir);
  $this->initAlgorithm();
}
```

10. Finally, we are able to define the method that actually generates the password. All it needs to do is to select an algorithm at random, and then loop through, calling the appropriate methods:

```
public function generate()
{
  $pwd = '';
  $key = random_int(0, count($this->algorithm) - 1);
  foreach ($this->algorithm[$key] as $method) {
    $pwd .= $this->$method();
  }
  return str_replace("\n", '', $pwd);
}

}
```

How it works...

First, you will need to place the code described in the previous recipe into a file called `PassGen.php` in the `Application\Security` folder. Now you can create a calling program called `chap_12_password_generate.php` that sets up autoloading, uses `PassGen`, and defines the location of the cache directory:

```
<?php
define('CACHE_DIR', __DIR__ . '/cache');
require __DIR__ . '/../Application/Autoload/Loader.php';
Application\Autoload\Loader::init(__DIR__ . '/..');
use Application\Security\PassGen;
```

Next, you will need to define an array of websites that will be used as a source for the word-base to be used in password generation. In this illustration, we will choose from the Project Gutenberg texts *Ulysses* (J. Joyce), *War and Peace* (L. Tolstoy), and *Pride and Prejudice* (J. Austen):

```
$source = [
  'https://www.gutenberg.org/files/4300/4300-0.txt',
  'https://www.gutenberg.org/files/2600/2600-h/2600-h.htm',
  'https://www.gutenberg.org/files/1342/1342-h/1342-h.htm',
];
```

Next, we create the `PassGen` instance, and run `generate()`:

```
$passGen = new PassGen($source, 4, CACHE_DIR);
echo $passGen->generate();
```

Here are a few example passwords produced by `PassGen`:

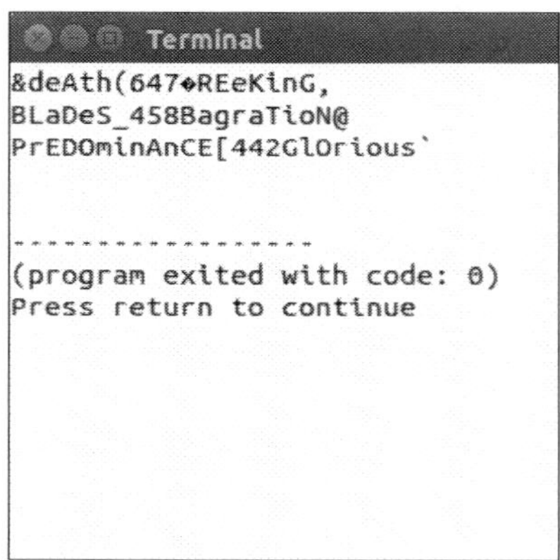

See also

An excellent article on how an attacker would approach cracking a password can be viewed at `http://arstechnica.com/security/2013/05/how-crackers-make-minced-meat-out-of-your-passwords/`. To find out more about brute force attacks you can refer to `https://www.owasp.org/index.php/Brute_force_attack`. For information on `oclHashcat`, see this page: `http://hashcat.net/oclhashcat/`.

Safeguarding forms with a CAPTCHA

CAPTCHA is actually an acronym for **Completely Automated Public Turing Test to Tell Computers and Humans Apart**. The technique is similar to the one presented in the preceding recipe, *Securing forms with a token*. The difference is that instead of storing the token in a hidden form input field, the token is rendered into a graphic that is difficult for an automated attack system to decipher. Also, the intent of a CAPTCHA is slightly different from a form token: it is designed to confirm that the web visitor is a human being, and not an automated system.

How to do it...

1. There are several approaches to CAPTCHA: presenting a question based on knowledge only a human would possess, text tricks, and a graphics image that needs to be interpreted.
2. The image approach presents web visitors with an image with heavily distorted letters and/or numbers. This approach can be complicated, however, in that it relies on the GD extension, which may not be available on all servers. The GD extension can be difficult to compile, and has heavy dependencies on various libraries that must be present on the host server.
3. The text approach is to present a series of letters and/or numbers, and give the web visitor a simple instruction such as *please type this backwards*. Another variation is to use ASCII "art" to form characters that a human web visitor is able to interpret.
4. Finally, you might have a question/answer approach with questions such as *The head is attached to the body by what body part*, and have answers such as *Arm*, *Leg*, and *Neck*. The downside to this approach is that an automated attack system will have a 1 in 3 chance of passing the test.

Generating a text CAPTCHA

1. For this illustration, we will start with the text approach, and follow with the image approach. In either case, we first need to define a class that generates the phrase to be presented (and decoded by the web visitor). For this purpose, we define an `Application\Captcha\Phrase` class. We also define properties and class constants used in the phrase generation process:

```
namespace Application\Captcha;
class Phrase
{
  const DEFAULT_LENGTH   = 5;
  const DEFAULT_NUMBERS  = '0123456789';
  const DEFAULT_UPPER    = 'ABCDEFGHJKLMNOPQRSTUVWXYZ';
  const DEFAULT_LOWER    = 'abcdefghijklmnopqrstuvwxyz';
```

```
const DEFAULT_SPECIAL  =
  '¬\`|!"£$%^&*()_-+={}[]:;@\'~#<,>.?/|\\';
const DEFAULT_SUPPRESS = ['O','l'];

protected $phrase;
protected $includeNumbers;
protected $includeUpper;
protected $includeLower;
protected $includeSpecial;
protected $otherChars;
protected $suppressChars;
protected $string;
protected $length;
```

2. The constructor, as you would expect, accepts values for the various properties, with defaults assigned so that an instance can be created without having to specify any parameters. The `$include*` flags are used to signal which character sets will be present in the base string from which the phrase will be generated. For example, if you wish to only have numbers, `$includeUpper` and `$includeLower` would both be set to `FALSE`. `$otherChars` is provided for extra flexibility. Finally, `$suppressChars` represents an array of characters that will be removed from the base string. The default removes uppercase `O` and lowercase `l`:

```
public function __construct(
  $length = NULL,
  $includeNumbers = TRUE,
  $includeUpper= TRUE,
  $includeLower= TRUE,
  $includeSpecial = FALSE,
  $otherChars = NULL,
  array $suppressChars = NULL)
  {
    $this->length = $length ?? self::DEFAULT_LENGTH;
    $this->includeNumbers = $includeNumbers;
    $this->includeUpper = $includeUpper;
    $this->includeLower = $includeLower;
    $this->includeSpecial = $includeSpecial;
    $this->otherChars = $otherChars;
    $this->suppressChars = $suppressChars
      ?? self::DEFAULT_SUPPRESS;
    $this->phrase = $this->generatePhrase();
  }
```

3. We then define a series of getters and setters, one for each property. Please note that we only show the first two in order to conserve space.

```
public function getString()
{
  return $this->string;
}

public function setString($string)
{
  $this->string = $string;
}

// other getters and setters not shown
```

4. We next need to define a method that initializes the base string. This consists of a series of simple if statements that check the various `$include*` flags and append to the base string as appropriate. At the end, we use `str_replace()` to remove the characters represented in `$suppressChars`:

```
public function initString()
{
  $string = '';
  if ($this->includeNumbers) {
      $string .= self::DEFAULT_NUMBERS;
  }
  if ($this->includeUpper) {
      $string .= self::DEFAULT_UPPER;
  }
  if ($this->includeLower) {
      $string .= self::DEFAULT_LOWER;
  }
  if ($this->includeSpecial) {
      $string .= self::DEFAULT_SPECIAL;
  }
  if ($this->otherChars) {
      $string .= $this->otherChars;
  }
  if ($this->suppressChars) {
      $string = str_replace(
        $this->suppressChars, '', $string);
  }
  return $string;
}
```

Best practice

Get rid of letters that can be confused with numbers (that is, the letter `o` can be confused with the number `0`, and a lowercase `l` can be confused with the number `1`.

5. We are now ready to define the core method that generates the random phrase that the CAPTCHA presents to website visitors. We set up a simple `for()` loop, and use the new PHP 7 `random_int()` function to jump around in the base string:

```
public function generatePhrase()
{
  $phrase = '';
  $this->string = $this->initString();
  $max = strlen($this->string) - 1;
  for ($x = 0; $x < $this->length; $x++) {
    $phrase .= substr(
      $this->string, random_int(0, $max), 1);
  }
  return $phrase;
}
}
```

6. Now we turn our attention away from the phrase and onto the class that will produce a text CAPTCHA. For this purpose, we first define an interface so that, in the future, we can create additional CAPTCHA classes that all make use of `Application\Captcha\Phrase`. Note that `getImage()` will return text, text art, or an actual image, depending on which class we decide to use:

```
namespace Application\Captcha;
interface CaptchaInterface
{
  public function getLabel();
  public function getImage();
  public function getPhrase();
}
```

7. For a text CAPTCHA, we define a `Application\Captcha\Reverse` class. The reason for this name is that this class produces not just text, but text in reverse. The `__construct()` method builds an instance of `Phrase`. Note that `getImage()` returns the phrase in reverse:

```
namespace Application\Captcha;
class Reverse implements CaptchaInterface
{
  const DEFAULT_LABEL = 'Type this in reverse';
  const DEFAULT_LENGTH = 6;
```

```
  protected $phrase;
  public function __construct(
    $label  = self::DEFAULT_LABEL,
    $length = self:: DEFAULT_LENGTH,
    $includeNumbers = TRUE,
    $includeUpper   = TRUE,
    $includeLower   = TRUE,
    $includeSpecial = FALSE,
    $otherChars     = NULL,
    array $suppressChars = NULL)
  {
    $this->label  = $label;
    $this->phrase = new Phrase(
      $length,
      $includeNumbers,
      $includeUpper,
      $includeLower,
      $includeSpecial,
      $otherChars,
      $suppressChars);
    }

  public function getLabel()
  {
    return $this->label;
  }

  public function getImage()
  {
    return strrev($this->phrase->getPhrase());
  }

  public function getPhrase()
  {
    return $this->phrase->getPhrase();
  }

}
```

Generating an image CAPTCHA

1. The image approach, as you can well imagine, is much more complicated. The phrase generation process is the same. The main difference is that not only do we need to imprint the phrase on a graphic, but we also need to distort each letter differently and introduce noise in the form of random dots.

2. We define a `Application\Captcha\Image` class that implements `CaptchaInterface`. The class constants and properties include not only those needed for phrase generation, but what is needed for image generation as well:

```
namespace Application\Captcha;
use DirectoryIterator;
class Image implements CaptchaInterface
{

  const DEFAULT_WIDTH = 200;
  const DEFAULT_HEIGHT = 50;
  const DEFAULT_LABEL = 'Enter this phrase';
  const DEFAULT_BG_COLOR = [255,255,255];
  const DEFAULT_URL = '/captcha';
  const IMAGE_PREFIX = 'CAPTCHA_';
  const IMAGE_SUFFIX = '.jpg';
  const IMAGE_EXP_TIME = 300;    // seconds
  const ERROR_REQUIRES_GD = 'Requires the GD extension + '
    .  ' the JPEG library';
  const ERROR_IMAGE = 'Unable to generate image';

  protected $phrase;
  protected $imageFn;
  protected $label;
  protected $imageWidth;
  protected $imageHeight;
  protected $imageRGB;
  protected $imageDir;
  protected $imageUrl;
```

3. The constructor needs to accept all the arguments required for phrase generation, as described in the previous steps. In addition, we need to accept arguments required for image generation. The two mandatory parameters are `$imageDir` and `$imageUrl`. The first is where the graphic will be written. The second is the base URL, after which we will append the generated filename. `$imageFont` is provided in case we want to provide TrueType fonts, which will produce a more secure CAPTCHA. Otherwise, we're limited to the default fonts which, to quote a line in a famous movie, *ain't a pretty sight*:

```
public function __construct(
  $imageDir,
  $imageUrl,
  $imageFont = NULL,
  $label = NULL,
  $length = NULL,
  $includeNumbers = TRUE,
```

```
    $includeUpper= TRUE,
    $includeLower= TRUE,
    $includeSpecial = FALSE,
    $otherChars = NULL,
    array $suppressChars = NULL,
    $imageWidth = NULL,
    $imageHeight = NULL,
    array $imageRGB = NULL
  )
  {
```

4. Next, still in the constructor, we check to see whether the `imagecreatetruecolor` function exists. If this comes back as `FALSE`, we know the GD extension is not available. Otherwise, we assign parameters to properties, generate the phrase, remove old images, and write out the CAPTCHA graphic:

```
if (!function_exists('imagecreatetruecolor')) {
    throw new \Exception(self::ERROR_REQUIRES_GD);
}
$this->imageDir    = $imageDir;
$this->imageUrl    = $imageUrl;
$this->imageFont   = $imageFont;
$this->label       = $label ?? self::DEFAULT_LABEL;
$this->imageRGB    = $imageRGB ?? self::DEFAULT_BG_COLOR;
$this->imageWidth = $imageWidth ?? self::DEFAULT_WIDTH;
$this->imageHeight= $imageHeight ?? self::DEFAULT_HEIGHT;
if (substr($imageUrl, -1, 1) == '/') {
    $imageUrl = substr($imageUrl, 0, -1);
}
$this->imageUrl = $imageUrl;
if (substr($imageDir, -1, 1) == DIRECTORY_SEPARATOR) {
    $imageDir = substr($imageDir, 0, -1);
}

$this->phrase = new Phrase(
  $length,
  $includeNumbers,
  $includeUpper,
  $includeLower,
  $includeSpecial,
  $otherChars,
  $suppressChars);
$this->removeOldImages();
$this->generateJpg();
}
```

5. The process of removing old images is extremely important; otherwise we will end up with a directory filled with expired CAPTCHA images! We use the `DirectoryIterator` class to scan the designated directory and check the access time. We calculate an old image file as one that is the current time minus the value specified by `IMAGE_EXP_TIME`:

```
public function removeOldImages()
{
  $old = time() - self::IMAGE_EXP_TIME;
  foreach (new DirectoryIterator($this->imageDir)
           as $fileInfo) {
    if($fileInfo->isDot()) continue;
    if ($fileInfo->getATime() < $old) {
      unlink($this->imageDir . DIRECTORY_SEPARATOR
             . $fileInfo->getFilename());
    }
  }
}
```

6. We are now ready to move on to the main show. First, we split the `$imageRGB` array into `$red`, `$green`, and `$blue`. We use the core `imagecreatetruecolor()` function to generate the base graphic with the width and height specified. We use the RGB values to colorize the background:

```
public function generateJpg()
{
  try {
      list($red,$green,$blue) = $this->imageRGB;
      $im = imagecreatetruecolor(
        $this->imageWidth, $this->imageHeight);
      $black = imagecolorallocate($im, 0, 0, 0);
      $imageBgColor = imagecolorallocate(
        $im, $red, $green, $blue);
      imagefilledrectangle($im, 0, 0, $this->imageWidth,
        $this->imageHeight, $imageBgColor);
```

7. Next, we define *x* and *y* margins based on image width and height. We then initialize variables to be used to write the phrase onto the graphic. We then loop a number of times that matches the length of the phrase:

```
$xMargin = (int) ($this->imageWidth * .1 + .5);
$yMargin = (int) ($this->imageHeight * .3 + .5);
$phrase = $this->getPhrase();
$max = strlen($phrase);
$count = 0;
$x = $xMargin;
$size = 5;
for ($i = 0; $i < $max; $i++) {
```

8. If `$imageFont` is specified, we are able to write each character with a different size and angle. We also need to adjust the x axis (that is, horizontal) value according to the size:

```
if ($this->imageFont) {
    $size = rand(12, 32);
    $angle = rand(0, 30);
    $y = rand($yMargin + $size, $this->imageHeight);
    imagettftext($im, $size, $angle, $x, $y, $black,
      $this->imageFont, $phrase[$i]);
    $x += (int) ($size  + rand(0,5));
```

9. Otherwise, we're stuck with the default fonts. We use the largest size of `5`, as smaller sizes are unreadable. We provide a low level of distortion by alternating between `imagechar()`, which writes the image normally, and `imagecharup()`, which writes it sideways:

```
} else {
    $y = rand(0, ($this->imageHeight - $yMargin));
    if ($count++ & 1) {
        imagechar($im, 5, $x, $y, $phrase[$i], $black);
    } else {
        imagecharup($im, 5, $x, $y, $phrase[$i], $black);
    }
    $x += (int) ($size * 1.2);
  }
} // end for ($i = 0; $i < $max; $i++)
```

10. Next we need to add noise in the form of random dots. This is necessary in order to make the image harder for automated systems to detect. It is also recommended that you add code to draw a few lines as well:

```
$numDots = rand(10, 999);
for ($i = 0; $i < $numDots; $i++) {
  imagesetpixel($im, rand(0, $this->imageWidth),
    rand(0, $this->imageHeight), $black);
}
```

11. We then create a random image filename using our old friend `md5()` with the date and a random number from `0` to `9999` as arguments. Note that we can safely use `md5()` as we are not trying to hide any secret information; we're merely interested in generating a unique filename quickly. We wipe out the image object as well to conserve memory:

```
$this->imageFn = self::IMAGE_PREFIX
. md5(date('YmdHis') . rand(0,9999))
. self::IMAGE_SUFFIX;
imagejpeg($im, $this->imageDir . DIRECTORY_SEPARATOR
```

```
    . $this->imageFn);
imagedestroy($im);
```

12. The entire construct is in a `try/catch` block. If an error or exception is thrown, we log the message and take the appropriate action:

```
} catch (\Throwable $e) {
    error_log(__METHOD__ . ':' . $e->getMessage());
    throw new \Exception(self::ERROR_IMAGE);
}
}
```

13. Finally, we define the methods required by the interface. Note that `getImage()` returns an HTML `<img>` tag, which can then be immediately displayed:

```
public function getLabel()
{
  return $this->label;
}

public function getImage()
{
  return sprintf('<img src="%s/%s" />',
    $this->imageUrl, $this->imageFn);
}

public function getPhrase()
{
  return $this->phrase->getPhrase();
}

}
```

How it works...

Be sure to define the classes discussed in this recipe, summarized in the following table:

Class	Subsection	The steps it appears in
`Application\Captcha\Phrase`	Generating a text CAPTCHA	1 - 5
`Application\Captcha\CaptchaInterface`		6
`Application\Captcha\Reverse`		7
`Application\Captcha\Image`	Generating an image CAPTCHA	2 - 13

Next, define a calling program called `chap_12_captcha_text.php` that implements a text CAPTCHA. You first need to set up autoloading and use the appropriate classes:

```
<?php
require __DIR__ . '/../Application/Autoload/Loader.php';
Application\Autoload\Loader::init(__DIR__ . '/..');
use Application\Captcha\Reverse;
```

After that, be sure to start the session. You would use appropriate measures to protect the session as well. To conserve space, we only show one simple measure, `session_regenerate_id()`:

```
session_start();
session_regenerate_id();
```

Next, you can define a function that creates the CAPTCHA; retrieves the phrase, label, and image (in this case, reverse text); and stores the value in the session:

```
function setCaptcha(&$phrase, &$label, &$image)
{
  $captcha = new Reverse();
  $phrase  = $captcha->getPhrase();
  $label   = $captcha->getLabel();
  $image   = $captcha->getImage();
  $_SESSION['phrase'] = $phrase;
}
```

Now is a good time to initialize variables and determine the `loggedIn` status:

```
$image      = '';
$label      = '';
$phrase     = $_SESSION['phrase'] ?? '';
$message    = '';
$info       = 'You Can Now See Super Secret Information!!!';
$loggedIn   = $_SESSION['isLoggedIn'] ?? FALSE;
$loggedUser = $_SESSION['user'] ?? 'guest';
```

You can then check to see whether the login button has been pressed. If so, check to see whether the CAPTCHA phrase has been entered. If not, initialize a message informing the user they need to enter the CAPTCHA phrase:

```
if (!empty($_POST['login'])) {
  if (empty($_POST['captcha'])) {
    $message = 'Enter Captcha Phrase and Login Information';
```

If the CAPTCHA phrase is present, check to see whether it matches what is stored in the session. If it doesn't match, proceed as if the form is invalid. Otherwise, process the login as you would have otherwise. For the purposes of this illustration, you can simulate a login by using hard-coded values for the username and password:

```
} else {
    if ($_POST['captcha'] == $phrase) {
        $username = 'test';
        $password = 'password';
        if ($_POST['user'] == $username
            && $_POST['pass'] == $password) {
            $loggedIn = TRUE;
            $_SESSION['user'] = strip_tags($username);
            $_SESSION['isLoggedIn'] = TRUE;
        } else {
            $message = 'Invalid Login';
        }
    } else {
        $message = 'Invalid Captcha';
    }
}
```

You might also want to add code for a logout option, as described in the *Safeguarding the PHP session* recipe:

```
} elseif (isset($_POST['logout'])) {
  session_unset();
  session_destroy();
  setcookie('PHPSESSID', 0, time() - 3600);
  header('Location: ' . $_SERVER['REQUEST_URI'] );
  exit;
}
```

You can then run `setCaptcha()`:

```
setCaptcha($phrase, $label, $image);
```

Lastly, don't forget the view logic, which, in this example, presents a basic login form. Inside the form tag, you'll need to add view logic to display the CAPTCHA and label:

```
<tr>
  <th><?= $label; ?></th>
  <td><?= $image; ?><input type="text" name="captcha" /></td>
</tr>
```

Here is the resulting output:

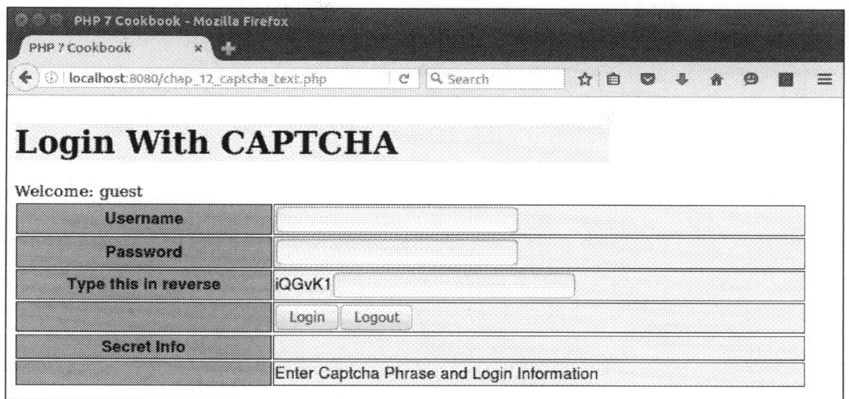

To demonstrate how to use the image CAPTCHA, copy the code from `chap_12_captcha_text.php` to `cha_12_captcha_image.php`. We define constants that represent the location of the directory in which we will write the CAPTCHA images. (Be sure to create this directory!) Otherwise, the autoloading and use statement structure is similar. Note that we also define a TrueType font. Differences are noted in **bold**:

```
<?php
define('IMAGE_DIR', __DIR__ . '/captcha');
define('IMAGE_URL', '/captcha');
define('IMAGE_FONT', __DIR__ . '/FreeSansBold.ttf');
require __DIR__ . '/../Application/Autoload/Loader.php';
Application\Autoload\Loader::init(__DIR__ . '/..');
use Application\Captcha\Image;

session_start();
session_regenerate_id();
```

Important!

Fonts can potentially be protected under copyright, trademark, patent, or other intellectual property laws. If you use a font for which you are not licensed, you and your customer could be held liable in court! Use an open source font, or one that is available on the web server for which you have a valid license.

Of course, in the `setCaptcha()` function, we use the `Image` class instead of `Reverse`:

```
function setCaptcha(&$phrase, &$label, &$image)
{
  $captcha = new Image(IMAGE_DIR, IMAGE_URL, IMAGE_FONT);
  $phrase  = $captcha->getPhrase();
```

```
    $label    = $captcha->getLabel();
    $image    = $captcha->getImage();
    $_SESSION['phrase'] = $phrase;
    return $captcha;
  }
```

Variable initialization is the same as the previous script, and login processing is identical to the previous script:

```
$image      = '';
$label      = '';
$phrase     = $_SESSION['phrase'] ?? '';
$message    = '';
$info       = 'You Can Now See Super Secret Information!!!';
$loggedIn   = $_SESSION['isLoggedIn'] ?? FALSE;
$loggedUser = $_SESSION['user'] ?? 'guest';

if (!empty($_POST['login'])) {

  // etc.  -- identical to chap_12_captcha_text.php
```

Even the view logic remains the same, as we are using `getImage()`, which, in the case of the image CAPTCHA, returns directly usable HTML. Here is the output using a TrueType font:

There's more...

If you are not inclined to use the preceding code to generate your own in-house CAPTCHA, there are plenty of libraries available. Most popular frameworks have this ability. Zend Framework, for example, has its Zend\Captcha component class. There is also reCAPTCHA, which is generally invoked as a service in which your application makes a call to an external website that generates the CAPTCHA and token for you. A good place to start looking is `http://www.captcha.net/` website.

See also

For more information on the protection of fonts as intellectual property, refer to the article present at `https://en.wikipedia.org/wiki/Intellectual_property_protection_of_typefaces`.

Encrypting/decrypting without mcrypt

It is a little-known fact among members of the general PHP community that the `mcrypt` extension, the core of most PHP-based encryption considered secure, is anything but secure. One of the biggest issues, from a security perspective, is that the `mcrypt` extension requires advanced knowledge of cryptography to successfully operate, which few programmers have. This leads to gross misuse and ultimately problems such as a 1 in 256 chance of data corruption. Not good odds. Furthermore, developer support for `libmcrypt`, the core library upon which the `mcrypt` extension is based, was *abandoned* in 2007, which means the code base is out-of-date, bug-ridden, and has no mechanism to apply patches. Accordingly, it is extremely important to understand how to perform strong encryption/decryption *without* using `mcrypt`!

How to do it...

1. The solution to the problem posed previously, in case you're wondering, is to use `openssl`. This extension is well maintained, and has modern and very strong encryption/decryption capabilities.

Important

In order to use any `openssl*` functions, the `openssl` PHP extension must be compiled and enabled! In addition, you will need to install the latest OpenSSL package on your web server.

2. First, you will need to determine which cipher methods are available on your installation. For this purpose, you can use the `openssl_get_cipher_methods()` command. Examples will include algorithms based on **Advanced Encryption Standard** (**AES**), **BlowFish** (**BF**), **CAMELLIA**, **CAST5**, **Data Encryption Standard** (**DES**), **Rivest Cipher** (**RC**) (also affectionately known as **Ron's Code**), and **SEED**. You will note that this method shows cipher methods duplicated in upper and lowercase.

3. Next, you will need to figure out which method is most appropriate for your needs. Here is a table that gives a quick summary of the various methods:

Method	**Published**	**Key size (bits)**	**Key block size (bytes)**	**Notes**
`camellia`	2000	128, 192, 256	16	Developed by Mitsubishi and NTT
`aes`	1998	128, 192, 256	16	Developed by Joan Daemen and Vincent Rijmen. Originally submitted as Rijndael
`seed`	1998	128	16	Developed by the Korea Information Security Agency
`cast5`	1996	40 to 128	8	Developed by Carlisle Adams and Stafford Tavares
`bf`	1993	1 to 448	8	Designed by Bruce Schneier
`rc2`	1987	8 to 1,024 defaults to 64	8	Designed by Ron Rivest (one of the core founders of RSA)
`des`	1977	56 (+8 parity bits)	8	Developed by IBM, based on work done by Horst Feistel

4. Another consideration is what your preferred block cipher **mode of operation is**. Common choices are summarized in this table:

Mode	**Stands For**	**Notes**
ECB	Electronic Code Book	Does not require **initialization vector** (**IV**); supports parallelization for both encryption and decryption; simple and fast; does not hide data patterns; not recommended!!!
CBC	Cipher Block Chaining	Requires IV; subsequent blocks, even if identical, are XOR'ed with previous block, resulting in better overall encryption; if the IVs are predictable, the first block can be decoded, leaving remaining message exposed; message must be padded to a multiple of the cipher block size; supports parallelization only for decryption
CFB	Cipher Feedback	Close relative of CBC, except that encryption is performed in reverse

Mode	Stands For	Notes
OFB	Output Feedback	Very symmetrical: encrypt and decrypt are the same; does not supports parallelization at all
CTR	Counter	Similar in operation to OFB; supports parallelization for both encryption and decryption
CCM	Counter with CBC-MAC	Derivative of CTR; only designed for block length of 128 bits; provides authentication and confidentiality; **CBC-MAC** stands for **Cipher Block Chaining - Message Authentication Code**
GCM	Galois/Counter Mode	Based on CTR mode; should use a different IV for each stream to be encrypted; exceptionally high throughput (compared to other modes); supports parallelization for both encryption and decryption
XTS	XEX-based Tweaked-codebook mode with ciphertext Stealing	Relatively new (2010) and fast; uses two keys; increases the amount of data that can be securely encrypted as one block

5. Before choosing a cipher method and mode, you will also need to determine whether the encrypted contents needs to be unencrypted outside of your PHP application. For example, if you are storing database credentials encrypted into a standalone text file, do you need to have the ability to decrypt from the command line? If so, make sure that the cipher method and operation mode you choose are supported by the target operating system.

6. The number of bytes supplied for the **IV** varies according to the cipher method chosen. For best results, use `random_bytes()` (new in PHP 7), which returns a true **CSPRNG** sequence of bytes. The length of the IV varies considerably. Try a size of 16 to start with. If a *warning* is generated, the correct number of bytes to be supplied for that algorithm will be shown, so adjust the size accordingly:

```
$iv   = random_bytes(16);
```

7. To perform encryption, use `openssl_encrypt()`. Here are the parameters that should be passed:

Parameter	Notes
Data	Plain text you need to encrypt.
Method	One of the methods you identified using `openssl_get_cipher_methods()`. identified as follows: *method - key_size - cipher_mode* So, for example, if you want a method of AES, a key size of 256, and GCM mode, you would enter `aes-256-gcm`.
Password	Although documented as *password*, this parameter can be viewed as a *key*. Use `random_bytes()` to generate a key with a number of bytes to match the desired key size.
Options	Until you gain more experience with `openssl` encryption, it is recommended you stick with the default value of `0`.
IV	Use `random_bytes()` to generate an IV with a number of bytes to match the cipher method.

8. As an example, suppose you wanted to choose the AES cipher method, a key size of 256, and XTS mode. Here is the code used to encrypt:

```
$plainText = 'Super Secret Credentials';
$key = random_bytes(16);
$method = 'aes-256-xts';
$cipherText = openssl_encrypt($plainText, $method, $key, 0, $iv);
```

9. To decrypt, use the same values for `$key` and `$iv`, along with the `openssl_decrypt()` function:

```
$plainText = openssl_decrypt($cipherText, $method, $key, 0, $iv);
```

How it works...

In order to see which cipher methods are available, create a PHP script called `chap_12_openssl_encryption.php` and run this command:

```
<?php
echo implode(', ', openssl_get_cipher_methods());
```

The output should look something like this:

```
Terminal
AES-128-CBC, AES-128-CFB, AES-128-CFB1, AES-128-CFB8, AES-128-CTR, AES-128-ECB,
AES-128-OFB, AES-128-XTS, AES-192-CBC, AES-192-CFB, AES-192-CFB1, AES-192-CFB8,
AES-192-CTR, AES-192-ECB, AES-192-OFB, AES-256-CBC, AES-256-CFB, AES-256-CFB1, A
ES-256-CFB8, AES-256-CTR, AES-256-ECB, AES-256-OFB, AES-256-XTS, BF-CBC, BF-CFB,
 BF-ECB, BF-OFB, CAMELLIA-128-CBC, CAMELLIA-128-CFB, CAMELLIA-128-CFB1, CAMELLIA
-128-CFB8, CAMELLIA-128-ECB, CAMELLIA-128-OFB, CAMELLIA-192-CBC, CAMELLIA-192-CF
B, CAMELLIA-192-CFB1, CAMELLIA-192-CFB8, CAMELLIA-192-ECB, CAMELLIA-192-OFB, CAM
ELLIA-256-CBC, CAMELLIA-256-CFB, CAMELLIA-256-CFB1, CAMELLIA-256-CFB8, CAMELLIA-
256-ECB, CAMELLIA-256-OFB, CAST5-CBC, CAST5-CFB, CAST5-ECB, CAST5-OFB, DES-CBC,
DES-CFB, DES-CFB1, DES-CFB8, DES-ECB, DES-EDE, DES-EDE-CBC, DES-EDE-CFB, DES-EDE
-OFB, DES-EDE3, DES-EDE3-CBC, DES-EDE3-CFB, DES-EDE3-CFB1, DES-EDE3-CFB8, DES-ED
E3-OFB, DES-OFB, DESX-CBC, RC2-40-CBC, RC2-64-CBC, RC2-CBC, RC2-CFB, RC2-ECB, RC
2-OFB, RC4, RC4-40, RC4-HMAC-MD5, SEED-CBC, SEED-CFB, SEED-ECB, SEED-OFB, aes-12
8-cbc, aes-128-cfb, aes-128-cfb1, aes-128-cfb8, aes-128-ctr, aes-128-ecb, aes-12
8-gcm, aes-128-ofb, aes-128-xts, aes-192-cbc, aes-192-cfb, aes-192-cfb1, aes-192
-cfb8, aes-192-ctr, aes-192-ecb, aes-192-gcm, aes-192-ofb, aes-256-cbc, aes-256-
cfb, aes-256-cfb1, aes-256-cfb8, aes-256-ctr, aes-256-ecb, aes-256-gcm, aes-256-
ofb, aes-256-xts, bf-cbc, bf-cfb, bf-ecb, bf-ofb, camellia-128-cbc, camellia-128
-cfb, camellia-128-cfb1, camellia-128-cfb8, camellia-128-ecb, camellia-128-ofb,
camellia-192-cbc, camellia-192-cfb, camellia-192-cfb1, camellia-192-cfb8, camell
ia-192-ecb, camellia-192-ofb, camellia-256-cbc, camellia-256-cfb, camellia-256-c
fb1, camellia-256-cfb8, camellia-256-ecb, camellia-256-ofb, cast5-cbc, cast5-cfb
, cast5-ecb, cast5-ofb, des-cbc, des-cfb, des-cfb1, des-cfb8, des-ecb, des-ede,
des-ede-cbc, des-ede-cfb, des-ede-ofb, des-ede3, des-ede3-cbc, des-ede3-cfb, des
-ede3-cfb1, des-ede3-cfb8, des-ede3-ofb, des-ofb, desx-cbc, id-aes128-GCM, id-ae
s192-GCM, id-aes256-GCM, rc2-40-cbc, rc2-64-cbc, rc2-cbc, rc2-cfb, rc2-ecb, rc2-
ofb, rc4, rc4-40, rc4-hmac-md5, seed-cbc, seed-cfb, seed-ecb, seed-ofb
```

Next, you can add values for the plain text to be encrypted, the method, key, and IV. As an example, try AES, with a key size of 256, using the XTS operating mode:

```
$plainText = 'Super Secret Credentials';
$method = 'aes-256-xts';
$key = random_bytes(16);
$iv  = random_bytes(16);
```

To encrypt, you can use `openssl_encrypt()`, specifying the parameters configured previously:

```
$cipherText = openssl_encrypt($plainText, $method, $key, 0, $iv);
```

You might also want to base 64-encode the result to make it more usable:

```
$cipherText = base64_encode($cipherText);
```

To decrypt, use the same `$key` and `$iv` values. Don't forget to un-encode the base 64 value first:

```
$plainText = openssl_decrypt(base64_decode($cipherText),
$method, $key, 0, $iv);
```

Here is the output showing the base 64-encoded cipher text, followed by the decrypted plain text:

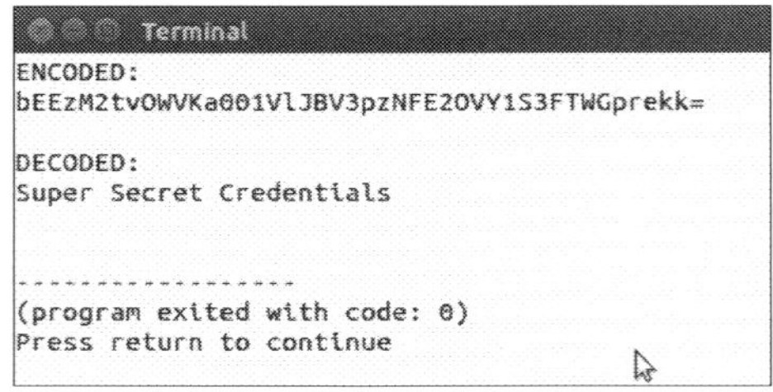

If you supply an incorrect number of bytes for the IV, for the cipher method chosen, a warning message will be shown:

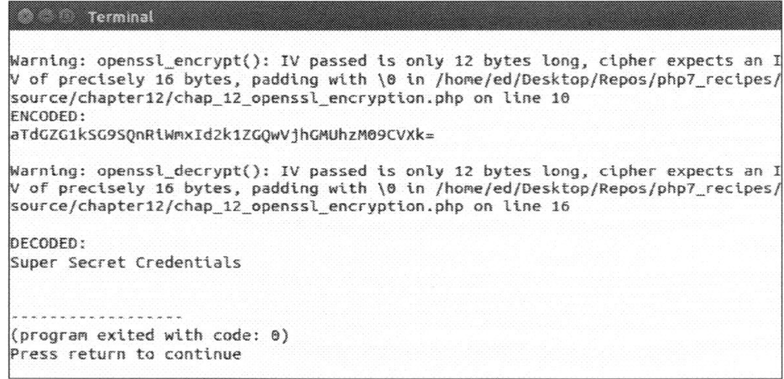

There's more...

In PHP 7, there was a problem when using `open_ssl_encrypt()` and `open_ssl_decrypt()` and the **Authenticated Encrypt with Associated Data** (**AEAD**) modes supported: GCM and CCM. Accordingly, in PHP 7.1, three extra parameters have been added to these functions, as follows:

Parameter	Description
`$tag`	Authentication tag passed by reference; variable value remains the same if authentication fails
`$aad`	Additional authentication data
`$tag_length`	4 to 16 for GCM mode; no limits for CCM mode; only for `open_ssl_encrypt()`

For more information, you can refer to `https://wiki.php.net/rfc/openssl_aead`.

See also

For an excellent discussion on why the `mcrypt` extension is being deprecated in PHP 7.1, please refer to the article at `https://wiki.php.net/rfc/mcrypt-viking-funeral`. For a good description of block cipher, which forms the basis for the various cipher methods, refer to the article present at `https://en.wikipedia.org/wiki/Block_cipher`. For an excellent description of AES, refer to `https://en.wikipedia.org/wiki/Advanced_Encryption_Standard`. A good article that describes encryption operation modes can be seen at `https://en.wikipedia.org/wiki/Block_cipher_mode_of_operation`.

For some of the newer modes, if the data to be encrypted is less than the block size, `openssl_decrypt()` will return no value. If you *pad* the data to be at least the block size, the problem goes away. Most of the modes implement internal padding so this is not an issue. With some of the newer modes (that is, `xts`) you might see this problem. Be sure to conduct tests on short strings of data less than eight characters before putting your code into production.

13
Best Practices, Testing, and Debugging

In this chapter, we will cover the following topics:

- Using Traits and Interfaces
- Universal exception handler
- Universal error handler
- Writing a simple test
- Writing a test suite
- Generating fake test data
- Customizing sessions using `session_start` parameters

Introduction

In this chapter, we will show you how traits and interfaces work together. Then, we turn our attention to the design of a fallback mechanism that will catch errors and exceptions in situations where you were not able (or forgot) to define specific `try/catch` blocks. We will then venture into the world of unit testing, showing you first how to write simple tests, and then how to group those tests together into test suites. Next, we define a class that lets you create any amount of generic test data. We close the chapter with a discussion of how to easily manage sessions using new PHP 7 features.

Using Traits and Interfaces

It is considered a best practice to make use of interfaces as a means of establishing the classification of a set of classes, and to guarantee the existence of certain methods. Traits and Interfaces often work together, and are an important aspect of implementation. Wherever you have a frequently used Interface that defines a method where the code does not change (such as a setter or getter), it is useful to also define a Trait that contains the actual code implementation.

How to do it...

1. For this example, we will use `ConnectionAwareInterface`, first presented in *Chapter 4, Working with PHP Object-Oriented Programming*. This interface defines a `setConnection()` method that sets a `$connection` property. Two classes in the `Application\Generic` namespace, `CountryList` and `CustomerList`, contain redundant code, which matches the method defined in the interface.
2. Here is what `CountryList` looks like before the change:

```
class CountryList
{
  protected $connection;
  protected $key   = 'iso3';
  protected $value = 'name';
  protected $table = 'iso_country_codes';

  public function setConnection(Connection $connection)
  {
    $this->connection = $connection;
  }
  public function list()
  {
    $list = [];
    $sql  = sprintf('SELECT %s,%s FROM %s', $this->key,
                    $this->value, $this->table);
    $stmt = $this->connection->pdo->query($sql);
    while ($item = $stmt->fetch(PDO::FETCH_ASSOC)) {
      $list[$item[$this->key]] =  $item[$this->value];
    }
    return $list;
  }

}
```

3. We will now move `list()` into a trait called `ListTrait`:

```
trait ListTrait
{
  public function list()
  {
    $list = [];
    $sql  = sprintf('SELECT %s,%s FROM %s',
                    $this->key, $this->value, $this->table);
    $stmt = $this->connection->pdo->query($sql);
    while ($item = $stmt->fetch(PDO::FETCH_ASSOC)) {
           $list[$item[$this->key]] = $item[$this->value];
    }
    return $list;
  }
}
```

4. We can then insert the code from `ListTrait` into a new class, `CountryListUsingTrait`, as shown next:

```
class CountryListUsingTrait
{
  use ListTrait;
  protected $connection;
  protected $key   = 'iso3';
  protected $value = 'name';
  protected $table = 'iso_country_codes';
  public function setConnection(Connection $connection)
  {
    $this->connection = $connection;
  }

}
```

5. Next, we observe that many classes need to set a connection instance. Again, this calls for a trait. This time, however, we place the trait in the `Application\Database` namespace. Here is the new trait:

```
namespace Application\Database;
trait ConnectionTrait
{
  protected $connection;
  public function setConnection(Connection $connection)
  {
```

```
        $this->connection = $connection;
      }
    }
```

6. Traits are often used to avoid duplication of code. It is often the case that you also need to identify the class that uses the trait. A good way to do this is to develop an interface that matches the trait. In this example, we will define `Application\Database\ConnectionAwareInterface`:

```
namespace Application\Database;
use Application\Database\Connection;
interface ConnectionAwareInterface
{
  public function setConnection(Connection $connection);
}
```

7. And here is the revised `CountryListUsingTrait` class. Note that as the new trait is affected by its location in the namespace, we needed to add a `use` statement at the top of the class. You will also note that we implement `ConnectionAwareInterface` to identify the fact that this class requires the method defined in the trait. Notice that we are taking advantage of the new PHP 7 group use syntax:

```
namespace Application\Generic;
use PDO;
use Application\Database\ {
Connection, ConnectionTrait, ConnectionAwareInterface
};
class CountryListUsingTrait implements ConnectionAwareInterface
{
  use ListTrait;
  use ConnectionTrait;

  protected $key   = 'iso3';
  protected $value = 'name';
  protected $table = 'iso_country_codes';

}
```

How it works...

First of all, make sure the classes developed in *Chapter 4, Working with PHP Object-Oriented Programming*, have been created. These include the `Application\Generic\CountryList` and `Application\Generic\CustomerList` classes discussed in *Chapter 4, Working with PHP Object-Oriented Programming*, in the recipe *Using interfaces*. Save each class in a new file in the `Application\Generic` folder as `CountryListUsingTrait.php` and `CustomerListUsingTrait.php`. Be sure to change the class names to match the new names of the files!

As discussed in step 3, remove the `list()` method from both `CountryListUsingTrait.php` and `CustomerListUsingTrait.php`. Add `use ListTrait;` in place of the method removed. Place the removed code into a separate file, in the same folder, called `ListTrait.php`.

You will also notice further duplication of code between the two list classes, in this case the `setConnection()` method. This calls for another trait!

Cut the `setConnection()` method out of both `CountryListUsingTrait.php` and `CustomerListUsingTrait.php` list classes, and place the removed code into a separate file called `ConnectionTrait.php`. As this trait is logically related to `ConnectionAwareInterface` and `Connection`, it makes sense to place the file in the `Application\Database` folder, and to specify its namespace accordingly.

Finally, define `Application\Database\ConnectionAwareInterface` as discussed in step 6. Here is the final `Application\Generic\CustomerListUsingTrait` class after all changes:

```
<?php
namespace Application\Generic;
use PDO;
use Application\Database\Connection;
use Application\Database\ConnectionTrait;
use Application\Database\ConnectionAwareInterface;
class CustomerListUsingTrait implements ConnectionAwareInterface
{

  use ListTrait;
  use ConnectionTrait;

  protected $key   = 'id';
  protected $value = 'name';
  protected $table = 'customer';
}
```

You can now copy the `chap_04_oop_simple_interfaces_example.php` file mentioned in *Chapter 4, Working with PHP Object-Oriented Programming*, to a new file called `chap_13_trait_and_interface.php`. Change the reference from `CountryList` to `CountryListUsingTrait`. Likewise, change the reference from `CustomerList` to `CustomerListUsingTrait`. Otherwise, the code can remain the same:

```
<?php
define('DB_CONFIG_FILE', '/../config/db.config.php');
require __DIR__ . '/../Application/Autoload/Loader.php';
Application\Autoload\Loader::init(__DIR__ . '/..');
$params = include __DIR__ . DB_CONFIG_FILE;
try {
    $list = Application\Generic\ListFactory::factory(
      new Application\Generic\CountryListUsingTrait(), $params);
    echo 'Country List' . PHP_EOL;
    foreach ($list->list() as $item) echo $item . ' ';
    $list = Application\Generic\ListFactory::factory(
      new Application\Generic\CustomerListUsingTrait(),
      $params);
    echo 'Customer List' . PHP_EOL;
    foreach ($list->list() as $item) echo $item . ' ';

} catch (Throwable $e) {
    echo $e->getMessage();
}
```

The output will be exactly as described in the *Using interfaces* recipe of *Chapter 4, Working with Object-Oriented Programming*. You can see the country list portion of the output in the following screenshot:

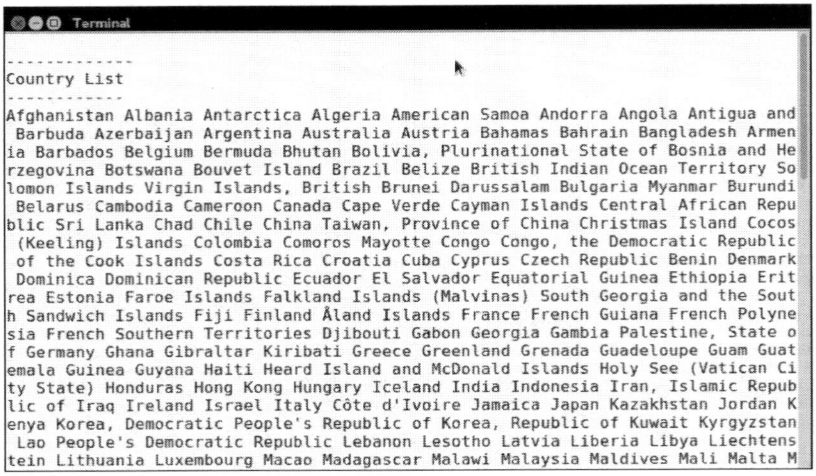

```
Terminal
-------------
Country List
------------
Afghanistan Albania Antarctica Algeria American Samoa Andorra Angola Antigua and
 Barbuda Azerbaijan Argentina Australia Austria Bahamas Bahrain Bangladesh Armen
ia Barbados Belgium Bermuda Bhutan Bolivia, Plurinational State of Bosnia and He
rzegovina Botswana Bouvet Island Brazil Belize British Indian Ocean Territory So
lomon Islands Virgin Islands, British Brunei Darussalam Bulgaria Myanmar Burundi
 Belarus Cambodia Cameroon Canada Cape Verde Cayman Islands Central African Repu
blic Sri Lanka Chad Chile China Taiwan, Province of China Christmas Island Cocos
 (Keeling) Islands Colombia Comoros Mayotte Congo Congo, the Democratic Republic
 of the Cook Islands Costa Rica Croatia Cuba Cyprus Czech Republic Benin Denmark
 Dominica Dominican Republic Ecuador El Salvador Equatorial Guinea Ethiopia Erit
rea Estonia Faroe Islands Falkland Islands (Malvinas) South Georgia and the Sout
h Sandwich Islands Fiji Finland Åland Islands France French Guiana French Polyne
sia French Southern Territories Djibouti Gabon Georgia Gambia Palestine, State o
f Germany Ghana Gibraltar Kiribati Greece Greenland Grenada Guadeloupe Guam Guat
emala Guinea Guyana Haiti Heard Island and McDonald Islands Holy See (Vatican Ci
ty State) Honduras Hong Kong Hungary Iceland India Indonesia Iran, Islamic Repub
lic of Iraq Ireland Israel Italy Côte d'Ivoire Jamaica Japan Kazakhstan Jordan K
enya Korea, Democratic People's Republic of Korea, Republic of Kuwait Kyrgyzstan
 Lao People's Democratic Republic Lebanon Lesotho Latvia Liberia Libya Liechtens
tein Lithuania Luxembourg Macao Madagascar Malawi Malaysia Maldives Mali Malta M
```

The next image displays the customer list portion of the output:

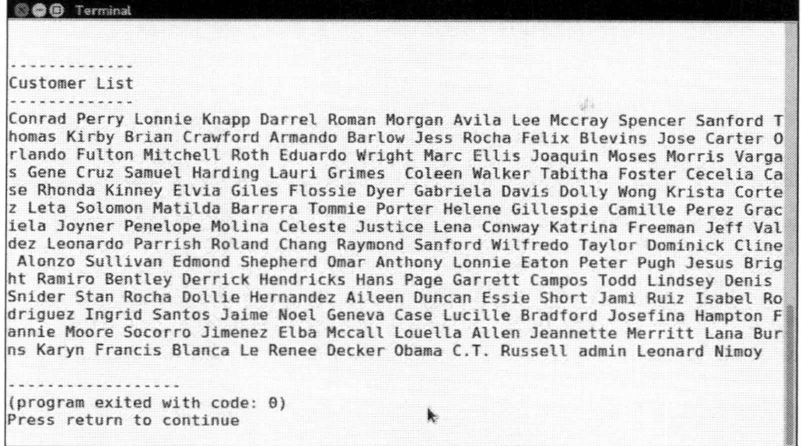

Universal exception handler

Exceptions are especially useful when used in conjunction with code in a `try/catch` block. Using this construct, however, can be awkward in some situations, making code virtually unreadable. Another consideration is that many classes end up throwing exceptions that you have not anticipated. In such cases, it would be highly desirable to have some sort of fallback exception handler.

How to do it...

1. First, we define a generic exception handling class, `Application\Error\Handler`:

```
namespace Application\Error;
class Handler
{
  // code goes here
}
```

2. We define properties that represents a log file. If the name is not supplied, it is named after the year, month, and day. In the constructor, we use `set_exception_handler()` to assign the `exceptionHandler()` method (in this class) as the fallback handler:

```
protected $logFile;
public function __construct(
  $logFileDir = NULL, $logFile = NULL)
```

```
{
  $logFile = $logFile    ?? date('Ymd') . '.log';
  $logFileDir = $logFileDir ?? __DIR__;
  $this->logFile = $logFileDir . '/' . $logFile;
  $this->logFile = str_replace('//', '/', $this-
    >logFile);
  set_exception_handler([$this,'exceptionHandler']);
}
```

3. Next, we define the `exceptionHandler()` method, which takes an `Exception` object as an argument. We record the date and time, the class name of the exception, and its message in the log file:

```
public function exceptionHandler($ex)
{
  $message = sprintf('%19s : %20s : %s' . PHP_EOL,
    date('Y-m-d H:i:s'), get_class($ex), $ex->getMessage());
  file_put_contents($this->logFile, $message, FILE_APPEND);
}
```

4. If we specifically put a `try/catch` block in our code, this will override our universal exception handler. If, on the other hand, we do not use try/catch and an exception is thrown, the universal exception handler will come into play.

Best practice

You should always use try/catch to trap exceptions and possibly continue in your application. The exception handler described here is only designed to allow your application to end "gracefully" in situations where exceptions thrown have not been caught.

How it works...

First, place the code shown in the preceding recipe into a `Handler.php` file in the `Application\Error` folder. Next, define a test class that will throw an exception. For the purposes of illustration, create an `Application\Error\ThrowsException` class that will throw an exception. As an example, set up a PDO instance with the error mode set to `PDO::ERRMODE_EXCEPTION`. You then craft an SQL statement that is guaranteed to fail:

```
namespace Application\Error;
use PDO;
class ThrowsException
{
  protected $result;
  public function __construct(array $config)
  {
    $dsn = $config['driver'] . ':';
```

```
        unset($config['driver']);
        foreach ($config as $key => $value) {
          $dsn .= $key . '=' . $value . ';';
        }
        $pdo = new PDO(
          $dsn,
          $config['user'],
          $config['password'],
          [PDO::ATTR_ERRMODE => PDO::ERRMODE_EXCEPTION]);
          $stmt = $pdo->query('This Is Not SQL');
          while ($row = $stmt->fetch(PDO::FETCH_ASSOC)) {
            $this->result[] = $row;
          }
      }
    }
```

Next, define a calling program called `chap_13_exception_handler.php` that sets up autoloading, uses the appropriate classes:

```
<?php
define('DB_CONFIG_FILE', __DIR__ . '/../config/db.config.php');
$config = include DB_CONFIG_FILE;
require __DIR__ . '/../Application/Autoload/Loader.php';
Application\Autoload\Loader::init(__DIR__ . '/..');
use Application\Error\ { Handler, ThrowsException };
```

At this point, if you create a `ThrowsException` instance without implementing the universal handler, a `Fatal Error` is generated as an exception has been thrown but not caught:

```
$throws1 = new ThrowsException($config);
```

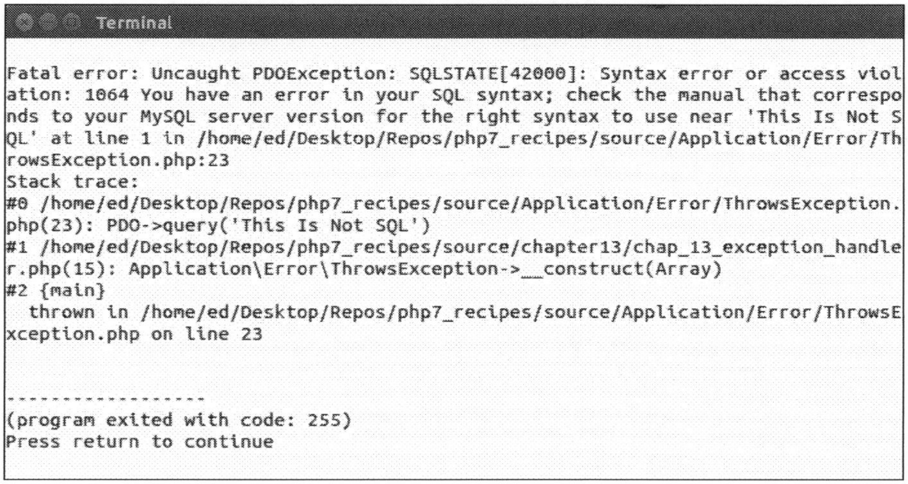

```
Terminal

Fatal error: Uncaught PDOException: SQLSTATE[42000]: Syntax error or access viol
ation: 1064 You have an error in your SQL syntax; check the manual that correspo
nds to your MySQL server version for the right syntax to use near 'This Is Not S
QL' at line 1 in /home/ed/Desktop/Repos/php7_recipes/source/Application/Error/Th
rowsException.php:23
Stack trace:
#0 /home/ed/Desktop/Repos/php7_recipes/source/Application/Error/ThrowsException.
php(23): PDO->query('This Is Not SQL')
#1 /home/ed/Desktop/Repos/php7_recipes/source/chapter13/chap_13_exception_handle
r.php(15): Application\Error\ThrowsException->__construct(Array)
#2 {main}
  thrown in /home/ed/Desktop/Repos/php7_recipes/source/Application/Error/ThrowsE
xception.php on line 23


------------------
(program exited with code: 255)
Press return to continue
```

If, on the other hand, you use a `try/catch` block, the exception will be caught and your application is allowed to continue, if it is stable enough:

```
try {
    $throws1 = new ThrowsException($config);
} catch (Exception $e) {
    echo 'Exception Caught: ' . get_class($e) . ':' . $e->getMessage()
    . PHP_EOL;
}
echo 'Application Continues ...' . PHP_EOL;
```

You will observe the following output:

```
Terminal
Exception Caught: PDOException:SQLSTATE[42000]: Syntax error or access violation
: 1064 You have an error in your SQL syntax; check the manual that corresponds t
o your MySQL server version for the right syntax to use near 'This Is Not SQL' a
t line 1
Application Continues ...


------------------
(program exited with code: 0)
Press return to continue
```

To demonstrate use of the exception handler, define a `Handler` instance, passing a parameter that represents the directory to contain log files, before the `try/catch` block. After `try/catch`, outside the block, create another instance of `ThrowsException`. When you run this sample program, you will notice that the first exception is caught inside the `try/catch` block, and the second exception is caught by the handler. You will also note that after the handler, the application ends:

```
$handler = new Handler(__DIR__ . '/logs');
try {
    $throws1 = new ThrowsException($config);
} catch (Exception $e) {
    echo 'Exception Caught: ' . get_class($e) . ':'
      . $e->getMessage() . PHP_EOL;
}
$throws1 = new ThrowsException($config);
echo 'Application Continues ...' . PHP_EOL;
```

Here is the output from the completed example program, along with the contents of the log file:

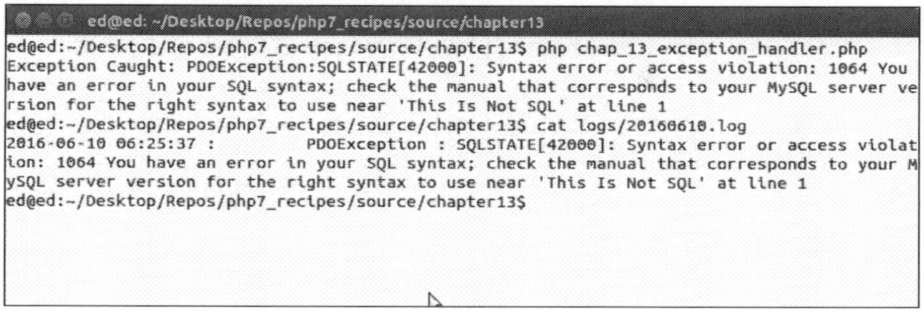

```
ed@ed:~/Desktop/Repos/php7_recipes/source/chapter13$ php chap_13_exception_handler.php
Exception Caught: PDOException:SQLSTATE[42000]: Syntax error or access violation: 1064 You
have an error in your SQL syntax; check the manual that corresponds to your MySQL server ve
rsion for the right syntax to use near 'This Is Not SQL' at line 1
ed@ed:~/Desktop/Repos/php7_recipes/source/chapter13$ cat logs/20160610.log
2016-06-10 06:25:37 :         PDOException : SQLSTATE[42000]: Syntax error or access violat
ion: 1064 You have an error in your SQL syntax; check the manual that corresponds to your M
ySQL server version for the right syntax to use near 'This Is Not SQL' at line 1
ed@ed:~/Desktop/Repos/php7_recipes/source/chapter13$
```

See also

- It might be a good idea to review the documentation on the `set_exception_handler()` function. Have a look, especially, at the comment (posted 7 years ago, but still pertinent) by Anonymous that clarifies how this function works: `http://php.net/manual/en/function.set-exception-handler.php`.

Universal error handler

The process of developing a universal error handler is quite similar to the preceding recipe. There are certain differences, however. First of all, in PHP 7, some errors are thrown and can be caught, whereas others simply stop your application dead in its tracks. To further confuse matters, some errors are treated like exceptions, whereas others are derived from the new PHP 7 `Error` class. Fortunately for us, in PHP 7, both `Error` and `Exception` implement a new interface called `Throwable`. Accordingly, if you are not sure whether your code will throw an `Exception` or an `Error`, simply catch an instance of `Throwable` and you'll catch both.

How to do it...

1. Modify the `Application\Error\Handler` class defined in the preceding recipe. In the constructor, set a new `errorHandler()` method as the default error handler:

```
public function __construct($logFileDir = NULL, $logFile = NULL)
{
  $logFile    = $logFile    ?? date('Ymd') . '.log';
  $logFileDir = $logFileDir ?? __DIR__;
  $this->logFile = $logFileDir . '/' . $logFile;
  $this->logFile = str_replace('//', '/', $this->logFile);
  set_exception_handler([$this,'exceptionHandler']);
  set_error_handler([$this, 'errorHandler']);
}
```

2. We then define the new method, using the documented parameters. As with our exception handler, we log information to a log file:

```
public function errorHandler($errno, $errstr, $errfile, $errline)
{
  $message = sprintf('ERROR: %s : %d : %s : %s : %s' . PHP_EOL,
    date('Y-m-d H:i:s'), $errno, $errstr, $errfile, $errline);
  file_put_contents($this->logFile, $message, FILE_APPEND);
}
```

3. Also, just to be able to distinguish errors from exceptions, add `EXCEPTION` to the message sent to the log file in the `exceptionHandler()` method:

```
public function exceptionHandler($ex)
{
  $message = sprintf('EXCEPTION: %19s : %20s : %s' . PHP_EOL,
    date('Y-m-d H:i:s'), get_class($ex), $ex->getMessage());
  file_put_contents($this->logFile, $message, FILE_APPEND);
}
```

How it works...

First, make the changes to `Application\Error\Handler` as defined previously. Next, create a class that throws an error that, for this illustration, could be defined as `Application\Error\ThrowsError`. For example, you could have a method that attempts a divide by zero operation, and another that attempts to parse non-PHP code using `eval()`:

```
<?php
namespace Application\Error;
class ThrowsError
{
  const NOT_PARSE = 'this will not parse';
  public function divideByZero()
  {
    $this->zero = 1 / 0;
  }
  public function willNotParse()
  {
    eval(self::NOT_PARSE);
  }
}
```

You can then define a calling program called `chap_13_error_throwable.php` that sets up autoloading, uses the appropriate classes, and creates an instance of `ThrowsError`:

```
<?php
require __DIR__ . '/../Application/Autoload/Loader.php';
Application\Autoload\Loader::init(__DIR__ . '/..');
```

```
use Application\Error\ { Handler, ThrowsError };
$error = new ThrowsError();
```

If you then call the two methods, without a try/catch block and without defining the universal error handler, the first method generates a `Warning`, whereas the second throws a `ParseError`:

```
$error->divideByZero();
$error->willNotParse();
echo 'Application continues ... ' . PHP_EOL;
```

Because this is an error, program execution stops, and you will not see `Application continues ...`:

```
Terminal

Warning: Division by zero in /home/ed/Desktop/Repos/php7_recipes/source/Applicat
ion/Error/ThrowsError.php on line 11

Parse error: syntax error, unexpected 'will' (T_STRING) in /home/ed/Desktop/Repo
s/php7_recipes/source/Application/Error/ThrowsError.php(15) : eval()'d code on l
ine 1


------------------
(program exited with code: 255)
Press return to continue
```

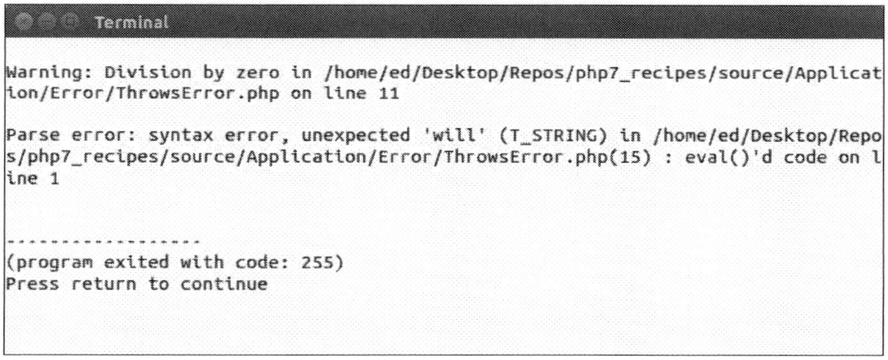

If you wrap the method calls in `try/catch` blocks and catch `Throwable`, the code execution continues:

```
try {
    $error->divideByZero();
} catch (Throwable $e) {
    echo 'Error Caught: ' . get_class($e) . ':'
      . $e->getMessage() . PHP_EOL;
}
try {
    $error->willNotParse();
} catch (Throwable $e) {
    echo 'Error Caught: ' . get_class($e) . ':'
    . $e->getMessage() . PHP_EOL;
}
echo 'Application continues ... ' . PHP_EOL;
```

From the following output, you will also note that the program exits with `code 0`, which tells us all is OK:

```
Warning: Division by zero in /home/ed/Desktop/Repos/php7_recipes/source/Applicat
ion/Error/ThrowsError.php on line 11
Error Caught: ParseError:syntax error, unexpected 'will' (T_STRING)
Application continues ...


------------------
(program exited with code: 0)
Press return to continue
```

Finally, after the `try/catch` blocks, run the errors again, moving the echo statement to the end. You will see in the output that the errors were caught, but in the log file, notice that `DivisionByZeroError` is caught by the exception handler, whereas the `ParseError` is caught by the error hander:

```
$handler = new Handler(__DIR__ . '/logs');
$error->divideByZero();
$error->willNotParse();
echo 'Application continues ... ' . PHP_EOL;
```

```
ed@ed:~/Desktop/Repos/php7_recipes/source/chapter13$ php chap_13_error_throwable.php

Warning: Division by zero in /home/ed/Desktop/Repos/php7_recipes/source/Application/Error/T
hrowsError.php on line 11
Error Caught: ParseError:syntax error, unexpected 'will' (T_STRING)
ed@ed:~/Desktop/Repos/php7_recipes/source/chapter13$ cat logs/20160610.log
ERROR     : 2016-06-10 07:16:00 : 2 : Division by zero : /home/ed/Desktop/Repos/php7_recipes
/source/Application/Error/ThrowsError.php : 11
EXCEPTION: 2016-06-10 07:16:00 :          ParseError : syntax error, unexpected identifier
 (T_STRING)
ed@ed:~/Desktop/Repos/php7_recipes/source/chapter13$
```

See also

- PHP 7.1 allows you to specify more than one class in the `catch ()` clause. So, instead of a single `Throwable` you could say `catch (Exception | Error $e) { xxx }`

Writing a simple test

The primary means of testing PHP code is to use **PHPUnit**, which is based on a methodology called **Unit Testing**. The philosophy behind unit testing is quite simple: you break down your code into the smallest possible logical units. You then test each unit in isolation to confirm that it performs as expected. These expectations are codified into a series of **assertions**. If all assertions return `TRUE`, then the unit has passed the test.

In the case of procedural PHP, a unit is a function. For OOP PHP, the unit is a method within a class.

How to do it...

1. The first order of business is to either install PHPUnit directly onto your development server, or download the source code, which is available in the form of a single **phar** (**PHP archive**) file. A quick visit to the official website for PHPUnit (`https://phpunit.de/`) lets us download right from the main page.
2. It is a best practice, however, to use a package manager to both install and maintain PHPUnit. For this purpose, we will use a package management program called **Composer**. To install Composer, visit the main website, `https://getcomposer.org/`, and follow the instructions on the download page. The current procedure, at the time of writing, is as follows. Note that you need to substitute the hash of the current version in place of `<hash>`:

```
php -r "copy('https://getcomposer.org/installer',
  'composer-setup.php');"
php -r "if (hash_file('SHA384', 'composer-setup.php')
  === '<hash>') {
    echo 'Installer verified';
} else {
    echo 'Installer corrupt'; unlink('composer-setup.php');
} echo PHP_EOL;"
php composer-setup.php
php -r "unlink('composer-setup.php');"
```

Best practice

The advantage of using a package management program such as Composer is that it will not only install, but can also be used to update any external software (such as PHPUnit) used by your application.

3. Next, we use Composer to install PHPUnit. This is accomplished by creating a `composer.json` file that contains a series of directives outlining project parameters and dependencies. A full description of these directives is beyond the scope of this book; however, for the purposes of this recipe, we create a minimal set of directives using the key parameter `require`. You will also note that the contents of the file are in **JavaScript Object Notation** (**JSON**) format:

```
{
  "require-dev": {
    "phpunit/phpunit": "*"
  }
}
```

4. To perform the installation from the command line, we run the following command. The output is shown just after:

```
php composer.phar install
```

```
ed@ed: ~/Desktop/Repos/php7_recipes/source/chapter13
ed@ed:~/Desktop/Repos/php7_recipes/source/chapter13$ php composer.phar install
Loading composer repositories with package information
Updating dependencies (including require-dev)
  - Installing myclabs/deep-copy (1.5.1)
    Loading from cache

  - Installing sebastian/version (2.0.0)
    Loading from cache

  - Installing sebastian/resource-operations (1.0.0)
    Loading from cache

  - Installing sebastian/recursion-context (1.0.2)
    Loading from cache

  - Installing sebastian/object-enumerator (1.0.0)
    Loading from cache

  - Installing sebastian/global-state (1.1.1)
    Loading from cache

  - Installing sebastian/exporter (1.2.1)
    Loading from cache
```

5. PHPUnit and its dependencies are placed in a `vendor` folder that Composer will create if it does not already exist. The primary command to invoke PHPUnit is then symbolically linked into the `vendor/bin` folder. If you place this folder in your `PATH`, all you need do is to run this command, which checks the version and incidentally confirms the installation:

```
phpunit --version
```

Running simple tests

1. For the purposes of this illustration, let's assume we have a `chap_13_unit_test_simple.php` file that contains the `add()` function:

```
<?php
function add($a = NULL, $b = NULL)
{
  return $a + $b;
}
```

2. Tests are then written as classes that extend `PHPUnit\Framework\TestCase`. If you are testing a library of functions, at the beginning of the test class, include the file that contains function definitions. You would then write methods that start with the word `test`, usually followed by the name of the function you are testing, and possibly some additional CamelCase words to further describe the test. For the purposes of this recipe, we will define a `SimpleTest` test class:

```
<?php
use PHPUnit\Framework\TestCase;
require_once __DIR__ . '/chap_13_unit_test_simple.php';
class SimpleTest extends TestCase
{
  // testXXX() methods go here
}
```

3. Assertions form the heart of any set of tests. The `See also` section gives you the documentation reference for the complete list of assertions. An assertion is a PHPUnit method that compares a known value against a value produced by that which you wish to test. An example is `assertEquals()`, which checks to see whether the first argument equals the second. The following example tests a method called `add()` and confirms **2** is the return value for `add(1,1)`:

```
public function testAdd()
{
  $this->assertEquals(2, add(1,1));
}
```

4. You can also test to see whether something is *not* true. This example asserts that 1 + 1 does not equal 3:

```
$this->assertNotEquals(3, add(1,1));
```

5. An assertion that is extremely useful when used to test a string is `assertRegExp()`. Assume, for this illustration, that we are testing a function that produces an HTML table out of a multidimensional array:

```
function table(array $a)
{
  $table = '<table>';
```

```
    foreach ($a as $row) {
      $table .= '<tr><td>';
      $table .= implode('</td><td>', $row);
      $table .= '</td></tr>';
    }
    $table .= '</table>';
    return $table;
  }
```

6. We can construct a simple test that confirms that the output contains `<table>`, one or more characters, followed by `</table>`. Further, we wish to confirm that a `<td>B</td>` element exists. When writing the test, we build a test array that consists of three sub-arrays containing the letters A–C, D—F, and G—I. We then pass the test array to the function, and run assertions against the result:

```
public function testTable()
{
  $a = [range('A', 'C'),range('D', 'F'),range('G','I')];
  $table = table($a);
  $this->assertRegExp('!^<table>.+</table>$!', $table);
  $this->assertRegExp('!<td>B</td>!', $table);
}
```

7. To test a class, instead of including a library of functions, simply include the file that defines the class to be tested. For the sake of illustration, let's take the library of functions shown previously and move them into a `Demo` class:

```
<?php
class Demo
{
  public function add($a, $b)
  {
    return $a + $b;
  }

  public function sub($a, $b)
  {
    return $a - $b;
  }
  // etc.
}
```

8. In our `SimpleClassTest` test class, instead of including the library file, we include the file that represents the `Demo` class. We need an instance of `Demo` in order to run tests. For this purpose, we use a specially designed `setup()` method, which is run before each test. Also, you will note a `teardown()` method, which is run immediately after each test:

```
<?php
use PHPUnit\Framework\TestCase;
require_once __DIR__ . '/Demo.php';
class SimpleClassTest extends TestCase
{
  protected $demo;
  public function setup()
  {
    $this->demo = new Demo();
  }
  public function teardown()
  {
    unset($this->demo);
  }
  public function testAdd()
  {
    $this->assertEquals(2, $this->demo->add(1,1));
  }
  public function testSub()
  {
    $this->assertEquals(0, $this->demo->sub(1,1));
  }
  // etc.
}
```

The reason why `setup()` and `teardown()` are run before and after each test is to ensure a fresh test environment. That way, the results of one test will not influence the results of another test.

Testing database Model classes

1. When testing a class, such as a Model class, that has database access, other considerations come into play. The main consideration is that you should run tests against a test database, not the real database used in production. A final point is that by using a test database, you can populate it in advance with appropriate, controlled data. `setup()` and `teardown()` could also be used to add or remove test data.

2. As an example of a class that uses the database, we will define a class `VisitorOps`. The new class will include methods to add, remove, and find visitors. Note that we've also added a method to return the latest SQL statement executed:

```
<?php
require __DIR__ . '/../Application/Database/Connection.php';
use Application\Database\Connection;
class VisitorOps
{

const TABLE_NAME = 'visitors';
protected $connection;
protected $sql;

public function __construct(array $config)
{
  $this->connection = new Connection($config);
}

public function getSql()
{
  return $this->sql;
}

public function findAll()
{
  $sql = 'SELECT * FROM ' . self::TABLE_NAME;
  $stmt = $this->runSql($sql);
  while ($row = $stmt->fetch(PDO::FETCH_ASSOC)) {
    yield $row;
  }
}

public function findById($id)
{
  $sql = 'SELECT * FROM ' . self::TABLE_NAME;
  $sql .= ' WHERE id = ?';
  $stmt = $this->runSql($sql, [$id]);
```

```
    return $stmt->fetch(PDO::FETCH_ASSOC);
  }

  public function removeById($id)
  {
    $sql = 'DELETE FROM ' . self::TABLE_NAME;
    $sql .= ' WHERE id = ?';
    return $this->runSql($sql, [$id]);
  }

  public function addVisitor($data)
  {
    $sql = 'INSERT INTO ' . self::TABLE_NAME;
    $sql .= ' (' . implode(',',array_keys($data)) . ') ';
    $sql .= ' VALUES ';
    $sql .= ' ( :' . implode(',:',array_keys($data)) . ') ';
    $this->runSql($sql, $data);
    return $this->connection->pdo->lastInsertId();
  }

  public function runSql($sql, $params = NULL)
  {
    $this->sql = $sql;
    try {
        $stmt = $this->connection->pdo->prepare($sql);
        $result = $stmt->execute($params);
    } catch (Throwable $e) {
        error_log(__METHOD__ . ':' . $e->getMessage());
        return FALSE;
    }
    return $stmt;
  }
  }
```

3. For tests that involve a database, it is recommended that you use a test database instead of the live production database. Accordingly, you will need an extra set of database connection parameters that can be used to establish a database connection in the `setup()` method.
4. It's possible that you wish to establish a consistent block of sample data. This could be inserted into the test database in the `setup()` method.
5. Finally, you may wish to reset the test database after each test, which is accomplished in the `teardown()` method.

Using mock classes

1. In some cases, the test will access complex components that require external resources. An example is a service class that needs access to a database. It is a best practice to minimize database access in a test suite. Another consideration is that we are not testing database access; we are only testing the functionality of one specific class. Accordingly, it is sometimes necessary to define **mock** classes that mimic the behavior of the their parent class, but that restrict access to external resources.

Best practice

Limit actual database access in your tests to the Model (or equivalent) classes. Otherwise, the time it takes to run the entire set of tests could become excessive.

2. In this case, for illustration, define a service class, `VisitorService`, which makes use of the `VisitorOps` class discussed earlier:

```
<?php
require_once __DIR__ . '/VisitorOps.php';
require_once __DIR__ . '/../Application/Database/Connection.php';
use Application\Database\Connection;
class VisitorService
{
  protected $visitorOps;
  public function __construct(array $config)
  {
    $this->visitorOps = new VisitorOps($config);
  }
  public function showAllVisitors()
  {
    $table = '<table>';
    foreach ($this->visitorOps->findAll() as $row) {
      $table .= '<tr><td>';
      $table .= implode('</td><td>', $row);
      $table .= '</td></tr>';
    }
    $table .= '</table>';
    return $table;
  }
```

3. For test purposes, we add a getter and setter for the `$visitorOps` property. This allows us to insert a mock class in place of the real `VisitorOps` class:

```
public function getVisitorOps()
{
  return $this->visitorOps;
```

```
}

public function setVisitorOps(VisitorOps $visitorOps)
{
  $this->visitorOps = $visitorOps;
}
} // closing brace for VisitorService
```

4. Next, we define a `VisitorOpsMock` mock class that mimics the functionality of its parent class. Class constants and properties are inherited. We then add mock test data, and a getter in case we need access to the test data later:

```
<?php
require_once __DIR__ . '/VisitorOps.php';
class VisitorOpsMock extends VisitorOps
{
  protected $testData;
  public function __construct()
  {
    $data = array();
    for ($x = 1; $x <= 3; $x++) {
      $data[$x]['id'] = $x;
      $data[$x]['email'] = $x . 'test@unlikelysource.com';
      $data[$x]['visit_date'] =
        '2000-0' . $x . '-0' . $x . ' 00:00:00';
      $data[$x]['comments'] = 'TEST ' . $x;
      $data[$x]['name'] = 'TEST ' . $x;
    }
    $this->testData = $data;
  }
  public function getTestData()
  {
    return $this->testData;
  }
```

5. Next, we override `findAll()` to return test data using `yield`, just as in the parent class. Note that we still build the SQL string, as this is what the parent class does:

```
public function findAll()
{
  $sql = 'SELECT * FROM ' . self::TABLE_NAME;
  foreach ($this->testData as $row) {
    yield $row;
  }
}
```

6. To mock `findById()` we simply return that array key from `$this->testData`. For `removeById()`, we unset the array key supplied as a parameter from `$this->testData`:

```
public function findById($id)
{
  $sql = 'SELECT * FROM ' . self::TABLE_NAME;
  $sql .= ' WHERE id = ?';
  return $this->testData[$id] ?? FALSE;
}
public function removeById($id)
{
  $sql = 'DELETE FROM ' . self::TABLE_NAME;
  $sql .= ' WHERE id = ?';
  if (empty($this->testData[$id])) {
      return 0;
  } else {
      unset($this->testData[$id]);
      return 1;
  }
}
```

7. Adding data is slightly more complicated in that we need to emulate the fact that the `id` parameter might not be supplied, as the database would normally auto-generate this for us. To get around this, we check for the `id` parameter. If not set, we find the largest array key and increment:

```
public function addVisitor($data)
{
  $sql = 'INSERT INTO ' . self::TABLE_NAME;
  $sql .= ' (' . implode(',',array_keys($data)) . ') ';
  $sql .= ' VALUES ';
  $sql .= ' ( :' . implode(',:',array_keys($data)) . ') ';
  if (!empty($data['id'])) {
      $id = $data['id'];
  } else {
      $keys = array_keys($this->testData);
      sort($keys);
      $id = end($keys) + 1;
      $data['id'] = $id;
  }
    $this->testData[$id] = $data;
    return 1;
  }

} // ending brace for the class VisitorOpsMock
```

Using anonymous classes as mock objects

1. A nice variation on mock objects involves the use of the new PHP 7 anonymous class in place of creating a formal class that defines mock functionality. The advantage of using an anonymous class is that you can extend an existing class, which makes the object appear legitimate. This approach is especially useful if you only need to override one or two methods.
2. For this illustration, we will modify `VisitorServiceTest.php` presented previously, calling it `VisitorServiceTestAnonClass.php`:

```
<?php
use PHPUnit\Framework\TestCase;
require_once __DIR__ . '/VisitorService.php';
require_once __DIR__ . '/VisitorOps.php';
class VisitorServiceTestAnonClass extends TestCase
{
  protected $visitorService;
  protected $dbConfig = [
    'driver'   => 'mysql',
    'host'     => 'localhost',
    'dbname'   => 'php7cookbook_test',
    'user'     => 'cook',
    'password' => 'book',
    'errmode'  => PDO::ERRMODE_EXCEPTION,
  ];
    protected $testData;
```

3. You will notice that in `setup()`, we define an anonymous class that extends `VisitorOps`. We only need to override the `findAll()` method:

```
public function setup()
{
  $data = array();
  for ($x = 1; $x <= 3; $x++) {
    $data[$x]['id'] = $x;
    $data[$x]['email'] = $x . 'test@unlikelysource.com';
    $data[$x]['visit_date'] =
      '2000-0' . $x . '-0' . $x . ' 00:00:00';
    $data[$x]['comments'] = 'TEST ' . $x;
    $data[$x]['name'] = 'TEST ' . $x;
  }
  $this->testData = $data;
  $this->visitorService =
    new VisitorService($this->dbConfig);
  $opsMock =
    new class ($this->testData) extends VisitorOps {
```

```
        protected $testData;
        public function __construct($testData)
        {
          $this->testData = $testData;
        }
        public function findAll()
        {
          return $this->testData;
        }
      };
      $this->visitorService->setVisitorOps($opsMock);
  }
```

4. Note that in `testShowAllVisitors()`, when `$this->visitorService->showAllVisitors()` is executed, the anonymous class is called by the visitor service, which in turn calls the overridden `findAll()`:

```
public function teardown()
{
  unset($this->visitorService);
}
public function testShowAllVisitors()
{
  $result = $this->visitorService->showAllVisitors();
  $this->assertRegExp('!^<table>.+</table>$!', $result);
  foreach ($this->testData as $key => $value) {
    $dataWeWant = '!<td>' . $key . '</td>!';
    $this->assertRegExp($dataWeWant, $result);
  }
}
}
```

Using Mock Builder

1. Another technique is to use `getMockBuilder()`. Although this approach does not allow a great deal of finite control over the mock object produced, it's extremely useful in situations where you only need to confirm that an object of a certain class is returned, and when a specified method is run, this method returns some expected value.

2. In the following example, we copied `VisitorServiceTestAnonClass`; the only difference is in how an instance of `VisitorOps` is supplied in `setup()`, in this case, using `getMockBuilder()`. Note that although we did not use `with()` in this example, it is used to feed controlled parameters to the mocked method:

```
<?php
use PHPUnit\Framework\TestCase;
require_once __DIR__ . '/VisitorService.php';
```

```
require_once __DIR__ . '/VisitorOps.php';
class VisitorServiceTestAnonMockBuilder extends TestCase
{
  // code is identical to VisitorServiceTestAnon
  public function setup()
  {
    $data = array();
    for ($x = 1; $x <= 3; $x++) {
      $data[$x]['id'] = $x;
      $data[$x]['email'] = $x . 'test@unlikelysource.com';
      $data[$x]['visit_date'] =
        '2000-0' . $x . '-0' . $x . ' 00:00:00';
      $data[$x]['comments'] = 'TEST ' . $x;
      $data[$x]['name'] = 'TEST ' . $x;
  }
  $this->testData = $data;
    $this->visitorService =
      new VisitorService($this->dbConfig);
    $opsMock = $this->getMockBuilder(VisitorOps::class)
                    ->setMethods(['findAll'])
                    ->disableOriginalConstructor()
                    ->getMock();
                    $opsMock->expects($this->once())
                    ->method('findAll')
                    ->with()
                    ->will($this->returnValue($this->testData));
                    $this->visitorService
                    ->setVisitorOps($opsMock);
  }
  // remaining code is the same
}
```

We have shown how to create simple one-off tests. In most cases, however, you will have many classes that need to be tested, preferably all at once. This is possible by developing a *test suite*, discussed in more detail in the next recipe.

How it works...

First, you need to install PHPUnit, as discussed in steps 1 to 5. Be sure to include `vendor/bin` in your PATH so that you can run PHPUnit from the command line.

Running simple tests

Next, define a `chap_13_unit_test_simple.php` program file with a series of simple functions, such as `add()`, `sub()` and so on, as discussed in step 1. You can then define a simple test class contained in `SimpleTest.php` as mentioned in steps 2 and 3.

Assuming `phpunit` is in your `PATH`, from a terminal window, change to the directory containing the code developed for this recipe, and run the following command:

`phpunit SimpleTest SimpleTest.php`

You should see the following output:

```
ed@ed: ~/Desktop/Repos/php7_recipes/source/chapter13
ed@ed:~/Desktop/Repos/php7_recipes/source/chapter13$ phpunit SimpleTest SimpleTest.php
PHPUnit 5.4.3 by Sebastian Bergmann and contributors.

.....                                                          5 / 5 (100%)

Time: 33 ms, Memory: 4.00MB

OK (5 tests, 9 assertions)
ed@ed:~/Desktop/Repos/php7_recipes/source/chapter13$
```

Make a change in `SimpleTest.php` so that the test will fail (step 4):

```
public function testDiv()
{
  $this->assertEquals(2, div(4, 2));
  $this->assertEquals(99, div(4, 0));
}
```

Here is the revised output:

```
ed@ed: ~/Desktop/Repos/php7_recipes/source/chapter13
ed@ed:~/Desktop/Repos/php7_recipes/source/chapter13$ phpunit SimpleTest SimpleTest.php
PHPUnit 5.4.3 by Sebastian Bergmann and contributors.

...F.                                                          5 / 5 (100%)

Time: 25 ms, Memory: 4.00MB

There was 1 failure:

1) SimpleTest::testDiv
Failed asserting that 0 matches expected 99.

/home/ed/Desktop/Repos/php7_recipes/source/chapter13/SimpleTest.php:28

FAILURES!
Tests: 5, Assertions: 9, Failures: 1.
ed@ed:~/Desktop/Repos/php7_recipes/source/chapter13$
```

Next, add the `table()` function to `chap_13_unit_test_simple.php` (step 5), and `testTable()` to `SimpleTest.php` (step 6). Re-run the unit test and observe the results.

To test a class, copy the functions developed in `chap_13_unit_test_simple.php` to a `Demo` class (step 7). After making the modifications to `SimpleTest.php` suggested in step 8, re-run the simple test and observe the results.

Testing database model classes

First, create an example class to be tested, `VisitorOps`, shown in step 2 in this subsection. You can now define a class we will call `SimpleDatabaseTest` to test `VisitorOps`. First of all, use `require_once` to load the class to test. (We will discuss how to incorporate autoloading in the next recipe!) Then define key properties, including test database configuration and test data. You could use `php7cookbook_test` as the test database:

```
<?php
use PHPUnit\Framework\TestCase;
require_once __DIR__ . '/VisitorOps.php';
class SimpleDatabaseTest extends TestCase
{
  protected $visitorOps;
  protected $dbConfig = [
    'driver'   => 'mysql',
    'host'     => 'localhost',
    'dbname'   => 'php7cookbook_test',
    'user'     => 'cook',
    'password' => 'book',
    'errmode'  => PDO::ERRMODE_EXCEPTION,
  ];
  protected $testData = [
    'id' => 1,
    'email' => 'test@unlikelysource.com',
    'visit_date' => '2000-01-01 00:00:00',
    'comments' => 'TEST',
    'name' => 'TEST'
  ];
}
```

Next, define `setup()`, which inserts the test data, and confirms that the last SQL statement was `INSERT`. You should also check to see whether the return value was positive:

```
public function setup()
{
  $this->visitorOps = new VisitorOps($this->dbConfig);
  $this->visitorOps->addVisitor($this->testData);
  $this->assertRegExp('/INSERT/', $this->visitorOps->getSql());
}
```

After that, define `teardown()`, which removes the test data and confirms that the query for `id = 1` comes back as `FALSE`:

```
public function teardown()
{
  $result = $this->visitorOps->removeById(1);
  $result = $this->visitorOps->findById(1);
  $this->assertEquals(FALSE, $result);
  unset($this->visitorOps);
}
```

The first test is for `findAll()`. First, confirm the data type of the result. You could take the topmost element using `current()`. We confirm there are five elements, that one of them is `name`, and that the value is the same as that in the test data:

```
public function testFindAll()
{
  $result = $this->visitorOps->findAll();
  $this->assertInstanceOf(Generator::class, $result);
  $top = $result->current();
  $this->assertCount(5, $top);
  $this->assertArrayHasKey('name', $top);
  $this->assertEquals($this->testData['name'], $top['name']);
}
```

The next test is for `findById()`. It is almost identical to `testFindAll()`:

```
public function testFindById()
{
  $result = $this->visitorOps->findById(1);
  $this->assertCount(5, $result);
  $this->assertArrayHasKey('name', $result);
  $this->assertEquals($this->testData['name'], $result['name']);
}
```

You do not need to bother with a test for `removeById()` as this is already done in `teardown()`. Likewise, there is no need to test `runSql()` as this is done as part of the other tests.

Using mock classes

First, define a `VisitorService` service class as described in steps 2 and 3 in this subsection. Next, define a `VisitorOpsMock` mock class, which is discussed in steps 4 to 7.

You are now in a position to develop a test, `VisitorServiceTest`, for the service class. Note that you need provide your own database configuration as it is a best practice to use a test database instead of the production version:

```
<?php
use PHPUnit\Framework\TestCase;
require_once __DIR__ . '/VisitorService.php';
require_once __DIR__ . '/VisitorOpsMock.php';

class VisitorServiceTest extends TestCase
{
  protected $visitorService;
  protected $dbConfig = [
    'driver'   => 'mysql',
    'host'     => 'localhost',
    'dbname'   => 'php7cookbook_test',
    'user'     => 'cook',
    'password' => 'book',
    'errmode'  => PDO::ERRMODE_EXCEPTION,
  ];
}
```

In `setup()`, create an instance of the service, and insert `VisitorOpsMock` in place of the original class:

```
public function setup()
{
  $this->visitorService = new VisitorService($this->dbConfig);
  $this->visitorService->setVisitorOps(new VisitorOpsMock());
}
public function teardown()
{
  unset($this->visitorService);
}
```

In our test, which produces an HTML table from the list of visitors, you can then look for certain elements, knowing what to expect in advance as you have control over the test data:

```
public function testShowAllVisitors()
{
  $result = $this->visitorService->showAllVisitors();
  $this->assertRegExp('!^<table>.+</table>$!', $result);
  $testData = $this->visitorService->getVisitorOps()->getTestData();
```

```
      foreach ($testData as $key => $value) {
        $dataWeWant = '!<td>' . $key . '</td>!';
        $this->assertRegExp($dataWeWant, $result);
      }
    }
  }
```

You might then wish to experiment with the variations suggested in the last two subsections, *Using Anonymous Classes as Mock Objects*, and *Using Mock Builder*.

There's more...

Other assertions test operations on numbers, strings, arrays, objects, files, JSON, and XML, as summarized in the following table:

Category	**Assertions**
General	`assertEquals()`, `assertFalse()`, `assertEmpty()`, `assertNull()`, `assertSame()`, `assertThat()`, `assertTrue()`
Numeric	`assertGreaterThan()`, `assertGreaterThanOrEqual()`, `assertLessThan()`, `assertLessThanOrEqual()`, `assertNan()`, `assertInfinite()`
String	`assertStringEndsWith()`, `assertStringEqualsFile()`, `assertStringStartsWith()`, `assertRegExp()`, `assertStringMatchesFormat()`, `assertStringMatchesFormatFile()`
Array/iterator	`assertArrayHasKey()`, `assertArraySubset()`, `assertContains()`, `assertContainsOnly()`, `assertContainsOnlyInstancesOf()`, `assertCount()`
File	`assertFileEquals()`, `assertFileExists()`
Objects	`assertClassHasAttribute()`, `assertClassHasStaticAttribute()`, `assertInstanceOf()`, `assertInternalType()`, `assertObjectHasAttribute()`
JSON	`assertJsonFileEqualsJsonFile()`, `assertJsonStringEqualsJsonFile()`, `assertJsonStringEqualsJsonString()`
XML	`assertEqualXMLStructure()`, `assertXmlFileEqualsXmlFile()`, `assertXmlStringEqualsXmlFile()`, `assertXmlStringEqualsXmlString()`

See also...

- For a good discussion on unit testing, have a look here: `https://en.wikipedia.org/wiki/Unit_testing`.
- For more information on `composer.json` file directives, see `https://getcomposer.org/doc/04-schema.md`.
- For a complete list of assertions, have a look at this PHPUnit documentation page:`https://phpunit.de/manual/current/en/phpunit-book.html#appendixes.assertions`.
- The PHPUnit documentation also goes into using `getMockBuilder()` in detail here: `https://phpunit.de/manual/current/en/phpunit-book.html#test-doubles.mock-objects`

Writing a test suite

You may have noticed after having read through the previous recipe that it can quickly become tedious to have to manually run `phpunit` and specify test classes and PHP filenames. This is especially true when dealing with applications that employ dozens or even hundreds of classes and files. The PHPUnit project has a built-in capability to handle running multiple tests with a single command. Such a set of tests is referred to as a **test suite**.

How to do it...

1. At its simplest, all you need to do is to move all the tests into a single folder:

   ```
   mkdir tests
   cp *Test.php tests
   ```

2. You'll need to adjust commands that include or require external files to account for the new location. The example shown (`SimpleTest`) was developed in the preceding recipe:

   ```
   <?php
   use PHPUnit\Framework\TestCase;
   require_once __DIR__ . '/../chap_13_unit_test_simple.php';

   class SimpleTest extends TestCase
   {
     // etc.
   ```

3. You can then simply run `phpunit` with the directory path as an argument. PHPUnit will then automatically run all tests in that folder. In this example, we assume there is a `tests` subdirectory:

   ```
   phpunit tests
   ```

4. You can use the `--bootstrap` option to specify a file that is executed prior to running the tests. A typical use for this option is to initiate autoloading:

   ```
   phpunit --boostrap tests_with_autoload/bootstrap.php tests
   ```

5. Here is the sample `bootstrap.php` file that implements autoloading:

   ```
   <?php
   require __DIR__ . '/../../Application/Autoload/Loader.php';
   Application\Autoload\Loader::init([__DIR__]);
   ```

6. Another possibility is to define one or more sets of tests using an XML configuration file. Here is an example that runs only the Simple* tests:

   ```
   <phpunit>
     <testsuites>
       <testsuite name="simple">
         <file>SimpleTest.php</file>
         <file>SimpleDbTest.php</file>
         <file>SimpleClassTest.php</file>
       </testsuite>
     </testsuites>
   </phpunit>
   ```

7. Here is another example that runs a test based on a directory and also specifies a bootstrap file:

   ```
   <phpunit bootstrap="bootstrap.php">
     <testsuites>
       <testsuite name="visitor">
         <directory>Simple</directory>
       </testsuite>
     </testsuites>
   </phpunit>
   ```

How it works...

Make sure all the tests discussed in the previous recipe, *Writing a simple test*, have been defined. You can then create a `tests` folder and move or copy all the `*Test.php` files into this folder. You'll then need to adjust the path in the `require_once` statements, as shown in step 2.

In order to demonstrate how PHPUnit can run all tests in a folder, from the directory containing the source code you defined for this chapter, run the following command:

```
phpunit tests
```

You should see the following output:

```
ed@ed: ~/Desktop/Repos/php7_recipes/source/chapter13
ed@ed:~/Desktop/Repos/php7_recipes/source/chapter13$ phpunit tests
PHPUnit 5.4.3 by Sebastian Bergmann and contributors.

............                                                    12 / 12 (100%)

Time: 53 ms, Memory: 4.00MB

OK (12 tests, 32 assertions)
ed@ed:~/Desktop/Repos/php7_recipes/source/chapter13$
```

To demonstrate the use of a autoloading via a bootstrap file, create a new tests_with_autoload directory. In this folder, define a bootstrap.php file with the code shown in step 5. Create two directories in tests_with_autoload: Demo and Simple.

From the directory containing the source code for this chapter, copy the file (discussed in step 12 of the previous recipe) into tests_with_autoload/Demo/Demo.php. After the opening <?php tag, add this line:

```
namespace Demo;
```

Next, copy the SimpleTest.php file to tests_with_autoload/Simple/ClassTest.php. (Notice the filename change!). You will need to change the first few lines to the following:

```
<?php
namespace Simple;
use Demo\Demo;
use PHPUnit\Framework\TestCase;

class ClassTest extends TestCase
{
  protected $demo;
  public function setup()
  {
    $this->demo = new Demo();
  }
// etc.
```

After that, create a tests_with_autoload/phpunit.xml file that pulls everything together:

```
<phpunit bootstrap="bootstrap.php">
  <testsuites>
    <testsuite name="visitor">
      <directory>Simple</directory>
    </testsuite>
```

```
    </testsuites>
</phpunit>
```

Finally, change to the directory that contains the code for this chapter. You can now run a unit test that incorporates a bootstrap file, along with autoloading and namespaces, as follows:

```
phpunit -c tests_with_autoload/phpunit.xml
```

The output should appear as follows:

```
ed@ed: ~/Desktop/Repos/php7_recipes/source/chapter13
ed@ed:~/Desktop/Repos/php7_recipes/source/chapter13$ phpunit -c tests_with_autoload/phpunit.xml
PHPUnit 5.4.3 by Sebastian Bergmann and contributors.

....                                                              4 / 4 (100%)

Time: 33 ms, Memory: 4.00MB

OK (4 tests, 6 assertions)
ed@ed:~/Desktop/Repos/php7_recipes/source/chapter13$
```

See also...

- For more information on writing PHPUnit test suites, have a look at this documentation page: `https://phpunit.de/manual/current/en/phpunit-book.html#organizing-tests.xml-configuration`.

Generating fake test data

Part of the testing and debugging process involves incorporating realistic test data. In some cases, especially when testing database access and producing benchmarks, large amounts of test data are needed. One way in which this can be accomplished is to incorporate a process of scraping data from websites, and then putting the data together in realistic, yet random, combinations to be inserted into a database.

How to do it...

1. The first step is to determine what data is needed in order to test your application. Another consideration is dose the website address an international audience, or will the market be primarily from a single country?
2. In order to produce a consistent fake data tool, it's extremely important to move the data from its source into a usable digital format. The first choice is a series of database tables. Another, not as attractive, alternative is a CSV file.

3. You may end up converting the data in stages. For example, you could pull data from a web page that lists country codes and country names into a text file.

AF Afghanistan	AG Algeria	AJ Azerbaijan
AL Albania	AM Armenia	AN Andorra
AO Angola	AR Argentina	AS Australia
AT Ashmore & Cartier Islands	AU Austria	AV Anguilla
AX Akrotiri	AY Antarctica	BA Bahrain
BB Barbados	BC Botswana	BD Bermuda
BE Belgium	BF Bahamas, The	BG Bangladesh
BH Belize	BK Bosnia & Herzegovina	BL Bolivia
BM Burma	BN Benin	BO Belarus
BP Soloman Islands	BR Brazil	BS Bassas Da India
BT Bhutan	BU Bulgaria	BV Bouvet Island
BX Brunei	BY Burundi	CA Canada
CB Cambodia	CD Chad	CE Sri Lanka
CF Congo	CG Congo (Dem. Republic of The)-(Zaire)	CH China
CI Chile	CJ Cayman Islands	CK Cocos (Keeling) Islands
CM Cameroon	CN Comoros	CO Colombia
CR Coral Sea Islands	CS Costa Rica	CT Central African Republic
CU Cuba	CV Cape Verde	CW Cook Islands

4. Since this list is short, it's easy to literally cut and paste this into a text file.

5. We can then do a search for " " and replace with "`\n`", which gives us this:

```
AA Aruba
AC Antigua & Barbuda
AE United Arab Emirates
AF Afghanistan
AG Algeria
AJ Azerbaijan
AL Albania
AM Armenia
AN Andorra
AO Angola
AR Argentina
AS Australia
AT Ashmore & Cartier Islands
AU Austria
AV Anguilla
AX Akrotiri
AY Antarctica
```

6. This can then be imported into a spreadsheet, which then lets you export to a CSV file. From there, it's a simple matter to import it into a database. phpMyAdmin, for example, has such a facility.

7. For the sake of this illustration, we will assume that we are generating data that will end up in the `prospects` table. Here is the SQL statement used to create this table:

```
CREATE TABLE 'prospects' (
  'id' int(11) NOT NULL AUTO_INCREMENT,
  'first_name' varchar(128) NOT NULL,
  'last_name' varchar(128) NOT NULL,
  'address' varchar(256) DEFAULT NULL,
```

```
  'city' varchar(64) DEFAULT NULL,
  'state_province' varchar(32) DEFAULT NULL,
  'postal_code' char(16) NOT NULL,
  'phone' varchar(16) NOT NULL,
  'country' char(2) NOT NULL,
  'email' varchar(250) NOT NULL,
  'status' char(8) DEFAULT NULL,
  'budget' decimal(10,2) DEFAULT NULL,
  'last_updated' datetime DEFAULT NULL,
  PRIMARY KEY ('id'),
  UNIQUE KEY 'UNIQ_35730C06E7927C74' ('email')
) ENGINE=InnoDB DEFAULT CHARSET=utf8;
```

8. Now it's time to create a class that is capable of generating fake data. We will then create methods to generate data for each of the fields shown above, except for `id`, which is auto-generated:

```
namespace Application\Test;

use PDO;
use Exception;
use DateTime;
use DateInterval;
use PDOException;
use SplFileObject;
use InvalidArgumentsException;
use Application\Database\Connection;

class FakeData
{
  // data generation methods here
}
```

9. Next, we define constants and properties that will be used as part of the process:

```
const MAX_LOOKUPS     = 10;
const SOURCE_FILE     = 'file';
const SOURCE_TABLE    = 'table';
const SOURCE_METHOD   = 'method';
const SOURCE_CALLBACK = 'callback';
const FILE_TYPE_CSV   = 'csv';
const FILE_TYPE_TXT   = 'txt';
const ERROR_DB        = 'ERROR: unable to read source table';
const ERROR_FILE      = 'ERROR: file not found';
const ERROR_COUNT     = 'ERROR: unable to ascertain count or ID
                        column missing';
```

```
const ERROR_UPLOAD     = 'ERROR: unable to upload file';
const ERROR_LOOKUP     = 'ERROR: unable to find any IDs in the
                         source table';

protected $connection;
protected $mapping;
protected $files;
protected $tables;
```

10. We then define properties that will be used to generate random letters, street names, and e-mail addresses. You can think of these arrays as seeds that can be modified and/or expanded to suite your needs. As an example, you might substitute street name fragments in Paris for a French audience:

```
protected $alpha = 'ABCDEFGHIJKLMNOPQRSTUVWXYZ';
protected $street1 = ['Amber','Blue','Bright','Broad','Burning',
  'Cinder','Clear','Dewy','Dusty','Easy']; // etc.
protected $street2 = ['Anchor','Apple','Autumn','Barn','Beacon',
  'Bear','Berry','Blossom','Bluff','Cider','Cloud']; // etc.
protected $street3 = ['Acres','Arbor','Avenue','Bank','Bend',
  'Canyon','Circle','Street'];
protected $email1 = ['northern','southern','eastern','western',
  'fast','midland','central'];
protected $email2 = ['telecom','telco','net','connect'];
protected $email3 = ['com','net'];
```

11. In the constructor, we accept a `Connection` object, used for database access, an array of mappings to the fake data:

```
public function __construct(Connection $conn, array $mapping)
{
  $this->connection = $conn;
  $this->mapping = $mapping;
}
```

12. To generate street names, rather than attempt to create a database table, it might be more efficient to use a set of seed arrays to generate random combinations. Here is an example of how this might work:

```
public function getAddress($entry)
{
  return random_int(1,999)
   . ' ' . $this->street1[array_rand($this->street1)]
   . ' ' . $this->street2[array_rand($this->street2)]
   . ' ' . $this->street3[array_rand($this->street3)];
}
```

13. Depending on the level of realism desired, you could also build a database table that matches postal codes to cities. Postal codes could also be randomly generated. Here is an example that generates postal codes for the UK:

```
public function getPostalCode($entry, $pattern = 1)
{
  return $this->alpha[random_int(0,25)]
    . $this->alpha[random_int(0,25)]
    . random_int(1, 99)
    . ' '
    . random_int(1, 9)
    . $this->alpha[random_int(0,25)]
    . $this->alpha[random_int(0,25)];
}
```

14. Fake e-mail generation can likewise use a set of seed arrays to produce random results. We could also program it to receive an existing `$entry` array, with parameters, and use those parameters to create the name portion of the address:

```
public function getEmail($entry, $params = NULL)
{
  $first = $entry[$params[0]] ?? $this->alpha[random_int(0,25)];
  $last  = $entry[$params[1]] ?? $this->alpha[random_int(0,25)];
  return $first[0] . '.' . $last
    . '@'
    . $this->email1[array_rand($this->email1)]
    . $this->email2[array_rand($this->email2)]
    . '.'
    . $this->email3[array_rand($this->email3)];
}
```

15. For date generation, one approach would be to accept as arguments an existing `$entry` array, with parameters. The parameters would be an array where the first value is a start date. The second parameter would be the maximum number of days to *subtract* from the start date. This effectively lets you return a random date from a range. Note that we use `DateTime::sub()` to subtract a random number of days. `sub()` requires a `DateInterval` instance, which we build using `P`, the random number of days, and then `'D'`:

```
public function getDate($entry, $params)
{
  list($fromDate, $maxDays) = $params;
  $date = new DateTime($fromDate);
  $date->sub(new DateInterval('P' . random_int(0, $maxDays) . 'D'));
  return $date->format('Y-m-d H:i:s');
}
```

16. As mentioned at the beginning of this recipe, the data sources we will use for fake data generation will vary. In some cases, as shown in the previous few steps, we use seed arrays, and build the fake data. In other cases, we might want to use a text or CSV file as a data source. Here is how such a method might look:

```
public function getEntryFromFile($name, $type)
{
  if (empty($this->files[$name])) {
      $this->pullFileData($name, $type);
  }
  return $this->files[$name][
  random_int(0, count($this->files[$name]))];
}
```

17. You will note that we first need to pull the file data into an array, which forms the return value. Here is the method that does that for us. We throw an `Exception` if the specified file is not found. The file type is identified as one of our class constants: `FILE_TYPE_TEXT` or `FILE_TYPE_CSV`. Depending on the type, we use either `fgetcsv()` or `fgets()`:

```
public function pullFileData($name, $type)
{
  if (!file_exists($name)) {
      throw new Exception(self::ERROR_FILE);
  }
  $fileObj = new SplFileObject($name, 'r');
  if ($type == self::FILE_TYPE_CSV) {
      while ($data = $fileObj->fgetcsv()) {
        $this->files[$name][] = trim($data);
      }
  } else {
      while ($data = $fileObj->fgets()) {
        $this->files[$name][] = trim($data);
      }
  }
```

18. Probably the most complicated aspect of this process is drawing random data from a database table. We accept as arguments the table name, the name of the column that comprises the primary key, an array that maps between the database column name in the lookup table, and the target column name:

```
public function getEntryFromTable($tableName, $idColumn, $mapping)
{
  $entry = array();
  try {
      if (empty($this->tables[$tableName])) {
```

```
        $sql  = 'SELECT ' . $idColumn . ' FROM ' . $tableName
          . ' ORDER BY ' . $idColumn . ' ASC LIMIT 1';
        $stmt = $this->connection->pdo->query($sql);
        $this->tables[$tableName]['first'] =
          $stmt->fetchColumn();
        $sql  = 'SELECT ' . $idColumn . ' FROM ' . $tableName
          . ' ORDER BY ' . $idColumn . ' DESC LIMIT 1';
        $stmt = $this->connection->pdo->query($sql);
        $this->tables[$tableName]['last'] =
          $stmt->fetchColumn();
    }
```

19. We are now in a position to set up the prepared statement and initialize a number of critical variables:

```
$result = FALSE;
$count = self::MAX_LOOKUPS;
$sql  = 'SELECT * FROM ' . $tableName
  . ' WHERE ' . $idColumn . ' = ?';
$stmt = $this->connection->pdo->prepare($sql);
```

20. The actual lookup we place inside a `do...while` loop. The reason for this is that we need to run the query at least once to achieve results. Only if we do not arrive at a result do we continue with the loop. We generate a random number between the lowest ID and the highest ID, and then use this in a parameter in the query. Notice that we also decrement a counter to prevent an endless loop. This is in case the IDs are not sequential, in which case we could accidentally generate an ID that does not exist. If we exceed the maximum attempts, still with no results, we throw an `Exception`:

```
do {
  $id = random_int($this->tables[$tableName]['first'],
    $this->tables[$tableName]['last']);
  $stmt->execute([$id]);
  $result = $stmt->fetch(PDO::FETCH_ASSOC);
} while ($count-- && !$result);
  if (!$result) {
      error_log(__METHOD__ . ':' . self::ERROR_LOOKUP);
      throw new Exception(self::ERROR_LOOKUP);
  }
} catch (PDOException $e) {
    error_log(__METHOD__ . ':' . $e->getMessage());
    throw new Exception(self::ERROR_DB);
}
```

21. We then use the mapping array to retrieve values from the source table using keys expected in the destination table:

```
foreach ($mapping as $key => $value) {
  $entry[$value] = $result[$key] ?? NULL;
}
return $entry;
}
```

22. The heart of this class is a `getRandomEntry()` method, which generates a single array of fake data. We loop through `$mapping` one entry at a time and examine the various parameters:

```
public function getRandomEntry()
{
  $entry = array();
  foreach ($this->mapping as $key => $value) {
    if (isset($value['source'])) {
      switch ($value['source']) {
```

23. The `source` parameter is used to implement what effectively serves as a Strategy Pattern. We support four different possibilities for `source`, all defined as class constants. The first one is `SOURCE_FILE`. In this case, we use the `getEntryFromFile()` method discussed previously:

```
        case self::SOURCE_FILE :
            $entry[$key] = $this->getEntryFromFile(
            $value['name'], $value['type']);
          break;
```

24. The callback option returns a value according to the callback supplied in the `$mapping` array:

```
        case self::SOURCE_CALLBACK :
            $entry[$key] = $value['name']();
          break;
```

25. The `SOURCE_TABLE` option uses the database table defined in `$mapping` as a lookup. Note that `getEntryFromTable()`, discussed previously, is able to return an array of values, which means we need to use `array_merge()` to consolidate the results:

```
        case self::SOURCE_TABLE :
            $result = $this->getEntryFromTable(
            $value['name'],$value['idCol'],$value['mapping']);
            $entry = array_merge($entry, $result);
          break;
```

26. The `SOURCE_METHOD` option, which is also the default, uses a method already included with this class. We check to see whether parameters are included, and, if so, add those to the method call. Note the use of `{}` to influence interpolation. If we made a `$this->$value['name']()` PHP 7 call, due to the Abstract Syntax Tree (AST) rewrite, it would interpolate like this, `${$this->$value}['name']()`, which is not what we want:

```
            case self::SOURCE_METHOD :
            default :
              if (!empty($value['params'])) {
                  $entry[$key] = $this->{$value['name']}(
                    $entry, $value['params']);
              } else {
                  $entry[$key] = $this->{$value['name']}($entry);
              }
            }
        }
      }
      return $entry;
    }
```

27. We define a method that loops through `getRandomEntry()` to produce multiple lines of fake data. We also add an option to insert to a destination table. If this option is enabled, we set up a prepared statement to insert, and also check to see whether we need to truncate any data currently in this table:

```
    public function generateData(
    $howMany, $destTableName = NULL, $truncateDestTable = FALSE)
    {
      try {
          if ($destTableName) {
            $sql = 'INSERT INTO ' . $destTableName
              . ' (' . implode(',', array_keys($this->mapping))
              . ') '. ' VALUES ' . ' (:'
              . implode(',:', array_keys($this->mapping)) . ')';
            $stmt = $this->connection->pdo->prepare($sql);
            if ($truncateDestTable) {
              $sql = 'DELETE FROM ' . $destTableName;
              $this->connection->pdo->query($sql);
            }
          }
      } catch (PDOException $e) {
          error_log(__METHOD__ . ':' . $e->getMessage());
          throw new Exception(self::ERROR_COUNT);
      }
```

28. Next, we loop through the number of lines of data requested, and run `getRandomEntry()`. If a database insert is requested, we execute the prepared statement in a `try/catch` block. In any event, we turn this method into a generator using the `yield` keyword:

```
for ($x = 0; $x < $howMany; $x++) {
  $entry = $this->getRandomEntry();
  if ($insert) {
    try {
        $stmt->execute($entry);
    } catch (PDOException $e) {
        error_log(__METHOD__ . ':' . $e->getMessage());
        throw new Exception(self::ERROR_DB);
    }
  }
  yield $entry;
}
}
```

Best practice

If the amount of data to be returned is massive, it's much better to yield the data as it is produced, thus saving the memory required for an array.

How it works...

The first thing to do is to ensure you have the data ready for random data generation. In this recipe, we will presume that the destination table is `prospects`, which has the following SQL database definition shown in step 7.

As a data source for names, you could create text files for first names and surnames. In this illustration, we will reference the `data/files` directory, and the files `first_names.txt` and `surnames.txt`. For city, state or province, postal code, and country, it might be useful to download the data from a source such as `http://www.geonames.org/`, and upload to a `world_city_data` table. For the remaining fields, such as address, e-mail, status, and so on, you could either use methods built into `FakeData`, or define callbacks.

Next, be sure to define `Application\Test\FakeData`, adding the content discussed in steps 8 to 29. After you have finished, create a calling program called `chap_13_fake_data.php`, which sets up autoloading and uses the appropriate classes. You should also define constants that match the path to the database configuration, and names files:

```
<?php
define('DB_CONFIG_FILE', __DIR__ . '/../config/db.config.php');
define('FIRST_NAME_FILE', __DIR__ . '/../data/files/first_names.txt');
define('LAST_NAME_FILE', __DIR__ . '/../data/files/surnames.txt');
```

```
require __DIR__ . '/../Application/Autoload/Loader.php';
Application\Autoload\Loader::init(__DIR__ . '/..');
use Application\Test\FakeData;
use Application\Database\Connection;
```

Next, define a mapping array that uses the column names in the destination table (prospects) as a key. You need to then define sub-keys for `source`, `name`, and any other parameters that are required. For starters, '`first_name`' and '`last_name`' will both use a file as a source, 'name' points to the name of the file, and '`type`' indicates a file type of text:

```
$mapping = [
  'first_name'   => ['source' => FakeData::SOURCE_FILE,
  'name'         => FIRST_NAME_FILE,
  'type'         => FakeData::FILE_TYPE_TXT],
  'last_name'    => ['source' => FakeData::SOURCE_FILE,
  'name'         => LAST_NAME_FILE,
  'type'         => FakeData::FILE_TYPE_TXT],
```

The `'address'`, `'email'`, and `'last_updated'` all use built-in methods as a data source. The last two also define parameters to be passed:

```
  'address'      => ['source' => FakeData::SOURCE_METHOD,
  'name'         => 'getAddress'],
  'email'        => ['source' => FakeData::SOURCE_METHOD,
  'name'         => 'getEmail',
  'params'       => ['first_name','last_name']],
  'last_updated' => ['source' => FakeData::SOURCE_METHOD,
  'name'         => 'getDate',
  'params'       => [date('Y-m-d'), 365*5]]
```

The `'phone'`, `'status'` and `'budget'` could all use callbacks to provide fake data:

```
  'phone'        => ['source' => FakeData::SOURCE_CALLBACK,
  'name'         => function () {
                    return sprintf('%3d-%3d-%4d', random_int(101,999),
                    random_int(101,999), random_int(0,9999)); }],
  'status'       => ['source' => FakeData::SOURCE_CALLBACK,
  'name'         => function () { $status = ['BEG','INT','ADV'];
                    return $status[rand(0,2)]; }],
  'budget'       => ['source' => FakeData::SOURCE_CALLBACK,
                     'name' => function() { return random_int(0, 99999)
                     + (random_int(0, 99) * .01); }]
```

And finally, `'city'` draws its data from a lookup table, which also gives you data for the fields listed in the `'mapping'` parameter. You can then leave those keys undefined. Notice that you should also specify the column representing the primary key for the table:

```
'city' => ['source' => FakeData::SOURCE_TABLE,
'name' => 'world_city_data',
'idCol' => 'id',
'mapping' => [
'city' => 'city',
'state_province' => 'state_province',
'postal_code_prefix' => 'postal_code',
'iso2' => 'country']
],
  'state_province'=> [],
  'postal_code'  => [],
  'country'    => [],
];
```

You can then define the destination table, a `Connection` instance, and create the `FakeData` instance. A `foreach()` loop will suffice to display a given number of entries:

```
$destTableName = 'prospects';
$conn = new Connection(include DB_CONFIG_FILE);
$fake = new FakeData($conn, $mapping);
foreach ($fake->generateData(10) as $row) {
  echo implode(':', $row) . PHP_EOL;
}
```

The output, for 10 rows, would look something like this:

```
Terminal
JONAS:ROTH:868 Golden Nectar Landing:Los Tanques:Durango:34674:MX:333-150-9473:J
.ROTH@southerntelecom.net:INT:91225.14:2013-01-23 00:00:00
QUENTIN:MORSE:261 Broad  Glen:Washington:District of Columbia:20227:US:178-296-1
510:Q.MORSE@southerntelco.com:INT:87721.42:2014-04-18 00:00:00
BELLE:DORSEY:625 Sunny Sky Terrace:Guardizela:Braga:4765-442:PT:464-925-4671:B.D
ORSEY@midlandtelecom.com:BEG:10635.27:2011-12-09 00:00:00
CORNELL:COBURN:569 Hazy Quail Chase:Gottumukkala:Andhra Pradesh:521180:IN:298-89
6-7184:C.COBURN@centralconnect.com:INT:83382.48:2015-04-19 00:00:00
SHANELL:WEST:960 Cotton Hickory Drive:Passinhos:Porto:4600-790:PT:628-313-7101:S
.WEST@westernconnect.net:ADV:77372.56:2015-09-24 00:00:00
GEARLDINE:TALBERT:337 Hazy Quail Valley:Ängelholm:Skåne:262 20:SE:559-906-5119:G
.TALBERT@midlandtelco.com:ADV:1993.02:2011-12-04 00:00:00
CLETA:BEASLEY:485 Dusty  Estates:Kamitobaiwanomotochou:Kyoutofu:601-8136:JP:615-
501-8316:C.BEASLEY@centralconnect.net:INT:38705.56:2016-03-29 00:00:00
DAINE:TYLER:501 Misty Deer Trace:Seringueiras:Rondonia:78990-00:BR:817-902-4758:
D.TYLER@fastconnect.net:ADV:61894.61:2012-10-05 00:00:00
MIESHA:SCANLON:620 Stony Creek Run:Indachou:Tottoriken:683-0027:JP:250-679-5497:
M.SCANLON@centralconnect.net:INT:96079.64:2013-08-31 00:00:00


------------------
(program exited with code: 0)
Press return to continue
```

There's more...

Here is a summary of websites with various lists of data that could be of use when generating test data:

Type of Data	URL	Notes
Names	`http://nameberry.com/`	
	`http://www.babynamewizard.com/international-names-lists-popular-names-from-around-the-world`	
Raw Name Lists	`http://deron.meranda.us/data/census-dist-female-first.txt`	US female first names
	`http://deron.meranda.us/data/census-dist-male-first.txt`	US male first names
	`http://www.avss.ucsb.edu/NameFema.HTM`	US female first names
	`http://www.avss.ucsb.edu/namemal.htm`	US male first names
Last Names	`http://names.mongabay.com/data/1000.html`	US surnames from census
	`http://surname.sofeminine.co.uk/w/surnames/most-common-surnames-in-great-britain.html`	British surnames
	`https://gist.github.com/subodhghulaxe/8148971`	List of US surnames in the form of a PHP array
	`http://www.dutchgenealogy.nl/tng/surnames-all.php`	Dutch surnames
	`http://www.worldvitalrecords.com/browsesurnames.aspx?l=A`	International surnames; just change the last letter(s) to get a list of names starting with that letter(s)
Cities	`http://www.travelgis.com/default.asp?framesrc=/cities/`	World cities

Type of Data	URL	Notes
	`https://www.maxmind.com/en/free-world-cities-database`	
	`https://github.com/David-Haim/CountriesToCitiesJSON`	
	`http://www.fallingrain.com/world/index.html`	
Postal Codes	`https://boutell.com/zipcodes/`	US only; includes cities, postal codes, latitude and longitude
	`http://www.geonames.org/export/`	International; city names, postal codes, EVERYTHING!; free download

Customizing sessions using session_start parameters

Up until PHP 7, in order to override `php.ini` settings for secure session management, you had to use a series of `ini_set()` commands. This approach is extremely annoying in that you also needed to know which settings were available, and being able to re-use the same settings in other applications was difficult. As of PHP 7, however, you can supply an array of parameters to the `session_start()` command, which immediately sets those values.

How to do it...

1. We start by developing an `Application\Security\SessOptions` class, which will hold session parameters and also have the ability to start the session. We also define a class constant in case invalid session options are passed:

```
namespace Application\Security;
use ReflectionClass;
use InvalidArgumentsException;
class SessOptions
{
  const ERROR_PARAMS = 'ERROR: invalid session options';
```

2. Next we scan the list of `php.ini` session directives (documented at `http://php.net/manual/en/session.configuration.php`). We are specifically looking for directives that, in the `Changeable` column, are marked `PHP_INI_ALL`. Such directives can be overridden at runtime, and are thus available as arguments to `session_start()`:

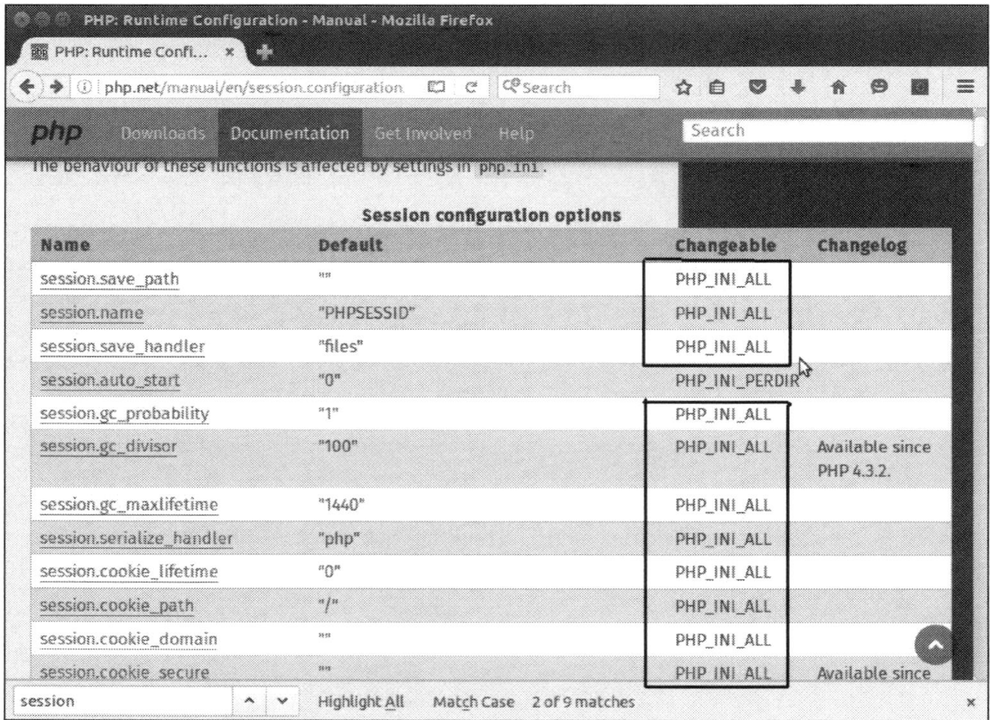

3. We then define these as class constants, which will make this class more usable for development purposes. Most decent code editors will be able to scan the class and give you a list of constants, making it easy to manage session settings. Please note that not all settings are shown, in order to conserve space in the book:

```
const SESS_OP_NAME         = 'name';
const SESS_OP_LAZY_WRITE   = 'lazy_write';  // AVAILABLE
  // SINCE PHP 7.0.0.
const SESS_OP_SAVE_PATH    = 'save_path';
const SESS_OP_SAVE_HANDLER = 'save_handler';
// etc.
```

4. We are then in a position to define the constructor, which accepts an array of `php.ini` session settings as an argument. We use `ReflectionClass` to get a list of class constants, and run the `$options` argument through a loop to confirm the setting is allowed. Also note the use of `array_flip()`, which flips keys and values, so that the actual values for our class constants form the array key, and the name of the class constant becomes the value:

```
protected $options;
protected $allowed;
public function __construct(array $options)
{
  $reflect = new ReflectionClass(get_class($this));
  $this->allowed = $reflect->getConstants();
  $this->allowed = array_flip($this->allowed);
  unset($this->allowed[self::ERROR_PARAMS]);
  foreach ($options as $key => $value) {
    if(!isset($this->allowed[$key])) {
      error_log(__METHOD__ . ':' . self::ERROR_PARAMS);
      throw new InvalidArgumentsException(
      self::ERROR_PARAMS);
    }
  }
  $this->options = $options;
}
```

5. We then close with two more methods; one gives us outside access to the allowed parameters, while the other starts the session:

```
public function getAllowed()
{
  return $this->allowed;
}

public function start()
{
  session_start($this->options);
}
```

How it works...

Place all the code discussed in this recipe into a `SessOptions.php` file in the `Application\Security` directory. You can then define a calling program called `chap_13_session_options.php` to test the new class, which sets up autoloading and uses the class:

```
<?php
require __DIR__ . '/../Application/Autoload/Loader.php';
Application\Autoload\Loader::init(__DIR__ . '/..');
use Application\Security\SessOptions;
```

Next, define an array that uses the class constants as keys, with values as desired to manage the session. Note that in the example shown here, session information is stored in a subdirectory, `session`, which you need to create:

```
$options = [
  SessOptions::SESS_OP_USE_ONLY_COOKIES => 1,
  SessOptions::SESS_OP_COOKIE_LIFETIME => 300,
  SessOptions::SESS_OP_COOKIE_HTTPONLY => 1,
  SessOptions::SESS_OP_NAME => 'UNLIKELYSOURCE',
  SessOptions::SESS_OP_SAVE_PATH => __DIR__ . '/session'
];
```

You can now create the `SessOptions` instance and run `start()` to start the session. You could use `phpinfo()` here to show some information on the session:

```
$sessOpt = new SessOptions($options);
$sessOpt->start();
$_SESSION['test'] = 'TEST';
phpinfo(INFO_VARIABLES);
```

If you look for information on cookies using your browser's developer tools, you will note the name is set to `UNLIKELYSOURCE` and the expiration time is 5 minutes from now:

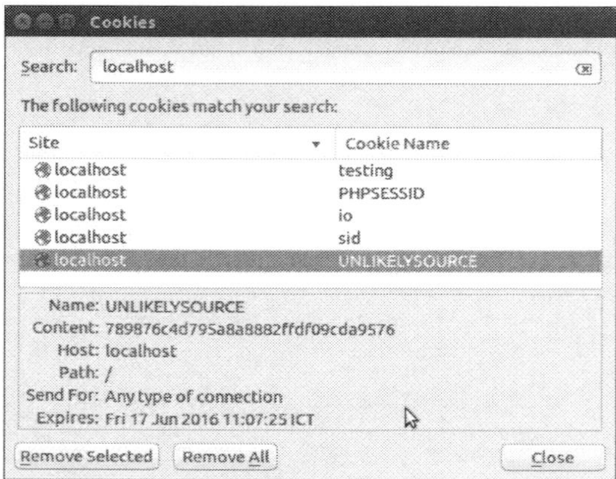

If you do a scan of the session directory, you will see that the session information has been stored there:

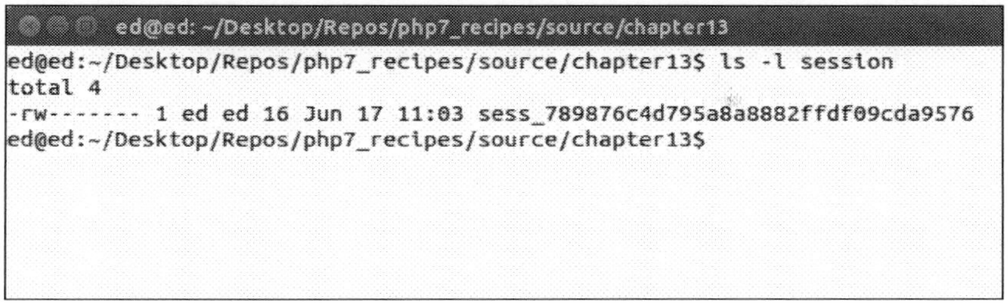

```
ed@ed: ~/Desktop/Repos/php7_recipes/source/chapter13
ed@ed:~/Desktop/Repos/php7_recipes/source/chapter13$ ls -l session
total 4
-rw------- 1 ed ed 16 Jun 17 11:03 sess_789876c4d795a8a8882ffdf09cda9576
ed@ed:~/Desktop/Repos/php7_recipes/source/chapter13$
```

See also...

- For more information on session-related php.ini directives, see this summary: http://php.net/manual/en/session.configuration.php

Defining PSR-7 Classes

In this appendix, we will cover the following topics:

- Implementing PSR-7 value object classes
- Developing a PSR-7 Request class
- Defining a PSR-7 Response class

Introduction

PHP Standard Recommendation number 7 (**PSR-7**) defines a number of interfaces, but does not provide actual implementations. Accordingly, we need to define concrete code implementations in order to start creating custom middleware.

Implementing PSR-7 value object classes

In order to work with PSR-7 requests and responses, we first need to define a series of value objects. These are classes that represent logical objects used in web-based activities such as URIs, file uploads, and streaming request or response bodies.

Getting ready

The source code for the PSR-7 interfaces is available as a `Composer` package. It is considered a best practice to use `Composer` to manage external software, including PSR-7 interfaces.

How to do it...

1. First of all, go to the following URL to obtain the latest versions of the PSR-7 interface definitions: `https://github.com/php-fig/http-message`. The source code is also available. At the time of writing, the following definitions are available:

Interface	**Extends**	**Notes**	**What the methods handle**
`MessageInterface`		Defines methods common to HTTP messages	Headers, message body (that is, content), and protocol
`RequestInterface`	`MessageInterface`	Represents requests generated by a client	The URI, HTTP method, and the request target
`ServerRequestInterface`	`RequestInterface`	Represents a request coming to a server from a client	Server and query parameters, cookies, uploaded files, and the parsed body
`ResponseInterface`	`MessageInterface`	Represents a response from the server to client	HTTP status code and reason
`StreamInterface`		Represents the data stream	Streaming behavior such as seek, tell, read, write, and so on
`UriInterface`		Represents the URI	Scheme (that is, HTTP, HTTPS), host, port, username, password (that is, for FTP), query parameters, path, and fragment
`UploadedFileInterface`		Deals with uploaded files	File size, media type, moving the file, and filename

2. Unfortunately, we will need to create concrete classes that implement these interfaces in order to utilize PSR-7. Fortunately, the interface classes are extensively documented internally through a series of comments. We will start with a separate class that contains useful constants:

Note that we take advantage of a new feature introduced in PHP 7 that allows us to define a constant as an array.

```
namespace Application\MiddleWare;
class Constants
{
  const HEADER_HOST    = 'Host';      // host header
  const HEADER_CONTENT_TYPE = 'Content-Type';
  const HEADER_CONTENT_LENGTH = 'Content-Length';

  const METHOD_GET     = 'get';
  const METHOD_POST    = 'post';
  const METHOD_PUT     = 'put';
  const METHOD_DELETE  = 'delete';
  const HTTP_METHODS   = ['get','put','post','delete'];

  const STANDARD_PORTS = [
    'ftp' => 21, 'ssh' => 22, 'http' => 80, 'https' => 443
  ];

  const CONTENT_TYPE_FORM_ENCODED =
    'application/x-www-form-urlencoded';
  const CONTENT_TYPE_MULTI_FORM    = 'multipart/form-data';
  const CONTENT_TYPE_JSON          = 'application/json';
  const CONTENT_TYPE_HAL_JSON      = 'application/hal+json';

  const DEFAULT_STATUS_CODE    = 200;
  const DEFAULT_BODY_STREAM    = 'php://input';
  const DEFAULT_REQUEST_TARGET = '/';

  const MODE_READ = 'r';
  const MODE_WRITE = 'w';

  // NOTE: not all error constants are shown to conserve space
  const ERROR_BAD = 'ERROR: ';
  const ERROR_UNKNOWN = 'ERROR: unknown';

  // NOTE: not all status codes are shown here!
  const STATUS_CODES = [
    200 => 'OK',
    301 => 'Moved Permanently',
    302 => 'Found',
    401 => 'Unauthorized',
    404 => 'Not Found',
    405 => 'Method Not Allowed',
    418 => 'I_m A Teapot',
    500 => 'Internal Server Error',
  ];
}
```

A complete list of HTTP status codes can be found here: `https://tools.ietf.org/html/rfc7231#section-6.1`.

3. Next, we will tackle classes that represent value objects used by other PSR-7 classes. For a start, here is the class that represents a URI. In the constructor, we accept a URI string as an argument, and break it down into its component parts using the `parse_url()` function:

```
namespace Application\MiddleWare;
use InvalidArgumentException;
use Psr\Http\Message\UriInterface;
class Uri implements UriInterface
{
  protected $uriString;
  protected $uriParts = array();

  public function __construct($uriString)
  {
    $this->uriParts = parse_url($uriString);
    if (!$this->uriParts) {
      throw new InvalidArgumentException(
        Constants::ERROR_INVALID_URI);
    }
    $this->uriString = $uriString;
  }
```

URI stands for **Uniform Resource Indicator**. This is what you would see at the top of your browser when making a request. For more information on what comprises a URI, have a look at `http://tools.ietf.org/html/rfc3986`.

4. Following the constructor, we define methods to access the component parts of the URI. The **scheme** represents a PHP wrapper (that is, HTTP, FTP, and so on):

```
public function getScheme()
{
  return strtolower($this->uriParts['scheme']) ?? '';
}
```

5. The **authority** represents the username (if present), the host, and optionally the port number:

```
public function getAuthority()
{
  $val = '';
  if (!empty($this->getUserInfo()))
  $val .= $this->getUserInfo() . '@';
```

```
    $val .= $this->uriParts['host'] ?? '';
    if (!empty($this->uriParts['port']))
    $val .= ':' . $this->uriParts['port'];
    return $val;
  }
```

6. **User info** represents the username (if present) and optionally the password. An example of when a password is used is when accessing an FTP website such as `ftp://username:password@website.com:/path`:

```
public function getUserInfo()
{
  if (empty($this->uriParts['user'])) {
    return '';
  }
  $val = $this->uriParts['user'];
  if (!empty($this->uriParts['pass']))
    $val .= ':' . $this->uriParts['pass'];
  return $val;
}
```

7. **Host** is the DNS address included in the URI:

```
public function getHost()
{
  if (empty($this->uriParts['host'])) {
    return '';
  }
  return strtolower($this->uriParts['host']);
}
```

8. **Port** is the HTTP port, if present. You will note if a port is listed in our `STANDARD_PORTS` constant, the return value is `NULL`, according to the requirements of PSR-7:

```
public function getPort()
{
  if (empty($this->uriParts['port'])) {
      return NULL;
  } else {
      if ($this->getScheme()) {
          if ($this->uriParts['port'] ==
              Constants::STANDARD_PORTS[$this->getScheme()]) {
              return NULL;
          }
      }
      return (int) $this->uriParts['port'];
  }
}
```

9. **Path** is the part of the URI that follows the DNS address. According to PSR-7, this must be encoded. We use the `rawurlencode()` PHP function as it is compliant with RFC 3986. We cannot just encode the entire path, however, as the path separator (that is, /) would also get encoded! Accordingly, we need to first break it up using `explode()`, encode the parts, and then reassemble it:

```
public function getPath()
{
  if (empty($this->urlParts['path'])) {
    return '';
  }
  return implode('/', array_map("rawurlencode",
               explode('/', $this->urlParts['path'])));
}
```

10. Next, we define a method to retrieve the `query` string (that is, from `$_GET`). These too must be URL-encoded. First, we define `getQueryParams()`, which breaks the query string into an associative array. You will note the reset option in case we wish to refresh the query parameters. We then define `getQuery()`, which takes the array and produces a proper URL-encoded string:

```
public function getQueryParams($reset = FALSE)
{
  if ($this->queryParams && !$reset) {
    return $this->queryParams;
  }
  $this->queryParams = [];
  if (!empty($this->uriParts['query'])) {
    foreach (explode('&', $this->uriParts['query']) as $keyPair) {
      list($param,$value) = explode('=',$keyPair);
      $this->queryParams[$param] = $value;
    }
  }
  return $this->queryParams;
}

public function getQuery()
{
  if (!$this->getQueryParams()) {
    return '';
  }
  $output = '';
  foreach ($this->getQueryParams() as $key => $value) {
    $output .= rawurlencode($key) . '='
```

```
        . rawurlencode($value) . '&';
    }
    return substr($output, 0, -1);
}
```

11. After that, we provide a method to return the `fragment` (that is, a # in the URI), and any part following it:

```
public function getFragment()
{
  if (empty($this->urlParts['fragment'])) {
    return '';
  }
  return rawurlencode($this->urlParts['fragment']);
}
```

12. Next, we define a series of `withXXX()` methods, which match the `getXXX()` methods described above. These methods are designed to add, replace, or remove properties associated with the request class (scheme, authority, user info, and so on). In addition, these methods return the current instance that allows us to use these methods in a series of successive calls (often referred to as the **fluent interface**). We start with `withScheme()`:

> You will note that an empty argument, according to PSR-7, signals the removal of that property. You will also note that we do not allow a scheme that does not match what is defined in our `Constants::STANDARD_PORTS` array.

```
public function withScheme($scheme)
{
  if (empty($scheme) && $this->getScheme()) {
      unset($this->uriParts['scheme']);
  } else {
      if (isset(STANDARD_PORTS[strtolower($scheme)])) {
          $this->uriParts['scheme'] = $scheme;
      } else {
          throw new InvalidArgumentException(
          Constants::ERROR_BAD . __METHOD__);
      }
  }
  return $this;
}
```

13. We then apply similar logic to methods that overwrite, add, or replace the user info, host, port, path, query, and fragment. Note that the `withQuery()` method resets the query parameters array. `withHost()`, `withPort()`, `withPath()`, and `withFragment()` use the same logic, but are not shown to conserve space:

```
public function withUserInfo($user, $password = null)
{
  if (empty($user) && $this->getUserInfo()) {
      unset($this->uriParts['user']);
  } else {
      $this->urlParts['user'] = $user;
      if ($password) {
          $this->urlParts['pass'] = $password;
      }
  }
  return $this;
}
// Not shown: withHost(),withPort(),withPath(),withFragment()

public function withQuery($query)
{
  if (empty($query) && $this->getQuery()) {
      unset($this->uriParts['query']);
  } else {
      $this->uriParts['query'] = $query;
  }
  // reset query params array
  $this->getQueryParams(TRUE);
  return $this;
}
```

14. Finally, we wrap up the `Application\MiddleWare\Uri` class with `__toString()`, which, when the object is used in a string context, returns a proper URI, assembled from `$uriParts`. We also define a convenience method, `getUriString()`, that simply calls `__toString()`:

```
public function __toString()
{
    $uri = ($this->getScheme())
      ? $this->getScheme() . '://' : '';
```

15. If the `authority` URI part is present, we add it. `authority` includes the user information, host, and port. Otherwise, we just append `host` and `port`:

```
if ($this->getAuthority()) {
    $uri .= $this->getAuthority();
} else {
```

```
        $uri .= ($this->getHost()) ? $this->getHost() : '';
        $uri .= ($this->getPort())
          ? ':' . $this->getPort() : '';
    }
```

16. Before adding `path`, we first check whether the first character is `/`. If not, we need to add this separator. We then add `query` and `fragment`, if present:

```
    $path = $this->getPath();
    if ($path) {
        if ($path[0] != '/') {
            $uri .= '/' . $path;
        } else {
            $uri .= $path;
        }
    }
    $uri .= ($this->getQuery())
      ? '?' . $this->getQuery() : '';
    $uri .= ($this->getFragment())
      ? '#' . $this->getFragment() : '';
    return $uri;
    }

    public function getUriString()
    {
      return $this->__toString();
    }

    }
```

Note the use of string dereferencing (that is, `$path[0]`), now part of PHP 7.

17. Next, we turn our attention to a class that represents the body of the message. As it is not known how large the body might be, PSR-7 recommends that the body should be treated as a **stream**. A stream is a resource that allows access to input and output sources in a linear fashion. In PHP, all file commands operate on top of the `Streams` sub-system, so this is a natural fit. PSR-7 formalizes this by way of `Psr\Http\Message\StreamInterface` that defines such methods as `read()`, `write()`, `seek()`, and so on. We now present `Application\MiddleWare\Stream` that we can use to represent the body of incoming or outgoing requests and/or responses:

```
    namespace Application\MiddleWare;
    use SplFileInfo;
    use Throwable;
```

```
use RuntimeException;
use Psr\Http\Message\StreamInterface;
class Stream implements StreamInterface
{
  protected $stream;
  protected $metadata;
  protected $info;
```

18. In the constructor, we open the stream using a simple `fopen()` command. We then use `stream_get_meta_data()` to get information on the stream. For other details, we create an `SplFileInfo` instance:

```
public function __construct($input, $mode = self::MODE_READ)
{
  $this->stream = fopen($input, $mode);
  $this->metadata = stream_get_meta_data($this->stream);
  $this->info = new SplFileInfo($input);
}
```

The reason why we chose `fopen()` over the more modern `SplFileObject` is that the latter does not allow direct access to the inner file resource object, and is therefore useless for this application.

19. We include two convenience methods that provide access to the resource, as well as access to the `SplFileInfo` instance:

```
public function getStream()
{
  return $this->stream;
}

public function getInfo()
{
  return $this->info;
}
```

20. Next, we define low-level core streaming methods:

```
public function read($length)
{
  if (!fread($this->stream, $length)) {
      throw new RuntimeException(
      self::ERROR_BAD . __METHOD__);
  }
}
```

```
public function write($string)
{
  if (!fwrite($this->stream, $string)) {
      throw new RuntimeException(
      self::ERROR_BAD . __METHOD__);
  }
}
public function rewind()
{
  if (!rewind($this->stream)) {
      throw new RuntimeException(
      self::ERROR_BAD . __METHOD__);
  }
}
public function eof()
{
  return eof($this->stream);
}
public function tell()
{
  try {
      return ftell($this->stream);
  } catch (Throwable $e) {
      throw new RuntimeException(
      self::ERROR_BAD . __METHOD__);
  }
}
public function seek($offset, $whence = SEEK_SET)
{
  try {
      fseek($this->stream, $offset, $whence);
  } catch (Throwable $e) {
      throw new RuntimeException(
      self::ERROR_BAD . __METHOD__);
  }
}
public function close()
{
  if ($this->stream) {
    fclose($this->stream);
  }
}
public function detach()
{
  return $this->close();
}
```

21. We also need to define informational methods that tell us about the stream:

```
public function getMetadata($key = null)
{
  if ($key) {
      return $this->metadata[$key] ?? NULL;
  } else {
      return $this->metadata;
  }
}
public function getSize()
{
  return $this->info->getSize();
}
public function isSeekable()
{
  return boolval($this->metadata['seekable']);
}
public function isWritable()
{
  return $this->stream->isWritable();
}
public function isReadable()
{
  return $this->info->isReadable();
}
```

22. Following PSR-7 guidelines, we then define `getContents()` and `__toString()` in order to dump the contents of the stream:

```
public function __toString()
{
  $this->rewind();
  return $this->getContents();
}

public function getContents()
{
  ob_start();
  if (!fpassthru($this->stream)) {
    throw new RuntimeException(
    self::ERROR_BAD . __METHOD__);
  }
  return ob_get_clean();
}
}
```

23. An important variation of the `Stream` class shown previously is `TextStream` that is designed for situations where the body is a string (that is, an array encoded as JSON) rather than a file. As we need to make absolutely certain that the incoming `$input` value is of the string data type, we invoke PHP 7 strict types just after the opening tag. We also identify a `$pos` property (that is, position) that will emulate a file pointer, but instead point to a position within the string:

```
<?php
declare(strict_types=1);
namespace Application\MiddleWare;
use Throwable;
use RuntimeException;
use SplFileInfo;
use Psr\Http\Message\StreamInterface;

class TextStream implements StreamInterface
{
  protected $stream;
  protected $pos = 0;
```

24. Most of the methods are quite simple and self-explanatory. The `$stream` property is the input string:

```
public function __construct(string $input)
{
  $this->stream = $input;
}
public function getStream()
{
  return $this->stream;
}
  public function getInfo()
{
  return NULL;
}
public function getContents()
{
  return $this->stream;
}
public function __toString()
{
  return $this->getContents();
}
public function getSize()
{
  return strlen($this->stream);
```

```
}
public function close()
{
  // do nothing: how can you "close" string???
}
public function detach()
{
  return $this->close();  // that is, do nothing!
}
```

25. To emulate streaming behavior, `tell()`, `eof()`, `seek()`, and so on, work with `$pos`:

```
public function tell()
{
  return $this->pos;
}
public function eof()
{
  return ($this->pos == strlen($this->stream));
}
public function isSeekable()
{
  return TRUE;
}
public function seek($offset, $whence = NULL)
{
  if ($offset < $this->getSize()) {
      $this->pos = $offset;
  } else {
      throw new RuntimeException(
        Constants::ERROR_BAD . __METHOD__);
  }
}
public function rewind()
{
  $this->pos = 0;
}
public function isWritable()
{
  return TRUE;
}
```

26. The `read()` and `write()` methods work with `$pos` and substrings:

```
public function write($string)
{
  $temp = substr($this->stream, 0, $this->pos);
  $this->stream = $temp . $string;
  $this->pos = strlen($this->stream);
}

public function isReadable()
{
  return TRUE;
}
public function read($length)
{
  return substr($this->stream, $this->pos, $length);
}
public function getMetadata($key = null)
{
  return NULL;
}

}
```

27. The last of the value objects to be presented is `Application\MiddleWare\UploadedFile`. As with the other classes, we first define properties that represent aspects of a file upload:

```
namespace Application\MiddleWare;
use RuntimeException;
use InvalidArgumentException;
use Psr\Http\Message\UploadedFileInterface;
class UploadedFile implements UploadedFileInterface
{

  protected $field;   // original name of file upload field
  protected $info;    // $_FILES[$field]
  protected $randomize;
  protected $movedName = '';
```

28. In the constructor, we allow the definition of the name attribute of the file upload form field, as well as the corresponding array in `$_FILES`. We add the last parameter to signal whether or not we want the class to generate a new random filename once the uploaded file is confirmed:

```
public function __construct(
  $field, array $info, $randomize = FALSE)
{
  $this->field = $field;
  $this->info = $info;
  $this->randomize = $randomize;
}
```

29. Next, we create a `Stream` class instance for the temporary or moved file:

```
public function getStream()
{
  if (!$this->stream) {
      if ($this->movedName) {
          $this->stream = new Stream($this->movedName);
      } else {
          $this->stream = new Stream($info['tmp_name']);
      }
  }
  return $this->stream;
}
```

30. The `moveTo()` method performs the actual file movement. Note the extensive series of safety checks to help prevent an injection attack. If randomize is not enabled, we use the original user-supplied filename:

```
public function moveTo($targetPath)
{
  if ($this->moved) {
      throw new Exception(Constants::ERROR_MOVE_DONE);
  }
  if (!file_exists($targetPath)) {
      throw new InvalidArgumentException(Constants::ERROR_BAD_DIR);
  }
  $tempFile = $this->info['tmp_name'] ?? FALSE;
  if (!$tempFile || !file_exists($tempFile)) {
      throw new Exception(Constants::ERROR_BAD_FILE);
  }
  if (!is_uploaded_file($tempFile)) {
      throw new Exception(Constants::ERROR_FILE_NOT);
  }
```

```
    if ($this->randomize) {
        $final = bin2hex(random_bytes(8)) . '.txt';
    } else {
        $final = $this->info['name'];
    }
    $final = $targetPath . '/' . $final;
    $final = str_replace('//', '/', $final);
    if (!move_uploaded_file($tempFile, $final)) {
        throw new RuntimeException(Constants::ERROR_MOVE_UNABLE);
    }
    $this->movedName = $final;
    return TRUE;
  }
```

31. We then provide access to the other parameters returned in `$_FILES` from the `$info` property. Please note that the return values from `getClientFilename()` and `getClientMediaType()` should be considered untrusted, as they originate from the outside. We also add a method to return the moved filename:

```
public function getMovedName()
{
  return $this->movedName ?? NULL;
}
public function getSize()
{
  return $this->info['size'] ?? NULL;
}
public function getError()
{
  if (!$this->moved) {
      return UPLOAD_ERR_OK;
  }
  return $this->info['error'];
}
public function getClientFilename()
{
  return $this->info['name'] ?? NULL;
}
public function getClientMediaType()
{
  return $this->info['type'] ?? NULL;
}

}
```

How it works...

First of all, go to `https://github.com/php-fig/http-message/tree/master/src`, the GitHub repository for the PSR-7 interfaces, and download them. Create a directory called `Psr/Http/Message` in `/path/to/source` and places the files there. Alternatively, you can visit `https://packagist.org/packages/psr/http-message` and install the source code using `Composer`. (For instructions on how to obtain and use `Composer`, you can visit `https://getcomposer.org/`.)

Then, go ahead and define the classes discussed previously, summarized in this table:

Class	**Steps discussed in**
`Application\MiddleWare\Constants`	2
`Application\MiddleWare\Uri`	3 to 16
`Application\MiddleWare\Stream`	17 to 22
`Application\MiddleWare\TextStream`	23 to 26
`Application\MiddleWare\UploadedFile`	27 to 31

Next, define a `chap_09_middleware_value_objects_uri.php` calling program that implements autoloading and uses the appropriate classes. Please note that if you use `Composer`, unless otherwise instructed, it will create a folder called `vendor`. `Composer` also adds its own autoloader, which you are free to use here:

```
<?php
require __DIR__ . '/../Application/Autoload/Loader.php';
Application\Autoload\Loader::init(__DIR__ . '/..');
use Application\MiddleWare\Uri;
```

You can then create a `Uri` instance and use the `with` methods to add parameters. You can then echo the `Uri` instance directly as `__toString()` is defined:

```
$uri = new Uri();
$uri->withScheme('https')
    ->withHost('localhost')
    ->withPort('8080')
    ->withPath('chap_09_middleware_value_objects_uri.php')
    ->withQuery('param=TEST');

echo $uri;
```

Here is the expected result:

```
https://localhost:8080/chap_09_middleware_value_objects.php?param=TEST

-----------------
(program exited with code: 0)
Press return to continue
```

Next, create a directory called `uploads` from `/path/to/source/for/this/chapter`. Go ahead and define another calling program, `chap_09_middleware_value_objects_file_upload.php`, that sets up autoloading and uses the appropriate classes:

```
<?php
define('TARGET_DIR', __DIR__ . '/uploads');
require __DIR__ . '/../Application/Autoload/Loader.php';
Application\Autoload\Loader::init(__DIR__ . '/..');
use Application\MiddleWare\UploadedFile;
```

Inside a `try...catch` block, check to see whether any files were uploaded. If so, loop through `$_FILES` and create `UploadedFile` instances where `tmp_name` is set. You can then use the `moveTo()` method to move the files to `TARGET_DIR`:

```
try {
    $message = '';
    $uploadedFiles = array();
    if (isset($_FILES)) {
        foreach ($_FILES as $key => $info) {
          if ($info['tmp_name']) {
              $uploadedFiles[$key] = new UploadedFile(
                                          $key, $info, TRUE);
              $uploadedFiles[$key]->moveTo(TARGET_DIR);
          }
        }
    }
} catch (Throwable $e) {
    $message =  $e->getMessage();
}
?>
```

In the view logic, display a simple file upload form. You could also use `phpinfo()` to display information about what was uploaded:

```
<form name="search" method="post"
  enctype="<?= Constants::CONTENT_TYPE_MULTI_FORM ?>">
<table class="display" cellspacing="0" width="100%">
    <tr><th>Upload 1</th><td><input type="file" name="upload_1" /></
td></tr>
    <tr><th>Upload 2</th><td><input type="file" name="upload_2" /></
td></tr>
    <tr><th>Upload 3</th><td><input type="file" name="upload_3" /></
td></tr>
    <tr><th> </th><td><input type="submit" /></td></tr>
</table>
</form>
<?= ($message) ? '<h1>' . $message . '</h1>' : ''; ?>
```

Next, if there were any uploaded files, you can display information on each one. You can also use `getStream()` followed by `getContents()` to display each file (assuming you're using short text files):

```
<?php if ($uploadedFiles) : ?>
<table class="display" cellspacing="0" width="100%">
    <tr>
        <th>Filename</th><th>Size</th>
      <th>Moved Filename</th><th>Text</th>
    </tr>
    <?php foreach ($uploadedFiles as $obj) : ?>
        <?php if ($obj->getMovedName()) : ?>
        <tr>
            <td><?= htmlspecialchars($obj->getClientFilename()) ?></td>
            <td><?= $obj->getSize() ?></td>
            <td><?= $obj->getMovedName() ?></td>
            <td><?= $obj->getStream()->getContents() ?></td>
        </tr>
        <?php endif; ?>
    <?php endforeach; ?>
</table>
<?php endif; ?>
<?php phpinfo(INFO_VARIABLES); ?>
```

Here is how the output might appear:

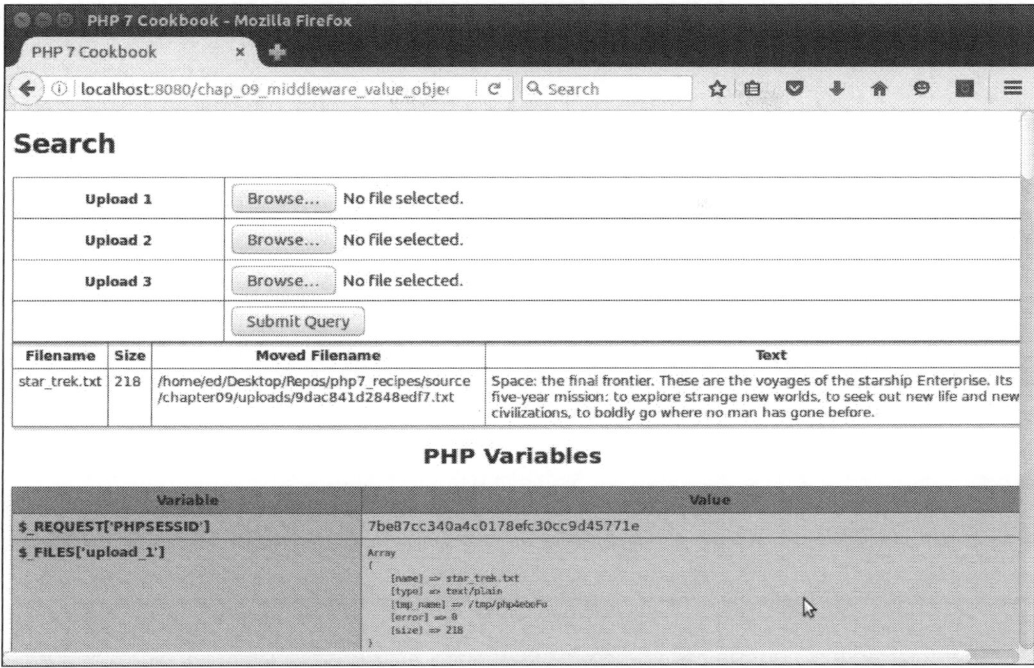

See also

- For more information on PSR, please have a look at `https://en.wikipedia.org/wiki/PHP_Standard_Recommendation`
- For information on PSR-7 specifically, here is the official description: `http://www.php-fig.org/psr/psr-7/`
- For information on PHP streams, take a look at `http://php.net/manual/en/book.stream.php`

Developing a PSR-7 Request class

One of the key characteristics of PSR-7 middleware is the use of **Request** and **Response** classes. When applied, this enables different blocks of software to perform together without sharing any specific knowledge between them. In this context, a request class should encompass all aspects of the original user request, including such items as browser settings, the original URL requested, parameters passed, and so forth.

How to do it...

1. First, be sure to define classes to represent the `Uri`, `Stream`, and `UploadedFile` value objects, as described in the previous recipe.
2. Now we are ready to define the core `Application\MiddleWare\Message` class. This class consumes `Stream` and `Uri` and implements `Psr\Http\Message\MessageInterface`. We first define properties for the key value objects, including those representing the message body (that is, a `StreamInterface` instance), version, and HTTP headers:

```
namespace Application\MiddleWare;
use Psr\Http\Message\ {
  MessageInterface,
  StreamInterface,
  UriInterface
};
class Message implements MessageInterface
{
  protected $body;
  protected $version;
  protected $httpHeaders = array();
```

3. Next, we have the `getBody()` method that represents a `StreamInterface` instance. A companion method, `withBody()`, returns the current `Message` instance and allows us to overwrite the current value of `body`:

```
public function getBody()
{
  if (!$this->body) {
      $this->body = new Stream(self::DEFAULT_BODY_STREAM);
  }
  return $this->body;
}
public function withBody(StreamInterface $body)
{
  if (!$body->isReadable()) {
      throw new InvalidArgumentException(
                self::ERROR_BODY_UNREADABLE);
  }
  $this->body = $body;
  return $this;
}
```

4. PSR-7 recommends that headers should be viewed as case-insensitive. Accordingly, we define a `findHeader()` method (not directly defined by `MessageInterface`) that locates a header using `stripos()`:

```
protected function findHeader($name)
{
  $found = FALSE;
  foreach (array_keys($this->getHeaders()) as $header) {
    if (stripos($header, $name) !== FALSE) {
        $found = $header;
        break;
    }
  }
  return $found;
}
```

5. The next method, not defined by PSR-7, is designed to populate the `$httpHeaders` property. This property is assumed to be an associative array where the key is the header, and the value is the string representing the header value. If there is more than one value, additional values separated by commas are appended to the string. There is an excellent `apache_request_headers()` PHP function from the Apache extension that produces headers if they are not already available in `$httpHeaders`:

```
protected function getHttpHeaders()
{
  if (!$this->httpHeaders) {
      if (function_exists('apache_request_headers')) {
          $this->httpHeaders = apache_request_headers();
      } else {
          $this->httpHeaders = $this->altApacheReqHeaders();
      }
  }
  return $this->httpHeaders;
}
```

6. If `apache_request_headers()` is not available (that is, the Apache extension is not enabled), we provide an alternative, `altApacheReqHeaders()`:

```
protected function altApacheReqHeaders()
{
  $headers = array();
  foreach ($_SERVER as $key => $value) {
    if (stripos($key, 'HTTP_') !== FALSE) {
        $headerKey = str_ireplace('HTTP_', '', $key);
        $headers[$this->explodeHeader($headerKey)] = $value;
```

```
        } elseif (stripos($key, 'CONTENT_') !== FALSE) {
            $headers[$this->explodeHeader($key)] = $value;
        }
    }
    return $headers;
}
protected function explodeHeader($header)
{
    $headerParts = explode('_', $header);
    $headerKey = ucwords(implode(' ', strtolower($headerParts)));
    return str_replace(' ', '-', $headerKey);
}
```

7. Implementing `getHeaders()` (required in PSR-7) is now a trivial loop through the `$httpHeaders` property produced by the `getHttpHeaders()` method discussed in step 4:

```
public function getHeaders()
{
    foreach ($this->getHttpHeaders() as $key => $value) {
        header($key . ': ' . $value);
    }
}
```

8. Again, we provide a series of `with` methods designed to overwrite or replace headers. Since there can be many headers, we also have a method that adds to the existing set of headers. The `withoutHeader()` method is used to remove a header instance. Notice the consistent use of `findHeader()`, mentioned in the previous step, to allow for case-insensitive handling of headers:

```
public function withHeader($name, $value)
{
    $found = $this->findHeader($name);
    if ($found) {
        $this->httpHeaders[$found] = $value;
    } else {
        $this->httpHeaders[$name] = $value;
    }
    return $this;
}

public function withAddedHeader($name, $value)
{
    $found = $this->findHeader($name);
    if ($found) {
```

```
        $this->httpHeaders[$found] .= $value;
    } else {
        $this->httpHeaders[$name] = $value;
    }
    return $this;
}

public function withoutHeader($name)
{
    $found = $this->findHeader($name);
    if ($found) {
        unset($this->httpHeaders[$found]);
    }
    return $this;
}
```

9. We then provide a series of useful header-related methods to confirm a header exists, retrieve a single header line, and retrieve a header in array form, as per PSR-7:

```
public function hasHeader($name)
{
    return boolval($this->findHeader($name));
}

public function getHeaderLine($name)
{
    $found = $this->findHeader($name);
    if ($found) {
        return $this->httpHeaders[$found];
    } else {
        return '';
    }
}

public function getHeader($name)
{
    $line = $this->getHeaderLine($name);
    if ($line) {
        return explode(',', $line);
    } else {
        return array();
    }
}
```

10. Finally, to round off header handling, we present `getHeadersAsString` that produces a single header string with the headers separated by `\r\n` for direct use with PHP stream contexts:

```
public function getHeadersAsString()
{
  $output = '';
  $headers = $this->getHeaders();
  if ($headers && is_array($headers)) {
      foreach ($headers as $key => $value) {
        if ($output) {
            $output .= "\r\n" . $key . ': ' . $value;
        } else {
            $output .= $key . ': ' . $value;
        }
      }
  }
  return $output;
}
```

11. Still within the `Message` class, we now turn our attention to version handling. According to PSR-7, the return value for the protocol version (that is, HTTP/1.1) should only be the numerical part. For this reason, we also provide `onlyVersion()` that strips off any non-digit character, allowing periods:

```
public function getProtocolVersion()
{
  if (!$this->version) {
      $this->version = $this->onlyVersion(
        $_SERVER['SERVER_PROTOCOL']);
  }
  return $this->version;
}

public function withProtocolVersion($version)
{
  $this->version = $this->onlyVersion($version);
  return $this;
}

protected function onlyVersion($version)
{
  if (!empty($version)) {
      return preg_replace('/[^0-9\.]/', '', $version);
  } else {
      return NULL;
```

```
    }
  }

  }
```

12. Finally, almost as an anticlimax, we are ready to define our `Request` class. It must be noted here, however, that we need to consider both out-bound as well as in-bound requests. That is to say, we need a class to represent an outgoing request a client will make to a server, as well as a request *received* from a client by a server. Accordingly, we provide `Application\MiddleWare\Request` (requests a client will make to a server), and `Application\MiddleWare\ServerRequest` (requests received from a client by a server). The good news is that most of our work has already been done: notice that our `Request` class extends `Message`. We also provide properties to represent the URI and HTTP method:

```
namespace Application\MiddleWare;

use InvalidArgumentException;
use Psr\Http\Message\ { RequestInterface, StreamInterface,
UriInterface };

class Request extends Message implements RequestInterface
{
  protected $uri;
  protected $method; // HTTP method
  protected $uriObj; // Psr\Http\Message\UriInterface instance
```

13. All properties in the constructor default to `NULL`, but we leave open the possibility of defining the appropriate arguments right away. We use the inherited `onlyVersion()` method to sanitize the version. We also define `checkMethod()` to make sure any method supplied is on our list of supported HTTP methods, defined as a constant array in `Constants`:

```
public function __construct($uri = NULL,
                            $method = NULL,
                            StreamInterface $body = NULL,
                            $headers = NULL,
                            $version = NULL)
{
  $this->uri = $uri;
  $this->body = $body;
  $this->method = $this->checkMethod($method);
  $this->httpHeaders = $headers;
  $this->version = $this->onlyVersion($version);
}
protected function checkMethod($method)
{
```

```
    if (!$method === NULL) {
        if (!in_array(strtolower($method), Constants::HTTP_METHODS)) {
            throw new InvalidArgumentException(
            Constants::ERROR_HTTP_METHOD);
        }
    }
    return $method;
}
```

14. We are going to interpret the request target as the originally requested URI in the form of a string. Bear in mind that our `Uri` class has methods that will parse this into its component parts, hence our provision of the `$uriObj` property. In the case of `withRequestTarget()`, notice that we run `getUri()` that performs the aforementioned parsing process:

```
public function getRequestTarget()
{
  return $this->uri ?? Constants::DEFAULT_REQUEST_TARGET;
}

public function withRequestTarget($requestTarget)
{
  $this->uri = $requestTarget;
  $this->getUri();
  return $this;
}
```

15. Our `get` and `with` methods, which represent the HTTP method, reveal no surprises. We use `checkMethod()`, used in the constructor as well, to ensure the method matches those we plan to support:

```
public function getMethod()
{
  return $this->method;
}

public function withMethod($method)
{
  $this->method = $this->checkMethod($method);
  return $this;
}
```

16. Finally, we have a `get` and `with` method for the URI. As mentioned in step 14, we retain the original request string in the `$uri` property and the newly parsed `Uri` instance in `$uriObj`. Note the extra flag to preserve any existing `Host` header:

```
public function getUri()
{
  if (!$this->uriObj) {
      $this->uriObj = new Uri($this->uri);
  }
  return $this->uriObj;
}

public function withUri(UriInterface $uri, $preserveHost = false)
{
  if ($preserveHost) {
    $found = $this->findHeader(Constants::HEADER_HOST);
    if (!$found && $uri->getHost()) {
      $this->httpHeaders[Constants::HEADER_HOST] = $uri->getHost();
    }
  } elseif ($uri->getHost()) {
      $this->httpHeaders[Constants::HEADER_HOST] = $uri->getHost();
  }
  $this->uri = $uri->__toString();
  return $this;
  }
}
```

17. The `ServerRequest` class extends `Request` and provides additional functionality to retrieve information of interest to a server handling an incoming request. We start by defining properties that will represent incoming data read from the various PHP `$_super-globals` (that is, `$_SERVER`, `$_POST`, and so on):

```
namespace Application\MiddleWare;
use Psr\Http\Message\ { ServerRequestInterface,
UploadedFileInterface } ;

class ServerRequest extends Request implements
ServerRequestInterface
{

  protected $serverParams;
  protected $cookies;
  protected $queryParams;
  protected $contentType;
```

```
  protected $parsedBody;
  protected $attributes;
  protected $method;
  protected $uploadedFileInfo;
  protected $uploadedFileObjs;
```

18. We then define a series of getters to pull super-global information. We do not show everything, to conserve space:

```
public function getServerParams()
{
  if (!$this->serverParams) {
      $this->serverParams = $_SERVER;
  }
  return $this->serverParams;
}
// getCookieParams() reads $_COOKIE
// getQueryParams() reads $_GET
// getUploadedFileInfo() reads $_FILES

public function getRequestMethod()
{
  $method = $this->getServerParams()['REQUEST_METHOD'] ?? '';
  $this->method = strtolower($method);
  return $this->method;
}

public function getContentType()
{
  if (!$this->contentType) {
      $this->contentType =
      $this->getServerParams()['CONTENT_TYPE'] ?? '';
      $this->contentType = strtolower($this->contentType);
  }
  return $this->contentType;
}
```

19. As uploaded files are supposed to be represented as independent `UploadedFile` objects (presented in the previous recipe), we also define a method that takes `$uploadedFileInfo` and creates `UploadedFile` objects:

```
public function getUploadedFiles()
{
  if (!$this->uploadedFileObjs) {
```

```
        foreach ($this->getUploadedFileInfo() as $field => $value) {
          $this->uploadedFileObjs[$field] =
          new UploadedFile($field, $value);
        }
      }
      return $this->uploadedFileObjs;
    }
```

20. As with the other classes defined previously, we provide `with` methods that add or overwrite properties and return the new instance:

```
public function withCookieParams(array $cookies)
{
  array_merge($this->getCookieParams(), $cookies);
  return $this;
}
public function withQueryParams(array $query)
{
  array_merge($this->getQueryParams(), $query);
  return $this;
}
public function withUploadedFiles(array $uploadedFiles)
{
  if (!count($uploadedFiles)) {
      throw new InvalidArgumentException(
      Constant::ERROR_NO_UPLOADED_FILES);
  }
  foreach ($uploadedFiles as $fileObj) {
    if (!$fileObj instanceof UploadedFileInterface) {
        throw new InvalidArgumentException(
        Constant::ERROR_INVALID_UPLOADED);
    }
  }
  $this->uploadedFileObjs = $uploadedFiles;
}
```

21. One important aspect of PSR-7 messages is that the body should also be available in a parsed manner, that is to say, a sort of structured representation rather than just a raw stream. Accordingly, we define `getParsedBody()` and its accompanying `with` method. The PSR-7 recommendations are quite specific when it comes to form posting. Note the series of `if` statements that check the `Content-Type` header as well as the method:

```
public function getParsedBody()
{
  if (!$this->parsedBody) {
```

```
            if (($this->getContentType() ==
                 Constants::CONTENT_TYPE_FORM_ENCODED
                 || $this->getContentType() ==
                 Constants::CONTENT_TYPE_MULTI_FORM)
                 && $this->getRequestMethod() ==
                 Constants::METHOD_POST)
            {
                $this->parsedBody = $_POST;
            } elseif ($this->getContentType() ==
                      Constants::CONTENT_TYPE_JSON
                      || $this->getContentType() ==
                      Constants::CONTENT_TYPE_HAL_JSON)
            {
                ini_set("allow_url_fopen", true);
                $this->parsedBody =
                  json_decode(file_get_contents('php://input'));
            } elseif (!empty($_REQUEST)) {
                $this->parsedBody = $_REQUEST;
            } else {
                ini_set("allow_url_fopen", true);
                $this->parsedBody = file_get_contents('php://input');
            }
        }
        return $this->parsedBody;
    }

    public function withParsedBody($data)
    {
      $this->parsedBody = $data;
      return $this;
    }
```

22. We also allow for attributes that are not precisely defined in PSR-7. Rather, we leave this open so that the developer can provide whatever is appropriate for the application. Notice the use of `withoutAttributes()` that allows you to remove attributes at will:

```
public function getAttributes()
{
  return $this->attributes;
}
public function getAttribute($name, $default = NULL)
{
  return $this->attributes[$name] ?? $default;
}
```

```
public function withAttribute($name, $value)
{
  $this->attributes[$name] = $value;
  return $this;
}
public function withoutAttribute($name)
{
  if (isset($this->attributes[$name])) {
      unset($this->attributes[$name]);
  }
  return $this;
}

}
```

23. Finally, in order to load the different properties from an in-bound request, we define `initialize()`, which is not in PSR-7, but is extremely convenient:

```
public function initialize()
{
  $this->getServerParams();
  $this->getCookieParams();
  $this->getQueryParams();
  $this->getUploadedFiles;
  $this->getRequestMethod();
  $this->getContentType();
  $this->getParsedBody();
  return $this;
}
```

How it works...

First, be sure to complete the preceding recipe, as the `Message` and `Request` classes consume `Uri`, `Stream`, and `UploadedFile` value objects. After that, go ahead and define the classes summarized in the following table:

Class	Steps they are discussed in
`Application\MiddleWare\Message`	2 to 9
`Application\MiddleWare\Request`	10 to 14
`Application\MiddleWare\ServerRequest`	15 to 20

After that, you can define a server program, `chap_09_middleware_server.php`, which sets up autoloading and uses the appropriate classes. This script will pull the incoming request into a `ServerRequest` instance, initialize it, and then use `var_dump()` to show what information was received:

```
<?php
require __DIR__ . '/../Application/Autoload/Loader.php';
Application\Autoload\Loader::init(__DIR__ . '/..');
use Application\MiddleWare\ServerRequest;

$request = new ServerRequest();
$request->initialize();
echo '<pre>', var_dump($request), '</pre>';
```

To run the server program, first change to the `/path/to/source/for/this/chapter folder`. You can then run the following command:

```
php -S localhost:8080 chap_09_middleware_server.php'
```

As for the client, first create a calling program, `chap_09_middleware_request.php`, that sets up autoloading, uses the appropriate classes, and defines the target server and a local text file:

```
<?php
define('READ_FILE', __DIR__ . '/gettysburg.txt');
define('TEST_SERVER', 'http://localhost:8080');
require __DIR__ . '/../Application/Autoload/Loader.php';
Application\Autoload\Loader::init(__DIR__ . '/..');
use Application\MiddleWare\ { Request, Stream, Constants };
```

Next, you can create a `Stream` instance using the text as a source. This will become the body of a new Request, which, in this case, mirrors what might be expected for a form posting:

```
$body = new Stream(READ_FILE);
```

You can then directly build a `Request` instance, supplying parameters as appropriate:

```
$request = new Request(
    TEST_SERVER,
    Constants::METHOD_POST,
    $body,
    [Constants::HEADER_CONTENT_TYPE =>
       Constants::CONTENT_TYPE_FORM_ENCODED,
       Constants::HEADER_CONTENT_LENGTH => $body->getSize()]
);
```

Alternatively, you can use the fluent interface syntax to produce exactly the same results:

```
$uriObj = new Uri(TEST_SERVER);
$request = new Request();
$request->withRequestTarget(TEST_SERVER)
        ->withMethod(Constants::METHOD_POST)
        ->withBody($body)
        ->withHeader(Constants::HEADER_CONTENT_TYPE,
            Constants::CONTENT_TYPE_FORM_ENCODED)
        ->withAddedHeader(
            Constants::HEADER_CONTENT_LENGTH, $body->getSize());
```

You can then set up a cURL resource to simulate a form posting, where the data parameter is the contents of the text file. You can follow that with `curl_init()`, `curl_exec()`, and so on, echoing the results:

```
$data = http_build_query(['data' =>
   $request->getBody()->getContents()]);
$defaults = array(
    CURLOPT_URL => $request->getUri()->getUriString(),
    CURLOPT_POST => true,
    CURLOPT_POSTFIELDS => $data,
);
$ch = curl_init();
curl_setopt_array($ch, $defaults);
$response = curl_exec($ch);
curl_close($ch);
```

Here is how the direct output might appear:

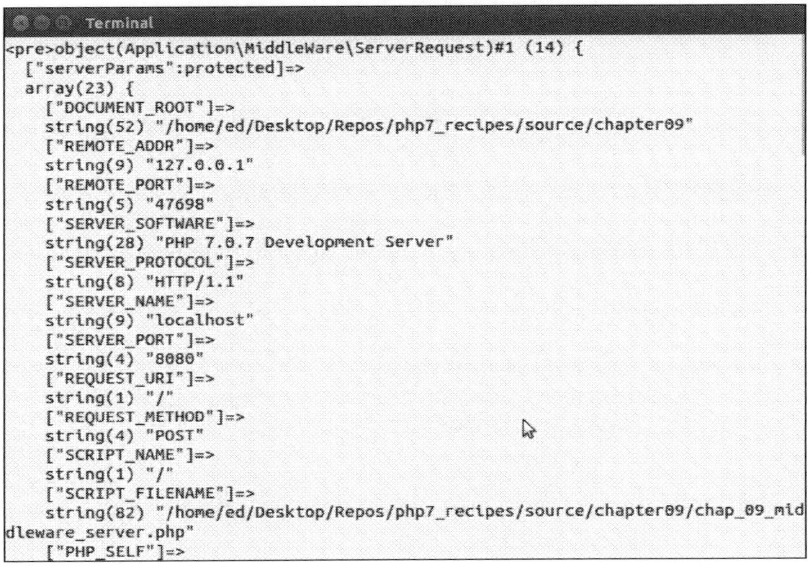

```
Terminal
<pre>object(Application\MiddleWare\ServerRequest)#1 (14) {
  ["serverParams":protected]=>
  array(23) {
    ["DOCUMENT_ROOT"]=>
    string(52) "/home/ed/Desktop/Repos/php7_recipes/source/chapter09"
    ["REMOTE_ADDR"]=>
    string(9) "127.0.0.1"
    ["REMOTE_PORT"]=>
    string(5) "47698"
    ["SERVER_SOFTWARE"]=>
    string(28) "PHP 7.0.7 Development Server"
    ["SERVER_PROTOCOL"]=>
    string(8) "HTTP/1.1"
    ["SERVER_NAME"]=>
    string(9) "localhost"
    ["SERVER_PORT"]=>
    string(4) "8080"
    ["REQUEST_URI"]=>
    string(1) "/"
    ["REQUEST_METHOD"]=>
    string(4) "POST"
    ["SCRIPT_NAME"]=>
    string(1) "/"
    ["SCRIPT_FILENAME"]=>
    string(82) "/home/ed/Desktop/Repos/php7_recipes/source/chapter09/chap_09_mid
dleware_server.php"
    ["PHP_SELF"]=>
```

See also

- An excellent article that shows example usage written by *Matthew Weir O'Phinney*, the editor of PSR-7 (also the lead architect for Zend Framework 1, 2, and 3), is available here: `https://mwop.net/blog/2015-01-26-psr-7-by-example.html`

Defining a PSR-7 Response class

The Response class represents outbound information returned to whatever entity made the original request. HTTP headers play an important role in this context as we need to know that format is requested by the client, usually in the incoming `Accept` header. We then need to set the appropriate `Content-Type` header in the Response class to match that format. Otherwise, the actual body of the response will be HTML, JSON, or whatever else has been requested (and delivered).

How to do it...

1. The `Response` class is actually much easier to implement than the `Request` class as we are only concerned with returning the response from the server to the client. Additionally, it extends our `Application\MiddleWare\Message` class where most of the work has been done. So, all that remains to be done is to define an `Application\MiddleWare\Response` class. As you will note, the only unique property is `$statusCode`:

```
namespace Application\MiddleWare;
use Psr\Http\Message\ { Constants, ResponseInterface,
StreamInterface };
class Response extends Message implements ResponseInterface
{
  protected $statusCode;
```

2. The constructor is not defined by PSR-7, but we provide it for convenience, allowing a developer to create a `Response` instance with all parts intact. We use methods from `Message` and constants from the `Constants` class to verify the arguments:

```
public function __construct($statusCode = NULL,
                            StreamInterface $body = NULL,
                            $headers = NULL,
                            $version = NULL)
{
  $this->body = $body;
  $this->status['code'] = $statusCode
    ?? Constants::DEFAULT_STATUS_CODE;
  $this->status['reason'] =
```

```
    Constants::STATUS_CODES[$statusCode] ?? '';
  $this->httpHeaders = $headers;
  $this->version = $this->onlyVersion($version);
  if ($statusCode) $this->setStatusCode();
}
```

3. We provide a nice way to set the HTTP status code, irrespective of any headers, using `http_response_code()`, available from PHP 5.4 onwards. As this work is on PHP 7, we are safe in the knowledge that this method exists:

```
public function setStatusCode()
{
  http_response_code($this->getStatusCode());
}
```

4. Otherwise, it is of interest to obtain the status code using the following method:

```
public function getStatusCode()
{
  return $this->status['code'];
}
```

5. As with the other PSR-7-based classes discussed in earlier recipes, we also define a `with` method that sets the status code and returns the current instance. Note the use of `STATUS_CODES` to confirm its existence:

```
public function withStatus($statusCode, $reasonPhrase = '')
{
  if (!isset(Constants::STATUS_CODES[$statusCode])) {
      throw new InvalidArgumentException(
      Constants::ERROR_INVALID_STATUS);
  }
  $this->status['code'] = $statusCode;
  $this->status['reason'] = ($reasonPhrase)
    ? Constants::STATUS_CODES[$statusCode] : NULL;
  $this->setStatusCode();
  return $this;
}
```

6. Finally, we define a method that returns the reason for the HTTP status, which is a short text phrase, in this example, based on RFC 7231. Note the use of the PHP 7 null coalesce operator `??` that returns the first non-null item out of three possible choices:

```
public function getReasonPhrase()
{
  return $this->status['reason']
```

```
            ?? Constants::STATUS_CODES[$this->status['code']]
            ?? '';
        }
    }
```

How it works...

First of all, be sure to define the classes discussed in the previous two recipes. After that, you can create another simple server program, `chap_09_middleware_server_with_response.php`, which sets up autoloading and uses the appropriate classes:

```
<?php
require __DIR__ . '/../Application/Autoload/Loader.php';
Application\Autoload\Loader::init(__DIR__ . '/..');
use Application\MiddleWare\ { Constants, ServerRequest, Response,
  Stream };
```

You can then define an array with key/value pairs, where the value points to a text file in the current directory to be used as content:

```
$data = [
  1 => 'churchill.txt',
  2 => 'gettysburg.txt',
  3 => 'star_trek.txt'
];
```

Next, inside a `try...catch` block, you can initialize some variables, initialize the server request, and set up a temporary filename:

```
try {

    $body['text'] = 'Initial State';
    $request = new ServerRequest();
    $request->initialize();
    $tempFile = bin2hex(random_bytes(8)) . '.txt';
    $code = 200;
```

After that, check to see whether the method is GET or POST. If it's GET, check to see whether an `id` parameter was passed. If so, return the body of the matching text file. Otherwise, return a list of text files:

```
if ($request->getMethod() == Constants::METHOD_GET) {
    $id = $request->getQueryParams()['id'] ?? NULL;
    $id = (int) $id;
    if ($id && $id <= count($data)) {
        $body['text'] = file_get_contents(
```

```
            __DIR__ . '/' . $data[$id]);
        } else {
            $body['text'] = $data;
        }
```

Otherwise, return a response indicating a success code 204 and the size of the request body received:

```
    } elseif ($request->getMethod() == Constants::METHOD_POST) {
        $size = $request->getBody()->getSize();
        $body['text'] = $size . ' bytes of data received';
        if ($size) {
            $code = 201;
        } else {
            $code = 204;
        }
    }
```

You can then catch any exceptions and report them with a status code of 500:

```
    } catch (Exception $e) {
        $code = 500;
        $body['text'] = 'ERROR: ' . $e->getMessage();
    }
```

The response needs to be wrapped in a stream, so you can write the body out to the temp file and create it as `Stream`. You can also set the `Content-Type` header to `application/json` and run `getHeaders()`, which outputs the current set of headers. After that, echo the body of the response. For this illustration, you could also dump the `Response` instance to confirm it was constructed correctly:

```
    try {
        file_put_contents($tempFile, json_encode($body));
        $body = new Stream($tempFile);
        $header[Constants::HEADER_CONTENT_TYPE] = 'application/json';
        $response = new Response($code, $body, $header);
        $response->getHeaders();
        echo $response->getBody()->getContents() . PHP_EOL;
        var_dump($response);
```

To wrap things up, catch any errors or exceptions using `Throwable`, and don't forget to delete the temp file:

```
    } catch (Throwable $e) {
        echo $e->getMessage();
    } finally {
       unlink($tempFile);
    }
```

To test, it's just a matter of opening a terminal window, changing to the `/path/to/source/for/this/chapter` directory, and running the following command:

```
php -S localhost:8080
```

From a browser, you can then call this program, adding an `id` parameter. You might consider opening the developer tools to monitor the response header. Here is an example of the expected output. Note the content type of `application/json`:

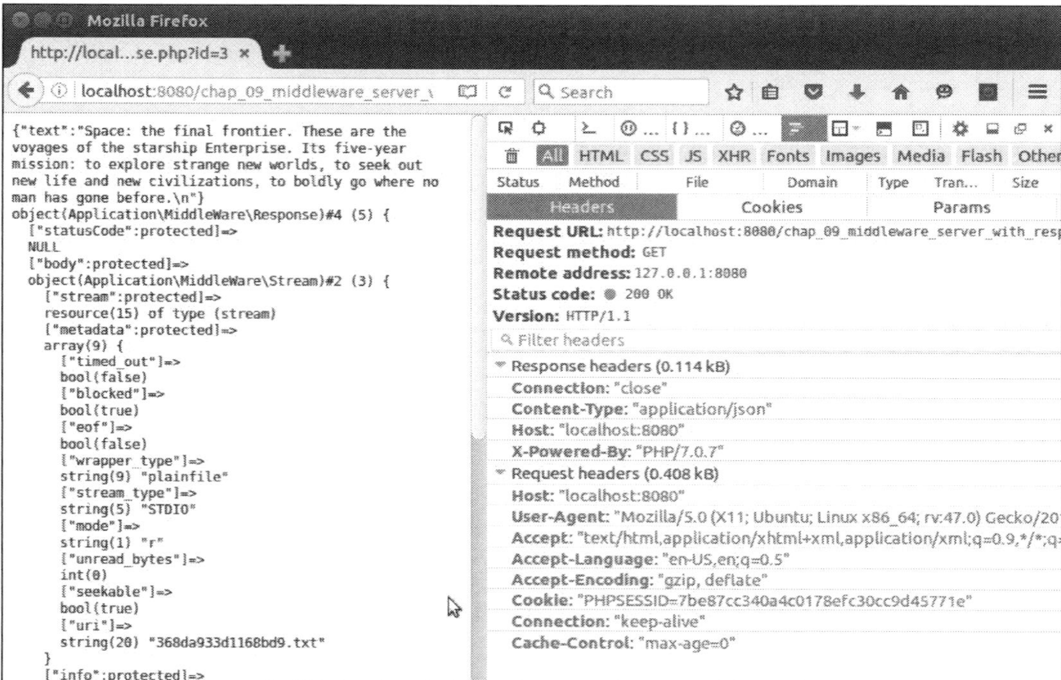

See also

- For more information on PSR, please visit `http://www.php-fig.org/psr/`.
- The following table summarizes the state of PSR-7 compliance at the time of writing. The frameworks not included in this table either do not have PSR-7 support at all, or lack documentation for PSR-7.

Framework	Website	Notes
Slim	http://www.slimframework.com/docs/concepts/value-objects.html	High PSR-7 compliance
Laravel/Lumen	https://lumen.laravel.com/docs/5.2/requests	High PSR-7 compliance
Zend Framework 3/ Expressive	https://framework.zend.com/blog/2016-06-28-zend-framework-3.html or https://zendframework.github.io/zend-expressive/ respectively	High PSR-7 compliance Also Diactoros, and Straigility
Zend Framework 2	https://github.com/zendframework/zend-psr7bridge	PSR-7 bridge available
Symfony	http://symfony.com/doc/current/cookbook/psr7.html	PSR-7 bridge available
Joomla	https://www.joomla.org	Limited PSR-7 support
Cake PHP	http://mark-story.com/posts/view/psr7-bridge-for-cakephp	PSR-7 support is in the roadmap and will use the bridge approach

- There are a number of PSR-7 middleware classes already available. The following table summarizes some of the more popular ones:

Middleware	Website	Notes
Guzzle	https://github.com/guzzle/psr7	HTTP message library
Relay	http://relayphp.com/	Dispatcher
Radar	https://github.com/radarphp/Radar.Project	Action/domain/ responder skeleton
NegotiationMiddleware	https://github.com/rszrama/negotiation-middleware	Content negotiation
psr7-csrf-middleware	https://packagist.org/packages/schnittstabil/psr7-csrf-middleware	Cross Site Request Forgery prevention
oauth2-server	http://alexbilbie.com/2016/04/league-oauth2-server-version-5-is-out	OAuth2 server which supports PSR-7
zend-diactoros	https://zendframework.github.io/zend-diactoros/	PSR-7 HTTP message implementation

Index

Symbols

A

N

O

P

Q

R

S

T

U

V

W

X

Y

Z

Printed in Great Britain
by Amazon